Limited Liability Company & Partnership Answer Book

Second Edition

This is a new edition of the Limited Liability Company & Partnership Answer Book. It replaces the First Edition. Please discard all previous editions and their supplements.

Limited Liability Company & Partnership Answer Book

Second Edition

Alson R. Martin

A PANEL PUBLICATION

This publication is designed to provide accurate and authoritative information in regard to the subject matter covered. It is sold with the understanding that the publisher is not engaged in rendering legal, accounting, or other professional services. If legal advice or other professional assistance is required, the services of a competent professional person should be sought.

—*From a Declaration of Principles* jointly adopted by a Committee of the American Bar Association and a Committee of Publishers and Associations.

Copyright © 2001 by PANEL PUBLISHERS
A Division of Aspen Publishers, Inc.
A Wolters Kluwer Company
www.panelpublishers.com

Permissions
Panel Publishers
1185 Avenue of the Americas
New York, NY 10036

ISBN 0-7355-1677-4

Printed in the United States of America
1 2 3 4 5 6 7 8 9 0

About Panel Publishers

Panel Publishers — comprising the former Prentice Hall Law & Business, Little, Brown and Company's Professional Division, and Wiley Law Publications — is a leading publisher of authoritative and timely treatises, practice manuals, information services, and journals written by specialists to assist attorneys, financial and tax advisors, and other business professionals. Our mission is to provide practical, solution-based how-to information keyed to the latest legislative, judicial, and regulatory developments.

We offer publications in the areas of compensation and benefits, pension, payroll, employment, civil rights, taxation, estate planning, and elder law.

Other Panel products on related topics include:
Asset Protection Journal
Asset Protection Strategies: Tax and Legal Aspects
Choice of Business Entity Answer Book
Closely Held Businesses in Estate Planning
Estate and Gift Tax Handbook
Failing and Failed Businesses
Federal Income Taxation of Debt Instruments
Federal and State Taxation of Limited Liability Companies
Federal Tax Course
Federal Tax Course Newsletter
Federal Taxation of Municipal Bonds
Income Taxation of Fiduciaries and Beneficiaries
International Taxation
Mergers, Acquisitions, and Buyouts
Multistate Corporate Tax Guide
The S Corporation Answer Book
The S Corporation: Planning and Operation
State and Local Taxation Answer Book
Structuring Venture Capital, Private Equity, and Entrepreneurial
    Transactions
Taxation of Compensation and Benefits
Taxation of the Entertainment Industry
Taxation of Investments Handbook
Valuation of Closely Held Businesses: Legal and Tax Aspects

PANEL PUBLISHERS
A Division of Aspen Publishers, Inc.
Practical Solutions for Legal and Business Professionals
www.panelpublishers.com

v

SUBSCRIPTION NOTICE

This Panel product is update periodically with supplements to reflect important changes in the subject matter. If you purchased this product directly from Panel Publishers, we have already recorded your subscription for this update service.

If, however, you purchased this product from a bookstore and wish to receive future updates and revised or related volumes billed separately with a 30-day examination review, please contact our Customer Service Department at 1-800-234-1660, or send your name, company name (if applicable), address, and the title of the product to:

Panel Publishers
A Division of Aspen Publishers, Inc.
7201 McKinney Circle
Frederick, MD 21704

About the Author

Alson R. Martin is a partner and co-Chair of Business and Finance Division of Shook, Hardy & Bacon L.L.P. in Overland Park, Kansas, with offices in Kansas City, Houston, Washington, D.C., Miami, Tampa, San Francisco, London, Geneva, Zurich, and Buenos Aires. Mr. Martin represents family, closely held, professional, and large private and publicly traded businesses.

He has been co-author of the book *Kansas Corporation Law & Practice (Including Tax Aspects)* (3rd ed. 1992). He is also technical editor of Panel's *401(k) Advisor*, a monthly newsletter. Mr. Martin is also author of a monthly newsletter published for a national study group of 185 tax advisors (attorneys, actuaries, and CPAs). Additionally, he has written many articles in various publications, including *The Journal of Taxation, Digest of Tax Articles, Journal of the Kansas Bar Association, The Financial Planner Magazine, The Practical Accountant Magazine, The Monthly Digest of Tax Articles, Tax Management Compensation Planning Journal, The Small Business Council of America Alert, ALI-ABA Course Materials, Journal of Taxation of Employee Benefits, ABA Tax Section Course Materials, American Bar Association Annual Meeting Materials, The Small Business Controller, The Financial Planner, Kansas Law Review*, and *The Journal of Pension Planning*.

Mr. Martin has been President, Tax Section, Kansas Bar Association and Chair, American Bar Association Personal Service Organizations (1984–96). He is a member, Closely Held Business Committee, Health Law Committee, and Limited Liability Task Force; President and Director of The Small Business Council of America; member, The ESOP Association Administration Advisory

Committee; Fellow, American College of Tax Counsel; and Life Member, American Tax Policy Institute. He also served as a Delegate and Chair of the Kansas Taxation Committee to the White House Conference on Small Business in June, 1995. He was a Trustee of Johnson County Community College from 1977–81.

Mr. Martin has been a faculty member for several ALI-ABA Courses, including "Estate Planning for the Family Business Owner", "Sophisticated Estate Planning Techniques", and the Annual Advanced Course of Study "Professional Service Organizations." He has also spoken on tax, estate planning, and business subjects to many businesses and professional organizations, including the following: national meeting of American Bar Association Tax Section, The ESOP Association Annual Convention, Creative Pension & Benefit Strategies, Kansas Bar Association Annual Meeting, Southern Federal Tax Conference, Notre Dame Estate Planning Symposium, Ohio Pension Conference, Georgia Tax Conference, Kansas Tax Conference, Mountain States Pension Conference, and numerous other professional groups, such as national meetings of Certified Professional Business Consultants, and state chapter meetings of Kansas and Missouri CPAs. Formerly an adjunct professor of law at both the University of Kansas and University of Missouri at K.C. Law Schools, Mr. Martin is listed in *The Best Lawyers in America, Guide to Leading U.S. Tax Lawyers*, and *The National Registry of Who's Who*™.

Mr. Martin graduated with Highest Distinction from Kansas University and was Phi Beta Kappa, a Summerfield Scholar, and Student Body President. He received his J.D., *cum laude*, and L.L.M. in taxation from New York University School of Law, where he was a Root Tilden Scholar and an editor of the *New York University Law Review*.

Acknowledgments

I could not have written this book without the help of many partners and associates at Shook, Hardy & Bacon L.L.P., as well as other colleagues. I would especially like to thank Michael Carson, Lance Pruitt, and Brian M. Jacques who, while working on their L.L.M. in taxation at the University of Missouri at Kansas City Law School, did much of the research on the recent developments covered in this book.

Introduction

The *Limited Liability Company & Partnership Answer Book, Second Edition* incorporates recent developments concerning limited liability companies (LLCs), limited liability partnerships (LLPs), and family limited partnerships (FLPs). It provides current information on how to tailor an LLC, LLP, or FLP to meet the specific requirements of such an organization. It also identifies the factors that are critical to success in establishing an LLC, LLP, or FLP, and outlines the important differences in tax treatment and among state statutes. Here is just a sample of the key issues that are covered in the book:

- The tax consequences of converting LLCs to and from multi-owner entities
- The effect of the use of a single or multi-membered LLC on a Section 1031 like-kind exchange
- How a family limited partnership or LLC can be used for business succession planning
- When a partnership or LLC interest is a security

The *Limited Liability Company & Partnership Answer Book, Second Edition* is intended to be useful and practical. To assist readers, important statutes, cases, and regulations are cited throughout the book.

As the reader is no doubt aware, substantial changes due to comprehensive state law and federal tax law changes with respect to all three entities requires rethinking past practices and choices.

It is not sufficient to form any of these entities today and review the tax and business issues tomorrow.

Emphasis throughout the book is on closely held entities. The forms have been updated based on the author's experience and law changes. I hope that you will find this book to be useful both as a resource for questions as well as a starting point for documentation. Of course, this book does not provide legal advice for specific situations, which should be sought from a competent professional.

Alson R. Martin
October 2000

How to Use This Book

The *Limited Liability Company & Partnership Answer Book, Second Edition* is designed for professionals who need quick and authoritative answers to questions on choosing the right business form, especially LLCs, LLPs, and FLPs. This book uses simple, straight forward language and avoids technical jargon wherever possible. The question and answer format, with its breadth of coverage and plain-language explanations, effectively conveys the complex subject matter of limited liability companies. In addition, the book provides appendix material and an extensive index.

List of Questions. A detailed list of questions follows the table of contents in the front of the book to help the reader locate areas of immediate interest. This list provides both the question number and the page on which it appears. A series of subheadings helps to group and organize the questions by topic within each chapter.

Question Numbers. The questions are numbered consecutively within each chapter (e.g., 2:1, 2:2, 2:3).

Appendices. For the reader's convenience, the following are provided: an updated analysis of LLCs by state; an updated member-managed LLC Operating Agreement; an updated manager-managed LLC Operating Agreement; a partnership agreement for a professional firm; a one-member LLC Operating Agreement; Check the Box Treasury Regulations; the Uniform Limited Liability Company Act; an updated family limited liability partnership agreement; and family limited partnership documents used in IRS audits.

Tables. In the back of the book are tables, or finding lists, provided for Internal Revenue Code and Treasury regulations sections, revenue rulings, revenue procedures, private letter rulings, notices, and court cases. References in the tables are to question numbers rather than page numbers.

Index. At the back of the book is an index provided as further aid to locating specific information. All references in the index are to question numbers rather than page numbers.

Table of Contents

CHAPTER **12**

List of Questions

Chapter 2 Formation

Comparing LLC Acts and Statutes

Forming the LLC

Chapter 3 Tax Classification

The "Check-the-Box" Regulations

Free Transferability of Interest

Enforcement of Commitments to Contribute Capital

Distributions

Chapter 5 Management and Control

The Operating Agreement

Manager-Managed LLCs

Choice of Member-Managed or Manager-Managed LLC

Fiduciary Duties and Duty of Care

Chapter 7 Taxation

Consequences to the LLC: Start-Up Decisions and Tax Elections

Partnership Operations

Single Member LLCs (SMLLC)

Large Partnerships, Publicly Traded Partnerships, and International Partnerships

Allocations Attributable to Nonrecourse Debt

Other Restrictions on the Allocation of LLC Income

Restrictions on the Use of LLC Losses by Members

Transfer of an LLC Interest

Termination and Liquidation of the LLC

Chapter 9 Securities and Bankruptcy Laws

Bankruptcy of a Member

Chapter 10 Specialized Uses in Business and Estate Planning

General Business Applications

Real Estate and Joint Ventures

Charitable and Non-Profit Activities

Health Care: Integrated Delivery Systems

Estate Planning

Chapter 11 Limited Liability Partnerships

In General

Choosing an LLP or an LLC

Extent of Liability Protection

Formation, Costs, and Operational Issues

LLPs and the Effects of Dissolution, Dissociation, and Termination

Chapter 12 Professional LLCs and LLPs: Comparison with General Partnerships and Professional Corporations

Fiscal Year, Medicare, Pensions, and Employee Benefits

Medical/Dental Insurance and Reimbursement Plans

Chapter 13 Family Limited Partnerships

Overview

Valuation Discounts

Chapter 1

Choice or Change of Entity

The limited liability company (LLC), while a relatively new form of business organization, is now widely used in the United States and other countries. It has unique attributes that make it the best entity to use in many, but not all, situations. This chapter describes the basic characteristics of the LLC and the other forms of business organizations recognized under state law in the United States today, and draws basic comparisons between the LLC and other entities. Chapter 1 focuses on choice-of-entity issues; comparisons with other types of entities are offered in later chapters, especially chapters 11 and 12.

Conducting Business as a Limited Liability Company

Q 1:1   What is an LLC?

The LLC is an organization formed under state law which, if properly structured and operated, shields the owners of the LLC (known as the "members") and the management (who may be the members or "managers") from personal liability for the debts and liabilities of the LLC. Entities like the LLC have existed in Europe and South America for some time. The German *Gesellschaft mit beschraenkter Haftung* (GmbH) and Brazilian *limitada* are foreign country versions of the LLC. The LLC, however, is a recent addition to the laws of most states in the United States – until 1990, only Wyoming (1977) and Florida (1982) had authorized the formation of LLCs in their states.

Q 1:2   Do all states recognize the LLC?

All 50 states and the District of Columbia have authorized the organization of LLCs. (See appendix A) Vermont, Massachusetts, and Hawaii were the last states to enact LLC acts.

Most LLC acts recognize LLCs formed in other states ("foreign" LLCs), and provide for the registration of the foreign LLC to do business in the state. [See appendix A; Draft Uniform Limited Liability Act (Uniform Act) §§ 1001-1013; Darrow, "Limited Liability Companies and S Corporations: Deciding Which is Optimal and Whether to Convert to LLC Status," 48 *Tax Law* 1, 2 (Fall 1994)]

Q 1:3   Can an LLC formed in one state conduct business in another state? Internationally?

Yes, as a general rule. The LLC statutes generally authorize the LLC to conduct business in the state in which it is formed, in other states, and internationally. Indeed, the Interstate Commerce Clause of the U.S. Constitution entitles an LLC formed in one state to conduct interstate commerce in all other states, and other states may not unreasonably burden the LLC's ability to transact interstate business. [US Cons art I, § 8, cl 3]

Q 1:4   Which state's law governs the operation of an LLC that conducts business in more than one state?

The provisions of most LLC statutes provide that the law of the place where the LLC was organized governs the organization, internal affairs, and liabilities of the members of the LLC, but generally limit the business of the LLC to those activities that may be conducted by a domestic LLC in the state. [Appendix A; Uniform

Act § 1001] However, some states do not specifically provide that the home state's law applies with respect to the liability of members. [Fla Stat § 608.505; Mont Code Ann § 35-8-1001; Pa Stat § 8981; SC Code Ann § 33-43-1001; Utah Code Ann § 48-2b-143; appendix A] In addition, the courts may apply foreign law in a veil-piercing case if the court sees veil-piercing as a type of statutory restriction on limited liability based on the disregard of formalities. However, if the veil-piercing is based on fraud, local law may apply.

Q 1:5   What happens if an LLC conducts business in a state that does not recognize foreign LLCs, or if the state questions a specific attribute or does not allow an LLC to conduct the specific business of the foreign LLC?

No direct legal precedents answer this question. *Thompson v. Schmitt* [274 SW 554, 560, 561 (Tex 1925)] addresses the conduct of business by a Massachusetts business trust in Texas. At that time, Texas did not statutorily recognize the business trust entity. The result of that case was disastrous for the owners of the trust. The Texas Supreme Court held that, because the Texas legislature had not authorized the use of a Massachusetts business trust as a legal form of business organization, the trust's beneficial holders were not shielded from personal liability for the trust's liabilities due to public policy.

One case addresses whether the limited liability protection of an LLC will be respected for causes of action arising in a state where the LLC has not been adopted. Before the New York LLC Act was adopted, a federal district court in New York "suggested" that the law of the place of origin of an LLC would apply if the LLC was properly organized. This court was analyzing a Lebanese LLC doing business in New York. [Abu-Nasser v Elders Futures, Inc, No. 88 Civ 7906, 1991 US Dist LEXIS 3794 (SDNY Mar 28, 1991)] The court thus implied that the foreign LLC would be respected as an LLC in New York; however, the court did not have to reach this conclusion.

Many LLC statutes provide that their law should be respected by the courts in other states, which provision may only have limited effect. [Merrill, "Treatment of Oregon Limited Liability Companies in States Without Limited Liability Company Statutes," 73 *Ore L Rev* 43 (1994)].

It is also necessary to review the LLC acts in states where the LLC's business will be conducted to ensure that those states recognize foreign LLCs, that is, those formed in other states, especially if the LLC is conducting a professional practice, insurance business, banking or other highly regulated business that may not be authorized in a state that otherwise allows other foreign LLCs to do business.

Q 1:6   Is there any limit on the number of members (owners) in an LLC?

No, there is no limit, although some states required at least two owners before the "check the box" treasury regulations came into effect. No LLC act limits the number of persons who may own an interest in a single LLC, although certain state and federal securities and income tax laws may be triggered based on the number of owners.

Q 1:7   Can an LLC have a corporate subsidiary?

Yes. No state prohibits an LLC from owning any or all of the stock of a corporation. All LLC statutes contain broad "powers" provisions and, for the most part, allow LLCs to conduct any business (and, impliedly, own any assets) that a business may lawfully own under the law of the relevant state. [Del Code Ann· tit 6, § 18-106; Mo Rev Stat § 347.710; Uniform Act § 112] An LLC, however, is not a permitted owner of an S corporation under the Internal Revenue Code. [IRC § 1361]

Q 1:8   Can any person or entity own an interest in an LLC?

Yes. Generally, any legally recognized "person" may own an interest in an LLC except a professional LLC, in which the ownership rules are more restrictive due to state law, licensing authority rules, or other regulations. The relevant state LLC act and other pertinent statues and regulations should be consulted. For example, the Missouri statue provides that any person may own an interest in an LLC and defines "person" to include individuals, partnerships, domestic or foreign limited partnerships, domestic or foreign LLCs, domestic or foreign corporations, trusts, business trusts, real estate investment trusts, estates, and other associations or business entities. [Mo Rev Stat § 347.015(15)] Uniform Act Sections 201 and 101(18) expand this definition by adding "government, government subdivision agency or instrumentality, or any other legal or commercial entity."

Q 1:9 Can an IRA invest in an LLC?

Yes, if permitted by the IRA document, absent a limitation in the LLC's articles of organization or operating agreement. An IRA cannot invest in collectibles, life insurance contracts, or make loans to its owner. An interest in an LLC is not an impermissible investment of an IRA. However, there are numerous issues and complexities that should be reviewed. For example, if the LLC that has checked the box to be taxed as a corporation and has made an "S" election, investment by an IRA will terminate the S election. [See the individual ownership requirements of § 1361(b)(1)(B)] Otherwise, since an LLC does not have the same restrictions on ownership that an S corporation, an LLC interest should be a permissible investment of an IRA.

Such an investment may not be advisable, however. The first issue is the prohibited transaction rules. A prohibited transaction will disqualify the tax exempt status of the IRA. Such a transaction will cause a constructive distribution of the IRA assets resulting in the IRA owner being taxed on the entire proceeds. Furthermore, the IRA owner may be subject to an early withdrawal penalty if he or she is younger than 59 $1/_2$ years.

Prohibited transactions occur when disqualified persons engage in specified types of self-dealing with the IRA. [§ 4975(c)] An owner of an IRA and beneficiaries of the IRA are disqualified persons. If the owner of an IRA has any dealings with or ownership in an LLC, then a prohibited transaction may occur. A host of issues arise in this context. For example, there might be a prohibited transaction if an IRA controlled an LLC and the LLC paid the IRA owner a salary, even if the salary represented reasonable compensation for services. However, one case has held the initial investment in a business not to be a prohibited transaction. [Swanson v. Comm., 106 TC 76 (1996)] In addition, the IRA may be subject to the unrelated business income tax discussed below.

Q 1:10   Can a retirement plan invest in an LLC?

Yes, but the same prohibited transaction issues and unrelated business income tax exist as are present for an IRA investment. However, qualified retirement plans, unlike IRAs, may own stock in an S corporation without terminating the S election. [IRC § 1361(c)(6)].

Q 1:11   What other tax issues exist for an investment in an LLC by an IRA or qualified retirement plan?

For IRAs and pension funds, it is unusual, although legal, to invest in a taxable investment. Investments by a tax exempt entity in a trade or business, or an investment with debt financing, operated through an entity taxed as a partnership creates taxation on net "unrelated business taxable income." Some pension funds as a matter of policy will not invest in a taxable transaction. Others will evaluate taxable investments by looking at the net after-tax returns. If the yield is acceptable in light of the additional expenses associated with the taxes, they will invest.

Notwithstanding its general exemption from federal income tax, a tax-exempt organization, described in sections 401(a) or 501(c) and exempt from tax under section 501(a), will generally be subject to the unrelated business income tax ("UBIT") in any taxable year to the extent that it has unrelated business taxable income ("UBTI"), less corresponding deductions, exceeding $1,000. Pursuant to section 512, such an organization may realize UBTI to the extent that it has income derived from either: (i) an "unrelated trade or business", as defined in section 513, carried on either directly by the organization or by any partnership in which it is a partner; or (ii) "debt-financed" property, under section 514, owned by the organization or any partnership in which it is a partner.

Many types of pass-through entities are generally permissible investments for exempt organizations, subject to this taxable income issue.

1. Limited Partnership

The limited partnership is one of the most common forms of pass-through investment vehicles used by pension funds and other exempt organizations. The limited partnership offers the maximum flexibility for management, control, and allocation of income and losses, while preserving limited liability for the investor. Under the limited partnership statutes effective in many states, the limited partners can play a fairly active role in the internal management decisions of the partnership, provided they do not act on behalf of the partnership with respect to non-partners.

An IRA, retirement plan, or other exempt organization that is a limited partner in a partnership will be subject to tax on any income derived from the unrelated trade or business activities of the partnership. [See Rev. Rul. 79-222, 1979-2 C.B. 236.] The exempt organization would be individually responsible for the filing of the UBTI tax returns and the payment of the tax. This includes tax filing and paying obligations in the states in which the partnership is doing business. Any exemptions or exclusions available to a partner will also apply to the partner's income from the partnership.

If the limited partnership is a publicly traded partnership ("PTP"), a tax-exempt partner's allocable share of its income will constitute UBTI regardless of the character of the income. [IRC § 512(c)(2).]

2. General Partnership

The general partnership is even more flexible than the limited partnership, but is seldom used by exempt organizations due to its joint and several liability risk.

3. Limited Liability Companies ("LLCs")

LLCs, unlike S corporations, generally have no restrictions on the kind of permissible owners and can generally own any kind of asset that a partnership could own. If classified as a partnership, an LLC can hold debt-financed real estate without incurring UBTI as long as it complies with section 514(c)(9). It is otherwise subject to the UBIT rules as is a partnership. If taxed as a regular "C" corporation, however, there is no UBIT tax because any taxable income is taxed at the corporate level.

Q 1:12   Can non-U.S. residents own an interest in an LLC?

Yes. Neither the IRS nor any state (except in states with corporate farming restrictions) prohibits nonresident aliens or foreign country business organizations from owning an interest in an LLC.

[See Uniform Act §§ 201 and 101(18), which do not restrict membership to U.S. persons.] None of these "persons," however, can own stock in an S corporation. [IRC § 1361(b)(1)(B)] Thus, an LLC is an obvious choice of organization if pass-through taxation is desired and any nonresident aliens will own an equity interest in the LLC. However, see Q 1:13 about the tax classification of LLCs in other countries.

Q 1:13   Is an LLC formed in the United States *and taxed as a partnership treated as a partnership for the tax purposes of another country's revenue laws?*

Not necessarily. For example, Canada may treat LLCs organized in the United States as corporations for Canadian tax purposes. [Arnold, "New Protocol to Canada-U.S. Treaty Addresses Estate Tax Issues, Limitations on Benefits and Mutual Assistance," 9 *Tax Notes Intl* 859 (Sept 18, 1994)] An analysis of the internal revenue law of each country and its tax treaties with the United States is beyond the scope of this book. The internal laws of each home country of a foreign investor in an LLC organized in the United States should be reviewed in connection with the investment in the LLC.

Defining Terms

Q 1:14   What is the terminology of an LLC?

Although not completely uniform, most LLC statutes commonly use the following nomenclature.

Members. The owner of an interest in an LLC is known as a member. To be a member, some LLC statutes require the person to be identified as a member in the Operating Agreement. [Mo Rev Stat § 347.113.1; Uniform Act § 406 (if an Operating Agreement is adopted)]

A person cannot be a member unless the person has received the prerequisite approval of the other members of the LLC. Uniform Act Section 601 requires unanimous consent for the direct admission of a member to the LLC, or majority (or otherwise agreed) consent for the transfer of a member's governance rights to another person who will be recognized as a member. [Uniform Act § 504; see, similarly, Prototype Act § 102(J)]

Articles. The LLC is formed by filing with the Secretary of State or similar official "Articles of Organization" containing basic information. The analogous corporate document is the Articles or Certificate of Incorporation. The analogous limited partnership document is the Certificate of Limited Partnership.

Operating Agreement. LLC acts generally require the members to adopt an agreement, usually referred to as an "Operating Agreement," providing the details about the operation of the company and the relationship of the members to each other. However, the Texas LLC Act refers to this agreement as the LLC's "Regulations," and Delaware refers to the "Limited Liability Company Agreement." [Tex Rev Civ Stat art 1528n, § 2.09; Del Code Ann tit 6, § 18-101(7)]

Uniform Act Section 406 provides for the adoption of an Operating Agreement by the unanimous consent of the members, but does not require the LLC to have an Operating Agreement. Prototype Act Section 102(K) does not require the Operating Agreement to be in writing.

Treasury Regulations Section 1.704-1(b)(2)(h) defines the partnership agreement as all agreements among the partners, or between one or more partners, or between one or more partners and the partnership, concerning the partnership and each partner's responsibilities, whether oral or written, and regardless of the title of the agreement. Thus, for tax purposes, all arrangements between one or more partners relating to the partnership, including options, buy-sell, or stop-loss arrangements, are considered part of the partnership agreement. In this book, references to the Operating Agreement are to the document referred to as such in the relevant LLC statute, which may include the "partnership agreement" referred to in Treasury Regulations Section 1.704-1(b)(2)(h). In some states the Operating Agreement may be oral, although use of a written agreement would help prevent differences of opinion over what the members intended, and provide guidance for the authority of the managers and members.

Interests. Members have interests in an LLC just as partners have interests in a partnership. LLCs do not issue shares of stock, although some LLC acts refer to "certificated interests." [Del Code Ann tit 6, § 18-702(c)]

Capital Account. For tax purposes, members of an LLC taxed as a partnership have a "capital account," which is an accounting and tax concept applicable to partnerships. In the case of an LLC, the capital account represents a member's (instead of a partner's) equity interest in the company. In this book, the capital account is defined by reference to the Code's definition; that is, a member's capital account is equal to that member's:

(a) capital contributions to the company (cash and net fair market value of property contributed), plus that member's allocable share of the company's income and gain each year (including tax-exempt income), less (b) distributions to the member by the company of cash or property (at net fair market value) and that member's allocable share of any tax losses, deductions, or IRC Section 705(a)(2)(B) expenditures. [Treas Reg § 1.704-1(b)(2)(iv)(b)]

Management. Under most statutes, the members can either designate "managers" or reserve management to themselves. Depending upon the powers given, the manager may function in a manner similar to that of a general partner. Uniform Act Section 301 provides that an LLC is managed by the members, unless the Articles vest management authority in one or more managers.

Choosing the "Right" Business Form: New Businesses

Q 1:15   Should a prospective business venture be operated through a C corporation, an S corporation, an LLC, a general partnership, a limited partnership (LP), a limited liability partnership (LLP), a limited liability limited partnership (LLLP), or a sole proprietorship?

The form of business organization to be used for a specific business or venture depends upon many factors. There is often no single right answer. There are differences, often significant, in each of the forms of business organization. Those differences should be considered carefully before selecting and forming the entity. State law and tax law (both state and federal) must also be reviewed.

When analyzing what form of business organization to use, many questions need to be answered, but the ten major questions are:

1. *Where will the business of the organization be conducted?* For example, is a foreign LLC recognized and treated appropriately for tax purposes in all of the states or other jurisdictions where the business will be conducted? (See appendices A and B.)

2. *Who will own the organization: individuals? corporations? trusts? U.S. residents? foreign citizens?* If corporations, LLCs, or nonresident aliens or certain trusts will be owners of the business, an S corporation is not an option. [IRC § 1361] However, the Small Business Job Protection Act of 1996 made qualified retirement plans (including qualified pension plans, profit sharing plans, 401(k) plans, and employee stock ownership plans (ESOPs)) and "electing small business trusts" (ESBTs) eligible as shareholders in S corporations. [Pub L No. 104-188, 104th Cong, 2d Sess §§ 1301-1317 (Aug 20, 1996); 69-Jan NY St BJ 54] Thus, if pass-through taxation and limited liability protection are desired and an S corporation is not an option, the LLC, LLP, LLLP, and limited partnership are the possible choices.

3. *How many owners will there be?* Thanks to the 1997 IRS "check-the-box" procedures, a single-member LLC may choose to be disregarded for tax purposes; although it will not be considered a partnership, it will be treated as a sole proprietorship and subjected to pass-through taxation. If there are more than 75 owners, the business cannot be conducted as an S corporation, because of the limit on the number of shareholders that an S corporation can have. [IRC § 1361] Husbands and wives (and their estates) are counted as one shareholder for purposes of determining the ownership of an S corporation. [IRC § 1361(b)(1)(A)]

4. *How do the owners expect to finance the venture's business?* If the venture will be financed with debt, an LLC, LLP, LLLP, or LP may be preferable to an S corporation because the members of an LLC may more often include a portion of the LLC's debt in the tax basis of their interest (see chapter 7). C or S corporation shareholders generally cannot include the entity's debt in the basis of their stock, even if they guarantee the debt.

If the business will want or need to retain significant earnings for future capital needs and if its tax bracket is significantly lower than that of its owners, a C corporation may be preferable to an LLC or S corporation. If the C corporation's retained earnings are reasonably necessary for the future use of the corporation, or less than $250,000 ($150,000 for personal service corporations), the Section 531 accumulated earnings tax will not apply. The shareholders of a regular C corporation are not subject to tax on income that is not distributed to them (although the C corporation is subject to tax to the extent that it has net taxable income not offset by credits or net operating losses).

LLC members, partners (LLP, LLLP, or otherwise), and S corporation shareholders are subject to tax on the entity's taxable income whether or not the business makes a distribution to the owners. Thus, if the business cannot or does not distribute all or a significant amount of its net earnings and needs to build its capital base for the future, LLC members, partners, and S corporation shareholders may pay tax on income they do not receive. This is not the case for shareholders in a regular corporation.

5. *Do the owners want flow-through (pass-through) taxation?* Flow-through taxation means the entity itself is not subject to tax; instead, all of the taxable income or loss flows through to the individual owners and is reported by them on their tax returns, regardless of the amount of the distributions of cash or property to the owners. The IRS "check-the box" regulations, however, allow LLCs to choose whether to be taxed as a partnership or as a corporation. [61 *Fed Reg* 21989 (1996); 57 *Taxn for Acct* 289] Should an "S" corporation choose to change its tax classification, however, it will be barred from changing to "S" status again for five years. [IRC §§ 1361-1380; *J Mo Bar* May-June 1997, 161; 57 *Taxn for Acct* 356, 365]

6. *Do the organizers of the business expect to incur net losses?* Many business ventures suffer losses in the first few years due to heavy start-up costs, front-loaded tax depreciation, and overhead in excess of revenue. If the owners have income from other sources, and they actively participate in the business of the entity, or have passive income from

other activities, the owners may desire to use an LLC or S corporation in which the losses flow through to the taxpayers, subject to limitations discussed in chapter 7. Regular C corporation losses do not flow through to the shareholders, because it is not a pass-through tax entity, but may be carried forward to later, or backward to earlier, taxable years of the C corporation to offset the C corporation's future (or past) taxable income. [IRC § 172]

An LLC may be better than an S corporation for the purpose of allowing losses to be used on the owners' tax returns. The ability of LLC members or S corporation shareholders to use the losses of the venture to reduce other taxable income is limited by their tax basis in their LLC interest or S corporation stock, as the case may be. If the business has debt, LLC members will have more tax basis (against which losses can be used) in their LLC interest than S corporation shareholders will have in their basis in their stock, because LLC members can include their share of the LLC's debt in their basis. An S corporation shareholder does not receive any benefit due to the S corporation's debt, unless the debt is owed by the S corporation to that shareholder. [IRC § 1367(b)(2)(B)]

7. *Do the owners of the organization want to create various classes of equity interests, or specially allocate the business income, losses, or other tax attributes to different owners?* S corporations can have only one class of stock. C corporations can have any number of classes of stock, but all of the holders of the same class of stock generally must be treated the same under state corporate law. LLCs treated as partnerships for tax purposes can allocate the LLC's income, gains, losses, deductions, credits, or other items among the members by almost any method desired, and may be inconsistent from one member to the next, as long as the allocations have "substantial economic effect" (see chapter 7). Thus, the LLC provides significant flexibility to the members in allocating the business's income and losses, which is not available to corporate shareholders.

8. *Are the owners concerned about limited liability?* Will the proposed business have contact or contracts with third parties? Is the business or investment subject to tort liability to third parties — for example, malpractice liability related to

a professional service business, or tort liability for injuries occurring on the business's real property?

9. *Do the owners of the business plan to offer employee benefits to owners who provide services? health insurance coverage? pension or profit sharing plans? cafeteria plans? other perks?* If employee benefits are desirable, there is a significant advantage to a C corporation's shareholder-employees over LLC member-employees and S corporation shareholder-employees who own more than 2 percent of the stock in the corporation (see chapter 7). An LLC, unless taxed as a corporation, cannot adopt an ESOP (employee stock ownership plan) due to the requirement that an ESOP own stock in a corporation. [IRC § 409(L)]

10. *Is the business regulated in a manner that dictates the form of business entity that must be used? Are there regulatory prohibitions against certain forms of business organization? Is it a law practice, or medical practice? Are their beneficial statutory or regulatory provisions of federal, state, or local law that apply or do not apply to particular forms of business entities?* Until the passage of the Small Business Job Protection Act of 1996, banks could not be organized as S corporations. However, under this law, financial institutions may take the form of S corporations so long as they do not account for bad debts by using the reserve method. [Pub L No 104-188, 104th Cong, 2d Sess §§ 1301-1317 (Aug 20, 1996); 25 *J Taxn for Law* 140]

Q 1:16   What is the difference between a C corporation and an S corporation?

All corporations formed under state law are C corporations unless they qualify, and make the election to be taxed, as an S corporation. They are known as C corporations because they are subject to tax under subchapter C of the Internal Revenue Code of 1986 (IRC), that is, Code Sections 301-385, as well as other provisions of the IRC, other than subchapter S. A C corporation, as an entity, is subject to tax on all of the corporation's taxable income. Shareholders also must include all dividends received from the corporation in their taxable income, although corporate shareholders may be able to exclude part or all of the dividends received. [IRC § 243] Thus, C corporation income is generally subject to two levels of tax, once to the corporation and again to shareholders on dividends paid to them.

Many closely held C corporations avoid the two layers of tax on their income by distributing all of their taxable income in the form of deductible salaries or bonuses. Although the income is taxable to the shareholder-employee, the corporation does not have any net taxable income to tax, thus only one level of tax is paid. However, this so-called "zeroing" out of income will not be respected by the IRS if the shareholders do not provide services to the corporation, or if the compensation is deemed "unreasonable," and thus not deductible under Code Section 162. Unreasonable compensation paid to shareholders is deemed a dividend, which is not deductible by the corporation, but is taxable to the recipient.

All state law partnerships, trusts, or LLCs taxed as an "association" (discussed in chapter 3) are taxed as C corporations under the IRC. [Treas Reg § 301.7701] However, they may make an "S" election.

An S corporation is a corporation formed under state law, but one that has made a special election to be treated as a "small business corporation" under subchapter S of the IRC. [IRC §§ 1361–1379] If qualified, so long as the S election remains in effect, the S corporation generally is not subject to tax, although there are certain exceptions to this rule. The net taxable income or loss of an S corporation flows through and is reported as taxable income or loss on the tax returns of the individual shareholders. S corporations, however, may be subject to tax on certain built-in gain items, passive income, distribution of appreciated property, and on certain other events. (See Panel Publishers, *The S Corporation Answer Book*, for a more specific discussion of the taxation of S corporations.)

In addition to the entity-level tax, many provisions of the IRC apply differently to C and S corporations. For example, generally a C corporation can obtain and deduct all of the cost of health insurance coverage and other fringe benefits for the C corporation's shareholder-employees as an ordinary and necessary business expense under Code Section 162, and such C corporation owner-employees have no taxable income on account of those benefits. Shareholder-employees of an S corporation who own stock constituting more than 2 percent of the corporation's issued and outstanding stock have taxable income on the portion of the corporation's expenses paid to provide health insurance coverage or certain other certain benefits to 2 percent shareholders. (See Code Section 1372, which provides that 2 percent shareholders are treated like partners in a partnership for the purposes of the fringe benefit rules; see chapter 7 for an analysis of these rules as they apply to members in an LLC taxed as a partnership.)

Q 1:17   What are the similarities and differences between a C corporation and an LLC?

C corporations and LLCs are similar in that both shield the owners of the entity from personal liability for the debts and obligations of the entity. Thus, generally for the owners of an LLC or a C corporation, the potential exposure to economic loss is limited to the amount of their investment in the organization. LLCs and corporations are formed by filing with the required state official, generally the Secretary of State.

Those situations generally are the only similarities, but there are many significant differences between a C corporation and an LLC:

Statutory Schemes. While C and S corporations are identical for state law purposes (other than perhaps state tax laws), C corporations and LLCs are separate legal entities and are governed by separate and distinct statutory provisions.

General Taxation. A C corporation is subject to tax on the corporation's net taxable income. An LLC can be taxed as a C corporation under the IRC or as a pass-through partnership for federal income tax purposes under subchapter K of the IRC. [IRC §§ 701–765]

Generally, the owners of the LLC can decide which federal income tax system they prefer, but must carefully structure the formation and ongoing operations of an LLC, to be taxed as a partnership for federal income tax purposes. The taxation for state purposes varies from state to state.

Fringe Benefit Taxation. Generally a C corporation can deduct fully the cost of health insurance and other qualified fringe benefits for all shareholder-employees, and they do not have taxable income attributable to those economic benefits. If an LLC is taxed as a partnership for federal income tax purposes, rules similar to the rules for S corporation 2 percent shareholders apply to all of the members of the LLC, regardless of the amount of their capital or profits interest in the LLC (with respect to fringe benefits provided by the LLC). [Treas Reg § 1.707-1(c)] A partner, even one who receives guaranteed payments, is not considered an "employee" under the IRC's various tax-free employee benefits, including Code Section 79 (group term life insurance), Code Sections 105 and 106 (accident and health plans), and Code Section 119 (meals and lodging). In addition, members cannot participate in a cafeteria plan sponsored by the LLC. [Prop Treas Reg § 1.125-1, A-4]

Capitalization. The LLC's financing options are much more flexible than those of a corporation. LLCs can have as many different classes of equity interests to which the members agree, and can discriminate freely within each class of interests with regard to voting, distributions, etc. Moreover, distinctions in equity interest do not have to be recorded in the Articles or necessarily disclosed to third parties, and can change as often as the members agree. Corporations can only issue classes of stock authorized in the Articles of Incorporation, and cannot discriminate among the holders of the same class of stock. [Revised Model Business Corporation Act (RMBCA) §§ 6.01, 6.02(c)]

Many LLC statutes authorize the LLC to issue interests in exchange for a broad range of types of property, and many authorize the issuance of interest in exchange for promissory notes or services to be performed in the future. [Uniform Act § 401; Fla Stat § 608-4211; Wyo Stat § 17-15-115; Colo Rev Stat § 7-80-102(4)] On the other hand, **Delaware**, for example, prohibits a corporation from issuing stock in exchange for a promissory note or services already rendered. [See Del Code Ann tit 8, § 152; but see RMBCA § 6.21(b) (stock may be issued for any tangible or intangible property or benefit to the corporation).] Delaware allows an LLC to issue an interest in exchange for a promissory note or services rendered or promise to perform future services. [Del Code Ann tit 6, § 18-501]

Further, corporations generally must have "surplus" equity to distribute a dividend to shareholders, whereas LLC's can make distributions to members at anytime so long as the distribution does not render the LLC insolvent. [Del Code Ann tit 8, § 170]

Finally, distributions that render the corporation or LLC insolvent are prohibited. Generally, if a corporation makes improper distributions, the board of directors, not "innocent" shareholders, are liable to third parties. However, in an LLC, members are liable for the return of improper distributions, whether or not they knew the distribution was improper.

Management. Corporations, other than statutory close corporations, must have a board of directors, whereas most LLCs can be managed by members or by a designated manager or managers. [Uniform Act § 301] Only **Minnesota** requires a "Board of Governors" similar to a corporate board of directors. [Minn Stat Ann § 322B.606]

Transferability of Interests. Before the "check-the-box" rules for tax classification, to be classified as a partnership for tax purposes, an LLC had to have at least two partnership tax characteristics, one of which is lack of free transferability of ownership interests. LLCs usually restrict the transfer of interests in the company. Indeed, most LLC statutes provide that members must approve any transfer of an interest, or the admission of new members, in some cases by unanimous consent. [Uniform Act § 504(b)(2) (requires majority approval to transfer of a member's governance rights)]

Corporations are just the opposite. Corporate statutes, except those governing professional corporations, do not restrict the sale or transfer of corporate stock by shareholders in any way. In addition, the sale of stock by shareholders does not affect the corporation's tax status or create a taxable event for the corporation. Corporate shareholders may agree to restrict the transfer of their stock. In fact, the shareholders of an S corporation should enter into an agreement to restrict the sale of their stock in the S corporation to ensure that the S election is not violated by the sale of stock to a corporation or other unqualified shareholder.

Continuity of Life. Corporations are perpetual, and under no circumstance will the occurrence of any event to a shareholder necessarily by state law terminate the existence of the corporation. An LLC, on the other hand, sometimes dissolves by statute upon the death, dissolution (ULLCA amended in 1996, excluding dissolution), bankruptcy, or other statutorily prescribed event at the member level. [Uniform Act § 801] Many states, however, expressly permit perpetual duration including Delaware, Florida, and Texas [6 Del. Code S. 18-801(1); Fla. Stat. S. 608.407(1)(b); and Tex. Rev. Civ. Stat. Ann. tit. 32 art. 1528n, S. 3.02(a)(2).] Other LLC acts have been amended to eliminate member dissolution as a default dissolution event.

Q 1:18   What are the differences between an LLC and a general partnership?

Assuming that the LLC is taxed as a partnership for federal income tax purposes, LLCs and general partnerships are both taxed as partnerships for federal income tax purposes. The key differences are described below.

Formation. LLCs are formed by filing Articles of Organization or a similar document with the Secretary of State or similar official.

There are no state law filing requirements for any organizational document of general partnerships except for trade name filings or applications for tax or employer numbers. Partnerships can be formed either by written agreement, orally or by inference. A partnership can be formed irrespective of the intent of the individuals.

Evidence of partnership includes: provisions or agreements about the sharing of income; death and disability (voluntary and involuntary retirement); funding with insurance; continuity and dissolution; pay in and pay out of capital (e.g. valuation of work in progress, capital accounts, when and in what for capital is paid in); how new partners are admitted; ownership of files and other papers and allocation of responsibility for patients or clients, rights of partners to manage and vote; resolution of disputes; limitations on nonpartnership activities; leaves of absence; expenses to be paid; accounting method, fiscal year; and financial policies.

Liability. The principal advantage of an LLC over a general partnership concerns the liability of the owners for the debts and other obligations of the business entity. As a partner in a general partnership, each partner is subject to joint and several *personal* liability for all of the partnership's liabilities. [Uniform Partnership Act (UPA) § 15] An act of a partner that is not for the carrying on of the business of the partnership in the usual way does not bind the partnership unless authorized by other partners. [UPA S. 20] The Revised Uniform Partnership Act (RUPA), limits the harshness of joint and several liability slightly by making the partners only secondarily liable for the liabilities of the partnership after the assets of the partnership. [RUPA S. 306]

No member of the LLC is liable personally for the debts or obligations of the LLC other than those specifically guaranteed or assumed by the particular LLC member, unless the LLC veil of liability protection can be pierced. For example, failing to use the name of the entity in the conduct of LLC business by a member, in many states, may operate in effect as a representation by the member that they are personally responsible for such acts or contracts, even though the member was acting on the LLC's behalf.

Fiduciary Duties of Members. RUPA provides that: "A partner's duty of care to the partnership and the other partners in the conduct and winding up of the partnership's business is limited to refraining from engaging in grossly negligent or reckless conduct, intentional misconduct, or a knowing violation of the law." [RUPA § 404(c)] Due to the relatively short existence of LLCs, the fiduciary standards for their members are not as clearly defined. However, it can be expected that LLC members may have similar fiduciary standards, with the possibility that standards for LLC members will be more stringent because the LLC members, as a general rule, are exposed to less personal liability. [Ribstein and Keating on Limited Liability Companies, § 9.11]

Rights of Members' Creditors. Generally, a creditor of both an LLC member and a partner may receive a charging order against their interests. A creditor of a partner, however, may take the additional step of seeking judicial dissolution of the partnership in order to compel distributions to the partner of assets in which the partner has an interest. In contrast, a creditor of an LLC member may not seek the judicial remedy of compulsory dissolution of the LLC in order to obtain assets which would be distributed to the member in dissolution.

Management and Authority. Generally each partner in a general partnership is an agent of the partnership and has statutory authority to represent and act on behalf of the partnership, including the ability to execute contracts that bind the general partnership. [UPA § 9(1)]

The same general rule applies to the members of an LLC under most LLC statutes, when the LLC is member-managed, although not all LLC statutes are uniform or explicit on this point. [See Uniform Act § 301; Del Code Ann tit 6, § 18-402; but see, e.g., Md Stat § 4A-401(a)(3) (which allows the Articles to limit a member's agency authority)] **Minnesota**, for example, requires an LLC to have a board of governors (i.e., in effect, managers, and is a notable exception to this rule) [Minn Stat Ann § 322B.606], although members, by unanimous vote, may take actions required by the statute to be taken by the governors.

Most LLCs can be managed by the members in their individual capacity or by one or more designated managers. If a manager is designated, the LLC statutes often provide that only the named managers have agency authority and the power to bind the LLC to a contract, and no member has that prerogative. [Mo Rev Stat § 347.065.2] However, many LLC statutes authorize the grant of agency authority to members in manager-managed LLCs. [Uniform Act § 301(c); NY Cons Law ch 576, § 412(b)(1)]

State Taxation. The fact that an LLC is taxed as a partnership for federal income tax purposes does not ensure that the LLC will be taxed as a partnership for state income tax purposes. For example, a few states impose an entity-level income tax on the LLC, whereas other states specifically provide that all LLCs are treated as partnerships for state tax purposes (see appendix B).

A general partnership under federal tax law is always taxed as a partnership for state income tax purposes, although a particular state (e.g., **New York**) may subject a general partnership to an entity-level tax. [NY Tax Law ch 60, art 23, § 701]

Allocation of Income and Distributions. Unless otherwise agreed, the general rule for a partnership is that each partner shares equally in the profit, losses, and distributions of the partnership. [UPA § 18] Uniform Act Section 404 contains a similar rule. To the contrary, unless otherwise agreed, members in an LLC in many states share in those items in proportion to the value of their capital contributions to the LLC. [Colo Rev Stat § 7-80-503, 504; NY Cons Law ch 576, §§ 503, 504; Va Code § 13.1-1029]

Q 1:19   What are the differences between an LLC and a limited partnership (LP)?

LLCs and LPs are very similar. Both must be structured and operated carefully to ensure that they are taxed as partnerships for federal income tax purposes. However, there are several significant distinctions.

General Partner Liability. While a limited partnership is not subject to the tax code ownership restrictions of an S corporation, a limited partnership must have at least one general partner who or which is liable for all of the debts of the partnership. In contrast, all of the members of an LLC normally are protected from personal liability, as are limited partners.

Participation in Management. The participation of limited partners in the management of a limited partnership can result in a loss of limited liability protection for that limited partner. [Revised Uniform Limited Partnership Act (RULPA) § 303] No similar restriction exists on the ability of LLC members to participate in the management of the LLC. All LLC members can participate in the management and control of the LLC, as members or as managers. [Uniform Act § 301]

RULPA has been revised, and the revision adopted by several states allows greater participation by limited partners in the management of the limited partnership.

For example, the **Delaware** RULPA allows a limited partner to exercise any power authorized in the partnership agreement or other written agreement. [Del Code Ann tit 6, § 17-302] The **Georgia** version of RULPA is even more liberal; it flatly states that a limited partner does not lose limited liability as a result of participating in the management or control of the business. [Ga Code Ann § 14-9-303].

Nevertheless, LLCs provide greater control, limited liability to all members, and are simpler to form and maintain.

Tax Ruling. To obtain an IRS ruling that a limited partnership is to be taxed as a partnership for federal income tax purposes, the limited partnership must make a representation that the general partners satisfy the minimum interest test and minimum capital tests of Sections 4.01–4.04 of Revenue Procedure 89-12. [1989-1 CB 798] This representation is necessary to obtain a ruling that the limited partnership does not have the corporate characteristic of limited liability, as discussed in chapter 3. In many cases, this will be critical in obtaining an IRS ruling that the limited partnership is to be taxed as a partnership for federal income tax purposes.

To satisfy the minimum interest test, the general partners collectively must have at least a 1 percent interest "in each material item of partnership income, gain, loss, deduction, or credit . . . at all times during the existence of the partnership, and the partnership agreement must expressly so provide." The limited partnership does not violate this representation by temporary lapses in compliance and failures to comply due to conformance with Code Section 704(b) or 704(c). Revenue Procedure 89-12 reduces the minimum interest test for limited partnerships with total capital contributions exceeding $50 million.

Revenue Procedure 89-12 also provides that, the general partners taken together must maintain a minimum capital account balance equal to the lesser of: 1 percent of the total positive capital account balances of the limited partnership, or $500,000. A general partner does not have to satisfy this test, if the general partner renders or will render substantial services to the partnership in his, her, or its capacity as a general partner, apart from services for which they are compensated with Code Section 707(c) guaranteed payments.

Because an LLC by statute has the corporate characteristic of limited liability (as defined by the IRS), only in certain circumstances will any member of an LLC be required to represent that it has a minimum net worth or is entitled to a prescribed minimum allocation of the LLC's income (see chapter 3). [Rev Proc 95-10, 1995-3 IRB 20] Only in certain circumstances will any particular LLC member obtain a favorable ruling.

Q 1:20 What are the differences between an LLC and a limited liability partnership (LLP)?

One principal difference between an LLC and an LLP is the level of limited liability protection for the owners of the entity. Generally, except for their own torts and debts they personally guarantee, members of an LLC are not personally liable for the debts or obligations of the LLC or the torts of any other member of the LLC.

In contrast, the original LLP statutes only shield each partner from the LLP's liabilities for the tort liabilities (malpractice) of another partner in the LLP. Each LLP partner thus remains liable for his or her own malpractice and, in many states, the partner remains liable for the malpractice of people he or she directly controls or supervises, as well as the LLP's general debts, including trade payables, loans, lease obligations, and other contract liabilities. The newer statutes in many states provide limited liability beyond the mere misconduct-type actions of other partners. [1997 Delaware Laws ch 114 (SB 115), approved June 30, 1997]

An LLP is a general partnership under state law that files specified articles with the secretary of state, and the statutory scheme is not complex. Some states also allow a limited partnership to become an LLP, which is known as an LLLP (a limited liability limited partnership). On the other hand, an LLC is not a partnership for state law (nontax) purposes, but a legal form of organization with distinct and unique statutory provisions.

The LLP has been enacted in every state. The LLP may in some states have to reregister as a limited liability partnership each time a partner dies or the entity otherwise dissolves, even if it is reconstituted by the remaining partners. The LLP might be more expensive, since filing fees in many states are per partner, not per entity. (See chapter 11 and appendix C.)

Q 1:21   What are the advantages of an LLC over an S corporation?

The S corporation is a corporation under state law that has made an election to be taxed under Subchapter S. Code Section 1371 provides that S corporations remain subject to the provisions of Subchapter C, to the extent Subchapter S does not apply. However, except as discussed below, an S corporation is not subject to any federal entity level of tax; income passes through, and is included in the taxable income of, each shareholder. Thus, the S corporation, like the LLC, protects each owner from personal liability for the entity's debts under state law, and there is generally only one level of tax on the business's income.

The flow-through taxation scheme under Subchapter S, however, is not identical to the partnership scheme under Subchapter K. There are many differences in the flow-through taxation of S corporations and LLCs taxed as partnerships.

Formation. Code Section 351 allows shareholders to transfer appreciated assets to a corporation tax free, but only if those shareholders are part of a "control group" of shareholders who own 80 percent of the voting stock or value of the stock in the corporation immediately after the transfer. There is no similar control requirement for transfers of appreciated property to an LLC. Any member of an LLC may, at any time, transfer appreciated property to an LLC tax free. [IRC § 721]

In forming a corporation, Code Section 357 requires a shareholder to report taxable income to the extent that the corporation assumes the shareholder's liabilities in excess of the shareholder's tax basis in any assets contributed to the corporation. On the other hand, in the context of an LLC, because a member's basis in his or her LLC interest includes that member's share of the LLC's liabilities, the member can avoid any gain attributable to debt assumed by the LLC in excess of the member's tax basis in the property contributed. [IRC § 752]

An LLC may be easier to form under federal and state securities laws because LLC interests in an LLC without managers are generally not securities, whereas shares of stock are securities and must comply with applicable exemption or registration rules. (See chapter 9.)

> **Example.** Assume that Philip, a member who has a one-third share in the profits and losses of an LLC, contributes assets to the LLC with a basis of $100, and the LLC assumes a $150 debt of Philip. Assume the debt is recourse to all three of the members, and their share of the debt is not changed by its transfer to the LLC. Philip is treated as receiving a $150 distribution of cash due to the LLC's assumption of his debt. [IRC § 752(b)] A member must recognize gain to the extent an LLC distributes cash in excess of the member's basis in his or her interest. [IRC § 731(a)] Nevertheless, because the debt is recourse to all of the members, and Philip is entitled to one-third of the LLC's losses, one-third, or $50, of the debt is allocated to the basis of Philip. [Treas Reg § 1.752-2] Thus, Philip's basis in his interest is equal to $100 (basis of assets contributed) plus $50 (share of LLC's recourse debt); the deemed $150 distribution to him does not exceed his basis in the LLC. Thus, he does not recognize gain on the LLC's assumption of debt in excess of his basis in the assets contributed.

Termination of Status. While an LLC can rarely lose its status as a partnership for tax purposes, the S corporation can forfeit the S election, and concomitantly pass-through taxation, immediately upon an event that causes the corporation to no longer meet the statutory requirements. [IRC § 1362(d)(2)] This could happen merely by altering the form of distributions or ownership of the corporation. It could also happen if the S corporation was originally a C corporation and, after making the S election, has excess passive earnings. [IRC §§ 1361(b), 1362(d)(3)] However, the Small Business Job Protection Act of 1996 granted the IRS (1) the power to validate late elections if there was reasonable cause behind the late election and (2) the retroactive power to correct an invalid but timely election. [Pub L No. 104-188, 104th Cong, 2d Sess §§ 1301-1317 (Aug 20, 1996)]

Flexible Capital Structure. An LLC, as a tax partnership, can have a variety of equity interests. On the other hand, an S corporation has stringent qualification rules. An S corporation:

- May not have more than one class of stock (and hence no special allocations of income and loss), although it can have voting and nonvoting stock and certain executive compensation plans similar to equity interests.

- May not have more than 75 individuals or qualified trusts as shareholders. The Small Business Job Protection Act of 1996 increased the maximum number of shareholders from 35 to 75. However, under the previous limit, the IRS reversed an earlier ruling and decided that two or more S corporations can join in a partnership without jeopardizing the old 35-shareholder rule. [Pub L No 104-188, 104th Cong, 2d Sess §§ 1301-1317 (Aug 20, 1996); Rev Rul 94-43, 1994-2 CB 198]

- Under the Small Business Job Protection Act of 1996, may own as much as 100 percent of the stock of a C corporation. In this case, the S corporation, however, will not be able to join in the filing of a consolidated return. [Pub L No. 104-188, 104th Cong, 2d Sess §§ 1301-1317 (Aug 20, 1996); 69-JAN NY St BJ 54] As long as the dividends from an 80 percent owned C corporation are related to earnings and profits from an active trade or business operations, they will be excluded from the definition of "passive income." [IRC § 1362(d); 25 *J Taxn for Law* 140, 142]

An S corporation is now allowed to own 100 percent (but not less) of a "qualified subchapter S subsidiary," in which case the existence of the subsidiary, for income tax purposes, is ignored; all assets, liabilities, income, deductions, and credit of the subsidiary are treated as if they belonged to the parent. [IRC § 1361(b)(3); 25 *J Taxn for Law* 140, 142] The parent S corporation must elect to treat the 100 percent subsidiary as a qualified Subchapter S subsidiary.

None of the above restrictions applies to an LLC, although the above-described changes to S corporations are a great improvement over prior law.

Allocations. An LLC can specially allocate income, loss, deductions, and other tax items in any manner specified in the Operating Agreement and change the allocations, as long as the allocations have "substantial economic effect." [IRC § 704(b); Treas Reg § 1.704-1(b)(2) (discussed in chapter 7)] An S corporation must apportion the corporation's income and loss per share per day, and cannot specially allocate net income or loss or particular deductions or other items. [IRC § 1377(a)]

Contribution of Appreciated or Depreciated Property. The S corporation may have an advantage over an LLC when owners contribute appreciated or depreciated property to the corporation. When a member contributes appreciated or depreciated property to the LLC, the LLC must specially allocate the unrealized gain or loss (and associated depreciation) to adjust for the difference between the member's basis in the property contributed and the property's fair market value. [IRC § 704(c); Treas Reg § 1.704-3] In addition, the disguised-sale rules of Code Section 707(b) and new Code Section 737 may cause the contributing member to recognize any unrealized gain inherent in an item of contributed property under circumstances that are discussed in chapter 7. There are no similar provisions in Subchapter S.

Termination. Code Section 708 provides that an LLC, if taxed as a partnership (and not an association taxable as a corporation), terminates if 50 percent or more of the LLC's interests are transferred in any 12-month period. Under current regulations, the LLC is deemed to distribute the LLC's property, and the members are deemed to recontribute the property to a new LLC for tax purposes. Upon recontribution, the new LLC's basis in the property is equal to each remaining member's pretermination basis in his or her LLC interest, and not the basis the LLC had in the property before the termination. [IRC § 708(b)] However, under the proposed regulations, the order of these designations is reversed; the LLC is deemed to transfer its assets and liabilities to a new LLC in exchange for an interest in the new LLC. The old LLC is then deemed to have distributed interests in the new LLC to the purchasing members and to the other members in liquidation. Although the final result remains the same, the tax consequences are significant; the members need not be concerned about gain recognition, a change in the LLC's basis, or a new seven-year period under Sections 704(c)(1)(B) and 737. Further, the IRS has ruled that the conversion of an interest in a partnership into an interest in an LLC does not qualify as a transfer for purposes of Section 708(b)(1)(B). [See Rev Rul 95-37, 1995-1 CB 130; Rev Rul 95-55, 1995-2 CB 313. For an excellent discussion of this topic, see 24 *J Real Est Taxn* 115] There is no comparable provision in Subchapter S.

Inside Basis Step-Up to Reflect Gain on Liquidation. Code Section 734 allows an LLC to make an election under Code Section 754 to step up the basis of the LLC's property when a member recognizes gain on the redemption of his, her, or its interest. Thus, the LLC can amortize and deduct the cost to redeem a member; on the other hand, since there is no comparable provision in Subchapter S, S corporation shareholders obtain no tax advantages in connection with the redemption of a shareholder.

Inside Basis Step-Up to Reflect Gain on Sale of Interest. Code Section 743 allows an LLC to make a comparable election under Code Section 754 for a new member who purchases his or her interest from another member or receives the interest after the death of a member. Thus, the new member benefits from a step-up in the basis of the LLC's property equal to the new member's "outside" basis in his or her interest in the LLC. There is no comparable provision under Subchapter S. (Note: The Section 734/754 and Section 743/754 elections are irrevocable once made. Thus, once elected, there is a danger that the LLC (and later members) may suffer from a step-down in the LLC's basis in the LLC's property.)

"Hot" Assets. When a member sells all or part of his, her, or its interest, or receives a disproportionate distribution, the member must recognize ordinary income to the extent of the member's share of accounts receivable, depreciation recapture, and other Section 751, or "hot," assets. [IRC § 751(a), (b)] There is no comparable provision in Subchapter S.

Distribution of Property In-Kind. Generally, neither the LLC, if taxed as a partnership, nor members recognize gain on the distribution of appreciated property. [IRC § 731(b)] Code Section 704(c) is an exception to this rule. Code Section 704(c) requires a member to report taxable income upon the distribution of property that had appreciated at the time the property was contributed to the LLC by that member if the property is distributed to another member within seven years of contribution. The recognized gain or loss is computed as if the property were sold for the property's fair market value at the time of distribution. Similarly, Code Section 737 requires a member to recognize up to the amount of any precontribution gain if the LLC distributes property (other than money) to the member, other than property contributed by that member, within seven years from the date the member contributes appreciated property to the LLC.

In addition, LLC members do not recognize gain on the liquidation of the company, unless the LLC distributes cash to the members in excess of each member's basis in his or her interest. [IRC § 731(a)]

An S corporation recognizes gain, which is passed through to the shareholders, on any distribution of appreciated property, including distributions in liquidation. [IRC §§ 311(b), 336] Although the income flows through to the shareholders, Subchapter C applies and the repeal of the *General Utilities doctrine under Code Section* 311(b) causes this result. [IRC § 1371]

Basis in Liabilities. The LLC has significant tax advantages over an S corporation in the use of the entity's liabilities by the owners. A member's tax basis in the member's interest includes a share of the LLC's debt to a third party. [IRC § 752] Conversely, the shareholder of an S corporation is not entitled to any increase in his or her stock basis on the S corporation's debts. If the shareholder, however, directly loans money to the S corporation, the shareholder can use the basis in the debt to absorb the S corporation's losses against the shareholder's other income. [IRC § 1367] The S corporation shareholder is not entitled to basis for the corporation's debts guaranteed by the shareholder. [See Panel's *S Corporation Answer Book*; see, e.g., Perry v Commr, 47 TC 159 (1966), *affd* 392 F 2d 458 (8th Cir 1968)] An LLC member may or may not be entitled to additional basis for guaranteeing the LLC's debt. [Treas Reg § 1.752-2(e)]

Basis is very important in the context of pass-through taxation. For example, LLC members and S corporation shareholders can use the entity's losses against other income only to the extent of tax basis in their interests, shares, and direct loans. [IRC §§ 704(d), 1366(d)] (The use of losses may also be limited by the Section 469 passive activity loss rules and the Section 465 at-risk rules, discussed in chapter 7.) Further, members and S corporation shareholders can receive cash distributions from the entity tax free to the extent of their tax bases in their interests, stock, and direct loans. [IRC §§ 731, 1366]

Employment Taxes. Generally, if the LLC is involved in a "trade or business" under Code Section 1402, each member is subject to self-employment tax on his or her distributive share of the LLC's income. [IRC § 1402] Wages and guaranteed payments paid to a member, however, are not subject to FICA if the member is subject to self-employment tax. [Rev Rul 69-184, 1969-1 CB 216] However, as discussed further in chapter 7, certain LLC members may not be subject to self-employment tax on their distributive share if they would be considered limited partners under state law and if the LLC were a limited partnership instead of an LLC. [Prop Treas Reg § 1.1402(a)-18] Otherwise, those members who are involved in the management of the business will be treated as general partners for purposes of the self-employment tax. [Prop Treas Reg § 1.1402(a)-18]

S corporation shareholders are not subject to self-employment tax on dividend distributions from the S corporation, but wages paid by the S corporation to a shareholder/employee are subject to the customary payroll taxes, and the S corporation must pay the employer's share of those taxes.

Thus, the distinction between an S corporation and LLC in this regard may be significant. For example, S corporation employee/shareholders can avoid the impact of this change by reducing their salaries and receiving a corresponding amount of dividend income from the S corporation in the form of dividend distributions. Dividend income is not wages or self-employment income subject to FICA or self-employment tax. [IRC § 1402(a)(2)] This technique, however, should be pursued cautiously. The IRS may attempt to recharacterize such "dividend" distributions as compensation, and has been successful in its challenges in the past. [Panel's *S Corporation Answer Book;* Rev Rul 74-44, 1974-1 CB 287; Radke v Commr,

895 F 2d 1196 (7th Cir 1990); Spicer Accounting, Inc v Commr, 918 F 2d 80 (9th Cir 1990)] Thus, compensation and dividend planning is very important, and S corporation shareholder/employees must be careful when they reduce their compensation and replace it with cash dividends to avoid the impact of the Social Security Medicare taxes.

Deduction for Liquidating Payments. Before 1993, any partnership, including an LLC taxed as such, could redeem a retiring or withdrawing member's interest and deduct (or otherwise reduce other members' distributive shares of income) the amount of the liquidation payment to the withdrawing member in exchange for that member's interest in the partnership's goodwill and unrealized receivables. [IRC § 736(a)] But see the discussion of new Code Section 736(b)(3), in chapter 7 below, which may alter this conclusion, except for partnerships in which capital is not a material income-producing factor. Under no circumstances may an S corporation deduct any portion of the payment (or the direct related expenses) to redeem a shareholder. [IRC § 162(k)]

Q 1:22   What are the advantages of an S corporation over an LLC?

Although an LLC generally offers many advantages over an S corporation, an S corporation may be desirable when:

- The owners want to use Code Section 1244. Code Section 1244 allows the initial owners of "small corporation" stock to claim an ordinary loss on the disposition of that stock, if the stock is sold at a loss.
- The owners want to distribute the business' cash in the form of corporate dividends, which are not subject to self-employment tax.
- The owners want to merge tax free with another corporation.

Q 1:23   What are the advantages of a general or limited partnership (LP) over an LLC?

Both a general and limited partnership might have a state tax advantage over an LLC in a few states. For example, Texas does not have an income tax, but does impose a franchise tax on LLCs formed or qualified to do business in Texas. If this is a critical factor in the choice of entity or state or organization, techniques are available to address some of the deficiencies of a general or limited partnership vis-a-vis the LLC.

For example, to avoid general partner liability, the general partner in a limited partnership, or all partners in a general partnership, could be S corporations—in which case, flow-through taxation could be preserved and additional liability protection obtained. But as discussed above, there are significant differences in the flow-through taxation of S corporations and partnerships which should be considered before pursuing this option. In addition, limited partners generally do not have the right to participate in management of an LP. Further, with each S corporation partner, there are significantly more administrative costs, for example, tax and accounting costs.

The limited partnership has a couple of additional advantages over an LLC, depending on the circumstances. As a result, these factors may outweigh any perceived tax or other advantage of the LLC. First, because limited partnerships have been in existence for several decades, there is a wealth of case law addressing most aspects of the operations of the limited partnership and the provisions of the Uniform Limited Partnership Act (ULPA) and the Revised Uniform Limited Partnership Act (RULPA). Either or both of those Acts have been adopted to some extent in every state. Thus, there is less variance in the ULPA and RULPA statutes adopted by most states than there is among LLC statutes.

Second, a term-of-years limited partnership may offer greater valuation discounts under state law, at least in states where an LLC member may withdraw as a matter of right under state law. This can be very significant for gift and estate tax purposes (see chapters 10 and 13).

Q 1:24   What are the advantages of an LLP over an LLC?

There are very few advantages of an LLP over an LLC. One advantage is the flexible nature of an LLP. Generally, an LLP is not a new entity but rather a partnership that files an election to be recognized in those states that have adopted the LLP. Thus, the same general partnership could be a general partnership in those states without LLP statutes and an LLP where recognized. An LLC is a separate entity for state law and state and federal tax purposes.

As discussed in detail in chapter 11, professional LLCs cannot qualify to do business in many states due to state professional credentialing restrictions for specific professions. In these situations, an LLP may be preferable.

Secondly, **Texas**, for example, imposes a franchise tax on LLCs, but does not impose a franchise tax on LLPs. The implication of this difference is discussed further in chapter 11, but could be a significant unnecessary cost.

Nevertheless, if a business can be conducted either as an LLC or LLP, and there is no significant state specific tax difference, a business should almost always be formed as an LLC rather than an LLP. But the use of a single entity for a professional multi-state practice has unique problems and limitations.

Q 1:25   When would it not be prudent to use an LLC?

LLCs are well-suited for entrepreneurial businesses with a small number of active investors. All members can enjoy limited liability protection while participating in the business. An LLC is also useful for family businesses that want to maintain control within the family, obtain the liability protection and tax benefits of a limited partnership, and restrict the transfer of voting rights outside the family.

Nevertheless, the state tax treatment of LLCs in states where the LLC proposes to do business should be considered, given the fact that a few states impose franchise or other taxes on LLCs (see appendix B).

Texas does not have an income tax, but does impose a franchise tax on LLCs formed or qualified to do business in Texas. The tax is equal to the greater of 0.25 percent of the LLC's taxable capital allocated to Texas, or 4.5 percent of the LLC's earned surplus allocable to Texas. [Tex Tax Code Ann § 171.001(d)(2)(A)] Capital for these purposes is the LLC's net assets, and earned surplus is based on the LLC's federal taxable income. [Tex Tax Code Ann § 171.002] Capital and earned surplus are apportioned to Texas based on the LLC's percentage of gross receipts attributable to Texas.

Florida, on the other hand, has amended its corporate income tax code to conform its treatment of LLCs to the treatment provided under federal tax law. Effective July 1, 1998, Florida joins the federal government and most other states by providing that an LLC formed under Florida law or qualified to do business in Florida as a foreign LLC is no longer subject to the state's corporate income tax if the LLC is classified as a partnership for federal income tax purposes. [Fla. Stat. ch. 608.505]

Although an LLC is no longer subject to Florida's state income tax, it nevertheless may cause the owners of an interest in an LLC to be subject to a Florida intangible tax. A nonresident is not subject to the tax. However, the problem arises when a Florida resident transfers real estate, which is exempt from the tax, to an FLP or an LLC. The FLP interest will be exempt from the tax for Florida residents with only publicly traded partnership interests being subject to the intangible tax on the individual's return. In contrast, the ownership interest in an LLC does not enjoy the same exemption. However, if all the entity owns is real estate, liability at the entity level won't cause a problem because realty assets are tax exempt. If, however, the entity owns taxable assets, various strategies could be advanced to protect the entity from being subject to the tax. For example, options include (1) the use of a non-Florida resident as a general partner, or (2) transfer the assets to a non-Florida irrevocable trust for a very short duration at the end of the calendar year.

In addition, an LLC, unless taxed as a corporation, cannot utilize an employee stock ownership plan or ESOP because ESOPs can only be established by corporations. [IRC § 409 (l)]

Q 1:26   When should an LLC be used over another form of business?

While the LLC is a good choice of entity for almost any type or form of business venture, the LLC is best suited for real estate investments, passive investments, or joint ventures between existing businesses, when:

1. There are not many investors;
2. Flow-through tax treatment is desirable;
3. Limited liability for investors is desired;
4. Fringe benefits for the owners who are also employees are not a material consideration; and
5. Management is to be performed by the owners or their elected representatives.

LLCs are often an excellent form of business organization for certain joint ventures and for medical services organizations, such as independent physician associations (IPAs), physician-hospital organizations (PHOs), management service organizations (MSOs), and other ventures being formed by medical service providers to strengthen their competitiveness in the managed care market, while maintaining independent practices. However, if nonprofit or charitable status is desired, the use of a not-for-profit corporation or trust may be preferable, because the LLC may not clearly be able to be formed on a not-for-profit basis under state law.

Q 1:27 Can professionals use an LLC?

While there may be a question in some states, many specifically have published authorization for professionals to use LLCs. [See, e.g., Kan Atty Gen Op No 92-23 (1992); NY Cons Law ch 576, § 1203(e)] California and Rhode Island prohibit the practice of professions through an LLC. [RI Gen Laws § 17-16-3] The California statute does not explicitly prohibit use of LLCs for the conduct of a professional service, but has reserved chapter 9 in the statute for future adoption of professional service LLCs (see chapter 12, below), and the California Secretary of State will not register professional service LLCs. Similarly, the Illinois LLC statute does not prohibit the practice of law through an LLC. (See chapter 12 for a detailed discussion of the use of the LLC by professionals.)

Choosing the "Right" Business Form: Existing Businesses

Q 1:28 Should all businesses convert to an LLC if it is the best entity?

No. Just because an LLC has advantages does not mean that under all circumstances it will be preferred to an S corporation or other entity. Moreover, converting a corporation to an LLC is usually not tax free. It is tested as a liquidation of the corporation. [Rev Rul 68-349, 1968-2 CB 143] If a future tax-free reorganization is desired, an LLC may be undesirable. Acquisition of an S corporation may qualify as a tax-free reorganization because only corporations may qualify. An acquisition of an LLC may not qualify as a tax-free reorganization. [See IRC § 368, which offers this treatment solely to corporations] In addition, an LLC cannot establish a tax-qualified employee stock ownership plan. Only a corporation can do so. [IRC § 409(l)]

Q 1:29   When should an entity convert to an LLC?

First, if it is the best form, and an existing corporation's net assets are not worth more than the shareholders' basis, there will be no tax and there could be a tax loss (an advantage to the owners) upon liquidation. Second, the limited liability of all members is an obvious advantage of an LLC over a general partnership.

The case of *Stoney Run Company v. Prudential-LMI Commercial Ins. Co.* [47 F 3d 34 (2d Cir 1995)] illustrates the value of a limited liability entity when the owners have substantial general liability insurance—even when the property they own is financed with nonrecourse debt. *Stoney Run* was a partnership that owned an apartment project in which several tenants were killed or injured by carbon monoxide resulting from a faulty heating and ventilation system. Suits were filed against the partnership and managing agent alleging negligent maintenance of the system. The insurer that issued the general liability insurance policy denied coverage on the basis of a standard pollution clause in the policy. While the result was favorable to the owners, an LLC would have insulated them individually had there been partnership liability.

Another situation in which the LLC provides an advantage over a general partnership is when the parties desire to preclude any one member from subjecting the entity to bankruptcy proceedings. Under the Bankruptcy Code, while unanimous consent of the general partners is required to file a voluntary petition on behalf of the partnership, it appears that any member has the power, even if he or she has agreed not to do so, to file an involuntary petition against the partnership. By contrast, shareholders who are not also creditors cannot file an involuntary petition against a corporation. The Bankruptcy Code does not refer to an LLC, but an LLC may come within the definition of "corporation." [11 USC § 101(9)]

Although an LLC has a number of advantages over a general partnership, at least in states that do not have a New York-type Registered LLP (RLLP) statute, a number of other factors appear to have influenced professional practice firms to remain general partnerships or to become RLLPs instead of LLCs. Among those factors are the following:

1. Easier regulatory and licensing compliance, particularly in the case of multistate practices;

2. Avoidance of revisiting existing partnership agreements;

3. Avoidance of compliance with securities law in some states;

4. Avoidance of employment discrimination and age discrimination laws that are not applicable to partnerships but may be applicable to LLCs;

5. Avoidance of entity-level taxes in some states; and

6. Availability of the favorable income tax rule under Code Section 736(b) for liquidation payments.

In the case of the conversion of a partnership, the general partners who become members on conversion will remain liable for preconversion partnership obligations. [For example, see, NY LLC Act § 1006(h)] Even if the act does not expressly provide, the result will be the same. [UPA § 36(i); Statewide Realty Co v Fidelity Management and Research Co, Inc, 611 A 2d 158 (NJ Sup Ct 1992)] A crucial question will be whether a particular obligation "arose" before or after the conversion. [For example, see, Citizens Bank of Mass v Parham-Woodman Medical Assn, 874 F Supp 705 (ED Va 1995) (the obligation under the loan documents arose when the loan documents were signed, not when the loan disbursements were made); Conklin Farm v Leibowitz, 140 NJ 417, 658 A 2d 1257 (1955)]

Q 1:30 Are there potential state tax disadvantages of the conversion itself?

Yes. The application of real estate transfer taxes on conversion will be a problem in some states. If conversion is effected pursuant to a statutory conversion provision, like New York's, in which title "remains vested in" the converted entity, the transfer taxes may not be applicable. [Schorr, *New York*, Limited Liability Companies & Partnerships, § 10:07(b) n1 (1994)] The New York City Department of Finance has ruled that a deed conveying real property to an LLC in which the parties conveying the property will have the same proportionate interest will be exempt from the

New York City real property transfer tax on the ground that it effects a mere change of identity or form of ownership or organization. [FLR 94-4391 (Dec 9, 1994)] A contrary position in the District of Columbia, which has a comparable conversion provision, has been reversed by a 1995 amendment to D.C. Code Section 29-1313.

However, in some states, even without a statutory conversion provision, the conversion of a partnership to an LLC without a change in the owners or their relative interests, when the conveyance of real property from the partnership to the LLC is involved, may nevertheless be exempt from the state and local documentary tax on deeds. [For example, see SC Dept of Revenue 95-9 (1995); Conn Dept of Revenue Servs PS 93(5.1) (May 19, 1995)]

The application of sales or use tax on the transfer of personal property should also be considered. In some states, the "occasional sale" exception may be available. A few states have expressly addressed the subject. [See, for example, Wis Dept of Revenue Pub No 119 VII D (Jan 1995) (no tax applicable if there is no change in ownership interests of members)] However, in some states an assumption of liabilities by the LLC upon a transfer of assets to an LLC may result in sales tax liability. [Lipmann, "State Tax Considerations of Conducting Business Through Alternative Entities," *State Tax Notes* 203-209 (July 17, 1995)]

In addition, as discussed previously, the tax consequences when converting from a corporation to an LLC (if allowed by state law) can be disastrous because it is treated as a corporate liquidation. [For a thorough discussion of the tax repercussions of such a move, see 25 *J Taxn for Law* 81]

Q 1:31 Can fiduciaries who are concerned about their liability benefit from an LLC?

Yes, in some states. Delaware and Georgia expressly authorize the parties to restrict those duties. [Del Code § 18-1101(c); Ga Code § 14-11-305(4)(A)] Even in states that do not authorize agreements limiting fiduciary duties, the parties should be free in LLCs, as they are in partnerships, to authorize the members to compete with the LLC and to engage in independent ventures without the constraints of the "corporate opportunity" doctrine.

Chapter 2

Formation

An LLC, like a corporation, limited partnership (LP), or limited liability partnership (LLP), has formal procedures that under state law must be followed. The statutory requirements vary among the states, and many of the LLC state statutes currently in force are not identical and, in fact, have significantly disparate provisions. The LLC is a separate legal entity, like a corporation or an LP. This chapter describes some of the major differences among the various LLC statutes currently in effect, and why it may be desirable to "shop around" and form the LLC in one state rather than another. This chapter also examines formation procedures in general, and discusses how to prepare the necessary documents, including the Articles and Operating Agreement.

Comparing LLC Acts and Statutes

Q 2:1   In what state should the LLC be organized?

The state where the LLC should be formed depends upon many factors. If the LLC will have a small number of investors and be operated in only one state, the LLC generally should be formed in that state in order to minimize the number of annual reports and filing fees required each year.

Although in many cases the LLC's business will be conducted in the same state where the LLC's members reside, sometimes that will not be the case. For example, if the LLC is being formed to hold real estate located solely in one state, the LLC probably should be formed in that state regardless of where the members reside. In any event, the local LLC statute and tax statutes should be reviewed carefully before forming the entity.

If the LLC will conduct business in several states or have a significant number of investors, the members may want to consider reviewing the LLC statutes of several states to determine which statute has the most desirable provisions. For example, the organizers may want to consider the following statutory provisions:

Management. Are there significant differences in the management or voting provisions of the statutes reviewed? For example, the extent to which the statute authorizes the LLC to indemnify managers for acts in their capacity as a manager should be considered, as well as limits on members' ability to act on behalf of the LLC. [See Uniform Act § 301; Prototype Act §§ 301, 404]

Withdrawal Rights. Do the various statutes allow members to withdraw from the LLC, and what are the consequences of withdrawal? Generally, the ability to limit the withdrawal of members is desirable from the LLC's and the owners' perspective. More important, what are the members' rights upon a withdrawal?

For example, the **Kansas** statute allows a member to withdraw, but that member's rights after a withdrawal, that is, the right to withdraw his or her capital or share of the LLC's value, is limited. [Kan Stat Ann § 17-7616]

In **Missouri**, Missouri Revised Statutes Section 347.121 allows a member to withdraw at any time upon 90 days prior written notice. The power to withdraw may be limited by the Operating Agreement, but each member always has the statutory right to withdraw; withdrawal, however, might be a breach of contract, that is, a breach of the Operating Agreement. In that event, the LLC may recover damages from the withdrawing member, and offset those damages against any distribution due to the withdrawing member. Nevertheless, if the LLC is continued after a withdrawal event by a member, and the Operating Agreement does not establish an amount or method for liquidating the withdrawn member's interest, Missouri Revised Statutes Section 347.103.2 requires the LLC to distribute to the withdrawn member their "fair value" as of the date of the withdrawal, based upon the withdrawing member's share of distributions.

If the withdrawal violates the Operating Agreement, Missouri Revised Statutes Section 347.103.2 protects the LLC by: (1) excluding from the fair value of the interest for this purpose any goodwill, and (2) allowing the LLC to reduce the value of the interest, by the amount of any damages suffered by the LLC or the LLC's members as a result of the breach of the Operating Agreement. This statute also allows the LLC to defer the necessary distributions, as may be approved by a court, to prevent the withdrawal from imposing an unreasonable hardship on the LLC.

Q 2:2   What are some of the other major differences among the various state LLC statutes?

Until the IRS issued the "check-the-box" regulations, practitioners previously classified LLC statutes in general as either "bulletproof" or "flexible," depending upon how the statute addressed the IRS's four corporate characteristics: (1) continuity of life, (2) free transferability of interests, (3) centralized management, and (4) limited liability. To be taxed as a partnership for federal income tax purposes, an LLC would be classified as a partnership only if it did not have more than two of the four corporate characteristics listed above. However, under the IRS "check-the-box" regulations, a LLC may freely select its own tax classification. Thus, the LLC may be taxed as a partnership or as a corporation as the situation requires.

Q 2:3   What was a "bulletproof" statute?

Before the IRS "check-the-box" tax classification procedure, bulletproof state statutes were enacted to ensure partnership tax status because they could not have either continuity of life or free transferability of interests. The statutes are bulletproof because the members cannot modify the statutory norm in the Articles or Operating Agreement or otherwise. (Colorado, Nevada, Virginia, and Wyoming statutes were originally bulletproof, although they all then modified their statutes to be "flexible.") Thus, LLCs that were formed in those "bulletproof" states, that comply with state law, were, for federal tax purposes, partnerships and could be classified by the IRS as associations taxable as C corporations. The cost for this protection, however, was the inelastic nature of the statutes. With the effectiveness of the "check-the-box" regulations, the utility of a bulletproof statute has disappeared. All new LLCs are now taxed as a sole proprietorship or partnership unless they elect to be taxed as a corporation.

Q 2:4   How do you determine if an LLC statute is bulletproof?

To determine if an LLC statute is bulletproof, examine the provisions that address dissolution and the transferability of interests to new members. If the statutory provisions require the unanimous consent of the (remaining) members to continue the business of the LLC after a dissolution event or to admit a new member, *and* the statutory provisions do not allow the members to alter those requirements in the Articles or Operating Agreement or otherwise, the statute is bulletproof.

The **Wyoming** statute was an example of a bulletproof statute, with the following provisions:

> Wisconsin Statutes Section 17-15-122. Interest in Company; Transferability of Interest.
>
> The interest of all members in a limited liability company constitutes the personal estate of the member, and may be transferred or assigned as provided in the operating agreement. However, if *all* of the other members of the limited liability company other than the member proposing to dispose

of his or its interest do not approve of the proposed transfer or assignment by *unanimous* written consent, the transferee of the member's interest shall have no right to participate in the management of the business and affairs of the limited liability company or to become a member. The transferee shall only be entitled to receive the share of profits or other compensation by way of income and the return of contributions, to which that member would otherwise be entitled. [emphasis supplied]

Wisconsin Statutes Section 17-15-123. Dissolution.

(a) A limited liability company organized under this chapter shall be dissolved upon the occurrence of any of the following events:

    (i) When the period fixed for the duration of the limited liability company shall expire;

    (ii) By the unanimous written agreement of all members; or

    (iii) Upon the death, retirement, resignation, expulsion, bankruptcy, dissolution of a member or occurrence of any other event which terminates the continued membership of a member in the limited liability company, unless the business of the limited liability company is continued by the consent of *all* the remaining members under a right to do so stated in the articles of organization of the limited liability company. [emphasis supplied]

(The Wyoming Statute was amended to be flexible as of July 1995.)

Q 2:5   What was a flexible LLC statute?

Flexible statutes allow the members to alter those dissolution and transferability provisions by agreement. Before "check-the-box," however, LLCs organized under flexible statutes could fail to be classified as partnerships. [See, for example, Rev Rul 93-38, 1993-1 CB 233 (Delaware); Rev Rul 93-49, 1993-2 CB 308 (Illinois); Rev Rul 93-50, 1993-2 CB 310 (West Virginia); Rev Rul 93-53, 1993-2 CB 312 (Florida)]

Q 2:6 Are the LLC acts similar to the Revised Uniform Limited Partnership Act (RULPA) and the Uniform Partnership Act (UPA)?

Yes, at least to a certain extent. Limited liability companies are hybrid entities, containing features both of business corporations and partnerships, many LLC statutes are modeled after RULPA, the UPA, or the state's own business corporation act. RULPA has been enacted in 48 states, and the UPA has been enacted in 49 states. In addition, a number of states have enacted a version of the Model Business Corporation Act. Thus, although there is little legal precedent specifically considering the provisions of LLC statutes, there is a significant number of court cases interpreting provisions of RULPA, the UPA, and state corporate statutes, which may be considered and applied by analogy in cases involving an LLC.

Q 2:7 Is there a uniform LLC act?

Yes. The uniform act is the Uniform Limited Liability Company Act (ULLCA), drafted by the National Conference of Commissioners on Uniform State Law. The initial draft of the ULLCA was approved in December 1994, but continues to be revised. [See Reynolds and Frost, "ULLCA Approved, But Revisions Continue," *J of Limited Liability Companies 184* (Spring 1995)] By 1996, **Hawaii, South Carolina, Vermont,** and **West Virginia** had adopted versions of the ULLCA. **Illinois** adopted its version based on the ULLCA in 1997.

Q 2:8 What is the Prototype LLC Act?

The Prototype Limited Liability Company Act (Prototype LLC Act) is a model LLC statute that has been prepared and adopted by the Working Group on the Prototype Limited Liability Company Act, Subcommittee on Limited Liability Companies, Committee on Partnerships and Unincorporated Business Organizations, Section of Business Law, American Bar Association. [Nov 19, 1992] Like the ULLCA, no state has adopted the Prototype LLC Act verbatim. However, several statutes, such as the **Missouri** LLC Act, are based in part on the Prototype Act.

Forming the LLC

Q 2:9 What do the owners of an LLC need to do in preparing for the formation of their LLC?

The formalities and tasks here are essentially the same as for a corporation.

The organizers of the LLC generally should hire a knowledgeable tax and business law attorney to assist in the formation of the LLC, specifically to prepare Articles of Organization and an Operating Agreement, to ensure that the LLC will accomplish the desired results. Because the LLC is a separate legal "person" the lawyer and organizers will need to prepare the necessary transfer documents to transfer the property that will be contributed to the capital of the LLC. Once the Articles are filed with the state, the members will need to:

- Obtain a new federal and state tax employer identification number;
- File workers' compensation and other employment related filings with the relevant states;
- Register with the state for the collection of sales tax, if applicable;
- Establish payroll procedures for employees and the payment of employment and trust fund taxes;
- Obtain insurance (e.g., property and casualty, business interruption, professional liability, workers' compensation, etc.); and
- Obtain necessary federal, state, and local licenses required, if any, for the business to be conducted.
- Open a bank account in the name of the LLC.
- File a "check-the-box" election if the LLC is to be taxed as a corporation.

Q 2:10 How do you form an LLC?

An LLC is formed by preparing and filing Articles of Organization, containing specific required information and perhaps optional information, signed by either an organizing member or other organizer. The signatures must be notarized, and the Articles are filed with the Secretary of State, or similar official, of the state in which the company is being formed. [Uniform Act §§ 202, 204; Prototype Act §§ 202, 204]

Q 2:11 What information must be included in the Articles of Organization?

While each state's law must be reviewed, most LLC acts require that the LLC Articles contain at least the following information:

Name of the Entity. The Articles must set forth the name of the LLC. The name must not be too similar to the name of any other LLC, corporation, limited partnership, or LLP registered with the Secretary of State of the state of organization. Many states have procedures for reserving names in advance of filing Articles of Organization and, in any event, a name should be at least cleared as available with the relevant Secretary of State before filing the Articles. [Uniform Act § 202(a)(1); Prototype Act § 202(A)]

With the caveats discussed above, the name of an LLC can be almost anything. Under most LLC Acts the name must include the words "limited company," or "limited liability company," or the abbreviation "L.C.," "L.L.C.," or, in some states, Ltd. [Uniform Act § 106; Prototype Act § 103(A); but see Mo Rev Stat § 347.020(2), which prohibits the use of "Ltd."] Generally the name cannot include the words "association," "corporation," "incorporated," "limited partnership," or "L.P." In addition, the name cannot include any words or abbreviation implying that the LLC is organized for any purpose not stated in the Articles or that the LLC is a governmental agency. [For example, see, Mo Rev Stat § 347.020.(2)]

Purpose. The Articles should state the LLC's purpose for organization. This may be specific or general, such as "Organized for the transaction of any or all lawful business for which a limited liability company may be organized under the laws of this state." [For example, see, Mo Rev Stat § 347.039.1 (2); Ala Code Ann § 10-12-10-(a)(3); neither the Uniform Act nor the Prototype Act require "purpose" to be included in the Articles]

State statutes typically provide that LLCs may engage in any lawful business or purpose while others permit the LLC to conduct activities that are lawful for other business entities. The trend is to permit LLCs to conduct any lawful business or activity. [See ULLCA § 112(a); Cal Corp Code § 17002; NY Partnership Law ch 34 § 201]

If the particular statute permits any lawful purpose, then the LLC should be allowed to engage in non-profit activities. However, some states add special limitations that says if the state's statutes contain special provisions for the formation of a designated type of corporation then an LLC can not be formed for the purpose for which the designated corporation may be formed. [For example, see, Ohio Rev Code § 1705.02] A similar result should follow if the LLC is allowed to engage in any lawful business although it is not definite on its face. [Ribstein and Keatinge on Limited Liability Companies § 4.10]

While these statutes seemingly provide LLCs a license to engage in a broad array of activities on their face, a careful practitioner should also inquire into constitutional and regulatory limits and their corresponding judicial interpretations in the state where LLC operation is desired. In **Oklahoma**, for instance, LLCs are permitted to "conduct business in any state for any lawful purpose, except the business of banking and insurance." Despite this broad language, an **Oklahoma** court ruled that an LLC could not receive a license to sell alcoholic beverages because the state constitution forbade "corporations, business trusts, and secret partnerships" from selling alcohol. Partnerships were permitted to obtain alcohol licenses, but the Court found that an LLC was not a partnership. [Meyer v Oklahoma Alcoholic Beverage Laws Enforcement Commission, 890 P2d 1361 (Okla Ct App 1995)] Note that if the **Oklahoma** statute permitted LLCs to engage in any activities lawful for partnerships a different result might have been warranted.

Registered Agent. The Articles must name a registered agent for the LLC in the state of formation, and must provide the registered agent's address, including street and number (in many cases a P.O. box is not acceptable). [Uniform Act § 202(a)(2); Prototype Act § 202(B)]

Duration. The Articles must, in many states, set a specific date on which the LLC will dissolve. It is acceptable in most states to provide a period of duration, for example, "sixty (60) years from the date this LLC is organized," instead of specifying a specific date for dissolution. [For example, see, Ala Code Ann § 10-12-10(a)(2) (which also authorizes perpetual existence)] Some states, however, require a specific date, for example, August 31, 2050. The emerging trend, however, is that duration need not be disclosed unless it is other than perpetual.

Management. In all states (other than Minnesota) the LLC can be managed by the LLC's members, or the members can designate managers. In most states, the Articles must set forth a statement that the LLC is to be managed by managers (if that is the case), otherwise the LLC will be deemed to be member-managed. [Uniform Act § 202(a)(5); Prototype Act § 202(A)] Alternatively, in a few states, unless the Articles state the LLC is member-managed, the LLC is deemed to be manager-managed.

To be clear, the Articles should always designate whether the LLC is member-managed or manager-managed.

Minnesota requires the LLC to be managed by a board of governors. Members may modify the powers and procedures for the Board of Governors in the Articles. [Minn Stat Ann §§ 322B.606, 322B.115] Delaware has a provision allowing the Articles to contain a limit on the presumption that managers are agents by virtue of being managers.

Continuation After an Event of Withdrawal. In some states, LLCs will dissolve upon the occurrence of certain "withdrawal" or "dissolution" events (e.g., death, dissolution, or bankruptcy of any member). The Articles should provide whether the remaining members have the right to continue the business of the LLC after such a withdrawal event, and under what conditions. Some state LLC acts require the remaining members to agree unanimously to continue the business of the LLC after a withdrawal event.

Most states, however, do not consider a withdrawal of a member a dissolution event and permit the LLC to continue its business without an affirmative agreement by the remaining members, unless the Articles or Operating Agreement otherwise provide.

Planning Pointer. A dissolution event may give members an option to get out of the business by not consenting to its continuance. If there are only a few members, and there is not a reasonable expectation that the LLC will ever have more than a few members, unanimous consent to continue the business after a dissolution event may be acceptable. If, however, there is a large number of members, the Articles probably should reduce the number of members whose consent is necessary to continue the business of the LLC. Otherwise, one member could hold the other members hostage, and force them to reorganize the LLC into a new LLC, which will not only cause significant administrative costs, but could have significant tax implications and costs (see chapter 7).

The *purpose* of the LLC is also relevant in analyzing a dissolution event. If the LLC is holding an investment for a small number of members, unanimous consent to continue the LLC after a dissolution event may be preferable, to allow members to withdraw their capital interest from the LLC's assets. If, however, the LLC is conducting a significant manufacturing or service business for the public, a lesser vote would be preferable, to help ensure that the business of the company will be continued.

Organizer. The Articles generally must identify the name (and sometimes the address) of each organizer and be signed by those organizers. [Uniform Act § 202(a)(3)] The organizer need not be a member or a manager in most states; in which case the buyer or anyone else can sign the Articles as the organizer. [Prototype Act §§ 201, 204(a)(3), 204(A)(3)]

Notary. The Articles should be notarized before filing. (Neither the Uniform Act nor the Prototype Act requires notarization. Generally, state securities offices require notarization of all documents filed.)

Other. The categories of information listed above are required in most states. Many states require that additional information be included in the Articles, much of which generally should be included in the Articles in any event.

Q 2:12   What additional information should be in the Articles?

Limited Liability. The Articles should contain a statement that the liability of the members is limited to their capital contributions.

Additional Members. The Articles should address the consent required to admit additional members to the LLC. States with bulletproof statutes, and many other states, require the unanimous consent of the members to admit an additional member. However, the preferable statutes allow the members to provide for a lesser vote by agreement. [Uniform Act § 504(b)(2); Prototype Act §§ 706(A), 801(A)(2); see also, e.g., Del Code Ann tit 6, § 18-30;

Mo Rev Stat § 347.113.2] When authorized by law, the Articles should state the consent required to admit additional members.

The vote required should be at least a majority in interest of the members other than the member, if any, proposing to transfer his, her, or its interest to another nonmember. "Majority in interest" is an IRS term defined in Revenue Procedure 94-46 [1994-28 IRB 129] and is critical in classifying the LLC as a partnership for tax purposes (see chapter 3).

Capital Contributions. The **Wyoming** LLC Act (one of the first LLC statutes enacted), for example, requires the organizer to disclose in the Articles the total amount of cash and the agreed value of property other than cash contributed in the initial formation of the company. [Wis Stat § 17-15-107] The Wyoming Act also requires the Articles to set forth any additional contributions the members have agreed to make, and the time or events upon the occurrence of which the additional capital will be contributed. [Wis Stat § 17-15-107]

While this is not required everywhere, the Articles should state that the contributions to the LLC will be based upon the agreement of the members as reflected in the Operating Agreement or otherwise. However, because the Articles are a public document, and anyone has the right to inspect them, the amount of, or forms of, contributions should not be included in the Articles unless required by statute.

Voting. LLC statutes are flexible in this regard, and generally the members can allocate voting rights, and those specified LLC actions requiring a vote, by agreement. However, the **Kansas** LLC Act, for example, states that each member has one vote unless otherwise provided in the Articles. [Kan Stat Ann 17-7612] Unless the LLC will always have equal members, it would be prudent to provide in the Articles that each member's voting rights are in proportion to their capital interest in the company. Otherwise, even if the members intend to maintain equal capital account balances, if an imbalance ever occurs, a member with less of an economic interest may have equal management control. For example, with one member/one vote, a 10 percent member would have an equal vote with a 50 percent member, which rarely would be acceptable. Moreover, this could affect the ability to discount the value of a member's interest for estate tax or other purposes (see chapter 10).

The voting provision may also set forth the affirmative vote of the members necessary to amend the Articles.

Other. The members may put any other provision in the Articles they want about the governance of the company, so long as the provision is not inconsistent with the law. Unusual items that members may want to add to the Articles include, for example, special classes of membership interests and special voting or management rights of specified members, depending upon the "deal" among the parties.

Care should be taken in adding optional provisions to the Articles, because of the formality and other requirements that must be followed to amend the Articles (Qs 2:13 and 2:14).

Q 2:13   When are the members required to amend the Articles?

Members must amend the Articles when the provisions of the current Articles are no longer consistent with the operation of the company. **Missouri**, for example, requires the members of an LLC to amend the Articles promptly (within 60 days) after a change in operations that is inconsistent with the Articles. [Uniform Act § 203(b); Mo Rev Stat § 347.041.2] For example, if the Articles state the LLC is managed by the members, and the members elect a manager, the Articles must be amended to reflect that change.

Although technically a change in the Articles, members are also required to file a form with the Secretary of State or similar official of each state where the LLC is registered upon a change in the name or address of the registered agent for the LLC in that state. This is generally done by completing a form provided by the relevant public office.

Q 2:14   How do the members amend the Articles?

To amend the Articles, LLCs must file "articles of amendment" with the Secretary of State of the state in which the LLC is organized. The articles of amendment should contain:

1. The name of the LLC;
2. The date the original Articles of Organization were filed; and
3. The statement of the amendment to the Articles.

[Uniform Act § 203; Prototype Act § 203]

Some states require a statement in the articles of amendment that the amendment has been approved by the members and managers as required by the LLC's Operating Agreement, unless the amendment is required by law (e.g., upon a change in the registered agent). [Mo Rev Stat § 347.041.1(5)]

Q 2:15   Who must sign the Articles of Organization, articles of amendment, and other filings with the applicable Secretary of State?

The acts generally provide that Articles of Organization may be signed by any person, whether or not a member, as organizer. [E.g., Mo Rev Stat § 347.037.1; Del Code Ann tit 6, § 18-201(a); Uniform Act § 204(a)(3); Prototype Act § 204(A)(3).] Following formation, most acts provide that, if the LLC is managed by a manager(s), the manager must sign filings with the state. If managed by members, a member must sign the filing. In either case, the document should indicate the signator's capacity. The LLC may also appoint an attorney-in-fact, which may be established through the provisions of the Operating Agreement, to sign documents to be filed with the state, and the LLC is not required to file a written power of attorney with the substantive documents filed with the state. [See Mo Rev Stat § 347.047; Uniform Act § 204; Prototype Act § 204.]

Many states do not require the power of attorney granted for the execution of these documents to be in writing, sworn, notarized, or otherwise acknowledged. [Del Code Ann tit 6, § 18-204(b); Uniform Act § 204(c)] However, each state's law should be reviewed before filing a document signed under a power of attorney.

Articles or a certificate of dissolution may need to be signed by all of the members, or at least the number of members required by the LLC's Operating Agreement to approve the dissolution of the LLC. [See Fla Stat § 648.408.(b)(3).]

Q 2:16   When should an LLC register in other states?

Most of the LLC statutes in force contain procedures for the registration of foreign LLCs. While the Interstate Commerce Clause of the U.S. Constitution prohibits states from unreasonably interfering with interstate commerce, states have the authority to regulate business within their borders. [US Const art I, § 8, cl 3] Thus, similar to corporate registration requirements, an LLC should register to do business in all states where it is doing business. The definition of "doing business" varies from state to state, and an LLC may be deemed to be doing business in one state but not in another where it conducts identical activities.

As discussed in more detail in chapter 12, professional LLCs will not be able to qualify to do business in many states due to state professional credentialing and licensing board rules (which are often statutory), even though those same states' LLC statutes do not restrict qualification.

Q 2:17 When is an LLC considered to be "doing" or "transacting" business in a state?

All of the LLC acts do not define what constitutes "doing business" in the state. The statutes that do define this term generally specify the term in the negative, by identifying those activities that are not considered to be "doing or transacting" business in the state, but also provide that this list is not all inclusive or exclusive. The following list contained in Uniform Act Section 1003, includes most of the common specific activities that states provide do not constitute "doing business" in that state:

1. Maintaining, defending, or settling a court action or proceeding;
2. Holding LLC meetings, or conducting any other activity with respect to the LLC's internal affairs;
3. Maintaining a bank account;
4. Contracting with independent contractors in the state to sell the LLC's products;
5. Soliciting or obtaining orders, through the mail or wire, or through employees, if the order is conditioned upon acceptance by the LLC in another state in which it is doing business;
6. Creating or acquiring indebtedness, mortgages, and security interests in property securing debt;
7. Collecting debts or enforcing mortgages, and security interests;

8. Holding, protecting, renting, maintaining and operating real or personal property seized upon a foreclosure of debt secured. (However, typically the ownership of income-producing real or personal property located in a state constitutes doing business in that state. [Uniform Act § 1003(b)] The Prototype Act provides that the ownership, without more, of real or personal property in a state does not constitute doing business in that state. [Prototype Act § 1008(A)(9); see also Iowa Stat § 490A.1407.2.(i); Va Stat § 13.1-1059(9)])

9. Conducting an isolated transaction that is completed within 30 days and that is not one in the course of repeated transactions of a like manner; or

10. Transacting business in interstate commerce.

The Prototype Act also contains favorable items designed to prevent the attribution to the LLC of the activities of other entities owned by the LLC in determining whether the LLC is doing business in the states where those other entities are doing business. As a result, an LLC is not considered doing business in a state, solely because the LLC owns (1) a controlling interest in a corporation that is doing business in that state, (2) a limited partnership interest in a limited partnership that is doing business in that state, or (3) is a member or manager of an LLC that is doing business in that state. [Prototype Act § 1008(B)(3)]

Many states have additional activities listed that do not constitute doing business. For example, **Virginia** provides that an LLC will not be considered doing business in the state if the LLC produces, directs, films, or provides crews or actors to motion picture feature films, television series or commercials, or promotional films; the activity conducted in the state is not continued for more than 90 days; and the films are processed, edited, marketed, and distributed outside of the state of Virginia. [Va Stat § 13.1-1059.A.11.]

Simply stated, if the LLC opens an office in a state, has a salesperson resident in a state, or regularly, other than by mail alone, solicits and transacts business in a state, the LLC most likely should officially register to do business in that state. The law of each respective state should be considered to determine if it is necessary to register or qualify to do business in a particular state or jurisdiction. To register, the LLC will need a "registered agent" who is a resident of that particular state (see Q 2:22).

Q 2:18   What are the consequences of not registering or qualifying to do business in a state where the LLC's activities constitute "doing business"?

The result can be significant. For instance, an LLC that does business in a state without first registering may be prohibited from bringing a legal action in the courts of that state or transacting any further business within the state. [Uniform Act § 1010; Prototype Act § 1007] In addition, the LLC may be subject to penalties, taxes, or other fees for failing to qualify to do business before conducting business in the state.

The failure to qualify should not, however, affect the limited liability of members or impair the validity of contracts executed by the LLC in the state [Uniform Act § 1010(b), (c); Prototype Act § 1007(B), (G)] Nevertheless, the LLC should qualify to do business in each state where its activities constitute "doing business" to avoid, perhaps expensive, retribution from the state, and possibly expensive legal battles over the validity of contracts executed in the state before the LLC qualified to do business.

Q 2:19   How many owners (members) are needed to form an LLC?

Every state allows one member LLCs except Massachusetts and the District of Columbia. The IRS in 1997 implemented "check-the-box" regulations, which allow single-member LLCs owed by individuals to be treated as sole proprietorships (a disregarded entity) for taxation purposes. Such entities will thus be subject to pass-through taxation as would a sole proprietorship. [Treas Reg § 301.7701-1(a)(4)]

It is also possible to have two members, even though they are related. There is no tax rule for treating a husband and wife as one owner, which would allow an LLC to be a disregarded entity if solely owned by them. Trusts or corporations can be members as well as individuals. Thus, it may be possible to have an LLC between an individual and a corporation in which that individual owns stock, or between an individual and a trust that benefits the individual. The "check-the-box" regulations allow substantial leeway in choosing the method by which the LLC will be taxed. [Treas Reg § 301.7701-3]

Q 2:20 Can one person own an LLC?

Yes, most states allow one-member LLCs, such as Missouri, Texas, and Colorado. [Uniform Act § 201, Mo Rev Stat § 347.017 (3), Colo Rev Stat § 7-80-203] In addition, the "check-the-box" regulations have simplified the tax concerns of single-member LLCs; such entities may choose to be disregarded as entities and will, therefore, be subjected to pass-through taxation. [Treas Reg § 301.7701-1(a)(4)]

Q 2:21 Do members need any third-party approvals to form an LLC?

No, unless the LLC will perform regulated professional services, in which case regulatory approval will usually be required before the LLC is formed.

However, if the proposed members already are conducting the business in another form of organization, and the business has contracts or debts, the proposed members most likely will need to obtain the consent of lenders, landlords, and other parties to contracts before transferring those assets and liabilities to an LLC.

For example, if two owners of real estate have a mortgage on the property, and they desire to form an LLC owned solely by them to hold the real estate, they must obtain the mortgagee's consent before transferring the property to the LLC. Otherwise, a deed of the real property to the LLC will trigger any "due on transfer" clause in the mortgage, and the lender may accelerate the remaining promissory note balance. This could be a tragic result if the current mortgage has a favorable interest rate, and the lender is looking for an excuse to eliminate the underlying debt.

Another example would relate to government approvals. For instance, two independent competitors may need to file a notice of their intent to enter a joint venture through an LLC under the Hart-Scott-Rodino Act, and obtain approval from the Federal Trade Commission and/or applicable state attorneys general offices (see chapter 10). For some business, the conversion to an LLC may trigger change of control provisions in executive compensation plans, debt instruments, or otherwise. This could cause significant nonvested compensation awards to become vested immediately, or cause lenders to accelerate the debt as discussed above.

In conclusion, all contracts and employee benefit plans of a business should be reviewed carefully for the effect of a conversion of the business to an LLC, before the LLC is formed.

Q 2:22 Who may serve as the LLC's registered agent?

Anyone (generally over the age of 18) or any entity can serve as a registered agent in most states, so long as they reside in the respective state and have a street address. Thus, an individual who resides in the state, or a corporation or other entity with an office in the state, may be a registered agent. Law firms will serve as a registered agent, and many have special subsidiaries solely for this purpose. There are also commercial services with offices in every state who will act as the registered agent for the LLC for an annual fee.

Q 2:23 How do you select a registered agent?

The person or entity who is to serve as the registered agent in a state must be a resident of that state. While any trusted member of the LLC who meets the age and residency requirements may serve, it may be best to use the company's law firm or their designated agent for this purpose. This not only keeps the law firm informed about the company's business, but also ensures that legal process, annual reports, and other "papers" served on the company's registered agent receive immediate attention and do not sit in the manager's or some member's in-box. Legal court filings served on an LLC's registered agent, annual reports, and other documents are time sensitive, and many require an immediate response. Thus, having the law firm serve as the registered agent ensures to the extent possible that the deadlines on these papers will be met. Registered agent services are also prompt and persistent in making sure that the company's members or managers respond timely to papers received by the service as the registered agent for the company.

Q 2:24   Does the LLC need registered agents in states other than the state of organization?

Yes, if the LLC does business in other states. To qualify to do business in a state, the LLC must designate a registered agent who resides in that state. [Uniform Act § 1007; Prototype Act § 1002]

Q 2:25   How much does it cost to form an LLC?

There is no fixed answer. Each state has an initial filing fee that can be expected to be at least $100. In addition, because the LLC is a new form of organization and the statutes in each state are different, sometimes significantly, it may be more expensive to form an LLC over a corporation. While most law firms have developed model Articles and Operating Agreements for their LLC clients to use, they will need to be edited and revised for each LLC formed. Thus, one of the advantages of the LLC—the flexibility of the members to alter the management and allocation of income—may result in additional legal fees necessary to prepare an Operating Agreement tailored for the distinctive economic conditions and management of each LLC. Corporations, on the other hand, have less flexibility and usually are formed with more standard articles and by-laws, and generally will have only special drafting needs if the shareholders want to implement a Shareholders' Agreement, which is often easier to prepare than an Operating Agreement.

Q 2:26   Do you need a lawyer to form an LLC?

It is not required, but the Articles and Operating Agreement are legally significant documents. Thus, the original investors retain a qualified tax lawyer and accountant to prepare and review the LLC's Articles and Operating Agreement before filing them with the state.

Q 2:27   Can an accountant form an LLC for a client?

No, unless the accountant is also an attorney. While as a practical matter accountants can form LLCs and prepare the necessary documents, this practice as a service to their clients likely will be considered the unauthorized practice of law, which is illegal and may subject the accountant to legal fines and state accounting licensing board disciplinary proceedings.

Converting an Existing Business to an LLC

Q 2:28 How is an existing partnership converted to an LLC?

An existing partnership can convert to an LLC simply by filing the required Articles and following the other requirements of the LLC act. (See chapter 7 for the tax consequences of such a conversion.)

Q 2:29 What is the effect of converting an existing partnership to an LLC?

Many LLC acts provide that the partnership does not dissolve upon converting to an LLC; the partnership's property and debts are transferred to the LLC by operation of law. [Uniform Act § 903 (debts only); Mo Rev Stat § 347.125.3, .4; Va Stat § 13.1-1067.1] While under such statutes it is not necessary to record deeds to effect the transfer of real estate, it would be prudent to file confirmatory deeds to this effect to ensure that the LLC's title to the property is clearly established. [WVa Stat § 31-1A-47 (requires filing of confirmatory deeds); especially under Uniform Act § 903, if applicable, (which does not provide that property automatically vests in the resulting LLC)] As discussed in Q 2:21, the partnership may need to obtain the consent of their mortgage lenders before recording a new deed for real property subject to a mortgage.

The LLC is, and its members (who were partners at the time of the conversion) remain, liable for the debts and claims against the partnership in existence before the conversion, to the extent that they were liable before the conversion. [See Town of Vernon v. Rumford Associates, 53 Conn. App. 785, 732 A.2d 779 (1999)] Thus, general partners remain liable for the partnership's pre-conversion debts. [Mo Rev Stat § 347.125.4]

Q 2:30   How do you convert an existing C or S corporation to an LLC?

The term "conversion" means the change of a business entity, by act of its owners, from one business organization form to another. This is often accomplished where shareholders of corporations wish to convert their corporations to LLCs under state law in order to be able to obtain federal tax classification as partnerships. However, exiting corporate solution without incurring a tax consequence with respect to appreciated assets is generally not possible.

There are generally five ways a conversion from a corporation into an LLC (taxed as a partnership) can be accomplished: (1) Liquidating the corporation first and then contributing the assets into a newly formed LLC. (2) The corporation's shareholders form a new LLC, contribute their corporate stock to the capital of the LLC, and then liquidate the corporation into the LLC. (3) Form an LLC with the corporation and its shareholders as members followed by a distribution of the corporation's LLC interest to its shareholders. (4) If permitted by state law, merge the corporation and the LLC with the business surviving as the LLC. [Uniform Act § 905; Prototype Act § 1204; Mo Rev Stat § 347.133] This fourth transaction will be treated for income tax purposes as if the corporation liquidated and its assets were then transferred by the shareholders to a new LLC. (5) Lastly, a corporation could sell its assets (subject to liabilities) to a new LLC.

Both from a practical and tax perspective, the second and fourth alternatives make the most sense from a C corporation's point of view. This avoids some of the inherent legal and tax problems involved in a corporate liquidation such as the transfer of assets to a new entity, recording costs and transfer taxes. With regard to an S corporation, alternative three would be ideal because the S corporation and its shareholders both need to be members of the LLC. As a result, the S corporation would not be required to terminate and subsequently liquidated, thereby deferring the liquidation tax indefinitely.

Where the LLC is to be taxed as a corporation, however, the reorganization provisions may be used to provide a tax free transition. [IRC § 368] For example, a private IRS letter ruling indicated that an S corporation that wanted to retain its status as an S corporation but operate as an LLC on the state level may do so by altering the Operating Agreement to ensure that the LLC is more corporate than noncorporate. The IRS agreed to treat the newly formed LLC as an S corporation for tax purposes even though it was recognized as an LLC on the state level and, therefore, the transformation occurred without any tax. [Ltr Rul 9636007; 85 *J Taxn* 375]

In Private Letter Ruling 199942009, the Service indicated that an S election under § 1362 would not terminate when an S corporation converted to a limited partnership under state law then elects to be taxed as an association (corporation), which in turn then made an S election. In this letter ruling, the two partners in the limited partnership were a SMLLC as a general partner and the owner of the SMLLC as an individual, being a limited partner.

Merging with LLCs and Other Entities

Q 2:31 Can an LLC merge with another LLC, corporation, or partnership?

Yes, in many states. Many LLC statutes authorize the merger of an LLC with another LLC, a partnership, a corporation, a trust, or a real estate investment trust. [See, e.g., Uniform Act § 904; Prototype Act § 1202 (but does not authorize merger with partnerships); Del Code Ann tit 6, § 18-209; Mo Rev Stat § 347.127.] Either the LLC or the other entity may be the survivor of such a merger. (See Q 7:78–Q 7:80 for the tax consequences of each of these mergers.)

For states that do not have a specific statute authorizing such a merger, an indirect merger can be accomplished by a transfer of stock, interests, or assets. [See Rev Rul 95-37, 1995-1 CB 130] A second method is the use of another state's merger statute. States such as Delaware have merger statutes that permit a merger or conversion of a domestic or foreign business entity to another entity. For example, Company X, a State A LLC, wants to merge with Company Y, a State A LLP. The desired result is for Company X and Company Y to become Company XY, a domestic LLC. If State A has no direct authorization for an LLC and LLP to merge, X and Y could determine if State A allows domestic and foreign entities to merge. Assuming State A has such a statute, then Y could form an LLP in Delaware (Company Z) and merge Y into Z. Z converts into an LLC under Delaware law, and then Z merges into X. Finally, if the state does not have merger provisions, but has adopted the Revised Uniform Partnership Act, the entity that is converting or merging can convert to a general partnership and the other entity can acquire all of its interests.

Q 2:32   What is the effect of a merger of an LLC?

In states where it is permitted, the survivor of a merger of an LLC and another entity will be entitled, by operation of law, to all of the property and subject to all of the liabilities of all of the entities merged. Like the conversion of a partnership, it is not necessary to record deeds to transfer real estate, but a confirmatory deed could be filed to clarify the chain of title. In addition, if an owner of one of the parties was liable for the debts of that party (e.g., a general partner) before the merger, the merger will not eliminate that liability. [Uniform Act § 905; Prototype Act § 1204; Del Code Ann tit 6, § 18-209(g)] The Delaware Code allows for more than one survivor to a merger.

Q 2:33   If an LLC is not the surviving entity of a merger, does that fact trigger a requirement to wind up the affairs of the LLC and distribute assets to creditors and members?

This issue is not adequately addressed in most statutes. In many states, the dissolution of an LLC triggers an obligation to distribute assets to members, which may be the only time a member, even a withdrawn member, can force the redemption of his, her or its interest in the LLC. [See, e.g., Kan Stat Ann § 17-7616.]

Arizona, **Delaware**, and **Oklahoma** specifically state that an LLC is not required to wind up its affairs, pay liabilities, or distribute assets following a merger of the LLC with another entity, even if the LLC is not the surviving entity in the merger. [Ariz Rev Stat Ann § 29-757(B); Delaware Code Ann tit 6, § 18-209(g) (last sentence); Ok Stat § 18-2054(G) (last sentence)]

Qualifying as a Foreign LLC

Q 2:34   Do the state LLC statutes allow a foreign LLC to do business in the state?

Yes, every state LLC statute provides for the operation of business within its state by foreign LLCs (see appendix A). Generally, the laws of the LLC's home jurisdiction will control the organization and internal affairs of the LLC. State statutes differ on the liability of members; some statutes provide that the LLC's home jurisdiction will determine liability, while other states provide that a foreign LLC is not entitled to any greater privileges than those available to domestic LLCs. Other states impose specific requirements on foreign LLCs to ensure that residents dealing with the foreign LLCs have adequate protection. [See, e.g., Wash Rev Code § 25.12.310 (foreign LLCs providing professional service must meet financial responsibility requirements or members face personal liability)]

LLCs conducting certain businesses, such as professional services, corporate forming, banking, insurance, etc., may not be able to qualify to do business in certain states due to provisions of the LLC statutes or other licensing entities, many of which have their own regulatory requirements.

Q 2:35   What constitutes "doing business" in another state?

Generally, state statutes do not provide a definition of "doing business" within a state. However, several states provide a list of activities that are not considered doing business in the state. These activities vary from state to state, but many states consider the following as secondary contacts:

1. Maintaining, defending, or settling any lawsuit or other legal proceeding;

2. Holding meetings of members or managers or carrying on other activities concerning internal affairs;

3. Maintaining bank accounts;

4. Maintaining offices or agencies for the transfer, exchange, and registration of a foreign LLC's securities or interests or maintaining trustees or depositories with respect to those securities or interests;

5. Selling goods through an independent contractor;

6. Soliciting or obtaining orders, whether by mail or employees or agents, if the orders require acceptance outside the state before a valid contract is formed;

7. Creating or acquiring indebtedness, mortgages, and security interests in real or personal property;

8. Securing or collecting debts or enforcing mortgages and security interests in property securing the debts;

9. Owning real or personal property;

10. Conducting an isolated transaction that is completed within a short period of time, such as 30 days, and is not a repeated transaction; or

11. Transacting business in interstate commerce.

Q 2:36   What are the consequences if an LLC is "doing business" in a state but is not registered as a foreign LLC?

There are several consequences if a particular state determines an LLC is doing business in the state without being registered as a foreign LLC. Some state statutes provide that the lack of registration will not subject the LLC members to personal liability. However, some state statutes do not mention personal liability. Presumably, the states that recognize domestic LLCs would also allow limited liability for the foreign LLC that did not register.

A foreign LLC without a certificate of authority to operate in the state will be unable to bring any action, suit, or proceeding in that state court. However, the LLC would remain liable for any act or contract entered into while it was operating in the state. Therefore, a party could bring an action against the LLC, and the lack of registration does not prevent the LLC from defending the action.

Most states provide that the secretary of state is the foreign LLC's registered agent for service of process if the LLC did not register with the state.

The LLC will still be liable for the registration fees, taxes, and penalties that it would have owed during the period of time it operated in the state. Many states, such as Illinois, impose penalties when an LLC transacts business in the state without being registered.

Q 2:37 How does an LLC register as a foreign LLC?

Each state statute provides specific guidelines for the registration procedure for that state for foreign LLCs, similar to those rules for foreign corporations. The issuance of the certificate of authority usually includes:

1. Name of the foreign LLC;
2. State of organization;
3. Date of formation;
4. Nature of business of purpose of LLC;
5. Address of the registered office and name of registered agent within the state;
6. Statement that the foreign LLC validly exists in the state of organization; and
7. Address of the office in the state of organization or the principal office.

The LLC is also required to pay a registration fee with its application (see appendix A). If any of the LLC information changes, the LLC should notify the state and file an amended application. Failure to update the registration could result in revocation of the foreign LLC's certificate of authority.

Q 2:38 Can a foreign LLC withdraw or revoke its foreign registration with a state?

Yes, the right of an LLC to transact business within a state may be terminated by either the LLC or the state. An LLC may withdraw from transacting business with a state by filing an application to withdraw. Generally, the LLC is required to declare it is not doing business within the state, surrender admission to transact business within the state, and revoke the authority of its registered agent to accept service of process. The LLC usually consents to the appointment of the secretary of state to accept service of process on behalf of the LLC. The state may terminate an LLC's right to transact business within the state. This is usually done in cases involving failure to file and pay the fees, misrepresentation or fraudulent statements of the application, or the secretary of state authorizes the revocation.

Neither the revocation nor withdrawal of the foreign LLC will relieve it for causes of action arising while the LLC was transacting business in the state.

Q 2:39   Are there any other consequences of registering as a foreign LLC?

Yes. The LLC may be subject to state income taxes if the state applies an entity-level tax on the LLC, and the state in question will be on notice that the members may be subject to state income taxes on their distributive share of income from the LLC (see appendix B).

Chapter 3

Tax Classification

This chapter analyzes the classification of an LLC for tax purposes. An LLC may be taxed as a partnership or as a corporation for federal income tax purposes. Most states treat an LLC as a partnership or a corporation based on the classification of the entity for federal tax purposes. A few states, however, tax the LLC entity itself, regardless of the LLC's federal tax classification. This chapter discusses the tests used in determining whether an LLC is a partnership or an association taxable as a corporation. It also discusses the IRS's "check-the-box" regulations which allow entities to make an election to be taxed as either a partnership or a corporation, thereby providing greater certainty as to their tax status.

The "Check-the-Box" Regulations

Q 3:1   How is an LLC treated for federal income tax purposes?

An LLC may be treated as a partnership or a corporation for federal income tax purposes. A partnership is defined as a syndicate, group, pool, joint venture, or other unincorporated organization that is not a trust, estate, or corporation. [IRC § 7701(a)(2)] Effective January 1, 1997, an LLC is treated as a partnership for tax purposes if it does not elect to be taxed as a corporation. It may also be taxed as a sole proprietorship or otherwise disregarded as an entity if the LLC has a single member under the "check-the-box" regulations.

Q 3:2   How is an LLC treated for state income tax purposes?

The various states are not consistent on the tax treatment of LLCs. Some states have their own rules. Some states follow the classification of the LLCs for federal tax purposes. Appendix B provides a listing of how each state currently classifies an LLC for state income tax purposes.

It is important to consider all of the state's LLC laws when contemplating formation. For example, Florida follows the federal rules for taxing LLCs and does not impose a personal income tax. Even though the corporate income taxes on LLCs were repealed, the interests in LLCs are subject to the Florida Intangible Personal Property Tax (FLINT).

Q 3:3   What is the effect of the final "check-the-box" regulations?

The starting point for analysis is the term *business entity*. The "check-the-box" Treasury regulations define a business entity as any entity recognized for federal income tax purposes that is not properly classified as a trust. [Treas Reg § 301.7701] A business entity with only one owner is classified as a corporation or is disregarded; if the entity is disregarded, its activities are treated in the same manner as a sole proprietorship, branch, or division of the owner. A business entity with two or more members may elect to be classified for federal tax purposes as either a corporation or a partnership.

Q 3:4   Can corporations "check-the-box" to be taxed as a partnership?

No. A corporation is an entity that:

1. Is organized under a federal or state statute, or under a statute of a federally recognized Indian tribe, if the statute describes or refers to the entity as incorporated or as a

corporation, body corporate, body politic, joint-stock company, or joint-stock association;

2. Elects to be classified under the regulations as an association taxable as a corporation;

3. Is an insurance company or an FDIC-insured bank;

4. Is a business entity owned by a state or a political sub-division thereof; or

5. Is one of the numerous foreign entities listed in the regulation.

If the business entity falls into one of the above categories, it cannot elect to be treated as a partnership for tax purposes.

Q 3:5 If no "check-the-box" election is made, what are the default rules for domestic entities, foreign entities, and existing entities?

Domestic Entities. Unless the regulations require classification as a corporation, a newly formed domestic entity will automatically be classified as a partnership for tax purposes if it has two or more members, unless an election is filed to classify the entity as an association (and thus, taxable as a corporation); no affirmative action need be taken by the entity to ensure partnership classification. Similarly, if that entity has a single member, it will not be treated as an entity separate from its owner for federal tax purposes unless an election is filed to classify that organization as an association. Comments to the Final Regulations indicate that an entity is not under single member ownership even if all the owners are under common control. [61 Fed Reg 66584 (Dec 18, 1996)] These default rules were aimed at matching the taxpayer's expectation and reducing the number of elections that would need to be filed. Although no election is required to be filed, a newly formed domestic entity may wish to file an election for protective purposes. A protective election is useful if there is doubt whether the entity is domestic or foreign. Foreign entities face different default rules under the "check-the-box" regulations (see below) so it may be advantageous for a new entity to protect itself with an election from a possible reclassification.

Foreign Entities. An entity is foreign if it is not organized pursuant to United States law or the law of any state or the District of Columbia. [Treas Reg § 301.7701-1(d)] A foreign entity will be classified as a corporation if it is designated as a "per se" corporation by the regulations. [See Treas Reg § 301.7701-2(b)(8)] If one or more of a foreign entity's members has personal liability, the entity will be classified as a partnership if it has two or more members, or it will be disregarded as a separate entity if it has a single owner. [Treas Reg § 301.7701-3(b)(2)(i)(A), (B)] Conversely, if all of the entity's members have limited liability, the entity's default classification will be that of an association. Under the "check-the-box" regulations, a member of a foreign entity has personal liability if that member is liable for all or part of an entity's debts and obligations based solely on the controlling statute or law pursuant to which the entity is organized, or if protection from personal liability is optional under the applicable law, the entity's organizational documents provide for personal liability. [Treas Reg § 301.7701-3(b)(2)(ii)]

In IRS Letter Ruling 9831007, a foreign limited liability company, which was a subsidiary of a domestic corporation, was authorized under Treas. Reg. § 301.7701-3(c)(2)(i)(B) to elect partnership classification on behalf of a foreign joint venture in which it was a participant. The joint venture was conducted through a limited liability entity under the local laws of the joint venture's country; thus, absent the election, it would have been classified as an association for U.S. tax purposes. The foreign limited liability company was authorized to make the election by the board of directors of the newly formed limited liability entity.

Existing Entities. Entities in existence before January 1, 1997 (the effective date of the final "check-the-box" regulations) that choose to retain their current classification would not be required to file an election. Rather, those entities would retain the classification claimed under the prior regulations, except that, if an eligible entity with a single owner claimed to be a partnership under the prior regulations, the entity would be disregarded as an entity separate from its owner under this default rule. However, a few state LLC statutes do not allow a one-member LLC.

A foreign entity is considered such an existing entity only if its classification immediately before the effective date of the regulations is relevant to any person for federal tax purposes; other foreign entities formed before the effective date of these regulations would be considered new entities at the time that their federal tax classification became relevant and, therefore, would be required to file a classification election or be classified under the general default rule described above.

Q 3:6   What about the classification of publicly traded partnerships?

As discussed in chapter 7, certain partnerships, including publicly traded partnerships, taxable mortgage pools, real estate mortgage investment conduits (REMICs), and qualified cost sharing agreements are taxed as corporations, not partnerships. [IRC §§ 7704, 7701(i), 860D(b); Treas Reg § 301.7701-1(b), (c)] These entities cannot make an election to be taxed as a partnership.

Q 3:7   Does the "check-the-box" rule apply retroactively to existing entities?

No (see SQ 3:5, above). Existing entities may, however, make the election. Adverse tax consequences could result from a change in classification of an existing entity. For example, if an entity previously taxed as a corporation elects to be classified as a partnership for tax purposes, the organization and its owners must recognize gain, if any, under the applicable rules of liquidation of corporations.

Q 3:8   What are the tax consequences for an LLC that makes an election to be taxed differently after January 1, 1997?

The election to be taxed differently will be treated as a conversion of the entity. Thus, for example, if an LLC that historically has been treated as a corporation makes an election to be taxed as a partnership, that election will be deemed a taxable conversion of the LLC from a corporation to a partnership. (See chapter 7 for a discussion of the tax consequences of the conversion of an LLC.) Generally, the LLC will be deemed to liquidate (with tax costs) and reconstitute itself as a partnership. The LLC would have to file a final return as a corporation and a first-year return as a partnership.

Q 3:9   How does an LLC elect under the "check-the-box" regulations?

An eligible entity may elect its classification by filing an election with the appropriate IRS Service Center. The regulations require that the election be made on Form 8832 and filed with the appropriate IRS Service Center. The election must be signed by either each member of the electing entity who is an owner at the time the election is filed, or any officer, manager, or member of the electing entity who is authorized to make the election and who represents to having such authorization under penalties of perjury. Any election which is to apply retroactively must also include the signature of any person who was an owner at the time for which the election is to be effective even though that individual may no longer be an owner at the time the election is made. The election will be effective on a date specified on Form 8832, or on the date filed if no such date is specified on Form 8832. The effective date specified on Form 8832 cannot be more than 75 days before the date the election was filed and cannot be more than 12 months after the date on which the election is filed. In addition to the original election, a business entity that makes an election must file a copy of its Form 8832 with its federal tax return for the year in which the election is effective. If the entity is not required to file a federal tax return, a copy of Form 8832 must be attached to the federal tax return of any direct or indirect owners of the entity.

Q 3:10   Do the "check-the-box" regulations apply to foreign organizations?

Yes (see SQ 3:5).

Q 3:11   How are employer identification numbers (EINs) handled?

If the entity already has an EIN, it will retain it if it retains its tax classification. Any organization without an EIN at the time it files its election, including an organization that had not previously been treated as a separate entity for federal tax purposes, must apply for an EIN on Form SS-4 when it files its election.

If a new single-member entity elects to be disregarded as an entity separate from its owner, then the taxpayer identifying number of its owner must be displayed on the election.

Q 3:12   Are there limits on changing elections and transition rules?

Yes. An eligible entity that makes an election to change its classification cannot change its classification by election again during the 60 months succeeding the effective date of the election. An existing entity that elects to change its classification as of the effective date of the regulations may elect, however, to change again within the first 60 months following the effective date. The 60-month limitation only applies to a change in classification by election. Thus, if a new eligible entity elects out of its default classification effective from its inception, that election is not a change in the entity's classification. However, the Commissioner may permit the entity to change its classification by election within the 60 months if more than 50 percent of the ownership interests in the entity as of the effective date of the subsequent election are owned by persons that did not own any interests in the entity on the filing date or on the effective date of the entity's prior election.

The "check-the-box" regulations provide that the IRS will not challenge the classification of an existing eligible entity, that was in existence before January 1, 1997, if:

1. The entity had a reasonable basis (within the meaning of Code Section 6662) for its claimed classification;
2. The entity and all members of the entity recognized the federal tax consequences of any change in the entity's classification within the 60 months before January 1, 1997; and
3. Neither the entity nor any member had been notified in writing on or before May 8, 1996 that the classification of the entity is under examination (in which case the entity's classification will be determined in the examination).

Q 3:13 What entities are considered to make a "deemed" election to be taxed as a corporation under the "check-the-box" regulations?

An entity that is exempt from taxation under Code Section 501(a) is treated as having made an election under the "check-the-box" regulations to be classified as an association. The election is effective as of the first day for which the tax exemption is claimed and remains in effect unless an election is made under the regulations after the entity's exempt status is withdrawn, rejected, or revoked. An entity that files on election under Code Section 856(c)(1) to be treated as a real estate investment trust is treated as having made an election under the "check-the-box" regulations to be classified as an association. Such election is effective as of the first day the entity is treated as a real estate investment trust.

Q 3:14   When should an entity elect to be taxed as an association?

A partnership or LLC treated as a partnership for tax purposes might consider electing to be taxed as an association in contemplation of a tax-free reorganization or restructuring with a publicly held corporation. This reclassification should be completed well in advance of any reorganization or restructuring. The effect of the reclassification would generally be governed by the tax-free incorporation rules established under Code Section 351, unless it is too close in line to a subsequent change of ownership, in which case the Section 351 "control" test may not be met. Such incorporation could, however, result in the recognition of tax if the entity's liabilities exceed the adjusted basis in the entity's assets or the adjusted basis of the members' interests. A reclassification from a partnership to a corporation should not be made in conjunction with a reorganization or as part of an agreed-upon plan, since such an agreement could run afoul the requirements of Code Section 351.

Q 3:15   Can an LLC elect whether to apply for a ruling under Revenue Procedure 89-12 or 95-10?

No. Revenue Procedure 95-10 specifically provides that Revenue Procedure 89-12 [1989-1 CB 798] no longer applies to LLCs.

Q 3:16   Does Revenue Procedure 95-10 apply to all LLCs?

Yes, except for one-member LLCs.

Q 3:17   Once issued, does a ruling under Revenue Procedure 95-10 apply indefinitely to an LLC?

No. If the LLC subsequently has only one member, the ruling is no longer effective as of the effective date the LLC terminates under Code Sections 708 and 736. In general, this would be the date when only one member is entitled to all of the income from the LLC. [Treas Reg §§ 1.708-1(b)(1)(i)(a), 1.736-1(a)(6)]

Q 3:18 Will an LLC necessarily fail to be classified as a partnership for tax purposes if it cannot satisfy the standards under Revenue Procedure 95-10?

No. An LLC may be classified as a partnership even if it cannot satisfy the Revenue Procedure 95-10 criteria, but the LLC will not be able to obtain an IRS ruling that the LLC is a partnership. Officially, there is no inference that an LLC that does not meet the Revenue Procedure 95-10 standards will not be treated as a partnership. [Comments of Monte Jackel, IRS deputy associate chief counsel (domestic-technical) at the January 24, 1995, New York State Bar Association Tax Section meeting, reported in February 13, 1995, *Tax Notes* at 932.]

Continuity of Life

Q 3:19 How does an LLC avoid "continuity of life"?

An LLC need no longer avoid "continuity of life" to be taxed as a partnership, effective January 1, 1997. An LLC avoids continuity of life if the death, insanity, bankruptcy, retirement, resignation, or expulsion of any member causes a dissolution of the organization, without any further action by the members. [Treas Reg § 301.7701-2(b)(1)] The enumerated event must occur with respect to a member, and not the LLC itself.

Q 3:20 What is a dissolution event?

A dissolution event is one of the circumstances under which an LLC will dissolve under the relevant state law or constituent documents of the LLC, upon the occurrence of that event with respect to a member of the LLC. The common dissolution events identified in the state statutes, IRS regulations, and Revenue Procedure 95-10 are: death, insanity, bankruptcy, retirement, resignation, or expulsion of a member. [See Uniform Act §§ 602, 801; Prototype Act §§ 802, 901]

Q 3:21 Does an LLC have to dissolve upon the occurrence of a dissolution event to avoid continuity of life?

No. Treasury Regulations Section 301.7701-2(b)(1) and state law generally provide that an LLC will dissolve upon the occurrence of a dissolution event unless the remaining members agree to continue the business of the LLC. While originally most state statutes required the members to approve a continuation of the LLC within 90 days of the date of the dissolution event, [Uniform Act § 801; Prototype Act § 901] newer statutes reverse this prescription and provide that the LLC continues unless the members affirmatively elect to dissolve it.

Q 3:22   Do all of the members have to consent to the continuation of the LLC after a dissolution event?

The answer to this question depends upon the relevant state law. In the states with the old "bulletproof" statutes, all of the members, other than the member who suffered the dissolution event, must consent to a continuation of the LLC. In "flexible" states, the LLC will be continued if at least a majority in interest of the remaining members agree to continue the LLC's business, although the members can provide in the Articles or Operating Agreement that a super-majority vote is required. [Uniform Act § 801; Prototype Act § 901]

Q 3:23   Will an LLC lack continuity of life if the remaining members can vote to prevent the dissolution of the LLC upon the occurrence of a dissolution event with respect to another member?

Yes, although continuity of life is now not a tax issue due to the "check-the-box" regulations. Originally, the IRS required that, to avoid the corporate characteristic of continuity of life, the remaining members must agree by unanimous consent to continue an LLC after a termination event. [Ltr Ruls 9219022, 9227033] However, the IRS has ruled an LLC lacks continuity of life if the controlling state statute or the Operating Agreement provides that the LLC dissolves upon the occurrence of a dissolution event unless a majority in interest of the remaining members vote to continue the LLC after the dissolution event.

Q 3:24   What is a "majority in interest"?

Revenue Procedure 94-46 [1994-28 IRB 129] defines majority in interest as a majority of the profits and a majority of the capital interests owned by the remaining members after a dissolution event. For these purposes, profits are determined and allocated based on any reasonable estimate of profits as of the date of the dissolution event; capital is determined as of the date of the dissolution event. [Rev Proc 95-10]

Q 3:25 Can an LLC lack continuity of life if the LLC's constituent documents do not identify all of the permitted dissolution events as events that will cause the dissolution of the LLC?

As a general rule, the LLC's constituent documents need no longer provide, for tax purposes, that the LLC will dissolve upon the dissolution events specified in Revenue Procedure 95-10. [1995-1 CB 501]

Under the old bulletproof statutes, the LLC's Articles and Operating Agreement provided that the LLC dissolved upon the occurrence of the events specified in the LLC act. Now states generally allow the members to identify those dissolution events, if any, that will automatically trigger a dissolution of the LLC. [Uniform Act § 801; Prototype Act § 901]

Nevertheless, if permissible under state law, before the advent of the "check-the-box" rules, the IRS ruled that an LLC lacks continuity of life, even though all of the dissolution events listed in Revenue Procedure 95-10 are not listed in the Articles and/or Operating Agreement of the LLC. [See Ltr Rul 9210019 (the IRS ruled an LLC did not have continuity of life, even though the only dissolution event for the LLC was the bankruptcy of a particular corporate member)]

Revenue Procedure 95-10 generally provides that all of the dissolution events must be identified as events that will cause the dissolution of the LLC. However, the IRS will rule an LLC lacks continuity of life, even though only one or more of the dissolution events are listed in the LLC's constituent documents, if the taxpayer clearly establishes to the IRS's satisfaction that there is a meaningful possibility of the occurrence of the events specified. [Rev Proc 95-10, § 5.01(4)] The Revenue Procedure does not define "meaningful" for these purposes. The relevant question should be whether or not the event chosen legally could happen, and not the likelihood of the occurrence of that event. For example, death could not be the sole triggering event, if all of the

LLC's members are corporations. [See Wirtz and Harris, "Assessing the Long-Awaited LLC Classification Guidelines," 51 *Taxes* 57 (Feb 1995)]

Q 3:26   In a member-managed LLC, do all of the members in the LLC have to be subject to the dissolution events?

Not today, only under the pre-1997 rules, if the LLC wanted an IRS ruling that the LLC does not have continuity of life. If member-managed, the IRS would not rule an LLC lacks continuity of life, unless the LLC dissolved upon the occurrence of a dissolution event with respect to any of the members. That is, the LLC's Articles or Operating Agreement could not provide that death is a dissolution event only upon the death of members A and B, not C. In this case, the death of A, B, or C must cause the dissolution of the LLC. [Rev Proc 95-10, § 5.01(2), 1995-1 CB 501] But this is no longer relevant for federal or state tax purposes.

Q 3:27   If the LLC has a designated manager who is not a member, do all of the members in the LLC have to be subject to the dissolution events?

No.

Q 3:28   If the LLC has designated managers who are also members in the LLC, did all of the members in the LLC have to be subject to the dissolution events?

No. If the LLC was managed by member-managers, the dissolution events must have applied equally to all of the member-managers, but it was not necessary that all members (other than member-managers) be subject to the occurrence of the dissolution events. [Rev Proc 95-10, § 5.01(1)]

Q 3:29   When did the IRS rule that an LLC managed by all of the members or by designated nonmember-managers lacks continuity of life?

Under the pre-1997 rules, an LLC lacked continuity of life if the controlling statute or Operating Agreement provided that the LLC would be dissolved upon the death, insanity, bankruptcy, retirement, resignation, or expulsion of any member without further action of the remaining members, unless the LLC was continued by the consent of at least a majority in interest of the remaining members. [Rev Proc 95-10, § 5.01(2), 1995-1 CB 501]

Q 3:30 When did the IRS rule an LLC managed by designated member-managers lacks continuity of life?

The IRS ruled an LLC lacks continuity of life if the controlling statute or Operating Agreement provided that the LLC dissolved upon the occurrence of a dissolution event to any one of the member-managers, unless the LLC was continued by the consent of at least a majority in interest of the remaining members. The IRS issued such rulings even though the Operating Agreement provides that the LLC does not dissolve upon the occurrence of a dissolution event with respect to a nonmanaging member. [Rev Proc 95-10, § 5.01(1)] However, the IRS issued this ruling only if the LLC satisfied defined minimum ownership and capital account tests, described in Qs 3:31 and 3:32.

This is a flexible standard that will be beneficial to many LLCs. The fewer persons that can cause an LLC to dissolve the better, from the LLC's perspective. Thus, for example, if the LLC dissolves only upon the death or dissolution of a member-manager, the death of a nonmanaging member would not cause the LLC to dissolve. This eliminates many of the administrative problems of a dissolution, and it eliminates the necessity of obtaining consent to continue the business after a dissolution event, along with the potential adverse tax consequences.

Q 3:31 What is the minimum ownership requirement under Revenue Procedure 95-10?

The IRS will not issue the ruling described in Q 3:29 or 3:32 with respect to member-managers under Revenue Procedure 95-10 unless the LLC's Operating Agreement expressly provides that all member-managers in the aggregate own at least a 1 percent interest in each material item of the LLC's income, gain, loss, deduction, or credit during the LLC's entire existence.

This requirement does not apply when the LLC dissolves upon a dissolution event with respect to any member, or when at least a majority of all members is required to approve the admission of a new member in connection with the transfer of an interest.

Q 3:32   What is the minimum capital account requirement under Revenue Procedure 95-10?

The IRS would not issue the ruling described in Q 3:29 or Q 3:33 with respect to member-managers under Revenue Procedure 95-10 unless the LLC's Operating Agreement expressly required the member-managers in the aggregate to maintain a minimum capital account balance equal to the lesser of 1 percent of the total positive capital account balances of all members *or* $500,000. To comply, the Operating Agreement required the member-managers to match, in the aggregate, contributions by nonmanager-members, in an amount equal to 1.01 percent of the nonmanager-member's contributions. [Rev Proc 95-10, § 4.04]

Q 3:33   Did temporary allocations that cause a violation of the minimum ownership requirement affect the IRS's ruling?

Code Sections 704(b) and 704(c) may affect the allocations of the LLC's income and loss, and cause the member-managers to receive less than a 1 percent interest in those items. The allocations, however, did not affect the IRS's ruling on continuity of life and free transferability of interest, as the case may be, so long as the allocation was temporary and the ruling request described why an allocation may be required under IRC Section 704(b) or 704(c). Otherwise, temporary allocations that cause the member-managers to receive less than 1 percent of the LLC's income and loss would affect the IRS's ruling, unless the LLC clearly establishes in the ruling request that the member-managers will have a material interest in the LLC's net profits and losses over the LLC's anticipated life. [Rev Proc 95-10, § 4.02]

The IRS stated in Revenue Procedure 95-10 that a profits interest will not be considered material, unless the profits allocation substantially exceeds 1 percent and will be in effect for a substantial period during which the LLC is expected to generate profits. For example, a 20 percent interest in profits that begins four years after the LLC's formation, which will continue for the LLC's life, generally would be considered material if the LLC is expected to generate profits for a substantial period of time beyond the initial four-year period. [Rev Proc 95-10, § 4.02]

Q 3:34   Are there any exceptions to the minimum ownership test?

Yes. If the LLC has total contributions in excess of $50 million, the member-managers are not required to have, in the aggregate, a 1 percent interest in the LLC's profits and losses. The Operating Agreement, however, must provide that the member-managers' percentage interest in those items equals 1 percent divided by a fraction, the numerator of which is total contributions and the denominator of which is $50 million, except for temporary allocations as explained in Q 3:33. [Rev Proc 95-10, § 4.03] For example, if members contribute $100 million to an LLC managed by member-managers, those member-managers must have a .5 percent interest in the LLC's income and losses at all times, except for temporary required allocations [.01/($100 million/$50 million)].

Q 3:35   Is there a minimum ownership percentage interest member-managers must have even if the LLC has total contributions in excess of $50 million?

Yes. Member-managers must have at least a .2 percent interest in the LLC's material items of income and loss during the LLC's life, regardless of the amount of the total contributions to the LLC.

Q 3:36   Are there any exceptions to the minimum capital account requirement?

Yes. If at least one member-manager contributes, or is obligated to contribute, substantial services to the LLC in their capacity as a member (other than services for which they will be paid), no member-manager is required to maintain the minimum capital account balance. [Rev Proc 95-10, § 4.04] Generally, the services must relate to the LLC's day-to-day operations, depending upon the nature of the LLC's activities, to qualify as substantial for the purposes of this standard. The IRS will scrutinize closely services performed in connection with the organization of the LLC in determining whether those services were substantial.

Nevertheless, the LLC's Operating Agreement must require the member-managers to contribute capital to the LLC upon dissolution of the LLC in an amount equal to the lesser of: the aggregate deficit capital account of the member-managers; *or* an amount equal to 1.01 percent of the nonmanager members' total contributions to the LLC, less the aggregate capital previously contributed to the LLC by the member-managers. [Rev Proc 95-10, § 4.05]

Q 3:37   What is the minimum capital account requirement if no member has a positive capital account?

If no member has a positive capital account, the member-managers are not required to have a positive capital account balance either. [Rev Proc 95-10, § 4.04]

Free Transferability of Interest

Q 3:38   How does an LLC avoid "free transferability of interest"?

While no longer necessary to achieve partnership tax status, the tax characteristic of free transferability of interest is avoided if members cannot assign their rights to participate in the management of the LLC without the consent of the other members. The state LLC statutes vary on the approval requirements. Some states allow members to agree, in the LLC's Operating Agreement, on the vote required to admit a member. [Uniform Act § 504(b)(2); Prototype § 706] States with bulletproof statutes require members to unanimously consent to the admission of a new member.

Revenue Procedure 95-10 [1995-1 CB 501] merely required approval of a new majority in interest for ruling purposes (see Q 3:43).

Q 3:39   Will an LLC have free transferability of interest if members can transfer the economic interest in their membership interest without the consent of the other members?

No. Treasury regulations and Revenue Procedure 95-10 are concerned with the free transferability of a member's right to participate in the management and affairs of the LLC, not the transfer of the members' economic interests in the LLC. [Treas Reg § 301.7701-2(e)(1); Rev Proc 95-10, § 5.02]

Q 3:40   Will an LLC have free transferability of interest if the transfer of interests is subject only to a right of first refusal by the other members before they transfer their interest in the LLC?

No. A modified form of free transferability exists if members can transfer all of their interest subject to a right of first refusal by the other members. Because an LLC formed under most of the state LLC statutes has the corporate characteristics of limited liability, the presence of this modified free transferability and one other corporate characteristic (e.g., centralized management) will cause the LLC to be classified as a corporation. (See, e.g., Letter Ruling 8828022 on a foreign LLC with continuity of life, centralized management, and modified transferability — classified as a corporation.) To date, this modified form of free transferability generally has not been a determinative factor in the existing partnership classification ruling.

This modified form of free transferability may become more important under those state LLC statutes that permit members to vary their liability for the LLC's debts if the IRS permits an analogous modified form of limited liability. If "modified" limited liability is possible (i.e., a member is liable for part, but not all, of the LLC's debts), an LLC could perhaps have modified free transferability of interest and remain classified as a partnership for tax purposes. Otherwise, if the LLC has limited liability, which will be the case in most instances, modified free transferability of interest may disqualify the LLC from partnership status, if the LLC also has centralized management.

Q 3:41   Are members required to obtain the unanimous consent of the other members before transferring their interests?

Not for tax purposes, but some bulletproof state statutes require such unanimity when the transferee is also to become a new member, not just an assignee. The IRS has taken the position that less than unanimous consent is sufficient to avoid free transferability. [Ltr Rul 9218078 (Jan 31, 1992) (**Texas** LLC—consent by manager or members owning two-thirds of the outstanding units); Rev Rul 93-91, 1993-2 CB 316; Rev Rul 93-92, 1993-2 CB 318; Ltr Rul 9219022 (unidentified state—consent of members holding majority of nontransferred profits); Treas Reg § 301.7701-3(b)(2), Ex (1) (unanimous consent of the general partners required); Rev Rul 88-79, 1988-2 CB 361 (A **Missouri** land trust lacked free transferability of interests when an assignee of a participant could become a substitute participant with the consent of a majority (by number) of the managers. If the parties provide that the consent to the transfer may not be unreasonably withheld, free transferability may exist.)]

Q 3:42   When will the IRS rule an LLC does not have free transferability of interests?

The IRS will no longer rule on this issue since it is irrelevant to tax treatment unless a foreign entity is involved. The IRS will rule that an LLC lacks free transferability of interest if each member, or those members who own more than 20 percent of all interest in the LLC's capital, income, and deductions, do not have the power to transfer to a nonmember all the attributes of a membership interest without the consent of at least a majority of the nontransferring members. [Rev Proc 95-10, § 5.01(2), 1995-1 CB 501]

Q 3:43   Is a majority of members different than a "majority in interest"?

For the purposes of approving free transferability of interests, a majority means a "majority of interest"; or a majority of either the capital or profits interests in the LLC; or a majority of members on a per capita basis. [Rev Proc 95-10, § 5.02(3)]

Q 3:44 **Will an LLC have free transferability of interest if the LLC's Operating Agreement requires members to obtain only the consent of the managers to approve the transfer of an interest?**

The IRS will rule an LLC lacks free transferability of interest if only the consent of the designated or elected member-manager is required to transfer an interest, if:

1. The controlling state statute or Operating Agreement requires the consent of at least a majority of the member-managers; and

2. The LLC satisfies the minimum ownership and capital account requirements set forth above (see Qs 3:31 and 3:32). [Rev Proc 95-10, § 5.02(1)]

Q 3:45 **Will an LLC lack free transferability of interest if members owning as much as 79.9 percent of the interest in the LLC can transfer their interest in the LLC without anyone's consent?**

Technically yes. Revenue procedure requires that only members who own, in the aggregate, more than 20 percent of the interest in the LLC obtain the requisite consent before they transfer their interest. Thus, if the Operating Agreement restricted the transferability of more than 20 percent of the interest in the LLC, the balance of the interests could be transferable without restriction. This presumes that the relevant state LLC statute would authorize such freedom, and presumes that a sufficient number of members would agree to restricting their transferability of interests even though the others can transfer at will. Freedom to transfer an interest would increase the value of that interest in the market and, therefore, would depress the value of those interests that could not be transferred without the requisite consent. Nevertheless, Revenue Procedure 95-10 appears to grant this flexibility. [See, similarly, Rev Proc 92-33, 1992-1 CB 782 (which provides the same general rule in the case of partnerships).]

Q 3:46   Will an LLC lack free transferability of interest if the Operating Agreement requires members to be reasonable when considering whether to approve the transfer of an interest?

The IRS will not rule an LLC lacks free transferability of interest unless the members (or member-managers, as the case may be) have a "meaningful" power to withhold their consent to the transfer of an interest. [Rev Proc 95-10, § 5.02(4)] The IRS explains this rule by providing that the power to withhold consent is not meaningful if the consent may not be withheld unreasonably. [Rev Proc 95-10, § 5.02(4)]

Therefore, the Operating Agreement should provide that members or member-managers may, at their sole and absolute discretion, withhold their consent to the transfer of an interest by a member. Otherwise, state law may impose an implied duty to act reasonably, which might prevent the IRS from issuing a favorable ruling.

Centralized Management

Q 3:47   What is centralized management?

An LLC has centralized management if any person or group of persons has continuing and exclusive authority to make the LLC's decisions necessary to the conduct of the LLC's business. [Treas Reg § 301.7701-2(c)(4)] Thus, for example, because a corporation has a board of directors, which govern the affairs of the corporation, a corporation has centralized management.

The designation of managers by an LLC generally restricts the members' ability to manage the LLC. For example, the selection of managers generally limits the members' agency authority. [Uniform Act § 301(b)] Consequently, an LLC generally will have this corporate characteristic if the LLC designates managers. Historically, the IRS has ruled that an LLC governed by managers has centralized management. [Rev Ruls 93-30, 1993-1 CB 231 and 93-38, 1993-1 CB 233] The IRS has taken the position that a manager-managed LLC has centralized management even if all members are managers. [Rev Rul 93-6, 1993-1

CB 229] Revenue Procedure 95-10 has altered this policy, as discussed below.

Q 3:48   When will the IRS rule an LLC does not have centralized management?

The IRS will rule an LLC lacks centralized management if either the controlling state statute or Operating Agreement provides that the LLC is managed by members exclusively in their membership capacity. [Rev Proc 95-10, § 5.03(1)]

Q 3:49   Will the IRS ever rule an LLC with designated managers does not have centralized management?

Yes. Contrary to prior rulings, the IRS will rule that an LLC with designated or elected managers lacks centralized management if the managers are also members and they own at least 20 percent of the LLC's total interests. [Rev Proc 95-10, § 5.03(2)] However, the IRS will not rule an LLC lacks centralized management if:

1. The member-managers are subject to periodic selections by members; or

2. The nonmanaging members have a substantially nonrestricted power to remove the member-managers.

The rationale behind this change in policy is twofold. First, Revenue Procedure 95-10 mirrors the requirement for limited partnerships to obtain a ruling that they do not have centralized management if the general partners own at least 20 percent of the total interests in the limited partnership. [Rev Proc 89-12, § 4.06] Second, consistent with the theory for limited partnerships, if the member-managers own a significant interest in the LLC, then they are managing the LLC not only for the nonmember managers but in their self-interest as significant equity participants in the LLC. Thus, they are acting less like "representatives" of the other members, and more in their own self-interest. That is the rationale behind the condition that the member-managers are not subject to periodic elections or the nonrestricted right of removal by the other members. If so, the member-managers would be acting in a representative capacity for the nonmanager-members, and less on their own behalf. In that case, they would be acting much like a board of directors, and thus resemble the centralized management of a corporation.

Limited Liability

Q 3:50   When do LLC members have "limited liability"?

An LLC has limited liability if, under local law, no member is personally liable for the LLC's debts and obligations. [Treas Reg § 301.7701-2(d)(1)] For these purposes, a member has personal liability if a creditor of the LLC has the right to require a member to satisfy a debt of the LLC to the extent that the LLC's assets are insufficient to satisfy the LLC's debt to that creditor. [Treas Reg § 301.7701-2(d)(1)]

Members and managers of an LLC are by statute generally not liable for the obligations of the LLC. However, there are circumstances under which members may become liable for the obligations of the LLC. For example, any person who purports to act on behalf of an LLC, without authority to do so, will be liable for any liabilities incurred or arising as a result of such actions. A member will also have liability with respect to that member's contributions to the LLC. [Uniform Act §§ 402, 409; Prototype Act § 502] Members and managers, however, are always liable for their own torts (see chapter 11), and the LLC members can lose their limited liability if the LLC does not use its proper name with third parties.

For example, it has been held under the Colorado notice provision [Colo Rev Stat 7-80-208] that because plaintiff did not know defendant was acting for an LLC, the statutory provision did not protect defendant from liability as a partially disclosed principal. [See Water, Wast and Land v Lanhan, 955 P2d 997 (Colo 1998)] The Colorado Supreme Court imposed liability on the agent manager because he disclosed only the initials "P.I.I." rather than the full name "Preferred Income Investors, LLC." Moreover, in applying principles of agency law, the court found sufficient evidence that plaintiff actually thought defendant was the principal. The court reasoned that to make filing of the articles alone enough to insulate the defendant from liability would be a significant departure from the common law, and, therefore, the legislature's intent to do so must be clearly expressed.

Q 3:51   Will the IRS ever rule an LLC does not have limited liability?

Yes. Although rarely applicable, the IRS will rule that an LLC lacks limited liability if these three conditions are satisfied:

1. At least one member assumes liability for all LLC obligations, pursuant to express statutory authority.
2. Generally, the assuming member's net worth is, and is expected to continue to be, at least 10 percent of the LLC's total capital contributions. If the assuming member cannot meet this requirement, the IRS may still rule that the LLC lacks limited liability if the assuming members demonstrate that they have substantial assets (other than the LLC interest) that could be reached by a creditor of the LLC.
3. The assuming members in the aggregate satisfy the minimum ownership tests and capital account requirements discussed in Qs 3:31 and 3:32. [Rev Proc 95-10, § 5.04]

Q 3:52   When would an LLC desire a ruling that it does not have limited liability?

Since the "check the box" tax election procedures were finalized, an LLC is generally presumed to be taxed as a partnership. IRS rulings are generally no longer sought by domestic LLC entities to be classified as a partnership. Limited liability is no longer an impediment to partnership tax status.

Q 3:53   How is an assuming member's net worth calculated for these purposes?

Revenue Procedure 95-10 provides that the principles of Revenue Procedure 92-88 [1992-2 CB 496] apply in calculating the net worth of the assuming member. Under those rules, the assuming member's assets are valued at fair market value, but excluding the value of the LLC interest owned by that person. In addition, if the value of an item of property is included in the calculation of the value of one member's assets, that property may not be taken into account in determining the net worth of any other assuming member. For example, the assets of spouses, both of whom are assuming members, may not be counted twice.

Q 3:54   What are the tax consequences of being classified as an "association" under the Internal Revenue Code?

An association is taxed as a C corporation under the Code. [IRC § 7701(a)(3)] (See chapters 1 and 11 for consequences of taxation as a C corporation.)

Q 3:55   When is an LLC treated as a partnership for state income tax purposes?

Whether an LLC is treated as a partnership for state income tax purposes depends on the state LLC statute by state tax law. Some states, such as **Colorado** and **Utah**, specifically state that LLCs are treated as partnerships. Appendix B provides a listing of how each state classifies an LLC for state income tax purposes.

Q 3:56   Is a one-member LLC treated as a partnership or an "association" under the Internal Revenue Code?

Under the "check-the-box" regulations, the one person LLC is not an entity, unless it elects to be taxed as a corporation, and is taxed as a sole proprietorship. The IRS will not issue a ruling on the classification of an LLC unless the LLC has at least two members. Any ruling will cease to apply if the LLC subsequently has only one member. [Rev Proc 95-10, § 4.01, 1995-1 CB 501]

The IRS previously treated one-person associations as corporations for tax purposes. [GCM 39395 (Aug 5, 1985)]

Q 3:57   How will a single member LLC, taxed as a disregarded entity for federal income tax purposes, be treated for state tax purposes?

Where state income tax law follows the federal rules, a single member LLC would be disregarded for state income tax purposes when disregarded for federal income tax purposes. However, at least two states have indicated that a single member LLC would be taxed as a partnership for state tax purposes. The New York Commissioner of Taxation and Finance in an advisory opinion for Arthur Anderson, LLP, interpreting the state's sales tax provisions, held that the LLC should be treated like a partnership. Arthur Anderson, LLP, TSB-A-99(7)S, 1/28/99. The commissioner relied upon S. 2(6) of the New York Tax Law which defines a partnership to include an LLC. Since the provision did not distinguish between disregarded single member LLCs and other LLCs, the commissioner reasoned that under New York Tax Law single member LLCs would be considered separate entities from their owner.

Another New York ruling, this time dealing with the excise tax on the furnishing of utility services, treats a single member LLC (rather than its member) as an entity subject to tax. New York Tax Law section 186-A imposes an excise tax on the gross operating income generated from the furnishing of utility services. In *Levin*, New York State Department of Taxation and Finance TSB-A-00(2)C, 1/28/00, P, a domestic limited partnership, was the sole member of a domestic LLC that owned an office building. The LLC charged its tenants for utility services. For purposes of Section 186-A, "utility" includes a person, and section 186-A2(b) of the Tax Law provides that "person" includes LLCs.

The advisory opinion concludes that an LLC, including a single-member LLC, that is providing a utility service is a "person" pursuant to section 186 and the LLC itself is liable for the tax imposed. The opinion further provides that P, the sole member of the LLC, will not be subject to tax, or be required to file a return under section 186-A of the Tax Law for the gross operating income of the LLC for which the LLC files a return and pays the tax imposed.

The Wisconsin Department of Revenue has similarly found that a single member LLC is not disregarded for state tax purposes by holding that a sale of equipment by a corporation to its single member LLC was a taxable sale under Wisconsin law. [Priv. Ltr. Rul. No. W9907001 (11/24/98), released in Wis. Dept. of Rev. Tax Bulletin No. 113, April 1999]

Chapter 4

Capital Contributions and Distributions

This chapter describes the capital formation of the LLC, that is, the types of property or services that may be contributed to an LLC in exchange for interests therein. It also discusses the ability to compromise or enforce obligations by members to contribute capital to the LLC. Finally, this chapter discusses the timing and restrictions on distributions of capital to members.

Formation

Q 4:1   How much capital must be contributed to the LLC?

Generally no minimum amount must be contributed to an LLC in exchange for an interest in the LLC. The question of adequate capitalization generally is left up to the agreement of the members. However, if a member receives a capital or profits interest in the LLC with a fair market value in excess of the fair market value of the capital contribution, the member may be subject to tax on receipt of that interest to the extent of the difference (see Qs 7:17 and 7:19).

Q 4:2   What type of property can be contributed to an LLC in exchange for a membership interest in an LLC?

The LLC acts are not uniform in this respect. Many LLC acts allow members to contribute almost anything of value in exchange for an interest, including cash, property, the right to use property, services performed or an agreement to perform services in the future, or a promissory note or other obligation to contribute capital in the future. However, some states limit capital contributions to cash or property [Fla Stat Ann § 608.4211; Wyo Stat § 17-15-115]; other states specifically prohibit the issuance of an interest in exchange for a promissory note or services to be rendered at a later date [SD Codified Laws Ann § 47-34-19]; and still others do not permit services to be contributed in exchange for an interest in an LLC. [Neb Stat § 21-2614]

Q 4:3   Can members obtain an interest in an LLC in exchange for a promissory note?

Many states either specifically allow this or do not specifically prohibit the issuance of an interest in exchange for a commitment to contribute capital. As discussed above, a few states prohibit the issuance of an interest in exchange for a promissory note.

Q 4:4   How does a member transfer property to the LLC?

Generally, the contributor should execute a bill of sale transferring any personal property to the LLC. If the property is real estate, the owner of the real estate should execute a deed transferring the real property to the LLC, and record that deed. (See Q 2:21 for the effect of an existing mortgage on real estate transferred to an LLC.) If the property consists of nontraded securities, for example, stocks and bonds, the owner of the securities should give the certificates to the LLC with an executed irrevocable stock power. If the securities are publicly traded, the LLC should register the ownership change with the applicable transfer agent. If the securities are not publicly traded, the LLC should register ownership of the securities with the appropriate official, such as the corporate secretary of the issuer.

If the member is contributing a promise to contribute cash or property in the future, the contributor should give to the LLC a negotiable promissory note to that effect, identifying the LLC as the initial payee or "holder." If the contributor is agreeing to perform services in the future, the contributor should execute a binding written agreement to that effect with the LLC, and the written agreement should set forth the value of the interest to be transferred to the member in exchange for services, for tax purposes. (See Q 7:19 for the tax consequences of a transfer of an interest in an LLC for services.)

If the LLC is taking property subject to an existing lien or other debt, the bill of sale transferring that property to the LLC should identify it. If the member is to be relieved, personally, of the debt encumbering any property contributed, the LLC should execute an "assumption agreement" assuming the debt. It may be necessary to obtain the lender's consent before the LLC assumes any debt of a member in order to prevent the debt from being accelerated. If the terms of the debt are favorable or the LLC cannot otherwise redeem or refinance the debt to be assumed, the LLC and member should attempt to obtain the lender's written consent before the LLC assumes the debt. Such assumption will not, by itself, relieve the member of the responsibility to pay the debt. Otherwise, the LLC should be prepared to pay off or refinance the debt if the lender has the right (and exercises that right) to call the debt due.

Q 4:5   Does the LLC issue "stock" or similar evidence of ownership?

There is no requirement to do so under state law. Capital contributions may merely be recorded in the LLC's books and records. However, no state LLC act prohibits the issuance of a certificate of ownership of an interest, and a few states specifically authorize the issuance of "certificated interests."

If certificates are issued, the LLC should put a legend on the instrument. The language in the legend should put third parties on notice that the interest represented by the certificates cannot be transferred without the consent of the other members as required in the LLC's Articles, for example, by all members or by a majority of members. The legend should refer to any documents that contain transfer restrictions, for example:

SUBJECT TO OPERATING AGREEMENT

The limited liability company interest represented by this certificate is subject to restrictions contained in an Operating Agreement dated as of the ___ day of _____, 200__, as amended from time to time, a copy of which is filed with the Company, and this interest cannot be sold, donated, transferred, pledged, hypothecated, transferred or otherwise disposed of except in accordance with the terms of that agreement.

Q 4:6   Does the LLC have to disclose capital contributions to the public?

Most LLC acts do not require disclosure. A few states, however, do. For example, the **Florida** and **Wyoming** LLC Acts require the members to report the total amount of all contributions, including any agreements to contribute capital in the future, in the Articles. [Fla Stat Ann § 608.407, Wyo Stat § 17-15-107]

Enforcement of Commitments to Contribute Capital

Q 4:7   Are oral promises to contribute capital to an LLC enforceable?

Not if prohibited by statute. [See, e.g., Mo Rev Stat § 359.755.]

Q 4:8   Can members enforce an agreement (in the Operating Agreement or otherwise) of the members to contribute additional capital to the LLC?

Many LLC acts specifically provide that a written agreement to contribute capital to the LLC is enforceable by the LLC. In addition, many statutes authorize members to agree to reduce or subordinate the interests of members who fail to satisfy obligations to contribute capital to the LLC. Damages may include the forfeiture of the defaulting member's interest. [See, e.g., Del Code Ann tit 6, § 18-502(c); Ga § 14-11-402; Fla Stat Ann § 608.4211(5).]

If the relevant statute does not address the question, it may be difficult to enforce an agreement among the members to forfeit a member's interest for failing to make an agreed contribution. While the Operating Agreement or other agreement of the members should be prepared to constitute a binding legal contract, many state partnership laws limit the ability to forfeit a partner's partnership interest under similar circumstances. Thus, a court might refer to the substantive partnership law of that state and not enforce a forfeiture of an LLC member's interest upon a default. However, an encumbrance on the interest, and an obligation to pay the amount with interest, should be enforceable, if provided in writing.

Q 4:9   Can members compromise another member's agreement to make a contribution to the LLC?

In some states (**Colorado, Florida, Kansas, Nevada, Texas, Utah, Virginia,** and **Wyoming**), if the other members agree (often the statute will require unanimous consent), an LLC may compromise the obligation of a member to make a contribution to the LLC's capital. [RULPA § 502(c)] However, in some states (Florida, Kansas, Nevada, Utah, and Wyoming), a creditor who extended credit to the LLC or whose claim arose before the date of the compromise may enforce the contribution obligation regardless of the compromise by the LLC and other members. In other states (Colorado, Texas, and Virginia), only creditors who relied on a member's pledge to lend money to the LLC may enforce that agreement following a compromise of the member's obligation by the LLC.

Q 4:10   Can creditors of the LLC enforce the terms of a member's obligation to contribute capital to the LLC?

The answer varies from state to state. In many states, members are liable directly to the LLC's creditors for the amount of their unsatisfied contribution obligations, but only if the creditor relied on the commitment. [Del Code Ann Title 6 § 18-502(b); Va Code Ann § 13.1-1027.C] Other states follow RULPA Section 17(3), which allows all creditors, whether or not they relied on the commitment, to enforce a member's agreement to contribute capital. Arizona specifically permits enforcement by a third-party creditor only if the LLC member agreed or the LLC assigned its interest in the member's obligation to the creditor. [Ariz Rev Stat Ann § 29-7028]

It is less clear whether creditors may enforce assessments made by the firm on its members. Recent cases in the limited partnership context suggest that creditors may be able to enforce obligations for additional contributions. [In re Securities Group, 74 F3d 1103 (CA 11 1966) (limited partners who sold interests before obligation to pay assessment was called by company were still liable to trustee in bankruptcy); Builders Steel v Hycore, Inc, 877 P2d 1168 (Okla Ct App 1994) (liability to creditor existed when obligation to pay assessment explicitly stated in certificate of organization)]

Distributions

Q 4:11   When can an LLC make distributions to members?

Absent any agreements with third parties restricting distributions, LLCs generally can distribute cash or property, whether income or capital, to the members as provided in the Operating Agreement, or otherwise agreed by the members. However, similar to corporate distribution statutes, most LLC acts prohibit any distributions to members if, following the distribution, the LLC's liabilities (other than liabilities to members) would exceed the value of the LLC's assets. [Kan Stat Ann § 17-7615] In determining the propriety of a distribution, the Uniform Limited Liability Company Act (ULLCA) and the **California** statute include liabilities the company owes to members except those providing for payment of principal and interest only if, and to the extent, payment of the distribution would be allowed under the statute. [Cal Corp Code § 17254; ULLCA § 406]

Most LLC statutes hold members liable to creditors for wrongful distributions although some states elect to treat wrongful distributions under their fraudulent conveyance statute. [See Md Code Corp & Ass'ns § 4A-101, et seq]

Q 4:12   How are distributions allocated among members?

Unless the members otherwise agree, most LLC statutes provide that distributions are shared in proportion to each member's contributions to the LLC. However, unlike an S corporation, which must make simultaneously equal distributions per share of stock, the LLC statutes generally allow members to discriminate in the timing and amount of distributions among one or more members in any manner they choose. Distributions are recognized for income tax purposes unless they do not have substantial economic effect.

Treasury Regulations Section 1.704-1(b)(2)(ii)(b) requires an LLC to make liquidating distributions in accordance with the positive capital account balances of the members. Accordingly, except upon liquidation, members can agree to make distributions per capita, proportionate to capital accounts, all to one or more members at any particular time, or by any other method they desire.

Q 4:13   Can a member demand that the LLC distribute specific property of the LLC to that member?

Unless otherwise provided in the Articles or Operating Agreement, a member has no right to demand and receive any specific LLC property. [Kan Stat Ann § 17-7615]

Q 4:14   Can an LLC force a member to accept a disproportionate amount of an in-kind distribution of property?

No. Unless the Articles or Operating Agreement provides otherwise, an LLC cannot force a member to accept a distribution of property in-kind, to the extent the portion of the asset to be distributed to the member exceeds that member's proportionate indirect interest in the property. [Kan Stat Ann § 17-7615]

Q 4:15   Can a member demand a distribution before withdrawing?

No, unless otherwise agreed by the members. Members should establish a mechanism—a voting requirement or objective criteria—for determining when the LLC will make distributions. The Operating Agreement should also allocate distributions among the various members or classes of interests.

Furthermore, it has been held that an allocation for income tax purposes did not create a legal right to a distribution. [Five Star Concrete, LLC v Klink, Inc, 693 NE 2d 583 (Ind App 1998)]

Q 4:16   Following a member's withdrawal, is the LLC required to return that member's capital account or share of the LLC's net worth?

The Uniform Act also allows the LLC to defer redemption of a member's interest when that member withdraws in violation of the Articles or Operating Agreement before the dissolution date set forth in the LLC's Articles. In that case, the LLC is not required to redeem a member's interest until the end of the term fixed in the Articles, but the deferred payment must include interest. [Uniform Act § 701(g)] A member can overcome this provision by persuading a court that an earlier buy-out of the member's interest would not cause "undue hardship" to the LLC.

Q 4:17   Is a member ever required to return a capital distribution to the LLC or the LLC's creditors?

The answer to this question depends, in many states, upon whether the recipient member knew a distribution was improper at the time of the distribution. For example, all LLC statutes forbid distributions to members, if the distribution would render the LLC insolvent.

Thus, in some states (**Colorado, Kansas, Nevada,** and **Texas**), if an LLC made a distribution to a member, and the member knew the distribution rendered the LLC insolvent, that member may be required to return to the LLC (or the LLC's creditors) an amount equal to the distribution.

The **Delaware** statute specifically defines knowledge as actual knowledge, rather than constructive knowledge. [Del Code Ann tit 6, § 18-101(5)]

Other states require members to return all wrongful distributions regardless of the member's knowledge.

Q 4:18   Can a member loan money to an LLC?

Yes. [See, e.g., Del Code Ann tit 6, § 18-108] Unless otherwise agreed, a member or manager has the statutory power in many states to lend money to the LLC or guarantee the LLC's debts. However, under fiduciary-duty principles, members should disclose their interest in any loan to the LLC, and should refrain from any vote approving the LLC's execution of a promissory note payable to a member, especially if the terms of the loan are not comparable with commercial loans from a third party. State LLC statutes do not often specify the extent to which the corporate or other fiduciary rules apply.

Unless the Operating Agreement provides a member with a unilateral right to make additional contributions, any advance by the member may be designated as a loan instead of a contribution. [Broyhill v DeLuca, 194 BR 65 (ED Va 1996)]

Q 4:19 Can a member borrow money from the LLC?

Yes. [See, e.g., Del Code Ann tit 6, § 18-108] However, the Operating Agreement should address this issue and set forth specific procedures for, or prohibitions against, lending money to members. If allowed, the members should consider requiring full disclosure and approval of some minimum number of the other members before the loan is made.

Q 4:20 What is the tax consequence to the member for a distribution from the LLC?

A current distribution (as opposed to a liquidating distribution) made to a member is generally not taxable. If the distribution exceeds the member's tax basis (see chapter 7) immediately before the distribution, the member must, however, recognize gain equal to the difference. A member will never recognize a loss because of a current distribution. (For the tax consequences of a liquidating distribution, see chapter 7.) The distribution will reduce the member's tax basis in his membership interest by the amount of money distributed or, if property is distributed, by the LLC's basis in the distributed property. [IRC § 733(2)] The Taxpayer Relief Act of 1997 altered the manner in which basis is allocated among properties received in both a liquidating distribution and a nonliquidating distribution in which the adjusted bases of the assets received exceed the member's outside basis.

Specifically, the Taxpayer Relief Act of 1997 modified IRC Section 732 by implementing a three-tier basis allocation process that takes into account the fair market value and any unrealized appreciation or depreciation of properties distributed by the LLC to a member. In addition, the IRS Restructuring and Reform Act of 1998 clarified that, for purposes of the allocation rules of IRC Section 732(c), "unrealized receivables" has the meaning given it in IRC Section 751(c) including the last two sentences of IRC Section 751(c), relating to items of property that give rise to ordinary income.

For non-liquidating distributions, the distributed property will generally have the same basis in the hands of the member as it did in the hands of the LLC before the distribution unless the adjusted basis in the property exceeds the member's outside basis in the LLC less cash received in the distribution. If the LLC's aggregate adjusted basis in the property distributed exceeds the partner's outside basis less cash received, the basis in the property is the member's outside basis less any cash received. (See chapter 7 generally for tax consequences.)

If the non-liquidating distribution consists of multiple properties and the LLC's aggregate basis in the assets exceeds the partner's basis in the membership interest ("outside basis"), basis must be allocated between the properties to the extent of the amount of the partner's outside basis. Section 732 provides two different rules in this case. First, if the LLC's basis in unrealized receivables and inventory exceeds the member's outside basis in the LLC, the difference is allocated initially to the receivables and inventory in proportion to any unrealized depreciation followed by an allocation in proportion to basis. In the event that the member's outside basis exceeds the LLC's basis in unrealized receivables and inventory, the difference is allocated to the nonreceivable and noninventory property in proportion to any unrealized depreciation followed by an allocation in proportion to the properties' basis.

If the distribution is in liquidation and the member's outside basis exceeds the LLC's basis in the property, the aggregate adjusted basis is determined by allocating the difference in basis among the LLC's nonreceivable and noninventory properties proportionately with respect to their fair market values. [IRC § 732(c)] This method, added by the Taxpayer Relief Act of 1997, represents a departure from the previous practice of first allocating basis to receivables and inventory followed by a proportionate allocation to the residuary property with respect to the LLC's basis in such property. If the distribution is in liquidation but the LLC's aggregate adjusted basis exceeds the member's outside basis, the basis is allocated in the same manner as if it were a non-liquidating distribution.

Q 4:21 How are distributions of marketable securities treated?

For purposes of Code Section 731, marketable securities are considered cash. Therefore, no loss may be recognized upon the distribution of marketable securities from an LLC to a member. This allows members to receive their share of appreciated marketable securities from the LLC without adverse tax consequences, unless the distribution exceeds the member's basis in the LLC interest.

Chapter 5

Management and Control

This chapter discusses the purpose and provisions of a typical Operating Agreement and it analyzes the powers of the members to govern and control the LLC, including the significance of electing a manager to manage the LLC as opposed to the members managing the LLC.

The Operating Agreement

Q 5:1   What is an Operating Agreement?

An Operating Agreement is a term contained in most LLC statutes to refer to an agreement among the members to govern the operations of the LLC's business, including the rights of members (and managers, if any) *vis-a-vis* each other. The **New York** LLC Act defines an Operating Agreement as "any written agreement of the members concerning the business of the limited liability company and the conduct of its affairs." [NY Partnership Law ch 34

§ 102(u)] The ULLCA provides that the Operating Agreement is the agreement, written or oral, providing for the "regulation of the affairs of the company, the conduct of its business and governing the relations among members, managers, and the limited liability company." [ULLCA § 101(13) (cross-referencing § 103)] The Florida and Texas LLC Acts refer to this document as the LLC's "regulations," and Delaware refers to the "limited liability company agreement." [Fla § 608.423; Texas arts 1528n, 2.09; Del Code Ann tit 6, § 18-101(6)]

All of the LLC acts allow the members, to some extent, to describe and define the members' and the managers' rights, authority, obligations, and duties in the Articles and in an Operating Agreement. Thus, whether or not the members are required to adopt a written Operating Agreement, the members should enter into a written agreement, consistent with their intent and the law of the state of the LLC's organization, containing at least some of the items discussed below.

While the members have wide latitude under the Operating Agreement in regulating the LLC, they may not contradict the LLC's articles of organization. Most statutes expressly state that the articles of organization control in the event of a direct conflict. [See, e.g., Cal Corp Code § 17005(f) (1994); NY Partnership Law ch 34 § 417]

> **Planning Pointer.** If the LLC does not adopt a written Operating Agreement in a state where it is not required, the LLC and the members will be subject to any "default" provisions of the relevant LLC statute. However, one of the advantages of the LLC is the members' ability to arrange their affairs almost any way they desire. Consequently, advisers should make sure that their clients are aware of the choices they have, especially with respect to management, withdrawal rights, the right to distributions, and the ability to alter many of the statutory provisions with respect to these and other items.

Q 5:2   What information should an Operating Agreement contain?

At a minimum, the Operating Agreement should have the following basic provisions:

- *Definitions.* It should establish a list of standardized, clearly defined terms or nomenclature relevant to the governance of the LLC.
- *Offices.* It should identify the LLC's registered office and principal place of business.
- *Permitted businesses of the company.* It should generally mirror the Articles and set forth the LLC's defined purpose and permitted business, and any vote of the members necessary to expand that purpose or business.
- *Management and officers.* It should address the management of the company, including provisions for the election of managers, if any, and indemnification of the members and managers active in the management of the LLC. In addition, if there are designated managers or officers, the Operating Agreement should set forth the extent of their authority.
- *Rights and meetings of members.* It should set forth the members' voting and other rights, any obligations to contribute additional capital, restrictions on withdrawal, etc. It should also contain procedures for meetings of the members, and the vote required of the members to make specified "major decisions" for the LLC. In addition, because some states' LLC statutes do not require either the purchase of a deceased member's share or the payment of that member's share to the decedent's estate, the agreement should make some provision for that eventuality.
- *Allocations, distributions, and reports.* This section should establish the basis for making distributions to members, including any prerequisites (e.g., specified member approval) that must be specified before making a distribution. Further, the agreement should also provide for any desired special allocations to members, if any, of the LLC's income, loss, deductions, credits, or other tax items, and further provide for their substantial economic effect.
- *Restrictions on transferability.* The LLC will often restrict the transferability of members' interests in the LLC to prevent unknown or unwanted third persons from acquiring an interest in the entity. The Operating Agreement should contain these restrictions or the Articles may contain them. If in the Articles, they can be amended by filing an amendment with

the Secretary of State or other appropriate office. Members may also want to enter into a buy-sell agreement which can be incorporated in the Operating Agreement or in a separate agreement among the members.

- *Dissolution and termination.* The LLC will dissolve upon certain events unless otherwise provided (see chapter 8). The Operating Agreement should follow the statute in this respect, and perhaps add additional dissolution events if so desired, or, alternatively, provide for the continued existence of the LLC despite the occurrence of a dissolution event. Thus, the Operating Agreement should also contain any rights by remaining members to continue the business of the LLC upon a dissolution event, including whatever vote is necessary. It should also set forth procedures for the payment of creditors and other events incident to a winding-up and liquidation of the LLC.

- *Miscellaneous provisions.* As a binding legal contract, the Operating Agreement should include the procedures that must be satisfied to amend the agreement, governing law, choice of law, and other such items. While many states do not require written Operating Agreements, the Operating Agreement should be written, to reduce disputes and ensure that the parties consider major issues. The Operating Agreement should always contain the standard integration clause, to ensure that the written Operating Agreement overrides any prior or later oral discussions or conduct, until it is formally amended, properly, in writing.

A copy of two sample Operating Agreements are attached as appendices F and G.

Q 5:3 Is an LLC required to have an Operating Agreement?

Not in all the states, and it may be an oral agreement in some states. However, several states, such as Missouri, require the members to adopt an Operating Agreement. The ULLCA, on the other hand, does not require an Operating Agreement. [ULLCA § 103] If required, it can be oral, unless required by state statute to be in writing. Some states, however, require that waiver of certain statutory provisions be in writing even if the Operating Agreement is permitted to be oral. [Colo Rev Stat § 7-80-108(3); 15 Pa Cons Stat § 8903] No state requires LLCs to file the Operating Agreement with the Secretary of State or similar state office.

Q 5:4   Should the Operating Agreement be written?

Of those states that require an Operating Agreement, only a few actually require a "written" Operating Agreement. [See Colo Rev Stat § 7-80-102(11); Nev Rev Stat § 86.101] However, an attorney should never advise clients to rely on an oral "operating agreement," and should always recommend to clients that they execute a written agreement to be certain that they understand their obligations and can later prove what they are, if there is disagreement.

Q 5:5   How is an oral Operating Agreement enforceable?

Yes, at least when oral contracts are enforceable. While most of the provisions of a typical Operating Agreement probably are not covered by the relevant state's statute of frauds, as a practical matter, it may be difficult to prove the terms of any oral Operating Agreement among an LLC's members.

Q 5:6   How is a written Operating Agreement enforceable?

Many state statutes specifically provide that the terms of the Operating Agreement may be enforced in court at law or in equity to the extent provided by law. [See Mo Rev Stat § 359.746.2; Del Code Ann tit 6, § 18-111.] The Operating Agreement establishes a binding legal contract among the parties to the agreement. Thus, the general law of contracts, as interpreted by the relevant state's courts, should apply to a breach-of-contract action with respect to the Operating Agreement. An enforceable arbitration procedure could also be specified.

Q 5:7   Can members specifically enforce the terms of the Operating Agreement?

Delaware law, for example, specifically provides that the members may, by agreement, impose "specified penalties or specified consequences" on members or managers who violate the terms of the "limited liability company agreement" (i.e., the Operating Agreement). [Del Code Ann tit 6, §§ 18-306, 18-405] Thus, if the members provide for specific performance, liquidated damages, or other equitable relief in their Operating Agreement, the Delaware courts should enforce those provisions absent some type of contractual defense.

Missouri, on the other hand, implies that specific performance may not be obtained in some cases to enforce a member's agreement to vote to continue the business of the LLC following an event of withdrawal by another member. Missouri allows specific enforcement if the members vote to continue the LLC *after* the event of withdrawal by the other member.

In some cases an argument by analogy to ordinary corporate management agreements might be made to enforce an LLC Operating Agreement. One case that gives a tremendous amount of deference to the owners' private agreement is Peck v. Horst, 264 P.2d 888 (Kan. 1953). In *Peck*, two owners of a corporation transferred their stock into a "voting trust and management agreement." The three trustees of this trust voted all the stock and controlled the corporation for a 10 year period. The trustees made all decisions with respect to the corporation, limited only by a requirement to act in the best interest of the two shareholders. The agreement even prohibited one stockholder from being physically on the premises. One of the shareholders challenged the agreement, but the court held that stockholders can waive any statutory provisions in the agreement, at least where the public interest and third parties are not harmed. The court applied a waiver theory on the facts which would extend to any party that assented to the agreement. A similar result was reached in Galler v. Galler, 203 N.E.2d 577 (Ill. 1964). In Galler, there was an agreement between two shareholders who owned 95 percent of the stock in a corporation. The corporation's four directors consisted of the two directors and their wives. If the corporation had an earned surplus of five million dollars or more, the agreement required dividends to be paid. Should one of the shareholders die, the widow designates a new director, despite a provision requiring the corporation to buy back decedent's stock to pay all estate and inheritance taxes. Even though such an arrangement would create an unequal balance in voting power and stock ownership, the Court held the agreement to be valid, noting that there was no harm to the public, creditors or any minority shareholders.

Q 5:8   Are all of the LLC's members required to consent to the terms of a written Operating Agreement?

Those states that require an Operating Agreement, either expressly or by implication, suggest that the initial Operating Agreement be adopted by all of the LLC's members at the time it is adopted. [See Mo Rev Stat § 359.746.1; Kan Stat Ann § 17-7613.]

A written Operating Agreement may bind only those members who have signed the document and transferees, as well as new members who have actual or constructive notice of the provisions. Thus, the members of an LLC should do what is necessary to ensure that each member has executed the agreement or an authorized counterpart to the agreement.

Q 5:9   Is an Operating Agreement effective against members who were not members at the time it was first adopted?

No, unless later members agree to be bound by the agreement, or, when they became members, they had actual or constructive notice. However, under most statutes, the consent of at least a majority of the members is required to admit a new member or a transferee of a member (as discussed in chapter 6) to the LLC. The Operating Agreement should require, as a condition to member-ship, that in addition to the required consent, a transferee or new member must execute and agree to be bound by the Operating Agreement or an authorized counterpart before they will be admitted to the LLC as a member. (A transferee is one who is assigned the LLC interest; therefore, he or she receives distribu-tions and profits. The transferee, however, is not a member of the LLC; therefore, he or she does not participate in managing the affairs of the LLC.)

Q 5:10   How many members must consent to amend a written Operating Agreement?

To be effective against all members, generally all members must consent to amend the Operating Agreement, unless otherwise provided in the Operating Agreement. Even if the Operating Agree-ment allows less than all of the members to amend it, it should require that amendments to change super-majority or unanimous voting provisions in the Operating Agreement be approved by an identical super-majority or unanimous vote, and specifically provide that an amendment is binding on all members and managers, even those who vote against it.

Q 5:11   Does an LLC have separate by-laws?

Generally not. The typical corporate by-law provisions (e.g., meetings of members, manager authority, etc.) are usually included in the LLC's Operating Agreement, which serves much the same function as corporate by-laws.

Management of the LLC

Q 5:12   Who governs the operations of the LLC?

In all states other than **Minnesota** (and formerly under the original **Colorado** statute), the members of an LLC have a choice whether to manage the LLC themselves or to designate a manager or managers for the LLC (see Q 5:28). Consequently, in most states the members must agree and provide for the mechanics of the governance of the LLC in the Operating Agreement and in the Articles (see Q 5:29).

Q 5:13   Do all managers and members have the same rights and duties with respect to the management of the entire company?

Not necessarily. Some states expressly allow the creation of distinct "series of interests" which permit members and managers to have separate powers and duties with respect to designated LLC property, obligations, and profits. [Del Code Ann tit 6, § 18-215; Iowa Code § 490A.305] These statutes also allow for liabilities resulting from the designated series to be charged only to that series insulating the rest of the company's assets if certain criteria are met including: maintenance of separate books and accounts with respect to each series and the disclosure of the limited liability of each series within the LLC. In addition, the Articles of Organization and Operating Agreement can create non-voting membership interests, superstatutory voting requirements as to specified issues, etc.

Q 5:14 Does an LLC have a board of directors?

Only **Minnesota** requires LLC's to have a board of directors, called a "board of governors" under the Minn Stat Ann LLC Act. [Minn Stat Ann § 322B.606] However, when an LLC has managers, they function in a fashion similar to corporate directors. If an LLC is manager-managed, and the members want to appoint one or more manager with special authority, the members should consider establishing a "board of managers" or an "executive committee" with procedures for adopting policies and implementing the members' and managers' decisions. The legality of this group would depend on state law.

Q 5:15 Does an LLC have officers?

Most LLC statutes do not provide for the appointment of officers. Nevertheless, members should be able to designate officers in the Operating Agreement to make clear who has authority and responsibility to carry out certain actions. If the LLC is to be managed by one manager, the manager could also hold a common, recognizable title, such as chief executive officer. These designations are understood to the outside world as designations of authority. In the business world, generally a person designated as a "manager" is not perceived as the highest level of authority in an organization, even though, by statute, the manager has executive authority in an LLC. Similarly, additional executive officers could be appointed with similar but lesser titles (e.g., chief financial officer, chief operating officer, secretary, treasurer, etc.).

If the LLC is to be managed by the members, statutorily or by common law, each member has actual or implied agency authority to represent and contract on behalf of the LLC. If a member-managed LLC appoints a chief executive officer, or other similarly designated person, whether a member or not, this fact could lead to an assertion that the LLC has "centralized management," and only such officer may act for the LLC. However, the appointment of an officer other than a manager should not impose upon an LLC the corporate characteristic of centralized management if all the members retain ultimate management agency authority, and if there is a designated officer or "managing member" in the Operating Agreement (under which the LLC is member-managed and has no managers, as such). Nevertheless, to be sure, if the members want to appoint officers but not be manager-managed, then the officers may be deemed to be managers, regardless of their title.

In a member-managed or manager-managed LLC, the members should consider designating one or more members or managers to hold the office of secretary and treasurer. The LLC statutes require the retention of certain documents, and the LLC will have bank accounts and tax returns to file. Both of these designated offices generally are recognized in the business community, and it would be useful to appoint individuals to act in these capacities to ensure that the LLC retains and keeps accurate records and financial information.

If any officers are appointed, the Operating Agreement should contain procedures for election, removal, and indemnification (and a clear job description) of each officer desired.

Finally, each entity taxed partnership should name a designated "Tax Matters Partner" for federal tax purposes. [IRC § 6231] The Operating Agreement should designate a partner to be the LLC's Tax Matters "Partner," which could be included in the treasurer's job description. This technique should work as a practical matter, although technically an LLC taxed as a partnership has no partners under state law.

Q 5:16   Do LLC acts require LLCs to maintain company records?

Many LLC acts follow Revised Uniform Limited Partnership Act (RULPA) Section 105 and require that the LLC maintain and retain a number of records. The statutes generally require the LLC to keep and make available to the members, upon reasonable request, these records:

- A copy of the Articles, Operating Agreement, and any minutes of meetings of the members;
- A current list of the name and address of each member and manager, if any;

- Financial information, including information generally included in a balance sheet, the agreed value of contributions or services rendered or to be rendered, and the status of any obligations of members to contribute additional capital;
- A true and correct copy of all of the LLC's tax filings, including federal, state, and local income tax returns and information returns; and
- The information necessary to determine a member's voting rights.

Many LLC statutes require the LLC to keep these records, and make them available for inspection by any member, at the LLC's principal place of business as designated in the Articles, if required, or in the Operating Agreement.

Q 5:17   Who has the authority to bind the LLC?

If manager-managed, generally only the LLC's managers generally have the ability to bind the LLC to a contract, unless they have authorized others to act on the LLC's behalf. If member-managed, each member generally has agency authority and can sign contracts that bind the LLC.

Member-Managed LLCs

Q 5:18   What is a member-managed LLC?

In a member-managed LLC the members have not designated a manager for the LLC in the Articles or Operating Agreement.

Q 5:19   Does each individual member have the authority to bind the LLC?

Yes, either explicitly by statute or implicitly under common law agency principles, unless the LLC is manager-managed. However, see Q 5:20 below on methods to limit this authority. If member-managed, every member generally could be an agent of the company, and bind the LLC contractually, including by signing contracts, so long as the member is apparently acting on behalf of the LLC in the LLC's usual business or affairs. [Mo Rev Stat § 359.738]

Q 5:20   Can you limit the agency authority of members to bind the LLC?

The LLC's Articles or Operating Agreement may restrict the authority of one or more members to bind the LLC. For instance, Missouri Revised Statutes Section 359.739 is an example of a statutory provision that is found in most LLC statutes, and states that no member, manager, or agent of an LLC can bind the LLC with persons who have actual knowledge of any restrictions on that member's (or other person's) ability to contract on the LLC's behalf. (See Q 5:30 for when a third party is deemed on notice of a restriction.)

Q 5:21   How do member-managed LLCs make and approve decisions?

In every state, the members are free to structure their management rights with respect to each other almost any way they choose. Thus, members should be able to delegate to another member (e.g., a "managing member") or committees of members the authority to make decisions and implement those decisions on behalf of the company, short of designating managers. Unless otherwise agreed or restricted by statutes (see Q 5:15), most decisions of the LLC in a member-managed LLC are subject to the approval of a majority of the members. However, contracts executed by a member with apparent authority to bind the LLC may be enforceable by third parties even if the members have not approved it. The LLC may have recourse to sue a member for damages who, without authority, binds the LLC to contract with a third party

Q 5:22   What is the basis for determining voting rights of the members?

In most states, unless otherwise agreed, members have voting rights in proportion to their capital contributions to the LLC. A few states have adopted the partnership default rule of one vote per member, unless the members establish a different rule for computing voting rights. [Ariz Rev Stat Ann § 29-681D; Kan Stat Ann § 17-7612; La Rev Stat § 12:1318(A)]

It should be noted that no LLC act requires every member to have voting rights, or to have an equal vote on each or any item subject to a vote of the members. The Operating Agreement should, therefore, describe the voting rights for each class of member, the decisions left to the members' approval, and the vote required (e.g., super-majority or unanimous) to approve those acts.

Q 5:23   What LLC decisions should require unanimous agreement or consent?

Certain LLC statutes, generally the original "bulletproof" statutes (see chapter 2), required members unanimously to consent to the continuation of the LLC following a dissolution event and/or the transfer of an interest to a nonmember.

The approval of the initial Operating Agreement will require unanimous consent. Otherwise, the members should be free to decide most questions without unanimous consent, unless otherwise required by state law. [See, e.g., NY Partnership Law ch 34 § 402(c), (d); Wis Stat § 183.0404(2)] State law requirements for unanimity often involve amendments to the articles of organization. [See Cal Corp Code § 171003(a)(2) (unanimity also required for amendment of operating agreement); Or Rev Stat § 63.444]

The requirement of unanimous consent dilutes the power of those who may have the largest stakes in the enterprise and subjects them to the will of the minority, however small. Thus, only in rare cases should the Operating Agreement require (or fail to reduce the vote for any statutory defaults that require unanimous consent, unless otherwise agreed) the unanimous vote of the members. Ultimately, it will depend on a judgment as to whether one is more worried about the tyranny of the majority (over the minority) or the tyranny of the minority (by blocking action desired by the majority).

Q 5:24   What LLC decisions should require at least majority consent?

The Articles and Operating Agreement should both require a vote of at least a "majority in interest" to approve the continuation of the business after a dissolution event. (See chapter 3 for a definition of "majority in interest.") Further, the Articles and Operating Agreement should require a majority vote to admit a transferee of a member's interest as a member of the LLC. [Rev Proc 95-10, 1995-3 IRB 20] (See chapter 3 for variations on the definition of "majority" for this purpose.) Unless the members have delegated all of their authority to the managers, most decisions requiring a vote should require a majority or super-statutory percentage vote, depending upon the particulars of the situation.

Q 5:25   Must an LLC have annual or regular meetings of the members?

No, although some of the first LLC statutes required the annual election of managers, if any. In addition, a few states, like Kansas and Minnesota, set forth detailed statutory provisions regarding meetings, including quorum, notice, and the issuance of proxies. [See Kan Stat Ann § 17-7613] The Operating Agreement should contain any mandatory statutory requirements for meetings, quorums, notices, and proxies, and otherwise establish procedures for calling meetings and transacting business at those meetings.

Q 5:26   Do members increase their exposure to personal liability for the LLC's debts by participating in the management of the LLC?

By statute, no, but as a practical matter, they do increase their exposure to claims. The LLC acts specifically address this issue and generally provide that no member is liable for the LLC's obligations solely by reason of acting in the member's capacity as a member in the LLC. Because members in a member-managed LLC have statutory agency authority, they have management authority, except as may be limited by the members in the Operating Agreement or otherwise.

By statute, if an LLC does not use its exact name, it may create statutory joint and several partnership-type liability for all members.

Thus, members need to be cognizant of establishing and maintaining formalities. For example, contracts executed by the member on the company's behalf should clearly indicate the member is signing in their agency capacity, and not personally. Thus, when signing documents, members should insist that the contract identifies the LLC as the contracting party, and the word "member" appears under the signatory line. For example:

Joe Sixpack, L.L.C. By: Joe Sixpack Title: Member

Q 5:27   Can an LLC indemnify a member?

Many LLC acts allow LLCs to indemnify members from liabilities while acting in their capacity as a member. Most statutes are silent, which should not prohibit LLCs from indemnifying members under the Operating Agreement or by other contract, to protect members active in the management of the LLC.

Manager-Managed LLCs

Q 5:28   Are LLCs required to have a manager?

At the time of this writing, only **Minnesota** requires their LLCs to have a "board of governors," which is comparable to having managers. [Minn Stat Ann § 322B.606] Even though a board of governors is required, the Minnesota LLC Act also provides for the sharing of management authority between members and the board. [Minn Stat Ann § 322B.606]

Until July 1, 1994, LLC's formed in **Colorado** were required to have a manager. [Colo Rev Stat § 7-80-401(1) (1990)] LLCs formed in Colorado before July 1, 1994 remain subject to the prior law, until all of the members make an election to apply the new law to their LLC. [Colo Rev Stat § 7-80-1101] Thus, until the members make the necessary election, the older Colorado LLCs must continue to have a manager.

All other states with LLC statutes allow the members to decide whether or not to designate the LLC as "manager-managed" or "member-managed."

Q 5:29   How does an LLC become manager-managed?

All LLC acts authorize the appointment of one or more managers to manage the LLC, instead of the members. In many states, an LLC is deemed to be member-managed, unless the Articles or

Operating Agreement specifically state the LLC is managed by a manager. [Kan Stat Ann § 17-7612; Mo Rev Stat § 347.079 (requires a statement in the Articles); Del Code Ann tit 6, § 18-402] In other states, the LLC is considered to be manager-managed, unless the articles specifically provide the LLC is managed by the members. [Texas LLC Act art 2:12]

Regardless of the statutory default, the members should indicate in the Articles and their Operating Agreement whether the LLC is manager-managed or member-managed.

Q 5:30   What is the statutory effect of a "manager-managed" LLC?

Generally, like general partners in a partnership, many LLC acts provide that all of the members of an LLC have agency authority to bind the LLC. [See Uniform Partnership Act (UPA) § 9(1); Kan Stat Ann § 17-7614; Mo Rev Stat § 359.738.1.] In those states, if the members elect to have a manager-managed LLC, the managers have the agency authority to bind the LLC, and the members do not.

The **Missouri** LLC Act provides a good example of the typical statutory provisions of the effect of a manager-managed LLC. Missouri Revised Statutes Section 359.738.2 provides that, if the LLC's Articles provide that the LLC is manager-managed, then:

- No member, acting as such, is an agent of the LLC;
- Every manager is an agent for the company, and has the statutory power, when apparently carrying on the LLC's usual business or affairs, to contractually bind the LLC, unless the members restrict that authority in the Articles, Operating Agreement, or otherwise, and the person with whom the manager is dealing knows of the limit on the manager's authority.

Thus, if a manager acts beyond the scope of his or her authority, but the affected third person had no knowledge of the manager's *ultra vires* act, the Missouri LLC statute, like many others, does not punish the third party.

It is not clear from the statute what kind of knowledge the person must have, or how much due diligence they must perform, to be protected by the statute. Analogizing to general principles of agency, it can be reasonably assumed that third parties would be deemed to be on notice if the manager's authority is restricted in the Articles (that are subject to public inspection), and the manager's actions with respect to that person are governed by those restrictions. [Restatement of Agency § 166] Thus, the LLC may be protected from the acts of managers outside the scope of their actual authority, if the Articles clearly limit the manager's power; but this will depend on whether state law deems all persons to have knowledge of publicly filed documents (even if a person has not in fact looked at it or understood it).

An act of a manager that is *not* for carrying on the LLC's usual business and affairs, does *not* bind the company, unless the Articles or Operating Agreement otherwise grants to the manager that authority. [Mo Rev Stat § 359.738.3]

Q 5:31   What authority does a member have in a manager-managed LLC?

Although most LLC acts limit the members' agency authority in a manager-managed LLC, members in a manager-managed LLC typically have rights similar to the rights of a shareholder in a corporation, unless otherwise agreed by the members. Thus, members usually have the right and the power to elect and remove the managers and the right to vote on major decisions.

Nevertheless, members in a manager-managed LLC may delegate to the manager all of their rights, and essentially abrogate their statutory rights and power (see Q 5:40). [See, e.g., Kan Stat Ann § 17-7614.]

Q 5:32   Who may be a manager?

The statutes generally do not establish qualifications for managers, other than **Colorado** and **Minnesota**. Colorado requires the manager to be at least 18 years of age if the manager is a natural person. [Colo Rev Stat 7-80-401(b)] Minnesota requires all managers to be *both* a natural person and at least 18 years of age. [Minn Stat Ann § 322B.67] Otherwise, any person, including a corporation, another LLC, professional management firm, trust, or partnership could be a manager.

Q 5:33   Does the manager have to be a resident of the state in which the LLC is formed?

No, unless the members otherwise impose this requirement in the Articles or the Operating Agreement, or, in certain states where professional LLCs are permitted (see chapter 12). Normally in a professional LLC, some or all members are required to be licensed under state law and may not otherwise legally be able to do business.

Q 5:34   How is (are) the initial manager(s) appointed?

As a practical matter, the initial manager will have to have the approval of all of the LLC's initial members. That is, in many states where the members must set forth in the Articles if the LLC is to be manager-managed, they must also name the initial manager in those Articles, or in the Operating Agreement. In either case, the initial members will have to at least agree with the person or persons named as the initial managers.

Q 5:35   Are the managers subject to periodic elections?

A few state LLC acts require the annual election of managers, unless otherwise agreed by the members. [NY Cons Law ch 576, § 413(a)] In most cases, the members may provide in the Operating Agreement procedures for periodic elections, resignation, removal, and election of successor managers.

Q 5:36   Can the members remove a manager without cause?

Unless otherwise agreed, LLC statutes authorize members to remove managers at any time with or without cause. If the Articles or Operating Agreement do not address the question, most statutes require the members to approve the election or removal of managers by at least a majority vote.

Q 5:37   Can a member be a manager?

In all states, the members may designate one or more members to be the LLC's manager.

Q 5:38 Does the manager have to be a member?

No, unless the LLC performs professional services. No state requires the members to select another member to be the manager (assuming the LLC is manager-managed) for general business LLCs. But a professional LLC must generally have a member as a manager, if a professional LLC is permitted by state law.

Q 5:39 Can all the members also be managers?

No state prohibits naming all the members to also be managers. Revenue Ruling 93-6 [1993-1 CB 229] ruled that an LLC had the corporate characteristic of centralized management when the five members were also the LLC's managers. However, the IRS has now altered its analysis of this issue. Under the "check-the-box" procedure [Treas Reg § 301.7701], the LLC does not need to acknowledge centralized management or other corporate characteristics in order to be taxed as a partnership.

Q 5:40 What powers may be delegated to the managers?

Except for any rights specifically reserved to the members by statute, the members can grant to the managers essentially unlimited authority to act on the LLC's behalf.

For tax classification purposes, members will no longer need to retain certain powers for continuing the LLC after a dissolution event and having the ability to restrict the transfers of interests in the LLC. Revenue Procedure 95-10 no longer generally is a concern due to the 1997 "check-the-box" procedure for LLC tax classification.

Q 5:41 Can an LLC indemnify a manager?

Yes. Many LLC acts specifically allow the LLC to indemnify and hold harmless managers from claims and demands against the manager in their capacity as manager. If the statute does not limit indemnification in any way, the members should consider limiting the indemnification of members and managers to acts or omissions that are not willful or (grossly) negligent.

Choice of Member-Managed or Manager-Managed LLC

Q 5:42   Should an LLC be "manager" managed or "member" managed?

The answer to this question depends on the facts and circumstances of each particular case.

An LLC probably should have one or more managers in the following situations, among others:

- If the LLC has a large number of members;
- If the LLC will be dealing with a large number of third parties, and the LLC has one or more members who are not actively involved in the LLC's business;
- If the LLC has issued interests to passive or silent members;
- If the LLC is formed by the patriarch or matriarch of a family business or investments, and he or she wants to retain full management control of the LLC, even though other family members (e.g., children or siblings) are issued interests; and
- If the LLC is a joint venture among two unaffiliated corporations that have other business interests, and the members want to retain a qualified person to operate the joint venture on their behalf.

In each of these cases, the appointment of a manager: (1) limits the ability of members to act beyond their authority, and may, depending on state law, prohibit members from binding the LLC to unwanted contracts; (2) provides more certainty to third parties wanting to contract with the LLC, who, if the LLC is not manager-managed, may insist upon the signature of all members before entering into a contract with the LLC; and (3) perhaps shelters the LLC from any *respondent* superior liability for torts by members who are not authorized to act on the LLC's behalf. [Mo Rev Stat § 359.743 (subjects an LLC to liability for all of the damages caused by a person acting in the ordinary course of the LLC's business or with apparent authority)]

If the LLC has only a few members, and the members will be involved actively in the business and affairs of the LLC, the members probably do not need a manager, but may choose to designate one if other LLC members want to attempt to avoid self-employment tax and can meet the IRS tests on this issue.

Q 5:43   When should an LLC not have a manager?

An LLC generally should not have a manager if the LLC wants to act as if it were a general partnership, and members want to share in important business decisions.

Q 5:44   What constitutes "notice" to an LLC?

Generally notice to any authorized person of the LLC is deemed notice to the LLC and, therefore, constitutes "knowledge" of the LLC. [See, e.g., Mo Rev Stat § 359.742] Some statutes do not specifically provide who constitutes an "authorized" person of an LLC; however, notice to a manager of a manager-managed LLC should constitute notice to the LLC. Missouri Revised Statutes Section 359.742 provides that notice to an authorized person does not constitute notice to the LLC, if the authorized person attempts (or consents) to defrauding the company.

Fiduciary Duties and Duty of Care

Q 5:45   Do the members have a duty of loyalty or fiduciary duty to each other?

Some LLC acts establish a fiduciary relationship among members with respect to the business of the LLC. For example, the Missouri LLC Act provides that every member or manager must account to the LLC for any profits or benefits derived by that person in connection with the business of the LLC or the use of the LLC's confidential information to that person's own advantage, without the informed consent of at least a majority (by number) of the disinterested members or managers. [Mo Rev Stat § 359.749.2] Thus, Missouri statute applies a "corporate opportunity" concept to the LLC. The members can waive application of this rule in the Operating Agreement. [Mo Rev Stat § 359.749.2]

Other states impose the manager's fiduciary duties to the LLC upon members for the purposes of defining the duty of loyalty between the members. [See, e.g., Ga Code Ann §§ 14-11-101(15), 14-11-304, 14-11-305(1)] States that follow this model generally require an Operating Agreement to provide for the division of internal power between members and the articles of organization to define agency power of the members with respect to third parties.

In addition to fiduciary duties, the ULLCA also references an obligation of "good faith and fair dealing" between the members. [ULLCA § 409(d)] Although not litigated extensively in the LLC context, the duty of good faith between partners generally applies more broadly than the fiduciary duties which govern partner relations. For example, an attempted sale of a limited partnership interest was held to be a "transfer" to attempt to subvert a right of first refusal held by another limited partner. This attempted sale was found to violate the implied duty of good faith between partners, although no fiduciary duty was violated. [Oregon RSA No 6, Inc v Castle Rock Cellular of Oregon Ltd. Partnership, 840 F Supp 770 (D Or 1993) (applying Oregon law)]

If not addressed by statute, the members should provide in the Operating Agreement any duty, such as the duty of loyalty, that they wish to apply to their LLC. In the case of an investor who is a passive member, a duty of loyalty or application of a "corporate opportunity" concept to that passive member may not be appropriate. The Missouri statute recognizes this concept. In the case of an LLC that is managed by managers, it provides that non-manager members do not have any duty to the LLC or the other members solely as a result of their status as a member, unless otherwise provided in the Operating Agreement. [Mo Rev Stat § 359.749.3] This exception specifically does not apply if the member obtains an unapproved profit or benefit derived in connection with the LLC's business or from confidential LLC information.

The ULLCA allows the Operating Agreement to reduce, but not eliminate, the duties of loyalty and care. [ULLCA § 103] The duty of loyalty cannot be eliminated, but the agreement can identify certain activities that do not violate the duty of loyalty, provided they are not unreasonable. The duty of care may not be unreasonably reduced under the ULLCA.

Q 5:46   What is the manager's duty of care?

Fiduciary principles would require managers and members (in the case of member-managed LLCs) to exercise good faith judgment, and only take management actions that they reasonably believe to be in the LLC's best interest. [See, e.g., Mo Rev Stat § 359.749.1]

Q 5:47   Does the "business judgment rule" apply to a manager's decisions?

In corporate law, the business judgment rule essentially shields an officer or director of a corporation from liability to the corporation or the corporation's creditors or owners from actions taken by that director or officer, when the particular act or decision was made in good faith, and in their reasonable judgment, in the corporation's best interest. [8 Del C § 141(a); see Smith v Van Gofkom, 488 A 2d 858 (Del 1985)]

The same protection should apply to members (if member-managed) or managers under many state LLC acts. In some states this rule is contained in state law. [Mo Rev Stat § 347.088] Thus, members or managers, as the case may be, are not liable for acts or omissions taken in the course of managing the LLC's business, if they take that act or omission in good faith and they reasonably believe that the act or omission was in the company's best interest.

If not provided by statute, members should consider applying the business judgment rule to their company in the Operating Agreement.

Q 5:48   Does the manager have any fiduciary duties or duty of loyalty to the LLC members?

The answer is not clear. Certain LLC acts are based on the Revised Uniform Limited Partnership Act, and do not address the fiduciary duties of members or managers. The California, Delaware, and Missouri LLC Acts, however, address this question. California provides that managers have the same fiduciary duties to the LLC and members as a partner has to a partnership and fellow partners, but those duties may be modified in the written

Operating Agreement. [Cal Code § 17153] Delaware provides that the LLC agreement can expand or restrict the fiduciary duties of the manager to the LLC. [Del Code Ann tit 6, § 18-110(c)] Missouri requires managers (and members acting in a management capacity) to fulfill their duties in good faith. The managers or members may not take advantage of any company opportunities but if they do, any profit or benefit derived will be held in trust for the benefit of the LLC. [Mo Rev Stat § 347.088] However, Missouri law also provides that a member in a manager-managed LLC (who is not a manager) has no duties to the LLC or other members, solely in his, her, or its capacity as a member. [Mo Rev Stat § 347.088.3]

Uniform Act. The Draft Uniform Limited Liability Act (Uniform Act) provides that managers owe the duty of loyalty and duty of care to members. [Uniform Act § 411] The statutory duty of loyalty consists of three main components:

- to account to the LLC and hold for it, as trustee, any property, profit, or benefit derived by the member without consent of the other members either in the winding up of the LLC business or from use of the LLC property;

- to refrain from dealing with the LLC on behalf of a party with interest adverse to the LLC without notice and consent of the other members; and

- to refrain from competing with the LLC without the notice and consent of the other members.

Managers violate the duty of care if they engage in grossly negligent, reckless, or intentional misconduct, or knowingly violate the law. [Uniform Act § 411]

ULLCA. Under the ULLCA, a manager has the duty of loyalty which includes the duty not to deal with the firm's property similar to the provision contained in the UPA § 21. Moreover, the manager also must refrain from both self-dealing and competition with the LLC. [ULLCA § 409(b)]

In conclusion, this question is largely unanswered in most states and, in many cases, may be subject to the case law of the relevant states by analogy. Therefore, the Operating Agreement should delineate any fiduciary duties of the managers and members to the LLC and each other. In some states, any consent to waiver of fiduciary duties by the members must be contained in a written Operating Agreement. [Cal Corp Code § 17005(d)] In many cases, when all members participate directly in the LLC's business and have relatively equal ownership interests, it may not be necessary to impose fiduciary duties on the members.

Q 5:49 Do managers have a duty to disclose information to members of an LLC?

Yes. Nearly all state statutes require managers to disclose their dealings to members of the LLC. These statutes also impose a duty upon the manager to maintain adequate books and records and grant members a right to inspect the book and records subject to reasonable limitations. Many states, however, do not expressly limit members' inspection rights to proper purposes although arguably this could be implied from the pertinent statutes or from analogy to the corporate and limited partnership contexts.

Q 5:50 What are the consequences of a breach of fiduciary duty where it exists?

In addition to any damages caused to the members or the company, managers or members who take an opportunity of the company for their own benefit without the informed consent of at least a majority of the other members must disgorge to the company the profits or benefits provided to them. [See, generally, Mo Rev Stat § 359.749.1.]

Derivative Suits

Q 5:51 Can a member file a derivative suit on behalf of the LLC?

The **Delaware** LLC Act specifically empowers each member to file an action in the Court of Chancery on behalf of their LLC if managers or the members with the authority to file the action fail to enforce the LLC's rights. [Del Code Ann tit 6, § 18-1001]

In a state with no specific statutory provision, the courts would determine whether such an action is permissible.

Q 5:52   What are the prerequisites for filing a Derivative Action?

Under Delaware Code Annotated title 6, Section 18-1002, following corporate law, a person must satisfy the following requirements before bringing a derivative suit:

- The person bringing the action must be a member of the LLC, both at the time the lawsuit is filed and either: (1) at the time the claim arose; or (2) at the time the claim arose, the person is the transferee of a member by operation of law or under the terms of the applicable Operating Agreement;
- The member filing the suit must set forth in the complaint attempts by the member to cause the manager or other members to file the action on the LLC's behalf, or set forth the reasons why the member believed those efforts would have been pointless.

Thus, similar to corporate derivative actions, the courts do not want to be involved in a derivative suit, unless the member filing the action first tried to force the persons with authority to prosecute the complaint or, at least, had a reasonable basis for deciding those efforts would have been ignored.

Q 5:53   Can a member who brings a derivative action recover expenses and attorney's fees?

Typically yes, if the suit is successful (whether by judgment or settlement), and if the court approves the payment to the plaintiff of reasonable expenses, including reasonable attorney's fees. [Del Code Ann tit 6, § 18-1004]

Other Litigation Issues Involving LLCs

Q 5:54   Can a member sue an LLC?

Yes. A member may sue the LLC or another member for legal or equitable relief. [ULCCA § 410(a)] An accounting is not required in order to bring suit. Moreover, California permits class action suits by members against an LLC. [Cal Corp Code § 17501]

Q 5:55   How is an LLC treated in Federal Courts for diversity purposes?

Courts will likely apply the aggregate theory to LLCs and examine the citizenship of each member in determining whether diversity of citizenship applies for the purposes of federal court jurisdiction. The U.S. Supreme Court applied this principle to limited partnerships in *Carden v. Arkoma Associates* and, in dictum, suggested that the same principle would apply to other unincorporated associations, including LLCs. [494 US 198 (1990)] Numerous Courts of Appeals have cited *Carden* in dismissing derivative suits in the partnership context because requisite joining of the partnership in the suit automatically destroyed diversity. [See, e.g., Bankston v Burch, 27 F3d 164 (CA5 1994)] At least one District Court has applied the *Carden* holding to LLCs. [See International Flavors and Textures, LLC v Gardner, 966 F Supp 552 (WD Mich 1997)]

Chapter 6

Members' Interests

This chapter discusses the ability of a member to assign or transfer an LLC interest and discusses the status of an assignee. This chapter also discusses the limited liability afforded a member and some situations in which limited liability might be lost.

Overview

Q 6:1   Who are the "members" in the LLC?

Only those persons who have been admitted to the LLC as a member are members in the company. In those states that require a written Operating Agreement, only those persons who have signed that agreement or been selected as a member, with the minimum required consent of the other members, are members.

Q 6:2   What is an "interest" in an LLC?

The LLC acts generally define an LLC interest to mean a member's share of the profits and losses of the company and the member's right to receive distributions of the company's assets.

Q 6:3   Are interests in an LLC represented by stock or other certificates of ownership?

Only a few LLC acts provide for the issuance of "certificates" to represent interests in an LLC. Although there is no prohibition against issuing certificated interests in other states, it is not customary to issue certificates (see Qs 6:5, 6:6).

A certificated interest may cause classification as a "security" for Uniform Commercial Code (UCC) or federal security law analysis although some state LLC statutes provide that statements of membership interest do not constitute securities. [See, e.g., ND Cent Code § 10-32-28(2); Tenn Code Ann § 48-215-101(b)] Other states address whether a certificated interest is a security in their adaptations of UCC Section 8-102. Revised UCC Section 8-102 excludes interests in LLCs from the definition of a security unless it is traded in securities markets or exchanges or the certificate provides that it is a security. Under the UCC, an interest in an LLC constitutes a financial asset if held in a securities account. **Maryland's** adaptation of this UCC provision excludes an LLC interest from the definition of "uncertificated security." [Md Comm Law § 8-102(1)(b)(v)] In comparison, the **Pennsylvania** version of the UCC deems a certificated LLC interest a "certificated security," and further provides that an uncertificated interest is an uncertificated security only if the interest is approved for trading in a recognized securities market or exchange. [13 Pa CSA § 8-102(s)]

Q 6:4   Is an interest personal property?

Every state LLC act defines the interest of each member to be personal property to that member. As personal property, the state statutes also make it clear that each member has an interest in the LLC itself but not in any specific property of the LLC.

Transferability of an Interest

Q 6:5   How are interests in an LLC transferred?

As personal property, an LLC interest may be transferred by a bill of sale, assignment, or comparable document. If the interests are documented with certificates, like stock certificates, it should be possible to transfer an interest by endorsing the certificate or by granting a power of attorney to the transferee or by granting a type of power like a stock power. To be effective the transferee must also cause the transfer of the interest to be reflected on the LLC's books. In any event, the transfer must first be approved under the LLC's requirements (e.g., approval of at least a majority in interest of members).

However, the transfer of an interest to a person does not by itself bestow the status of a member in the LLC (see Q 6:6). Rather, the transferee is merely an assignee of certain economic rights unless the other members by a requisite vote approve the transfer of a membership interest.

Q 6:6   Can a member assign his or her interest in an LLC without anyone's consent?

In many cases yes, although the transferee will be an assignee and not a member. Only members can vote and exercise other rights of members, but an assignee, like a member, may receive distributions of cash or property.

The Operating Agreement articles, or statute may limit the power of a member in an LLC to transfer an LLC interest in whole or in part. Some state LLC acts prohibit a member from transferring that member's own interest without the consent of all of the other members. Consent may be inferred by a failure to object to a transfer, and the failure to follow formalities by one individual, such as signing an amended Operating Agreement, may not be raised as objection by another member at a later date. [In re DeLuca (Broyhill v DeLuca), 194 BR 65 (ED Va 1996)] Many of the newer statutes require only majority consent, or allow the members to alter the statute's requirement for unanimous consent. In addition, any attempted transfer may be void if: (1) right-of-first-refusal restrictions in the Articles or Operating Agreement have not been complied with, or (2) a transfer of an interest in a professional LLC is attempted to a person or entity not licensed or otherwise eligible for membership.

In conclusion, while it may be possible to transfer the interest to someone without the consent of the other members, the transferee of that interest will not be a member unless the transferee has satisfied the statutory and any other requirements to obtain the status of a member.

Q 6:7   What rights does a member have following the assignment of that member's interest to a nonmember who is not admitted to the LLC?

As a general rule, an assigning member ceases to be a member of an LLC upon the assignment of a complete interest to a third party, regardless of the status of the assignee. Thus, even if the assignee is not admitted to the LLC as a member, the assignor loses all rights to management and distributions.

Q 6:8   What obligations does a member have following the assignment of that member's interest to another person?

Under most LLC acts, a member is not relieved of obligations to contribute capital or perform services for the LLC, except post-transfer obligations, once the assignee is admitted as a member. A member is also not relieved of the obligation to return any wrongful distributions (e.g., distributions that rendered the LLC insolvent). In addition, any member guarantees of liability will remain in effect unless canceled by the affected creditor.

Q 6:9   Do non-assignor members have any duties towards assignees?

There is no contractual relationship between the assignee and the remaining members. Moreover, the assignee does not possess a member's rights or duties to the remaining members because, technically, the assignee is not a member. Given these factors, it is arguable that the remaining non-assignor members have no duties towards an assignee. [Ribstein and Keatinge on Limited Liability Companies, § 7.04]

In the partnership context, some courts have held that an assignee could not dispute decisions of the partner-assignor which adversely affected the flow of money to the assignee. [Bauer v The Bloomfield Company/Holden Joint Venture, 849 P 2d 1365 (Alaska 1993)] However, an assignee which is a dissociated member or deceased members' estate might compel a different result. [Ribstein & Keatinge on Limited Liability Companies, § 7.04]

Q 6:10 Can members pledge or encumber their interest in an LLC without the consent of the other members?

The LLC acts generally do not forbid the pledge or encumbrance of an interest in an LLC. Indeed, many provide that a member does not cease to be a member upon a pledge, encumbrance, or other grant of a security interest in an LLC, unless otherwise agreed by the members. [See, e.g., Del Code Ann tit 6, § 18-702(b)(2); Mo Rev Stat § 359.771.1.]

To avoid the inconvenience or disruption of dealing with the creditors of each member, the members should consider restricting the pledge of a member's interest in the LLC, at least without the other members' consent. Every member's interest should secure their contribution obligations to the LLC, if any. If members are allowed to pledge or otherwise encumber their interest to a third-party creditor, the third party's rights to the interest will be that of an assignee unless the transferee becomes a member. This does not prevent a creditor from obtaining a "charging order" against a member's interest in an LLC to satisfy a judgment against a member-debtor (but see Qs 6:11 and 6:12).

Q 6:11 What rights do creditors have upon the exercise of their security interest in a member's LLC interest?

A creditor with an assignment of, or charging order against, a member's interest has the same rights as an assignee who has not been admitted as a member to the LLC. The LLC acts uniformly adopt this rule, which follows Revised Uniform Limited Partnership Act (RULPA) Section 703. A creditor or judgment creditor of a member is entitled to a "charging order" against the interest, but no more. Accordingly, a creditor who has seized a member's LLC interest to satisfy the member's personal debts does not thereby become a member in the LLC, unless admitted by the other members pursuant to the procedures required for any other transferee of an interest. Consequently, a judgment creditor cannot:

- Exercise management rights,
- Force a distribution,
- Require the redemption of a member's interest, or
- Seize any specific property of the LLC.

However, there are occasions when a creditor may pierce the limited liability veil of the LLC. If there are sufficient grounds to pierce the entity veil, then the creditor will be able to reach the LLC assets directly. The Service has stated this as their position in Chief Counsel Advice 199930013. Further, the Service says the fact that an entity is disregarded as an entity separate from the taxpayer does not change the analysis.

The IRS will defer to state law principles as to what property a taxpayer has an interest for tax collection purposes. If the sole member's interest is involuntarily assigned to the creditor, and the creditor/assignee only receives the economic rights, the debtor/member still has the management rights in the LLC. However, this may present a problem in the sense that there is less of an incentive for the member/manager to manage the LLC if none of the profits will accrue to him. Any compensation paid by the LLC for the benefit of a member or manager would be subject to attachment and garnishment by the creditor.

Q 6:12   What is a "charging order"?

A charging order is a statutory remedy of a creditor when the creditor is unable to force a partner or LLC member to assign his or her partnership interest to the creditor. A charging order is neither an assignment nor an attachment. It is a court order, somewhat like a garnishment, that directs the partnership or LLC to make any distributions it would have made to the partner or member to the creditor. The theory behind this rule is that, to allow a creditor access to the partnership or LLC assets and records as a result of the creditor's claim against one partner/member, would disrupt entity's business to the detriment of the other owners, especially if management rights were also involved. It is thus used to protect the business and the other owners.

A creditor may also be able to foreclose on the debtor's partnership interest. A judgment lien, by itself, does not constitute a charging order or a lien. Such lien must be perfected through a charging order. [See RUPA § 504] While a judgment creditor of a partner/member may not proceed directly against the entity, the creditor may set aside as fraudulent a transfer of assets by a judgment debtor to or from a partnership or LLC in which the judgment debtor is an owner if the transfer is made to hinder, delay, or defraud creditors of the partner.

Q 6:13 Will a charging order afford the same protection in a single member LLC?

One purpose of a charging order is to protect other partners or owners from interruption of business activities as a result of an attachment of partnership or LLC assets. When the claim is against someone who owns a single member LLC interest, such a purpose would appear to be inapplicable. The Service analyzed this in terms of who owns the property. [Chief Counsel Advise 199930013] An LLC interest is defined by most states as the member's share of the profits and losses and rights to distribution of the assets. Thus, the distributions to the member would clearly be available for attachment. The right to attach the assets of the LLC directly depends on the ability to pierce the corporate veil.

The issue becomes more complicated when personal use assets are transferred into an LLC. There are at least two approaches to attacking a transfer into a single member LLC. The first is whether or not there is a legitimate business purpose. Under this approach, if there is not a valid business reason that a nonbusiness asset is transferred into an existing or new LLC, then the veil could be disregarded. However, the Uniform Limited Liability Company Act states that an LLC can be organized for any lawful purpose. There does not have to be any business purpose in forming an LLC under this approach. Under this rationale, it would seem that nonbusiness LLCs and LLCs with a business purpose but owning nonbusiness assets will be protected. In addition, the transfer of business assets for a business purpose, but done solely with the intent to hide assets from a creditor would seem to be under less scrutiny providing an avenue for fraud.

Furthermore, a remedy is already available to the creditor. The holder of an LLC interest has an equity interest in that LLC. As long as there was not some kind of gift or transfer for less than full and adequate consideration, that equity interest in the LLC is certainly available to the creditor. For example, if the LLC asset consisted of a vacation home that is owned by more than one person, courts might be reluctant to allow an innocent LLC member to have to liquidate to pay the other member's debts, but the creditor could obtain a charging order as to the debtor's interest in the LLC.

It may make sense to analyze these transfers in terms of whether or not there is fraudulent transfer. Oftentimes, the timing of the transaction is a good indicator of whether or not there is some intent to hinder, defraud, or delay a creditor. Under the approach, the analysis would not involve the LLC but whether the asset transfer itself is fraudulent.

Q 6:14 What is the tax status of an assignee (including a creditor assignee) of an LLC interest?

Because the assignee of a member's interest in an LLC is entitled to the economic rights (e.g., allocations of income and loss, and to distributions) of their assignor, the assignee of an interest in an LLC treated as a partnership for federal income tax purposes may be treated as a member (partner) for tax purposes. [Rev Rul 77-137, 1977-1 CB 178] The ruling provides that an assignee may be treated as a partner if the owner assigns irrevocably to another the right to share in the profits and losses of the organization and to receive all distributions, including liquidating distributions, to which the transferring owner would have been entitled had the assignment not been made. In the ruling, the assigning partner agreed to exercise any residual powers remaining solely in favor of and in the interest of the assignee. In addition, the assignee, although not formally admitted to membership, acquired substantially all of the dominion and control over the interest and, for Federal income tax purposes, was treated as a substituted partner.

The holder of a charging order may, however, hold an interest that is similar to a garnishment or may foreclose the entire interest. In determining whether the holder will be treated as a partner, it is necessary to compare the interest held by the creditor with that of the debtor/partner. Where the charging order is similar to a garnishment, the debtor/partner/member could be treated as the partner, thus being required to include the distributive share of income and loss and entitled to a deduction if the payment of the judgment would give rise to a deduction. In the case of the foreclosure of a partnership or LLC interest pursuant to a charging order, whether the judgment creditor or the debtor/partner will be treated as the owner will turn on the retained interest of the debtor after the foreclosure. The only guidance on this subject suggests that if the debtor retains a governance interest which does not have to be exercised for the benefit of the assignee, the debtor is still treated as the partner (or member). [See Treas Reg 1.704-1(e)(2)(ix)] Presumably, under this analysis, if under the statute or agreement, the debtor/partner's interest in the entity is extinguished by the foreclosure, the creditor should be treated as the partner.

The implications of this conclusion extend beyond the allocation of income and deductions from the LLC. Presumably, if the debtor is still treated as the owner, there is no disposition of the partnership or LLC interest or the claim, thus, the debtor would not recognize gain or loss on the foreclosure until the interest is terminated. It would seem highly inconsistent to treat the debtor as the owner for purposes of a distributive share, but not for purposes of transfer of the interest.

Q 6:15   Can a member transfer the voting rights inherent in an LLC interest without transferring the economic interest in the LLC?

Yes, if the state statute provides for the grant of a proxy by one member to another person to exercise that member's right to vote. [See, e.g., Del Code Ann tit 6, § 18-302(c).] In addition, this issue is separate and apart from the ability of a member to delegate authority to a manager or another person, as is allowed, at least within specified limits under all LLC acts.

Q 6:16   Can a member transfer economic rights in an LLC, without transferring management rights?

Yes. Generally this is all a member can transfer without the other members' required consent. In addition, unless otherwise agreed by the members, any transfer of part or all of a member's interest in an LLC will cause that member to cease to be a member in the LLC if the transferee becomes a substitute member (see Q 6:7).

Q 6:17   What rights does a transferee or assignee of an interest have with respect to the LLC?

Unless otherwise agreed in advance by the members, the transferee of a member's interest, who is not admitted as a member, has no rights to participate in the management and affairs of the LLC. A nonmember transferee obtains the transferor member's rights to share in the company's profits and losses, to receive distributions, and allocations of income, gain, loss, deductions, tax credits or any other item allocable to the assignor member.

An assignee or transferee receives only the economic rights of the assignor member. If that member's rights to the LLC's income and losses were not in proportion to the size of the interest, the transferee of that interest would not be entitled to anything more or less, regardless of the size of the interest received.

Q 6:18   Does a transferee of an interest in an LLC have any obligations if not admitted to the LLC as a member?

Generally, no. An assignee or transferee of a member's interest that does not become a member does not have any liability as a member solely as a result of the assignment of an interest.

To dissuade assignees from accepting the assignment of an interest, the Operating Agreement could provide that the assignee of an interest be subject to all of the obligations of a member, including the obligation to make additional capital contributions to the LLC, whether or not the assignee is admitted to the company as a member. It is unclear if such a provision would be enforceable. However, an LLC should be able to offset against any distributions payable to an assignee of an interest, the amount of any capital calls allocable to that interest due under the Operating Agreement, at least if an offset provision is included either in the Articles or Operating Agreement.

Q 6:19   Does a transferee of an interest, who is admitted as a member, have any obligations to the LLC?

A transferee-member has, to the extent assigned, all of the rights and obligations of the transferor and the other members, to the extent provided in the Articles, the Operating Agreement, and the applicable statutes. It should be noted that an assignee who is admitted as a member may be liable for any unsatisfied obligations of the assignor to contribute capital to the LLC.

Consequently, before purchasing an interest in an LLC, a person should obtain a signed estoppel from the LLC that the assigning member has no unsatisfied obligations to the company.

Withdrawal

Q 6:20   Does a member have an unlimited right to resign from an LLC?

No. The LLC acts vary on whether a member has the right to resign from an LLC at any time. Under most statutes, unless otherwise agreed by the members, a member has the right to resign from the LLC upon a specified period of notice (e.g., **Missouri** requires 90 days notice, **Delaware** requires six months). [Mo Rev Stat § 359.775; Del Code Ann tit 6, § 18-603]

However, the statutes vary somewhat on the power to prohibit member's from resigning. For instance, the Delaware LLC Act allows members to prohibit by agreement any withdrawal or transfer of their interest before the dissolution and winding up of the company. [Del Code Ann tit 6, § 18-603] On the other hand, Missouri allows members to restrict the power but not the right to resign. That is, regardless of the members' agreement, a member can resign upon the required notice. However, if the members agreed not to resign, and a member breaches that agreement, the Missouri LLC Act allows the LLC to offset from any distributions due, including in redemption of the withdrawn member's interest, any damages caused by the wrongful withdrawal. [Mo Rev Stat § 359.775]

If the LLC act is similar to the Missouri Act in this regard, members who agree not to resign should include that agreement in the written Operating Agreement. The members may want to require withdrawing members to pay liquidated damages upon resignation, if the members expect it would be impossible to calculate the damage caused by a member's withdrawal.

It should be noted that, while a member may have the right in many cases to resign, that does not necessarily mean the member has a right to force the LLC to redeem its interest or to otherwise withdraw its capital from the LLC. The **Kansas** statute, for example, does not confer such a right. Other statutes may, however, allow a withdrawing member to receive "fair value" or other designated measure of value upon withdrawal (see Q 6:21).

Q 6:21   Can a member force the LLC to redeem that member's interest in the LLC?

Yes, in many states, but not all. However, in most states, the LLC's Operating Agreement can restrict each member's ability to force the LLC to redeem that member's interest. (See Qs 4:15 and 4:16 which describe the ability of a member to force a distribution from the LLC.) The Operating Agreement should address this question.

Q 6:22   Can a member's creditors force the LLC to redeem that member's interest in the LLC?

Generally no, unless the Operating Agreement gives to them this right. All of the LLC acts provide that a creditor who acquires a member's interest in an LLC is only an assignee of that interest. (See Q 6:11 on charging orders, and Q 6:17 on the limited rights of an assignee, including a creditor-assignee, of a member's interest.)

Q 6:23   Can a member force the LLC to distribute specific property to that member?

No. All of the LLC acts limit a member's ability to force distributions in any event and state that a member has no direct interest in any of the assets of that LLC (see Q 6:21).

Limited Liability

Q 6:24   Are LLC members personally liable for the LLC's debts and obligations?

All of the LLC acts in one form or another provide that no manager or member is personally liable for the debts or liabilities of an LLC solely as a result of that person's status as a manager or a member. Moreover, members do not become liable for the LLC's debts or liabilities solely as a result of participating in the management of the LLC. For example, in a suit against an LLC and an individual member where no personal misconduct is alleged against the individual member, the member would not be a proper party to the suit. [See Page et al v Roscoe, LLC et al, 497 SE2d 422 (CANC 1998) (case remanded to determine whether plaintiffs should be sanctioned for naming the member as a defendant)] However, individuals are always liable for their own "torts," and the LLC may be as well if the member was acting within the scope of the LLC's business (see chapter 12 and Q 6:25).

It sometimes may be difficult to distinguish individual liability for personal wrongs and for liabilities of the business. For example, **Hawaii** blurs the distinction between individual and vicarious liability by providing that violation of a statutory penal provision "shall be deemed to be also that of the individual members, managers, or agents of the limited liability company who have authorized, ordered, or done any of the acts constituting in whole or in part the violation." [Haw Rev Stat § 480-17(b)]

Q 6:25   When are members personally liable for the debts and obligations of the LLC?

Despite the broad protection from personal liability, managers and members can become liable for the LLC's obligations and liabilities created by their own tortious acts or omissions. This exposure to liability is not unlike the exposure of corporate officers, directors, and employees (in some cases) due to personal liability for their own wrongful acts or omissions.

Most LLC statutes also provide that the LLC is required to use a specific indication of its status in its legal name, such as LC, LLC, Limited Company, or Limited Liability Company. Failure to follow this statutory requirement could lead to the loss of the statutory limited liability benefit.

In addition, members and managers can, by their conduct, imply personal responsibility for an LLC's obligations, and if reasonably relied upon by third parties, may be held personally liable for those debts. For example, a member-manager of an LLC was held personally liable to a third party under agency law principles because he failed to disclose the name of the LLC for which he was acting and that his principal was an LLC. [Water, Waste, and Land v Lanham, 955 P2d 997 (Colo 1998)] Moreover, the state statutory provision providing that LLC articles of organization provide constructive notice of matter required to be stated in them was not intended to override applicable agency law. Consequently, whenever managers or members are acting on behalf of an LLC, the managers or members, as the case may be, should make it clear they are acting on the LLC's behalf and not personally. For example, managers and members should execute contracts on the LLC's behalf only if the contract is in the name of the LLC, and the signatory line clearly identifies their status, as follows:

[Manager-Managed] [Member-Managed]

Auburn Tiger, LLC Kansas Jayhawk, LLC

By: Terry Bowden By: Roy Williams

Title: Manager Title: Member

(See chapter 5 on the ability of the LLC to indemnify members and managers.)

Members may also, by agreement with a third party, guarantee all or a portion of the LLC's debts. In addition, the certificate of articles may provide for member liability in limited, specified cases. The **California** statute requires any agreement or statement of member liability in the certificate to expressly reference the statute which governs member liability. [Cal Corp Code § 17101(c)(2), (e); Cal Corp Code § 17158 (for manager liability)] **New York** expressly notes that guarantees by members do not require a statement of lack of member liability in the certificate. [NY Partnership Law ch 34, §§ 609(b), 611] On the other hand, the ULLCA and some states such as **Iowa**, **Tennessee**, and **Utah** require member liability be expressly included in the certificate so that the validity of a member guarantee in the absence of a provision in the certificate is questionable.

Q 6:26   Does the LLC insulate a member from personal liability for his or her own torts or malpractice (whether brought under tort or contract)?

No LLC act, corporation act, or limited partnership act protects an individual from liability for his or her own torts or malpractice.

Q 6:27 Does the LLC insulate a member from personal liability for the torts or malpractice of a manager, employee, or other member of the LLC?

Yes, in many states, at least to a large extent. Some LLC acts (e.g., **Utah, Montana,** and **South Carolina**) specifically provide this protection. Arguably, this protection applies in all states. However, a member is liable for his or her own "torts," such as damage caused by negligently driving a vehicle during the scope of employment or in some cases through acts or omissions of those employees or other members under their direct supervision or control (see chapter 12).

The answer to this question also depends upon the law applicable to the various professionals under state law. For example, in **Hawaii**, while lawyers may practice law in an LLC, the Supreme Court of Hawaii, in its role as the regulator of the state bar, has held that all of the shareholders of a law firm professional corporation are liable for the malpractice of each of their fellow shareholders. [Petition of Bar Association of Hawaii, 516 P 2d 1267 (1973)] The Georgia Supreme Court, by contrast, overruled a similar result it previously reached in *First Bank & Trust Co v Zagoria.* [302 SE 2d 674 (1983)] *Zagoria* stated that the Georgia Supreme Court, rather than the legislative enabling act, determines the ability of lawyers to insulate themselves from personal liability for the acts of other shareholders in their professional corporation. [Henderson v HSI Financial Services, Inc, 471 SE 2d 885 (1996)] The court recognized that under its regulatory powers, while the Georgia Supreme Court defines whether lawyers may practice their profession in a partnership, professional corporation, or other group structure, the relevant statutes govern whether a particular form of business provides its members with exemptions from personal liability. [Henderson at 886] Georgia Code Section 14-11-314 provides that the Georgia LLC Act does not alter the law applicable to the liability for professional services rendered in that state. Thus, *Henderson* apparently would apply to law firm LLCs as well, and thus members would appear to be shielded from the malpractice liability of their fellow members (see chapter 12).

Washington imposes personal liability on foreign LLCs rendering professional services if certain financial responsibilities are not met. [Wash Rev Code § 25.15.310]

Q 6:28   Can a creditor "pierce the limited liability veil" of an LLC?

In the corporate context, a large body of case law has developed with respect to the ability of a corporation's creditors to attach the personal assets of shareholders in closely held corporations in many circumstances. The courts have established a number of factors that, if present, will allow creditors to pierce the corporate veil of liability protection. Generally, creditors can pierce the veil when shareholders do not follow corporate formalities and the corporation is, in essence, the alter ego of the shareholders. In addition, often courts will pierce the veil when the corporation has been thinly capitalized, especially in cases of tort liability, where the victim does not voluntarily choose to contract with a limited liability entity.

Because the LLC is relatively new, case law will be slow to develop. In addition, the corporate cases may be distinguishable because of the statutory ability of LLCs to be more flexible and less structured than corporations. For example, corporate statutes generally require a board of directors and officers, and do not provide for the direct participation in management by shareholders. On the other hand, in the LLC context, the owners or members directly participate in management, unless a manager is designated, and there is no statutory requirement for a board of directors or manager (except in **Minnesota**, see Q 5:14). Some state statutes are requiring the application of corporate standards to determine if the limited liability veil should be pierced. [See Cal Corp Code § 17101; Me Rev Stat Ann tit 13 § 645(3)] On the other hand some states, such as California, will not consider the fact that a meeting was not called in establishing personal liability of a member if meetings were not required by the Operating Agreement. [See Cal Corp Code § 17101(b)]

Nevertheless, it may be prudent to provide in the Operating Agreement for annual meetings of the members, and the retention of minutes, to establish that the LLC and the LLC's members are abiding by some "separateness," by following formal procedures for operating and governing the LLC. However, it would be worse to require such meetings but not hold them than not to have a provision for annual meetings.

It should be noted that **Georgia** has addressed this issue in its LLC Act. Georgia Code Section 14-11-314 states:

The failure of a limited liability company to observe formalities relating to the exercise of its powers or the management of its business and affairs is *not* grounds for imposing personal liability on a member, manager, agent, or employee of the limited liability company for liabilities of the limited liability company.

[See also Prototype Act § 405(D), which contains a similar provision with respect to the failure to maintain required records.] Thus, while this does not discount all of the common law factors that may result in a court piercing the limited liability veil in favor of a creditor of the LLC, the Georgia Act and Prototype Act increase the certainty of limited personal liability for members of an LLC governed by those statutes where adopted.

In one important respect, LLCs may be more likely to create liability for members due to LLC entity debts because many LLC statutes, unlike corporate statutes generally, expressly condition limited liability on the use of the precise LLC name (see Q 6:25).

In *Ditty v. Checkrite, Ltd., Inc.,* [973 F Supp 1320 (D Utah 1997)] the court refused to pierce the veil of a law firm LLC to impose liability on an attorney in the firm. The court reasoned that the mere fact that the defendant was the sole owner and the president of the firm and took the major active role in it was "at best, only marginally probative of the factors considered when determining whether to pierce the corporate veil," and that there was no evidence of improper organization under the Utah Limited Liability Company Act.

Property of the LLC

Q 6:29   What constitutes property of the LLC?

Most LLC acts provide that real and personal property owned or purchased by the LLC constitutes the property of the LLC and not the property of any individual member. In addition, some LLC acts (e.g., Mo Rev Stat Sections 359.763.3., 4) contain language similar to the Uniform Partnership Act [UPA § 8], and provide a litany of rules to determine when property is deemed to be owned by the LLC. These rules are as follows:

1. Property is presumed to be owned by the LLC if acquired in the LLC's name;

2. Property is presumed to be owned by the LLC if purchased with the LLC's funds, even if acquired in the name of a member, manager, or other person;

3. Property is presumed not to be the property of the LLC, if purchased by someone with his or her own funds (or at least not the LLC's funds), and is not acquired in the name of the LLC, even though the property may be used in, or in connection with, the LLC's business; and

4. Real and other property, the ownership of which customarily is a matter of public record, may not be considered to be the LLC's property to the prejudice of a nonmember who does not have actual knowledge that the LLC actually owns the property.

If possible, the LLC's records should clearly document the ownership of the LLC's property for tax, liability, and other purposes. Many state LLC statutes, in fact, make this a mandatory obligation although they do not prescribe the consequences for a failure to comply. **Oklahoma** is one exception and uses rules similar to those in the Uniform Partnership Act. [Okla Stat tit 18, § 2019.1] Some state LLC statutes that follow the Prototype Act do have rules similar to the partnership rules which address this issue. In addition, if public recording is customary, as in the case of real estate and automobiles, the LLC and the members should, to the extent possible, properly record the LLC's title to this property.

Q 6:30   Can an LLC own real property?

All LLC acts specifically authorize the LLC to own real estate. In fact, this is a very common use of the LLC.

Members' Interests, Employment Discrimination, and Worker's Compensation

Q 6:31   Do employment discrimination laws apply to members of an LLC?

It is unclear at the present time. There are two areas of discrimination law which may apply: (1) The Age Employment Discrimination Act, and (2) Title VII of the Civil Rights Act prohibiting discrimination based on "race, color, religion, sex, or national origin." While it is obvious that these laws will apply with respect to non-member employees, the application to members is less certain.

Generally, true partners are not considered employees for employment discrimination purposes. Shareholders in a professional corporation, however, have been found to be employees by some courts although this result is not universal. [Strother v Southern California Permanente Medical Group, 79 F 3d 859 (9th Cir 1996)] Moreover, in the partnership context, some courts will look beyond the formalities and examine the substance of the relationship between a "partner" and the partnership. In other words, if an individual formally designated as a partner is actually treated in an employee-like fashion, the partner may actually be considered an employee for discrimination purposes.

The fact that LLC members are not actually partners is another technical distinction which may cloud the issue. It has been suggested the classification of an LLC as a non-partnership may actually serve as a presumption that members are employees. [See Ribstein and Keatinge on Limited Liability Companies, § 14.05] The ability of an LLC to be either member-managed or manager-managed also adds an additional layer of uncertainty. A member in a manager-managed LLC may, in effect, be treated more like an employee than a member in a member-managed LLC. Distinctions even arise between a manager-managed LLC and a general or limited liability partnership with management committees because true partners have more ability to bind the partnership and participate in management than LLC members under the relevant default rules.

Q 6:32   How are LLC members classified for purposes of worker compensation laws?

It varies from state to state. Some states have taken clear positions on the issue while others have not. In states that have spoken to the issue, two patterns have emerged. First, some states permit LLC members to be considered employees for worker compensation purposes if they so elect. [See, e.g., Ind Code § 22-3-6-1] On the other hand, members are treated as employees with the ability to opt out of coverage. [See, e.g., Colo Rev Stat § 8-41-202 (members with greater than 10 percent interest may opt out)]

In states which have not addressed the issue, one must attempt to draw parallels from partnership classification. Generally, partners are treated as co-owners ineligible for coverage under worker compensation laws although exceptions do exist. As with the analysis regarding LLC members and employment discrimination law (see Q 6:31 above), there are some differences between LLCs and general partnerships which may give rise to divergent conclusions—particularly with manager-managed LLCs.

Chapter 7

Taxation

This chapter discusses the federal taxation of the LLC (including conversions of entities into LLCs) and its members, from formation to liquidation and dissolution. Most LLCs are structured to be taxed as a partnership or, if a single owner entity, a sole proprietor or disregarded entity for federal income tax purposes. This chapter, therefore, focuses on the federal income taxation of a partnership and its partners under Subchapter K of the Internal Revenue Code of 1986 (IRC), as applied to the LLC, including tax issues unique to an LLC. Although most LLCs are taxed as a partnership, they may be taxable as a regular C or "S" corporation (or, technically, as an association taxable as a corporation for federal income tax purposes). In this chapter, it is assumed that the LLC is taxed as a partnership, sole proprietorship or disregarded completely, and not taxed as a corporation, for federal income tax purposes.

Introduction

Q 7:1   Is an LLC subject to income tax?

If the LLC is taxed as a partnership, sole proprietorship or a one-owner disregarded entity if a single member LLC ("SMLLC") the LLC is not subject to federal income tax at the entity level. [IRC § 701] Rather, all income and losses pass through to each member. Members, if taxed as partners, in turn receive a Form K-1 from the LLC and report their share of the LLC's income, losses, deductions, and credits on their individual income tax returns. [IRC § 702] Sole proprietor LLCs, if permitted by state law, may be taxed as sole proprietorships under the final "check-the-box" regulations, whereby LLC items would be reported on Schedule "C" or "E" of the owner's personal income tax return. A SMLLC owned by a corporation is taxed as if an unincorporated division of that corporation.

Tax Basis

Q 7:2   What is tax basis?

Basis is a tax concept that determines whether any taxable disposition of property creates a realized and a recognized gain or loss. It is often the amount of cash and the basis of property a person has invested in another piece of property, which may be adjusted by several factors. A taxpayer is, absent an exception, generally subject to tax on the sale or exchange of property if the cash or fair market value of property received exceeds that taxpayer's tax basis in the property transferred. Basis also can relate to other basis or values. For example, property inherited from a decedent generally has a basis equal to its fair market value at the date of death or alternate valuation date; while a donee generally inherits the basis of a living donor.

For an LLC taxed as a partnership, basis is important for another reason. Members can deduct certain losses of an LLC allocated to them to the extent of their tax basis in their LLC interest, subject to limitations discussed below. [IRC § 704(d)] A member's tax basis in an LLC interest can never be less than zero; although one often hears the term "negative basis," the term actually means a deficit capital account, which can trigger tax (often depreciation recapture) upon sale, foreclosure, gift, or other nondeath transfer.

Q 7:3   How is a member's tax basis in an LLC interest calculated?

A member's tax basis in an LLC interest initially is equal to the amount of cash and adjusted tax basis of property contributed by that member to the LLC in exchange for the LLC interest. [IRC § 722] If the member purchased the interest from another member, the purchasing member's tax basis initially would be equal to the amount of cash or fair market value of property transferred in exchange for the interest. [IRC §§ 742, 1101] A member's tax basis also includes any portion of the LLC's liabilities, unless (1) the debt is nonrecourse to that member and another member is personally liable for all of the debt, or the debt is not qualified [IRC § 752]; or (2) the member is not at risk. [IRC § 465]

A member's interest in an LLC is adjusted from time to time as follows:

1. Increased by the member's distributive share of the LLC's income and tax-exempt income;
2. Increased by the member's share of the LLC's recourse (and, in some cases, qualified nonrecourse) liabilities for which no other member is personally liable (see Qs 7:4–7:6 and Qs 7:58–7:67 on how the LLC's debt is allocable to each member's basis);

3. Decreased by the member's distributive share of the LLC's losses and nondeductible expenses, which are not properly chargeable to capital accounts; and

4. Decreased by any distributions to the member.

[IRC §§ 705, 722, 752; Treas Reg §§ 1.752-2(e)(1), 1.704-2(b)(4)]

Q 7:4   What LLC liabilities are allocable to a member's basis under Code Section 752?

"Liability" is not defined specifically in Code Section 752 or in the underlying regulations. Generally, the LLC's Section 752 liabilities include those obligations of the LLC that create or increase the LLC's basis in any LLC asset. [Rev Rul 88-77, 1988-2 CB 129] For example, it would include LLC debts for which the LLC is not entitled to a direct deduction for principal payments on that debt.

Accrued but unpaid expenses may be considered a liability includible in the member's basis if the LLC uses the accrual method of accounting. [LaRue v Commr, 90 TC 465,478 (1988); see also Rev Rul 88-77 (in which the IRS ruled a cash-basis partnership's accrued but unpaid expenses are not liabilities for Section 752 purposes)]

The IRS ruled that the liability generated by a short sale of securities is a liability for Section 752 purposes that may increase each member's tax basis. [Rev Rul 95-26, 1995-1 CB 131]

Q 7:5   What portion of the LLC's recourse liabilities are included in a member's tax basis in the LLC?

A liability is recourse for tax purposes if any member or related person bears the economic risk of loss for that liability. [Treas Reg § 1.752-2; see Treas Reg § 1.752-4(b) (for the definition of related person)]

Each member's share of the LLC's recourse liabilities is based on that member's (or related person's) economic risk of loss on the recourse liabilities. Generally, a member bears the economic risk of loss for a recourse liability to the extent that (upon an assumed liquidation of the LLC) the member or related person would have an obligation to repay any of the LLC's creditors (or make a contribution to the LLC) but would not be entitled to a reimbursement from another member or related person of another member. [Treas Reg § 1.752-2(b)] In determining this liability, all relevant statutes and contractual arrangements among the members are taken into account, and the actual economic ability of the member to satisfy such obligation is ignored. For instance, if a member guaranteed an LLC's liability, and no other member is otherwise liable or personally guaranteed that debt, all of that liability would be included in the member's tax basis. [Treas Reg § 1.752-2(b)(2); see also Treas Reg § 1.752-2(d)(2), -2(f), Exs 3, 4] However, if the member's risk of loss on the guarantee was limited, only the maximum amount of potential liability would be included in the member's basis. The balance of the debt would be allocated to all other eligible members under the general rule discussed below. If no member bears any economic burden with respect to the debt, the debt is characterized as non-recourse debt (see Q 7:6, below).

Although there are numerous exceptions, as a general rule, if an LLC's recourse liability is recourse against all members, then each member's allocable share of the liability is included in basis to the extent of that member's distributive share of the LLC's losses and to the extent to which that member would be required to restore a deficit capital account balance on the deemed liquidation of the LLC. [Treas Reg § 1.752-2(b), -2(f), Ex 1]

Q 7:6 What portion of the LLC's nonrecourse liabilities are includible in a member's tax basis in the LLC?

A nonrecourse liability is a debt for which the member (or related person) of the LLC does not bear an economic risk of loss. [Treas Reg § 1.752-1(a)(2)]

If nonrecourse, the basis attributable to the debt is allocable to members in accordance with their share of the LLC's minimum gain and Section 704(c) minimum gain (see Q 7:69 *et seq*) The balance generally is allocated to members in accordance with their distributive share of the LLC's profits. [Treas Reg § 1.752-3(a)]

Q 7:7 What happens if a member guarantees a nonrecourse debt?

If a member guarantees an otherwise nonrecourse debt of the LLC, that debt is considered recourse to the guarantor, and all of the basis attributable to that debt is allocated to that member. [Treas Reg §§ 1.752-1(a)(1), -2(a)] In addition, nonrecourse debt owed to a member or related party is treated as recourse debt. The member to whom the debt is owed is treated as bearing the entire risk of loss because such member would be the sole loser if the LLC failed to pay the debt.

Q 7:8 Does a member have a different basis in interests acquired at different times or for separate classes of interests in an LLC, if the member owns more than one class of interest in the LLC?

No, not in an LLC taxed as a partnership. Revenue Ruling 84-53 [1984-1 CB 159] holds that a partner has a single unified basis in a partnership interest, even though the partner may own more than one class of interest (e.g., a preferred interest and a subordinate or common interest, or two or more interests acquired at different times).

Q 7:9 When is a member's basis in an LLC interest determined?

Basis is determined when a member's or LLC's tax consequences depend on the member's tax basis in the LLC. Generally, basis is redetermined at the end of the LLC's tax year, upon the sale or exchange of the member's interest, or upon a liquidation or other distribution of property by the LLC to the member.

Capital Accounts and Other Items

Q 7:10 What are capital accounts?

A member's capital account reflects the value, that is the equity, of a member in the LLC. The capital account is continually adjusted to reflect the operations of the LLC. Maintaining the capital account is essential in reflecting the economic arrangement among the members which, in turn, is essential in satisfying the substantial-economic-effect test (see Q 7:43).

Q 7:11   What is the difference between a member's tax basis and capital account?

At least three important distinctions may be made between tax basis and capital accounts:

1. *Basis versus fair market value.* If a member acquires an interest in an LLC by contributing property other than cash, the tax basis in the LLC interest is equal to the tax basis in the property contributed. The capital account, however, is equal to the fair market value of the property contributed.

2. *Liabilities.* A member's tax basis in an LLC may include all or a portion of the amount of the LLC's liabilities. Because capital accounts reflect a member's gross, not net, equity in the LLC, capital accounts do not include a member's allocable share of the LLC's liabilities, even if the member has guaranteed the debt.

3. *"Negative basis."* A member's tax basis in an LLC interest cannot be negative. [IRC § 704(d)] A member's capital account, however, can be negative, and, as discussed above, is often called "negative basis" in common parlance, although technically it does not exist. Commonly, negative basis is caused by depreciation deductions allocated in excess of basis.

Q 7:12   How is a member's capital account computed?

A member's capital account is, in the case of a new LLC, the amount of cash and fair market value of property contributed by the member to the LLC. A member's valuation of contributed property, distributed property, or property otherwise revalued by the LLC generally will be accepted if agreed to in an arm's-length negotiation and the members have sufficiently adverse interests. [Treas Reg § 1.704-1(b)(2)(iv)(h)] If a member who contributes property receives an interest in the LLC that is not proportionate to the fair market value, this constitutes a gift (if among relatives) or compensation.

A member's capital account is increased by the member's distributive share of the LLC's taxable and tax-exempt income and gain.

A member's capital account is decreased by the amount of cash and fair market value of property distributed by the LLC to the member, and by the member's distributive share of the LLC's losses and deductions. [Treas Reg § 1.704-1(b)(2)(iv)]

Q 7:13   What is the initial capital account of a member who acquires an interest from another member as opposed to the LLC?

A new member acquires the capital account (or pro rata portion thereof) attributable to the transferring member's interest in the LLC. [Treas Reg § 1.704-1(b)(2)(iv)(1)] An LLC interest represents a direct interest in the underlying LLC assets, unlike a shareholder's interest in a corporation. The transferee member generally succeeds to the transferor's capital account and to all the inside tax attributes of the transferor's interest, such as built-in gain or loss under Code Section 704(c) about a Section 754 election.

Q 7:14   Is a member's capital account ever adjusted to reflect changes in the fair market value of the LLC's property?

Yes. Upon the admission of a new member or the withdrawal of an existing member, the capital accounts of the members may be adjusted to reflect changes in the fair market value of the LLC's assets. [Treas Reg § 1.704-1(b)(2)(iv)(f), -1(b)(2)(m)]

Q 7:15   Is a member's capital account adjusted upon receipt of a Section 707(c) guaranteed payment from the LLC?

A Section 707(c) payment is income to the member and either deductible or capitalized by the LLC, depending upon the nature of the payment. If deductible by the LLC, each recipient member's capital account is affected by the guaranteed payment to the extent of that member's distributive share of the LLC's deductions, losses, or other items attributable to the guaranteed payment. [Treas Reg

§ 1.704-1(b)(2)(iv)(a)] The charge is solely against the member's capital account only if there is a valid special allocation of the entire deduction to that member. [IRC § 704]

Q 7:16 What is the effect on a member's basis of an obligation to make a capital contribution?

The basis for the partnership interest of a limited partner or a member of a limited liability company may be increased if the partner/member has an obligation to make an additional contribution to partnership capital. The partnership agreement/limited liability company agreement documents the amount of capital that the limited partners/members are to contribute initially. In addition, the limited partners/members may be required by the agreement to contribute a stated amount of additional capital at a later date.

The regulations allow the partner to increase basis to the extent of the partner's share (determined by the economic risk of loss) of full recourse liabilities, limited to the maximum amount of additional capital the partner is obligated to contribute. [Treas Reg § 1.752-2(b)(3) and (4)] While such treatment is clear for obligations that are fixed in amount and payable on a specified date, obligations that are subject to less specific requirements pose some uncertainties. Thus, if a limited partner's original contribution was $15,000 and she was obligated by the agreement to contribute an additional $10,000 at a later date, her share of the partnership's full recourse liabilities determined pursuant to her economic risk of loss, up to a total of $25,000, could constitute basis.

Formation and Consequences to the Members

Q 7:17 What constitutes operating as a partnership for purposes of federal income tax?

Section 761 of the Internal Revenue Code provides that a partnership includes a syndicate, group, pool, joint venture or other unincorporated organization through or by means of which any business, financial operation or venture is carried on, which is not a corporation, trust or estate. Income Tax Regulation Section

1.761-1(a) provides that a joint venture undertaken merely to share expenses is not a partnership. Mere co-ownership of property that is maintained, kept in repair, and rented or leased does not constitute a partnership. Tenants in common, however, may be partners if they actively carry on a trade, business or financial operation, or venture and divide the profits thereof. In *Commissioner v. Culbertson*, 337 U.S. 733 (1949), the Supreme Court set forth the following test. The determination of whether a partnership exists is to be made by considering whether, in view of the parties' actions, the parties in good faith and acting with a business purpose intended to join together in the present conduct of the enterprise. The Tax Court later set forth a list of factors to be considered in making such a determination in *Luna v. Commissioner* 42 T.C. 1067 (1964). Those factors set forth in *Luna* are:

> The agreement of the parties and their conduct in executing its terms; the contributions, if any, which each party had made to the venture; the parties' control over income and capital and the right of each to make withdrawals; whether each party was a principal and co-proprietor, sharing a mutual proprietary interest in the net profits and having an obligation to share losses, or whether one party was the agent or employee of the other, receiving for his services contingent compensation in the form of a percentage of income; whether business was conducted in the joint names of the parties; whether the parties filed federal partnership returns or otherwise represented to respondent or to persons with whom they dealt that they were joint ventures; whether separate books of account were maintained for the venture; and whether the parties exercised mutual control over the assumed mutual responsibilities for the enterprise.

The Service has applied the guidelines set forth above in two Technical Advise Memorandums finding a partnership in one instance and not in another. In TAM 199907029, the IRS rejected use by individual partners of a tax-free real estate exchange, based on their asserted separation of partnership operations from property ownership. The co-owners of an apartment building filed partnership returns for more than 20 years showing the property as a partnership asset, opened a joint bank account, paid property expenses through their joint account and eventually entered into a "partnership agreement." The service concluded they were in fact partners for tax purposes and the property was a partnership asset despite the manner in which title was held. Three of the four tax-payers elected to use Section 1033. They agreed they intended to be partners only to building operations, not ownership. However, they had consistently listed the building and mortgage interest as a partnership asset and a partnership liability, respectively, on the partnership's tax returns.

In *TAM 199922014*, the IRS found that a service arrangement involving a fee based on net profits and a considerable amount of business and management collaboration was nevertheless not a partnership. P was a corporation engaged in the business of providing turnkey office operation and financial management services to professional service organizations ("Service Groups"). Before providing services to a Service Group, P forms a subsidiary ("P Sub") that enters into an asset purchase agreement and a service agreement with the Service Group. Under the asset purchase agreement, P Sub acquires from the Service Group all the assets and properties, tangible and intangible, used in the Service Group's business (including equipment, accounts receivable, cash, and inventory), and assumes certain of the Service Group's obligations and contracts with vendors. Under the service agreement, P Sub agrees to provide the Service Group with offices, facilities, equipment, supplies, support personnel, and management and financial advisory services. The facilities provided under the service agreement include the assets transferred by the Service Group to P Sub under the asset purchase agreement. In addition to providing the facilities and offices, P Sub is responsible for all costs of repairs, maintenance and improvements, utility expenses, normal janitorial services, refuse disposal and all other costs and expenses reasonably incurred in conducting operations in the facilities and offices. P Sub also is responsible for paying any associated expenses such as real or personal property lease or sublease expenses, taxes and insurance. The Service Group reimburses P Sub for all of these expenses.

P Sub is prohibited by law from participating in the core component of Service Group's business — the provision of professional services — which is the primary income producing activity of the Service Group. The Service Group retains the sole authority to direct the business, professional, and ethical aspects of its business practice and remains responsible for the hiring and firing of professionals and all issues related to the conduct of its business practice. Matters involving the internal agreements and finances of the Service Group, including the distribution of professional service income among the individual professionals in the Service Group, tax planning, pension and investment planning, and expenses relating to internal business matters remain the sole responsibility of the Service Group.

P Sub and the Service Group form a policy board which is responsible for developing management and administrative policies for the overall operation of the facilities and offices. P Sub and the Service Group have equal representation on the policy board. The policy board is responsible for decisions on capital improvements and expansions, annual budgets, advertising and other administrative matters. The policy board coordinates the services that P Sub provides and manages the contractual relationship between the Service Group and P Sub, but does not control or coordinate the provision of the Service Group's business services.

P Sub purchases the Service Group's accounts receivable on an ongoing month-by-month basis. If, after acquiring the receivables, P Sub collects any amounts in excess of the amount paid for the receivables, or if it cannot collect the entire amount it paid for the receivables, P Sub accounts for those differences by means of a rolling average computation that adjusts subsequent payments made to the Service Group for the next month's receivables. The purpose of the rolling average computation is to credit the Service Group with all amounts collected on the receivables and to place the entire burden of uncollected accounts on the Service Group.

P Sub receives three types of payments under the service agreement:

1. P Sub is reimbursed for certain direct expenses it incurs in providing the services delineated under the service agreement;
2. P Sub receives a fee for the use of the real and personal property owned by P Sub and leased to the Service Group; and
3. P receives a fee equal to a percentage of net income of the Service Group.

The service agreement expressly states that P Sub will act as an independent contractor, not as a partner. Neither P Sub nor the Service Group holds itself out to third parties as a partner in a partnership. The facilities and offices retain the name of the Service Group. Moreover, even though some of P Sub's employees interact with clients in the Service Group's offices, the clients are not told that these individuals are P Sub's employees. P Sub handles all collection actions, such as client billing, on behalf of the Service Group and in the Service Group's name. The P Sub name does not appear in any correspondence with clients, other companies, etc. In all correspondence, the Service Group is listed as the provider of the business services. Moreover, the Service Group remains solely responsible for the compensation of its professional personnel, who are paid by the Service Group from funds received from P for accounts receivable. P Sub and the Service Group maintain separate books and records; however, consistent with the bookkeeping aspects of the service agreement, an employee of P Sub maintains the Service Group's books and records.

Under these facts, which involve very close integration of business and management and significant sharing of net income, the National Office concluded that the arrangement between P Sub and the Service Group is not a tax partnership, relying in part on the "intent" test in *Commissioner v. Culbertson,* 337 US 733 (1949): "The best evidence of the intent of parties is any written document signed by the parties that defines their relationship." Regarding intent, the fact that the parties did not hold themselves out as partners and the fact that the parties were prohibited under local laws and rules from being partners were important. The IRS likely would have ruled in favor of partnership status, however, if the parties had contracted for the same rights and obligations and called the arrangement a partnership or if they had routinely held themselves out as partners.

Q 7:18 What are the tax consequences to the members upon the formation of the LLC?

Generally, a person does not recognize gain or loss on property or cash contributed to an LLC in exchange for an interest in the LLC. [IRC § 721] The member's basis in the LLC interest is equal to the amount of the cash and the member's adjusted tax basis in the property contributed. [IRC § 722] If the property contributed to the LLC is a capital or business asset, the member's holding period for the property will "tack" and become the member's deemed holding period. If the property transferred to the LLC would produce ordinary income upon sale by the member, there is no tacking of the holding period; therefore, the holding period of the member's LLC interest begins when the LLC interest is received. [IRC § 1223(1)]

Q 7:19   Can a member recognize gain on the contribution of appreciated property to an LLC?

Yes. First, a member recognizes gain if: (1) appreciated property is contributed to the LLC; (2) the LLC assumes debt encumbering the property in excess of the member's total basis in the LLC interest; and (3) the member has a smaller percentage of the debt immediately after the transfer to the LLC than before. [See IRC §§ 731(a)(1), 752(b); Treas Reg § 1.752-1(c)] However, a member's basis includes the allocable share (in accordance with the ratio of shared losses) of the LLC's debt. Thus, unlike a transfer to a corporation, the transfer by a member of assets with a basis less than the debt transferred to the LLC does not, absent a reduction of the sharing of debt liability, create a taxable event as it would in a corporation. [IRC § 357(c)]

Second, if the LLC sells a contributed asset that had built-in gain (or loss) at the time of the contribution, that is, the fair market value of the asset exceeded (or is less than) the member's tax basis in the property at the time of the contribution, Code Section 704(c) requires that gain (or loss) to be allocated to the contributing member. (See Q 7:24 for a more detailed discussion of Code Section 704(c).)

Third, if the LLC would be considered an investment company under Code Section 351 (e) (assuming the LLC is taxed as a corporation, not a partnership), the member would recognize built-in gain (but not recognize a loss) upon contribution of property to that LLC. [IRC § 721(b)]

Sections 351(e) and 721(b) were originally enacted to prevent taxpayers from diversifying their assets through the use of so-called "swap funds" or "exchange funds" without paying current tax. A partnership with privately placed securities and less than 80 percent of the partnership's assets constituting publicly traded stock or securities, would qualify—a so-called swap fund without income tax, and the balance of the assets constituted privately placed securities.

The Taxpayer Relief Act of 1997 modified the definition of an investment company by expanding substantially the types of assets that must be taken into account for purposes of determining whether a corporation is an investment company. Under new Code Section 351(e), the term "investment company" includes any corporation if more than 80 percent of its assets by value consist of stock and securities (regardless of whether they are publicly traded), money, financial instruments, foreign currency, interests in REITs, RICs, common trust funds, and publicly traded partnerships, certain interests in precious metals, certain interests in entities that hold such items, and other assets specified in the regulations. The act does not modify any of the other provisions of Treasury Regulations Section 1.351-1(c), including the rule that only assets held for investment are considered in making the determination and the "look through" rule that applies if the entity owns at least 50 percent of either the combined voting power of all classes of voting stock or the total value of all stock of the subsidiary. [See, e.g., Ltr Rul 9617017]

These provisions apply to all transfers after June 8, 1997, in taxable years ending after such date, except for transfers of a fixed amount of securities made pursuant to a binding written contract in effect on June 8, 1997.

A transfer to an investment company triggering gain recognition under Section 721(b) occurs if two conditions are met:

1. The transfer results in diversification; and
2. The transferee is an entity, more than 80 percent of the value of whose assets (excluding cash and nonconvertible debt obligations) are held for investment and are readily marketable stock or securities.

Prior to the Taxpayer Relief Act of 1997, readily marketable securities were defined as "convertible debentures, convertible preferred stock, warrants, and other stock rights if the stock for which they may be converted or exchanged is readily marketable." [Treas Reg § 1.351-1(c)(3)] This definition of readily marketable securities did not have an impact on many investment or business partnerships.

The Taxpayer Relief Act broadens the definition of a transfer of an investment company:

(A) by taking into account all stock and securities held by the company, and

(B) by treating as stock and securities
  (i) money
  (ii) stock and other equity interests in a corporation
  (iii) any foreign currency
  (iv) any interest in a real estate investment trust
  (v) interests in precious metals, unless metal is used or held in the active conduct of a trade or business
  (vi) interest in an entity if substantially all of its assets are from the preceding clauses above or clause (vii) below
  (vii) any other asset specified by the IRS in its regulations

[IRC § 351(e), as amended by the Taxpayer Relief Act of 1997] The precise impact of this change is unclear because the regulations continue to refer to the "readily tradeable security" rule. If the items enumerated above now constitute a "security," but the test under the regulations otherwise is intended to be unchanged, the task becomes one of determining if the above items are readily tradable. If the assets are not readily tradable, either by exclusion from the definition of "readily tradeable security" in Treasury Regulations § 1.351-1(c)(3) or under the facts and circumstances, the cash serves to reduce the assets which are considered marketable securities. Cash arguably is not readily marketable, under the regulation definition, because there is no economic incentive to trade cash for cash and, thus, no exchange exists.

Alternatively, if the change was intended to eliminate the marketability requirement so that all securities are taken into account, any transfer of property to a partnership with greater than 80 percent of its assets in cash and/or other listed assets has the potential to trigger gain or loss. The legislative history suggests that Congress intended the second approach. The Senate Report to the proposed changes states that Congress did not intend to override the traditional rules that (1) only assets held for investment are considered; (2) pursuant to Treasury Regulations Section 1.351-1(c)(4), assets of subsidiaries are treated as owned proportionately by parent entities with a greater than 50 percent interest; (3) plans with respect to the entity's assets be considered at the time of transfer under Treasury Regulations Section 1.351-1(c)(2); and (4) contributions result in diversification under Treasury Regulations Section 1.351-1(c)(1)(i). A footnote to this passage, after stating that money counts under the 80 percent test, indicates that under a plan of contribution to an entity of both money and non-securities, the investment company determination is to be made after the plan is fully implemented. Assuming that money is excludable from the definition of readily marketable security, this signifies that the readily marketable requirement was meant to be overridden, because a contribution of money subsequent to a contribution of non-security property, if considered in tandem, would not increase the likelihood that an entity is an investment company. This shows that Congress intended the contribution of money to have the effect of making an entity more like an investment company, and is to be added to the stock and securities for the 80 percent rule.

Diversification results if nonidentical assets are not insignificant in relation to the total assets transferred. [Treas Reg § 1.351-1(c)(1)] A partner with a one percent interest is disregarded. The regulations provide an example that 1.96 percent of the total assets is insignificant. But larger percentage amounts raise the diversification issue. For example, in an exchange for interests in a newly formed partnership *AB*, *A* contributes appreciated Intel stock worth $890 and *B* contributes $110 in cash. For purposes of the investment company rule, cash is a nonidentical asset and is a significant part (11 percent) of the assets transferred. The contributions result in diversification, and *A* fully recognizes his gain realized on the contribution of the Intel stock to the partnership. [Rev Rul 87-9, 1987-1 CB 133]

If the LLC is considered as an "investment partnership", the rules under § 731 relating to gains on distributions of marketable securities will not apply if made to an "eligible partner". An "eligible partner is any partner who did not contribute any asset to the partnership other than those assets defined in a transfer of an investment company. [IRC § 731(c)(3)(C)(iii)(I)]

Fourth, a member, after a transfer to an LLC taxed as a partnership, may be required to recognize built-in gain if that member is treated as having made a disguised sale of the property under Treasury Regulations Section 1.707-3 or under Code Section 737. (See Qs 7:29 and 7:30 on disguised sales and Code Section 737.) In addition, if the property is inventory or other trade or business property, any sale by the LLC within five years will generate ordinary income rather than capital gain.

Fifth, a contributing member was, under former Code Sections 1491 and 1494, subject to a 35 percent excise tax on the built-in gain of appreciated property contributed to a foreign LLC. The Taxpayer Relief Act of 1997 repealed Code Sections 1491 and 1494, generally effective for transfers made on or after August 5, 1997. Under former Code Section 1491, a U.S. person that contributed appreciated property to a foreign partnership generally was required to pay an excise tax in an amount equal to 35 percent of the unrealized appreciation inherent in such property at the time of the contribution.

Under former section 1494, if a U.S. person transferred property to a foreign partnership, such person was required to file an information return with respect to such transfer. If such a return was not filed, the statute required the transferor to pay an excise tax in an amount equal to 35 percent of the value of the property, even if the property was not appreciated (such as capital contribution of cash).

Q 7:20   Can a member recognize a loss on the contribution of property to an LLC?

No. [IRC § 721(a)]

Q 7:21   Is a member subject to tax on the contribution of services in exchange for an interest in the LLC?

The answer depends in part on whether the interest received in exchange for the services (or a promise to perform future services) is a capital interest or a profits interest and, if a mere profits interest, whether it can be valued. A capital interest is an interest in the LLC's underlying assets, as well as a right to share in the LLC's distributions of income and losses under the Operating Agreement. [Treas Reg § 1.704-1(e)(1)(v); Mark IV Pictures Inc v Commr, 969 F 2d 669 (8th Cir 1992), aff'g, 60 TCM 1171 (1990); Rev Proc 93-27,

1993-2 CB 343, § 2.01] A profits interest is a right to receive an allocation of certain LLC income (even though the holder may not have an immediate right to a distribution), but does not represent a share in the LLC's assets. [Treas Reg § 1.704-1(b)(2)(ii)(b)(1), (iv)(b)]

If a person contributes services in exchange for an LLC capital interest that is not subject to restrictions, the member would recognize ordinary income to the extent of the fair market value of the interest received. [Treas Reg § 1.721-1(b)(1)] The income is reportable by the member, and the LLC is entitled to a deduction for the year in which the capital interest is transferred to the member. If the capital interest is subject to restrictions, however, Section 83 principles apply in deferring recognition of income (and the corresponding LLC deduction) until those restrictions lapse; the value of the interest received and corresponding amount of taxable income is determined at that later time when the lapse occurs, and not upon receipt [Treas Reg § 1.721-1(b)(1)], unless the member sooner makes a Section 83(b) election.

A person receiving a restricted capital interest may make a Section 83(b) election to treat the value of the interest received as ordinary income in the year of receipt, despite the restrictions. [Treas Reg § 1.83-2] A person may want to make this election (which must be made within 30 days of receipt of the interest) if there is an expectation that the interest will significantly appreciate, since any subsequent appreciation is subject to tax at capital gains tax rates upon a transfer, instead of ordinary income rates. [Treas Reg § 1.83-2(a)]

Upon receipt of only a profits interest in exchange for services, the result depends on the circumstances. The major issues are the valuation of the interest and the appropriateness of taxing a speculative right to receive income in the future. In *Campbell v. United States*, [943 F 2d 815 (8th Cir 1991), *rev'g* 59 TCM 236 (1990)] the court held that the receipt of a profits interest in exchange for services is not taxable if the value of the interest was too speculative to tax. The *Campbell* decision, however, does not foreclose taxation of a profits interest if the value of the interest is reasonably ascertainable.

The IRS has issued guidance on this question. Revenue Procedure 93-27 [1993-2 CB 343] provides that the IRS agrees not to attempt to tax a taxpayer upon receipt of a profits interest in exchange for services, unless:

1. The interest received entitles the holder to a substantially certain and predictable stream of income from the LLC's asset, e.g., high-quality debt securities or a net lease; or

2. The member transfers the profits interest within two years of receipt; or

3. The interest is publicly traded, within the meaning of Code Section 7704(b) (relating to publicly traded partnerships).

If the taxpayer is not taxed as provided above, the question remains whether the value of the profits interest is reasonably calculable. If so, the amount of income recognized equals the fair market value of the LLC interest transferred, either at the time the transfer is made for past services, or at the time the services have been rendered, in the case of future services. [Treas Reg § 1.721-1(b)(1); Campbell v Commr, 943 F 2d 815 (8th Cir 1991)]

If a member is to perform services in the future, it is common to either (1) delay the issuance of the partnership interest until the services are complete or (2) issue a forfeitable LLC interest. Upon a delayed issuance, a service member recognizes income, and the LLC obtains a deduction when the interest is issued. The income recognized and the amount deducted is determined by the fair market value of the interest received at that time. [IRC § 83] If a forfeitable LLC interest is issued before all the services are rendered, and if the member will forfeit all or a portion of the interest if the services are not performed, the service member will recognize income, and the LLC will get a deduction, when the forfeitability lapses. The amount of income recognition and tax deduction is equal to the fair market value of the interest at the time the forfeitability lapses. However, as noted above, the person receiving the forfeitable LLC interest may make a Section 83(b) election to treat the value of the interest received as ordinary income in the year of receipt, despite the risk of forfeiture.

In contrast to an S Corporation, there is no second class of stock issue with respect to an LLC so the individuals receiving a forfeitable LLC interest would be subject to any limitations set forth in the underlying documents. Presumably, any items actually allocated to them prior to the elimination of the risk of forfeiture would be reflected on the Schedule K-1. In addition, the documentation should state what interest if any they have in profits for purposes of the creation of a tax basis in their LLC interest through the nonrecourse debt of the LLC.

If the LLC holds property other than money at the time an LLC interest is issued to a service member, it is treated as if the LLC had transferred a portion of that property to the service member in payment of services, with the service member then contributing that portion back to the LLC in return for an LLC interest. If at that time any of the property has a fair market value greater than its inside basis, the LLC will recognize gain on the transfer to the service member.

Q 7:22 What are the effects of compensating an employee for services with an interest in the LLC?

An interest in an LLC could be an interest in both capital and profits or solely profits, as discussed above. If the interest in the LLC is issued to the employee without any restrictions, then the individual will not thereafter be a common law employee of the LLC but will be a member. If the LLC member receives a distributive share of income, the character of such income will depend on its character at the partnership level. Any salary or other guaranteed payments will constitute ordinary income. A person with such an interest should be a member because the interest issued is subject to the same entrepreneurial risks as the other members. If the LLC has appreciated assets, the LLC would recognize gain on the issuance of the interest. A service member should receive an upward adjustment in basis if this is applicable. For ease of administration, a capital account book-up prior to the transfer should clarify the value of such interests.

When an employee becomes a member, the LLC will be unable to deduct the cost of health insurance for the individual. The money paid for health insurance will be included in the individual's gross income. The employee will be able to take an above the line § 162(l) deduction to the extent allowed in the Code. [IRC § 162(l)] The employee will be ineligible for unemployment insurance. Depending upon state law, the individual might also be ineligible for worker's compensation.

By restricting the employee's rights, employee status can be maintained, where desired. First, if the intent is to provide the employee with a "stake" in the company, a bonus determined by the percentage of the LLC's profits would provide the same incentive without jeopardizing the employee status. The employee would therefore not gain any continuing interest, but would only receive a share of the profits while employed.

Second, the employee's right to the LLC interest could be restricted in a manner it which it would be subject to forfeiture for a period of time. This could be accomplished by providing for forfeiture of this interest if employment is terminated within a specific period. This would forestall the loss of employee status provided an election is not made under § 83(b), until the interest is no longer subject to a substantial risk of forfeiture.

Third, an individual could continue to be an employee of an affiliated or member corporation while becoming a member of the LLC.

Q 7:23   What is the difference between a profits interest and a phantom ownership arrangement?

A phantom ownership arrangement is a contractual right tied in a defined way to the profitability of the LLC. Such an arrangement would likely be treated as a deferred compensation plan generating ordinary income when received, which often occurs after the individual is no longer working for the LLC. On the other hand, a profits interest is a property interest generally existing for the life of the partnership. Thus, a service performer who has only a phantom ownership arrangement would not be considered a member for tax purposes, while one who has a profits interest could be considered a member depending upon certain factors. [See Rev Proc 93-27, 1993-2 CB 343]

Q 7:24   What are the tax consequences of contributing appreciated property to the LLC?

A member does not generally recognize gain on the contribution of appreciated property (i.e., property with a fair market value in excess of tax basis) to an LLC in exchange for a membership interest. [IRC § 721] However, the investment company may require gain recognition [See Q7:19 above], and Code Section 704(c) requires the LLC to allocate among the members income, gain, loss, and deductions on the contributed property in a specified manner to take into account the difference between the fair market value of the property at the time of the contribution and the adjusted basis; the purpose of the requirements is to prevent shifting precontribution income or loss among members in an LLC in a manner different from that which would occur if the asset were sold for cash and the proceeds contributed to the LLC.

Code Section 704(c), therefore, requires the LLC to allocate any precontribution gain or loss to the member who contributed the property, upon the sale of that property by the LLC to a third party. The contributing member is required to report the gain (or loss) upon a distribution in kind by the LLC of the built-in gain (loss) property to another member within seven years of the contribution with respect to property contributed to the partnership prior to June 8, 1997. [IRC § 704(c)(1)(B)] Any other post-contribution gain or loss is allocated to all the members in accordance with the Operating Agreement.

Taxpayers were able to avoid Code Section 704(c)(1)(B) by simply redeeming the contributing partner's interest in the partnership for property other than the contributed property. In 1992, Congress enacted Code Section 737, which generally required a partner to recognize gain if such partner contributed built-in gain property to a partnership and, within five (now seven) years after the contribution, received a distribution from the partnership of property other than the property contributed by such partner.

The Taxpayer Relief Act of 1997 extends the five-year period to seven years, effective for property contributed to a partnership after June 8, 1997, subject to an exception for property contributed to a partnership pursuant to a written binding contract in effect on June 8, 1997.

The contributing member's capital account reflects the fair market value of the property, while the member's tax basis in the LLC interest only includes the member's adjusted basis of the property. This causes a difference between book basis and tax basis. As a result, any depreciation deductions must be allocated, like taxable loss, to the noncontributing member, to reduce the book/tax disparity. Treasury Regulations Sections 1.704-3(b), (c), (d) contain allocation methods for eliminating the book/tax disparity of property contributed to an LLC.

Subchapter S does not contain a provision comparable with Code Section 704(c). Thus, subchapter S shareholders can shift the tax consequences of built-in gain and built-in loss property among the various shareholders in an S corporation; members in an LLC cannot. This could be significant, depending on the nature of the organization's business and the tax position of the various owners. It can work to shift taxable income from one owner to another, whether or not this result is intended. However, the IRS takes the position that "dealer" property, which would trigger ordinary income upon sale by the shareholder who owns it, continues to remain trade or business property if contributed to an S corporation. But any gain is taxed pro rata to all S shareholders upon sale, due to the single-class-of-stock rule.

Q 7:25   What is the "ceiling rule"?

Treasury Regulations Section 1.704-3 generally requires an LLC to allocate: (1) to the noncontributing members — equal amounts of book and tax depreciation on appreciated property contributed to the LLC; and (2) to the contributing member — any precontribution gain or loss on the contributed property. This is done to eliminate or reduce the book/tax disparity among the members. However, the LLC cannot allocate more income, gain, loss, or deduction on an item of contributed property than the LLC itself recognizes on that property (the "ceiling rule"). [Treas Reg § 1.704-3(b)(1)] "Curative allocations," discussed in Q 7:26, may also be appropriate. The ceiling rule can be illustrated as follows:

Example 7-1. *A* and *B* form the *AB* LLC. *A* contributes depreciable property with an adjusted basis of $4,000 and fair market value of $10,000 to the LLC. *B* contributes $10,000 cash to the LLC. The depreciable property is accounted for using the straight-line depreciation method over ten years, with no salvage value ($1,000 per year). *A* and *B* share income and losses equally. For book purposes, the property depreciates $1,000 per year, with $500 allocated to both *A* and *B*. For tax purposes, however, the LLC can deduct only $400 per year ($4,000 basis × 10 percent). Treasury Regulations Section 1.704-3(b)(1) requires the LLC to allocate all of the tax depreciation to *B*. The ceiling rule prevents the LLC from allocating more than the $400 tax depreciation to *B* for tax purposes. Thus, following the allocation, *B* has a capital account of $9,500 ($10,000 contribution less $500 book depreciation) and a $9,600 tax basis ($10,000 basis less $400 tax depreciation); *A* has a $9,500 capital account ($10,000 less $500 book depreciation) and a $4,000 basis ($4,000 basis less $0 tax depreciation).

Q 7:26   What are "curative allocations"?

If the ceiling rule applies and causes a distortion in the book and tax accounting of the members, the LLC may make a curative allocation of income, gain, loss, or deduction to the noncontributing members to make up for a tax allocation that is less than the book allocation.

> **Example 7-2.** Assume the same facts as Example 7-1; however, if the LLC has other depreciable property, the LLC could allocate the book depreciation on that other property equally ($500 each) between *A* and *B*, but shift $100 of other tax depreciation on that property to *B*, to offset the impact of the ceiling rule, which limits the tax depreciation on the asset in question to *B* of $400. [Treas Reg § 1.704-3(c)]

Q 7:27   What are remedial allocations?

A remedial allocation is similar to a curative allocation; it is a method to offset the impact of the ceiling rule under Code Section 704(c) of book/tax disparities. Under the remedial allocation method, if the ceiling rule applies, the LLC can allocate income, gain, loss, or deduction to the noncontributing member in an amount equal to the impact of the ceiling rule, and make a corresponding allocation of income, gain, loss, or deduction to the contributing member. [Treas Reg § 1.704-3(d)]

> **Example 7-3.** Assume the same facts as Example 7-1; however, instead of using the curative allocations, the LLC uses remedial allocations to eliminate the effect of the ceiling rule. The ceiling rule caused *B* to receive $100 less tax depreciation than book depreciation. The LLC could use the remedial allocation to eliminate the impact of the ceiling rule, by allocating $100 of tax depreciation to *B* and, at the same time, allocating $100 of ordinary income to *A*.

Q 7:28   Which method, curative or remedial, should an LLC use to eliminate book/tax disparity under Code Section 704(c)?

There is no correct answer. The relative tax positions of each member in an LLC will affect which method in the Treasury regulations is selected.

Q 7:29   What is a "disguised sale"?

A disguised sale is a transaction in which one member contributes appreciated property to an LLC, and the LLC distributes cash or other assets to that member. Certain transactions, although nontaxable in form when tested solely under Code Sections 721 and 731, are viewed as, in substance, equivalent to a sale of the property to the other members in the LLC. The IRS lost a number of cases attempting to recharacterize these transactions as sales. [See Otey v Commr, 70 TC 312, *aff'd per curiam*, 634 F 2d 1046 (6th Cir 1980); Park Realty Co v Commr, 77 TC 412, *acq* 1982-2 CB 2; Jupiter Corp v US, 2 Cl Ct 61 (1983); but see Colonade Condominium, Inc v Commr, 91 TC 793 (1988) (in which the IRS was successful)]

To eliminate the disguised-sale tax-deferral technique, Congress enacted Code Section 707(a)(2)(B) in 1984, which provides that a transaction will be treated as a sale under Code Section 1001 if a member (directly or indirectly) transfers cash or property to an LLC, and there is a related direct or indirect transfer of cash or property by the LLC to that member or another member. The assumption of liabilities by the LLC from a member may also be considered a related distribution of cash and thus a disguised sale in certain circumstances. [Treas Reg §§ 1.707-3, -5]

Whether or not a transaction is a disguised sale is dependent upon a facts-and-circumstances test. [Treas Reg § 1.707-3] Treasury Regulations Section 1.707-3 identifies a number of transactions presumed to be disguised sales and establishes a window of time during which that presumption applies. [Treas Reg §§ 1.707-3(c)(1), -3(f), Exs 3, 4] If a member contributes property to an LLC, followed by a distribution (other than distributions of operating income) of cash or other assets to the contributing member within two years of the initial contribution, a disguised sale occurs. Contributions followed by a distribution more than two years from the date of the contribution are presumed to be outside the scope of Code Section 707(a)(2)(B). [Treas Reg § 1.707-3(c)(1), -3(f)]

When a member contributes encumbered property to an LLC, it is treated as a simultaneous transfer of the property to the LLC by the member, and the LLC's distribution of cash to the member, to the extent of the contributing member, is relieved of a share of the liability (see Q 7:17). The transfer of encumbered property will not, however, be treated as a disguised sale if the encumbrance is a "qualified liability" and there is no other transfer to the contributing member that would bring the transaction under Code Section 707(a)(2)(B) apart from the encumbrances. A "qualified liability" is:

1. a liability incurred more than two years before the transfer;
2. a liability that, based on all facts and circumstances, was not incurred in anticipation of the transfer;
3. a liability, the proceeds of which are directly traceable to capital expenditures for the property (such as acquisition debt); or
4. trade payables incurred in the ordinary course of business and transferred in connection with the transfer of the LLC of substantially all of the assets used in the business.

Q 7:30 Are there other IRC provisions that recharacterize as taxable transactions transfers involving entities taxed as partnerships?

Yes. Code Section 704(c)(1)(B) generally requires a member to recognize any unallocated pre-contribution gain or loss on property contributed to the LLC, upon a distribution of that property to another member within seven years of the contribution. As discussed in Q 7:29, it is presumed that any distribution (or relief from debt liability) to a contributing member (other than operating cash flow distributions) within two years from the date of the contribution will be treated as a disguised sale under Code Section 707(a)(2)(B) and Treasury Regulations Section 1.707-3. Code Section 704(c)(1)(B) deals with property distributed by the LLC to other members within seven years after the contribution from another member.

Code Section 737 was enacted by Congress in 1992 to remedy a related perceived loophole and, in effect, reaches a similar result to the Code Section 707 disguised sale. Code Section 737 requires a contributing member to recognize the net built-in gain (but not loss) on any property contributed to the LLC, if the LLC distributes other property back to that member within seven years from the date of the original contribution. The contributing member is not, however, required to recognize pre-contribution gain if the LLC merely redistributes the contributed property to the member who contributed that property. [IRC § 737(d)(1)] Code Section 737 does not apply to constructive distributions of property upon a termination of the LLC under Code Section 708. [Treas Reg § 1.737-2(a)]

Thus, while the result of each of the three code sections [IRC §§ 704(c)(1)(B), 707(a)(2)(B), 737(d)(1)] is similar, the sections apply in different circumstances. The purpose of each of the sections is to prevent the assignment of income to other members, or the deferral of income by the contributing member, through the literal application of tax provisions to transactions that, if done outside a partnership, would constitute a taxable sale of assets.

Q 7:31   Is a post-formation contribution of property to an LLC treated differently than the original contribution of property upon formation of the LLC by the founding members?

No. Unlike Code Section 351, which applies to the transfer of property to a corporation (including an S corporation) in exchange for stock, the general rules on contributing property to an LLC taxed as a partnership apply to any contribution, made at any time, by any member, regardless of how small that member's interest. In contrast, a taxpayer contributing appreciated property to a corporation must recognize gain on the property, unless immediately after the transaction the taxpayer is, or is a part of the group, in "control" of the corporation (i.e., 80 percent ownership of voting shares and the shares outstanding of the corporation). [IRC §§ 351(a), 368(c)] There is no control test under Code Section 721.

Consequences to the LLC: Start-Up Decisions and Tax Elections

Q 7:32 What are the tax consequences to an LLC upon the contribution of property?

An LLC does not recognize gain or loss upon receipt of property, including cash, in exchange for an interest in the LLC. [IRC § 721(a)] This rule applies whether property is contributed to the LLC upon formation or to an existing and operating LLC (see Q 7:31). Property, in this context, includes, but is not limited to, cash, tangible and intangible personal property, accounts receivable, licenses, patents, contract rights, and installment notes. The LLC's basis in the contributed property equals the adjusted basis of the property in the hands of the member at the time of the contribution. [IRC § 723] Additionally, the LLC's holding period for the property is equal to the holding period of the member that contributed the property. [IRC § 1223(2)]

Q 7:33 Can the LLC or its members deduct in the year of formation the expenses incurred to organize the LLC?

No. Code Sections 263 and 709 require the LLC to capitalize these expenses, which include legal and accounting fees for planning, as well as drafting the LLC's Articles, Operating Agreement, and other "formation" expenses such as applying for taxpayer identification numbers. The LLC may amortize and deduct certain organizational costs over 60 months. [IRC § 709(b)(1); Rev Rul 87-111, 1987-2 CB 160]

Q 7:34 Can the LLC elect a taxable year other than a calendar year?

Yes, but only to a limited extent. [IRC § 706] Because of the ability to defer tax due to a deemed taxable distribution at the end of the fiscal year, the IRC requires an LLC to use the same tax year as the LLC's members. [IRC § 706(b)(1)(B)] If the LLC's members are all individuals, the LLC must use a calendar year, except in the unusual circumstance that members file individual returns on a fiscal year. If members have different tax years, the LLC must use the tax year of the members who own more than 50 percent of the LLC's capital and profits interests. [IRC §§ 706(b)(1)(B)(i), (b)(4)] If a majority of the members do not have the same taxable year, the LLC must use the taxable year of the "principal members," that is, each of those members who owns 5 percent or more of the LLC's capital and profits interests. [IRC § 706(b)(1)(B)(ii)]

The LLC may also use any other taxable year, if it can establish to the IRS's satisfaction that it has a valid business purpose, other than the deferral of tax to the members. [IRC § 706(b)(1)(C)] If the tax deferral is no longer than three months, the LLC may adopt a different taxable year; however, the LLC will have to pay tax to the IRS as if the tax year selected did not qualify for deferral, to compensate for the benefits of the tax deferral. [IRC §§ 444(a), (b), (c), 7519]

Q 7:35   Can an LLC use the cash basis, rather than the accrual, method of accounting?

Sometimes. Code Section 703 allows an LLC to adopt a method of accounting different from that used by the LLC's members. However, even if the cash basis is used, other code sections may prevent the LLC from deducting many prepaid expenses, like prepaid interest, farming expenses, and rent in certain cases, as they are paid. (See Code Sections 461(g), 464, 467; see also the Section 1272-1274 rules, which may require a cash-basis taxpayer to accrue original issue discount on certain debt instruments.)

If, however, the LLC is considered a tax shelter, which would require it to have losses, or has a C corporation, other than a personal service corporation as a member, it cannot use the cash basis of accounting. [IRC § 448] Code Section 448(d)(3) defines a tax shelter in part as a non-C corporation enterprise that, at any time, had been offered for sale in an offering required to be registered with any federal or state agencies that regulate the sale of securities. This definition is further expanded by Temporary Treasury Regulations Section 1.448-1T(b)(2), which provides that, an offering is required to be registered with a federal or state agency if, under federal or state law, failure to file an exemption notice would violate the law (whether or not the notice is actually filed).

An S corporation is not treated as a tax shelter merely because it is required to file an exemption notice from securities registration, if all corporations formed in the particular state are also required to do so. [IRC § 448(d)(3)] However, Code Section 448(d)(3) does not similarly exempt limited partnerships or LLCs.

Nevertheless, because of the expansion of LLC statutes, the IRS has issued letter rulings on the ability of LLCs to use the cash method of accounting. It appears, however, that either the states in question do not have any specific securities registration requirement for these companies, or the IRS has ignored this provision in temporary regulations. In Letter Rulings 9321047 and 9415005, Arizona and Delaware law firms were allowed to use the cash method when practicing as LLCs. The focus of both letter rulings was on aspects of tax shelter treatment, particularly treatment as a syndicate under Temporary Treasury Regulations Section 1.448-1T(b)(3), which addresses whether 35 percent or more of the LLC's losses would be allocated to "limited entrepreneurs," a statutory term.

A literal reading of Temporary Treasury Regulations Section 1.448-1T(b) would prohibit an LLC from using the cash method of accounting in many states. The Committee reports on the 1988 change in Code Section 448(d)(3) for S corporations indicate that Congress intended to focus on entities that are required to register their securities in a public offering, not on those entities in states that require securities registration whether or not the securities are issued in a private or public setting. The approach taken by the IRS in letter rulings, even though they cannot be relied upon by anyone other than the taxpayer to whom they are addressed, should provide some comfort. [IRC § 6110(j)]

Nevertheless, practitioners should be aware that, if an LLC is required to file a notice with the state securities commission for LLC interests issued, the LLC may be forced to use the accrual method of accounting.

Q 7:36   Can an ordinary asset in the hands of a member be converted into a capital asset in the LLC?

Generally, no. If, the sale of an asset would generate ordinary income in the hands of the contributing member, that asset will continue to be an ordinary asset after contribution to an LLC. [IRC § 724] Thus, for example, a member's unrealized receivables and inventory will continue to be treated as such after being contributed to the LLC.

However, inventory may lose this taint if the LLC continues to hold the property five years after the contribution. [IRC § 724(b)]

Likewise, if a member contributes an asset with an adjusted basis in excess of the fair market value of the asset at the time of the contribution, the disposition of the asset at a loss will be a capital loss to the extent of the member's built-in loss at the time of the contribution, if the LLC disposes of the asset within five years from the date of the contribution. [IRC § 724(c)] The built-in capital loss must be allocated to the contributing member. [IRC § 704(c)]

The same analysis may not apply to contributions to an S corporation. Treasury Regulations Section 1.1375-1(d) applies a subjective test instead of the mandatory treatment for an LLC under Code Section 724. Thus, a shareholder's ordinary asset may be treated as a capital asset of the S corporation, at least if the asset was not contributed to the S corporation for the purpose of converting the character of the asset.

Partnership Operations

Q 7:37   Does an LLC file a federal income tax return?

Yes, unless it is a one-member LLC taxed as a disregarded entity or sole proprietorship. The LLC, if taxed as a sole proprietorship, files on Schedule E of the Form 1040, the personal tax return, and if taxed as a partnership, is required to file Form 1065 (Partnership Tax Return) annually. An LLC owned by one entity (a "SMLLC") has its income, gain, losses, deductions and credits reported on its owner's return. Form 1065 is only an informational return, and the LLC must issue a separate Form K-1 to each individual member, which separately states specific items that may be treated differently by each individual member. [IRC § 702] For example, the LLC must itemize capital gains and losses, charitable contributions, dividends, and foreign taxes.

Q 7:38   Is the character of income determined at the LLC or member level?

At the LLC level, except as provided in Code Section 724, discussed in Q 7:36. The character of income or loss (as ordinary or capital) and deductions or credits are determined at the LLC level, and do not depend upon how they would be determined if incurred directly by one or more members. [IRC § 702(b)] However, as discussed in Q 7:37, each member's net tax consequences for the LLC's capital gains or losses, charitable contributions, and other items will depend upon that member's individual tax situation.

Q 7:39 How is the LLC's income, gains, losses, deductions, and credits allocated among the members?

LLC statutes and the IRC allow members, within limits (see Q 7:41), to allocate the LLC's income, losses, deductions, and the like, in any manner agreed by the members. Without an agreement, each member's distributive share of the LLC's tax items should be allocated in accordance with each member's economic interest in the LLC. [IRC § 704(a), (b)] The LLC, however, is not required to allocate all items identically. Therefore, except as discussed in Q 7:41, the LLC can allocate gains differently than losses, and deductions differently among each member, or make any other allocation it wants.

Q 7:40 Does Section 1032 provide advantages for the corporate partner who contributes its own stock to a partnership or LLC, and then the partnership uses the stock to acquire property or compensate for services?

Yes. Section 1032 allows for nonrecognition treatment to a corporation on the receipt of property in exchange for its own stock. Thus, upon the initial contribution of stock to a partnership in exchange for partnership interests, the corporation would recognize no gain or loss. Furthermore, when the partnership uses the stock to acquire property or compensate services, the corporation will not recognize gain with respect to the distribution of stock and receive an increase in basis to the extent of gain realized by the partnership.

Revenue Ruling 99-57 [1999-51 IRB 678] addresses this issue which is sometimes referred to as the "zero basis" problem. The ruling gives the example of a corporate partner, A, and an individual, B, form the AB partnership. A contributes its own stock with a basis of zero and a fair market value of $100 and B contributes a piece of land with a basis and fair market value of $100. No gain or loss will be recognized on the contribution under section 721(a). The AB partnership will have a zero basis in the stock under section 723. Each partner receives a 50 percent partnership interest, with A's basis at zero and B's basis at $100. Under the partnership agreement, each partner will be allocated an equal share of all partnership items.

After the value of the stock increases to $120, the AB partnership acquires property from C with a fair market value of $60 for 50 shares of A stock and also exchanges 50 shares of A stock to D in exchange for services by D valued at $60. AB realizes $120 in gain because the basis in the stock is $0. $100 of the gain would be allocated to A under Section 704(c) since A contributed stock with a zero basis. The $20 in appreciation will be split equally between A and B. Thus, A would recognize $110 in gain. The Ruling also explains:

> Section 1032 is intended to prevent a corporation from recognizing gain or loss when dealing in its own stock. Under § (704(b) and 704(c), a corporate partner contributing its own stock generally will be allocated an amount of gain attributable to its stock that corresponds to its economic interest in the stock held by the partnership. Accordingly, use of the aggregate theory of partnerships is appropriate in determining the application of § 1032 with respect to gain allocated to a corporate partner. Under § 1032, A's share of the gain resulting from AB's exchange of A stock will not be subject to tax. In addition, A increases its basis in its partnership interest in AB under § 705 by $110x, the amount equal to A's share of the gain resulting from AB's exchange of A stock, thereby preserving the nonrecognition result of the transaction in accordance with the policy underlying § 1032.

The contribution of stock by a corporate partner to a partnership in exchange for partnership interests will not result in gain recognition by the partner if the stock is exchanged later in a taxable transaction. Under Section 704, the partnership will realize gain that will be allocated to the partners according to the partnership agreement. Section 1032 provides that the corporate partner will not recognize the allocation of realized gain from the exchange of stock. In addition, Section 705 gives the corporate partner an increase in basis equal to the amount of gain resulting from the exchange of stock by the partnership.

Q 7:41 Are there any restrictions on the manner in which the LLC allocates income, losses, deductions, and the like, to the members?

Yes. There are at least five restrictions on the allocation of the LLC's income and losses.

1. Pre-contribution gains and losses. Code Section 704(c) (see Q 7:35) requires an LLC to allocate to the contributing member any built-in pre-contribution gain or loss attributable to an asset contributed by that member (see Q 7:20).

2. Assignment of service income. Code Section 704(e) prohibits an LLC from allocating to the donee of an interest in an LLC, the LLC's income attributable to the reasonable compensation for services performed by the donor member before the gift of the interest to the donee.

3. Pre-membership income or loss. Code Section 706(d) prohibits an LLC from allocating income and deductions attributable to a period before a person acquired interest in the LLC. Code Section 706(d)(2) requires cash-basis LLCs to allocate the LLC's distributive items on a daily basis if there is a shift or transfer of the LLC's interests.

4. Substantial economic effect. As discussed in Q 7:37, if the LLC allocates any item of income, loss, deduction, or credit in a manner other than in accordance with the member's economic interest in the LLC, those allocations must have substantial economic effect. Otherwise, the IRS will require the LLC to re-allocate those distributive shares in accordance with the members' economic interests.

5. Pre-contribution trade or business property. See Q 7:36.

[IRC § 704(b); Treas Reg § 1.704-1(b)(1)(i)]

Q 7:42 Are there special rules regarding aggregation of income and losses for securities partnerships?

Yes. An LLC operating as a securities partnership can make a reverse Section 704(c) allocation on an aggregate basis with regard to qualified financial assets using any reasonable approach under Section 704(c). This enables the LLC to offset aggregate built in gains with built in losses when it is clear that the purpose is not to shift tax consequences among the members of the LLC. A reverse Section 704(c) allocation is a revaluation of property to adjust the capital accounts of the partners. The allocation must comply with the requirements set out in Treasury Regulations Section 1.704-1(b)(2)(iv)(f). The special rule for securities partnerships, as well as the definition of what is a qualified financial asset, is set out in Treasury Regulations Section 1.704-3(e)(3). [See also PLR 199909025]

Q 7:43   What is economic effect?

A tax allocation has economic effect if the member who receives the allocation also receives or bears any corresponding economic benefit or burden. [Treas Reg § 1.704-1(b)(2)(ii)(a)] For example, if tax depreciation on an asset is specially allocated to a member, any corresponding recapture income on the sale of that asset must be allocated to that member.

For special allocations to have economic effect, the IRS requires that the Operating Agreement or other agreement among the members contain these three provisions:

1. *Capital accounts.* The LLC must maintain a capital account for each member at all times under the rules set forth in Treasury Regulations Section 1.704-1(b)(2)(iv).

2. *Liquidating distributions.* The LLC must distribute the LLC's assets upon liquidation to the members in accordance with their positive capital account balances, after taking into account all capital account adjustments for the LLC's tax year during which the LLC liquidates. The liquidating distributions must be made by the end of the taxable year during which the LLC liquidates (or if later, within 90 days after the date of the liquidation). [Treas Reg § 1.704-1(b)(2)(ii)(b)(2)]

3. *Restoration of deficit capital accounts.* If a member has a negative capital account, that member must contribute to the LLC's capital account upon liquidation of that member's interest the amount of the negative balance. The Operating Agreement or other agreement must make this an unconditional obligation on each member. In addition, the agreement must require the member to make this contribution by the end of the taxable year during which the member's interest is liquidated (or, if later, within 90 days after the date of the

liquidation). The amount contributed by the member under this requirement must be paid to the LLC's creditors upon liquidation of the LLC or must be distributed to the other members in accordance with their positive capital account balance. [Treas Reg § 1.704-1(b)(2)(ii)(b)(3)]

In Revenue Ruling 99-43, 1999-42 IRB 506, the Service held that a special allocation lacked substantiality when the partners amended the partnership agreement to specially allocate cancellation of indebtedness income and book items from a related revaluation after the event creating such items had occurred, even though the overall effect of the special allocation on the partners capital account did not differ substantially from the economic effects of the original allocations in the partnership agreement. Under the facts of the Revenue Ruling, the partnership attempted to allocate the resulting cancellation of indebtedness entirely to a partner who was technically insolvent under IRC § 108. This was a shifting and a transitory allocation under § 1.704-1(b)(2)(iii)(C) and § 1.704-1(b)(2)(iii)(B), in that the overall tax liability of the partners would be less if the special allocation was allowed. The Service thus held that the allocations should be reallocated according to the partners' interest in the partnership. [§ 1.704-1(b)(3)]

Q 7:44   Will the IRS respect special allocations of LLC items even if each member is not required to restore negative capital account balance?

Yes. Treasury Regulations Section 1.704-1(b)(2)(ii)(d) sets forth the "alternate economic effect" test, which is an option to the standard economic effect test. Under the alternate economic effect test, special allocations will be respected as having economic effect if the Operating Agreement or other agreement requires the LLC to maintain capital accounts, make liquidating distributions in accordance with positive capital account balances, and the agreement contains a qualified income offset (see Q 7:45).

If the LLC relies upon this standard for economic effect, allocations will have economic effect only to the extent that the allocations do not reduce a member's capital account below the amount the member has agreed, or is otherwise obligated to restore as of the end of the LLC's taxable year to which the allocation relates.

Q 7:45   What is a "qualified income offset"?

A qualified income offset is a contractual provision that requires the LLC to allocate income, including gross income, to a member as quickly as possible to restore any negative capital account caused by any unexpected allocations of losses and deductions to that member. [Treas Reg § 1.704-1(b)(2)(d)(4)-(6)] Thus, the LLC must specially allocate income, including gross income if necessary, to a member, to eliminate any negative balance in that member's capital account caused by these three allocations or distributions to that member:

1. Oil and gas depletion allowances;
2. Allocations attributable to services rendered by a member [see, e.g., IRC § 704(e)], or shifts in the member's interest in the LLC during the taxable year [IRC § 706(d)], or income or loss realized by the LLC upon the distribution of unrealized receivables or substantially appreciated inventory to another member of the LLC in exchange for that member's interest in the LLC's other assets [see Treas Reg § 1.751-1(b)(2)(ii)]; or
3. Distributions to the member in excess of any reasonably expected increases in the member's capital account, other than increases under a minimum gain charge back (see Q 7:70), unless the distribution is made from the proceeds of nonrecourse debt allocable to an increase in the LLC's minimum gain. [Treas Reg § 1.704-1(b)(2)(d)(4)-(6)]

A valid qualified income offset provision requires a priority of income or gain that overrides the general showing arrangement to which the members have agreed. Since the qualified income offset provision is triggered, by definition, by the occurrence of unexpected events, its inclusion in the LLC Operating Agreement necessarily creates an element of unpredictability. For this reason, many people prefer not to include a qualified income offset provision in the agreement.

Single Member LLCs (SMLLC)

Q 7:46   What is a SMLLC?

A SMLLC or single member limited liability company is simply an LLC in which one individual or entity owns 100 percent of the ownership interest of the LLC. Pursuant to Treasury Regulations

Section 301. 7701-3, in the absence of an election to be classified as an association, a domestic SMLLC is disregarded as an entity separate from its owner for federal income tax purposes.

Q 7:47 Does a SMLLC need an operating agreement?

At this time, this question is largely unanswered. The term agreement suggests the reconciliation of two or more different interests. In a SMLLC, there is really only one interest, that of the owner. Furthermore, the operating agreement would be both ineffective and unnecessary to control the internal operation of the LLC. As the sole member, the owner would be able to operate the LLC in any manner desired and go virtually unchallenged. Since the owner would control all the voting rights as well, the owner could simply amend any operating agreement to suit his whim as needed.

Thus any need for an operating agreement would not appear to arise from a need for internal control. There are however, three reasons why an operating agreement might be worthwhile. First, an operating agreement can set forth the assets of the LLC, and be used to help segregate the owners' personal assets from the claims of LLC creditors. Secondly, by providing for reasonable compensation to the owner for services rendered to the LLC, the operating agreement might provide some protection against claims by creditors that distributions made when the LLC was technically insolvent were wrongful distributions. Lastly, many LLC statutes provide for dissolution of an LLC if the LLC does not have a member for a certain duration of time. By providing an alternative provision in the operating agreement, the statutory provision can be overridden. This alternative provision can prevent breach of contract claims and unanticipated exposure to liability which could result from an unanticipated dissolution. For these reasons, it would be prudent to establish an operating agreement for SMLLCs.

Q 7:48 How would the sale of a SMLLC which is disregarded for federal income tax purposes be treated?

Since the SMLLC is not recognized for federal income tax purposes, the owner of the SMLLC would be viewed as owning the assets of the LLC. The owner for income tax purposes cannot merely convey its interest in the LLC. Rather, the owner would be deemed to have conveyed each asset individually. Thus upon sale, the owner would recognize a gain or a loss on each item. [Rev Rul 99-5] It is unclear what an election to be taxed as an association would have upon this treatment. Presumably, the conversion to an association would be a tax-free transaction under Section 351. After this transfer, the owner would then be able to convey the interest in the LLC. It is likely, however, that the service might apply the step-transaction principles to this type of transaction if it occurred shortly before the sale.

Q 7:49   What are the tax consequences of converting SMLLCs to and from multi-owner entities?

Depending upon the fact pattern involved, the tax consequences can vary. The IRS has issued two rulings on the tax consequences of converting domestic SMLLCs to and from multi-owner entities classified as partnerships for federal tax purposes. [Rev Rul 99-5, 1999-5 IRB 8; Rev Rul 99-6, 1999-6 IRB 6]

Revenue Ruling 99-5 discusses two fact situations involving conversions from SMLLCs, disregarded as separate entities for tax purposes, to multi-owner entities classified as partnerships. The fact patterns involve: (1) the sale by the sole member of a 50-percent interest in the LLC, and (2) the exchange of a 50-percent interest in the LLC for a capital contribution made directly to the LLC. In the first situation, the LLC, which, for federal tax purposes, is disregarded as an entity separate from its owner, is converted to a partnership when the new member purchases a 50-percent interest in the disregarded entity from the original member. As a result, the original member recognizes gain or loss from the deemed sale of an interest to the new member under Code Section 1001. Under Code Section 721(a), no gain or loss is recognized by either member as a result of the conversion of the disregarded entity to a partnership. In the second situation, the LLC is converted from an entity that is disregarded as an entity separate from its owner to a partnership when a new member contributes cash to the LLC. The contribution is treated as a contribution to a partnership in exchange for an ownership interest in the partnership. Thus, this transaction will be tax-free except to the extent any liabilities contributed to the partnership exceed the basis of its assets.

Revenue Ruling 99-6, by contrast, discusses the tax consequences of converting a multi-member LLC classified as a partnership to a single-member LLC. It discusses two different fact patterns involving: (1) the sale of one member's interest in a two-member LLC to the other member, and (2) the sale of the entire interests by both members of a two-membered LLC to an unrelated third person, who continues the business as a single-member LLC. In each case, the partnership is terminated upon completion of the transaction and a liquidating distribution of the partnership assets is deemed to have been made. Accordingly, the selling partner must treat the transaction as the sale of a partnership interest under Treasury Regulations Section 1.741-1(b) and therefore must report any gain or loss resulting from the sale. [IRC § 741] As for the purchasing partner, the partnership is deemed to make a liquidating distribution of all its assets to the two partners, and following this distribution, the purchasing partner is treated as acquiring the assets deemed to have been distributed to the selling partner in liquidation of the partnership interest. The basis in these assets generally will be the purchase price paid to the selling partner. Moreover, the purchasing partner is considered to receive a distribution of those assets attributable to his former interest in the partnership. As a result, the purchasing partner must recognize gain or loss, if any, on the deemed distribution of the assets to the extent required by Code Section 731(a).

Q 7:50 In a SMLLC which is disregarded for federal income tax purposes, what is the proper method of reporting federal employment tax obligations?

Pursuant to IRS bulletin Notice 99-6, the Internal Revenue Service will accept reporting of payment of employment taxes in two different manners. First, calculation, reporting and payment of all employment tax obligations with respect to employees of a disregarded entity may be made by its owner and under the owner's name and taxpayer identification number. Secondly, calculation, reporting and payment of all employment tax obligations may be made by the state law entity with respect to its employees under its own name and taxpayer identification number. The notice provides that irrespective of the manner of reporting selected by the limited liability company, the owner will remain personally liable for the employment tax.

Q 7:51   Is the owner of a SMLLC personally liable for employment taxes incurred by the limited liability company?

Under the "check-the-box" regulations, a business entity with a single owner will be treated as a disregarded entity for federal income tax purposes, unless an election is made by the limited liability company to be taxed as an association. [Treas Reg § 301.7701-3(b)(1)] Letter Ruling 199922053 and Cumulative Bulletin Notice 99-6, advise that the owner of a limited liability company will be personally liable for employment tax obligations because the limited liability company is disregarded for federal tax purposes.

Q 7:52   May the IRS collect an individual's federal income tax liability from a SMLLC, if the LLC is treated as a disregarded entity for federal income tax purposes?

No. Pursuant to the "check-the-box" regulations a limited liability company with a single owner may elect to be classified as an association (and taxed similar to a corporation) or to be disregarded as an entity separate from it's owner. [Treas Reg § 301.7701-3(b)(1)] If the limited liability company elects to be disregarded, the owner would report the income from the limited liability company on the taxpayers personal income tax return as if operating as a sole proprietorship.

State law will determine the nature of a person's interest in property for determining whether the tax lien or levy attaches. [United States v National Bank of Commerce, 472 US 713 (1985); Aquilino v United States, 363 US 509 (1960); United States v Bess, 357 US 51 (1958)] In Chief Counsel Advise memorandum 199930013, the service noted that pursuant to West Virginia state law, the taxpayer holds no interest in the property of the limited liability company. Since the property is not the property of the taxpayer, the service cannot levy against that property to satisfy a tax assessed solely against the taxpayer.

The Memorandum discusses two possible methods of collection of the tax from the LLC. First, the service suggests attaching the taxpayers "transferable distributional interest". Secondly, the Service recommends filing alter ego liens through application of the "piercing the corporate veil" concept to limited liability companies. The service references a 1994 law review article for suggested factors for consideration. [Fox, *Piercing the Veil of Limited Liability Companies*, 62 Geo Wash L Rev 1143 (1994)] The article indicates that failure to adhere to corporate formalities and lack of separation may not apply in piercing the limited liability company's veil. By the very nature of limited liability companies, they are intended not to require the formalities of corporations and are intended to allow member management. The article concludes that inadequate capitalization alone can be sufficient for piercing the limited liability company's veil.

The Chief Counsel Advise Memorandum directs that piercing the limited liability company's veil can be considered on a case-by-case basis. The Service indicates that it believes the most important factor may be that the limited liability company is being used to evade the payment of taxes, such as where the income earned by the taxpayer is being paid directly to the limited liability company.

Q 7:53   Can a SMLLC treated as a disregarded entity be effectively used as an alternative to a corporate subsidiary?

Yes, using a SMLLC which is disregarded for federal income tax purposes as a subsidiary corporation provides limited liability to the parent corporation and prevents the need to file a consolidated return. Use of a disregarded SMLLC can also be an effective means of avoiding the separate return limitation year rules in a consolidated return. The parent corporation might also be able to aggregate the income, gain, deductions, loses and credits.

There are two methods available to convert a subsidiary into a SMLLC. In states that provide for a merger of a corporation into a LLC, the subsidiary can merge into the LLC and then terminate the subsidiary. In Private Letter Ruling 9822037, the service indicated that a merger of a corporation owned by a single owner into a SMLLC owned by the same individual would be viewed as a liquidation of the corporation.

Under the second method, the subsidiary forms a SMLLC, and transfers all of its assets to the SMLLC, under Code Section 721. Then, the subsidiary liquidates into the parent under Code Section 332. The service would be unable to argue that there were ever two owners of the SMLLC. This two step transaction should be possible without federal income tax recognition.

Although state laws allow for SMLLCs, not all states follow the federal regulations for classification of SMLLCs. Some states look to the SMLLC's member to determine the state tax treatment. Other states, such as Delaware, treat all LLCs as partnerships. Delaware, New Hampshire and Texas require that a corporate member file a state income tax return. Since the states fail to have any kind of uniform treatment, individuals who are considering use of a SMLLC should carefully examine the states they anticipate operating in, and those states' treatment of SMLLCs.

Q 7:54   How will the use of a SMLLC effect a Section 1031 like-kind exchange?

With the advent of the new "check-the-box" regulations, a business entity with only one owner is classified as a corporation or is disregarded as an entity separate from its owners. Under Treasury Regulations Section 301.7701-3(b)(1)(ii), a domestic eligible entity with a single owner is disregarded as an entity separate from its owners unless it elects to be treated as a corporation under Treasury Regulations Section 301.7701-3(c). Therefore, in a Section 1031 like-kind exchange, it may be possible to transfer or "drop-down" the replacement asset into a single-member LLC and still qualify for nonrecognition treatment.

In Private Letter Ruling 9807013, the taxpayer, a limited partnership with two partners, requested a ruling as to whether the receipt of replacement properties by the taxpayer's SMLLC will be treated as the receipt of real property by the taxpayer for purposes of qualifying for nonrecognition of gain under Code Section 1031. In a favorable ruling for the taxpayer, the IRS concluded that the LLC receipt of the replacement property would be treated as the receipt of real property directly by the taxpayer for purposes of qualifying for nonrecognition of gain under Code Section 1031. The IRS provided no reasoning other than stating that, under Treasury Regulations Section 301.7701-2(c)(2), a business entity that has a single owner and is not a corporation is disregarded as an entity separate from its owner for federal tax purposes. Accordingly, the assets of the SMLLC are treated as the assets of the taxpayer.

There are, however, many situations where SMLLCs may not be feasible or desirable to a third party. For example, many lenders now require that borrowers form a "single purpose 'bankruptcy remote' entity" ("SPBRE") to borrow the funds and hold the property. This bankruptcy remote protection is being required by lenders in an effort to curb past behavior on the part of borrowers who declared bankruptcy in an effort to delay or hinder the lender's ability to foreclose on the collateral. However, this protection being sought by lenders has resulted in much complexity and additional expense in the area of like-kind exchanges under Code Section 1031. For example, by the lender requiring the holder of the financed property (i.e., the replacement property) to be a newly formed SPBRE, the lender will cause the recipient of the property to be an entity for local law purposes different from the entity that transferred the relinquished property.

There have been a few situations where lenders have permitted SMLLCs that have a manager who can veto a bankruptcy filing or a sale of all the assets and who is contractually obligated to take into account the interests of the lender. Depending upon the size of the deal, lenders may feel uncomfortable with only contractual protection that may or may not be subject to being set aside in a bankruptcy proceeding.

The challenge, then, is to select an SPBRE that meets the stringent requirements of the lender, yet will be treated as a non-entity by the Service, so that the transferor of the relinquished property is treated as the recipient of the replacement property. Until recently, the only possible alternatives included the Illinois land trusts, Delaware business trusts, various imputations of LLCs or a complete election out of Subchapter K, all of which carry various risks and additional expenses. Now, however, there is a viable alternative which permits the disregarding of a two-member LLC where one of the members has no economic interest. [Ltr Rul 9911033]

In Private Letter Ruling 19911033, the taxpayer was a grantor of a trust who, under Code Section 671, was treated as the owner of the trust's assets, and who wished to exchange real property held by the trust for other real property in accordance with the deferred exchange provisions of Code Section 1031(a)(3). The trustees of the trust assigned their rights in a contract to sell the real property to a qualified intermediary. To satisfy the lender's requirement that legal title to the property be held by a bankruptcy-remote entity, the trust formed an LLC with the trustees and a corporation wholly owned by the trust as members. One of the members of the board of directors of the corporation would be a representative of the lender. The trust would have a 100 percent interest in the profits, losses, and capital of the LLC, while the corporation would have no interest in the LLC's profits, losses, or capital. The corporation would be designated a "manager" in the LLC agreement which required a unanimous vote of its board of directors together with that of the trust, before certain action could be taken with respect to the secured property. All other decisions of the LLC would be made solely by the trust. The replacement property was then transferred directly to the LLC.

In determining if the parties intended to enter into a partnership, the Service reasoned, that based on the LLC agreement, the trust and the corporation did not enter into the LLC agreement with the intention of operating a business and sharing profits and losses therefrom. The corporation's sole limited purpose for becoming a member of the LLC was to prevent the trust from voluntarily placing the LLC into bankruptcy. The corporation had no interest in the LLC's profits or losses and did not manage the enterprise or have any management rights other than the limited rights enumerated in the LLC agreement. Therefore, the IRS held that the LLC would not be treated as a partnership, but instead treated as an entity owned solely by the trust.

The Service also determined that so long as the LLC doesn't elect to be treated as an association taxable as a corporation, it will be disregarded as an entity separate from the trust. As a result, the acquisition of the replacement property by the LLC will be treated as a direct acquisition by the trust under Code Section 1031(a)(3). [See also Ltr Rul 199914006, discussed in Q7:56]

Q 7:55   Are SMLLCs an effective method of segregating the liability of numerous assets in an LLC or FLP?

Yes, a SMLLC can be effectively used as a means of asset protection and risk segregation. The disregarded nature of SMLLC will eliminate the need to file an additional federal tax return. The LLC which will hold all the assets is generally referred to as the big LLC. When transferring assets to the big LLC, in order to prevent the assets of the big LLC from potentially be liable for the asset, the owner should place the item into a SMLLC prior to contribution. Then the entire membership interest should be transferred to the big LLC in exchange for a membership interest. If less then the entire interest is transferred to the big LLC, then the big LLC will be deemed to have purchased a portion of the single members interest in the underlying assets. [Rev Rul 99-5, 1999-5 IRB 8] Thus the big LLC could be viewed as owning the subject property and the purposes of using a SMLLC would be frustrated.

Q 7:56 When can an multi-member LLC be disregarded like a SMLLC for federal income tax purposes?

A multi-member LLC will be disregarded for federal income tax purpose when only one member supplies both the economic means and the management needs of the business and no partnership is found to exist. The Supreme Court defined a partnership as the joining together of two or more individuals to operate a business and share in its profits and losses. [Commissioner v Culbertson, 337 US 733 (1949)] The Tax Court set fourth a seven-factor test for determining whether a partnership had been formed in *Luna v. Commissioner.* [42 TC 1067 (1964)] The service relied on both of these cases to find that a multi-member LLC could be disregarded for federal income tax purposes in Private Letter Rulings 199914006 and 199911033 (discussed in the preceding question). In Private Letter Ruling 199914006, the taxpayer was the two member LLC. One member was compensated with a one-time fee for joining the LLC. This member possessed no rights in either the capital or the income of the LLC nor did the member hold any managerial rights. The member's sole right as a member, was the ability to vote on any decision to engage in any business beyond the stated purpose of the LLC, to file a voluntary or involuntary petition for bankruptcy, to voluntarily dissolve, liquidate, consolidate, merge with any other entity, sell substantially all of the LLC assets, or to amend the LLC's certificate of formation. The operating agreement provided that a unanimous vote of the shareholders was required to engage in these activities. The member was also obligated to continue the operation of the LLC in the event of bankruptcy of the other member. In finding that the LLC should be disregarded, the service held that it was not a partnership, since the two members did not enter into an agreement to share profits and losses.

The facts in Private Letter Ruling 199911033 indicate that a lender of the LLC had required the joining of an additional member. The facts of Private Letter Ruling 199914006, also suggest that the joining of the second member might have been necessitated by a lender. The question then becomes, is the exception created by these two letter rulings limited to situations in which a second member is necessitated by a lender. Or, would a multi-member providing with one members interest being limited in a similar type of manner as set forth in the letter rulings, in those states which require two members to form an LLC also be disregarded? There are no bright lines to the boundaries of this exception. Therefore, in order to ensure qualification under this exception, planning should be restricted to the facts of the letter rulings.

Q 7:57   How will a SMLLC taxed as a disregarded entity for federal income tax purposes be treated for state tax purposes?

Treatment of SMLLCs under state law is largely untested. Where state income tax law follows the federal rules, a SMLLC would be disregarded for state income tax purposes when disregarded for federal income tax purposes. However, at least one state's department of taxation and finance has indicated that a single member LLC would be taxed as a partnership for state tax purposes. The New York Commissioner of Taxation and Finance in an advisory opinion for Arthur Anderson, LLP, interpreting the state's sales tax provisions, held that the LLC should be treated like a partnership. Arthur Anderson, LLP, TSB-A-99(7)S, 1/28/99. The commissioner relied upon S. 2(6) of the New York Tax Law which defines a partnership to include an LLC. Since this provision did not distinguish between disregarded SMLLCs and other LLCs, the commissioner reasoned that under New York Tax Law, SMLLCs would be considered entities separate from their owner.

Large Partnerships, Publicly Traded Partnerships, and International Partnerships

Q 7:58 How does the Taxpayer Relief Act of 1997 address the treatment of electing large partnerships?

The act adds, for tax years beginning in 1998, a new Part IV to Subchapter K that addresses the treatment of "electing large partnerships". [IRC § 771] An electing large partnership is generally an entity separate from its partners. Part IV explicitly provides that Parts I through III of Subchapter K (Code Sections 701 through 761) are inapplicable to electing large partnerships to the extent such provisions are inconsistent with the provisions of Part IV. [IRC § 771] Electing large partnerships generally are required to report only a net income or net loss figure to their partners. Carved out from this general rule, however, are a number of items for which partners must separately account. For example:

- income or loss from passive activities;
- income or loss from nonpassive activities;
- net capital gain or loss to the extent allocable to passive or nonpassive activities;
- tax-exempt interest;
- net alternative minimum tax adjustments, separately computed for passive and nonpassive activities;
- general business, low-income housing, rehabilitation, and nonconventional fuel credits, and foreign income taxes; and
- any other items determined by the Secretary of the Treasury (the "secretary") to be appropriate for separate treatment.

Q 7:59 What are the basic criteria for a partnership to be an electing large partnership?

An electing large partnership is any partnership (other than a service or commodities partnership) with at least 100 partners in the year preceding the year with respect to which the election is made. [IRC § 775(a)(1)] The number of partners will generally be determined by counting only those persons who hold their interests through other partnerships. The election, once made, is binding for all future years and may not be revoked without the consent of the secretary.

Q 7:60   How is a publicly traded partnership classified for tax purposes?

Since 1988, a publicly traded partnership generally has been classified as an association taxable as a corporation unless at least 90 percent of the partnership's gross income is "passive-type" income and the partnership is neither registered as a management company or unit investment trust under the Investment Company Act of 1940 (the "ICA") nor treated as a "business development company" pursuant to an election under the ICA. [IRC § 7704(a),(c)]

The Omnibus Budget Reconciliation Act of 1987, however, contains a special "grandfather" rule providing that certain publicly traded partnerships in existence on December 17, 1987, would not be classified as associations taxable as corporations until taxable years beginning after December 31, 1997. [Pub L No 100-203, § 10211(c)] Even though the "grandfather" period has expired, under the 1997 Taxpayer Relief Act, these publicly traded partnerships can continue their status as partnerships if they so elect and consent to the application of a 3.5 percent tax on their gross income from the active conduct of trades and businesses. [IRC § 7704(g)] In addition, the 1998 Restructuring Act makes it clear that the 3.5 percent gross income tax is paid by the partnership, not by the partners in their separate or individual capacities.

Q 7:61   How does the Taxpayer Relief Act of 1997 affect contributions to international joint ventures?

The act repeals Code Sections 1491 and 1494 generally effective for transfers made on or after August 5, 1997. Under former Code Section 1491, a U.S. person that contributed appreciated property to a foreign partnership generally was required to pay an excise tax in an amount equal to 35 percent of the unrealized appreciation inherent in such property at the time of the contribution.

Under former Code Section 1494, if a U.S. person transferred property to a foreign partnership, such person was required to file an information return with respect to such transfer. If such a return was not filed, the statute required the transferor to pay an excise tax in an amount equal to 35 percent of the value of the property, even if the property was not appreciated (such as a capital contribution of cash).

Q 7:62 How does Code Section 721(c) affect foreign partnerships?

The Taxpayer Relief Act of 1997 enacted new Code Section 721(c) to the Code. The legislative history does not provide any indication of what Congress intended to achieve by enacting Code Section 721(c), although it seems likely it was intended to take the place of Code Section 1496. While repealing the automatic toll charge on outbound transfers to foreign partnerships imposed by former Code Section 1491, the act grants the Treasury Department the authority to promulgate regulations requiring a contributing partner to recognize gain on the contribution of appreciated property to a partnership (whether foreign or domestic) if the built-in gain, when recognized, will be includable in the gross income of a person other than a U.S. person.

Regulations under Code Section 721(c) should be concerned largely with situations in which a person contributes appreciated property to a partnership with one or more foreign partners and Code Section 704(c)(1)(A) (along with Code Sections 704(c)(1)(B) and 737) may fail to ensure that built-in gain is allocated to the contributing partner.

Therefore, it is hoped that any regulations promulgated under Code Section 721(c) will be narrow. Such regulations should apply only to contributions of built-in gain property to partnerships with foreign partners if it is reasonably anticipated at the time of the contribution that the "ceiling rule" will be implicated with respect to the contributed property and will affect one or more foreign partners.

The ceiling rule provides that, for any taxable year, the total taxable income, gain, loss, or deduction allocated to the partners with respect to a particular asset cannot exceed the total partnership taxable income, gain, loss, or deduction with respect to that asset for the taxable year, regardless of the amount of the partnership's "book" items with respect to that asset for such year. [See Treas Reg § 1.704-3(c)] The traditional method with curative allocations generally permits a partnership that encounters the ceiling rule with respect to a particular asset (the "limited asset") to take tax items from another asset (the "reduced asset") and allocate those items to the noncontributing partners to the extent that such partners would not have received an equal amount of tax and book items with respect to the limited asset without such taking.

Q 7:63   Is a U.S. person subject to reporting requirements with respect to transfers of property to foreign partnerships, and if so, what are the penalties for failure to comply with the requirements?

Yes. The Taxpayer Relief Act of 1997 amends Code Section 6038B(a)(1) which mandates reporting under certain conditions. Under Code Sections 6038(a) and 6038B(b)(1) and as to transfers made after August 5, 1997, U.S. persons must report these contributions of property to foreign partnerships if: (1) the U.S. partner transferring the property holds, directly or indirectly, at least a 10-percent interest in the partnership; or (2) the fair market value of the property contributed, when added to the fair market value of any other property transferred by such person (or a related person) to the partnership during the 12-month period ending on the date of the transfer, exceeds $100,000.

The act modifies Code Section 6038B to exact a penalty for failure to comply with the aforementioned reporting requirements. Pursuant to Code Section 6038B(c) failure to comply results in a penalty "equal to 10 percent of the fair market value of the property at the time of the exchange (and, in the case of a contribution (to a foreign partnership), such person shall recognize gain as if the contributed property had been sold for such value at the time of the contribution). Subsection (c) does provide a $100,000 limit on this penalty unless the reporting failure was intentional.

Q 7:64   How does the Taxpayer Relief Act of 1997 affect the Stock and Securities Trading Safe Harbor with respect to foreign corporations and nonresident aliens?

Prior to the act, foreign persons trading securities and stocks for their own accounts would not be treated as being engaged in a U.S. trade or business so long as the securities trading partnership's principal office was outside of the United States. This principal office requirement was required in order to meet the safe harbor of Code Section 864(b)(2)(A)(ii).

The act modifies the above code section by repealing the principal office requirement that the office be located outside the United States. This area of investment had been problematic to investors due in part to the Treasury Regulation promulgated to interpret old Code Section 864(b)(2)(A)(ii). Specifically, Treasury Regulations Section 1.864-2(c)(2)(iii) contained 10 activities which if conducted abroad would warrant a finding that the partnership did not have its principal office in the United States, which would then satisfy the safe harbor. With the repeal of the principal office location requirement, foreign investment gross receipts attributable to periods after December 31, 1997 can no longer be recharacterized under Treasury Regulations Section 1.864-2(c)(2)(iii) as income connected with a U.S. trade or business.

Q 7:65   Does the Taxpayer Relief Act of 1997 affect transfers of intangibles to foreign partnerships?

Yes. Under former Code Section 367, a transfer of an intangible to a corporation was treated as a deemed sale for a stream of royalty payments over the useful life, and as such, was sourced as U.S. income. The act repeals the sourcing portion of the above rule. The income is treated under present Code Section 367 as foreign source income to the extent that the income represents a licensing or sales agreement. [IRC § 367(d)(2)(C)]

Regulations under Code Section 367 have been promulgated which reflect that Code Section 367(d) will be applied to foreign partnerships involving a like transfer of intangibles. The legislative history reflects such application to foreign partnerships stating:

The bill repeals the rule that treats as U.S. source income any deemed royalty arising under Section 367(d). Under the bill, in the case of a transfer of intangible property to a foreign corporation, the deemed royalty payments under Section 367(d) are treated as foreign source income to the same extent that an actual royalty payment would be considered to be foreign source income. Regulatory authority is granted to provide similar treatment in the case of a transfer of intangible property to a foreign partnership.

[Senate Finance Committee Report, 1997 Taxpayer Legislation: Law, Explanation and Analysis, CCH 11,760]

Allocations Attributable to Nonrecourse Debt

Q 7:66 What is a nonrecourse deduction?

A nonrecourse deduction is an LLC tax deduction or a Section 705(a)(2)(B) expenditure attributable to the LLC's nonrecourse debt. [Treas Reg § 1.704-2(b)(1)] Perhaps the most common nonrecourse deduction is tax depreciation of an asset that secures the LLC's nonrecourse debt.

An LLC has nonrecourse deductions each year to the extent that the LLC has a net increase in minimum gain (see Q 7:69) during a tax year, reduced by the amount of the LLC distributions of proceeds from nonrecourse liabilities (which generated the additional minimum gain) to the members. [Treas Reg § 1.704-2(c)] However, generally, refinancings, conversions of debt, and other changes to debt instruments do not generate nonrecourse deductions. [Treas Reg § 1.704-2(c)]

Q 7:67 Do allocations of nonrecourse deductions have substantial economic effect?

No. Nonrecourse debt of an LLC is the LLC's debt for which no member or related person bears the economic risk of loss. This means that those persons are not personally liable for the debt. [Treas Reg §§ 1.704-2(b)(3),1.752-1(a)(2)]

If lenders do not require members to guarantee the LLC's debt, the LLC's debt will be "nonrecourse" for these purposes. Nevertheless, the debt will be included in one or more members' tax basis in their LLC interest (see Q 7:6). As a result, they will be entitled to share in losses attributable to depreciation and other items attributable to the debt; however, these allocations cannot have economic effect because the lender, not the members, bears the economic burdens on the allocations. That is, while members will be entitled to the tax benefits attributable to the depreciation of an asset purchased with nonrecourse debt, if the LLC does not repay the debt in full, the lender, not the members, will suffer the real economic loss.

Nevertheless, the IRS will respect allocations of LLC losses and deductions attributable to nonrecourse deductions, if the allocations are made in accordance with each member's interest in the LLC. [See Q7:68 and Treas Reg § 1.704-2(b)(1)]

Q 7:68 When will the IRS respect allocations of nonrecourse debt?

Tax benefits arising from nonrecourse debt will be honored by the IRS if the LLC satisfies this four-part test in Treasury Regulations Section 1.704-2(e):

1. The LLC must maintain capital accounts, and the Operating Agreement must require the LLC's assets to be distributed to the members in accordance with their positive capital account balances upon liquidation of the LLC.

2. The LLC Operating Agreement must require that nonrecourse deductions be divided among the members, consistent with the allocation of some other significant item attributable to the asset that is encumbered by the nonrecourse debt that gives rise to the deduction. For example, some other "significant item" could include income attributable to the lease or sale of the encumbered property.

3. The LLC Operating Agreement must require the LLC to allocate partnership minimum gain to the members with negative capital accounts generated by: (a) the allocations of nonrecourse deductions to them, or (b) distributions of the proceeds from a nonrecourse liability to them, upon an increase in the LLC's minimum gain. This is generally referred to as a minimum gain charge back (see Q 7:63 and 7:69-75).

4. The LLC's other material allocations and capital account adjustments have substantial economic effect under Treasury Regulations Section 1.704-2(e)(4).

Q 7:69   What is minimum gain?

An LLC has minimum gain to the extent that the principal balance of a nonrecourse debt secured by an asset exceeds the LLC's adjusted basis in that asset. [Treas Reg § 1.704-2(d)] The aggregate amount of the LLC's minimum gain at any one time is determined by subtracting the principal balance of all of the LLC's nonrecourse debt at that time from the LLC's adjusted tax basis of the property securing that debt. [Treas Reg § 1.704-2(d)(1)]

Q 7:70   How does an LLC determine if it has a net increase or decrease in minimum gain?

The net increase or decrease in the LLC's minimum gain is determined by subtracting the amount of the LLC's aggregate minimum gain at the end of the tax year from the balance of the LLC's minimum gain at the end of the immediately preceding tax year. [Treas Reg § 1.704-2(d)(1)]

Generally, an LLC will incur a decrease in minimum gain upon the sale of an asset that had been subject to a nonrecourse liability, or when the LLC makes principal payments on nonrecourse debt.

Q 7:71   What is a minimum gain chargeback?

A minimum gain charge back is an allocation of the LLC's income to the members to the extent of their share of the LLC's net decrease in the LLC's minimum gain, as defined in Treasury Regulations Section 1.704-2(g). [Treas Reg § 1.704-2(f)(1)]

For example, if the LLC sells a depreciable asset secured by non-recourse debt or repays principal on that debt, the LLC may be required to allocate income to the members to the extent that their capital accounts were reduced below zero by the nonrecourse deductions attributable to that asset or debt.

LLC Operating Agreements may contain a minimum gain charge back. A common minimum gain charge back provision is as follows:

If there is a net decrease in Company Minimum Gain for a fiscal year, then there shall be allocated to each Member items of income and gain for that year equal to that Member's share of the net decrease in Minimum Gain (as determined under Treasury Regulations Section 1.704-2(g)(2)), subject to the exceptions set forth in Treasury Regulations Section 1.704-2(f)(2), (3), and (5), provided, that if the Company has any discretion as to an exception set forth pursuant to Treasury Regulations Section 1.704-2(f)(5), the Tax Matters Member may exercise such discretion on behalf of the Company. The Tax Matters Member shall, if the application of the Minimum Gain charge back requirement would cause a distortion in the economic arrangement among the Members, ask the Commissioner to waive the Minimum Gain charge back requirement pursuant to Treasury Regulations Section 1.704-2(f)(4). The foregoing is intended to be a "Minimum Gain Charge back" provision as described in Treasury Regulations Section 1.704-2(f) and shall be interpreted and applied in all respects in accordance with that Regulations Section.

The definitions section of the Operating Agreement should define minimum gain as follows:

"Minimum Gain" shall have the meaning set forth in Treasury Regulations Section 1.704-2(d).

Q 7:72 When is the LLC required to allocate minimum gain to the members?

An LLC is required to allocate minimum gain only if the LLC has a net decrease in the company's aggregate minimum gain from one tax year to the next. [Treas Reg § 1.704-2(f)(1)] There are exceptions to this rule, including net decreases caused by certain debt conversions or refinancings following capital contributions or, if waived by the Commissioner of the IRS, the minimum gain charge back distorts the members' economic arrangement. [See Treas Reg §§ 1.704-2(f)(2)-(4)] For example, if a member contributes capital to the LLC, and the LLC uses that capital to repay a nonrecourse liability or increase the basis of an encumbered asset (e.g., by making capital improvements), either event would cause a decrease in LLC minimum gain; therefore, that member is not subject to a minimum gain charge back. [Treas Reg § 1.704-2(f)(3)]

Q 7:73   What is member nonrecourse debt?

Member nonrecourse debt is a nonrecourse debt of the LLC for which a member or related person, as defined in Treasury Regulations Section 1.752-4(b), bears the economic risk of loss under Treasury Regulations Section 1.752-2. For example, a member nonrecourse debt includes any LLC nonrecourse debt that a member (or related person) has guaranteed or for which the member is the actual creditor. [Treas Reg § 1.704-2(b)(4)]

Q 7:74   What is the consequence of member nonrecourse debt?

All nonrecourse deductions attributable to member nonrecourse debt must be allocated to that member. [Treas Reg § 1.704-2(i)] If more than one member bears the economic risk of loss on that debt, the allocable nonrecourse deductions must be allocated among those members according to the ratio in which they bear the risk of loss. [Treas Reg § 1.704-2(i)]

Q 7:75   Are members with member nonrecourse debt subject to a minimum gain chargeback?

Generally, yes. Similar to the minimum gain charge back, members with member nonrecourse debt must be subject to a member nonrecourse debt minimum gain charge back upon a net decrease in the LLC's member nonrecourse debt as of the end of the taxable year. [Treas Reg § 1.704-2(i)(4)]

In addition to the exceptions listed for the general minimum gain charge back, a member is not subject to a member nonrecourse debt minimum gain charge back upon the conversion of the member nonrecourse debt to a straight nonrecourse debt of the LLC. [Treas Reg § 1.704-2(i)(4)]

The LLC's Operating Agreement should contain a member nonrecourse debt minimum gain charge back provision similar to the following:

> If during a fiscal year there is a net decrease in Member Nonrecourse Debt Minimum Gain, then, in addition to the amounts, if any, allocated pursuant to the preceding paragraph, any Member with a share of that Member Nonrecourse Debt Minimum Gain (as determined under Treasury Regulations Section 1.704-

2(i)(5)) as of the beginning of the fiscal year shall, subject to the exceptions set forth in Treasury Regulations Section 1.704-2(i)(4), be allocated items of income and gain for the year (and, if necessary, for succeeding years) equal to that Member's share of the net decrease in the Member Nonrecourse Debt Minimum Gain. The Tax Matters Member shall, if the application of the Member Nonrecourse Debt Minimum Gain charge back requirement would cause a distortion in the economic arrangement among the Members, ask the IRS Commissioner to waive the Minimum Gain charge back requirement pursuant to Treasury Regulations Sections 1.704-2(f)(4) and 1.704-2(i)(4). The foregoing is intended to be the "charge back of Member Nonrecourse Debt Minimum Gain" required by Treasury Regulations Section 1.704-2(i)(4) and shall be interpreted and applied in all respects in accordance with that Regulations Section.

Other Restrictions on the Allocation of LLC Income

Q 7:76 Can family members use an LLC to assign income attributable to the services or property of one family member to other family members?

No. Code Section 704(e) prevents the assignment of income among family members, and is generally known as the "family partnership rules." The LLC's income cannot be allocated to donee family members, unless the donor receives an allocation of income commensurate with the value of the donor's services to the LLC. [Treas Reg § 1.704-1(e)(1)(ii)] Likewise, the LLC's income from income-producing assets can be allocated only to those family members who have a bona fide interest in the LLC's capital. [IRC § 704(e)(1); Treas Reg § 1.704-1(e)(1)(v)]

Q 7:77 Can new members be allocated income and losses the LLC accrued before the date the member was admitted to the LLC?

No. Code Section 706 requires the LLC to allocate the LLC's income and losses as to prevent the assignment of income from old members to new members. For these purposes, even cash-basis LLCs are placed on the accrual basis for certain items. [See IRC § 706(d)(2)]

Restrictions on the Use of LLC Losses by Members

Q 7:78   Can LLC members deduct the LLC's tax losses?

Generally, yes, but only if the LLC is engaged in an activity for profit [IRS § 183], and meets other rules discussed below. Although not dispositive, Code Section 183 contains a presumption, known as the "hobby loss" rule. A taxpayer is presumed to be engaged in an activity for profit if the income from the activity exceeds the deductions attributable to that activity for any three years out of a consecutive five-year period. [IRC § 183(d)]

An LLC member can only deduct LLC tax losses to the extent of the member's tax basis in the member's LLC interest at the end of the tax year in which the loss occurred. (See Q 7:2 et seq.) [IRS § 704(d)] A loss that cannot be deducted because of tax basis limitation can be carried forward by the member and deducted in a later year when the member obtains additional tax basis, such as by liability allocation or contributions.

Q 7:79   Is a member's use of the LLC's losses to offset income from other sources limited in any way?

Yes. A member's ability to use the LLC's losses is limited first by the amount of that member's tax basis in interest in the LLC. Second, even if the member has sufficient tax basis, they may not be entitled to use those losses to the extent that the Section 465 at-risk rules and Section 469 passive activity rules limit the use of the LLC's losses by that member (see Qs 7:72 and 7:74).

Q 7:80   How do the at-risk rules of Code Section 465 apply to an LLC?

In general, a member can only deduct losses from an activity to the extent that the member has an amount at risk at the close of the taxable year. In the LLC context, the at-risk rules apply at the member level, not the LLC level. Any amount that cannot be deducted by a member because of the at-risk rule is suspended and carried forward to a later year in which the member's at-risk amount increases to a sufficient level to absorb the suspended loss. The amount at risk equals:

1. The amount of cash contributed by the member; *plus*
2. The adjusted basis of property contributed by the member; *plus*
3. The member's proportionate share of the LLC's income; *less*
4. The member's proportionate share of the LLC's losses; *less*
5. Any distributions to the member; *plus*
6. The amount of the LLC's debt for which the member is personally liable.

Therefore, nonrecourse debt can increase a member's tax basis in the LLC interest, but the debt will not be included in the calculation of the amount at risk unless it is qualified nonrecourse financing. In general, qualified nonrecourse financing requires that:

- the debt be obtained with respect to the holding of real property,
- the lender be a "qualified person,"
- no other person may be liable for the debt, AND
- the debt not be convertible.

[IRC § 465(b)(6)] A lender does not count as a qualified person if: (1) the lender sold the property to the taxpayer; (2) the lender is related to the taxpayer and the loan is not commercially reasonable; or (3) the lender receives a fee in connection with the sale of the land.

In August 1998, the IRS issued final regulations under the Section 465(b)(6) qualified nonrecourse financing exception to the at-risk rules. [Treas Reg § 1.465-27] The final regulations essentially adopted the same basic approach as the proposed regulations in providing that LLC financing can meet the tests for qualified nonrecourse financing in certain circumstances, even if the LLC is "personally liable" for repayment of the financing. The final regulations also provide additional guidance that expands the scope of the proposed rules to cover a greater range of nonrecourse financings. For example, they allow taxpayers to secure a qualified nonrecourse loan with property other than real property and incidental property (subject to a 10 percent cap) and to borrow on a nonrecourse basis without providing a direct security interest in the underlying real property. In addition, the final regulations provide much needed guidance concerning issues raised by the use of tiered partnerships and single member LLCs. Generally, these additions in the final regulations are pro-taxpayer; and, as a result, it should be easier for members of LLCs and other partnerships to meet the tests for the qualified nonrecourse financing exception.

The final regulations have a generous effective date. While they are effective for financings incurred on or after August 4, 1998, they also allow taxpayers to apply them retroactively for any financing incurred before August 4, 1998. The Preamble to the final regulations notes that if a taxpayer applies the regulations retroactively, the IRS will require the taxpayer to reduce the amounts at risk, but only to the extent that application of the regulations increases the losses allowed for tax years ending before August 4, 1998.

The LLC's losses allocated to a member are not deductible by the member on that member's individual income tax return, if the losses exceed the amount by which the member is at risk. [IRC § 465(a)(1)] Any losses not deductible because of the at-risk limitation may be carried forward. [IRC § 465(a)(2)] If the amount at risk falls below zero because of cash distributions, a member must include in income an amount equal to the negative amount at risk.

Q 7:81 Is a member at risk for the debts of the LLC that are guaranteed by that member?

Even if a member is at risk for the LLC debt due to becoming a guarantor, the member may not be at risk for tax purposes. A member is not at risk, under Code Section 465, if the member has a right of indemnification. The member is not at risk until the member makes payment to the creditor, as guarantor, and has exhausted all legal rights against the primary obligor. [See Prop Treas Reg § 1.465-6(d)]

Even if the member agrees in writing not to seek indemnification from others, the member may still not be at risk for tax purposes. Local law might still allow the member to have a right of indemnification. [See Brand v Commr, 81 TC 821 (1982); and Bjecke v US, 677 F Supp 633 (D ND 1987)]

Q 7:82   How do the passive activity loss rules of Code Section 469 apply to an LLC?

Code Section 469 prevents all taxpayers who are individuals, estates, trusts, closely held C corporations, or personal service corporations from deducting losses from passive activities to the extent that the losses exceed the taxpayer's income from passive activities. A passive activity is a trade or business in which the LLC member, including a professional corporation, individual, partnership, or other LLC, does not materially participate, or any rental activity. [IRC § 469(c)] The Section 469 passive activity loss rules apply in addition to the Section 465 at-risk rules. In addition, the passive activity rule applies at the member level and not at the LLC level.

Passive activity losses that cannot be deducted in the current tax year are suspended and carried forward until the member has sufficient income from passive activities to deduct them, or until the member disposes of the passive activity. [IRC § 469(g)] Upon the disposition of a passive activity in a taxable transaction, all losses suspended under Code Section 469 may be deducted without regard to the amount of the passive activity income of the member. [IRC § 469(g)(1)]

An individual LLC member materially participates in an activity if he or she satisfies one of these seven tests:

1. The individual participates for more than 500 hours in the passive activity during the taxable year;

2. The individual's participation constitutes substantially all of the participation in the activity by all participants during the year;

3. The individual participates for more than 100 hours but not less than any other individual;

4. The activity is a significant participation activity and the individual's cumulative number of hours for participation in all significant participation activities exceeds 500 hours;

5. The individual materially participated (more than 500 hours for limited partners) in the activity for five of the ten immediately preceding taxable years;

6. The activity is a service activity, and the individual materially participated (more than 500 hours for limited partners) in any three preceding years; or

7. Based on all of the facts and circumstances, the individual participates in the activity on a regular, continuous, and substantial basis.

[Temp Treas Reg § 1.469-5T(a)]

Only three of the above tests apply to limited partners — tests (1), (5), and (6). Although the IRS has failed to address this issue adequately, it seems inappropriate, at least if there are no managers, to apply the limited-partners tests to LLC members, since LLCs are designed to permit active involvement by LLC members. LLC members are, for this purpose, more analogous to S corporation shareholders. Therefore, it would be appropriate to apply to LLC members the same material participation tests that apply to S corporation shareholders. However, it is unclear whether LLC members and member-managers would be subject to the more stringent rules of limited partners.

Q 7:83   Do the anti-abuse rules of Treasury Regulations Section 1.701-2 apply to an LLC?

Yes, if taxed as a partnership. The anti-abuse regulations apply to all transactions involving a partnership that occur on or after May 12, 1994. [Treas Reg § 1.701-2(g)] The anti-abuse regulations were adopted to curb the use of partnerships for tax-avoidance purposes, and have been criticized as being too vague, broad, and extending beyond Congress's intent. Presumably, the IRS could apply the anti-abuse rules to LLCs, if the LLCs are classified as partnerships for federal tax purposes and if the LLC is used for a tax-avoidance purpose. The IRS will recast a transaction if a partnership is formed, or availed of in connection with a transaction, in which (1) a principal purpose is to reduce substantially the present value of the members' aggregate federal tax liability; and (2) the tax reduction is inconsistent with the intent of subchapter K. [Treas Reg § 1.701-2(b)]

The intent of subchapter K can be found in these three requirements:

1. The LLC is bona fide, and each LLC transaction or series of transactions are entered into for a substantial business purpose. Cases have denied partnership status for income tax

purposes on business purpose grounds; [See Byers v Commr, 199 F 2d 273 (8th Cir 1952); Form Builders, Inc v Commr, 58 TCM (CCH) 1415 (1990)]

2. The substance of each LLC transaction will govern rather than form; and

3. The tax consequences to each member of LLC operations and of transactions between the member and the LLC must reflect the member's economic agreement and the member's taxable income. [Treas Reg § 1.701-2(a)]

Q 7:84   What is a tax shelter?

A tax shelter is any investment about which any person could reasonably infer that the "tax shelter ratio" (see Q 7:85) as of the close of any of the first five years ending after the date on which the investment is offered for sale may be greater than two to one, that is, losses are at least twice as large as gains. Additionally, an investment is a "tax shelter" only if the investment interest is:

1. required to be registered under a federal or state law regulating securities; or

2. sold pursuant to an exemption from registration requiring filing of a notice with a federal or state agency regulating the offering or sale of securities; or

3. is a substantial investment.

[IRC § 6111(c)(1)]

A substantial investment would include an amount of more than $250,000 offered for sale and at least five investors are expected. [See Temp Treas Reg § 301.6111-1T, Q&A 22]

Q 7:85   What is the tax shelter ratio?

A tax shelter ratio is computed as follows:

1. the aggregate amount of the deductions and 350 percent of the credits that are represented to be potentially allowable by any investor for all periods up to, and including, the close of the year; divided by

2. the investment base (i.e., the amount of money and the adjusted basis of other property, reduced by any liabilities) contributed by the investor as of the close of the year.

[IRC § 6111(c)(2), (3)]

Q 7:86   When is an LLC required to register as a tax shelter?

A "tax shelter organizer" is required to register a tax shelter with the IRS not later than the day on which the first offering for sale of interests in the tax shelter occurs. [IRC § 6111(a)(1)] A tax shelter organizer is the person who is principally responsible for organizing the tax shelter. If no organizer registers the tax shelter, the duty then falls on the person who participates in the sale or management of the investment. [IRC § 6111(d)(1)]

Transfer of an LLC Interest

Q 7:87   What are the tax consequences on the sale of an LLC interest?

A member recognizes capital gain or loss on the sale of the LLC interest. [IRC § 741] The amount of the gain or loss equals the amount realized, less the member's tax basis in the LLC interest. The amount realized equals any cash received, plus the fair market value of any property received, plus the selling member's proportionate share of the LLC's liabilities. [IRC § 752(d)]

As a general rule, a partner that disposes of an interest in a partnership recognizes gain from the sale or exchange of a capital asset. Code Section 751(a), however, generally requires a partner that sells or exchanges an interest in a partnership to recognize ordinary income rather than capital gain if the partnership owns assets that, if disposed of, would yield ordinary income. Similarly, under Code Section 751(b), a distribution from a partnership may be treated as a sale of assets between the partner and the partnership if the distributee partner receives ordinary income assets in exchange for its interest in other partnership property (or receives other partnership property in exchange for its interest in partnership ordinary income assets).

Under former law, Code Sections 751(a) and (b) were implicated only if the partnership held "substantially appreciated" inventory or "unrealized receivables." For this purpose, a partnership's inventory was "substantially appreciated" if its fair market value exceeded 120 percent of its adjusted basis.

The Taxpayer Relief Act of 1997 repeals the requirement that inventory be substantially appreciated before the application of Code Section 751(a) is triggered. This change will require more taxpayers to treat as ordinary income a portion of the gain recognized on the sale or exchange of partnership interests. Significantly, however, the act retains the substantial appreciation requirement for distributions under Code Section 751(b).

The tax basis of the transferee member's share of the LLC's property could be increased or decreased to reflect the selling member's gain or loss on the transaction if a Section 754/743(b) election is in effect. This election procedure must be authorized by the LLC (when taxed as a partnership) and not the individual member.

As discussed in Q 7:77, the LLC's income and deductions are allocated between the selling member and transferee under Code Section 706 for the period before and after the transfer of the interest.

Q 7:88   What are the tax consequences upon the death of a member?

Upon the death of a member, the member's estate is entitled to a basis in the member's interest equal to the fair market value of the interest on the date of the member's death. [IRC § 1014] However, the estate is not entitled to a basis adjustment for the member's interest in a cash-basis LLC's zero-basis receivables. Income earned or realized but not reported by a decedent as of the date of his or her death (e.g., cash-basis receivables) is treated as income in respect of a decedent (commonly referred to as IRD). [IRC § 691] The estate must report IRD as income upon collection, and the estate cannot adjust the basis of the decedent member's interest in the LLC to avoid this income. [See Quick Trust v Commr, 54 TC 1336 (1970), aff'd, 444 F 2d 90 (8th Cir 1971); Woodhall v Commr, 28 TCM 1438 (1969), aff'd, 454 F 2d 226 (9th Cir 1972)]

If the Operating Agreement or a separate buy-sell agreement requires the redemption of a member's interest at death, that portion of the redemption attributable to a cash-basis LLC's accounts receivable is treated as a Section 736(a) payment (i.e., a guaranteed payment or distributive share payment), and is IRD. [IRC § 753]

For partnership taxable years beginning in or before 1997, the taxable year of the deceased member (the decedent) closes as of the date of death, but the LLC's tax year does not terminate on the death of a member, unless the LLC terminates under Code Section 708. [IRC § 706(c)(1); Treas Reg § 1.706-1(c)(3)(i)] Therefore, through partnership tax years beginning in 1997 or before, the decedent's successor reports the LLC's income for the entire year, including that portion of the year during which the decedent was alive. [Treas Reg § 1.706-1(c)(3)(ii)]

Effective for partnership tax years beginning after December 31, 1997, the partnership tax year ends upon the date of death of a partner with respect to that partner. [IRC § 706 (c)(2)(A)] Under old law, the taxable year of a partnership closed with respect to a partner whose entire interest was sold, exchanged, or liquidated but generally did not close on the death of a partner. This old law was modified by the Taxpayer Relief Act of 1997 which provides this new blanket rule. Therefore, tax items of income, loss, etc. up to the date of death will be reported on the final Form 1040 and post-death items will be included in the first Form 1041 of the estate (or trust), or other successor in interest. The successor to a decedent may be entitled to an adjustment to the basis of the LLC's assets if a Section 743(b)/754 election is in effect or made.

Alternatively, Code Section 732(d) permits a decedent's estate or other successor-in-interest to obtain the effect of a Section 743(b) adjustment for property distributed within two years of the date of death, even if a Section 754 election is not in effect. The Section 732(d) election produces an adjustment in the basis of the distributed property at the LLC level immediately prior to the distribution. If the Section 732(d) election is available, it may have advantages over a Section 754 election because no action on the part of the LLC or any consent of the surviving members is required. Also, a Section 732(d) election will have no effect upon subsequent distributions to the surviving members or subsequent transfer by them, and the LLC is not required to maintain separate basis accounts.

Termination and Liquidation of the LLC

Q 7:89 When does an LLC terminate for tax purposes?

An LLC terminates for tax purposes if no part of the LLC's business continues to be conducted. If 50 percent or more of the total interest in capital and profits in the LLC is sold or exchanged within a 12-month period, the LLC will terminate. [IRC § 708(b)] Successive sales of the same LLC interest are not counted twice in the 12-month period.

Q 7:90 What are the tax consequences of a termination of the LLC?

Upon an event that causes the technical termination of an LLC under Code Section 708, the LLC is treated as if it contributed all of its assets and liabilities to a "new" LLC in exchange for an interest in the new entity. The "old" LLC is then deemed to distribute interests in the "new" LLC to the purchaser and the other remaining partners, either for the continuation of the business or its dissolution and winding up.

The deemed contribution of assets to the "new" LLC and the distribution of the "new" LLC interests to the partners of the "old" LLC are disregarded for purposes of maintaining capital accounts. [Treas Reg § 1.708-1(b)(1)(iv)] Furthermore, the LLC continues to use the same employer identification number. [Treas Reg § 301.6109-1(h)(1)] The LLC also retains the same holding period for property with built-in gain or loss. [Treas Reg § 1.704-4(a)(4)(ii),-4(c)(3)] The regulations provide for a five-year holding period; however, this does not reflect the change to a seven-year holding period made to Section 704(c)(1)(B) by the Taxpayer Relief Act of 1997. One change which may result, however, is that the partnership may elect a new allocation method under Code Section 704(c). [Treas Reg § 1.704-3(a)(2)]

A member may recognize gain or loss on a liquidating distribution from the LLC if the cash and marketable securities received from the liquidating distribution exceeds the member's tax basis in the LLC interest. No loss is recognized by the member unless the member receives only cash, unrealized receivables, or inventory in the distribution, to the extent that the member's adjusted basis in the LLC interest exceeds the value of the property received in the distribution. [IRC § 731(a)(2)]

Q 7:91   What are the member's tax consequences of a liquidation of his, her, or its interest?

A liquidation of a member's interest is defined as a single distribution or a series of distributions by an LLC to a member that results in a termination of the distributee's entire interest in the LLC. [Treas Reg § 1.761-1(d)] A member recognizes gain if the amount of cash and marketable securities distributed in liquidation of that member's interest exceeds the member's tax basis in their LLC interest. [IRC § 731(a)(1)] Similarly, a taxable gain can occur if the termination of interest relieves the member of debt, which is treated as a distribution of cash. [Monahan v Commr, 1994 TCM 201 (1994), aff'd, 86 F3d 1162 (9th Cir 1996)] A loss may be recognized by a member on a liquidating distribution, but only if the property distributed consists of only money, unrealized receivables, and inventory. [IRC § 731(a)(2)]

If the distribution is comprised of substantially appreciated inventory and the distributee-member relinquishes his right to other LLC property, then the distribution is treated as a sale or exchange and the distributee will recognize income on the portion of the distribution beyond his proportionate share. [IRC § 751(b)] Substantially appreciated inventory was redefined by the Taxpayer Relief Act to encompass inventory items which have a fair market value in excess of 120 percent of its adjusted basis. [IRC § 751(b)(3)] The income recognized by the distributee will be ordinary to the extent of the difference between the fair market value of the inventory received and the adjusted basis of LLC property relinquished in the exchange. [Treas Reg § 1.751-1(b)(3)(iii)]

Effective for distributions occurring after August 5, 1997, the determination of a distributee partner's basis in property distributed to it by a partnership depends on whether the distribution is a liquidating distribution or a current distribution. [IRC § 732] Generally, a substituted basis rule applies to property distributed to a partner in liquidation of a partner's interest. The partner's basis in the distributed property equals the partner's adjusted basis in its partnership interest (as reduced by any money distributed in the same transaction).

The Taxpayer Relief Act of 1997 modifies Code Section 732 by implementing a three-tier basis allocation process that takes into account the fair market value and any unrealized appreciation or depreciation of properties distributed by the partnership to a partner. In addition, the IRS Restructuring and Reform Act of 1998 clarifies that for purposes of the allocation rules of Code Section 732(c), "unrealized receivables" has the meaning given it in Code Section 751(c) including the last two sentences of Code Section 751(c), relating to items of property that give rise to ordinary income.

Q 7:92   What are the tax consequences to the LLC upon the liquidation of a member's interest in the LLC?

The LLC does not recognize any gain or loss upon the liquidation of a member's LLC interest. [IRC § 731(a)]

Generally, the LLC cannot deduct the payments to a member in redemption of their interest. [IRC § 736] However, the LLC may be entitled to adjust the basis of the LLC's assets to reflect the amount of the payment made to a member in exchange for the member's interest in the LLC, if the LLC has a Section 754/734 election in effect.

Before January 5, 1993, Code Section 736(b)(2) provided that, payments to a partner in liquidation allocable to the partnership's unrealized receivables and goodwill (unless, for goodwill, the partnership agreement provided otherwise), were not treated as payments for partnership property, but were treated as ordinary income to the partner and deductible by the partnership. Code Section 736(b)(3), enacted in 1993, now provides that this rule only applies to the extent that the redeeming partner is a general partner and capital is not a material income-producing factor for the partnership. The legislative history indicates that Code Section 736(b)(2) continues to apply to professional practices (e.g., doctors, dentist, lawyers, and accountants), and that Code Section 736(b)(3) was not intended to alter the partnership's deduction for payments to a liquidating professional practice partner allocable to unrealized receivables and goodwill.

Q 7:93   **Are members in a professional practice LLC or partners in a professional practice LLP "general partners" for the purposes of Code Section 736(b)(3); that is, can a professional practice LLC or LLP deduct payments to a liquidating member to the extent allocable to unrealized receivables or goodwill?**

There is, as of the date of this publication, no authority on this point to analyze since the enactment of Code Section 736(b)(3), which addressed liquidating payments to partners. Under Code Section 736(b)(3) the partnership may deduct such payments to "general partners" only when capital is not a material income-producing factor. However, the IRS, on December 28, 1994, issued proposed regulations under Code Section 1402 that addressed when a member of an LLC will be treated as a limited partner under Code Section 1402(a)(13).

Code Section 1402(a)(13) excludes from self-employment income a limited partner's distributive share of the limited partnership's income, except to the extent of Section 707(c) payments to the limited partner for services actually rendered. The IRS has issued Proposed Treasury Regulations Section 1.1402(a)-18, which provides that a member in an LLC will be treated as a limited partner for these purposes if: (1) the member is not a manager of the LLC; and (2) the LLC could have been formed as a limited partnership in the jurisdiction in which the LLC was formed, and the relevant member would have been classified as a limited partner. A moratorium was placed on these regulations until June 30, 1998, by TRA 1997. If the LLC is managed by the members, then no member could qualify as a "limited partner" for these purposes, except in a few states, such as Georgia.

It is reasonable to assume that the IRS might apply a similar test to Code Sections 736(b)(3) and 736(b)(2). In many states partners of professional practices would not qualify as limited partners. Applying the proposed regulations' test, each member or LLP partner in a professional practice LLC or LLP likely would, under most states' partnership rules, be treated as a general partner under Code Section 736(b)(3), even if that partner were classified by the partnership as a limited partner. In that case, payments to the liquidating member or LLP partner that are allocable to the LLC's or LLP's unrealized receivables and goodwill (unless, for goodwill, the Operating Agreement or LLP agreement provides otherwise) should be deductible by the LLC or LLP. Those payments should be treated as ordinary income to the departing member or LLP partner, and therefore, would constitute self-employment income. However, the deduction issue under Code Section 736(b)(3) for the LLC is not clear due to its use of the term "general partner."

Q 7:94 Can an LLC amortize as goodwill under Code Section 197 the amount of any payments made to a member in redemption of interest in the LLC in excess of that member's interest in the fair market value of the LLC's assets?

Yes, to the extent that the LLC makes a Section 754/734 basis adjustment that is not allocable to the LLC's other assets. [Temp Treas Reg § 1.197-1T(b)(8)] However, because Code Section 197 requires amortization and deduction of goodwill over 15 years, it will be better to allocate the redemption price to other, more quickly depreciable property, to the extent possible. In addition, if the Section 736(b)(3) limitation does not apply, the LLC should be able to deduct all of this payment in the year of the distribution, instead of over 15 years.

Q 7:95 What are the tax consequences of a liquidation of the LLC?

The LLC will not recognize gain or loss upon the liquidation of the LLC. [IRC § 731(b)] The rules discussed in Q 7:89 for the liquidation of a member's interest in the LLC apply to the redemption of a member's interest in connection with the entire liquidation of the LLC. It should be noted that, as discussed in Q 7:43, the final distribution of the LLC's assets upon a liquidation of the LLC must be made in accordance with the positive capital account balances of the members in the LLC.

Conversion of a Corporation or Partnership to an LLC

Q 7:96   What are the tax consequences of converting a corporation into an LLC?

The conversion of a corporation into an LLC is treated as a liquidation of the corporation followed by a contribution of the assets to the LLC. The corporation will recognize gain equal to the excess of the fair market value over the basis of the corporation's assets. [IRC § 336] The shareholders will also recognize gain to the extent that the fair market value of the assets contributed to the LLC exceed their basis in their stock. [IRC §§ 331, 1001] Gain recognized by an S corporation on liquidation is passed through and taxed to the S corporation's shareholders, which increases their stock basis. [IRC § 1367(a)] The shareholders will also be subject to tax on the amount, if any, by which the fair market value of the assets distributed exceeds their stock basis, as adjusted. [IRC §§ 1371(a)(1), 331] The S corporation could be subject to built-in gains tax upon the S corporation's liquidation. [IRC § 1374] The shareholders of the corporation will have a basis in their LLC interest equal to the fair market value of the corporation's assets at the time of the conversion, as a result of the gain recognized on the conversion.

Q 7:97   What are the tax consequences of converting a partnership into an LLC?

A conversion from a partnership to an LLC will be tax free except to the extent that the partnership's liabilities exceed the basis of its assets. [IRC §§ 721(a), 752; see also Ltr Ruls 9350013, 9029019, 9119029; Ltr Rul 9501033 (conversion of a Maryland general partnership into a Maryland LLC, classified as a partnership for tax purposes, does not result in gain to the members provided there is no change in the partners' share of liabilities as a result of the conversion)] The conversion will not result in a termination of the partnership under Code Section 708(b). [Ltr Rul 9432018; Rev Rul 84-52, 1984-1 CB 157; Ltr Rul 9424036, as supplemented by Ltr Rul 9448026 (conversion of a general partnership into an LLC will not result in termination), Ltr Rul 9443024 (conversion of limited partnership to an LLC will not result in a termination)] The LLC, if taxed as a partnership, may continue to use the partnership's old tax identification number because it is the same entity for tax purposes. [Rev Rul 95-37, 1995-1 CB 130] Further, the partners' holding periods for their respective interests in the LLC include the holding periods of their respective interests in the partnership; the tax year of the partnership did not close with respect to the partners as a result of the conversion; and the LLC's basis in the assets it received from the partnership was the same as the partnership's basis in those assets. [Ltr Rul 9841030]

If the conversion causes a member to be relieved of some or all liability for the partnership's debts, that member may recognize taxable income to the extent of the debt relief. Also, a general partner may recognize gain if the general partner is relieved of liabilities, which are not allocated to that partner's basis in LLC interest following the conversion to an LLC. [Ltr Rul 9432018; Rev Rul 84-52, 1984-1 CB 157]

Q 7:98   What are the tax consequences of merging a corporation into an LLC? An LLC into a corporation?

Some state LLC statutes permit LLCs to merge with other entities, including corporations. [See, e.g., Va Code § 13-1-1070] While merging with, or converting to or from, another organization that is taxed as a partnership may not have adverse tax consequences, a merger of a corporation into an LLC, with the LLC surviving, will be treated as a taxable liquidation of the corporation, causing the C or S corporation to recognize gain on the distribution of assets with fair market values in excess of basis.

Similarly, the merger of an LLC with a corporation, with the corporation surviving, is treated like a conversion of an LLC to a corporation. Thus, the conversion may be treated as:

1. the distribution of the LLC's assets (subject to its liabilities) to members, and the contribution of those assets to a new corporation;

2. a contribution of the LLC's assets to the corporation in exchange for stock, and a liquidating distribution of that stock to members; or

3. a contribution of members' interests to the corporation in exchange for stock (resulting in a termination of the LLC), and a liquidation of the LLC into the corporation.

The tax consequences may differ for each separate form of this transaction, depending upon the LLC's assets and liabilities and relative tax positions of each member. Therefore, each form should be reviewed, and documentation should be prepared to follow the most desirable form.

Employee Benefits

Q 7:99   Can the LLC provide tax-free benefits to employees?

Yes. To the extent otherwise authorized by the Code, an LLC can provide tax-free benefits, including Section 79 group term life insurance, disability, health insurance and reimbursement under Code Sections 105 and 106, and cafeteria plans under Code Section 125, and other benefits to non-member employees.

Q 7:100   Can an LLC provide tax-free employee benefits to members?

No, not for health, life, disability, and other fringe benefits excluded from taxable income only for "employees" under various Internal Revenue Code provisions. The LLC's cost of benefits to members is treated as Section 707(c) guaranteed payments to the members. [See Treas Reg § 1.707-1(c); Prop Treas Reg § 1.125-1, Q&A 4] As a result, the cost of these benefits is included in the recipient member's ordinary taxable income. A member may deduct 40 percent of the cost of health insurance in 1997, 45% in 1998-99, 50% in 2000-01, 60% in 2002, 80% in 2003-05, 90% in 2006, and 100% in 2007. [IRC § 162(l) (deduction permanently reinstated in April, 1995); see also Rev Rul 91-26, 1991-1 CB 184 (for a discussion of the federal income tax consequences upon the payment of health insurance premiums on behalf of a partner)]

Qualified Retirement Plans

Q 7:101   What is a qualified retirement plan?

A qualified retirement plan is a pension or profit sharing plan that satisfies the extensive and complex requirements under Code Section 401. (See, generally, Panel Publishers, *The Pension Answer Book*, 10th ed., for an in-depth analysis of pension plans.)

There are many types of qualified retirement plans, but all plans can be classified as either a defined contribution plan or a defined benefit plan. Generally, a defined contribution plan is a plan in which the employer, and perhaps employees, contribute to the plan from time to time, but the amount of the benefits distributable by the plan are derived solely from the contributions (plus earnings and less losses on those contributions) to the plan on behalf of the individual employee; moreover, there is no guaranteed benefit to the employee under the plan's terms. There is no maximum limit on benefits, but there is a per-participant limit on contributing under Code Section 415(c). A defined benefit plan establishes a set benefit to be paid by the plan to the participant at the time provided for payment by the plan. Employers and, in some cases, employees contribute to defined benefit plans, but the contribution is based on the amount necessary to pay the promised benefit to employees, based on an actuarial calculation and assumed earnings rates. Benefits cannot exceed specified limits under Code Section 415(b).

The Taxpayer Relief Act of 1997 eliminated one of the several remaining differences between corporate and partnership plans. For self-employed individuals, employer matching contributions will not be treated as elective deferrals for tax years beginning in 1997 for SIMPLE plans and in 1998 for 401(k) plans. [IRC § 402(g)]

Q 7:102   Can an LLC adopt a qualified retirement plan?

Yes. The Code does not require a business to be incorporated to adopt a qualified retirement plan. Thus, an LLC can adopt a qualified retirement plan.

Q 7:103 What are the advantages of a qualified retirement plan?

A qualified retirement plan provides significant tax advantages to employers and employees. Within limits, the employer can deduct contributions to the plan on behalf of employees. [IRC § 404] Employees are not subject to tax on the contributions to the plan by their employer until the plan makes a distribution to the employee. [IRC § 402] Current earnings of the plan are also not taxed. [IRC § 501]

Q 7:104 Can members participate in the LLC's qualified retirement plans?

Yes, if the LLC conducts a trade or business and the member has "net earnings from self-employment." [Ltr Rul 9432018; IRC § 401(c)(2)(A); Treas Reg § 1.1402(c)-1] A general partner's distributive share of the partnership's income is "net earnings from self-employment," whether or not the general partner renders services to the general partnership. [IRC § 1402(a)] However, for Section 401 purposes, the net earnings only include trade or business income of a partnership if a material amount of the partnership's income is produced by personal services provided by the taxpayer. [IRC § 401(a)(2)(A)(i)]

As a result, only those members who have earned income from providing services in the conduct of the LLC's trade or business may participate in the LLC's qualified retirement plan. [See Treas Reg § 1.401-10(c)(3); Frick, 56 TCM 1368 (1989); Pugh, 49 TCM 748 (1985); Frick, 50 TCM 1334 (1985)]

Q 7:105 How much can an LLC contribute to a qualified retirement plan on behalf of a member?

Code Section 415(c) limits the annual amount that an employer may contribute to a defined contribution plan (or combination of plans) on behalf of any participant, including a member, to the lesser of $30,000 (as indexed for inflation) or 25 percent of qualified compensation. There is no statutory limit on the amount that may be contributed to a defined benefit plan, rather Code Section 415 limits the maximum benefit payable to a participant under the plan.

For these purposes, qualified compensation is limited to $150,000, as adjusted for inflation after 1994. Thus, regardless of the actual compensation payable to an employee, or a member's earnings from self-employment from an LLC, the LLC can not consider compensation or earnings from self-employment in excess of this statutory compensation limit.

Q 7:106   How is a member's earnings from self-employment calculated under the Section 415(c) limitation on contributions to a qualified retirement plan?

A member's net earnings from self-employment, in determining how much an LLC can contribute to a qualified plan on a member's behalf, are reduced by: (1) the actual amount of the contribution made on behalf of the self-employed individual; and (2) the member's tax deduction for one half of the self-employment tax paid by the individual member. [IRC §§ 415(c)(3)(B), 401(c)(2)(A)] Thus, the effective maximum contribution rate on behalf of a member is 20 percent of compensation, not 25 percent. If the LLC only has a profit sharing plan, the maximum effective contribution rate is approximately 12 to 13 percent, as opposed to 15 percent in the case of corporate employees (see Panel Publishers, *The Pension Answer Book*).

Q 7:107   Is there a difference between a corporation and an LLC with respect to qualified retirement plan contributions on behalf of owner employees?

Yes. This is one of the tax advantages of a corporation over an LLC. As discussed in Q 7:106, members in an LLC are treated as self-employed in calculating the maximum contribution by the LLC on behalf of the employer. Employee-shareholders are not similarly treated, and thus should be entitled to the maximum 15 percent to 25 percent of compensation contributions, depending on the type of plan, whereas LLC members can deduct about 12 percent to 20 percent of compensation.

In addition, contributions by a corporation to a pension plan on behalf of a shareholder-employee are not subject to FICA or Medicare tax, whereas all of an LLC's members' distributive share of the LLC is subject to FICA (subject to the annual cap) and unlimited Medicare tax. [See GCM 39807]

Q 7:108 Are there any differences between the operation of a qualified retirement plan by an LLC and a corporation?

Yes. The Tax Equity and Fiscal Responsibility Act of 1982 (TEFRA) was intended to bring about parity between corporate and noncorporate retirement plans. Before TEFRA, one of the most important tax reasons for incorporating the closely held business or professional practice was to take advantage of the special tax treatment for corporate retirement plans. After TEFRA, retirement plan advantages alone were no longer the motivating factor to incorporate. However, corporate plans still retain significant advantages over plans available to partners, LLC (if taxed as a partnership) members, or proprietors (commonly referred to as "Keogh" plans). Some of these advantages are:

1. Payments attributable to medical insurance, health insurance, or disability insurance are not deductible for Keogh plans. [IRC § 404(e)] Code Section 404 allows a deduction for these expenses from corporate plans.

2. Self-employed individuals are not "separated from service" for purposes of Code Section 402(e)(4). Thus, there may be no ten-year forward averaging before age 59-1/2, except for distributions upon disability or death. [IRC § 402(e)(4)(A)] However, if a plan is terminated, there can be a rollover distribution into an IRA by a self-employed person. [Rev Rul 78-404, 1978-2 CB 156] Without a plan termination, however, no rollover distribution may be possible by a self-employed person to a qualified plan—only to an IRA (and a technical reading of the IRC would require five years of active participation for an IRA rollover by a self-employed person before age 59-1/2). Corporate employees who separate from service with a corporation may take their retirement benefits or may roll them over to an IRA or another corporate plan. [IRC §§ 402(a)(5)(E)(ii), 408(d)(3)(A)(iii)]

3. Employee-participants in a corporate plan can borrow from the plan, while owner-employees of Keogh plans and shareholder-employees of subchapter S plans are forbidden from borrowing. [IRC § 4975(d)]

4. An LLC taxed as a partnership or sole proprietorship may not sponsor an employee stock ownership plan [IRC § 4975(e)(7)] because it is not a corporation and does not have stock. [IRC § 409(l)]

5. The exemption from the 10 percent early distribution penalty for persons separating from service at or after age 55 does not literally apply to self-employed individuals. [IRC § 72(t)]

6. The funding of a Keogh plan cannot create a net operating loss, unlike the funding of a corporate plan.

7. Tax-free disability payments are possible for corporate employees under Code Section 105(c) and the authority of the *Wood* and *Masterson* cases. [Wood v US, 590 F 2d 321 (9th Cir 1979); Masterson v US, 478 F Supp 454 (ND Ill 1979)]

8. Employer contributions for "employees" are not subject to social security or Medicare tax because they are not wages. [IRC § 1402]

Q 7:109 Can an LLC contribute as much to a qualified retirement plan on behalf of members, as a corporation could on behalf of shareholder-employees?

TEFRA abolished many special Keogh plan limitations, such as the bank trustee requirement, 100 percent vesting, the requirement of a definite formula for a profit sharing plan, the mandatory consent to participate by an owner-employee, limitations upon social security integration, the five-year restriction on participation in the event of a premature distribution, the defined benefit plan limitations that existed under former Code Section 401(j), and the excise tax for excess contributions under former Code Section 4972. Perhaps most important, the deduction limits and contribution limits for Keogh plans are the same as those for corporate plans for fiscal years beginning in 1984. In essence, corporate and Keogh plan participants may contribute the lesser of a percentage of income or $30,000 (indexed) to defined contribution retirement plans. On the other hand, defined benefit plans may provide for benefits not exceeding the lesser of $120,000 (indexed) per year or 100 percent of income; however, if a defined benefit normal retirement age is less than age 62, the benefit must be reduced below $120,000. [IRC §§ 404, 415]

Q 7:110 Can the LLC adopt a nonqualified retirement plan?

Yes, although it would not prevent current tax to the owner making the deferral, unlike an owner who is an employee of a regular C corporation.

Q 7:111 Can an LLC adopt a qualified ESOP?

No. An ESOP, or employee stock ownership plan, is a type of qualified retirement plan in which the funds contributed to the plan are invested in employer securities. Code Section 409(l) defines employer securities to include common stock and, in certain cases, convertible preferred stock. "Employer securities," however, does not include an interest in a partnership or an LLC. Thus, an ESOP cannot own an interest in an LLC.

Q 7:112 Can employees of an LLC participate in an ESOP adopted by a corporation that owns an interest in the LLC?

No. While the employees of all corporations in a controlled group of corporations may participate in the ESOP of any of the corporations, an LLC, classified as a partnership for tax purposes, cannot be a member of a controlled group of corporations. [IRC § 409(l)(4); GCM 39880; Ltr Rul 9236042 (in which the IRS ruled that the employees of a partnership could not participate in an ESOP maintained by a corporation that owned an interest in the partnership)]

Self-Employment Tax

Q 7:113 Are members subject to self-employment tax on distributive shares of the LLC's income?

In 1997, the Treasury withdrew its proposed regulations submitted in 1994 regarding classification of members of unincorporated entities as either general or limited partners, and offered a new set of proposed regulations in their place.

Under the 1997 proposed regulations, an LLC member will be classified as a limited partner unless one of four tests is met in which case the member will be a general partner. The four tests are:

1. *The Liability Test.* The member faces personal liability for claims against the LLC.
2. *The Authority Test.* This requires that the member has the authority to create binding contracts on behalf of the LLC.

3. *The Participation Test.* Here the member must participate more than 500 hours per year in the business of the LLC.

4. *The Personal Services Test.* The member must provide greater than a *de minimis* amount of services on behalf of the business of the LLC, and the business must involve the areas of health, law, engineering, architecture, accounting, actuarial science, or consulting.

In a departure from the 1994 proposed regulations, the 1997 regulations permit a member's distributive share to be taxed as a limited partner's distributive share under certain circumstances. The 1997 proposed regulations set forth two alternative tests which may serve to reclassify a distributive share of a general partner's to one of a limited partner's. They are:

1. *The Two Classes of Interest Test.* This test applies to distributive shares with respect to a second class of interest which may be held by an individual who is otherwise classified as a general partner. This class of interest is also required to be held by individuals who qualify as limited partners and the rights and obligations with respect to the second class of interest must be identical. Note that this test does not apply to a member treated as general partner by virtue of the Personal Services Test.

2. *The Single Class of Interest Test.* This test only applies to members classified as general partners under the Participation Test. If the member's rights and obligations with respect to that interest are identical to that of other members classified as limited partners and those other members have a "substantial continuing interest" in the LLC, the member's distributive share will be taxed as one of a limited partner and not of a general partner. The regulations provide that 20 percent ownership of a particular class of interest constitutes a substantial continuing interest. For purposes of the test, members' interest may be identical even though one is classified as a general partner who provides services to the LLC and the others as limited partners who do not.

Neither the Code nor the Regulations expressly purport to limit the reclassification of a distributive share from one flowing to a general partner to one flowing to a limited partner on the basis of whether the payment is guaranteed instead of payment that is merely remuneration for services. A careful practitioner, however, may provide for a guaranteed payment in order to comply with the spirit of the regulation which attempts to distinguish between compensation for services and returns on capital.

The 1997 Proposed Regulations have been accompanied by intense criticism on the ground that they eliminate the benefits of being a limited partner in state law limited partnerships. As a result, Congress prohibited the issuance of any further regulations and suspended the effectiveness of the 1997 proposed regulations until July 1, 1998. [Taxpayer Relief Act of 1997 (PL 105-34 § 935] This criticism on the basis of limited partnership concerns may be somewhat misguided because (1) limited liability companies have replaced the use of limited partnerships in many instances and (2) the application to limited partnerships is, in reality, extremely limited. The very nature of limited partnerships provides limited liability to limited partners and prevents limited partners from binding the partnership. Thus, the only practical applications would be to those limited partnerships who have at least one member who spends more than 500 hours in the business of the limited partnership and has a second class of interest with differing rights and obligations than the limited partners and to those limited partners in a service partnership. Another possible application of the new regulation would be the extremely rare instance where all members of a limited partnership participate more than 500 hours which would result in the treatment of all of them as limited partners instead of general partners for purposes of the distributive share.

There is no authority, however, that members of manager-managed LLCs are limited partners. In general, the LLC is treated as a partnership for federal tax purposes. The LLC members have limited liability. Limited Liability is the essence of being a limited partner. In addition, if it is a manager-managed LLC, those members who are not managers have limits on their control of the LLC's day-to-day operations. Thus, nonmanager members in a manager-managed LLC are similar to limited partners and arguably should be classified as limited partners for section 1402(a)(13) purposes.

It would, however, be a misconception to assume that the owners of an interest in an organization that does not meet the state law definition of a limited partnership but is treated as a partnership under the broad definition of the code and the check-the-box regulations have to be classified as being either general partners or limited partners. Although limited partners may be referred to in several other sections of the code, section 1402(a)(13) appears to be the only place where status as a limited partner is crucial to a tax consequence.

Although other code sections may provide examples of defining a limited partner, resorting to the state law definition could be a viable approach. In *Estella G. Johnson v. Commissioner*, T.C. Memo. 1990-461, 90 TNT 178-13, the Tax Court stated that "limited partnerships are creatures of agreement cast in the form prescribed by State Law. The taxpayer's argument [that her working interest in an oil well was equivalent to limited partner's interest and did not produce self-employment income] was rejected because she and the other working interest owners did not take the necessary steps to comply with state law." However, members of an LLC are not "limited partners" as that term is defined under state law. Their status is created by an entirely different piece of legislation than the limited partnership act.

One solution to this controversy would be a rule that treats reasonable compensation for services from all entities taxed as a partnership as self-employment income. The problem with such a rule is that of separating compensation for services from return of capital. One technique used by passthrough organizations is to separate their capital and their services into two or more separate entities. In appropriate situations, this can also help accomplish other income tax and estate planning goals. Thus, the equipment and premises used in the activity can be owned by an investment entity and leased to the operating entity. [See Edwin D Davis, *et ux* v Commissioner, 64 TC 1034 (1975)] This type of structure should allow the profit of the separate entities to escape self-employment tax.

Q 7:114 Are members in an LLC that owns rental property subject to self-employment tax on rental income?

Generally, the answer is no. However, if the rentals are received in the course of a trade or business as a real estate dealer, then they are subject to self-employment tax. [Treas Reg § 1.1402(a)(1)] One is involved in the trade or business of a real estate dealer when the individual engages in the buying and/or selling of real estate to customers for profit. Simply holding real estate for investment or speculation purposes will not classify members of an LLC as being in the trade or business of a real estate dealer. The rule changes when the rental income is derived from farm land.

Rental income from farm land is included in gross income for self-employment tax purposes if two conditions are met: (1) the rentals are acquired under an agreement that provides for production of "agricultural or horticultural commodities" on the land, and (2) the owner or lessor materially participates in the production or management thereof. [IRC § 1402(a)(1)] Under these circumstances, the rental proceeds are included in the recipients gross income as "farm rental income" and subject to self-employment taxation. [Treas Reg § 1.1402(a)-4(b)(ii)]

Other Tax Issues

Q 7:115 Can members deduct unreimbursed business expenses paid on behalf of the LLC?

Yes. If a member incurs unreimbursed business expenses incurred on an LLC business, the member may deduct those expenses as follows. If an individual member has a right to reimbursement but forgoes that right, the member can deduct business expenses under Code Section 67 as a miscellaneous itemized expense on Schedule A, Form 1040. The deduction is limited to expenses in excess of 2 percent of the member's adjusted gross income. [IRC § 67] On the other hand, if the member has no right to reimbursement for the expense, the member may deduct those expenses from his, her, or its distributive share of the LLC's income "above the line," on the individual tax return, but only if the LLC is taxed as a partnership. [Ltr Rul 9316003]

Q 7:116 Must an LLC be taxed as a partnership?

No. An LLC could be taxed as a corporation, if the LLC elects corporate status under the "check-the-box" regulations (see chapter 3). [IRC § 7701; Treas Reg § 301.7701-2(a)(1); Ltr Rul 9636007; see also Pillow, Schmalz, and Starr, "Check-the-Box Proposed Regs. Simplify the Entity Classification Process," 85 *J Tax* 72 (Aug 1996)] A one-owner LLC will be taxed as a sole proprietorship or disregarded entity unless it elects to be taxed as a regular corporation.

Specified unincorporated organizations may also make a special election to be excluded from Subchapter K of the IRC, if:

1. The LLC is used for investment purposes only, and not for the active conduct of a trade or business; or

2. The LLC is used for the joint production, extraction, or use of property, but not for the purpose of selling services or property produced or extracted.

[IRC § 761; Treas Reg § 1.761-2]

To be excluded from subchapter K, the LLC's members must be able to compute their income without the necessity of computing the LLC's income in the aggregate. [Treas Reg § 1.761-2(a)(1)] In Field Service Advise Memorandum 199923017, the Service indicated that "[g]enerally, the service does not allow entities formed under a state's partnership or limited partnership laws to elect out of subchapter K." The service went on to strictly construe Treasury Regulations Section 1.761-2(a)(2)(ii), which provides that investing partners "reserve the right separately to dispose of their shares of any property acquired or retained, to require the ability to demand and receive any distributions at will." The memorandum denied an election out of subchapter K to a limited partnership, because the partners had "no right to demand and receive any distribution from a limited partnership in any form other than cash." This position is contrary to the position previously taken by the service in GCM 38025, September 20, 1979. In that memorandum, the service concluded that it is sufficient for the participants to reserve either the right to take property in kind or retain the right to separately dispose of their share. This election must be filed with the LLC's timely filed Form 1065 for the first taxable year for which the LLC wants to be excluded from subchapter K. Thus, partnerships that own property in the partnership's name cannot elect out of Subchapter K under Code Section 761(a), under the "small business" rules since the partners do not "own the property as co-owners."

Q 7:117   What are the tax consequences of a corporation owning an interest in an LLC?

A corporation, as a member of an LLC, will receive its proportionate share of the LLC's gain, income, losses, deductions, and credits. Such amounts are reportable on the corporation's income tax return, and are subject to the federal tax rates for corporations.

Q 7:118 How are passive corporate owners of a flow-through entity treated for state tax purposes in the state where the entity is doing business?

Flow through entities such as the LLC and LLP are tools often utilized by corporations for structuring joint ventures. These entities provide flow-through taxation while providing limited liability. A key factor that is often under appreciated is the state tax consequences. The state tax consequences should be carefully considered in the planning phase of any such transaction.

Most states currently recognize that a passive owner is not subject to state privilege taxes merely due to the corporations holding of an interest in a flow-through entity. Privilege taxes are typically limited to those "doing business" with the state. Thus a passive owner in a flow-through entity would not be considered "doing business" within a state were the entity operated. Some states however, apply an aggregate or agency theory to find a passive owner as "doing business" within the state. [Conn Gen Stat § 12-214 (1997)]

State corporate income tax can also be a trap for the unwary. Many states such as Alabama model their income tax statute after the federal system. They tax corporations that have income derived from, or the source of which is derived from the state imposing the tax. [Ala Code § 40-14-41 (1997)] Thus, many passive corporate owners are taxed in states where their only nexus with the state is the corporation's ownership interest in the flow-through entity. Other states, however, have found that passive corporate owners of flow-through entities exempt from income taxation. [GA Comp R & Regs 560-7-8-.34 (1998)]

Q 7:119 What are the tax consequences of an LLC owning an interest in a corporation?

An LLC, as a shareholder in a corporation, will not have any tax consequences unless the LLC receives a dividend distribution from the corporation or the LLC disposes of its stock in the corporation. Provided that the LLC is taxed as a partnership for tax purposes, the LLC cannot take a deduction for dividends received from another corporation under Code Section 243. Any dividends received from the corporation are reported by the LLC to the members, in proportion to their interests in the LLC. The dividends retain the character of investment/portfolio income when allocated to each member.

Q 7:120 May an LLC own stock in an S corporation?

No. An LLC may not own stock in an S corporation without causing the revocation of the corporation's S election. An LLC is not a qualified shareholder of an S corporation. [IRC § 1361(b)]

Q 7:121 May an S corporation own an interest in an LLC?

Yes. An S corporation may own an interest in an LLC. An S corporation, as a member of an LLC, will receive its proportionate share of the LLC's income, losses, deductions, and credits. Those items are reportable on the S corporation's income tax return and, in turn, passed through proportionately to each shareholder of the S corporation.

Q 7:122 May an LLC participate in a Section 1031 like-kind exchange?

An LLC may participate in a like-kind exchange if the LLC satisfies the Section 1031 requirements. Generally, no gain or loss is recognized on the exchange of property. Three tests must be met:

1. Both the property surrendered and the property received are held either for productive use in a trade or business, or for investment;

2. The property surrendered and the property received are of "like-kind"; and

3. The exchange is a reciprocal transfer of properties as distinguished from a sale and repurchase.

[IRC § 1031(a)(1)]

If the like-kind property is not received directly from the transferor of the LLC's property, Code Section 1031 and underlying Treasury regulations establish a procedure for the implementation of a deferred or three-party like-kind exchange. To summarize these rules, the proceeds of the first closing must be delivered by the transferee of the LLC's property to a "qualified trust" or "qualified intermediary" as defined in Treasury Regulations Section 1.1031-1(k). Then, those proceeds must be used to purchase replacement property, which must be identified within 45 days from the date the old property was relinquished. The identification requirement can be met by designating the property to be received in the contract between the parties. Additionally, the replacement property must be received by the LLC on the earlier of: (1) the date that is 180 days after the old property was relinquished; or (2) the due date of the LLC transferor's tax return. [IRC § 1031(a)(3)]

Each exchange of property can have up to three replacement properties designated to it of any fair market value or any number of properties as long as their aggregate fair market value does not exceed 200 percent of the aggregate fair market value of all the relinquished properties. Generally, if the taxpayer or LLC has identified more properties as replacements than is permitted by the Internal Revenue Code, the transaction is treated as if no replacement property had been identified (i.e., gain will then be recognized on the exchange). [Treas Reg § 1.1031(k)-1(c)(4)] Thus, how the transaction is structured could become important for an LLC desiring to transfer multiple properties. For example, if the LLC wanted to transfer two parcels of property and designate three replacement properties for each, the transaction must be structured in such a way that will classify it as two exchanges.

There are many methods that can be used in structuring an exchange that will increase the chance of having it classified as a multiple transaction, including:

1. Acquiring different buyers for each parcel;
2. Using separate contracts for the sale;
3. Using separate escrow agents and brokers for each sale;
4. Increasing the amount of time between each transfer; and
5. Advertising each property separately.

There are other factors used by the IRS and the courts in determining whether the disposition of multiple properties will constitute a single or multiple exchange that are not in control of the transferor, including: (1) proximity of the properties (the greater the distance apart, the greater the chance of multiple transaction classification); and (2) whether the properties transferred were or are going to be used in a single business operation. These methods and factors mentioned are not separately conclusive, nor are they a complete list.

The like-kind exchange rules do not apply to certain property, including partnership interests or securities. [IRC § 1031(a)(2)] An owner of a one member LLC may exchange his interest for the interest in a different one member LLC if the underlying assets of the LLC would allow Section 1031 treatment. This is possible because the separate existence of a one-member LLC will be ignored unless it elects to be taxable as a corporation. [Ltr Rul 9751012]

An issue particularly relevant in the context of an LLC is how long the taxpayer must hold the property, or replacement property, to qualify for Section 1031 treatment. The IRS ruled that Code Section 1031 did not apply to an individual taxpayer who exchanged like-kind real estate but immediately transferred the replacement property to a wholly owned corporation. [Rev Rul 75-292, 1975-2 CB 333] Similarly, Code Section 1031 did not apply to an individual taxpayer who received real estate from a corporation upon liquidation of the corporation and then immediately exchanged the property for like-kind property. [Rev Rul 77-337, 1977-2 CB 305]

The courts have been more lenient, and have held that Code Section 1031 applies on facts similar to those in Revenue Rulings 75-292 and 77-337. [Magneson v Commr, 81 TC 767 (1983), aff'd, 753 F 2d 1490 (9th Cir 1985); Bolker v Commr, 81 TC 782 (1983), aff'd, 760 F 2d 1039 (9th Cir 1985), but see Chase v Commr, 92 TC 874 (1989)]

An LLC and a member are distinct and separate taxpayers. An individual taxpayer could therefore not enter into a deferred like-kind exchange and then have the replacement property transferred directly to an LLC owned by the taxpayer, unless it is a SMLLC which is disregarded for federal income tax purposes. [Ltr Rul 9807013] In a like-kind exchange, the transferor of the relinquished property and the transferee of the replacement property must be the same. Consequently, it may be prudent to transfer relinquished property to an LLC well before entering into a contract for a like-kind exchange of that property, if the taxpayer wants to hold the replacement property in an LLC. The longer the property is owned by the LLC before entering the like-kind exchange agreement, the better. The replacement property could be transferred to an LLC after completing the like-kind exchange, but the taxpayer must be cautious and will have to rely on the *Magneson* case, which the IRS may not follow outside of the Ninth Circuit. Thus, it may be prudent to hold the property individually for a "cooling" period, perhaps a year or longer, to be safe.

Q 7:123 May an LLC convert to an LP while proceeds from the sale of property are held by a qualified intermediate and have the LP be treated as both the transferor and the transferee for purposes of § 1031?

In Private Letter Ruling 199935065, the Service considered where an LLC liquidated to its members then the members immediately transferred the assets and liabilities to the newly formed LP. In the newly formed LP all partners hold both general and limited partner interests. The partners interest in capital, losses and profits were the same percentages as had been held in the LLC. The service held that under Code Section 708, the LP would be considered for federal income tax purposes a continuation of the LLC and that the LP would be treated as both the transferor and the transferee for purposes of § 1031.

Q 7:124 Who are "responsible persons" in the LLC for employment tax matters?

The IRS can assert a penalty under Code Section 6672 against a responsible person if employment taxes are not remitted to the government. A "person" is defined as any officer or employee of a corporation, or a member or employee of a partnership who, as officer, employee, or member, is under a duty to remit employment taxes on behalf of the entity. [IRC § 6671(b)] However, that list of persons is not all inclusive. Additionally, the definition of responsible person is broad and all encompassing.

Certain state law provisions could allow collection of the employment taxes from general partners, even if those partners do not meet the stringent requirements of Code Section 6672. Therefore, direct assessment can be made against partners, and other responsible persons. Presumably, any person, including LLC members, who qualify as responsible persons could be liable for the penalty under Code Section 6672. It is unclear whether the LLC members, solely in their capacity as members, could be deemed responsible persons. However, if the member is directly responsible for the payment of the LLC's payroll (including taxes), is the treasurer and directs the payment of payroll, or directs or participates in a decision to instruct some other person not to pay the LLC's payroll taxes, that member could be considered a responsible person and face personal liability for the back payroll taxes, plus a 100 percent penalty.

Q 7:125   What is a "tax matters member"?

A tax matters member is similar to tax matters partner (TMP). A partnership must have a TMP. A TMP can be a general partner designated by the partnership. If the partnership does not designate a TMP, the general partner with the largest profits interest at the close of the year will be the TMP. If no TMP is designated, and it is impractical to use the largest profits interest, the IRS will select a TMP. [IRC § 6231(a)(7)]

A proposed Treasury regulation that pertains to the designation of a TMP for an LLC was issued in October 1995. Under the proposed regulation, a member-manager of LLC would be considered to be a general partner for purposes of Code Section 6231(a)(7). [Prop Treas Reg § 301.6231(a)(7)-2(a)] As a result, the member-manager could be designated as the tax matters member for the LLC. For LLCs with no member-manager, any of the members could serve as the tax matters member for the LLC. As a practical matter, the LLC documents should name a tax matters member. If none is named and the LLC does not have a member-manager, presumably the member with the largest profit interest might be selected by the IRS as the tax matters member.

Q 7:126   When do state, as opposed to federal, tax issues become important?

It is essential to determine the state tax consequences of the choice of entity. The choice will affect the taxation of the entity itself and may have important consequences for the owners of the entity.

Q 7:127   Do states classify and tax unincorporated organizations as partnerships, corporations, or otherwise?

States may elect to classify LLCs for state tax purposes in three different ways. First, the LLC may be classified as a corporation. Second, states may elect to classify LLCs as partnerships for state income tax purposes regardless of how the LLC is treated for federal tax purposes. [See Colo Rev Stat § 39-22-201.5 (1991) (applying to Colorado LLCs only); Md Ann Code § 10-102.1 (1992); and Utah Code Ann § 48-2b-157 (1991)] The final, and most common, approach is to classify the LLC in a manner consistent with the LLC's classification for federal income tax purposes. [See, e.g., California Senate Bill 1234 (directing state regulatory agency to issue regulations in accordance with the check-the-box regulations)]

Most states do not impose taxes on general partnerships. Exceptions include the Illinois personal property replacement tax on the net income of business organizations [Ill Ann Stat ch 35 §§ 5-205(b)]; the New Hampshire business profits tax [NH Rev Stat § 77:14]; the Tennessee tax on bond interest and stock dividends received by partnerships [Tenn Code Ann § 67-2-102]; the District of Columbia unincorporated business tax, which excludes most personal service businesses [DC Code Ann § 47-1808.3]; the West Virginia business franchise tax [W Va Code § 11-23-6]; the Hawaii gross income tax [Haw Rev Stat § 237-1]; and New York City unincorporated business tax. [NYC Code §§ 11-502(a), and 503] Michigan passed legislation in 1999 to phase out the single business tax over the next 23 years. [Mich. H.B. 4745; Mich Comp Laws § 208.6]

Due in part to the check the box regulations, specific entity taxation of LLCs is present in only one state. Texas imposes corporate income or franchise taxes on LLCs. Several other states, such as Illinois and California, impose significant filing fees. The Texas franchise tax is in part an income tax and applies to LLCs but not partnerships, nor does it apply to an LLC that is a limited partner in a limited partnership. Even after adopting the federal system, LLCs remain subject to the Capital Stock and Franchise Tax.

Q 7:128   How is an owner of a multistate business taxed?

Most states have asserted jurisdiction to tax nonresident partners based on the aggregate theory of partnership [Appeal of HF Ahmanson & Co, Cal BOE, 1965 Cal Tax LEXIS 38 (Apr 5, 1965)

("In California a partnership, unlike a corporation, is considered to be not a legal entity but an association of individuals.")], or the concept that any partner present in the state is an agent of the nonresident partner so that the nonresident is present through an agent. [Chapman v Browne, 48 NYS 2d 598, 268 AD 806 (NY App Div, 3d Dept 1944)] Thus, a nonresident partner will generally be taxable even if the nonresident has no other ties to the taxing state. This is in contrast with the treatment of nonresident shareholders in C corporations, who will not be subject to state tax unless some other nexus exists with the state.

Q 7:129   How is the multistate business itself taxed?

The rules for corporations and certain other multistate businesses are complex. If a corporation is subject to taxation on its distributive share of income and loss from an incorporated organization it owns, there are several questions of allocation and apportionment that must be addressed. As noted above, a state may only tax a non-resident if the income is fairly apportioned. Thus, it is important to determine how much of the income of the partnership is properly apportioned to the taxing state. This constitutional limitation precludes a state from taxing more than the corporation's income that is properly attributable to the partner's direct and indirect (including through the partnership) business activities in a state. [Homart Development Co v Norberg, 529 A 2d 115 (RI 1987)] Thus, it is important to determine how much of the income of the partnership is properly apportioned to the taxing state.

Q 7:130   What are the rules for allocation?

The Uniform Division of Income for Tax Purposes Act ["UDITPA" §§ 9, 10, 13 and 15] sets forth a three-factor test for the allocation of income by comparing the dollar value within the state with the dollar value everywhere of the taxpayer's payroll, property, and sales. Not all states follow this approach, and others do not count all three factors or double weight one of the factors in determining the allocation. If the taxpayer operates more than one business, the application of the factors to a business will turn on the activities that are part of the same business, known in tax parlance as the determination of whether activities are "unitary" with each other. If various activities are unitary they will be considered together to determine the appropriate factors on which to allocate income, and the income from all the activities are combined and apportioned together. Some of the elements that will be applied to determine whether the activities are unitary include whether:

1. Unity of ownership exists among the activities;

2. The various activities are functionally integrated; and

3. The activities contribute to or are dependent on one another.

[Container Corp of America, 463 US 159 at 166-167 (1983)]

States vary in whether they include the factors from a partnership in which the corporation is a general partner in the computation of the unitary factors. If they do not include the partnership's factors, it may be possible to use a partnership to reduce the factors allocable to the taxing state by putting businesses with considerable factors into an unincorporated business.

Q 7:131 How is an estate or trust's distributable net income and accounting income affected by holding an interest in an LLC?

An LLC allocates its income and loss to its members based upon the members' distributive share. Because LLCs are pure conduits for tax purposes, a member's distributive share of LLC profits is currently includable in the member's gross income, whether or not the LLC actually distributes the profits. LLC distributions are an independent phenomenon which may or may not have any bearing on the current pass-through of LLC tax attributes. Distributable net income (DNI) is defined as the taxable income (as defined in Code Section 63) of an estate or trust, with certain adjustments. A distributive share of the LLC gross income is includable in determining taxable income and is treated as if received directly by the estate or trust holding the LLC interest. [IRC §§ 61-63] It is, therefore, includable in an estate or trust member's DNI, whether or not the LLC made an actual distribution.

The effect of including the distributive share of LLC income in DNI of an estate or trust and of allocating tax liability attributable to such distributive share to an estate or trust or its beneficiaries is uncertain. The main difficulty lies in the lack of coordination between the subchapter K tax rules and the principal/income allocation rules under local law.

Under Code Section 643(b), "income" is defined as income determined under the terms of the governing instrument and applicable local law. This is not a tax concept. In measuring the amounts that an income beneficiary is entitled to receive as income, the Revised (1962) Uniform Principal and Income Act (the "Revised Act") appears to operate strictly on a cash basis, not on an accrual or pass-through basis.

Only LLC distributions actually received by the trust or estate that are properly considered to constitute income for fiduciary accounting purposes would be treated as Section 643(b) income, the distribution of which can carry out the taxable income of the trust to its beneficiaries under the DNI mechanism. Since income, as determined under local law, includes "receipt," it would appear that, if an estate or trust owning an LLC interest does not receive an actual distribution, it has not received any local law income, only taxable income, and there is, accordingly, no income required to be distributed currently that can carry out DNI to a beneficiary.

If the fiduciary of the trust, including a simple trust or a complex trust required to distribute all of its income currently, determines that it has not received any income for accounting purposes from the LLC under the governing instrument or local law, and does not otherwise make distributions to beneficiaries that carry out the DNI of the trust attributable to the LLC distributive share, the trust will be liable for the tax on the distributive share. The fiduciary must then determine whether the tax should be charged to income or principal.

Q 7:132   What special tax issues do large LLCs face?

LLCs may, for tax purposes, qualify as publicly traded partnerships if members may trade their interests on a recognized securities exchange. Under Code Section 7704, publicly traded partnerships are taxed as corporations. However, when the publicly traded partnership rules were adopted in 1987, a 10 year grandfather clause allowed publicly traded partnerships to continue to be taxed as partnerships provided that they did not add a substantial new line of business. The Taxpayer Relief Act extended the grandfather provision but added a surtax of 3.5 percent on gross income from active trade or business activities. Thus, a publicly traded LLC which may have this grandfathered status by virtue of its conversion from a publicly traded partnership, must now face the additional tax as well as exercising caution not to add a substantial new line of business unless it is willing to forfeit its status as a partnership for tax purposes.

Additionally, the Taxpayer Relief Act permits simplified reporting for "electing large partnerships" with greater than 100 members. This new legislation allows individual LLC members to compute income as if an LLC level 754 election was made. In general terms, this permits items of income usually computed separately at the partner level to be done at the partnership level while virtually all elections relating to the computation of income are made at the partner level.

Q 7:133 What is the income tax effect of the death of an LLC member?

The Taxpayer Relief Act provides that an LLC's tax year closes with respect to a decedent member at the date of death. [PL No 105-34 § 1246] This allows all proportionate amounts of income or loss to be included on the decedent's final income tax return for years after 1997. Prior to the Taxpayer Relief Act, the death of a member did not close the tax year of the LLC with respect to the member's interest which resulted in the LLC's gain or loss being reflected on the decedent's estate or trust income tax return.

Options, Warrants, and Convertible Units of Interests

Q 7:134 Why would an LLC use options with respect to its interests?

One reason is to compensate service providers. The use of options, warrants or convertible interests generally allows a service member a period of time to exercise an option without immediate realization of income because options are not yet "property" within the meaning of Code Section 83. Section 83 deals with the transfer of property in connection with the performance of services. If the option has no connection with compensation for services then Code Section 83 will not apply. Furthermore, depending on the type of interest given, the option holder may avoid taxation upon the exercise of the option. [See Q 7:136]

Q 7:135   Is there a taxable event with respect to the issuance an option?

Generally, an option or warrant for an LLC interest is not taxable upon its issuance. An option or warrant for an LLC profits only or regular capital interest is not likely to fall under the definition of property. [See Treas Reg § 1.83-(a)(2)] Thus, the employee would not realize income, and the LLC would not be entitled to a deduction.

Certain stock options that have a readily ascertainable fair market value will be governed by Code Section 83. [See Treas Reg § 1.83-7] Stock options are considered to have a readily ascertainable fair market value if the options themselves are:

1. Actively traded on an established market; or
2. Transferable by the option holder, immediately and in full, not subject to any restriction or condition (other than a lien or other condition to secure the payment of the purchase price) which has a significant effect upon the fair market value of the option, and the fair market value of the option privilege is readily ascertainable under the meaning of Treasury Regulations Section 1.83-7(b)(3).

[Treas Reg § 1.83-7(b)(1-2)]

An option might have certain consequences upon issuance if the purchase price is significantly lower than the fair market value of the LLC interest. If the difference in price is significant enough, then the option holder may be treated as owner of the interest. [See Rev Rul 82-150, 1982-2 CB 150] In Revenue Ruling 82-150, the option's exercise price was $30,000 and the value of the stock subject to the option was $100,000. The option holder paid $70,000 for the option. The IRS applied substance over form and allocated 100 percent of the income pro rata to the option holder.

Q 7:136 Is there a taxable event with respect to the exercise of an option or warrant?

In some cases, there is a taxable event upon the exercise of an option. The first determination that must be made is if the interest acquired when the option or warrant is exercised is a capital interest or a profits interest being purchased with the option. [See Q 7:21] Upon the exercise of an option or warrant of a capital interest given as compensation, there would be income to the option holder and a compensation deduction to the LLC. The amount of income realized upon the exercise of the option or warrant would be the fair market value of the option holder's interest in the LLC less any amount the option holder paid for the interest. [See IRC § 83] For example, *A* and *B* are 50/50 owners of the *AB* LLC, which consists of assets with a basis and fair market value of $1,000. *A* and *B* give their employee *C* an option exercisable for one year to purchase a one third interest in the *AB* LLC for $500. The option itself has no readily ascertainable fair market value. *C* exercises the option four months later when the LLC assets are worth $1600. *C* now has a one third interest in $2100. The $2100 represents the fair market value of all the LLC's assets which consist of $1600 plus the purchase price of $500.

If the option given is for a pure profits interest, the exercise of an option to acquire such an interest may avoid taxation. The analysis depends on whether it is given for services and whether Code Section 83 governs, but in either case, the exercise of an option to purchase profits interests will likely yield the same result. The safe harbor provisions of Revenue Procedure 93-27 [1993-2 CB 343] provide that the interest does not constitute property within the meaning of Code Section 83 if three conditions are met. In Revenue Procedure 93-27, the Service announced they would not tax the receipt of profits interest given as compensation as long as the interest provides no certain and predictable stream of income, there is no transfer of the interest within two years of the receipt, and the interest is not publicly traded within the meaning of Code Section 7704(b). If Code Section 83 were to govern, then the option holder would recognize gain in the amount of the fair market value of the profits interest that would most likely be zero.

These concepts become important especially if the service member (or potential service member) wants to take advantage of a

Section 83(b) election. As discussed in Q 7:21, a Section 83(b) election is where the service partner would include in income the value of such interest transferred over any amounts paid for the interest. A Section 83(b) election can only be made after exercise of the option or warrant as the grant of the option or warrant itself does not have a readily ascertainable fair market value. [See IRC § 83(e)(3)] The advantage of such an election is the possible ability to include gross income currently and be able to recognize income at a later date as either capital or ordinary depending on the nature of the gain to the LLC. Section 83 will only apply to the transfers of property. Some commentators suggest that when a profits interest is issued, the contribution of capital by the recipient of the interest could make the profits interest more akin to a capital interest, increasing the likelihood that the interest is property under the meaning of Section 83. However, if the tests of Revenue Procedure 93-27 are met, there will be no tax.

Q 7:137 How are the members capital accounts adjusted upon the exercise of an option?

Upon the exercise of an option to purchase a capital interest given as compensation to a service member, the LLC would receive a deduction for a compensation and the service member would have an initial capital account of the amount paid for the interest. The other capital accounts would be reduced by any appreciation attributable to the service member. In the example in Q 7:136 above, *C* paid $500 for an interest worth $700. Thus, $200 shifted from *A* and *B* to *C*, which would reduce *A*'s and *B*'s capital account by $100 each.

The question becomes more troublesome if the option is not used in connection with a service member. Using the same example in Q 7:136 except *C* is not a service member but rather purchases the option for $30. *C*, upon the exercise of the option for $500, has a one third interest in an LLC with assets of $2130. *C* has paid $530 for the right to receive (if the LLC were liquidated) $710. The question now is how to allocate the $180. Treasury Regulations Section 1.704-1(b)(2)(iv) does not directly address the issue of capital account reallocation upon the exercise of an option or warrant. As to *A* and *B*, Section 721(a), which states that a partnership or its partners will not recognize gain when exchanging a partnership interest for property, applies. The question now becomes what to do with C's capital account. One solution is for C to recognize $180 in gain, which is the immediate increase in his capital account. While recognition would be the case if the option was given to the service member as discussed above or gratuitously given, this would be inconsistent with Code Section 721(a). Another method is a "book-up". [See Treas Reg 1.704-1(b)(2)(iv)(f)] A book-up is a revaluation of property that can occur on a specified event or events to accurately reflect the partners capital accounts. Such events are specified in the operating agreements, meaning that if this issue is not addressed, this regulation will not apply.

Since this issue is not directly addressed by the regulations, the fall back provisions of Treasury Regulations Section 1.704-1(b)(2)(iv)(q) would most likely come into play. This regulation provides for situations where guidance is lacking by stating that adjustments will not be considered maintained properly unless the adjustments are made in a manner that:

1. Maintains equality between the aggregate governing capital accounts of the partners and the amount of partnership capital reflected on the partnership's balance sheet, as computed for book purposes,
2. Is consistent with the underlying economic arrangement of the partners, and
3. Is based, wherever practicable, on Federal tax accounting principles.

Thus, C's capital account would receive a "book-up" in the amount of the unbooked appreciation from $530 to $710. C's outside basis in his LLC interest would remain $530.

Q 7:138 Do convertible LLC interests have an effect on capital accounts upon conversion?

Probably not. Conversion rights are most likely defined in the Operating Agreement. In the option situation discussed in the previous questions, the exercise of the option was an exchange of property LLC interests. Convertible interests are not new assets or property coming into the LLC, but rather existing interests that can be changed in form. This is more akin to a profit sharing arrangement. Upon liquidation, the member will be taxed on his or her interest. It could be argued that any unrealized appreciation that shifts upon the exercise of a conversion right has already accrued to that member.

If the conversion is treated as an exchange, it does not necessarily mean that there is a taxable event. The Service has ruled that a conversion of a partnership interest into an LLC interest is not a transfer for purposes of Code Section 708 (b)(1)(B). [See Rev Rul 95-37, 1995-1 CB 130]

Q 7:139   How can an LLC avoid the uncertainties of options, warrants and convertible units?

One method is not to give the holder of an option or a convertible LLC unit an immediate right to capital, but require all future income be used to replenish the capital account. While this solves the problem in capital account adjustments, it places a risk on the exercising member if the LLC does not have sufficient future profits to allocate. Another method is to allocate all losses or deductions to nonexercising members first until the accounts are balanced. Yet another way would be to allocate any appreciation in LLC assets first to the exercising member. This would be done if there is a book up in the future. Therefore, the Operating Agreement could include a provision for a book up after a specified period of time after the exercise of the option or conversion right to allow some time for additional appreciation in case a book up was done close in time to the exercise.

For the convertible LLC unit, it may be advisable to place in the Operating Agreement a mandatory conversion event. One suggestion is a mandatory conversion when the conversion from one type of unit to another would yield a higher return of capital. An example would be where someone holds a preferred convertible LLC unit that would be more valuable if converted to a common unit because the common units are yielding a higher return. The risk to the holder of the convertible unit is the risk if the LLC becomes unprofitable in the future, the benefit of any priority in distribution is lost.

Chapter 8

Dissolution

This chapter discusses the concept of a dissolution of the LLC, and sets forth the conditions upon which the LLC is dissolved. This chapter also discusses the consequences of a dissolution and the ability to continue the business of the LLC after a dissolution event. Finally, this chapter distinguishes a dissolution of the company from a liquidation of the company, and describes the process of winding up the LLC.

Dissolution Events

Q 8:1   When does an LLC dissolve?

Most LLC acts provide that an LLC dissolves upon the occurrence of one or more of the following events:

- The arrival of the date set forth in the Articles as the last date for the existence of the LLC;

- By agreement, typically unanimous, of the members of the LLC;

- Upon the occurrence of a dissolution event with respect to a member, unless the business of the LLC is continued as described in Q 8:4; and

- Some state LLC acts contain a procedure for a judicial disso-lution of the LLC. [See, e.g., Del Code Ann tit 6, § 18-802.]

Finally, some state statutes provide that the members may set forth in the Operating Agreement additional events upon the occur-rence of which the LLC will be dissolved.

Q 8:2   What is an event of withdrawal, dissolution, or dissociation by a member?

These terms are used interchangeably in the various statutes and in this book. Most LLC acts define each of the following as a separate LLC dissolution event:

- Death or dissolution of a member;
- Retirement or resignation of a member;
- Expulsion of a member; and
- Bankruptcy of a member.

Expulsion of a member from an LLC can occur in various ways. For example, in *Gee et al. v. Bullock*, [1996 WL 9377009 (RI Super 1996)] the defendant formed an LLC under the Rhode Island LLC Act with two plaintiffs to operate a retail pasta business. The defendant agreed to sign an Operating Agreement but later refused to do so. After certain business disputes, defendant locked the plaintiffs out and fraudulently transferred LLC assets to a corpora-tion she owned. The court, in applying the Rhode Island LLC act then in effect, held the lockout constituted an expulsion of the plaintiffs and thus triggered the dissolution of the LLC. As a result, the plaintiffs were entitled to the fair value of their LLC interest and, because of her wrongful actions, the defendant was not entitled to manage the LLC's wind-up and dissolution, which instead was entrusted to a third-party trustee.

Several states also provide that the occurrence of one or more of the following constitutes a dissolution event:

- The insanity or other incompetence of a member;
- The assignment of assets by a member to creditors; and
- A catchall, which provides that the LLC dissolves upon any other event that terminates the continued membership of a member in the LLC, for example, an assignment of its interest to a third party.

Finally, some state LLC statutes also permit dissolution on "illegal, oppressive, fraudulent, or unfairly prejudicial conduct." [ULLCA § 801(54)]

Q 8:3   Is voluntary withdrawal permitted, and if so, are there any limits that apply?

Voluntary withdrawal by members is permitted in most states. **Colorado** provides that the withdrawn member has no management rights and, as a result, no fiduciary duties to the other members. However, withdrawn members are owed fiduciary duties following withdrawal until they are paid for their interests. [Colo Rev Stat § 7-80-603]

Some states place restrictions on the timing of withdrawal. The **Washington** LLC statute provides that, absent a provision in the Operating Agreement, withdrawal requires unanimous consent prior to dissolution and winding up. [Wash Rev Code § 25.15.130(3)]

Q 8:4   Does the LLC automatically dissolve upon the occurrence of a dissolution event?

Yes, unless the remaining members vote to continue the business of the LLC. Originally, many states with "bulletproof" statutes required the unanimous consent of the remaining members to continue the business of the LLC following a dissolution event. Most states are now more flexible and provide that unanimous consent is not required, at least if the members agree otherwise in the Articles or the Operating Agreement.

For tax purposes, to continue to be taxed as a partnership, there must be at least two remaining members.

One should note, however, that in some jurisdictions it might be possible to have a court-appointed receiver following the occurrence of dissolution events without a request for the actual dissolution of the LLC. [Diaz v Fernandez, 910 P 2d 96 (Colo App 1995) (owners of 49 percent interest were successful in getting receiver appointed without dissolution)]

Q 8:5   How much time do the members have to decide whether to continue the business of the LLC following a dissolution event, without suffering a dissolution?

Most statutes require the remaining members to make a decision within 90 days following a dissolution event, to avoid suffering a dissolution of the LLC.

Q 8:6   What is the tax significance of a dissolution of the LLC?

The courts and IRS have identified continuity of life as a characteristic of a corporation. That is, a corporation's life is continuous and could be perpetual, regardless of the death or any other dissolution event with respect to a shareholder. A partnership's continued existence, however, is dependent upon the continued existence of the partners of the partnership. Both the Uniform Partnership Act (UPA) and the Revised Uniform Limited Partnership Act (RULPA) state that a partnership dissolves upon the occurrence of one of the dissolution events described above (see Q 8:1). Consequently, the courts and the IRS have concluded that, to distinguish hybrid business organizations, continuity of life is a distinguishing feature between a corporation and a partnership.

But for income tax purposes, dissolution has no significance per se to the LLC or its members. It may or may not involve a termination of partnership income tax status. [See Q 7:63 and IRC § 708]

Members' Rights Upon a Dissolution Event

Q 8:7   What rights and obligations does a member have who suffers a dissolution event or event of withdrawal?

The answer to this question varies widely among the states. In many states, a withdrawing member is entitled only to the distributions and rights granted to them under the operating or other agreement, if any. In some states, a withdrawing member is entitled to the return of his or her capital or the redemption of his or her interest at fair value. [See chapter 4; see also ULLCA §§ 701, 702 for intricate procedure regarding buy-out right of a member's interest] The right to a redemption of interest is limited in all states where the redemption would render the LLC insolvent. Finally, many states also allow the LLC to defer redemption of a member's interest when the payment would be unreasonably burdensome on the LLC.

Members may also be subject to certain obligations upon a withdrawal. For instance, their withdrawal generally does not release them from obligations to contribute capital due before the date of their withdrawal. In addition, several states provide for the payment of damages (and the set-off of these damages against distributions due) by members who withdraw in violation of an agreement not to withdraw from the LLC.

The simple voluntary resignation of a member may be a dissolution event, which gives rise to certain obligations on the LLC in many states. However, in many cases, those rights and obligations may be altered by the agreement of the members. Consequently, members should consider limiting the ability of a member to resign and clearly establishing the rights and obligations of a member upon their resignation. In addition, the Operating Agreement or buy-sell agreement should conclusively establish a mechanism for the valuation of each member's interest and the payment of the distribution over time, if authorized by law.

⚹ 8:8 What rights do the remaining members have following an event of withdrawal by a member?

All states allow the remaining members to continue the business of the LLC following a dissolution event of another member. If the LLC is continued, the LLC is not dissolved.

If the relevant LLC act requires the redemption of a withdrawn member's interest, those same statutes generally establish a court procedure to defer distributions to withdrawn members if those payments would cause an unreasonable hardship on the LLC and remaining members.

⚹ 8:9 Can the nonwithdrawing members continue the LLC or the business of the LLC following an event of withdrawal?

Generally yes, under the applicable statute or under a right set forth in the Articles to continue the business of the LLC following a dissolution event.

Q 8:10   Is unanimous consent required to continue an LLC following an event of withdrawal by a member?

Yes, under a few statutes. Other flexible statutes allow the members to continue the business of the LLC under a right set forth in the Articles or upon the approval of a lesser number of members as agreed in advance.

However, if authorized by state law, the members could reduce the vote necessary to continue the business of the LLC following a dissolution event to the vote of a "majority in interest."

Q 8:11   Should the Articles require unanimous consent of the remaining members to continue the LLC following a dissolution event?

Generally no, unless required by the applicable state statute. If unanimous consent is required, the LLC could be forced by any remaining member into the costly procedure of dissolving for state law and tax purposes, regardless of the size of the remaining member's interest. For example, a member holding the smallest of interests could cause the LLC to dissolve by refusing to consent to the continuation of the LLC's business following a dissolution event suffered by another member.

In addition, all LLC acts allow members to withdraw their capital upon a dissolution of the LLC, to the extent the LLC has assets in excess of the LLC's liabilities as of the date of dissolution. Thus, the LLC's capital may be reduced dramatically, even though the majority members desire to continue the LLC's business.

Consequently, if acceptable under state law, most LLCs should reduce the vote required to continue the business to a "majority in interest" as defined in Revenue Procedure 94-46 [1994-2CB 688].

Process of Dissolution

Q 8:12   How is the LLC dissolved?

If dissolution is desirable or unavoidable, LLC acts require the LLC to file with the applicable state official (typically, the Secretary of State) a notice of intent to dissolve and/or articles of dissolution. Many states also require an LLC in the process of dissolving to notify the LLC's creditors during a specified time period before formal dissolution.

Q 8:13   What is the difference between a dissolution and liquidation of the LLC?

A dissolution of the LLC is a technical statutory term which defines the termination of the LLC's existence for state law purposes. An LLC may suffer a dissolution event but not actually liquidate, if the members elect to continue the business of the LLC. The liquidation of the LLC is the actual process of discontinuing all of the LLC's business and distributing the LLC's assets to creditors and members.

A third related but different concept is the termination of the LLC for tax purposes under Code Section 708 (see Q 7:63). The LLC may terminate for tax purposes but neither dissolve nor liquidate.

Q 8:14   What are the consequences of a dissolution of the LLC?

Upon the dissolution of the LLC, the LLC's business is wound up and is liquidated.

Q 8:15   How is an LLC wound up?

The process of winding up an LLC requires the disposition of assets, the payment of creditors, and if there are any assets remaining, distributions to members in liquidation of their interests. Many states provide for an accounting of the LLC's assets and liabilities in connection with the liquidation of the LLC.

One of the single largest issues in connection with the winding-up of an LLC is the value of the LLC's assets. If it is desirable to liquidate hard assets, obviously the cash or value of other property received in exchange for the asset establishes the value for that asset. However, many LLCs may hold illiquid real estate or other unmarketable assets, and the LLC's creditors and members may debate the value of those assets for the purposes of debt payments and final distributions to members.

As a result, the members should consider including in the Operating Agreement a mechanism for valuing nonpublicly traded assets for the purpose of liquidating distributions. If nothing else, the members could agree to a procedure for selecting appraisers to value assets conclusively that is binding on the members vis-à-vis each other. On the other hand, the members could impose on each other an obligation to arbitrate any such questions.

Q 8:16   Who has the authority to wind up the LLC?

Generally, the LLC acts bestow on the members or managers designated to wind up the affairs of the LLC implied actual authority to carry on the business of winding up the affairs of the LLC. Someone will need authority to sell assets, pay debts, collect accounts receivable, and perform or provide for the performance of any outstanding contractual obligations. Withdrawn members may be prohibited in some states from winding up the LLC. [Jim Avalon Investments, LLC v Nischan, 1997 WL 133939 (Conn Super 1997)] Trustees in bankruptcy, however, may have the authority to wind up an LLC's affairs. [In re DeLuca (JTB Enterprises, LC v D&B Venture, LC), 194 BR 79 (ED Va 1996)]

However, as discussed in chapter 5, all members in a member-managed LLC, and all managers in a manager-managed LLC, generally have agency powers and apparent authority, even while the LLC is winding up following a dissolution event. As a result, the Operating Agreement should address the winding-up process and designate those persons responsible for the winding up of the LLC and limit the authority of all other members and managers. The Operating Agreement should also determine if those involved in the winding-up process will be compensated for their services.

Q 8:17   What rights do the LLC's creditors have following a dissolution of the LLC?

Generally nonmember creditors have priority over members, including members who have loaned money to the LLC.

Q 8:18   Do the LLC's creditors have the right to force members to contribute additional capital to the LLC following dissolution, to satisfy the LLC's debts?

Generally no, unless the members' contractual pledges to the LLC have not been satisfied or compromised by the LLC and other members, or the member has received a wrongful distribution. (But see chapter 4.) Even then, many LLC acts allow only those creditors who relied on the commitments to enforce the obligations.

Q 8:19   Are the members required to notify anyone of a dissolution of the LLC? Of a liquidation?

If the LLC suffers a dissolution event, but the remaining members vote to continue the LLC's business, the LLC acts do not require any disclosure of the dissolution event. However, the LLC contractually may have an obligation to notify creditors of the event.

If the LLC does not continue in business, many LLC statutes require the LLC to notify creditors of the dissolution and liquidation. As a practical matter, members will have to notify all creditors if they have assets to distribute, otherwise third parties and members may not receive clean title to these assets.

Chapter 9

Securities and Bankruptcy Laws

This chapter reviews how the federal and state securities laws apply to LLCs and their members. It analyzes whether an interest in an LLC is a security, and the common registration exemptions that apply to offering and issuing securities. This chapter also reviews how the U.S. Bankruptcy Code may apply to an LLC, and the effect of a bankruptcy of an LLC on the LLC's business. It considers the impact of a bankruptcy of a member on the LLC and on the relationship of the bankrupt member to the LLC and other members. Finally, this chapter offers general principles that lenders should consider when preparing to make a loan to an LLC or to an LLC member, secured by their LLC interest.

Securities Laws

Q 9:1   Is an LLC interest a security under the federal and state securities laws?

Yes or no, depending upon the circumstances. Section 2(1) of the Securities Act of 1933 (1933 Act) [15 USC § 77b(1)] defines a security under the federal laws to include stocks, certificates of interest in a profit-sharing arrangement, and investment contracts (see Q 9:5).

Q 9:2   What is an investment contract?

An investment contract under the 1933 Act has been defined as:

> a contract, transaction or scheme whereby a person invests his money in a common enterprise and is led to expect profits solely from the efforts of the promoter or a third party, it being material whether the shares in the enterprise are evidenced by formal certificates or by nominal interests in the physical assets employed in the enterprise.

[SEC v WJ Howey Co, 328 US 293, 298, 299 (1946), *rehg den,* 329 US 819 (1946)]

The *Howey* test, the most widely used test for investment contracts, contains four elements to determine the existence of an investment contract: (1) investment of money, (2) in a common enterprise, (3) with the expectation of profits, (4) solely from the efforts of others. The first three elements exist in every business involving more than one person or entity. For LLCs, the phrase "solely from the efforts of others" must be considered. With regard to a single member LLC, the "solely" requirement would seem to preclude an interest of a SMLLC from ever being a security. While the "solely" requirement has not been expressly removed from the *Howey test,* the Supreme Court has not mandated a literal interpretation. [See United Housing Foundation v. Forman, 423 US 837 (1975)] The Supreme Court rephrased the *Howey* test of a security as an "investment in a common venture premised on a reasonable expectation of profits to be derived from the entrepreneurial or managerial efforts of others." [Forman at 852]

Therefore, if a member engages in substantial daily management of the LLC, the profits are dependent on the member's efforts, not those of a third party. Thus, a security is not indicated. On the other hand, if the member is excluded from management decisions, the profits are dependent substantially on third parties and a security could be established. [See SEC v Vision Communications, Inc, No 94-0615 (DDC May 11, 1994); SEC v Parkersburg Wireless Ltd Liab Co, No 94-1079 (DDC May 16, 1994); SEC v

Knoxville LLC, No 94-1073 B (SD CA Jul 11, 1996); SEC v Irwin Harry Bloch, litigation of release No 14511, 59 SEC docket 931, 1995 WL 317420 (SEC) (May 25, 1995); SEC v United Communications Ltd, litigation of release No 14477, 59 SEC docket 424, 1995 WL 254714 (SEC) (Apr 24, 1995); SEC v American Interactive Group, LLC, litigation release No 14462, 59 SEC docket 203, 1995 WL 229088 (SEC) (Apr 10, 1995); SEC v Future Vision Direct Mktg, Inc, litigation of release No 14384, 58 SEC docket 1716, 1995 WL 25731 (SEC) (Jan 18, 1995)]

Q 9:3   Is an interest in an LLC an investment contract?

Generally, LLCs represent a pooling of assets with the expectation of profits. Thus, the critical issue is whether the expected profits will be produced by the efforts of others. No one single, easily applied standard exists for determining whether an interest in an LLC is a security.

In the member-managed LLC, each member generally has agency authority to act on behalf of the LLC and to participate in managing the LLC's activities. The legal precedents that address whether a general partnership interest is a security should, therefore, apply to an LLC managed by members rather than managers. Member-managed LLCs are much like a general partnership: like general partners, each investor has agency authority and the power to participate in governing the enterprise.

Q 9:4   When is a partnership or LLC interest a security under Federal law?

A member-managed LLC is very similar to a general partnership. A general partnership interest is usually not a security, because all partners in a general partnership have the ability to participate in management decisions. The Fifth Circuit Court of Appeals, however, has held that a general partner or investor in a joint venture can establish that an interest is a security if:

1. The partnership agreement limits the authority of the general partner or joint venturer in question in a manner similar to the limits placed on a limited partner under a limited partnership agreement; or

2. The general partner or joint venturer is so inexperienced and unknowledgeable in business affairs that he or she is incapable of exercising his or her authority intelligently; or

3. The general partner or joint venturer is so dependent on the unique skills or ability of the promoter or manager that he or she could not remove the managing partner or manage the partnership or joint venture alone.

[Williamson v Tucker, 645 F 2d 404 (5th Cir 1981), *cert den*, 454 US 897 (1981); see also SEC v Glenn W Turner Enter, Inc, 474 F 2d 476 (9th Cir 1973), *cert den*, 414 US 8211 (1973); Koch v Hankins, 928 F 2d 1471 (9th Cir 1991); Hocking v Dubois, 885 F 2d 1449 (9th Cir 1989), *cert den*, 494 US 1078 (1989); Matek v Murat, 862 F 2d 720 (9th Cir 1988); Banghart v Hollywood Gen Partnership, 902 F 2d 805 (10th Cir 1990); Maritan v Birmingham Properties, 875 F 2d 1451 (10th Cir 1989)]

The Third Circuit and Fourth Circuit have applied more objective criteria in determining whether a general partnership interest is a security, by considering the legal rights of the general partner investor under the Uniform Partnership Act (UPA) and partnership agreement, especially with respect to the power to remove a managing general partner. [Goodwin v Elkins & Co, 730 F 2d 99 (3d Cir 1984), *cert den*, 469 US 831 (1984); Rivanna Trawlers Unlimited v Thompson Trawlers, Inc, 840 F 2d 236 (4th Cir 1988)]

The objective criteria applied by the Third and Fourth Circuits have been expanded upon by some circuits by the admission of extrinsic evidence to establish whether a general partner investor could exercise its power to, say, remove a managing general partner. [Ribstein and Keatinge on limited liability companies. See also Koch v Hankins (928 F2d 1471 (9th Cir 1991)) (question of fact whether partners could exercise control over the overall enterprise); Stone v Kirk, 8 F 3d 1079 (6th Cir 1993)] However, in Halden v. Hagopian [928 F 2d 1115 (9th Cir 1992)] the court, in applying *Koch*, did not find a security in the general partnership agreement and required a strong showing of lack of business expertise sufficient to use those powers.

Consequently, in member-managed LLCs, members may be able to invoke the *Williamson* analysis in persuading a court that their interest in the LLC is a security, especially when they have a small interest and are passive investors. However, promoters may be able to invoke the terms of the governing LLC statute, the Articles, and the Operating Agreement in defending an unwanted characterization that an LLC interest is a security, using the *Goodwin* and *Rivanna* reasoning. [See Lion, "Wrapping up LLCs: Two Frequent Questions," 4 *Bus Law Today*, ABA Section of Business Law, 63, 64 (Mar/Apr 1995)]

Conversely, a limited partnership interest usually is a security because a valid limited partnership agreement is structured so that limited partners cannot participate in management. Manager-managed LLCs are likely to be treated in the same way as to members' investments. Therefore, to avoid security treatment, careful structuring of the LLC and the Articles of Organization and the Operating Agreement becomes critical.

A few courts have directly addressed the issue of whether interests in LLCs are securities. LLC interests are securities when the interests are sold to numerous unsophisticated investors. [E.g., SEC v Parkersburg Wireless LLC, 991 F Supp 6 (DDC 1997)]

In an LLC in which management is centralized and the members have significant voting and veto powers, it has been held that such an interest is a security even if the investor had significant theoretical control power, but was unable realistically to use such power. [SEC v Aqua-Sonic Prods Corp, 687 F 2d 577 (2d Cir 1982), *cert den*, 459 US 1086 (1982)]

Parkersburg did not base its conclusion on the fact that Parkersburg was a "manager-managed" LLC. The courts applied the general partner tests to the interests even though a member in a manager-managed LLC does not have the same statutory management authority as does a member in a member-managed LLC. If this approach is followed by other courts, the substance of the relationship among the members rather than the labels "member-managed" or "manager-managed" will be the determinative factor in ruling whether interests are securities.

However, in *Keith v. Black Diamond Advisors, Inc.* [1999 WL 124454 (SDNY, March 8, 1999)], the plaintiff sued for violations of federal securities laws under Sections 10(b) and 29(b) of the Securities Exchange Act of 1934 (the "Exchange Act"), 15 U.S.C. §§ 78j(b) and 78cc(b), and Rule 10b-5 promulgated thereunder,

17 C.F.R. § 240.10b-5. The court held that whether the New York LLC interests were securities was determined by the control the members could exercise over the LLC. The New York Limited Liability Company Law grants members many powers. Their control was contrary to the passivity contemplated under the *Howey* test.

While the plaintiff urged the court to consider "economic realities," the court reviewed the legal structure of the investment. The plaintiff could have exercised control, and the decision whether an interest is a security is not based on the choice by a member to remain passive. Where the member has power to participate in management, the interest is not a security due to the lack of action by the investor.

Q 9:5   Do states follow the 1933 Act's definition of security?

In many states, yes, but the states follow four different approaches. Thus, the law of each state must be reviewed carefully. While states differ on how they classify LLC interests, there are generally four categories of treatment. The first category of states follows a Howey/Forman analysis. The second group is made up of states with a specific state statute classifying LLC interests as securities. The third group of states classify LLC interests as securities with an exception relating to member management. The final group is made up of a variety of states that may or may not directly address the issue by statute, but the analysis is based on something other than the Howey/Forman analysis.

The definition of security in the Uniform Securities Act [§ 101(16)] is virtually identical to the federal definition of stock. Except for the added language regarding limited partnership interests and various option securities, this section follows the 1956 Act provision. That provision in turn was substantially identical to § 2(1) of the Securities Act of 1933. The Uniform Act Committee determined to retain the essential parts of the existing definition because it has been broadly construed in federal and state courts and seems adequate generally to embrace most investment vehicles that the human mind can conceive. With respect to the specific, more traditional instruments included within the definition, for example, the courts have used a "plain meaning" approach; that is, does the particular instrument possess the usual characteristics associated with the instrument? If so, then the relevant securities act applies. [See, e.g., Landreth Timber Company v Landreth, 471 US 681 (1985)] For other specific instruments, the "unless the content otherwise requires" language may require a further inquiry. The burden, however, still will be on the person claiming that the instrument is not a security to establish either that such instrument does not possess the essential attributes or that it bears a strong family resemblance to those instruments not commonly understood as being securities (e.g., notes issued in truly mercantile transactions as opposed to notes issued to investors). [See Exchange National Bank of Chicago v Touche Ross & Co, 544 F 2d 1126 (2d Cir 1976), *op mod*, 746 F 2d 930 (2d Cir 1984), *cert den*, 469 US 884 (1984)]

The following states have adopted the Uniform Securities Act with 1988 amendments: Alabama, Code 1975 §§ 8-6-1 to 8-6-33; Alaska, As. 45.55.010 *et seq*.; Arkansas, A.C.A. §§ 23-42-101 to 23-42-508; Colorado, West C.R.S.A. §§ 11-51-101 to 11-51-908; Connecticut, C.G.S.A. §§ 36(b)-2 to 36(b)-33; Delaware, 6 Del. C. §§ 7301 to 7330; District of Columbia, D.C. Code 1981 §§ 2-2601 to 2-2618; Hawaii, H.R.S. §§ 485-1 to 485-25; Idaho, I.C. § 30-1401 *et seq*; Indiana, West A.I.C. 23-2-1-1 to 23-2-1-24; Iowa, I.C.A. §§ 502.101 to 502.614; Kansas, K.S.A. 17-1252 to 17-1275; Kentucky, K.R.S. 292.310 to 292.550, 292.991; Maine, 32 M.R.S.A. §§ 10101 to 10711; Maryland, Code Corporations and Associations, §§ 11-101 to 11-805; Massachusetts, M.G.L.A.C. 110A, §§ 101 to 417, Michigan, M.C.L.A. §§ 451.501 to 451.818; Minnesota, M.S.A. §§ 80A.01 to 80A.31; Mississippi, Code 1972, §§ 75-71-101 to 75-71-735; Missouri, A.M.S. §§ 409.101 to 409.418; Montana, M.C.A. 30-10-101 to 30-10-308; Nebraska, R.R.S. 1943, §§ 8-1101 to 8-1123; Nevada, N.R.S. 90.211 to 90.860; New Hampshire, R.S.A. 421-B:1 to 421-B:34; New Jersey, N.J.S.A. 49:3-47 to 49:3-76; New Mexico, N.M.S.A. 19798, §§ 55-13B-1 to 58-13B-57; North Carolina, G.S. §§ 78A-1 to 78A-65; Oklahoma, 71 Okl. St. Ann. §§ 1 to 16, 101 to 103, 201 to 204, 301 to 307, 401 to 413, 501, 502, 701 to 703; Oregon, O.R.S. 59.005 *et seq*.; Pennsylvania, 70 P.S. §§ 1-101 to 1-704; Puerto Rico, 10 L.P.R.A. §§ 851 to 895; Rhode Island, Gen. Laws 1956, §§ 7-11-101 to 7-11-806; South Carolina, Code 1976, §§ 35-1-10 to 35-1-1590; South Dakota, S.D.C.L. 47-31A-101 to 47-31A-420; Utah, U.C.A. 1953, 621-1-1 to 621-1-30; Vermont, 9 V.S.A.

§§ 4201 to 4241; Virginia, Code 1950, §§ 13.1-501 to 13.1-527.3; Washington, West R.C.W.A. 21.20.005 to 21.20.940; West Virginia, Code, 32-1-101 to 32-4-418; Wisconsin, W.S.A. 551.01 to 551.69; Wyoming, W.S. 1997, §§ 17-4-101 to 17-4-131.

States following the Howey/Forman analysis do not have specific statutory guidance on the issue. Instead, the courts have applied the Howey test in situations in determining whether the interests in question were securities. Conceivably, any state with no direct proclamation as to the status of LLC interests as securities could fall into this category by future judicial interpretation. The prevailing factor in these cases seems to be the ability to participate in or affect the day-to-day operations of the LLC.

In *People v. Riggle* [96 CA 1476 (Colo App 1998) (not selected for official publication)], the court considered whether interests in *Parkersburg* were "securities" for Colorado law purposes. If the interests in *Parkersburg* were securities, the court stated that a fact finder might find that (1) the number of members necessary to remove the manager would make removing the manager by members impractical, (2) the number of members would make management impractical, (3) the business in which the LLC was to engage was very specialized, and (4) the operating agreement stated that it was in the member's best interest to engage a manager. Based on the number of interests sold and the limited competence of the members to conduct wireless cable business, the court found that "there was sufficient evidence to establish that the membership interests being sold by defendant were investments (sic) contracts and, therefore, securities within the meaning of the pertinent statutes."

The Colorado court cited Williamson v Tucker, 645 F 2d 404 (5th Cir 1981) and other cases dealing with the characterization of general partnership interests as securities. In doing so, the court stated that a membership interest in a manager-managed LLC, in which the members had the ability to assume management by a majority vote, would be determined to be a security by looking less at the members' actual exercise of management than at the following factors: (1) whether the members have contracted away their control, (2) whether the member is so inexperienced that he or she is incapable of exercising managerial powers, or (3) whether the member is so dependent on some unique entrepreneurial or managerial ability of the manager that, realistically, that manager cannot be replaced and the members cannot exercise meaningful managerial powers. The opinion suggests that if a member could exercise management rights and was not restricted by the items listed above, but chooses not to, the interest would not be a security.

In *Nutek Information Systems, Inc. v. Arizona Corporation Commission* [281 Ariz Adv Rep 34, 1998 WL 767176 (Ariz App Div 1, 1998)], the Arizona Court of Appeals ruled that membership interests in member-managed Texas limited liability companies ("LLCs") involved in telecommunications would be treated as securities under the Arizona securities law. Interests in LLCs were not specifically included in the statutory definition of securities under the Arizona Securities Act, so the court analyzed whether the interests were "investment contracts." The court applied the *Williamson* test, stating that the plaintiff arguing that a general partnership interest (or an interest in an LLC) is a security "has a difficult burden to overcome."

Nevertheless, the court found that members in the LLC did not have control for several reasons. First, management agreements between the LLC and a promoter, in place before investors became members, gave the management functions to a third party. Second, the members were large in number and geographically dispersed. Third, the investors did not have the technical expertise to manage the LLC. They had to rely on others to run the LLC's business.

The Arizona Corporation Commission ("Commission") and the court ruled that the investors could not exercise effective management because they lacked telecommunications expertise. While noting a split in authority, the court determined that the investors' technical skill should be measured by reference to the specific business of the LLC, citing *Williamson* that the general partner's knowledge and experience be measured. The court observed that members of LLCs do not have individual liability for the obligations of the LLC. Therefore, they have less incentive to be as involved as does a general partner who has personal liability for the partnership obligations it reasoned. The court would not extend the "strong presumption" that partnership interests are not securities (under *Rivanna Trawlers*) to LLC interests.

The Arizona court, as in *Parkersburg*, found that the larger number and geographic diversity of the members made it difficult to participate in the management of the business. The court's discussion of expertise and the differences between LLCs and partnerships may be *dicta*. But logically the court's holdings in these areas would mean that closely held enterprises are securities even if members actively participate because the investors are not expert in the business, or elect to operate in a limited liability form.

Sometimes the state will have a case directly on point stating that the state will approach this issue under the Howey/Forman analysis. [See Activator Supply Co. v. Wurth, 722 P.2d 1081 (Kan. 1986)] Some states have statutes that leave the question open for the Howey/Forman analysis to examine.

Georgia. Statute provides that: "Nothing in this chapter shall be construed as establishing that a limited liability company interest is not a security." [Ga Code Ann § 14-11-1107(n)]

The second category of states have taken specific action to address LLCs under their securities laws. A number of state statutes expressly address whether LLC interests are securities. The following states are examples of the specific treatment of LLCs as securities.

Alaska. Security means . . . a limited liability company interest. [Alaska Stat § 45.55.130(12)]

New Mexico. Unless the context requires otherwise, security means . . . any interest in a limited liability company. . . . [NM Stat Ann § 58-13B-2(v)]

Ohio. It is flatly stated that a "security means any . . . membership interest in a limited liability company. . . ." [Ohio Rev Code Ann § 1707.01(D)]

Vermont. States that security includes . . . any membership interest in a limited liability company. . . . [Vt Stat Ann tit 9 § 4202a(14)]

The third category treats the LLC interests as securities unless the taxpayer can otherwise show management participation. Some states require all members to manage the LLC in order to avoid treatment of the interests as securities.

California. Security means any . . . interest in a limited liability company and any class or series of such interests (including any fractional or other interest in such interest), except a membership interest in a limited liability company in which the person claiming this exception can prove that all of the members are actively engaged in the management of the limited liability company; provided that evidence that members vote or have the right to vote or the right to information concerning the business and affairs of the limited liability company, or the right to participate in management, shall not establish without more, that all members are actively engaged in the management of the limited liability company. [Cal Corp Code § 25019]

Indiana. "Security means an interest in a limited liability company and any class or series of an interest in a limited liability company (including any fractional or other interest in an interest in a limited liability company). . . . Security does not include . . . an interest in a limited liability company if the person claiming that the interest is not a security can prove that all of the members of the limited liability company are actively engaged in the management of the limited liability company." [Ind Code Ann § 23-2-1-1(k)]

Iowa. An LLC is a security unless the person claiming it is not a security can prove that all of the members are actively engaged in management. [Iowa Code § 502.102.14]

Other states require some member management to avoid security classification, but are unclear as to how much.

Nebraska. A security expressly includes LLC interests unless the member enters into a written commitment to be engaged actively and directly in the management of the LLC, and members of the LLC are actively engaged in the management (although it is unclear whether all members must enter into written commitments to actively manage). [Neb Rev Stat § 8-1101(13)]

Some states will analyze the interest not only by the corporation, but by the purchaser.

Pennsylvania. Statute takes the approach of federal case law. Pennsylvania provides: "a security means any . . . membership interest in a limited liability company of any class or series, including any fractional or other interest in such interest unless extended by clause (v) . . . security does not include . . . (v) a membership interest in a limited liability company where all of the following conditions are satisfied: (A) the membership interest is in a company that is not managed by managers; (B) the purchaser of the membership interest enters into a written commitment to be engaged actively and directly in the management of the company; and (C) the purchaser of the membership interest, in fact, does participate actively and directly in the management of the company." [Pa Stat Ann tit 70, § 1-102(t)]

The final category consists of states that address the issue, directly or indirectly, by a method different from those listed above. Some states are ambiguous in that there are statutes on the issue, but the ultimate result is most likely a Howey/Forman analysis.

Michigan. An interest in a limited liability company is a security to the same extent as an interest in a corporation, partnership, or limited partnership is a security. [Mich Comp Laws Ann § 450.5103]

Other states create a rebuttable presumption.

Missouri. The rebuttable presumption is that an LLC interest is not a security if management is not vested in one or more managers. [Mo Ann Stat § 347.185]

Some states consider the interests as securities unless the LLC can fall under an exception

Utah. An LLC interest is a security unless the LLC: (1) qualifies as a family LLC; (2) has five members or less; or (3) individual claiming exception can prove that all members are active in management. [Utah Code Ann § 61-1-13]

Wisconsin. States that a security is presumed to include an interest in a limited liability company (organized under Wisconsin law) if the right to manage the limited liability company is vested in one or more managers or if the aggregate number of lenders of the limited liability company after the interest is sold exceeds 35. Securities not presumed to include an interest in a limited liability company (organized under Wisconsin law) if the aggregate number of members of the limited liability company, after the interest is sold, does not exceed a designated number of members and the right to manage the limited liability company is vested in its members. [Wis Stat Ann § 551.02(13)(c)]

[See MA Sargent and A Ghais, "Securities Law Development: State Treatment of LLC Interests as Securities," 2 J *Limited Liability Com-*

panies 184 (Spring 1996) [Note that this article contains charts which show the treatment of LLC interests under state securities laws. An up-to-date version of these charts exists on the Internet via the Blue Sky Law Home Page, http://www.law.ab.umd.edu/marshall/bluesky; Welle, "Limited Liability Company Interests as Securities: An Analysis of Federal and State Actions Against Limited Liability Companies Under the Securities Laws," 73 *Denv U L Rev* 425, 495-505 (1996)]

Q 9:6   Who is an underwriter under the securities laws?

Section 1(11) of the 1933 Act defines an underwriter as follows:

> The term "underwriter" means any person who has purchased from an issuer with a view to, or offers or sells for an issuer in connection with, the distribution of any security, or participates or has a direct or indirect participation in any such undertaking, or participates or has a participation in the direct or indirect underwriting of any such undertaking; but such term shall not include a person whose interest is limited to a commission from an underwriter or dealer not in excess of the usual and customary distributors' or sellers' commission. As used in this paragraph the term "issuer" shall include, in addition to an issuer, any person directly or indirectly controlling or controlled by the issuer, or any person under direct or indirect common control with the issuer.

In this context the LLC (and perhaps current members) would be an "issuer"; the issuer is not normally itself an underwriter. While investment banks are typically underwriters of securities, a manager or other promoter may be considered an underwriter as well, at least if he or she is in the trade or business of selling interests in new enterprises.

The Uniform Securities Act, used as a guide for state laws, does not contain a definition of "underwriter."

Q 9:7   What is Rule 144?

U.S. Securities and Exchange Commission (SEC) Rule 144 entitled "[p]ersons deemed not to be engaged in a distribution and therefore not underwriters" provides a safe harbor. Those persons who satisfy the conditions of the rule are not underwriters. [17

CFR § 230.144 as amended 61 FR 21356-59 (1996) and 62 FR 9242-70 (1997)] Rule 144 generally applies to persons, like members, who received the securities being sold directly from the issuer in a private placement transaction in which the interests were exempt from registrations. Rule 144 is designed to allow those persons to sell their securities to third persons but avoid being classified as an underwriter under the 1933 Act. As a result, they can sell securities owned by them to third parties without registering the securities. [SEC Rule 144(b)] Rule 144 may apply if:

1. There is adequate current public information about the issuer at the time the securities are being sold. This requires an LLC to issue extensive reports similar to those required under the Securities and Exchange Act of 1934 (1934 Act). [SEC Rule 144(c)] Consequently, many LLCs are not able, nor desire, to take advantage of this rule.

2. The LLC interests sold under Rule 144 are restricted securities, and they have been held by the seller for a minimum of one year. [SEC Rule 144(d) as amended 62 FR 9242-70 (1997)]

3. Interests in the LLC sold during the preceding three-month period have been fewer than, generally, the greater of: (a) 1 percent of the class of securities outstanding, or (b) the average weekly trading volume of the class of securities during the preceding four weeks. [SEC Rule 144(e)] as amended 62 FR 9242-70 (1997)]

4. The LLC interests are sold through broker transactions or directly to a market maker. [SEC Rule 144(f)]

5. The seller files a notice on Form 144 about the proposed sale with the SEC. [SEC Rule 144(h)]

Because of the extensive requirements, it is unlikely that many LLCs, or holders of LLC interests, will attempt to sell their interests in the LLC under Rule 144.

Q 9:8   What is the significance of being deemed an underwriter?

If the seller of the securities is an underwriter of the securities, the securities must be registered before the underwriter can sell those securities to third parties. [1933 Act § 77d(1)] To avoid underwriter status, it must be established that the person who wants to sell unregistered securities did not purchase those securities from the issuer for the purpose of distributing them to the public. It must also be established that the seller is not: (1) offering or selling the securities for the issuer; (2) directly or indirectly assisting anyone else to sell the issuer's unregistered securities to the public; or (3) participating, directly or indirectly, in the underwriting of an undertaking by the issuer to sell unregistered securities to the public. [1933 Act §§ 77d(3)(A)-(C)]

Q 9:9 When will members want to characterize their interest in the LLC as a security?

Passive investor LLC members may attempt to characterize their interest as a security if the LLC fails and the investors lose some or all of their investment. If the LLC interest is a security, and the LLC interests are not registered or exempt from registration, the holder of the interest may be entitled to rescind the investment and obtain a return of the funds paid for the LLC interest, plus interest. In addition, unless the LLC offering was wholly intrastate, the federal securities laws may apply, and investors will have the right to sue in federal court.

Further, even if properly registered or exempt from registration, federal and state securities laws, as well as the common law, may impose anti-fraud liability upon persons involved in the offering. Promoters may be personally liable for such conduct if the offering documents or any oral statements in connection with the offer or sale of interest in the LLC contain material omissions or misrepresentations of fact. [See Sargent, "Are LLC Interests Securities?," 1 *J Limited Liability Companies* 34, 35 (Summer 1994).] As a practical matter, therefore, a private placement memorandum disclosing material facts is often prepared to rebut later claims by dissatisfied investors that they were misled about the risks of their investment.

Q 9:10 What is the effect of state blue sky securities laws on the issuance of interests in an LLC?

Even if an LLC interest is not a security or is exempt from registration under federal securities laws, the law of each state where an LLC interest will be sold must be considered in determining whether the LLC interest is a security and, whether registration is required. Because most LLC statutes have only recently been enacted, many states have not yet amended their securities laws to address the issuance of LLC interests, especially in the context of limited offering exemptions (see Qs 9:5 and 9:16). However, it should be expected that such interests will be treated like stock in a corporation or like partnership interests.

Q 9:11   When does the organizer of an LLC need to register the interest in the LLC with federal or state securities regulatory authorities?

Unless an exemption applies, all LLC interests that constitute securities must be registered before they may be offered or sold. If no exemption applies, the issuer must register the LLC interests under the federal and state securities laws where the LLC interests will be offered. A number of limited-offering exemptions, however, should apply with respect to most LLC offerings (see Q 9:12). These rules provide an exemption not for the securities themselves but only for the transactions by which such securities are sold or offered for sale.

Q 9:12   What common exemptions for registration of securities apply to LLCs?

Section 4(2) of the Securities Act of 1933 provides a general exempting from registration for "transactions by an issuer not involving any public offering." Sales to sophisticated investors with access to company information who can fend for themselves are exempt. As the number of security owners increases and their relationship to management becomes more remote, it becomes more difficult to prove compliance with this statutory exemption.

Section 3(a)(11) of the 1933 Act also exempts from federal registration any security offered and sold only to those persons who reside within a single state or territory, when the issuer is a resident of, and doing business in, that state. [See also SEC Rule 147, 17 CFR § 230.147 (1996).]

Regulation D [SEC Rules 501-508; 17 CFR §§ 230.501-508 (1996)] provides a number of different exemptions so that an LLC will not have to register interests in the LLC before offering and selling those interests. Rule 504 exempts offerings of less than $1 million; Rule 505 applies to offerings for less than $5 million with 35 or fewer non- accredited investors, plus an unlimited number of accredited investors. Rule 506 exempts transactions by an issuer that do not involve a public offering. Regulation D applies only if there is no advertising or public solicitation in connection with the transaction as to Rules 505 and 506. Rule 504 offerings of up to $1 million in a 12-month period may use general solicitation and advertising.

Form D must be filed with the SEC within 15 days after the first sale subject to Rule 504, 505, or 506. No federal filing fee is required.

Q 9:13 Who is considered an accredited investor?

The following are classified as accredited investors under Rule 501(a):

1. Any bank or savings and loan, whether acting in its individual capacity or as a fiduciary (e.g., for a trust); any broker dealer registered under the 1934 Act; any insurance company; any investment company or business development company registered as defined under the Investment Company Act of 1940; any small business investment company licensed by the Small Business Administration; any governmental employee benefit plan with at least $5 million in assets; any ERISA employee benefit plan, provided the investment decision is made by a plan fiduciary—that is, a bank, savings and loan, insurance company, or registered investment adviser—if the ERISA plan has more than $5 million in assets or is a self-directed plan in which the investment decisions are made solely by accredited investors.

2. Any private business development company as defined in Section 202(a)(22) of the Investment Advisers Act of 1940.

3. Any organization described in Code Section 501(c)(3), corporation, business trust, or partnership, not formed for the specific purpose of acquiring the securities offered, with more than $5 million in total assets.

4. Any director, executive director, or general partner in the issuer of the securities being offered or sold, or any director, executive officer, or general partner of that issuer.

5. Any natural person whose individual net worth, or joint net worth with that person's spouse, at the time of the purchase, exceeds $1 million.

6. Any natural person who had an individual income in excess of $200,000 in each of the two most recent prior years, or joint income with that person's spouse in excess of $300,000 in each of those two years, if that person also has a reasonable expectation of reaching the same income level in the current year.

7. Any trust, with total assets in excess of $5 million, not formed for the specific purpose of acquiring the securities offered, whose purchase is directed by a sophisticated person as described in Rule 506.

8. Any entity in which all of the equity owners are accredited investors.

An issuer must be able to prove that an investor was an accredited investor at the time of sale, by obtaining documentation or by otherwise reasonably believing that the investor is accredited, after inquiry. [SEC Release No 6389]

Q 9:14   What is the SEC's small business initiative?

The Small Business Investment Incentive Act of 1980 may be beneficial to LLCs. The small business initiative led to the development of Regulation D by the SEC in 1982. Regulation D coordinates the following limited-offering exemptions that apply to the offering and sale of securities, including interests in LLCs classified as securities:

Rule 504. All offerings of less than $1 million in any 12-month period are exempt from registration under the 1933 Act. As a result, all offerings of securities for less than $1 million are subject only to the relevant state securities laws. The exemption, however, does not apply to a "development stage" company that does not have a specific business plan or acquisition target; nor does it apply to an investment company, or a company subject to the 1934 Act's reporting requirements. As stated previously, all Regulation D offerings must not involve advertising or public solicitation, and investors must agree not to resell the securities.

Regulation A. Regulation A exempts registration of up to $5 million worth of certain securities offered in any 12-month period. Regulation A also allows certain pre-registration activity to gauge investor interest after a Form A-1 offering statement has been filed with the SEC and before incurring the expense of preparing the offering materials that must be filed, even though the securities are exempt from registration. No sale of securities under Regulation A can occur until a Form A-1 offering statement has been qualified and a final Offering Circular is delivered.

Form SB-2 and Regulation S-B. These provide for less-complex disclosure and simpler registration procedures for the offering and sale of securities by U.S. and Canadian issuers with less than $25 million of revenues in the preceding fiscal year and less than $25 million of securities already issued to the public.

Trust Indenture Act Regulations. Debt securities sold to the public generally must comply with the provisions of the Trust Indenture Act of 1939. Under that statute, issuers of debt instruments sold to the public must have an independent trustee to protect the interests of investors in the debt instruments, and there must be an indenture. The SEC, however, exempts debt offerings of less than $5 million from having to have an indenture, and a qualified indenture is not required for offerings up to $10 million.

Q 9:15   What is Rule 701?

SEC Rule 701 [17 CFR § 230.701 (1996)] exempts from registration securities issued by non-publicly-traded companies to employees, directors, officers, and consultants in exchange for bona fide services under a written compensatory plan or contract, including stock options. The amount of interests that may be issued is limited, and a notice must be filed with the SEC. [SEC Rule 702, 17 CFR § 230.702 (1996)]

Q 9:16   Are there also state exemptions to the registration of securities?

Yes. Many states have adopted the Uniform Limited Offering Exemption, which mirrors and provides for simultaneous compliance with Rules 505 and 506 under SEC Regulation D. [See, e.g., Kan Admin Regs § 81-5-6; Mo Code Regs tit 15, 30-54.210.]

In addition, many states also have their own statutory exemptions. For example, **Kansas** and **Missouri** have an isolated-transaction exemption. Kansas exempts from registration up to five sales of a security by an issuer or non-issuer during any 12-month period. [Kan Stat Ann § 17-1261(a); Kan Admin Regs § 81-5-3] Missouri has a single transaction exemption that applies only to issuers. [Mo Rev Stat § 409.402(b)(1)]

Kansas and Missouri also have limited-offering exemptions, similar to the law of many states. A Kansas issuer may issue securities to up to 20 investors in any 12-month period, without registration. [Kan Stat Ann § 17-1262(l)] Sales under the isolated-transaction exemption are counted toward the limited-offering exemption. [Kan Admin Regs § 81-5-3(e)] Kansas specifically provides that sales of LLC interests classified as securities may be included under these exemptions. [Kan Stat Ann § 17-1262(m)] Missouri's limited-offering exemption is broader than the Kansas exemption. In Missouri, issuers may issue securities to up to 25 persons regardless of their residence. [Mo Rev Stat § 409.402(b)(9); Mo Code Regs tit 15, 30-54.130] Missouri also has a separate exemption that applies to the sale of securities to up to 15 Missouri residents in a 12-month period. [Mo Rev Stat § 409.402(b)(10); Mo Code Regs tit 15, 30-54.140]

The examples provided above are only a few of the provisions of state securities laws that may exempt the registration of LLC interests that are considered securities.

Q 9:17   Do the 1933 and 1934 Acts and state securities laws apply to an LLC interest if the interest is exempt from registration?

If LLC interests are securities, the offer and sale of those securities are subject to the anti-fraud provisions of the 1933 Act and 1934 Act, and similar state statutes, even if they are exempt from registration. [1933 Act §§ 12(2), 17(a); 15 USC §§ 77l(2), 77q(a); 1934 Act § 10(b); 15 USC § 78j(b)] There are similar provisions under state securities laws.

LLC interests that are not required to be registered under the 1934 Act will not be subject to the proxy Section 14 of the 1934 Act [15 USC § 78N] or short-swing trading rules, Section 16(b) of the 1934 Act. [15 USC § 78P] Registration is required for companies that are listed on an exchange or have total assets exceeding $1 million and equity securities held by more than 750 people. [1933 Act § 12(a), (g); 15 USC § 78L(a), (g)]

Q 9:18   Will the SEC or state securities commissioners provide guidance on whether an interest in an LLC is a security or not?

Perhaps. The SEC and most state securities commissioners have procedures established to obtain private "no-action" letters to provide guidance on various matters under their respective securities laws. However no SEC no-action letters are known that address LLC interests in any way.

The **Kansas** Securities Commissioner, however, ruled that LLC interests were not securities, when the issuing LLC was organized to operate an independent practice association (IPA) among physicians. The Kansas Securities Commissioner reached that conclusion because each of the participating physicians would be actively involved in managing and operating the IPA, and would earn income through the IPA commensurate with the services provided by them to IPA patients.

Q 9:19   Can an LLC go public?

Yes. The IRC classifies a publicly traded LLC as a publicly traded partnership, in which case the LLC is taxed as a corporation, not a partnership. [IRC § 7704] A publicly traded partnership is a partnership whose interests are traded on an established securities market, or are readily tradeable on a secondary market (or the substantial equivalent). [IRC § 7704(b)] In addition, an LLC that has more than 500 members could also be classified as a corporation for tax purposes. [IRS Notice 88-75, 1988-2 CB 386]

Q 9:20   What are the tax consequences of being considered publicly traded for tax purposes?

As of the first day an LLC is publicly traded and treated as a corporation under Code Section 7704, the LLC will be treated as if the LLC contributed all of its assets (subject to liabilities) to a corporation in exchange for the stock in the corporation, and the stock is distributed to the members in liquidation of the LLC. [IRC § 7704(f)] The LLC may also have to use the accrual method of tax accounting if and when it is taxed as a corporation on account of becoming a publicly traded partnership. [IRC § 448]

Bankruptcy Laws

Q 9:21 May an LLC apply for protection from creditors under the U.S. Bankruptcy Code?

Probably yes. Only an entity that is a "debtor" may file a petition for protection under the U.S. Bankruptcy Code. [11 USC § 101 *et. seq.*] Only a "person" may be a debtor. [11 USC §§ 301, 303] Most commentators believe that an LLC is a person under the Bankruptcy Code, because the statute defines person to include an individual, partnership, and a corporation, and the use of the word "includes" evidences an intent not to limit the statutory definition of person to the forms of business entities listed. [11 USC §§ 101(41), 102(3); see also Kornberg, Schorr, Antonoff, "Treatment of LLCs Under Chapter 11 of the Bankruptcy Code," 1 *J Limited Liability Companies* 17 (Summer 1994)]

Q 9:22 Which chapters of the Bankruptcy Code apply to LLCs?

Assuming an LLC can be a debtor under the Bankruptcy Code, an LLC is eligible to file a Chapter 7 bankruptcy (liquidation) and a Chapter 11 bankruptcy (reorganization).

Q 9:23 Is an LLC treated like a partnership or corporation under the Bankruptcy Code?

The Bankruptcy Code treats partnerships and corporations differently. [See, e.g., 11 USC §§ 502(a), 508(b), 723.] The Bankruptcy Code does not define partnership for these purposes, but does define a corporation to include a partnership organized under a law that makes only the capital subscribed responsible for the debts of that association. [11 USC §§ 101, 101(9)(A)(ii)] Most LLCs should fit within this definition, except when the LLC forfeits its limited liability under state law (e.g., by failing to use its proper name, including its designation as an LLC) or under the limited circumstances when the members of an LLC have agreed to be fully liable for the LLC's debts and liabilities. [See, e.g., Del Code Ann tit 6, § 18-303(b) (which specifically contemplates a member personally assuming the LLC's liabilities)]

Nevertheless, many LLC interests of members who are not managers are also much like a limited partnership, especially manager-managed LLCs, and the Bankruptcy Code explicitly excludes a limited partnership from the definition of a corporation. [11 USC § 101(9)(B)] Limited partnerships may, like corporations, file for bankruptcy or reorganization.

If treated as a corporation, the LLC should not be subject to the rule that holds general partners personally liable for the debtor's liabilities. [11 USC § 723]

If regarded as a partnership, LLC members may be liable for contribution obligations. [11 USC § 723]

Furthermore, the Uniform Partnership Act, which applies in the absence of any definition in the Bankruptcy Code, excludes from the definition of "partnership" companies "formed under any other statute." [UPA § 6(2)] Also under UPA Section 6(1) and RUPA Section 101(4), a partnership must have at least two members. However, designating LLCs as corporations is not without uncertainty. Their close resemblance to limited partnerships may exclude them from corporate treatment under the bankruptcy code.

Further, a one-member LLC may not be either an individual, partnership, or corporation, and so may not be a "person" [11 USC § 101(41)] eligible for relief in bankruptcy. [11 USC § 109(b), (d), or (f)] [See Blakemore, "Limited Liability Companies and the Bankruptcy Code: A Technical Review," *Am Bankr Inst J* 12 (June 1994)]

Q 9:24 What effect has the new check-the-box regulation had upon this treatment?

Under the check-the-box regulations, all domestic eligible entities having two or more members are considered a partnership, without the necessity of election or other action, unless the entity affirms to elect to be treated as a corporation. [26 CFR § 301.7701-3(b)(1)(i)] Member domestic eligible organizations will be "invisible" for tax purposes. [26 CFR § 301.7701-3(b)(1)(ii)] An eligible entity will be treated as a partnership (if it has two or more owners) or will be disregarded (if it has one owner) under the new regulations unless in either case it elects to be treated as a corporation. An eligible entity is any business entity other than those set out in regulation. [26 CFR §§ 301.7701-2(b)(3) thru 301.7701-2(b)(6)]

Under the check-the-box tax classification rule, an LLC and other unincorporated firms have partnership tax treatment even if they have corporate features. To the extent that LLCs currently are distinguishable from corporations and are treated like partnerships for securities and bankruptcy purposes, changing LLC statutes to adopt more corporate-like features may change this treatment. In particular, adopting corporate-like centralized management, either by statute or customized agreements, undercuts the argument for treating LLCs as nonsecurities under federal and state law and for treating LLC members like partners rather than employees. Also, free transfer of interests may make LLC interests look more like securities. To the extent that check-the-box leads to changes in statutory default rules, this may weaken the argument for presuming that LLCs are partnerships for security purposes. According, any such statute and contractual change should be approached with caution and full appreciation of the regulatory implications of such changes.

Q 9:25   Who has the authority to file a bankruptcy petition on behalf of an LLC?

There is no clear answer to this question. The LLC's Operating Agreement should contain a specific grant of authority to either the managers or members (including the number of members who must consent) to file a bankruptcy petition. In the absence of specific authority in the Operating Agreement or Articles, the answer will depend upon whether the LLC is manager-managed or member-managed.

A bankruptcy court might conclude that a member-managed LLC requires the consent of all members before a voluntary petition is filed on behalf of the LLC, which is the general rule for partnerships, even though the LLC is otherwise treated as a corporation. [See Bankruptcy Rule 1004(a).]

However, if it is treated like a general partnership, a petition approved by less than all the partners is treated as an involuntary proceeding. [11 USC § 303(b)(3)] It is also not clear whether, in a member-managed LLC, the court will apply a majority-vote provision in the applicable statute or will instead assume that unanimity is required to enter bankruptcy by analogy to dissolution by member vote. In *In re DeLuca* [(JTB Enterprises LC v D&B Venture LC) 194 BR 79 (Bankr ED Va 1996)], it was held that the decision to file a bankruptcy was a major decision requiring a member vote. The court had held in an earlier action arising out of the same bankruptcy that a bankrupt member lacked authority to file a Chapter 11 bankruptcy on behalf of the LLC. [In re DeLuca (Broyhill v DeLuca), 194 BR 65 (Bankr ED Va 1996)] In the case of *In re Phillips* [966 F 2d 926 (5th Cir 1992)] it was held that a bankrupt general partner who was winding up a limited partnership lacked authority to file a Chapter 11 petition on behalf of the limited partnership. [See Blakemore, "Limited Liability Companies and the Bankruptcy Code: A Technical Review," *Am Bankr Inst J* 12 (Jun 1994).]

In a manager-managed LLC, the managers should have the authority to file a bankruptcy petition, even in the absence of a specific grant of this authority in the Articles or Operating Agreement. [Uniform Act §§ 301(b), (c); Prototype Act § 301] Nevertheless, filing a bankruptcy petition may be an act outside the usual conduct of the LLC's business. Consequently, without explicit authority in the Articles or Operating Agreement, the manager's filing of a bankruptcy petition for the LLC may not be effective.

The answer to the question of who has authority to authorize a bankruptcy filing may affect how creditors proceed against the LLC. For example, upon the filing of a bankruptcy petition, the Bankruptcy Code places an automatic stay on most proceedings against a debtor and the debtor's property. [11 USC § 362(b)] If a creditor ignores the filing and continues to proceed against the LLC based upon a belief that the bankruptcy was unauthorized, the creditor risks violating the automatic stay. A creditor may be subject to money damages, including punitive damages, and the equitable subordination of its claims against the LLC, if it violates the automatic stay. [In re Zartun, 30 BR 543 (Bankr 9th Cir 1983); In re Jacobs, 100 BR 357 (Bankr D Ohio 1989)]

Q 9:26   May an LLC be forced into bankruptcy?

Yes. An involuntary bankruptcy case can be initiated under a variety of conditions. If creditors assert that the debtor LLC is not paying its debts they can force the LLC into involuntary bankruptcy. At least three creditors with debts totaling $5,000 or more must join in the petition. However, if the debtor has fewer than 12 creditors, one or more may file the petition as long as the claim(s) total at least $10,000. Members of the LLC are not creditors just because they hold an interest in the LLC. In addition, an involuntary bankruptcy petition may be filed by fewer than all the members without consent of the remaining members. If an involuntary case is opposed by the entity, a hearing will be held and the petitioner must prove that the debtor is not paying its disputed debts when due.

Q 9:27   What should a creditor do to determine if a member or manager has the authority to file a bankruptcy petition?

If a creditor prefers to pursue its claims against an LLC outside bankruptcy rules, a creditor who believes that the person who filed the bankruptcy petition did not have the authority to do so should seek to dismiss the petition under the Bankruptcy Code. [11 USC § 1112; Kornberg at 19 (Q 9:21)] This may be the only prudent way to ensure that individual actions by creditors against an LLC will not violate the Bankruptcy Code's automatic stay.

Q 9:28   Can an LLC continue to conduct business after a Chapter 11 bankruptcy filing?

Probably. If an LLC can file a Chapter 11 petition to reorganize, an LLC can thereafter continue to conduct business as a debtor in possession, subject to the supervision of the bankruptcy court. [11 USC §§ 1104(a), 1107, 1108]

Q 9:29   Does an LLC owe a fiduciary duty to creditors?

When an entity becomes insolvent, its fiduciary duty to owners is extended to creditors and employees by federal bankruptcy law. [Kornberg at 21 (Q 9:21); Commodity Futures Trading Commr v

Weintraub, 471 US 343 (1985); In re Albion Disposal, Inc, 152 Bankr 794, 816 (Bankr DNY 1993)] Thus, while an LLC is operating as a debtor in possession, the LLC has a duty to maximize the value of the LLC's business and assets for members, creditors, employees, and others. Consequently, the operations of the LLC as a debtor in possession are subject to the bankruptcy court's supervision, and the LLC must submit periodic reports of operations, income, and expenses to the court. [11 USC § 704(8)]

Q 9:30 Is a member's property part of an LLC's bankruptcy estate?

No. The property of an LLC is separate and distinct from the property of each member. [Uniform Act §§ 207, 208; Prototype Act § 501] Thus, a member's property should not be part of the LLC's bankruptcy estate. Likewise, creditors generally will not be subject to the automatic stay against the property of individual members who have not filed personal bankruptcy. At least one court has, however, applied 11 U.S.C. § 105, to enjoin a suit against a general partner. The court indicated this action was appropriate in order to permit the partners to focus their energies and attention on the partnership reorganization, without having the distraction of the creditors collection efforts. *Litchfield Co. v. Anchor Bank,* 135 N. G. 797 (W.D.N.C. 1992). Also, unless members have personally guaranteed the LLC's debts, they have received impermissible distributions, or they have not made all mandatory capital contributions, they should not be subject to personal liability to the LLC's creditors. [Uniform Act § 304]

Q 9:31 May an LLC use its property to conduct business after the filing of bankruptcy?

If the LLC is a debtor in possession, the LLC may use its assets in the ordinary course of business, subject to the general supervision of the court and the business-judgment rule. [11 USC § 363(b)(1); In re Integrated Resources, Inc, 147 Bankr 650 (Bankr DNY 1992)] This rule does not apply to cash and cash equivalents that have been pledged as specific security to a secured creditor, unless the court or creditor consents. [11 USC § 363(c)(2)]

Q 9:32   May an LLC sell assets outside of the ordinary course of business while in bankruptcy?

Yes, but only if approved by the bankruptcy court. The court generally will approve the sale, if the LLC establishes a good reason for the transaction. [In re Lionel Corp, 722 F 2d 1063 (2d Cir 1983); In re Coughlin, 27 BR 632 (Bankr 1st Cir 1983)] However, a sale of all of the LLC's assets will be subject to extra scrutiny. [In re Chateaugay Corp, 973 F 2d 141 (2d Cir 1992); In re Thomson McKinnon Secs, Inc, 120 BR 301 (Bankr DNY 1990)]

Q 9:33   Who is an insider of an LLC under the Bankruptcy Code?

Officers and directors of a corporation, and general partners of a partnership, are classified as insiders under the Bankruptcy Code. [11 USC § 101(3)(A)] It is not clear whether members or managers of an LLC would be considered insiders. Members likely would be considered insiders in a member-managed LLC, and managers probably are the only insiders in manager-managed LLCs.

Q 9:34   Does the bankruptcy of an LLC cause a dissolution of the LLC under state law?

Probably not, although this is not a settled issue. By analogy to partnerships, at least one case held that the bankruptcy of a partnership did not result in the termination of that partnership under state law. [In re Safren, 65 BR 566 (Bankr D Cal 1986)] Furthermore, an LLC which has been dissolved by operation of state law is not eligible for chapter 11 reorganization. [C-TC 9th Avenue Partnership, 113 F 3d 1304 (2d Cir 1997)]

Q 9:35   What are the consequences to the LLC's other members of the bankruptcy of a member?

Generally, the first stated consequence is the dissolution of the LLC under state law and the LLC's Articles or Operating Agreement. All LLC statutes provide that an LLC dissolves upon the bankruptcy of a member, unless the remaining members consent (with unanimous consent required in some states or by agreement) to the continuation of the LLC. [Uniform Act § 801; Prototype Act

§ 901] The requirement of dissolution under the relevant statute and LLC documents is critical in finding that the LLC does not have continuity of life for tax purposes (see chapter 3).

Bankruptcy of a Member

Q 9:36 Are the dissolution provisions in the LLC's Articles and Operating Agreement enforceable upon the bankruptcy of a member?

Despite the state law provisions that mandate the dissolution of an LLC upon bankruptcy of a member, many bankruptcy courts have refused to enforce similar provisions under partnership agreements and the UPA. These courts have concluded that the dissolution provisions are *ipso facto* clauses, that is, contract or statutory terms designed to terminate or modify a contract when one of the parties to the contract files bankruptcy. [In re Safren, 65 BR 566 (Bankr D Cal 1986); In re Rittenhouse Carpet, Inc, 56 BR 131 (Bankr D Pa 1985); In re Minton Group, Inc, 27 BR 385 (Bankr DNY 1983) *affd* 46 BR 222 (Bankr D NY 1985)] *Ipso facto* clauses are against public policy and are invalid under the Bankruptcy Code. [11 USC §§ 365(b)(2), 365(e)(1), 541(c)(1), 1124(2)(A)]

A Nebraska bankruptcy court has held that a bankruptcy filing of an LLC member does not automatically dissolve the LLC or terminate the debtor-member's membership interest in the LLC. [In re Dougherty Construction, Inc, 188 BR 607, 609 (Bankr D Neb 1995)] A Virginia Bankruptcy court cited *Dougherty*, but declined to follow that ruling. [In re Deluca, 194 BR 79 (Bankr ED Va. 1996)] In that case the court held that the operating agreement which gave control to the Deluca's was dissolved as a result of the Deluca's Chapter 11 filing.

Q 9:37 Should payment of an LLC's liabilities by a member guarantor be treated as cancellation of debt or as a contribution to capital?

This will be treated as a contribution to capital. Often due to necessity, an LLC member's guarantee will be required in order for the LLC to acquired the requisite financing needed by LLC. In a private letter ruling, the Service indicated that, in a partnership, this payment would be treated as a contribution to capital. [Ltr Rul. 199921008] The letter ruling indicated that the initial guarantee of the loan would result in an increase in the basis in that partner's partnership interest, due to an increased share of the responsibility for the partnership's liability pursuant to § 722. Any subsequent payment would further increase the partner's basis, as a contribution to capital under § 722. The resulting decline in partnership liability would decrease that partner's partnership interest pursuant to § 752(b). This approach should also apply to LLCs taxed as a pass-through entity.

Q 9:38   What are the consequences if a court refuses to enforce the dissolution provisions of the LLC's governing statutes and documents?

The remaining members may not be able to terminate the bankrupt member's rights under the agreement. [Kornberg at 23 (Q 9:21)] In addition, the LLC and remaining members may not be able to enforce a buy-sell provision that requires the sale of a member's interest upon a bankruptcy.

Members should consider the implications of such a requirement carefully before they insert it in an Operating Agreement or otherwise. If the Operating Agreement required the LLC to redeem a member's interest upon filing for bankruptcy, that member's creditors likely will force the member into bankruptcy to liquidate the member's interest. Consequently, this reduces the member's ability to negotiate with creditors and avoid bankruptcy. Similarly, if the Operating Agreement grants to the LLC and remaining members the option to purchase a bankrupt member's interest, that will also likely cause creditors to force the member into bankruptcy in hope of triggering the buyout. However, this may be desirable from the LLC and remaining members' perspective, to avoid the incon-venience and expense associated with a bankrupt member.

If the court will not enforce the dissolution provisions, and the member assumes the Operating Agreement (as an executory contract; see Q 9:36), the bankrupt member may be entitled to retain an interest in the LLC and enforce the agreement on the other members (see Q 9:38).

Q 9:39   What is an "executory contract"?

An executory contract is generally defined as a contract under which both sides have material obligations remaining to be performed.

Q 9:40   What is the effect of an executory contract in bankruptcy?

Debtors in bankruptcy have the right to assume, assign, or reject executory contracts. [11 USC §§ 365, 1123(b)(2)] A debtor is deemed to have breached the contract if it rejects it; the nonbreaching party to the contract may have a claim for damages which is treated as a pre-petition claim against the debtor's estate. [11 USC § 502(g)]

Q 9:41   Is an Operating Agreement an executory contract?

Probably yes. The majority of courts have held that partnership agreements are executory contracts. Therefore, bankrupt members may be able to reject the Operating Agreement, or assume the agreement and hold it binding against the nonbankrupt members. [In re Cardinal Industries, Inc, 116 BR 964 (Bankr D Ohio 1990); In re Priestly, 93 BR 253 (Bankr DNM 1988)] If assumed, the bankrupt member must cure any defaults by the member under the agreement (other than provisions addressing insolvency or bankruptcy) and must provide adequate assurance that the member will perform in the future. [11 USC § 365(b)(1)] This creates a tension between maximizing the value of the debtor-member's bankruptcy estate and the interest of the remaining members to choose their own business associates. The trustee of the debtor-member may want to assume the executory contract and participate in the management of the LLC. The remaining members may assess the *ipso facto* provisions and attempt to prevent the trustee from assuming or assigning the contract under 11 USC Sections 365(c) and 365(e).

Q 9:42   Can the LLC prevent a bankrupt member from assuming and assigning rights under the Operating Agreement?

Probably yes. Nondebtors to an agreement are allowed to reject the assumption and assignment of an executory contract by the debtor, if the nondebtor is not required to accept performance of the agreement by anyone other than the debtor. [11 USC § 365(c)(1)] All LLC statutes provide, and the Articles and Operating Agreement should provide, that a member may not transfer management rights in the LLC to a nonmember without the consent of the other members. (In some cases unanimous consent is required.) Therefore, the LLC and other members cannot be forced to accept performance under an Operating Agreement by anyone other than a member. Consequently, Operating Agreements should fall squarely under 11 USC Section 365(c)(1) and should not be subject to being assumed and assigned by a debtor member, without the nondebtor members' consent. This would allow the remaining LLC members to squeeze out the debtor-member, which would diminish the value of that member's bankruptcy estate. Otherwise, the bankruptcy trustee could assume and assign the contract, forcing the admission of a new and unwanted member into the LLC.

This analysis only prevents the assumption and assignment of the Operating Agreement. The bankrupt member can assume the Operating Agreement without the remaining members' consent. [In re Cardinal Industries, Inc, 116 BR 964 (Bankr D Ohio 1990, citing H Rep No 1195, 96th Cong, 2d Sess (1990)]

Q 9:43 Can a bankrupt member's creditors acquire the member's economic interests in the LLC?

Yes, but that is all the creditors are entitled to without the other members' consent. A creditor who acquires a member's economic interest in an LLC generally is entitled only to a "charging order" against the bankrupt member's economic interest. [Uniform Act § 502; Prototype Act § 704(A)] A charging order entitles the holder of the charging order to receive only the bankrupt member's allocations of profit and loss and distributions made by the LLC after the charging order becomes effective.

Q 9:44 Can a Trustee in Bankruptcy sell a member's interest?

The answer will depend on the existence and enforceability of any restrictions in the operating agreement. Case law interpretations of the Bankruptcy Code seem to indicate that the trustee has power over the debtor's property free of any restrictions implicated by the bankruptcy. [See 11 USC §§ 363 and 541; see also Connolly v Nuthatch Hill Associates (In re Manning), 831 F 2d 205 (agreement giving partner 75% of capital account is a modification); In re DeLuca (Broyhill v DeLuca, 180 BR 65 (BC ED Va 1996) (bankruptcy estate has economic interest in firm as an assignee despite fact it may not continue as a partner)]

Q 9:45 Can an LLC be an insider of an individual debtor?

Yes. The Bankruptcy Court held so in *In re Barman,* 237 B.R. 342 (Bankr ED Mich 1999). In *Barman,* the Court applied the standards for determining the insider status of a corporation. Under the Bankruptcy Code, an insider of a debtor-individual includes a corporation in which the debtor is a director, officer, person in control or an affiliate. [11 USC 102(31)] If an individual were to be considered an insider of the company under the Bankruptcy Code, so that any transaction between that individual and the company would not be considered arms length and require close scrutiny, then the company is considered an affiliate of the individual. The legislative history of § 101(31) of the Bankruptcy Code suggests that an insider is someone who "has a sufficiently close relationship with the debtor that his conduct is made subject to closer scrutiny than those dealing at arms' length with the debtor." [H Rep. No. 595, 95th Congress. 2d session 312 (1978)] Because the debtor in *Barman* owned a one third voting interest of the LLC, the debtor would be considered analogous to a director, officer or person in control. This qualified the LLC as an affiliate of the debtor making the LLC an insider.

Chapter 10

Specialized Uses in Business and Estate Planning

This chapter reviews how the LLC may be used in operating specific businesses other than professional practices, which are discussed in chapter 12. This chapter also analyzes the possible benefits of the use of an LLC in estate planning.

General Business Applications

Q 10:1 What types of business are best suited for an LLC?

An LLC is useful for investments in which a limitation on investors' liability is desired. The LLC may be used by virtually any type of business. Certain limitations on the LLC entity, however, may make it unsuitable for a business in certain circumstances. For instance, while there is no limit on the number of investors, as a practical matter, because of the necessity to limit the transferability of interests, and the inability to "go public" with the interests and retain partnership taxation, the LLC remains best suited for closely held businesses, real estate ventures, joint ventures, and affiliations of persons who do not necessarily expect returns based on the increase in the value of their interests but on cash flow from the entity.

Q 10:2 Can an LLC be used for natural resource exploration?

Yes. [See Maxfield, O'Connor, and Wolf, "New Oil and Gas Exploration Vehicle: The Limited Liability Company," 38 *Rocky Mtn Min L Inst* (1992)] The ability of the LLC to be treated as a partnership makes the LLC particularly useful for the special allocation of intangible drilling costs.

Q 10:3 Can an LLC engage in the farming business?

Yes, but a few states, discussed below, prohibit or limit an LLC, at least one that is not family owned, from owning agricultural land, to prevent foreign or large corporate owners of the state's agricultural land. If there are no prohibitions under state law, the LLC is an ideal vehicle for owning a farm or ranch. The LLC shields the owners from extensive liability risks inherent in the ownership of real property (see Q 10:4); moreover, multiple member-farmers could specially allocate the income and expenses of different crops, while splitting the income on mutually worked crops or animals. The family farmer may be able to reduce estate taxes significantly and preserve more of the farm's assets for future generations. In bad years, the LLC will allow any losses to be deducted by members who participate in the business, to the extent of their tax basis.

Iowa, Kansas, Minnesota, and **Oklahoma** each have prohibited the ownership of agricultural land by LLCs or have authorized only certain family LLCs to own agricultural land. [Kan Stat Ann §§ 17-5903, 17-5904 prohibit LLCs from owning agricultural land except as allowed by exceptions to the Kansas corporate farming rules; Iowa Code Ann § 172C.3A originally prohibited LLC farm ownership, but has enacted an exception for "family farm limited liability companies"; see also Minn Stat § 500.24(3); Ok Stat Ann § tit 18, § 955(a)(5)]

Real Estate and Joint Ventures

Q 10:4 Are LLCs suitable for real estate investments?

Yes. LLCs taxed as partnerships are an excellent form of business organization for the ownership of real property. Owners of real estate are subject to risks of liability above and beyond mortgage liability, such as tort liability, environmental liability under the Comprehensive Environmental Response, Compensation, and Liability Act (CERCLA), and public access liability and expenses under the American with Disabilities Act (ADA), etc. [CERCLA, 42 USC § 9607(a); ADA, 42 USC §§ 12101-12213] The traditional entity for real estate investment has been the general or limited partnership. The LLC is superior to both of those entities because no LLC member must be liable personally for the LLC's debts and liabilities, and all members in an LLC can participate fully in the business of the LLC without jeopardizing their limited liability shield. However, as discussed in more detail in chapter 12, it should be remembered that members are personally liable for damage they create due to their own negligence or other tort.

Once a corporation owns real estate, all future appreciation will be subject to tax upon the distribution of the property to members, even if the corporation is an S corporation. The distribution of property from a corporation, including an S corporation, is subject to tax to the extent that the fair market value of the property exceeds the corporation's adjusted tax basis in the real estate. [IRC § 311(b)] Neither the LLC nor the members are subject to tax on the distribution of property (other than cash) from the LLC to the members, except in certain circumstances related to pre-contribution gain on assets contributed to the LLC by one or more members. [IRC §§ 704, 737] Finally, refinancing proceeds can be distributed tax free from an LLC taxed as a partnership but not from a corporation (see chapter 7). [IRC § 301]

Members are entitled to include in their tax basis the LLC's debt, even if the debt is nonrecourse. [IRC § 752] S corporation shareholders cannot include the corporation's debt in the basis of their stock. This is important in the early years of real estate development because it increases the members' ability to use any losses suffered by the LLC against other sources of income. [IRC § 704(d)] In addition, loan refinancing proceeds cannot be distributed without tax from a C corporation, but they may be from an LLC taxed as a partnership. Finally, members are considered at risk under Code Section 465 (which further increases the ability to use the LLC's losses) for their share of the LLC's "qualified nonrecourse financing." [IRC § 465(b)(6)]

Q 10:5 What is qualified nonrecourse financing?

Qualified nonrecourse financing is debt:

1. That is borrowed from a qualified person and that is used in the activity of holding real property (other than mineral property) and is secured by the real property;

2. For which no person is personally liable for repayment; and

3. That is not convertible into equity.

[IRC § 465(b)(6)]

A qualified person is defined as anyone actively engaged in the business of lending money and is not the seller (or a related person of the seller) of the real property in question, or anyone who receives a fee attributable to the investor's investment in the property. If the lender is related to any of the LLC's members, the terms of the debt must be commercially reasonable and comparable to those available to nonrelated third persons. [IRC §§ 465(b)(6)(D), 49(a)(1)(D)(iv)]

Q 10:6 What are some other tax advantages to using an LLC for real estate investment?

Code Section 469 was amended in 1993 to liberalize the use of losses by taxpayers in the real property business (also available to S corporation shareholders).

Rental income is not considered to be net earnings from self-employment (i.e., self-employment income). Thus S corporation shareholders and LLC members are treated identically in this regard. [IRC § 1402(a)(1)] Social security and Medicare taxes are not applicable to passive rental income [IRC §1402], but they are also not considered to be compensation income eligible for a qualified retirement plan contribution (see chapter 7). [IRC § 414(b)]

Q 10:7 Can an LLC obtain title insurance?

Yes. An LLC will need to review the terms of any proposed title insurance policies carefully. Similar to general partnerships, LLCs technically dissolve upon the death, dissolution, bankruptcy, withdrawal, or other statutory or contractual events (see chapter 7). In

Fairway Development Co. v. Title Insurance Company [621 F Supp 120 (ND Ohio 1985)] a partnership technically dissolved upon a change in the partners in the partnership, although the remaining partners continued the partnership. Nevertheless, the court found that the resulting partnership was not the same as the partnership named in the title insurance held by the venture on some real property. Consequently, the resulting partnership did not have a cause of action following the failure of title in the property. In response, title companies now will issue "fairway endorsements," which extend the coverage under the title policy covering real estate owned by partnerships to successor partnerships and to dissolved partnerships. LLCs should consider obtaining fairway endorsements, although, unlike some partnerships, a new LLC is not created when a member terminates an interest or a new member is added.

Q 10:8 Can an LLC be used for joint ventures by unrelated corporations, other business entities, or other LLCs?

Yes. S corporations cannot have corporate shareholders, and limited partners in a limited partnership generally cannot participate in management of the limited partnership. In addition, corporations cannot file a consolidated tax return (which enables affiliated corporations to net their earnings and losses for tax purposes) with a corporation, unless the parent corporation owns at least 80 percent of the vote and value of the stock of the subsidiary. [IRC § 1504] Consequently, the LLC is an ideal business organization for joint ventures between corporations, other business entities, and LLCs themselves, for these three reasons:

1. The income and losses of the LLC flow through to each member, and may be allocated specially to one member or another.

2. The venturer, as a member of an LLC, does not have any liability for the LLC's debts and liabilities, unless it guarantees or otherwise assumes those debts.

3. Each joint venture member can participate fully in the management of the LLC without jeopardizing limited liability protection.

One difference in using a corporation to establish a joint venture is the dividends-received deduction. Although the distributee corporation is subject to tax, corporation shareholders of another corporation are entitled to a dividends-received deduction ranging from 70 percent to 100 percent of the dividend, depending on how much stock the distributee corporation owns. [IRC § 243] This deduction applies only to corporations and does not apply to LLCs. However, the fact that there is only one level of tax should, in most corporate joint venture situations, make up for the loss of the dividends-received deduction.

Q 10:9   Are LLC ventures subject to Hart-Scot-Rodino filing?

Yes. Like corporate joint ventures, LLC joint ventures may be subject to a Hart-Scot-Rodino filing with the FTC, depending on the circumstances, to allow for antitrust review.

Q 10:10   Are LLCs suitable for venture capital or leverage-buyout (LBO) deals?

Yes. Because of the significant flexibility in the ownership, capitalization, and allocation of income and losses, LLCs should be considered for use in venture capital transactions. One disadvantage of the LLC, however, is the inability to "go public," because of the restrictions on the transferability of interest under all LLC statutes, and because publicly traded LLCs are taxed as associations taxable as a corporation. [IRC § 7704] But the LLC can incorporate on a tax-free basis before issuing stock to public investors, although the "control" test should be carefully examined. [IRC § 351]

LLCs currently are treated more favorably than partnerships under the national bank lending limits. Federal law prohibits a national bank (as distinguished from a state-chartered bank) from lending more than 15 percent of the bank's unimpaired capital and surplus to a single person. [12 USC § 85] Loans to one person may be attributed to others, and in the case of partnerships, a loan to the partnership is considered a loan to each of the general partners in the partnership. Therefore, lenders must aggregate loans made to partnerships and the individual general partners of that partnership to determine if the bank complies with the lending limit. [48 Fed Reg 15844, 15848 (Apr 12, 1983)] The Office of the Comptroller of the Currency (OCC) has ruled, however, that an LLC is not subject to the partnership rule. [OCC Interpretive Ltr 602 (Aug 13, 1992)] Thus, a national bank could lend up to 15 percent of its capital to an LLC and make additional loans to each of the LLC's members.

An LLC is subject to the corporate group rules. [12 CFR § 32.5(b)(3)] The corporate group rules prohibit a national bank from lending more than 50 percent of the bank's unimpaired capital and surplus to a single corporate group, including LLCs and the LLC's members and subsidiaries in which the LLC owns at least 50 percent of the entity's voting stock.

Q 10:11   Can an LLC be used for international transactions?

Generally, yes. The LLC is useful for investments by nonresident aliens because they cannot own stock in an S corporation. [IRC § 1362] Thus, to attain limited liability and pass-through taxation, the LLC is the best alternative. In addition, the LLC is older and similar to many non-U.S. entities. Central and South American countries have *limitadas*, France has the *Société à responsabilité limitée* (SARL), Germany has the *Gesellschaft mit beschraenkter Haftung* (GmbH), and Italy has the SpA. If the LLC is used for outbound transactions in other countries, practitioners must review the laws of those countries in determining if the LLC's limited liability protection will be respected and if any registration is required. Local tax law and tax treaties must also be reviewed in determining how the LLC will be taxed, and if the LLC must withhold against any distributions back to the United States.

Q 10:12   Can an LLC be a bank?

Most states require banks to be corporations. Some states have amended their laws to allow banks to be formed as LLCs. [See, e.g., Del Stat Ann tit 6, § 18-106.] Some states do not specifically prohibit an LLC from the banking business in the LLC statute, but the state banking statutes must be reviewed. (see Q 10:13)

Q 10:13   Can an LLC be an insurance company?

Some states prohibit an LLC from selling insurance. [Del Stat Ann tit 6, § 18-106] However, a few states are allowing LLCs to market and sell certain lines of insurance. For example, effective February 1, 1999, Pennsylvania LLCs, although still prohibited from being organized for the purpose of banking or insurance, may be organized by one or more banks or a banking organization for the sole purposes of marketing and selling title insurance. Further, as long as an insurance agency is licensed in Pennsylvania, it too may be organized as an LLC. [Act 124 (HB 1479), Laws 1998]

Q 10:14 Can an LLC be used for investment clubs and vacation home ownership among unrelated parties?

Yes. The LLC is an ideal choice of entity for the ownership of vacation rental homes. The LLC limits the liability of the members who own the LLC. This is particularly important when the vacation home is routinely rented to third parties. To obtain the tax benefits incident to ownership of a vacation rental home, the members may not use the LLC for more than the greater of 14 days, or 10 percent of the number of days during the taxable year for which the unit is rented for fair rental value. [IRC §§ 280A(d)(1)(A), (B)] This rule applies in the aggregate to all members; thus the LLC members are entitled collectively to use the vacation home for only 14 days. [IRC § 280A(d)(2)]

Charitable and Non-Profit Activities

Q 10:15 Can an LLC be a tax-exempt organization under Code Section 501(c)(3)?

Yes, but only if it is taxed as a corporation. Under the "check-the-box" regulations (see chapter 3), an LLC cannot attain tax-exempt status and a tax classification as a partnership because the regulations specifically state that the organization cannot be a Section 501(c)(3) entity. The regulations also contain a provision that states that any organization that has been determined to be, or claims to be, exempt from tax under Code Section 501(c)(3) will be treated as having elected to be treated as an association taxable as a corporation. Such provision would foreclose a charitable organization formed as an LLC from being granted exempt status under Code Section 501(c)(3) while maintaining flow-through tax treatment. Flow-through tax treatment could be significant tax treatment to a Section 501(c)(3) LLC in order to meet the members' public support tests.

Q 10:16   Can an LLC be used for a joint venture between a tax-exempt entity and a for-profit entity?

Yes, if the Operating Agreement is properly structured and certain requirements are met. The LLC must pass a two-pronged test established by the courts and the IRS. [GCM 39005 (June 28, 1983); Plumstead Theatre Society v. Commr, 74 TC 1324, *affd* 675 F 2d 244 (9th Cir 1982)] The first prong requires an evaluation of the purpose of the LLC, while the second prong requires an evaluation of the structural aspects of the LLC, including specific business and financial characteristics.

The first prong of the test requires that the activity of the LLC serve a recognized charitable purpose. The second prong of the test involves three questions: (1) does the LLC expose charitable assets to unnecessary or unwarranted risks?; (2) can the charitable organization operate the LLC exclusively in furtherance of its charitable purposes?; and (3) do the activities or structure of the LLC have the effect of conferring a private benefit on the for-profit members?

First, a charitable member's assets may be at risk by either exposure to liability for the LLC's debts and obligations, or by virtue of a guarantee, indemnity, or penalty provisions in the Operating Agreement. Because an LLC provides all of its members with limited liability (if operated correctly), the charitable member need not place any amount at risk beyond that initially invested or subsequently contributed. This fact generally allows this "exposure test" to be met. The Operating Agreement often contains a provision for additional capital contributions. Any capital calls should apply equally to the for-profit and tax-exempt members. Any provision requiring additional capital contributions solely from the tax-exempt member and not from the for-profit members could result in a private benefit and cause the "exposure test" not to be met. Any penalty provision should be reasonable under the facts and circumstances. Other provisions of the Operating Agreement the IRS may find problematic include: a guarantee for the charitable member to fund loss reserves, a requirement that the charitable member allocate all or a part of the capital contributions to another member; indemnification for losses sustained; or a guarantee to another member of a minimum investment return.

Second, in order for the LLC to be operated exclusively for a charitable purpose, the charitable member should have control over the daily activities of the LLC. Without this control, the IRS could determine that a private benefit might occur. Therefore, the charitable member should always be a managing member. If the for-profit members have the power to amend the Operating Agreement without the consent of the charitable member, the IRS could determine that the tax-exempt member does not actually have control of the LLC. In addition, if the charitable member can be removed from its management position without cause, or if its position is subject to periodic elections, the required control might be absent.

Special attention should be made for the LLC involving a private foundation. Private foundations are subject to the excess business holding rules of Code Section 4943 which restricts the interest held by the private foundation to 20 percent in any one entity. Private foundation members could run afoul of this rule if a member fails to make a capital contribution and the failure results in a change in the pro rata interests of the members. A private foundation has 90 days to divest itself of an excess interest if Code Section 4943 is violated. This would be difficult considering the transfer restrictions for a member's interest in an LLC.

Thus, the IRS has ruled that a tax-exempt member does not jeopardize its tax-exempt status if it forms an LLC with a for-profit member. [Rev Rul 98-15, 1998-1 CB 718; Ltr Rul 9517029] The language of the Operating Agreement (guarantee provisions, designation of control over operations, and capital calls) played a key role in the IRS' holding and determination that the exempt members continued its exempt status. However, in Revenue Ruling 98-15, the Service appears to have reiterated an organizational test for joint ventures involving a tax-exempt member, at least as to "whole hospital" joint ventures, consisting of the following requirements:

- The nonprofit member must be in control of the LLC's governing board, without regard to its percentage ownership interest in the LLC, i.e., even if it owns less than 50 percent of the ownership interests.
- The nonprofit member must be able to initiate action to serve new exempt purpose needs.
- Neither the for-profit corporation nor a subsidiary of the for-profit corporation can serve as manager of the LLC, even if terms and conditions of the management contract are entirely reasonable.
- LLC executives cannot be insiders of the for-profit corporation.

In addition to the requirements above, there appears to be an additional requirement that the LLC's governing documents provide that the governing board has a specific fiduciary duty to operate the LLC in a manner that furthers charitable purposes and that this duty overrides any state law fiduciary duty to operate the LLC for the financial benefit of its owners. This requirement seems justified because absent such an override, the LLC governing board would have a fiduciary duty to consider the financial benefit of the LLC's members over any charitable purposes.

Health Care: Integrated Delivery Systems

Q 10:17   Can an LLC be used for the operation of a physician hospital organization (PHO), management service organization (MSO), independent practice association (IPA), or other form of medical provider integration?

Yes, the LLC is an excellent choice of entity for these organizations. [See Paul, Levine, and Sfekas, *Limited Liability Companies Provide New Planning Opportunities for Health Care Alliances*, 1993; Prentice-Hall] There are at least four advantages to using an LLC for an integrated delivery system:

1. *Flexible management structure.* All investors may have management rights.
2. *Pass-through taxation.* In many cases the LLC will receive only sufficient income to pay the following administrative ex-

penses: general administrative costs, peer and quality review costs, the cost to operate a credentialing standards board, and the costs of a board or committee to negotiate contracts with third-party payors. Most of the economic benefits flow through or around the LLC to providers in exchange for health care services.

3. *Liability protection.* As discussed in chapter 12, many LLC statutes shield members from contract and tort liability of other members; members generally are liable only for their own torts and the torts of those they supervise and control.

4. *Diversification of ownership.* Health care providers, professional practice groups, and administrative and other persons may, under state professional corporation law, be able to own an interest in an LLC but not another professional corporation.

Many integrated delivery models generally have little, if any, net taxable income; C corporations, therefore, may also be useful alternatives, but only if permitted under the state professional corporation law. C corporations have an advantage over LLCs because the C corporation can provide tax-free fringe benefits to shareholder-employees. However, in many of these cases, that will not be a concern, because the physician and the hospital's independent practices and services remain separate. Thus, each separate health care provider can determine separate employee fringe benefits to the extent that they can afford those expenses. Moreover, unlike S corporations, there are no limits on the nationality or number of investors there may be. This is particularly important when a critical mass of providers is necessary to make an IPA or PHO viable and successful.

Q 10:18   Can tax-exempt hospitals participate in LLCs?

Yes. Two issues, however, must be discussed. First, state LLC law must allow an LLC to be formed for a nonprofit purpose, unless the LLC is formed as a for-profit entity. Second, the IRS has ruled that a tax-exempt hospital may forfeit its tax exemption if the hospital participates with an entity that allows part or all of the exempt hospital's income to inure to the benefit of those members, in violation of Code Section 501(c)(3). The IRS and the courts have, however, approved tax-exempt entities' ownership of for-profit subsidiaries in certain situations. [See Rev Rul 98-15 and Q 10:16] The LLC should not be viewed any differently, so long as the hospital receives a return from the LLC commensurate with its investment and receives fair market compensation for the services provided to the patients.

If the investment in a PHO LLC does not jeopardize the hospital's tax exemption, and the LLC's activity is conduct that the hospital could have performed itself, the LLC's income should not be considered unrelated trade or business income. [IRC § 512(c)(1)] Hospitals probably will be able to take advantage of this provision to avoid tax on the hospital's distributive share of the LLC's income, if any.

Q 10:19 Are LLC interests in a PHO's securities under federal and state securities laws?

They may be (see chapter 9).

Estate Planning

Q 10:20 Is an LLC favorable for estate planning purposes?

Several tax and nontax benefits exist in using an LLC for holding a business for the benefit of transferring it to family members upon ultimate disposition. Because income is passed through to LLC members, the tax benefits may be lower than for trusts, since trusts attain the highest marginal tax rate of taxable income at only $7,500. Further, using an LLC may reduce estate, gift, and transfer tax due to minority and marketability discounts. [Rev Rul 93-12, 1993-1 CB 202] However, those discounts are not as large as an LLC permitting a member to liquidate an interest in an LLC as in a corporation or limited partnership for a term of years because those entities have a lack of marketability where not publicly traded and no obligation to repurchase their interests exists.

From a nontax standpoint, all members of an LLC have limited liability. Further, management flexibility in the LLC could help in carrying out a family's estate plan.

Q 10:21   Is an LLC more favorable than an S corporation for estate planning purposes?

Estate planning for owners of an S corporation is severely lim-ited if the S corporation survives and prospers. Business succession is limited because certain trusts, family limited partnerships, and family LLCs cannot be shareholders in an S corporation. An LLC, in contrast, has no restrictions on the number of members or on the type of member allowed. Additionally, an LLC can have as many classes of membership interests as desired.

An LLC can make special allocations of income, losses, deduc-tions, and credits (assuming it has economic effect; see chapter 7), whereas an S corporation cannot. Additionally, the members of an LLC can use the liabilities of an LLC to increase their basis, thereby allowing them to deduct flow-through losses.

Q 10:22   What is the effect on the LLC and the members' LLC interest upon the death of a member?

An LLC dissolves upon the death of a member. However, the remaining members may vote to continue the business of the LLC. Whether unanimous consent or only a majority consent is neces-sary will depend upon the state LLC statute and the Operating Agreement (see chapter 8).

If the LLC does not dissolve, the outside basis of the LLC (i.e., the members' LLC interest) is stepped up to fair market value upon the death of a member. [IRC § 1014] If the LLC makes a Section 754/743 election, the assets of the LLC will also be stepped up. This will reduce the gain that the LLC must recognize upon the disposition of the LLC's assets (see chapter 7 and Q 10:23).

Q 10:23   Can an LLC make an election under Code Sections 754/743 upon the death of one of its members?

Yes. A member's outside basis in the LLC interest is that mem-ber's basis in the LLC interest itself. The inside basis is the mem-ber's share of the LLC's basis in its assets. When an LLC interest is transferred, the LLC can elect, under Code Sections 754 and 743, to have the inside basis of the new member adjusted, so that it equals the amount the member paid for the interest. The election is also available when a member dies, and the member's interest is passed to a beneficiary. At death, the beneficiary's outside basis in the LLC interest equals the fair market value on the date of death (or six months after the date of death, if the alternate valuation date is used). [IRC § 1014] If a Section 754/743 election is made, the beneficiary's share of the LLC's assets also equals the fair market value on the valuation date. The result is that only the appreciation after the date of death is taxed to the beneficiary upon a disposition of the LLC's assets or upon a disposition of the LLC interest itself.

Q 10:24   Is the transfer of an LLC interest subject to Code Section 2036(b)?

No. Under Code Section 2036(b), stock transferred during life is included in the donor's gross estate if: (1) the donor retained the right to vote the transferred shares; and (2) at any time within three years of death, the donor owned at least 20 percent of the voting stock of the corporation. In determining the 20 percent ownership requirement, the constructive ownership rules of Code Section 318 apply. This can cause a problem for estate taxation purposes, for family businesses.

For example, if a family member transfers 25 percent of the stock in a family corporation to another family member, but retains the voting rights, the full value of the stock is included in the transferor's gross estate. Due to the constructive ownership rules, the transferor is deemed to still own the 25 percent interest in the corporation and to retain the voting rights to the interest. This can cause interference with estate planning for donors with stock in a corporation. The problem can be eliminated, however, if the family business was organized as an LLC. Code Section 2036(b) only applies to stock in corporations and not to ownership interests in an LLC. Therefore, LLCs structured as a partnership for tax purposes are not subject to this rule.

Q 10:25   Is an LLC more favorable than an irrevocable life insurance trust for estate planning purposes?

Not necessarily. An irrevocable life insurance trust can safely be used to exclude policy proceeds from the life of the insured, the insured's spouse, and the insured's family, at least when structured properly. Like an irrevocable life insurance trust (ILIT), an LLC could purchase a life insurance policy with cash provided by the insured, in exchange for a membership interest or as contributions to the LLC. The insured retains control over the management of the LLC, including control over the investments and cash value. The family could then own the balance of the interests in the LLC. These LLC interests could be obtained as outright gifts, and if properly structured, could fall within the $10,000 annual gift exclusion. Even though the insured retains management authority, the policy proceeds, upon the death of the insured, would be included in the insured's gross estate only up to the insured's percentage interest in the LLC, provided the policy proceeds were paid to the LLC (unless the insured could exercise incidents of ownership in the life insurance policy through the LLC).

The Operating Agreement could allow for amendments or a termination of the LLC, if family circumstances change. This feature is not generally available in an ILIT. Because distributions in kind may be made to fund a distribution upon termination, certain members may receive the policy or policy proceeds while other members receive other assets.

As stated above, it is more beneficial to tax the LLC income at the member's individual tax rates since those rates are often lower than the maximum income tax rates for small amounts of taxable income. The LLC could opt to distribute enough cash to the members in order to pay their income taxes and retain the remaining income in the LLC.

Q 10:26 Is an LLC interest subject to discounts for lack of marketability and minority interests?

Yes. Depending upon the restrictions on transfers in the Operating Agreement and the type of assets held, an LLC interest may be reduced, for gift-giving purposes, due to the lack of marketability and minority interests. The IRS has recognized that such discounts are appropriate in family situations. [Rev Rul 93-12, 1993-1 CB 202] Additionally, a provision in state law that prevents the LLC from liquidating upon a dissolution event could give rise to a discount due to the restriction on a member's ability to liquidate and obtain the capital. [Harrison v Commr, 52 TC Memo (CCH) 1306

(1987); and Estate of Watts v Commr, TCM 1985-595 (1985)] However, in certain family-controlled LLCs, unlike family corporations or family limited partnerships, discounts for restrictions on liquidation may be disregarded for valuations under Code Section 2704(b) (see Q 10:27).

Prior to the advent of the check-the-box regulations, dissociation of a member typically precipitated dissolution of the LLC so that continuity of interest did not exist and the LLC could be taxed under subchapter K. The check-the-box regulations have eliminated the necessity for this requirement in the LLC articles of organization or operating agreement. As a result, if the state LLC statute provides that death does not cause dissolution and the members do not possess a default right to be repaid contributions, discounts with respect to LLC interests will be permissible notwithstanding Section 2704(b) of the Internal Revenue Code (see Q 10:27).

The LLC interest must be allowed based upon what a willing buyer and willing seller would buy and sell the LLC interest for, with full knowledge of all relevant facts. [Treas Reg §§ 20.2031-1(b), 25.2512-(f)(2)] It is also clear that, for gift-giving purposes, the interest is valued in the hands of the recipient, and not what the transferor owned. [Alanson Found v Commr, 674 F 2d 761 (9th Cir 1981), 81-2 USTC, 13,438]

In applying a minority discount, the key is to value the LLC interest based upon the price a willing buyer would pay a willing seller for that particular interest. [TAM 9432001] Therefore, if a member holds a 65 percent interest in an LLC, and gifts 10 percent to a transferee, a minority discount would presumably apply even though the transferor continues to hold a 55 percent interest in the LLC.

The IRS has ruled, however, that a minority discount is not automatic. Rather, other factors will be reviewed and are relevant in determining the value of the gift. These factors can include who the transferee is, what the transferee already owns, and what others have previously received. [TAM 9436005]

Q 10:27   Is an LLC interest subject to Code Section 2704(b)?

If a member cannot force the LLC to liquidate the member's interest, the transfer of the LLC interest will give rise to a discount equal to that in a corporation or family limited partnership for a term of years since the member cannot by state law obtain "fair value." The valuation, for gift-giving purposes, is based upon the interest in the LLC as a going concern, and the gift is not valued based upon its liquidation value.

However, under Code Section 2704(b), if there is a transfer of an interest among family members, and the transferor and members of the transferor's family control the LLC, certain "applicable restrictions" on a member's liquidation rights are disregarded for valuation purposes. These applicable restrictions include a restriction that lapses after the transfer or a restriction that can be removed, in whole or in part, by the transferor or any member of the transferor's family, or any restriction imposed, or required to be imposed, by state or federal law. [IRC §2704(b)] This Code section was enacted in an attempt to allow discounts only for those restrictions that are meaningful. If a restriction was imposed to get a discounted value upon a transfer, but the restriction could be removed or had no substance due to family ownership, no discount would be allowed. Some states have enacted statutes to circumvent Code Section 2704(b).

If the Operating Agreement is to be disregarded (for purposes of a member's liquidation rights), then the applicable state LLC statute would apply. In many states, the LLC statutes provide that any member can receive, within a reasonable time, the "fair value" of the member's interest in the LLC. [Rev Stat Gen Laws 1956 (1992 Reenactment) § 7-16-29; Mo Rev Stat § 347.103(2); and PLLCA § 602] This would severely limit any discount, since the member would have an immediate right to receive the value of the capital interest.

Some states require a waiting period before a member can receive a return of capital. This waiting period diminishes any discount, but probably does not eliminate it all together.

Arizona has specifically enacted a provision directly to limit the effects of Code Section 2704(b). The provision states that, if the withdrawing member is a family member of a family-controlled LLC, the distributions that the withdrawn member is entitled to receive are based on the lesser of: a complete wind up of the LLC *or* the member's right to anticipated future distributions if the LLC were to continue for 25 years. [Ariz Rev Stat § 329-

707(C)] This section allows members to use LLCs for estate planning without eliminating any valuation discounts because of Code Section 2704(b).

Q 10:28   After "check-the-box" is implemented (see chapter 3), can an individual, a corporation, an LLC or other entity form a one-owner LLC?

Yes, if state law permits. State LLC statutes currently allow LLCs either to be formed with only one member [see, e.g., Colo Rev Stat Ann § 7-80-203; Mo Rev Stat § 347.037] or to continue to exist if the number of members falls to one. [NC Gen Stats § 57C-6-01(4)]

Chapter 11

Limited Liability Partnerships

The limited liability partnership, or LLP, is not a separate form of business organization; rather, it is a form of registration of a general partnership but without some or all of the joint and several liability for the partners which otherwise exists with a general partnership. It is currently (as this book goes to press) recognized in most states. Existing LLP statutes differ, however, in some fundamental ways. This chapter describes the characteristics of an LLP, and compares an LLP to an LLC.

In General

Q 11:1 What is a limited liability partnership (LLP) or registered LLP (RLLP)?

A limited liability partnership (LLP) is a general partnership (in some states it may also be a limited partnership) that has, pursuant to state law, filed an application with the Secretary of

State in the state of the LLP's organization to be treated as an LLP. Existing general partnerships can convert to an LLP by filing with the state. When a professional partnership so registers, it is sometimes called an "RLLP" or a registered limited liability partnership. A limited partnership that so registers is an LLLP, a limited liability limited partnership which limits the liability of the general partners. Currently, fourteen states by statute authorize the LLLP.

All LLP acts are designed to limit the liability exposure of partners while preserving the partnership's tax status. In all acts, the partnership does not lose its partnership status and remains controlled by its state's partnership laws except to the extent the LLP statute so specifies. Furthermore, the partnership does not become a new legal entity upon filing with the appropriate state agency.

Q 11:2   Is an LLP considered an entity or is it considered as an aggregate of its members?

Much like a general partnership, the answer is unclear for LLPs formed under the UPA although the limited liability feature of an LLP leans towards classification as an entity. For LLPs formed in states which have adopted the RUPA, the LLP is clearly classified as an entity. [RUPA § 201]

Q 11:3   How many states have adopted the LLP?

All fifty states and the District of Columbia have enacted statutes allowing limited liability partnerships.

California, Nevada, Oregon, and **New York** allow only professional firms to have LLP status. The Limited Liability Partnership Acts in each jurisdiction were adopted generally as amendments to the partnership law of those jurisdictions. Accordingly, the limited liability partnership provisions are codified at scattered locations from the general partnership law and statutes.

The location of each statute within each jurisdiction is as follows:

- Alabama (Ala. Code §§ 10-8A-101 to 10-8A-109 (Supp. 1997));
- Alaska (Alaska Stat. §§ 32.05);

- Arizona (Ariz. Rev. Stat. Ann. §§ 29-244 to 29-257 (W. Supp. 1995));
- Arkansas (Ark. Code Ann. §§ 4-42-703);
- California (Cal. Corp. Code §§ 15002-15058 (West. Supp. 1996));
- Colorado (Colo. Rev. Stat. §§ 7-60-141 to 7-62-1104 (Supp. 1996));
- Connecticut (Conn. Gen. Stat. Ann. §§ 34-40 to 34-81z (West. Supp. 1996));
- Delaware (Del. Code Ann. tit. 6, §§ 1502-47, 17-214 (1993 and Supp. 1995));
- District of Columbia (D.C. Code Ann. § 1107, §§ 41-151.1 to 41-161.6);
- Florida (Fla. Stat. Ann. Chs. 620-78 to 620-789 (West. Supp. 1996));
- Georgia (Ga. Code Ann. §§ 14-8-2 to 14-8-64 (Supp. 1996));
- Hawaii (Haw. Rev. Stat. §§ 425-151 to 425-180);
- Idaho (Id. Code §§ 53-302 to 53-504) (Supp. 1995));
- Illinois (Ill. Comp. Stat. Ann. 805/205-2 to 805/205-40 (West. 1996));
- Indiana (Ind. Code Ann. §§ 23-4-1-2 to 23-4-1-52 (Michie Supp. 1996));
- Iowa (Iowa Code Ann. §§ 486.2 to 486.46 (West. Supp. 1996));
- Kansas (Kan. Stat. Ann. §§ 56-302 to 56-347, 56-1a102 (1994 and Supp. 1995)); Id. §§ 17-2708, 17-7606 (1995));
- Kentucky (Ky. Rev. Stat. Ann. §§ 275.015, 362.155 to 362.605 (Banks.—Baldwin Supp. 1995)); Louisiana (La. Rev. Stat. Ann. §§ 9:3431 – 9:3435 (West. Supp. 1996)); Id. § 12:117 (West. 1994 and Supp. 1996));
- Maine (Act of April 10, 1996, Ch. 633, 1996 Me. Legis. Serv. 552 (West));
- Maryland (Md. Code Ann., Bus. Occ. and Prof. § 1-101 (Supp. 1995) and Md. Code Ann., Corps. and Ass'ns §§ 1-203 to 10-102 (Supp. 1995));
- Massachusetts (1995 Mass. Adv. Legis. Serv. 281 (Law Co-op));

- Michigan (Mich. Comp. Laws Ann. §§ 449.15-48 (West. Supp. 1996));
- Minnesota (Minn. Stat. Ann. §§ 319A. 02-12 (West 1996), §§ 323.02-47 (West. 1995 and Supp. 1996));
- Mississippi (Miss. Code Ann. §§ 79-12-3 to 79-12-177 (Supp. 1995));
- Missouri (Mo. Rev. Stat. §§ 358.020-510 (Supp. 1995));
- Montana (Mont. Code Ann. §§ 35-10-102 to 35-10-710 (1995));
- Nebraska (L.B. 681, §§ 198 to 214, 94th Leg., 2d Sess., 1996 Neb. Laws 190, 245-51 (Codified as amended at Neb. Rev. Stat. §§ 67-301 to 67-346));
- Nevada (Nev. Rev. Stat. Ann. §§ 87.020-.560 (Michie 1995));
- New Hampshire (Act effective Aug. 9, 1996, Ch. 212, 1995 at N.H. H.B. 580));
- New Jersey (N.J. Stat. Ann. §§ 42:1-2 to 42:1-49 (West. Supp. 1996));
- New Mexico (N.M. Stat. Ann. §§ 54-1-1 to 54-1-48 (Michie Supp. 1996));
- New York (N.Y. Partnership Law §§ 2-71, 121-1500 to 121-1503 (McKinney Supp. 1996));
- North Carolina (N.C. Gen. Stat. §§ 55B-9, 59-32 to 59-84.3 (1995));
- North Dakota (N.D. Cent. Code §§ 45-22-01 to 45-22-27 (Supp. 1995));
- Ohio (Ohio Rev. Code Ann. §§ 1775.05-1777.03 (Banks. — Baldwin 1994));
- Oklahoma (Act effective Nov. 1, 1996, Ch. 223, 1996 Okla. Sess. Law Serv. 871 (West));
- Oregon (Act effective Jan. 1, 1996, Ch. 689, 1995 Or. Laws 2075));
- Pennsylvania (Pa. Cons. Stat. Ann. §§ 8201-21 (West 1995));
- Rhode Island (Act of Aug. 6, 1996, Ch. 96-270, 1995 R.I. H.B. 8082));
- South Carolina (S.C. Code Ann. §§ 33-41-20 to 33-41-1210 (Law. Co-op. Supp. 1995));

- South Dakota (S.D. Codified Laws §§ 48-1-1 to 48-1-111 (Michie Supp. 1995));
- Tennessee (Tenn. Code Ann. §§ 61-1-101 to 147 (Supp. 1995));
- Texas (Tex. Rev. Civ. Stat. Ann. art. 6132a-1 to 6132b-10.04 (West. Supp. 1996));
- Utah (Utah Code Ann. §§ 48-1 to 48-48 (Supp. 1996));
- Virginia (Va. Code Ann. §§ 50-43.1 to 50-73.78, 54.1-3902 (Michie Supp. 1995));
- Washington (Wash. Rev. Code Ann. §§ 25.04.700-.750 (West. Supp. 1996));
- West Virginia (WV. Code § 47B-1-1 to § 47-11-5);
- Wisconsin (Act of Dec. 1, 1995, act 97, 1995-96 Wis. Legis. Serv. 871 (West));
- Wyoming (Wyo. Stat. §§ 17-21-1101 to 17-21-1105).

Q 11:4   What caused the LLP to be created?

The LLP first appeared in Texas in 1991 with the purpose of shielding general partners of general partnerships (primarily law and accounting firms) from personal liability for negligence based torts committed by other partners. Partners continued to be liable for the torts committed by those whom they supervised or directed, and the LLP was required to carry at least $100,000 in liability insurance to cover tortious acts. Not all professional firms, especially those doing business in multiple states can legally operate in each such state as a professional corporation, limited liability company, or general business corporation.

By 1993, the LLP gained popularity with adoptions in various forms by **Delaware,** the **District of Columbia, Louisiana,** and **North Carolina.** Delaware had the broadest and most innovative LLP statute at this time. **Delaware** adopted several changes to the original Texas version:

- Greater protection from wrongful acts and omissions of other partners.
- Imposing supervisory liability for only "direct" supervision.
- Requiring minimum liability insurance of $1 million.

- Granting express authorization for LLPs to engage in activities outside of the state.
- Deferring to the state Supreme Court for a determination of law firm eligibility for limited liability status.
- Limiting the maximum registration fees to the amount corporations paid in franchise taxes.

In 1994, **Minnesota** and **New York** adopted LLP statutes which included enhanced limited liability parallel to corporations by protecting against vicarious liability for all partnership liabilities regardless of their nature. [Minn Stat Ann § 323.14(2); NY Partnership Law § 26(b)] The **Minnesota** statute is unique because it protects partners for liability for directed or supervised conduct. In response to the creation of such a wide liability shield, the **Minnesota** statute permits piercing the LLP veil but excepts a failure to follow formalities as a ground for arguing the veil should be pierced. [Minn Stat Ann § 323.14(3); see also ND Cent Code § 44-22-09 for a similar provision] Under the **Minnesota** statute, a partner is liable for distributions received when the LLP was insolvent. [Minn Stat Ann § 323.14(5)]

The **New York** statute retains liability for actions of a partner in a supervisory capacity and, as stated above, limits the protection to professional firms. [NY Partnership Law §§ 26(c) and 121-1500(a)] **New York** also requires publication of notice of the firm's LLP status in two newspapers for six weeks following registration. [NY Partnership Law § 121-1500(a)] **Delaware** amended its LLP act in 1994 to protect partners from contract claims and specifying that partners are not liable for contributions to the partnership or indemnification to other partners due to liabilities of the partnership if the partner would not otherwise be liable under the LLP statute. [Del Code Ann tit 6, § 1515(b)] A partner under the **Delaware** act was still liable for that partner's own actions and for the actions of others that partner supervised.

After 1994, the clamoring began for statutes which extended **New York's** broad liability shield to all partnerships, not merely professional firms, without potential partner liability for receipt of distributions while the LLP was insolvent as under the **Minnesota** act. **Georgia** became the first jurisdiction to enact such a statute in 1995. [Ga Code Ann § 14-8-15(a)] Moreover, the ABA advocated such a provision in its Prototype LLC Act.

Q 11:5   Are there distinct LLP acts in most states?

As noted above, an LLP is not a separate form of business entity, unlike an LLC. It is a general partnership with limited liability status. Accordingly, most LLP provisions are included in a state's partnership law.

Prior to 1995, all states, except Texas, integrated LLP provisions in their form of the UPA. This began to change as states started to adopt versions of the RUPA promulgated in 1994. In 1996, the RUPA was amended to include specific provisions pertaining to LLPs as a result of their rapid proliferation. A Prototype LLP Act was promulgated by the ABA in 1995 as a proposal to integrate LLP provisions into the RUPA. States with LLP provisions embodied in pre-amendment versions of the RUPA include: **Montana, Wyoming,** and **Texas.**

States which had adopted versions of the RUPA with the LLP amendments by 1997 are: **Alabama, Arizona, California, Connecticut, Florida, New Mexico, North Dakota, Virginia,** and **West Virginia.** The balance of the states included their LLP provisions in their versions of the UPA.

The integration of LLP provisions into the different types of partnership acts may have subtle, but important, implications, particularly with respect to choice-of-law provisions (see SQs 11:15.4 and 11:15.5).

Choosing an LLP or an LLC

Q 11:6   What are the differences between an LLP and an LLC?

The principal difference between an LLP and an LLC is the degree of protection from liability of the owners of the entity. A member of an LLC generally is not personally liable for the debts or obligations of the LLC or the torts of any other members of the LLC. Members of an LLC, like owners of any type of entity, remain liable for their own torts (such as malpractice or other negligence, fraud, or misrepresentation) and for debts that they personally guarantee.

The original LLP statutes were designed to shield a general partner (especially professionals) from joint and several liability for the malpractice of another partner in the LLP. An LLP partner is not individually liable for debts and obligations of the LLP arising from errors, omissions, negligence, incompetence, or malfeasance attributable to the LLP and committed by the LLP's other partners, employees, agents, or representatives, at least if that partner did not supervise or negligently fail to supervise the wrongdoer. In some states, LLP partners remain liable for: their own individual malpractice or other negligence or tort liability; liability of those persons they directly control; and the LLP's contract obligations, such as general debts, including trade payables, loans, and lease obligations. Some LLP statutes, however, also protect against liability for contract obligations that are not personally guaranteed by the partner (see chapter 12).

The management function of an LLP is performed by general partners with strong default rules providing for equality with respect to fiduciary, management, and financial rights. There are usually no required officers, although an LLP may have a managing partner or others deemed necessary by a specific partnership. With an LLC, the management function is performed by managers unless it is reserved to its members. The management of an LLP is governed by the partnership agreement. An LLC is governed under state law. The filing requirements for an LLP requires a certificate to be filed with the secretary of state. For an LLC, articles of organization must be filed. Absent anything in the partnership agreement, partners in an LLP will be entitled to an equal share of profits and losses regardless of their contributions according to the default rules. RUPA allows for oral modificaions to the partnership agreement. [RUPA § 101(7)] If a state's LLC act requires a written operating agreement and written amendments, the ability to change profit shares may require more effort. The ULLCA allows for oral operating agreements. [ULLCA § 103]

Default provisions in RUPA require a majority vote of partners in an LLP as to decisions in the ordinary course of business. Matters outside the ordinary course of business will require unanimous consent of all partners. [See RUPA § 401(j)] Such provisions of an LLC may depend on whether or not the LLC is member-managed or manager-managed.

Further, the term of an LLP is governed by the partnership agreement, and may be indefinite. The term of an LLC can vary, although the LLC term can be amended or it can be reconstituted if it dissolves. Many state LLC statutes have no term requirement.

The management of a partnership is by its general partners. In a limited partnership, the general partners must usually be disclosed in the certificate. [See RULPA §§ 101(5), 201(a)(3), 202(b), 207(2)] This provides notice to creditors as to the identity of the general partners. On the other hand, an LLC in many states need not disclose the identity of its managers.

The division between general and limited partners tends to be somewhat clearer in a limited partnership than that of managers and members in an LLC. In a closely held LLC, even if the members delegate the power to bind the firm to designated managers, they may have significant expectations of participating and control. Thus, even in the absence of a provision in the Operating Agreement, a court may allow an LLC member to initiate certain actions in a centrally managed LLC. However, with regard to a limited partnership, such participation and control is inconsistent with the basic governance structure.

An LLP in many states must file a renewal application annually, or upon a change in partners, with the secretary of state. Such a renewal application must be accompanied by an annual fee and updated information on the LLP. In contrast, an LLC once it is filed with the secretary of state forms a business entity and does not have to refile annually (except for an annual report) to keep that entity's status current.

Q 11:7   When is an LLP partner liable for the torts of others?

The standard for this vicarious liability varies from state to state. All LLP statutes impose liability if the partner committed the misconduct or directed or directly controlled the conduct.

There is some question as to the level of supervision or control that is necessary to give rise to vicarious liability. Some state courts rely upon *respondeat superior* analysis in determining when a partner in an LLP will be liable for the torts of others. [See Oberzon v Smith, 254 Kan 846, 869 P 2d 682 (1994).]

An LLP statute may require both supervision and control before an LLP will be liable for the conduct of one of the LLP's employees. [See Iowa Stat Ann 56-315(c).] As a result, a department head or managing partner may not be liable for the conduct of anyone else working in a department or for a partner's client, unless that partner worked directly with, and controlled the work of, an LLP employee working on the matter.

Colorado, Georgia, Indiana, Kentucky, Louisiana, and Utah's LLP statutes do not provide for supervisor liability. [Colo. Rev. Stat. Ann. S. 7-60-155(2)(a)(West Supp. 1997); GA Code Ann. S. 14-8-15(c)(Supp. 1998); Ind. Code Ann. S. 23-4-1-15(3)(Michie Supp. 1997); KY Rev. Stat. Ann. art. S.362.220 (Banks-Baldwin Supp. 1997); LA Rev. Stat. Ann. S.9.3431 (West Supp. 1998); Utah Code Ann. S. 48-1-12 (1998)]

Q 11:8   Which partnerships are best suited to be an LLP?

Generally, an LLP is best suited for professionals (e.g., accountants, doctors, and lawyers) to attempt to limit their personal liability (see chapter 12 for a more detailed discussion) if an LLC or professional corporation cannot be used, or if it or its members are taxed more favorably than an LLC or PC. However, an LLP may or may not be preferable to a professional corporation or LLC for tax or liability protection purposes, depending on the exact facts and circumstances of the organization in question. However, conversion to an LLP by a general partnership is easiest since the LLP remains a partnership under state law.

Q 11:9   Why use an LLP instead of an LLC?

An LLP generally is preferable to an LLC in several instances, for example, when the LLC cannot be used by the particular business or profession because of statutory or regulatory prohibitions in one or more states where it transacts business, or when the state imposes more tax on LLCs than on LLPs. In many states the statute or professional licensing authorities (or both) prohibit, or have not expressly authorized, the practice of a profession through an LLC. For example, in Illinois and New Mexico, the state supreme court has not authorized LLCs to provide legal services. Rhode Island LLC statutes specifically prohibit the practice of a profession through an LLC. Several states, including Alabama, Arkansas, Arizona, Delaware, Georgia, Idaho, Indiana, Iowa, Kansas, Michigan, Minnesota, Missouri, Montana, Nebraska, New Hampshire, Oregon, Utah, Virginia, and Wyoming have provisions within the state statute specifically allowing professionals to practice as an LLC.

As an example of state tax differences, Texas imposes a type of income tax on LLCs through its franchise tax, based on the LLC's net earnings. A Texas LLP, however, is not subject to this tax on capital. From this perspective, it is preferable in Texas to practice a profession through an LLP as opposed to an LLC.

An LLP may be preferable because it avoids, or at least reduces, the need to revisit the partnership's existing written agreements, whereas the use of an LLC would require many issues to be reviewed, renegotiated, and new documents to be prepared. In addition, in some professions, individuals may be able to be a "principal" in a partnership, and treated and taxed as a partner, but not a member in an LLC. For example, a computer specialist could be a principal and treated as a partner in an accounting firm, but could not in many states be a member in an LLC if not a CPA.

Another aspect where an LLP may have an advantage over an LLC is with respect to employment regulation. Generally, partners are considered co-owners, and accordingly, are not covered by employment discrimination and worker compensation laws. [See Q 11:47] Although neither statutory nor judicial pronouncements are well defined, LLC members are arguably more like employees, particularly in manager-managed LLCs. If LLC members are classified as employees, the LLC may be saddled with higher costs in an attempt to comply with these provisions and to make restitution for any violation.

LLPs also have an advantage over LLCs concerning distributions made when the entity is insolvent or will be rendered insolvent due to the distribution. Many LLC statutes specifically give creditors remedies against both members who receive and members who authorize such distributions. LLPs do not typically present the same problem due the historical origins of LLPs.

Co-owner status in an LLP may also serve to limit the applicability of federal and state securities laws. Having the status of a co-owner greatly diminishes the possibility that the partnership agreement is an investment contract, and thus a security (see chapter 9 for a detailed discussion of securities law). This may serve to eliminate costs associated with registration of the member's interest as a security if no exemptions from registration apply. In contrast, some state securities laws consider a member's LLC interest as a security. Moreover, a member-managed LLC more closely resembles an investment contract under federal and state securities laws.

While the possible exception of LLPs from employment and securities laws may be beneficial to the partnership in terms of reduced expenses needed for compliance, it serves to strip partners of possible legal remedies in the event of unscrupulous activities by other partners. Accordingly, the use of an LLP to circumvent possible application of these laws should be carefully weighed against the possible adverse consequences to individual partners.

Q 11:10 Why use an LLC instead of an LLP?

Because some LLPs are intended to shield partners only from their fellow partners' negligence and malpractice, but not from joint and several liability for contract debts (rent, loans, etc.), the LLC, which limits all liability, is always preferable to an LLP for liability purposes. Thus, if an LLC is allowed in a state for a business, profession, or investment, and there are no unique taxes on the LLC that are not imposed on the LLP, the LLC will almost always be the more preferable choice, except if the entity does business (in the corporate sense) in certain other states that do not allow the LLC to perform that business or profession. In addition, malpractice in many states can result in a breach of implied contract claim, which might not be protected by the LLP.

An LLC also provides greater capacity to restrict nonmanaging members from binding the firm. In an LLP, a partner can bind the firm as to third parties in any ordinary matter. An LLC may restrict non-managing members from possessing agency powers, thus providing for more streamlined management.

An LLC may be more effective for restricting the power of a firm member to disassociate, depending on state law. Both LLC and partnership statutes provide default rules for a member to exit the firm. However, with LLPs, an attempt to circumvent the default rule is not permitted. [RUPA § 103(b)(6)] In contrast, most LLC statutes allow restrictions on the right of members to exit the firm.

While the prohibition on dissociation may be problematic in terms of operation of the firm when members disagree, such a restriction allows greater discounts on member's interests for tax purposes, especially for estate and gift tax valuations.

In a limited partnership, if the general partner is a corporation, adoption of the proper structure under IRS regulations achieves limited liability and pass-through tax treatment. [IRC § 7701] A limited partner in an LLLP (a limited liability limited partnership), however, in many states may lose limited liability protection if the limited partner participates in the control or management of the partnership business. By contrast, unless he or she has otherwise agreed, no member of an LLC will be personally liable for the LLC's obligations, and all members may participate in the control of the business.

Q 11:11   What are the differences between an LLP and a limited partnership (LP)?

No partner in an LLP is liable for all debts of the partnership, whereas the general partner in a limited partnership is liable for all the debts of the partnership. In contrast, limited partners in an LP are not liable for any debts of the partnership while partners in an LLP, under some statutes, are liable for the partnership's debts in contract.

The effect of the degree of management on liability is also an important difference. In LLPs, the degree of management is irrelevant in determining liability unless that partner directly supervises the activity which causes liability. With LPs, if a limited partner participates in management, that partner may become liable for all the firm's debts, similar to the liability of a general partner.

Extent of Liability Protection

Q 11:12   What level of protection against liability does an LLP give its partners?

The scope of limited liability protection varies considerably in each state under each state's LLP statute. However, areas of uniformity exist. In all states a partner is personally liable for his or her own negligence or misconduct. The scope of protection partners have from liability also varies under each state's LLP statute. However, common areas of protection exist, such as from other partners' negligence, malpractice, malfeasance, or torts.

The LLP statutes in those states that initially passed LLP statutes, such as Texas, only gave protection to non-negligent partners from errors, omissions, negligence, incompetence, or malfeasance of the other parties. [For example, Tex Art 6132b-3.08(2) (1993); NC Gen Stat § 59-45(b) (1993).] These states are generally referred to as having a first generation LLP Statute. The states that continue to have first generation LLP statutes include Arizona, Iowa, Louisiana, North Carolina, Pennsylvania, South Carolina, Texas and Utah. Accordingly, partners could be held vicariously liable for the wrongful actions of other partners if the non-negligent partner had notice or knowledge of the misconduct and did nothing to try to prevent it, or, be held joint and severally liable for any debts or obligations derived from other causes. This meant that partners were still personally liable on such things as commercial debts, contract liabilities, and contract-based claims arising from the wrongdoing of other limited partners.

Minnesota then passed an LLP statute which broadened the scope of limited liability to the partners of an LLP. For example, limited liability partners were protected both directly and indirectly from personal liability for all debts and obligations of the partnership which included both torts and commercial contracts, making them like LLCs for this purpose. These statutes are generally referred to as the second generation LLP statutes.

The National Conference of Commissioners on Uniform State Laws (NCCUSL) adopted the following provision in respect of the extent of limited liability of limited liability partners.

"An obligation of a partnership incurred while the partnership is a limited liability partnership whether arising in contract, tort or otherwise is solely the obligation of the partnership. A partner is not personally liable directly or indirectly including by way of contribution or otherwise for such partnership obligation solely by reason of being or so acting as a partner. This subsection shall apply notwithstanding anything inconsistent in the partnership agreement that existed immediately before the vote required to become a limited liability partnership under Section 100(b)." [NCCUSL Draft LLP Amendments to RUPA § 306(c) (Jul 12-19, 1996)]

However, personal liability continues to exist for limited liability partners in respect of debts and obligations arising from a partner's own negligence or tortious conduct in all LLP statutes. Further, under most statutes a partner remains liable for the wrongdoing of those under the partner's direct supervision and control. Colorado, Georgia, Indiana, Kentucky, Louisiana and Utah's do not provide for supervisor liability. [Colo. Rev. Stat. Ann. § 7-60-155(2)(a) (West Supp. 1997); GA Code Ann. § 14-8-15(c) (Supp. 1998); Ind. Code Ann. § 23-4-1-15(3) (Michie Supp. 1997); KY Rev. Stat. Ann. art. § 362.220 (Banks-Baldwin Supp. 1997); LA. Rev. Stat. Ann. § 9.3431 (West Supp. 1998); Utah Code Ann. § 48-1-12 (1998)]

Formation, Costs, and Operational Issues

Q 11:13   How do you register an LLP?

To form an LLP, an application must be filed with the state. Each state statute requires the LLP application to be executed by at least a majority in interest of the partners or by one or more partners authorized to do so by the partners.

State LLP statutes generally require that the application include:

1. *Name.* The partnership's name, which typically must include either the words "registered limited liability partnership" or the abbreviation "LLP." Most states require that these designations be at the end of the LLP's name.

2. *Partners.* The number of partners at the time of the application.

3. *Activity.* A description of the partnership's business.

4. *Other items.* Some states have additional requirements, such as the partnership's federal tax number, address, and registered office or agent. For example, Virginia requires the filing of a certified copy of the partnership's locally filed partnership certificate, and New York requires publication.

Generally, a filing fee must be paid to the state. The filing fees can run the range of $200 per partner (1993 Texas statute) to a flat $100 filing fee (Louisiana, Virginia, and North Carolina). Additionally, the LLP could be required to pay an annual renewal fee. The annual renewal fees are not tied to a tax return filing date, but rather to the original filing of the LLP's application.

Additionally, an LLP that performs business in another state could be required to register with the state as a foreign LLP and pay a filing fee, which could be very expensive.

The registration is generally effective upon filing, although several states allow the partnership to specify a later date upon which LLP status is to take effect. [See, e.g., Fla Stat § 620.78; Off Code of Ga § 14-8-62; Ann Code of Md, Corps & Ass'ns § 9-801]

Most LLP laws provide that the registration lasts for a one-year period. [But see Idaho Code § 53-343 (registration effective until withdrawal); Ann Code of Md, Corps & Ass'ns § 9-801 (registration effective until withdrawal); McKinney's Consol Laws of NY, Partnership Law § 121-500 (biennial registration requirements)] In some states, the LLP will be required to file a renewal application in order to remain an LLP. [See, e.g., Iowa Code § 486.44; Kent Rev Stat § 362-555; Minn Stat Ann § 323.44] The renewal application typically has to contain the same information as the original application. [See, e.g., Del Code tit 6, § 1545; Fla Stat § 620.78; Ill Comp Stat, Ch. 805, Act 205, § 8.1] The execution, filing, and fee requirements may be the same as well. By filing a renewal application, the partnership may remain an LLP for another renewable one-year period.

Other states, rather than requiring a renewal application, provide that a registered limited liability partnership must file an annual notice or report and pay an annual fee. [See, e.g., Colo Rev Stat § 7-60-149; NJ Stat § 42:1-44; Wash SB No. 5374, Laws of 1995, § 3] In the annual notice or report, the partnership must indicate changes in information since the last filing. [See, e.g., N Mex Stat § 54-1-44; Tenn SB No 193, Laws of 1995, § 9; Wash SB No 5374, Laws of 1995, § 3] The statutes requiring annual fees and notices provide that a failure to file or pay the fee will result in a revocation of the partnership's registration. [See, e.g.,

Colo Rev Stat § 7-60-182; N Mex Stat § 54-1-44; Ohio Rev Code § 1775.63]

An LLP can also voluntarily cancel or withdraw its registration. This is done by filing a written withdrawal notice with the secretary of state. [See, e.g., Fla Stat § 620.785; Minn Stat Ann § 323.44; NJ Stat § 42:1-44.] By making this filing, the partnership does not dissolve. However, it will no longer be an LLP. Because of the serious consequences of withdrawal, some states provide that the decision must be approved by all of the partners (unless the partnership agreement provides otherwise). [See Colo Rev Stat § 7-50-144; Minn Stat Ann § 323.44.]

Q 11:14 What are the consequences of an LLP failing to renew its registration?

An LLP's status expires generally one year after the date of registration. An RLLP must file a renewal application annually with the secretary of state. This registration must be accompanied by an annual renewal fee and updated information. If a renewal filing is not made, the business will be treated as a traditional general partnership by default, which subjects the partners to joint and several liability for all debts and obligations of the partnership. The subsequent failure to refile does not dissolve the partnership. However, it could put the partners at risk of the more traditional personal liability.

A number of LLP statutes contain "savings clauses" which protect partners from the inadvertent lapse of an LLP status. Such provisions require the secretary of state to provide written notice to the partnership that it has failed to pay fees or file reports. The notice also warns the partnership that its LLP partnership status will be revoked after a specified period of time unless the filing fee and penalties are forthcoming within that time period.

Under the NCCUSL draft LLP amendments, an NCCUSL partnership is given a two-year grace period in which it can reactivate its LLP status by filing and paying appropriate fees. At that time the liability protection will relate back and provide the LLP liability protection throughout the lapsed period.

Q 11:15   What types of specific voting requirements exist for conversion from a general partnership to an LLP and what are the consequences to the members of LLP registration?

In the absence of a provision in the partnership agreement, state LLP statutes provide a default rule for an election of LLP status. All of the states require at least a majority-in-interest or majority of the partners with some states requiring unanimous consent.

If mere majority approval is required to convert a general partnership into an LLP, liability may shift between members without approval of the members assuming the liability. In a general partnership, liability is borne jointly and severally among all the partners. If LLP status is elected potential liabilities are redistributed from all partners to those partners who have direct supervisory and monitoring responsibilities. Some commentators submit that partners assuming the added liability potential must approve the conversion to LLP status. [Bromberg and Ribstein on Limited Liability Partnerships § 2.04(b)] Others point out that statutes permitting such a redistribution of liability potential in contravention of the contract between partners embodied in the partnership agreement and without consent of all parties may contradict the Contacts Clause of the United States Constitution. [US Constitution, Article I, § 10: No state shall . . . pass any . . . Law impairing the obligation of contracts; see Henry N Butler & Larry E Ribstein, The Contract Clause and the Corporation, 55 Brook L Rev 767 (1989)]

Q 11:16   What are the consequences if the registration of the LLP is defective?

The failure to comply with the technical requirements of the statute may cause the limited liability shield to be disregarded. However, the harsh effects of this possibility may be mitigated in one of two ways. First, many LLP statutes permit "substantial compliance." [See, e.g, Del Code Ann tit 6 § 1515(b)] For substantial compliance to apply, the errors must have been made with a good faith effort towards compliance.

Another possible theory in favor of limited liability is LLP by estoppel. This occurs when the alleged LLP holds itself out as such and the third party contracts with the firm on the assumption that it is, in fact, an LLP. Although not heavily litigated in the LLP context, the doctrine is clearly established in corporate law and may similarly apply to LLPs. [See, e.g, Cranson v IBM Corp, 200 A 2d 33 (Md 1964); Harry Rich Corp v Feinberg, 518 So 2d 377 (Fla Dist Ct App 1987); and HF Phillipsborn & Co v Suson 322 NE 2d 45 (Ill 1975)]

Q 11:17   What must an LLP do in order to maintain its status?

It must continue to comply with the statutory requirements. These typically include the maintenance of liability insurance (if applicable), the maintenance of registration, the proper disclosure of LLP status to third parties, and proper authorization of LLP status by the appropriate number of partners. Ideally, these measures should be assigned to one or more members in the partnership agreement because proper designation of the responsibility for compliance will increase the likelihood that compliance will occur.

Q 11:18   What are the possible consequences if the composition of the LLP changes?

The **Texas** LLP statute contains specific provisions that contemplate amendments when partners are added to the partnership. Texas imposes an additional fee upon the addition of partners.

State LLP statutes generally do not address the technical question of what happens to an LLP when a partner dies or otherwise withdraws from the partnership. As a general rule, a partnership formed under the Uniform Partnership Act is legally dissolved when those events occur. Even if the business of the dissolved partnership is continued, the dissolution of the partnership involves the creation of a new partnership for state law (although not usually federal tax) purposes. It may be possible for a party challenging a partnership's LLP status to claim that the partners of the "new" partnership are not entitled to the benefit of the old partnership's LLP status. A completely new registration by a continuing partnership every time the partnership undergoes a technical dissolution should eliminate any problem, but it would be tedious, time consuming, and expensive. It could be very expensive for partnerships that register in several states.

Q 11:19 How does the limited liability shield apply to new members of a pre-existing LLP?

A new member is not liable for LLP obligations incurred by the LLP before admission of the new partner. [UPA § 17; RUPA § 306(b)]

Q 11:20 How is a limited liability partnership treated for tax purposes?

An LLP is generally treated as a partnership for state and federal tax purposes (see chapter 3). Most professional LLPs will be general partnerships before filing an application to become an LLP. The mere fact that the partners are shielded from liability for the malpractice of other partners will normally not change the LLP's tax classification to one of an association taxable as a corporation.

The IRS has ruled that converting from a general partnership to an LLP will not result in a termination of the partnership under Code Section 708. [Ltr Ruls 9426037, 9507014] The IRS noted that this conversion is analogous to converting a general partnership into a limited partnership. [Rev Rul 84-52, 1984-1 CB 157] Thus, for tax purposes, the entity is the same and may continue to use the same federal partnership employer identification number.

Under Code Section 708(a) [(1986), as amended], a partnership continues to exist for federal income tax purposes until it is terminated. Under Code Section 708(b) a partnership is terminated if: there is a complete cessation of business [IRC § 708(b)(1)(A)]; a reduction in the number of partners to one through either withdrawal, death, or transfer of partnership interest among the partners [IRC § 708(b)(1)(A); Treas Reg §§ 1.708-1(b)(1)(i), 301.7701-3(a)]; or the sale or exchange of more than 50 percent of the interest in the partnership capital or its profits in any 12-month period. [IRC § 708(b)(1)(B); Prop Treas Reg § 1.708-1.708-1(b)(1)(iv)]

A termination under Code Section 708(b)(1)(A) results in a partnership ceasing to exist for tax purposes. As a consequence, there is a deemed distribution to the partners of the assets of the partnership in a liquidation to which Code Sections 731 and 732 apply. A partnership that terminates as a consequence of one partner buying the interests of the others terminates immediately following the purchase. [Treas Reg § 1.708-1(b)(1)(iv)]

Whether a termination event occurs under Code Section 708(b)(1)(B) will depend upon whether the transfer is a sale or exchange and whether the transferred interests constitute at least 50 percent of the total interest in partnership capital and profits. A termination under this section will distribute all the partnership assets immediately after the sale that triggered the termination to its partners. Immediately following the distribution the partners are deemed to recontribute the assets to a new partnership. Such a distribution of property is treated for federal tax purposes as an actual distribution. However, the proposed regulations have a significant effect on these two transactions. A termination under the proposed regulations will transfer all the partnership assets and liabilities immediately on the sale triggering the termination to a new partnership in exchange for all of the interests in the new partnership. Immediately following the transfer, the terminated partnership is deemed to distribute interest in the new partnership to the partners of the terminated partnership in liquidation of the terminated partnership. Accordingly, the proposed regulations do not give rise to a deemed distribution of partnership assets, or a consequential liability for federal tax purposes. However, federal tax liability may still exist in respect to a termination that does not flow from an assets distribution.

Q 11:21   Is malpractice insurance required to obtain LLP status?

Several of the earlier statutes require insurance or an escrow account covering claims with respect to which the partners are not jointly liable. Most of the more recent statutes, as well as the prototype statute, do not require insurance, leaving issues of insurance for professionals to the statutes dealing with specific professions and occupations. [See e.g, Mass Gen L ch 108, § 45(8)]

Some states require a fixed amount of liability insurance coverage. Delaware provides that an LLP must carry at least $1 million of liability insurance to cover the kinds of negligence, wrongful acts, and misconduct for which liability is limited. It also provides that instead of insurance, the LLP can provide $1 million of funds specifically designated and segregated for the satisfaction of judgments based on those acts for which liability is limited, by deposit in trust or bank escrow of cash, certificates of deposit, or U.S. Treasury obligations, or a bank letter of credit or insurance company bond. [Del Code tit 6 § 1546] Likewise, **Alaska** and **Oklahoma** also require $1 million in liability insurance. [Alaska Stat § 32.05.416; Okla Stat tit 54, § 407 (deductible must not be greater than 10% unless other security is present)] Other states have lesser requirements: **New Mexico** requires LLPs to carry at least $500,000 of liability insurance (or in segregated and designated funds) per occurrence [N Mex Stat § 54-1-47]; **Connecticut** requires $250,000 in coverage [Conn Gen Stat § 34-53(4)]; **South Carolina** requires $100,000 beyond any deductible or the amount required by licensing authorities [SC Code Ann § 33-41-1130(A)(1) – (2)]; **Texas** requires $100,000 [Tex Rev Civ Stat Ann art 6132b-§ 45-C(1)]; and the **District of Columbia** requires the greater of $100,000 or the largest amount an individual partner carries. [DC Code Ann § 46(a)] In **Washington,** professional LLPs must carry insurance coverage in a range of $1 million to $3 million depending on the size and nature of the business. [Wash Rev Code § 25.04.730(5)]

The other common approach is to tie the amount of coverage required to a formula taking into account the number of partners in the LLP. **Florida** requires at least $100,000 multiplied by the number of general partners in excess of one, but no less than $200,000 or more than $3 million. [Fla Stat § 620.82] In **California,** the standard is $100,000 per person with a cap of $5 million for accounting firms and $7.5 million for law firms or, alternatively, a confirmation of partnership net worth in excess of $10 million. Similarly, **Hawaii** requires either $100,000 per licensed partner up to $5 million or $10 million in partnership net worth. [Haw Rev Stat § 425-BB] The requirement in **Rhode Island** is $50,000 per professional, but not less than $100,000 and with a cap of $500,000. The deductible per claim must be less than $25,000 multiplied by the number of professionals. [RI Gen L § 7-12-58]

A failure to adhere to the insurance requirement will result in a loss of limited liability up to the amount that would have been covered if the insurance had been in place. [Alaska Stat § 32.05.416; Okla Stat tit 54, § 407; Wash Rev Code § 25.04.730(5)] If the LLP makes a false claim of insurance coverage, joint and several liability results for all debts. [Haw Rev Stat § 425-BB]

Q 11:22   What are the different types of names that an LLP uses?

In different states the terms limited liability partnership (LLP) and registered limited liability partnership (RLLP) are used. **Ohio** uses the term "registered partnership having limited liability" (PLL). In most states, the designation as an LLP or RLLP must be used in order to raise the limited liability shield in contract dealings with third parties. Failure to do so serves as a misrepresentation of the firm's status and estoppel will apply as to bar a defense of limited liability. Some state statutes excuse the failure to disclose LLP status if the third party did not rely on the firm's apparent general partnership status in signing the contract. The disclosure of LLP status is largely irrelevant with respect to tort creditors because the reliance element will generally be lacking.

Q 11:23   Is foreign qualification of LLP status necessary and, if so, how is it obtained?

A number of states also have provisions dealing with foreign registered limited liability partnerships. The laws provide that before transacting business in the state, a foreign LLP has to register with the appropriate state official. [See, e.g., Colo Rev Stat § 7-60-144; Fla Stat § 620.84; Off Code of Ga § 14-8-45; Ky Rev Stat § 362.585; N Mex Stat § 54-1-46; McKinney's Consol Laws of NY, Partnership Law § 121-1502; Code of Va § 50-43.7] **Delaware, Idaho, Illinois, Iowa,** and **Utah,** however, permit a foreign LLP to transact business without registration.

The information that must be included in a foreign LLP's registration form is generally the same as that required for a domestic LLP, with the addition of the state and date of formation. [See, e.g., Fla Stat § 620.84; Kent Rev Stat § 362.585; Minn Stat Ann § 323.48]

A foreign LLP also has to meet renewal/annual notice requirements to maintain its registration in the foreign state. In several states, foreign LLPs are subject to biennial registration requirements. [See, e.g., N Mex Stat § 54-1-46; McKinney's Consol Laws of NY, Partnership Law § 121-1503; Tenn SB No 193, Laws of 1995, § 9]

None of the states define what activities constitute "transacting business" in the state. However, a few statutes contain a list of activities that an LLP can engage in without being considered doing business in the state. [See, e.g., Ariz Rev Stat § 29-254; Off Code of Ga § 14-8-45; Ann Code of Md, Corps & Ass'ns § 9-909; McKinney's Consol Laws of NY, Partnership Law § 121-1502; N Dak Cent Code § 45-22-21] New York's law, for example provides that:

A foreign limited liability partnership shall not be considered to be carrying on or conducting or transacting business or activities in this state by reason of carrying on in this state any one or more of the following activities:

(i)   maintaining or defending any action or proceeding, whether judicial, administrative, arbitrative or otherwise, or effecting settlement thereof or the settlement of claims or disputes;

(ii) holding meetings of its partners; or

(iii) maintaining bank accounts.

[McKinney's Consol Laws of NY, Partnership Law § 121-1502]

Q 11:24   What is the definition of a "foreign" LLP?

Most states define a foreign LLP as a firm registered as an LLP in another jurisdiction and formed by an agreement governed by the laws of that jurisdiction. Complexities arise in the few states that endeavor to define "LLP" in terms of similarities to domestic LLPs instead of merely accepting the foreign state's designation of LLP status. [See, e.g., Ohio Rev Code Ann § 1775.05(C); Va Code Ann § 73.79] For instance, a state whose LLP statute provides partial protection may not consider a foreign firm an LLP if it purports to have limited liability for both contract and torts under its home state's law. Moreover, an LLP formed in a state with a complete shield for both tort and contract liabilities may exceed the statutory definition for limited liability in some states. [See Ky Rev Stat ch 275.015]

Even if the partnership agreement is governed by the laws of another state, some states will classify an LLP as "domestic" rather than "foreign" if the LLP is registered under the laws of that state. [See, e.g., Ohio Rev Code Ann § 1775.04(A); Va Code

Ann § 50-73.79] These types of statutes may permit an LLP to enjoy more favorable laws of one state while taking advantage of lower registration or administrative costs of other states. The opportunities for this form of "jurisdiction shopping" is dwindling as more states adopt the RUPA with the 1996 LLP amendments which strictly apply the registration state's law.

Q 11:25 What are the consequences of a failure to register a foreign LLP?

Typically, the primary penalties for a failure to register are a prohibition to sue in the state's courts and the ability of third parties to substitute service of process on the secretary of state instead of a designated agent of the LLP in lawsuits filed against the LLP. [See, e.g., Colo Rev Stat § 7-60-144; Fla Stat § 620.84; Off Code of Ga § 14-8-564]

North Dakota, however, takes a more drastic approach and strips the limited liability shield of partners and imposes personal liability for a failure to register. [ND Cent Code § 45-22-20]

Q 11:26 Which state's law applies to foreign LLPs?

With respect to the internal affairs of the LLP and the liability of the partners, the state of formation will govern the LLP in the vast majority of states. [See, e.g., Ariz Rev Stat Ann § 29-246; DC Code § 41-147; Md Code Ann, Corps & Ass'ns § 9-901; Minn Stat Ann § 323.48]

In contrast, local law will apply to most other instances, including regulatory matters. Often foreign LLPs' activities are limited to those permissible for a domestic LLP. Moreover, liability limitations on domestic LLPs will apply to foreign LLPs regardless of their liability protection in their formation or registration state. Any professional licensing requirements placed on domestic LLPs which provide professional services will be imposed of foreign LLPs as well. [See, e.g., Fla Stat Ann § 620.84(8); Mo Rev Stat § 358.440(19)(1); Nev Rev Stat § 87.560(2); Ore Rev Stat § 68.760(3)]

Q 11:27   What are the choice of law default rules under the 1994 RUPA for foreign LLPs?

Under the 1994 pre-LLP RUPA, the state where the LLP has its chief executive office governs "relations among the partners and between the partnership." [RUPA § 106 (1994)] This may not be the state of formation or even the state where the dispute arose. The law of the state where the dispute arose, however, would apply to legal disputes involving the LLP members and third parties. [RUPA § 103(b)(9) (1994) (partnership agreement cannot effect rights of third parties)] Uncertainty exists, however, when an LLP's internal affairs and its disputes with third parties are interrelated. For instance, an LLP may be liable to a third party which would be governed in a registration state where the obligation arose. This obligation may be satisfied by enforcing a delinquent capital contribution which would qualify as a dispute between the partner and the partnership to be decided under the law where the chief executive office is located. It is not clear which state's law would apply in this situation.

It is important to note that, under the 1994 version, the LLP may waive the RUPA choice-of-law provision and choose to be governed by the law of any state.

Finally, there is a question of whether the 1994 version RUPA applies at all to foreign LLPs because § 202 disqualifies as a partnership an association "formed under a statute other than this [Act], a predecessor statute, or comparable statute of another jurisdiction. . . ." [Bromberg & Ribstein on Limited Liability Partnerships § 6.03(a)] It has been suggested that a foreign LLP may not be formed under that state's version of the RUPA and, therefore, may be only an association and not a "partnership" for RUPA purposes. [See Bromberg & Ribstein on Limited Liability Partnerships § 6.04(a)]

Q 11:28   What are the choice-of-law default rules under the 1996 amended version of the RUPA?

Under the amended 1996 version of the RUPA, laws of the formation state govern the internal affairs of a foreign LLP. [RUPA § 1101 (1996)] Moreover, the 1996 RUPA expressly states that the registration state's law governs the LLP's debts and obligations to third parties within the registration state. [RUPA § 106(b) (1996)] This still does not address the issue of whether the formation state's or registration state's law applies when the obligation to a third party is interrelated to a dispute between the partners and the LLP (see SQ 11:14.4). The amended RUPA also provides that the law of the registration state "governs relations among the partners and between the partners and the partnership. . . ." [RUPA § 106(b) (1996)] This language presumably includes LLPs and implies that § 1101 is applicable to use the law of the LLP's formation state to govern its internal affairs. In contrast to the 1994 version, the ability to waive these choice-of-law provisions in the partnership agreement is not permitted. [RUPA § 103(b)(9) (1996)]

Practitioners should be wary of some states which have haphazardly added the foreign LLP provisions to their RUPA version. In these states there may be conflicting statutory authority requiring the use of the law of both the state where the LLP's chief executive office is located and the state of formation as required by § 1101 under the 1996 amendment. [See, e.g, Fla Stat Ann § 620.84; NM Stat Ann § 54-1-16] Other states have adopted only the LLP provisions and reconciled the new additions with their version of the RUPA. **Montana** provides the formation jurisdiction applies "notwithstanding" the general choice-of-law provision although the jurisdiction of "formation" is not clearly defined and may possibly include a state specified in the partnership agreement or the state where the chief executive office is located. [Mont Code Ann § 35-10-710(5)] **West Virginia** specifies that the internal affairs of an LLP are governed by the law of the state where the LLP is registered. [W Va Code § 47B-10-4(f)]

Q 11:29 Under an LLP, are an individual owner's liabilities limited to those created by the individual's own acts or improper supervision?

No, under the Uniform Partnership Act, each partner has the obligation to indemnify the partnership [UPA § 18(a)] for losses. In addition, the UPA also provides that a partner be indemnified by the partnership for all losses, expenses, and obligations incurred by a partner. [UPA §§ 18(b), (c)] Thus, when an LLP is adopted, these provisions should be negated. Otherwise, the adoption of an LLP will accomplish very little, since the partners will remain jointly and severally liable through the indemnification process. In addition, partners' liability may not be reduced in any practical way, since each time an indemnification occurs, it may create a greater pool of assets that a creditor may reach. Thus, liabilities and indemnifications are a significant problem in any limited liability entity, including an LLP; however, in an LLP they are generally required by statute, unless specifically eliminated in the partnership agreement.

Q 11:30 How is an LLP classified under the Bankruptcy Code?

It is not clear whether an LLP is classified as a partnership or corporation. The definition of a corporation under the Bankruptcy Code includes an "association having a power or privilege that a private corporation, but not an individual or partnership, possesses . . . but does not include a limited partnership." [11 USC § 101(9)] The limited liability privilege gives credence to the argument that the LLP should be classified as a corporation under the Bankruptcy Code. On the other hand, the fact that LLPs are clearly partnerships under state law, that limited partnerships are not corporations under the Bankruptcy Code, and that state law liability limitations on partnership contribution obligations are respected under the Bankruptcy Code all serve to swing the pendulum in favor of partnership classification.

Q 11:31 Does an LLP afford any protection if the LLP partnership files for bankruptcy?

Yes. Section 212 of the Bankruptcy Reform Act of 1994 [PL 103-394] amended Section 723(a) of the U.S. Bankruptcy Act to provide that a partner is only liable to the trustee in bankruptcy "to the extent that under applicable nonbankruptcy law such general partner is personally liable for such deficiency." A partner in a registered limited liability partnership would only be liable in bankruptcy to the extent that a partner would be liable for a deficiency under the registered limited liability statute under that the partnership was organized.

Q 11:32 Are LLP owners liable when operations or distributions render the entity insolvent?

If an LLP provides limited malpractice protection, the partners normally remain liable to reimburse the LLP for any liabilities, as stated above under the Uniform Partnership Act (Q 11:15) due to the partners' statutory indemnity liabilities (unless negated in the partnership agreement). The **Minnesota** LLP statute expressly deals with this issue by providing that a partner in an LLP is liable for two years for any distributions that would have been illegal had the LLP been a corporation. [Minn Stat § 323.14 subd 5 (1994)]

Q 11:33 Can a partnership considering LLP status register in a state other than its principal place of business, and if so, what factors should be considered?

Generally, yes. A partnership considering LLP status should look to the protection from liability the various state statutes provide in choosing which state to register. It is important, however, to consider how the state where the partnership's operations are centered treats foreign LLPs. The opportunity to forum shop for the most advantageous LLP statute may be limited by local restrictions concerning the limited liability treatment of certain types of business. This is particularly true with partnerships providing professional services where state regulatory and licensing authorities may have stringent guidelines on the form of business and the prerequisites for limited liability of partners. Variations in the cost of registration should also be considered.

Q 11:34 Are there other types of LLP statutes that provide greater protection to partners?

Yes. State statutes which provide the greatest protection are those which shield against both tort and contract liability. These include: New York, Ohio, California, Colorado, Georgia, Hawaii, Idaho, Indiana, Maryland, Massachusetts, Missouri, Montana, North Dakota, Oregon, South Dakota, Minnesota, and Virginia.

The New York law provides full liability protection for torts and contracts. The New York statute also adds additional language shielding partners from debts and obligations chargeable to partners in addition to those chargeable to the partnership by reason of being such a partner or acting in such capacity in the conduct of the other business or activities of the registered LLP. However, New York law only allows certain professional partnerships to become LLPs and then only after publication of notices, in addition to central filing. [NY Partnership Law §§ 26(b)-(f)] Those states that restrict the use of LLPs by attorneys or require a rule of court are Delaware, Florida, Illinois, Indiana, Kentucky, Massachusetts, Nevada, New Jersey, and Wisconsin. The Minnesota LLP statute is not limited to professionals. It may be used by any business or profession. [Minn Stat § 323.14 (1994)]

The Virginia LLP Act has been amended as follows:

A partner in a registered limited liability partnership is not individually liable directly or indirectly, including by way of indemnification, contribution or otherwise, for the debts, obligations and liabilities chargeable to the partnership, whether sounding in tort, contract or otherwise, arising from the negligence, malpractice, wrongful acts or misconduct committed while the partnership is a registered limited liability partnership and in the course of the partnership business by another partner, employee, agent or representative of the partnership. [Va Code Ann 50-15.B]

Nevertheless, even this protection will not protect against the partner's own negligence, malpractice, wrongful acts, or other misconduct, including supervisory liability. [Va Code Ann § 50-5.C.; see also, Del Code Ann § 1515(b)] UPA Section 15(b) also makes all partners jointly liable for partnership obligations, including the obligation to indemnify a negligent or otherwise liable partner.

States with the strongest liability shields typically provide for continued LLP status if a change in membership occurs. [See, e.g., Del Code Ann tit 6 § 1546(a)] Additionally, **New York, Colorado, Georgia, Indiana, Maryland, Missouri, Montana, North Dakota, Oregon,** and **South Dakota** provide the added safeguard of permitting LLP status to continue in the event of dissolution.

Although providing limited liability to both torts and contracts, the **Colorado, Minnesota,** and **North Dakota** statutes do impose liability for distributions received by partners when the LLP is insolvent. [Colo Rev Stat § 7-60-146-147; Minn Stat Ann § 323.14(5); and ND Cent Code § 44-22-10]

Q 11:35 Does the creation of an LLP terminate the existence of the underlying state law partnership and create a new partnership for purposes of Code Section 708(b)?

No. Letter Ruling 9325043 (March 29, 1993) has so ruled. This ruling notes that the state law partnership entity remains in existence. It may continue to use the same federal tax identification number. The IRS has so ruled with respect to LLCs that are created from partnerships and remain partnerships. [See Rev Rul 95-37, 1995-1 CB 130]

Q 11:36 Is there any negative tax impact when a general partnership registers with the state to form an LLP?

No. The IRS has ruled on several occasions that the registration will be treated in the same manner as a conversion by a general partnership into a limited partnership, which has no tax impact if nothing else is changed in terms of the partners' sharing in profits and losses. [Ltr Ruls 9229016, 9420028, 9424036, 9423037, 9424038, 9423040]

Q 11:37 Is an LLP able to use the cash method of accounting like other general partnerships?

Yes. This is an important issue for professionals, since the use of cash-method accounting does not require them to pay tax until they collect their outstanding billings. Likewise, they cannot deduct obligations until they pay for them. The IRS has privately ruled on several occasions that an LLP can use the cash-basis method of accounting in the same fashion as a general partnership. [Ltr Ruls 9420028, 9424036, 9423037, 9424038, 9423040]

Q 11:38 Will an LLP general partner be treated as a general partner for purposes of net income from self-employment?

Yes, as a general rule. [IRC § 1402(a); Prop Treas Reg § 1.1402(a)-18] If such income is not so treated, the partner will not have Social Security or Medicare tax liability; however, the practice will also not be able to make a retirement plan contribution on the partner's behalf. The 1997 Taxpayer Relief Act suspended the application of the proposed regulation through June 30, 1998.

Code Section 1402(a)(13) provides that the "distributive share of any item of income or loss of a limited partner, as such, other than guaranteed payments" are to be excluded from earnings for self-employment tax purposes. This means that self-employment tax is generally not owed by limited partners. It also means, however, that such income is not included in determining the amount of contributions to or the benefit from, a tax-qualified retirement plan. [IRC § 401(c)] Thus, until the treatment of members in LLPs is clarified, benefit issues may be raised that would not be present in a general partnership that is not an LLP.

This provision was originally designed to prevent passive investors in limited partnerships from including investment income in earnings on which Social Security benefits are based. Should this rule apply to LLCs, such as professional service LLCs, in which most members would be actively involved in the business? Limited partnerships may avoid application of the rule by paying guaranteed payments to limited partners, so presumably LLCs could as well. One private ruling has held that members of a personal service LLC will not be treated as limited partners under Code Section 1402(a)(13). [Ltr Rul 9432018 ("Also, the members' distributive shares of income are not exempted from net earnings from self-employment by Section 1402(a)(13). Therefore, A's distributive share of the income and loss described in Code Section 702(a)(8) from any trade or business carried on by LLC shall be includible in computing the net earnings from self-employment of A.")] In a later ruling, the service appears to indicate that the amount of participation might be a consideration in determining treatment under Section 1402(a)(13). [Ltr Rul 9452024] Proposed Treasury Regulations Section 1.1402(a)-18 would increase the application of SECA taxes to these distributions. Its application was suspended by the 1997 Taxpayer Relief Act through June 30, 1998.

Q 11:39 Is it possible to create an LLP that would result in a taxable event?

Yes. If the allocation of debt were changed at the same time that a partnership registered to become an LLP, then a deemed distribution could be said to occur. [IRC § 752]

Q 11:40   Can a professional corporation convert into an LLP or an LLC without tax consequences if the conversion is expressly provided by state statute?

No, unless there would be no tax on the corporation and shareholders if the corporation were liquidated. This is treated, for tax purposes, as if it were a liquidation and then a recontribution by the individual shareholders into the new entity. Thus, liquidation tax occurs, if it applies, whether the entity is a C corporation or an S corporation.

Q 11:41   Can a non-profit organization form an LLP?

No. Under UPA § 6(1) and RUPA § 202, a profit motive is an essential element for classification as a partnership. By negative implication, non-profit organizations are excluded from the definition of a partnership.

Q 11:42   Can a sole proprietor form an LLP?

No. By definition, a partnership consists of "two or more persons." [UPA § 6(1); RUPA § 202] The sole proprietor seeking the benefits of limited liability may still incorporate, or alternatively in some states, form an LLC.

LLPs and the Effects of Dissolution, Dissociation, and Termination

Q 11:43   What happens to an LLP upon the dissociation of a member?

If the LLP statute if based on the UPA, a dissociation of a partner dissolves the partnership. [UPA § 31] The limited liability shield should remain while the partnership winds up its affairs because, under § 30 of the UPA, the partnership remains in existence during the winding up process. The disassociated partner, on the other hand, loses the limited liability shield with respect to post-dissociation debts.

In contrast, the dissociation of a partner does not cause dissolution under LLP statutes based upon the RUPA. [RUPA §§ 601, 603]

Thus, the LLP registration will remain effective only until it is canceled or revoked. [RUPA § 1001(d)]

Q 11:44   What happens to a partner's responsibility for pre-existing liabilities following dissociation?

Under both the UPA and RUPA, the partner is still liable for debts existing prior to dissociation or termination. Theoretically, the liability under a state adopting the RUPA may be greater because the RUPA holds partners liable for "obligations" and not merely liabilities. [RUPA § 703(a)]

Conversions and Mergers

Q 11:45   Are LLPs permitted to merge with other partnerships?

Yes, under the RUPA. [See, generally, RUPA Art 9] The RUPA, however, has conflicting provisions with respect to the continuing effectiveness of an LLP registration following the merger. Section 904 treats the merging LLP as "the same entity that existed before the conversion," suggesting that the registration would remain effective. In contrast, § 906 references the cessation of the merging partnerships "separate existences" which indicates that the registration would not carry over to the new partnership. An argument can be made that the registration continues because § 1001(d) provides that registration is effective until cancellation or revocation. [Bromberg & Ribstein on Limited Liability Partnerships § 3.12(c)]

No merger provisions exist in the UPA. Therefore, a merger would effectively consist of a dissolution of one partnership with a subsequent sale to the surviving firm.

Application of Securities and Employment Discrimination Law to LLPs

Q 11:46   Do LLP interests qualify as securities?

Probably not. Generally, partners are considered co-owners of the partnership and by definition participate in the management of the firm. Thus, an LLP interest will generally not be an "investment contract" because as a co-owner, the partner will not be relying on the efforts of others. In extremely rare circumstances, an LLP interest may meet the **Williamson** test and be classified as a security if a partner has virtually no control of the partnership's management so as to be compared with a limited partner.

Q 11:47   Does employment discrimination law apply to partners in an LLP?

Generally, no. However, an LLP may have to comply with employment discrimination laws at the partner level in limited circumstances. If an individual is a partner in both substance and form, that individual will considered a co-owner and employment discrimination laws will not apply to that person. If, however, an individual is labeled a "partner" but has little or no control in the management of a firm and is treated functionally as an employee, some courts have been willing to look beyond the formal designation of "partner" and hold the individual was an employee protected by discrimination laws. [Strother v Southern California Permanente Medical Group, 79 F 3d 859 (9th Cir 1996] In **Strother,** the alleged partner's compensation was based solely on individual performance and the partner was also subject to discipline for inadequate job performance.

Chapter 12

Professional LLCs and LLPs: Comparison with General Partnerships and Professional Corporations

This chapter discusses the types of entities used by professionals to practice their professions, focusing on LLCs and LLPs, and comparing them to professional corporations. This chapter also analyzes the liability for malpractice of professionals who practice as members of an LLC or as partners in an LLP. Many of the issues are state specific, and a conclusion that is correct in one state may be inappropriate in another.

General Partnership of Professionals: No Longer the Preferred Practice Entity

Q 12:1   What are the significant factors that determine a general partnership?

Vicarious Liability. In a general partnership, each partner is personally, jointly, and severally liable for the acts of the other partners in pursuit of partnership business and for the liabilities of the partnership under the Uniform Partnership Act (UPA). [UPA § 15; Prophit v McSween, 347 So 2d 11 (1977)]

General Rule. A professional who is a partner of a general partnership is liable for his or her own professional errors and omissions and for those of his or her partners and associates, provided that the tortious wrong or contractual breach occurred during the performance of services within the scope (or apparent scope) of the partnership's business. [See UPA §§ 13-15; Zimmerman v Hogg & Allen, 209 SE 2d 795 (1974)] The professional's actual knowledge of the event or act causing the alleged malpractice injury is not necessary. All acts performed within the scope of its business are committed with the professional's imputed knowledge. [Buder v Denver Natl Bank, 157 F 2d 520 (1945)] In short, the partners are liable even if they do not participate in the wrong, ratify it, or have knowledge of it, as long as it occurred in the ordinary course of the professional's partnership business. [UPA § 13]

Q 12:2   What are the exceptions to joint and several liability among partners?

Vicarious liability is not imposed on partners when the act committed by one of the partners is not within the ordinary course of the partnership's business, such as a claim for malicious prosection [Jackson v Jackson, 201 SE 2d 722 (1974)] or when the partner acts outside the ordinary business and does so without authority from the other partners. Thus, an act of a partner that is not for the carrying on of the business of the partnership in the usual way does not bind the partnership unless authorized by other partners. [UPA § 20] Moreover, if the partner has acted in an unauthorized manner, the innocent partners are not deemed to have ratified the actions of the rogue professional unless, in the absence of actual overt ratification, their actions or lack thereof are convincing as to their knowledge: ". . . [the] remaining partners [must] have more than suspicion or gossip that an agreement has been entered into; there must be more than a hint as to its terms, and there must be detailed knowledge of its provisions so that it can be said that by their [the remaining partners'] silence there was acquiescence, ratification or estoppel." [In re Lester, 386 NYS 2d 509 (1976)]

Q 12:3   Does dissolution of a general partnership terminate partners' liability?

Dissolution of the partnership does not discharge a partner's liability based upon happenings during the partnership's existence. [Burnside v McCrary, 384 So 2d 1292 (1980)] The duty to a client by a lawyer for purposes of liability attaches at the time of retention. [Redman v Walters, 88 Cal App 3d 448 (1979)]

Q 12:4   What is the effect of a partner's withdrawal?

Authority is split on a former partner's liability to the client for legal malpractice that occurred after the partner left with respect to a matter in that the firm was retained before the departure. In *Redman,* liability was imposed; in *Burnside,* it was not. Neither holding negates the proposition of *Welsh v. Carrol* [378 So 2d 1255 (1979)]; that is, all partners of the firm are liable for the firm's malpractice except for those who specifically withdrew from the partnership before the assumption of the duty in question or the liability alleged.

In *Redman,* a partner's liability to the client can only be terminated when the client knows of, and consents to, the partner's withdrawal, which terminates the partner's individual obligation. While this may be practical for small partnerships, it is not when partners are so numerous that they are unknown to the client. Moreover, this rule places an onerous burden on the withdrawing partner when he or she wants to withdraw under circumstances that are unfriendly or adversarial to the partnership; if the surviving partners accede to the withdrawal, they will be increasing their own liability to the client and thus may be unwilling to lend support to the withdrawal's presentation to the client, regardless of reasonability. Pragmatically, the client will consult with the remaining partners about the withdrawal and base the decision on all facts and circumstances, including the liability issue.

> **Example 12-1.** If X practices accounting in a partnership with Y, and Y commits malpractice, damaging a third party, then X, Y, and the partnership would all be liable. If a general partnership owns real estate and the partnership borrows money, all partners are liable, jointly and severally, to repay that note, absent limits within the note.

Q 12:5   What is the importance of an Operating Agreement with respect to the withdrawal of a member?

The importance of the Operating Agreement's terms with respect to the withdrawal of a member cannot be overestimated. For example, the Operating Agreement should deal with work in progress and its value. In general, the court will not look outside the Operating Agreement unless the agreement is ambiguous, in which case it may look at the entire agreement and consider its object, nature and purpose.

If the business of an LLC continues following withdrawal of a member, the withdrawing member will be entitled to receive any distributions to which he or she is entitled upon withdrawal under the provisions of the Operating Agreement. [See, e.g., Mo Rev Stat § 347.103.2] In one such case, a court construed an Operating Agreement of a law firm organized as an LLC. [See Goldstein and Price, LC v Tonkin & Mondl, LC, 1998 WL 312244 (Mo App June 16, 1998)] In *Goldstein and Price*, the withdrawing member argued that fees earned by the LLC for work in progress was an obligation owed severally to the members of the LLC, and as such, should be apportioned in accordance with the actual contribution of each lawyer to the eventual result. The trial court agreed with the withdrawn member and applied *quantum meruit* to apportion the fee between the LLC and the member. However, the court of appeals disagreed with this interpretation and held that the withdrawing member's share of the fee, to the extent earned while he was a member of the LLC, is determined by the allocation rules contained in the LLC's Operating Agreement as orally amended by all of the members. The appeals court reasoned that *quantum meruit* has no application when an express agreement governs the parties' rights and obligations.

Q 12:6   Can persons practice a profession together and inadvertently create a *de facto* partnership?

Yes. A *de facto* partnership, and its accompanying shared joint and several liability, can arise if people or entities hold themselves out as partners; thus great care should be taken in office sharing and other joint arrangements. Three methods by which a partnership can be created or inferred for purposes of liability are by agreement of the parties, by appearance, and by conduct.

Partnerships may be written, oral, or implied, though if implied, the plaintiff must allege and prove that he or she was injured by the conduct of the professionals and misled by the appearance of a partnership. [Collins v Levine, 274 SE 2d 841 (1980)]

Evidence of a partnership includes: provisions or agreements about the sharing of income; death and disability (voluntary and involuntary retirement); funding with insurance; continuity and firm dissolution; pay in and pay out of firm capital (e.g., valuation of work in progress, capital accounts, when and in what form capital is paid in); how new partners are admitted; ownership of files and other papers and allocation of responsibility for patients or clients; rights of partners to manage and vote; resolution of disputes; limitations on nonpartnership activities; leaves of absence; expenses to be paid; accounting method; fiscal year; and financial policies.

Q 12:7   Is intent to form a partnership required for a partnership to exist?

No. Liability as partners can occur through partnerships that exist for the purpose of liability to the client, regardless of the intent of the professionals. These implied or *de facto* partnerships can be creatures of economic arrangements, such as sharing of office space, income, expenses, and common letterhead, without any formal practice entity. This type of practice association can cause joint liability for professionals associated with the individual committing malpractice. [Myers v Aragonia, 318 A 2d 263 (1974)] The determining factor will be how the association appears to the client.

In *Joseph v. Greater New Guide Baptist Church, Inc.* [194 So 2d 127 (1966)] sharing office space and expenses and using a joint name did not create a *de facto* partnership. However, in *Van Dyke v. Bixby*, [388 Mass 663, 448 NE 2d 353 (1983)] on similar facts, the court let the jury decide whether a partnership existed.

Q 12:8   Do firms or practices that work jointly on projects become jointly and severally liable?

Possibly. Two unsettled areas of vicarious *de facto* partnership liability exist in multifirm joint ventures. For attorneys, *Ortiz v. Barrett* [278 SE 2d 833 (1981)] stands for two propositions: (1) when the role of the local counsel is largely passive, courts will be reluctant to impose vicarious liability for the errors of outside counsel, and (2) when outside and local counsel are more nearly equal in responsibilities, a client proving injury will likely be permitted to hold both attorneys jointly and severally liable. In both instances the performance of the professionals involved will be measured by the same standard of care. However, local counsel will only be liabile for errors in performing tasks required by the lead counsel. The issue of tort responsibility of local counsel for the malpractice of out-of-state or associated counsel continues to be a gray area. [For an overview of the problems and suggested solutions to the question as it relates to federal district courts see: "Local Associated Counsel in the Federal District Courts: A Call for Change," 67 *Cornell L Rev* 345 (1982)]

Multifirm joint ventures are practice vehicles designed to allow a firm to expand its market share or to compete with firms that possess greater capabilities. This is a different concept than associating counsel, who has a required expertise or qualification for a limited period of time (litigation) or project (syndication). The multifirm joint venture is an ongoing association of firms that has as its goal an ongoing economic relationship. By virtue of this pooling of expertise, each member firm is given access to the collective talent in marketing its own expertise in other geographical areas, and can share in the marketing, management, and professional contacts of the associated firms.

The multifirm entity issue is new to the courts, but courts may not interpret the vehicle in light of what the member firms believe they are, but rather, what their clients reasonably believe them to be. If their appearance is such that the client could conclude that their association is the equivalent to a national or regional professional firm, then a court could hold all members of the association liable for the malpractice of one. The issue will not necessarily be decided on what the professional firms intended to project as their collective image, but rather what the client was lead to believe by the conduct and appearance of the association as a whole.

Characteristics of the Corporation for Professionals

Q 12:9 How are corporations different from general partnerships as to liability?

In a corporation, the individual committing a tort (such as malpractice) would be liable (as would a partner), and the corporation itself would also be liable under the rule of *respondeat superior*, if the act was within the scope of employment (as would a partnership). However, it is a standard principle of corporate law that the other shareholders and employees of the corporation, who are not directly involved in the wrongful act, would not be personally liable, unlike partners of a general partnership, who are jointly and severally liable for all partnership liabilities. As a result, the corporation serves to insulate shareholders from personal liability for the wrongful acts of employees or other shareholders and from corporate contractual obligations.

Q 12:10 Can the corporate limited liability veil be pierced to create owner liability?

Yes. The non-acting shareholders can nonetheless be personally liable to a creditor who is able to "pierce the corporate veil." But piercing the veil is very, very difficult to do. Courts have generally focused on the following criteria in determining whether a creditor can pierce the corporate veil:

1. Undercapitalization;
2. Failure to observe corporate formalities;
3. Siphoning of corporate funds by the shareholders;
4. Nonfunctioning officers and directors;

5. Absence of corporate records;

6. Commingled personal and corporate records and assets;

7. Failure to hold out to the public as a corporation; and

8. Use of the corporate entity in promoting injustice or fraud.

[See Amoco Chemicals Corp v Bach, 222 Kan 589, 567 P 2d 1337 (1977); and Mackey v Burke, 751 F 2d 322 (10th Cir 1984) (similar considerations apply when there is liability from a subsidiary in connection with determining whether the parent corporation should also be liable)]

Q 12:11 Do professionals who are shareholders have liability for actions other than their own?

Yes, they may have *supervisory liability*. Directors, officers, and other responsible parties can be personally liable if they have been negligent in supervising or overseeing corporate employees. Generally, directors and officers are not liable for tortious acts of officers, agents, or employees of the corporation unless they participated in, directed, supervised, or authorized the wrongful act. [18B Am Jur 2d *Corporations* § 1879 (1985); 90 ALR 3d 916 § 2 (1979)] Directors and officers are not liable if they could not, in exercise of ordinary and reasonable supervision, have detected wrongdoing of subordinate officers. [18B Am Jur 2d *Corporations* § 1879 (1985)] Directors or officers of a corporation do not incur personal liability for its acts merely by reason of their official character; however, if an officer commits or participates in commission of a wrongful act, he or she is liable to injured third persons. [Kansas Comm on Civil Rights v Serv Envelope Co, Inc, 233 Kan 20 (1983)]

Professional Corporation Statutes: Similarities and Differences

Q 12:12 Why have professional corporations become so popular?

Professional corporations (PCs), also known as professional service corporations (PSCs), exist in all states and are subject to a special provision which generally provides that the incorporation must not affect any law, duty, right, or privilege arising out of the professional relationship, such as liability or the confidentiality of communications. Therefore, incorporation of a professional does not affect the liability that a professional would have for his or her own malpractice. Nevertheless, incorporating a professional practice can protect a professional's personal non-exempt assets for malpractice committed by another professional in the same corporation, and will usually limit the professional's personal liability for ordinary business debts, absent a personal guarantee.

Q 12:13   Are there different types of professional limited liability in different states?

Yes. The law governing whether a professional operating in a PC is liable for the malpractice of a co-shareholder varies from state to state. These laws can be divided into four broad categories. [Comment, "Shareholder Liability in Professional Legal Corporations: A Survey of the States," 47 *Pitt L Rev* 817 (1986)]

Category 1: Unlimited liability states. A few states, like **Oregon,** do not protect the shareholder of a professional corporation from acts of another shareholder in performance of that shareholder's professional service. In some such states it may, however, be possible for a professional to practice through a general business corporation. In those states, a crucial issue is what constitutes the "provision of professional services." [Annot, 31 ALR 4th 898 (1984)] If liability is found related to the provision of professional services, each professional who is a shareholder in the PC is jointly and severally liable for the acts of any other shareholder. Nevertheless, to a great extent, these states follow the majority view that professional corporation shareholders are not personally liable for the corporation's ordinary business debts. [See Birt v St Mary Mercy Hosp, Inc, 370 NE 2d 379 (Ind App 1977); In re Florida Bar, 133 So 2d 554 (Fla 1961); In re Rhode Island Bar Ass'n, 263 A 2d 692 (RI 1970); Fure v Sherman Hosp, 371 NE 2d 143 (Ill App 1977); Connell v Hayden, 443 NYS 2d 383 (1981); but see *contra*, Nelson v Patrick, 326 SE 2d (NC 1985); Boyd v Badenhausen, 556 SW 2d 896 (Ky 1977)]

Category 2: Limited liability states. About 20 percent of the states, like **Alabama** and **Nevada,** provide almost complete personal liability protection for professional corporation shareholders from the acts of their co-shareholders and the corporation's ordinary business debts. [See ABA Formal Opin 303] Under the law of those states, a professional generally is shielded from liability for the misdeeds of another shareholder, provided the professional did not participate in those acts. [Cleveland v Williams, 441 So 2d 919 (Ala Civ App 1983)] Although a state's PC statute may grant broad protection, the state's courts may alter that protection and increase potential liability among PC shareholders, especially when lawyers incorporate. [See Haw Rev Stat § 416-153; but see, *Petition of Bar Assoc,* 516 P 2d 1267 (1973); and Hawaii Supreme Court Rule 24. Also note Henderson v HSI Financial Services, Inc, 471 SE 2d 885 (1986), (overruling First Bank & Trust v. Zagoria, 302 SE 2d 674 (1983) to the extent it states that the Georgia Supreme Court, rather than the legislative enabling act, determines the ability of lawyers to insulate themselves from personal liability for the acts of other shareholders in their professional corporation]

Category 3: Supervisory liability states. A common professional corporation statute is a statute like **New York**'s, which imposes liability on the shareholder of a professional corporation for that shareholder's misconduct and the misconduct of any person under that shareholder's direct supervision and control while performing professional services. [NY Bus Corp Law § 1505] These states also generally protect shareholders from personal liability for the corporation's ordinary business debts. [See "Professional Corporation Stockholders' Nonmalpractice Liability," 50 ALR 4th 1276; We're Associates v Cohen, Stracher & Bloom, PC, 65 NY 2d 148, 480 NE 2d 357, 50 ALR 4th 1269 (1985); but see *contra* Infosearch, Inc v Horowitz, 459 NYS 2d 348 (1982)]

Category 4: Savings clause states. Many states' PC statutes have a "savings clause," that is, a clause providing that nothing in the statute affects the liability between the professional and the client for services performed for that client. In several states, this clause is the only provision regarding a PC shareholder's liability. [Cal Corp Code § 13410; Ohio Rev Code Ann § 17856.04] Thus, the extent of a shareholder's liability in these states for the acts of a co-shareholder is left to the judiciary. In **North Carolina** and **Ohio** (due to a constitutional provision), courts have held that professional corporation shareholders have personal liability for the acts of all shareholders providing professional services and the corporation's ordinary business debts. [Zimmerman v

Hogg & Allen, 207 SE 2d 267, *rev'd on other grounds*, 209 SE 2d 795 (1974); South High Dev, Ltd v Weiner, Lippe & Cromley Co, 445 NE 2d 1106 (1983)]

Conclusion. The law is not settled in every state about the extent to which a professional corporation provides limited liability. The practitioner must examine the law carefully in a particular state before counseling a client to incorporate a professional practice. A practitioner should also document business reasons, other than just tax and limited liability, for incorporation. [Sargent v Commr, 929 F 2d 1252 (8th Cir 1991) (where the IRS unsuccessfully tried to challenge the validity of a professional hockey player's corporation); see also East End Memorial Ass'n v Egerman, 514 So 2d 38 (Ala 1987) (where creditors challenged a corporation's validity)]

Q 12:14 Can a PC with limited liability lose this protection?

Yes. The rules for piercing the veil discussed above, and supervisory liability can also apply to the PC. In addition, doctrines, such as agency and apparent authority, can render individual owners of corporations personally liable for corporate debts when they hold themselves out as individuals or noncorporate entities. [Mark Peterson Dental Lab, Inc v Kral, 458 NE 2d 1290 (Ohio App 1983) (dentist operating through a PC held personally liable for services rendered when service order forms did not clearly indicate that a corporate entity was involved)]

Q 12:15 Can national firms use a PC?

Not easily. One of the drawbacks to operating as a single professional corporation or an LLC is the difficulty (sometimes the impossibility) in qualifying the single professional entity to do business in all other states. If the professional practice spans several states, and a professional's professional corporation could not qualify in some states because of, for example, a state requirement that all PC owners be licensed to practice in that state, this fact is a practical bar to incorporating. Even if the professional corporation can qualify to do business in other states, there are additional administrative concerns.

One Entity. If a law firm is practicing in three states, to be recognized as a PSC in each of the three states would require compliance with the PSC statutes of each of those states. If the law of one state does not recognize foreign PSCs, a foreign PSC would be required to qualify to do business as a regular business corporation, in which case it may violate the jurisdiction's unauthorized-practice-of-law rules or may be disregarded as a corporate entity for purposes of limiting liability.

Q 12:16 Can the problem of the multistate PC be cured?

Sometimes, but not always. For example, in **Rhode Island,** Supreme Court Rule 41 states that a professional service corporation may not engage in the practice of law unless and until it applies to, and receives from, the court a *license* to operate under the Professional Service Corporation Law, and only so long as the license remains in good standing. Furthermore, Section 11-27-5 of the Rhode Island General Laws restricts the practice of law to those duly admitted members of the Rhode Island Bar. Thus, it appears that a PSC must do more than just qualify to do business to engage in the practice of law in Rhode Island. [Taylor v Branham, 35 Fla 297, 17 So 552 (1895); Herbert H Pape, Inc v Finch, 102 Fla 425, 136 So 496 (1931)]

Separate Entity in Separate State (with Partnership, LLC, or RLLP as Umbrella Entity). The problem of not being able to qualify as a foreign PSC under the laws of a particular state can often be cured by forming a second PSC in that state in compliance with the laws of that state. The problem here is that, not all of the shareholders of the first PSC may be eligible to be shareholders of the second PSC, if, for instance, the state PSC statute requires that all shareholders of a PSC be licensed in the state of incorporation.

Problems in creating a partnership of PSCs with a separate corporation for each state in which the firm practices include:

1. Deterrent to firm unity;
2. Notification of creditors;
3. Loss of flexibility for allocating income for state income tax purposes; and
4. Voting issues (by corporations versus by owners).

Partnership of One-Owner/Employee PSCs. As an alternative to forming a partnership of PSCs with one PSC formed in each state in which the firm conducts its practice, individual partners might form their own PSCs. Problems that exist with a partnership of individual PSCs include:

1. Creditors might require personal guarantees by the shareholders of the PSC.
2. The corporate veil might be easier to pierce.
3. The PSC might have to qualify to practice in other jurisdictions where the shareholder is admitted because the partnership is operating in those jurisdictions.
4. The burden of each corporation properly documenting its transactions and filing state and federal tax returns, as well as the requirement in many situations to file more than one state income tax return.

The LLC for Professionals

Q 12:17   What are the characteristics of an LLC when used by professionals for their profession?

General Rule. The limited liability company (LLC), which is a creature of state statute, operates much like a corporation for purposes of providing the protection of the corporate veil, so that members are not personally liable for wrongful acts or debts of the company. Therefore, an LLC generally offers the limited liability advantage of an S corporation without the Section 1361 restrictions on ownership. In addition, the LLC can be structured to provide pass-through taxation like that enjoyed by a partnership.

Formation. All states have LLC statutes. Like a limited partnership, an LLC is generally taxed like a partnership under the Code, although not all states permit professionals to practice through an LLC. LLC statutes or other authority may allow professionals to operate through an LLC.

Multistate Practice Problems. To facilitate use of the LLC form by professional service firms engaged in interstate practice, state LLC legislation should, but often does not, contain provisions that: authorize the use of LLCs by professionals; limit the personal liability of LLC members for the LLC's debts and obligations; provide sufficient organizational flexibility; and facilitate interstate practice to qualify an LLC or a PC to do business in many states.

Authorization to Render Professional Services. LLC legislation in many states clearly authorizes LLCs to offer professional services. For example, the **Utah, Virginia, Missouri, Kansas, Iowa,** and **Arizona** statutes all provide for use of the LLC form by professionals.

Some state LLC acts neither expressly permit nor prohibit the formation of professional service LLCs. The **Colorado, Florida, Minnesota, Nevada, Oklahoma, Wyoming,** and **Texas** LLC Acts all fall into this category. Therefore, there may be uncertainty as to whether a professional group can form an LLC in these states. In addition, the state agency that regulates the profession in question may place restrictions on its members as to forming an LLC in that state for the practice of that profession.

California and **Rhode Island** statutes bar LLCs from providing professional services; the restriction in California applies to anyone requiring a license.

While **Kentucky** does not prohibit professionals from using an LLC, the Kentucky Supreme Court initially rejected a proposed rule that would have expressly permitted the use of an LLC, LLP, or professional service corporation by attorneys. This position was changed on Feburary 1, 2000. The proposed Supreme Court Rule 3.130, Rule 5.7 provided:

> A lawyer may practice with, in the form of, or as a partner, shareholder, member, manager, employer or agent of, a general partnership, a registered limited liability partnership, a professional service corporation or a limited liability company. In each case, the practice of law with or in the form of such entity shall be subject to these Rules and the statutes governing the formation and operation of such entity.

The Kentucky Supreme Court initially rejected the proposed rule because "the members of the Supreme Court of Kentucky do not agree that lawyers can so limit their liability."

See appendix H.

Q 12:18 Are LLCs for professionals as well developed legally under state law as PCs?

No.

Conflicts with Existing Professional Regulations. Many state regulations do not explicitly recognize the LLC as an acceptable organizational form for professional service firms. State accountancy rules, for example, authorize CPAs to practice through sole proprietorships, partnerships, or professional corporations. State LLC legislation could contain a "repealer" provision that amends and supersedes state laws to the extent they would bar professionals from forming LLCs. Alternatively, the LLC legislation could contain technical provisions amending or superseding specific restrictions in professional licensing regulations. Over time, state regulations will be conformed to the statutes to allow professionals to use the LLC, at least where the state statutes permit professional LLCs.

Kansas Attorney General Opinion 92-23 [Feb 14, 1992] allows accountants to practice through an LLC if it is organized and operated in conformity with the ownership rules of state professional corporation law. [But see Early Detection Center v Wilson, 248 Kan 869, 811 P 2d 860 (1991)]

Professional Liability. Each state LLC statute contains a general provision protecting members against personal liability for debts and obligations of the LLC. Professional service firms require additional assurance, however, that the rules relating to professional liability are unambiguous.

Most state LLC acts provide that LLC members are not personally liable for company debts and obligations and are not proper parties to an action against the company "solely by reason of" their status as members. The argument might be made that liability for professional malpractice derives primarily from the professional/client (or patient) relationship and not "solely by reason of" membership in the LLC. Thus, general liability provisions should be clearly stated so as not to be subject to judicial interpretation, limiting the limited liability, which could result in joint and several liability, as in a general partnership.

Qualifications to Do Business. State LLC legislation can facilitate interstate practice by: specifically empowering domestic LLCs to operate and exercise the powers granted by the statute outside of the state; providing that the LLC act determines the rights and obligations of LLCs operating in interstate commerce, except as otherwise provided by law; and specifying that other states recognize and afford constitutional full faith and credit to LLCs organized under its provisions. The **Nevada** and **Texas** LLC Acts contain this latter type of provision. Although such statutory language may not be binding on other states, it may influence a foreign court's choice-of-law analysis.

Some states, however, expressly prohibit foreign LLCs from powers not granted to domestic LLCs. The **Illinois** and **Louisiana** LLC Acts, for example, contain such provisions. Such restrictive language bars foreign professional service LLCs from operating in states that do not permit professionals to form domestic LLCs. Moreover, some states require that foreign professional service LLCs comply with certain requirements applicable to domestic LLCs in order to retain limited liability status for its members. [See Wash Rev Code § 25.15.310]

The LLP for Professionals

Q 12:19   What is the registered limited liability partnership?

Texas, Louisiana, Delaware, North Carolina, and the **District of Columbia** were the first jurisdictions to enact statutes allowing limited liability partnerships. With the passage of the **Vermont** legislation (effective January 1, 1999) all fifty states and the District of Columbia have now enacted statutes allowing limited liability partnerships. **Rhode Island** places restrictions on the eligibility of professional firms to use an LLP. In Rhode Island, accountants are the only profession allowed to use LLPs. [RI Gen Laws § 7-12-31.1(2)] In contrast, **California, Nevada, New York,** and **Oregon** require that only professionals may form LLPs. These entities provide limited liability as to certain claims (if certain requirements are met), but are a general partnership for all other purposes.

Under the original Texas LLP statute, for example, liability could be eliminated for the partners not participating in an occurrence of malpractice if they had no notice of facts and circumstances that suggested their partner could commit malpractice, such as notice of senility, incompetence, chronic sleep deprivation, conflict of interest, etc. If a partnership is formed as an LLP (or RLLP), plaintiffs could attempt to bring every partner in the partnership into the litigation under this type of notice theory.

Using Two Entities

Q 12:20   Why do some practices use more than one entity?

Some professional organizations use two or more entities. For example, it is seldom advantageous, and indeed generally disadvantageous (for tax and liability purposes) to own real estate in the practice entity. Typically, that is owned in another entity that is designed to be taxed as a partnership. In addition, equipment and other assets are also often owned in another entity, especially when a regular C corporation is used to minimize or eliminate double taxation upon the sale of the practice. Payments to the professionals themselves are often in the form of a non-compete payment directly to the professional, which only creates one level of tax to the sellers, even in a regular C corporation, and avoids the double-taxation problem when C corporations sell their assets and liquidate, a problem that has existed since the Tax Reform Act of 1986 and the repeal of *General Utilities*.

Multistate Professional Practices

Q 12:21   Do multistate professional practices have special problems?

Yes. Multistate practices have trouble in many states with one or more types of limited liability entities and often cannot use them. This is because many states restrict ownership exclusively to people licensed and practicing in that state, which is impossible in a multistate organization. However, such an entity may be a partner in a larger firm that has offices outside the state. Thus, the partnership of professional corporations (or its cousins, the limited liability company or the limited liability partnership including professional corporations) may have individual incorporated professionals or entire offices with multiple owners which themselves are incorporated.

The larger the firm, the more likely the firm will have difficulty in changing from a partnership philosophy to a corporate philosophy or vice versa. While logically this should not be true, it is, nevertheless, in the author's experience. Small firms have much less difficulty in making the transition, perhaps because there are fewer egos to stroke and fewer political and tactical concerns.

Engineering firms are also unique in many ways. Many are organized as general business corporations rather than professional corporations (and some are also organized as general partnerships or LLCs). Many state laws are more favorable toward engineers than any other profession, in terms of ability to use a general business corporation, which is not possible for many professionals in most states due to a form of the "corporate practice of a profession" prohibition. This prohibition exists in some states by statute, and in others by state case law.

Specific Types of Professional Liability

Q 12:22 What liability does a limited liability entity protect against?

A limited liability entity, when it works as well as possible, protects a professional against contract debts (lease, loans, etc.) and the joint and several liability created by other professionals' acts or omissions. It does not protect the entity itself, nor does it protect the professional who violates his or her duty to a client or patient.

Any negligence or breach of the professional's duty to a client or patient may generate liability for that professional which cannot be removed or limited by using a limited liability entity. Thus, the professionals who commit an act or omission that amounts to malpractice and damages a client or patient may not escape liability through the use of any entity. It is the other owners of the entity who are not involved in the tortious acts or omissions, who escape liability.

The entity itself is also liable for the actual wrongs of a professional on the theory of *respondent superior*, the theory that applies and makes an employer liable for any wrong committed by an employee in the act of doing the employer's business, absent special circumstances (such as the employee's intentional torts, such as assault, at least if unforeseen by the employer). However, an entity is not liable for the acts of an independent contractor unless they involve inherently dangerous activity. [Restatement (Second) of Agency § 219]

Q 12:23 What types of liability does a professional face?

Tort. By entering into a relationship with the client or patient, the professional undertakes a duty to perform services competently. If the professional is negligent in the performance of those duties, the professional will be liable in tort to the client or patient. Generally the agent who commits a tort is not relieved of liability for that tort because the agent is acting for a principal. Some courts have held purely economic losses cannot be recovered in a tort. Tort law applies in situations in which a duty exists wholly apart from contractual undertakings. In *Collins v. Reynard* [607 NE 2d 1185, 1186 (Ill 1992)] the Illinois Supreme Court held that a legal malpractice action could be maintained in tort or in contract, and that economic damages are recoverable. Although this may resolve the question of the recovery of economic losses, in light of the subsequent discussion of LLPs, the distinction between tort and contract may still be significant. Cases have held that a professional's breach of implied warranty is a "hybrid of the standard tort claim for malpractice sounding in negligence," and that "when a duty to take care arises from a contract, or irrespective of a contract, the action is one in tort." [FDIC v Clark, 978 F 2d 1541, 1551, 1552 (10th Cir 1992)]

Contract. The professional who has entered into a contractual relationship with a client or patient has a duty to perform the contract. The cause of action for breach of contract has been recognized as a separate cause of action for legal malpractice. A representation by a lawyer that the lawyer will attain a specific result may give rise to a duty to fulfill that representation.

Breach of Fiduciary Duty. Because clients repose special trust and confidence in attorneys, and, because attorneys act as agents for their clients, attorneys owe their clients fiduciary duties. [See Restatement (Second) Torts § 874 (liability for breach of fiduciary duty); Restatement of the Law Governing Lawyers § 71, cmt c.] Under traditional view of agency, the breach of a fiduciary duty to a principal is actionable by the principal, but an agent is not liable to third parties for harm to the pecuniary interest of a third party that results from the agent's failure to perform duties for his or her principal. As an employee owes a duty to an employer and a partner owes a duty to the partnership and other partners, so an attorney, by virtue of the attorney's relationship of trust and confidence, owes a fiduciary duty to the client. These fiduciary duties include protecting confidences, loyalty (avoiding certain conflicts of interest and refraining from using powers arising from the lawyer-client relationship adversely to the client), informing the client, safeguarding the client's property and documents, and obedience (acting only within the lawyer's authority). [Restatement of the Law Governing Lawyers § 72, cmt f]

Violation of Statutes and Rules. To the extent professionals participate in violations of statutes, civil or criminal, such attorneys may be subject to liability for such actions. [In re Am Continental Corp/Lincoln Sav Loan Sec Litig, 794 F Supp 1424 (D Ariz 1992) (allowing claims against Jones, Day, Reavis, & Pogue to proceed to trial under Sections 10(b) and 11 of the Securities Exchange Act of 1934 and the Racketeering Influenced and Corrupt Organizations Act (RICO); In re Fishbein, Katzman, Fisher & Kaye, Scholer, Fierman, Hays & Handler, OTS AP-92-19 (1992)]

Q 12:24 What types of liability do professionals have that other business owners also have?

The owners of a professional practice have the same liability for nonprofessional obligations of the organization, such as lease obligations, guarantees of debt, and the like, as do nonprofessionals. A few cases, however, hold that lawyers have liability as partners despite their legal structure, but those cases are typical of only a few states and are not true in the majority of states. [We're Associates Co v Cohen, Stracher & Bloom, PC 65 NY 2d 148, 490 NY Supp 2d 743, 480 NE 2d 357, 50 *ALR* 4th 1269 (NY Ct App, 1985) (owners of professional corporation not personally liable for the lease obligations of corporation; joint liability under professional corporation provisions of corporation statute related only to professional services); with Zimmerman v Hogg & Allen, 22 NC App 544, 207 SE 2d 267, *rev's on other grounds*, 286 NC 24, 209 SE 2d 795 (1974); and Nelson v Patrick, 73 NC App 1, 326 SE 2d 45 (1985) (both holding shareholders in a professional corporation liable as partners)]

Issues in Using the LLP

Q 12:25   What is the nature of an LLP (also known as an RLLP)?

A limited liability partnership is not a new entity but rather a general partnership that has registered with the secretary of state by filing an appropriate document. An LLP is the same general partnership that existed before the filing of the registration with the secretary of state. An LLP does not incur costs and taxes attendant to transfer of assets, and the LLP is able to take advantage of the rules developed for general partnerships. (This form of entity is discussed in more detail in chapter 11.)

Q 12:26   Are the filing fees a significant consideration in choosing an LLP versus a PC or LLC?

Yes, in some states more than others. Many states impose a per-partner fee, and the filing fees could get onerous for a multistate LLP, especially when it is considered that a new LLP technically exists each time an owner is added or subtracted. Under the Uniform Partnership Act (UPA), which is in effect in some form in all states, the legal identity of the partnership changes (i.e., the new partnership is formed) on the admission or disassociation of a partner; hence, a new partnership is formed. [See, e.g., Fairway Dev Corp v Title Ins Co of Minnesota, 621 F Supp 120 (ND Ohio 1985)] The **Texas** Act requires an annual fee of $200 per partner per year. [Texas RUPA, § 3.08(b), as added by 1993 Texas Ch 917; 1993 Texas House Bill 273 (approved June 19, 1993)] Most states impose a flat annual fee, but the **Delaware, Illinois, Kansas,** and **Pennsylvania** statutes base their registration fee on the number of partners. [Del Code Ann tit 6, § 1544(c) ($100 per partner); Ill Ann Stat ch 805, para 205/8.1(c) ($100 for each partner, but not in excess of

$5,000); Kansas ($75 for each partner whose principal office is in Kansas); 15 Pa Consol Stat § 8221 ($200 per Pennsylvania general)]

Q 12:27 In an LLP, what changes are there in the direct liability of partners?

The short answer is that there are none. All LLP statutes provide that, in one way or another, but notwithstanding the limits on liability of the other partners in the LLP, each partner remains liable for his or her own errors, omissions, negligence, incompetence, or malfeasance, including the negligence, wrongful acts, or misconduct of any person under the partner's direct supervision and control. [Ariz Rev Stat Ann § 29-915 (c); Conn Gen Stat Ann § 34-53; Del Code Ann tit 6, § 1515(c); DC Code Ann § 41-146(a) (1993) (partner also liable if partner had notice of the errors, omissions, negligence, incompetence, or malpractice at the time of occurrence); Ill Ann Stat ch 805, para 205/15 (c); Kan Stat Ann § 56-315; Ohio Rev Code Ann § 1775.14 (A)(2) (partner liable if in direct supervision or control of wrongdoer); Md Code Ann, Corps & Ass'ns § 9-307(2)(C)(1) (partner liable for negligent or wrongful act or omission of another partner, employee, or agent of the partnership if the partner is negligent in appointing, supervising, or cooperating with the other partner, employee, or agent); NY Partnership Law § 26(C) (partner liable for persons under partner's direct supervision and control); NC Gen Stat § 59-45 (partner liable if "directly involved in the specific activity in which the errors, omissions, negligence, incompetence, or malfeasance)]

Q 12:28 What is the limited liability protection in multistate operations of an LLP?

This is unclear because (1) the states that do have LLP statutes have varying provisions from state to state; and (2) certain states lack provisions regarding choice of law. With professional firms, state licensing authorities also have further restrictions beyond the state's general LLP provisions. Some states, such as New York, expressly manifest an intent that their laws govern LLPs organized in that state and be given full faith and credit by other states. [NY Partnership Law § 121-1503(a)] But this provision may not be recognized by another state unless perhaps the professional and client contract to use New York law to interpret their contract. However, states which consider contractual choice-of-law agreements with respect to limited liability protection an ethical issue for professional firms may not be inclined to honor such an agreement.

Q 12:29 What liability protection does an LLP statute provide?

Subject to the limitations on protection for the partner himself or herself for negligence or failure to supervise, the states differ on other types of liability. In some states, such as the original Texas statute, the vicarious liability protection is limited to malpractice claims filed as negligence claims. [Tex Rev Civ Stat Art 6132b § 15] This would not literally extend to malpractice claims that are framed in terms of breach of expressed or implied contract, nor would it include other contract obligations such as breach of lease, guarantee, etc. Thus, it is possible that these statutes offer very little protection. One commentator had stated: "The statutory words have a distinct torts flavor and appear not to cover any contractual liability. Plaintiffs will probably try to plead their cases in ways to avoid the statutory words." [Source and Comments by Alan R Bromberg — 1992 Amendments, following tit 105, art 6132b § 15 (1991 Supp)] Some states provide protection against tort claims but not contract claims, while many states protect partners of LLPs from tort and contract claims (**Alabama, California, Colorado, Georgia, Idaho, Indiana, Maryland, Massachusetts, Minnesota, Missouri, Montana, New York, North Dakota, Oregon, South Dakota,** and **Wisconsin**).

Hence, many LLP acts designed to provide protection for malpractice leave partners and LLPs jointly and severally liable for malpractice claims framed in contract as well as all other contract claims, such as breach of lease agreements, etc. Significantly, many professional firms have failed, such as the Laventhol & Horovath accounting firm and the Finley, Kumbel law firm, because of contractual liabilities and not malpractice liabilities (although potential malpractice liabilities may have, in some cases, speeded the departure of partners, which created exposure to contract liabilities).

The term "malfeasance" is used in some LLP statutes. It is possible to argue that malfeasance relates to malpractice, whether the claim is made in tort or in contract. [FDIC v Clark, 978 F 2d 1541 (10th Cir 1992) (suggesting that even if the relationship between a professional and the client originates in contract, malpractice still sounds in tort)] However, the cases are in conflict on this point, and liability exposure in this type of LLP statute is certainly unclear and not as well protected as in an LLC or a professional corporation (except in those few states that do not allow professionals to use an LLC or a professional corporation to limit liability).

Q 12:30 In general, does the LLC, professional corporation, or LLP offer the most liability protection?

In some states, the LLP offers the least liability protection, for the reasons discussed above. The LLP may not protect even against all malpractice claims if framed in contract. It does not, in many states, protect against regular contract or guaranty claims. In addition, the partners remain liable for indemnification obligations under state law (unless negated in their agreement) under indemnity theories, requiring reimbursement of the partnership and partners for losses. Other liabilities, such as environmental liability, employment law liability for sexual harassment, and the like, must be considered in this context. Thus, the LLP offers the least protection of any professional liability vehicle as a general matter except in states such as **Minnesota, Missouri, New York** and **Virginia,** where the LLP statute is similar to the LLC statute for liability limitation purposes.

Q 12:31 How does the LLP entity compare with other entities as a general matter?

Members in an LLP may continue to call each other "partners" because they are. An LLP, as discussed above, is subject to the same rules as a general partnership for contribution and indemnity liability by partners, both to other partners and to the partnership itself. As to third parties, a partner in an LLP may have the same type of liability as a regular partnership for contractual obligations, which may include some malpractice liabilities. Thus, the liability of partners under most LLP statutes is greater than that of shareholders in a regular or professional corporation. It is also greater than that of members in an LLC.

Q 12:32 What about severance pay and accounts receivable payments to general partners—are they treated in the same way for a general partnership versus an LLP?

This is unclear but very important. This ambiguity is one of the biggest reasons why a general partnership may want to consider the use of a professional corporation rather than an LLP or an LLC when income payments (in addition to capital payments) are made to former partners.

The Revenue Reconciliation Act of 1993. Code Section 736(b)(3) repeals the provision allowing a partnership to take an ordinary deduction for payments to retiring or deceased partners. Under Code Section 736(b)(3), the deduction is still available for a "general partner" in a partnership in which capital is not a material income-producing factor. The Conference Report makes clear that this exception is intended to allow professional practices to continue to use this provisions. Obviously, to the extent LLCs and LLPs are used by professionals for a practice, the question will be whether the congressional intent for this exception extends to them and treats such members or limited liability general partners as a "general partner in a partnership."

Q 12:33 If there are problems with the use of the LLP entity, why have big accounting and law firms chosen to use this entity?

Professional accounting firms, law firms and other professionals have been subject to a significant increase in malpractice liability exposure. They have, to varying degrees, an intense interest in taking whatever actions are prudent to minimize this liability. The professional corporation and the LLC involve the creation of a new entity and require registration in states that allow them. In addition, the state professional licensing organizations impose restrictions that make it impossible to do business in all states by multistate firms operated as a PC or LLC.

The LLP, on the other hand, requires no change in the underlying general partnership entity because LLP status is achieved by a partnership merely by state registration. It also allows principals (such as non-CPA members) to maintain their same status, which is not the case in an LLC (where state requirements prohibit non-CPA, nonattorney members from being owners). Thus, LLC non-CPA or non-attorney principals are not able to receive a K-1 due to lack of member status in most states with an LLC. Keep in mind that the professional corporation has been around for three decades but has not been able to be used by multistate firms doing business in all 50 states, and the LLC has the same problem, due to local qualification requirements. Hence, the LLP, even though imperfect, may be the best choice for these businesses, but may not be the best choice for other practices that do not operate in so many states.

Issues in Using the LLC

Q 12:34   Is the LLC a good alternative to an LLP or a PC?

Yes, but its limited liability attributes may not be any better than those of the professional corporation. In some circumstances, it may not be as advantageous, especially for tax purposes.

Advantages. Perhaps the biggest advantage of the LLC over a professional corporation is that, for existing general partnerships, the creation and use of an LLC is a less drastic change than the adoption of a professional corporation format. The LLC can be structured to continue to be taxed as the same general partnership. The same tax identification number can be used. [Rev Rul 95-37, 1995-1 CB 130] The LLC need not have managers but may only have members, which are equivalent to partners (and then can use an executive committee of all members and a managing member, much like what is done by a general partnership).

On the other hand, the professional corporation can also be structured so that its operation is very analogous to the large general partnership. For example, all partners can be shareholders and directors. The executive committee could be the board of directors, and the managing partner can become the president.

Approximately 13 states do not recognize a subchapter S corporation for tax purposes. Of course, the LLC would be preferable to a flow-through to a subchapter S corporation for organizations with more than 75 owners because they could not qualify for subchapter S status due to the stock ownership requirement of subchapter S corporations. [IRC § 1361] There is no limit to 75 owners in LLCs. In addition, LLCs have no structure to be taxed as a partnership, and have no possible problem with unreasonable compensation, personal holding company status, the accumulated earnings tax, or other problems that the professional corporation may experience. However, the professional corporation attributes are usually not a problem in practice and are generally easily avoided by the literally thousands of professional corporations in operation throughout the United States.

It should be noted that qualifying to do business in states other than the state of the LLC creation is difficult for LLCs and PCs in many instances. While some states have complete reciprocity, others have limits on various things, such as the name that can be used (e.g., there may be a requirement that the name of an existing state owner be included in the firm name, at least in that state), the owners all need to be licensed to practice in the state in question (which will render the multistate PC or LLC impossible in many instances), and other restrictions which make the use of various states difficult. It should be noted that engineers have special statutes in many states, which allow them to use professional corporations or even general business corporations, and to use them on a multistate basis. However, physicians, lawyers, accountants, and others have more restrictive professional licensing requirements which are separate and distinct from the state statute itself.

Authorization to Render Professional Services. Ideally, state LLC legislation should clearly authorize LLCs to offer professional services. The **Utah, Virginia, Kansas, Iowa,** and **Arizona** statutes, for example, all provide for use of the LLC form by professionals. The **Missouri, New York,** and **Pennsylvania** state legislatures permit professional service LLCs.

Several state LLC acts neither expressly permit nor prohibit the formation of professional service LLCs. Such a neutral approach may be acceptable, although not preferable. For such instances, the state legislature or appropriate professional regulatory bodies would need to amend professional regulations to allow the use of LLCs, as was the case in **Texas.**

California and **Rhode Island** statutes bar LLCs from providing professional services.

Conflicts with Existing Professional Regulations. Existing state regulatory schemes typically do not recognize the LLC as an acceptable organizational form for professional service firms. Most state accountancy laws, for example, authorize CPAs to practice only through sole proprietorships, partnerships, or professional corporations. State LLC legislation could contain a "repealer" provision that amends and supersedes state laws to the extent they would bar professionals from forming LLCs. Alternatively, the LLC legislation could contain technical provisions amending or superseding specific restrictions in professional licensing legislation and regulations.

Kansas Attorney General Opinion 92-23 [Feb 14, 1992] allows accountants to practice through an LLC if it is organized and operated in conformity with the state professional corporation law. [But see Early Detection Center v Wilson, 248 Kan 869, 811 P2d 860 (1991)]

Professional Liability. Each state LLC statute contains a general provision protecting members against unlimited personal liability for debts and obligations of the LLC. Professional service firms require additional assurance, however, and the rules relating to professional liability are unambiguous. Several state LLC acts provide that LLC members are not personally liable for company debts and obligations and are not proper parties to an action against the company "solely by reason of" their status as members. In light of the current laws not limiting the liability of professionals, the argument might be made that liability for professional malpractice derives primarily from the professional/client (or patient) relationship and not "solely by reason of" membership in the LLC. Thus, general liability provisions should be clearly stated so as not to be subject to unwarranted judicial interpretation.

Interstate Operations of LLCs. State LLC legislation can facilitate interstate practice by: specifically empowering domestic LLCs to operate and exercise the powers granted by the statute outside the state; providing that the LLC act determines the rights and obligations of domestic LLCs operating in interstate commerce, except as otherwise prohibited by law; and conveying the intent of the legislature that other states recognize and afford constitutional full faith and credit to LLCs organized under its provisions. The **Nevada** and **Texas** LLC Acts contain this latter type of provision. Although such statutory language may not be binding on other states, it may influence a foreign court's choice-of-law analysis.

Some states, however, expressly prohibit foreign LLCs from exercising powers not granted to domestic LLCs. The **Illinois** and **Louisiana** LLC Acts, for example, contain such provisions. Such restrictive language bars foreign professional service LLCs from operating in states that do not permit professionals to form domestic LLCs.

Tax Treatment of LLPs and LLCs. The tax treatment of LLPs and LLCs are virtually identical. LLPs may have a slight advantage in terms of the deductibility of severance and accounts receivable payments to deceased or dissociating partners if IRC § 736(b)(3) applies to LLPs but not LLCs. Section 736 relates to severance payments to general partners and it is not clear at the present time whether a partner in an LLP qualifies as a general partner under this provision (see Q 12:32). Partners in an LLP are more likely to qualify under IRC § 736 than an LLC member because of the presumption that LLP partners share management responsibilities. LLC members do not benefit from such a presumption—particularly if the LLC is manager-managed and the non-manager members more closely resemble limited rather than general partners.

Q 12:35   Is cash-basis accounting always available for an LLC?

No. Code Section 446(c) permits the use of the cash or accrual method, generally.

Code Section 448(a) provides that the following taxpayers must use the accrual method and cannot use the cash method:

- C corporations
- Partnerships with a C corporation partner
- Tax shelters

Code Section 461(i)(3) provides that a tax shelter is:

1. Any enterprise, if interests are offered in a registered offering;
2. Any tax shelter [IRC § 6662(d)(2)(C)]; or
3. Any "syndicate."

Code Section 1256(e)(3)(B) provides that a syndicate is anything other than a C corporation in which greater than 35 percent of the losses are allocated to either limited partners or limited "entrepreneurs." [IRC § 464(e)(2)]

Code Section 464(e)(2) defines a "limited entrepreneur" as a person who:

1. Is not a limited partner; and

2. Does not actively participate in management.

What are the members of an LLC? If they are treated as limited partners, then, since *all* losses are allocated to "limited partners," the cash method is not allowed. If they are treated as limited entrepreneurs, then it would be necessary to determine who is participating in management. Only if greater than 35 percent of the members are nonparticipating, however, would the cash method be required.

All IRS rulings on this issue to date are private letter rulings and, while favorable, cannot be relied upon by other LLCs to assure the use of cash-basis accounting.

Q 12:36 When is the professional corporation (PC) a useful alternative, and what are the factors that cause a professional corporation to be used in lieu of the general partnership, the LLC, or the LLP?

The PC (or professional service corporation (PSC)) is useful for professionals who practice in one or a few states and prefer to maximize tax advantages.

Issues in Using the PC

Q 12:37 Why has the PC become so popular as a vehicle to limit liability in most states?

Limitation of personal liability is generally the primary reason professionals choose to incorporate. Skyrocketing malpractice rates, potential uninsured liability for punitive damages, and fellow employees' (and partners') actions are all reasons for incorporation. In one case, the U.S. Supreme Court upheld a $2.2 million treble damage antitrust award against a physician and all of his partners, a result that could have been avoided by the partners by incorporation. [Patrick v Burget, 108 S Ct 1658 (1988)]

In a general partnership of professionals, each general partner is liable for the liabilities of the partnership, including the torts (such as automobile accidents) of other partners and employees which occur within the scope of their employment. On the other hand, a shareholder-employee of a professional corporation is generally liable only to the extent of the professional's investment in the stock of the corporation, except for the professional's own malpractice and that of others under the professional's direct supervision. [Boyd v Badenhausen, 556 SW 2d 896 (Ky 1977); Kurzner v US, 413 F 2d 97, 107 (5th Cir 1969); In re Rhode Island Bar Ass'n, 106 RI 752, 263 A 2d 692 (1970); We're Associates Co v Cohen, Scratcher & Bloom, PC, 65 NY 2d 148 (1985); Stewart v Coffman, 748 P 2d 579 (Utah App 1988); Jones v Teilborg, 727 P 2d 18 (Ariz 1986); East End Memorial Ass'n v Egerman, 514 So 2d 38 (Ala 1987); Birt v St Mary Mercy Hosp of Gary, Inc, 370 NE 2d 379 (Ind App 1977) (holding a nontreating physician not liable for the tort of a fellow professional shareholder); In re Florida Bar, 133 S 2d 554 (Fla 1961) (upon petition by the Florida Bar Association, held that shareholders in a legal professional corporation would not be liable for professional misdeeds of the other shareholders); In re Rhode Island Bar Ass'n, 263 A 2d 692 (RI 1970) (this court approved limited liability for attorneys in professional corporations only if they carry mandatory liability insurance)]

Two cases involving medical malpractice persuasively argue that there is no liability by individual shareholders for corporate debts occurring as a result of medical malpractice by other shareholders. [Fure v Sherman Hosp, 55 Ill App 3d 572, 371 NE 2d 143 (1977); Connell v Hayden, 83 AD 2d 30, 443 NYS 2d 383 (1981)] In *Fure v. Sherman Hospital*, a doctor who was a shareholder in a professional corporation was being used for an act of negligence of another doctor-shareholder in the same corporation. The innocent doctor did not participate in any of the acts of negligence or hold any supervisory control over the other shareholder doctor.

The court ruled that, a professional service corporation is liable, like any other corporation, for the torts of its officers or employees when acting in those capacities. However, the rule is that no action can be maintained against any other employee unless that other employee can be considered a wrongdoer. An employee is liable for injury to third persons when, and only when, that employee breaches some duty to a third person. At common law, a servant is not vicariously liable for the negligence of a co-employee. [Fure v Sherman Hosp at 396]

In a few states such as **Ohio,** limited liability for professional actions (as opposed to limited liability for other corporate debts) does not exist. In addition, in the states where professional corporation limited liability is recognized, it can be destroyed if the individual shareholders sign agreements personally rather than in their capacity as agents of the corporation. [See Coffee v Iman, 728 P 2d 376 (Colo 1986); see generally, Annot 39 *ALR* 4th 556 (1985).]

Many courts have held that general corporate law principles of liability apply to professional corporations. For example, in *McGuire v. Seifers* [235 Kan 368, 681 P 2d 1025 (1984)] the **Kansas** Supreme Court held that a professional corporation is subject to the general corporation laws of Kansas, except as specifically provided in the professional corporation law. The general corporation law requires that a corporation be held vicariously liable for the acts of its professional employees, according to *McGuire*. This same principle applies to partnerships. This case might also mean that the professional corporation gives double coverage for malpractice liability through the Health Care Stabilization Fund, in that the professional corporation and the individual physician will each be separately insured. The *McGuire* case held that a private malpractice carrier must pay separately up to each policy limit for the individual physician and the professional corporation.

Even professionals who share office space and expenses, but not income, and not partners for tax purposes, may be considered to be partners for state law liability purposes, if they have indicia of a partnership, such as shared bank accounts, use of a common name, common billing, and so forth. [Van Dyke v Bixby, 388 Mass 663, 448 NE 2d 353 (1983)]

These factors and others mean that, as a general rule, the corporation will have only a small number of shareholders, one class of stock, and modest capital investments. Unless the corporation owns a building (that, if owned, should almost always be owned in a separate partnership or limited liability company), its major assets will be furniture, fixtures, accounts receivable, and work in process. Occasionally, centralization of management may be a significant benefit of incorporation, such as in the case of an older professional who will let a younger professional own stock, but never more than 49 percent. Usually, though, the professionals will want the very opposite; namely, management similar to that of a partnership and no free transferability of shares.

Corporate continuity of enterprise makes it much easier for a single professional's practice to be wound up after his or her death. No special court permission or accounting is required. The corporation can collect its receivables and, within limits, take advantage of its ability to spread the tax liability between the corporation and its shareholders through proper timing of the liquidation procedure.

Q 12:38 Can a professional corporation, like an LLC, vary voting requirements depending on the type of issue?

Yes. The articles of incorporation may include superstatutory voting requirements (also called veto provisions) for the directors and stockholders, either generally or by class or series, and for holders of other securities entitled to vote. The advantage of superstatutory voting requirements is that they afford greater protection to minority interests. On the other hand, such provisions enhance the possibility of corporate deadlock. Most attorneys tend to shy away from unanimity or large majority voting provisions in the articles of incorporation, preferring to treat such provisions selectively in shareholder agreements. Having such provisions in the articles imposes a permanency that, for example, may be undesirable in the event of a division of ownership upon death.

Q 12:39 What are some of the tax advantages of the PC generally not available to the LLC (unless the LLC elects to be taxed like a corporation)?

There are several such advantages.

Section 1244 Plans. Loss incurred upon a sale of common stock or upon the bankruptcy or liquidation of the corporation is treated as a capital loss for income tax purposes, unless the rules of Code Section 1244 apply. Code Section 1244 permits individuals (as opposed to trusts or estates) to claim an ordinary loss of up to $50,000 for any taxable year for single taxpayers ($100,000 in the case of married taxpayers filing a joint tax return) if stock meeting the requirements of that section is disposed of at a loss. [IRC § 1244(b)] The requirements of Code Section 1244 are as follows:

1. A small business corporation, eligible for Section 1244 treatment, is one in that the aggregate amount of money and other property received by the corporation for stock as a contribution to capital and as paid-in surplus does not exceed $1 million. This determination is made as of the time of the issuance of the stock in question. It includes amounts received for the stock and for all other stock previously issued. [IRC § 1244(c)(3)(A)] The value of property other than money received by the corporation for stock is an amount equal to the adjusted basis to the corporation of the property for determining gain, reduced by any liability to which the property was subject or that was assumed by the corporation. This determination is made as of the time the property was received by the corporation. [IRC § 1244(c)(3)(B)]

2. The equity capital limitation has been repealed. After November 6, 1978, a corporation can issue additional Section 1244 stock without regard to its equity capitalization. Consequently, a qualifying corporation may issue Section 1244 stock without regard to the amount of its equity capital, up to $1 million, reduced by the amount received for any common stock already issued.

3. The requirement that a written plan be in existence to issue Section 1244 stock has been repealed.

4. Section 1244 no longer requires that there be no prior offering of stock before a valid Section 1244 issuance may occur. Indeed, stock may qualify for Section 1244 treatment even if the corporation has been doing business for quite some time. However, there must be a legitimate business purpose for the issuance of Section 1244 stock. [Hill v Commr, 51 TC 621 (1969); Morgan v Commr, 46 TC 878 (1966)] If stock is issued in contemplation of dissolution or for the purpose of affording shareholders an ordinary loss when the cessation

of corporate business is imminent, Section 1244 treatment will be denied. [Nelson v Commr, 1984 TC Memo 465]

5. Another decision indicates that Code Section 1244 may be limited to "largely an operating company," terms that may be narrower than the statute itself seems to require. [H L Davenport, 70 TC No 86 (1979)]

If a loss occurs, it is deductible as an ordinary loss only if the corporation, during its past five years of existence, had less than 50 percent of its income from passive investment sources, sales, exchanges of stock, or securities, and the stock was not acquired for property (in a tax-free exchange) with a basis in excess of its value at the time of acquisition.

Q 12:40 Is the LLC preferable to a PC with respect to Section 351 transfers upon organization?

Yes. The LLC is also created tax free under Code Section 721 if taxed as a partnership. Code Section 721 does not contain an 80 percent ownership requirement. In addition, debts can be greater than the adjusted basis of the assets transferred into the LLC without triggering current income tax. The only way that debts can create income tax upon creation is if they are shifted, so that one party is relieved of certain indebtedness in the creation of the LLC. [IRC §§ 721, 752]

Section 351 Transfers. Gain or loss generally goes unrecognized upon a transfer of assets to a corporation if the tests of Code Section 351 are met. The three methods by which a partnership can accomplish such a transfer are set forth in Revenue Ruling 84-111. [1984-2 CB 88]

The requirements of Code Section 351 may be summarily stated as follows. The transfer must be of property solely in exchange for stock of the transferee corporation, and immediately after the exchange the transferors must own at least 80 percent of the voting power of all classes and 80 percent or more of the total number of shares of all classes of stock. [IRC § 368(c)] If, in addition to stock, the shareholder receives money or "other property," then gain, if any, must be recognized, but only to the extent of the money or the value of any other property received. [IRC § 351(b)] Under the

Omnibus Reconciliation Act of 1989, debt securities cannot be received tax free upon incorporation after October 2, 1989.

It is generally advantageous to make use of Section 351 provisions. Losses are not recognized for tax purposes when the transfers are between a shareholder and a corporation in which the shareholders own more than 50 percent of the stock [IRC § 267] and gains are treated as ordinary income (if the transferor owns more than 80 percent in value of the stock). [IRC § 1239] Attribution rules are applied under both sections, so that stock owned by family members is deemed to be owned by the transferor. Any situation in which the attribution rules might be a problem should be examined carefully.

Of course, in situations where the rules of Code Section 351 do not apply, the recapture rules applicable to depreciable property [IRC § 1245] and accelerated depreciation on real estate [IRC § 1250] may require recognition of ordinary income to the transferors if the sale is at a price above their tax basis in the assets transferred.

Some have argued that accounts receivable should not be transferred to a new corporation in an Section 351 transaction, for fear that the transfer might be regarded as an anticipatory assignment of income; that fear, however, is unfounded. [See Biblin, "Assignments of Income in Connection with Incorporating and Liquidating Corporation," 1969 *So Calif Tax Inst* 383] There should be no problem of income recognition on accounts receivable if all other business assets are also transferred to the corporation. Of course, the preincorporation accounts receivable may simply be retained by the individuals who earned them.

Some argue that accounts payable transferred to a corporation cannot be treated as a business deduction when paid by the corporation. The theory is that the payments are attributable to liabilities incurred before incorporation, and hence are capital expenditures. That idea has not prevailed, however, and would be inappropriate in view of the basic policy of Code Section 351, which is to treat a new corporation as a continuation of the previous business.

There are problems, however, if the corporation assumes liabilities, such as a mortgage on an office building, which exceed the total tax basis of the assets transferred to it. In that case, Code Section 357(c) applies; income is recognized, at the time of the transfer, to the extent that the liabilities exceed basis. The corporation may not be required to recognize income, however, when the excess liabilities do not represent a mortgage (e.g., regular accounts payable). [Bongiovanni v Commr, 73-1 USTC ¶9133 (2d Cir 1972); see also Donald D Focht, 68 TC 223 (1977); but cf. Orr v Commr, 78 TC 75 (1982) (the transfer of customer deposits results in gain to the transferor on the theory that a customer deposit is not an "accounts payable" type of liability)]

Under the Omnibus Budget and Reconciliation Act of 1989, for transfers made after October 2, 1989, securities received in a Section 351 transaction will be treated as boot. The Act deleted the reference to "securities" in Section 351(a),(b),(d),(e),(g). Nonrecognition treatment, therefore, will be accorded only when property is transferred solely in exchange for stock of the transferee corporation. Therefore, any discussion of whether a note is a security is moot because all debt obligations, whether securities or nonsecurities, will be treated as boot.

The incorporated professional generally wants a retirement plan immediately. The only way sufficient cash can be generated to start business with a significant salary and with the ability to fund a retirement plan, is to transfer receivables into the business. Generally the office equipment, fixtures, supplies, receivables, and a little cash will be transferred to the corporation by bill of sale in exchange for all of the stock being issued.

Usually no investment credit is recaptured when business assets are transferred to a corporation in a Section 351 transaction, even when some assets are leased to the corporation by the shareholders. [Rev Rul 83-65, 1983-1 CB 10]

Two revenue rulings holding that income need not be recognized when accounts payable are assumed by a new corporation. [Rev Rul 80-199, 1980-2 CB 122; Rev Rul 80-198, 1980-2 CB 133] If less than the entire practice is incorporated, there can be Section 351 qualification problems. [Ltr Rul 8139073]

There is another potential problem if the corporation elects to be taxed under subchapter S of the tax code: notes given to shareholders in exchange for property can be treated as a second class of stock, disqualifying the corporation from S eligibility. Relevant to the discussion of debt being treated as a second class of stock is

Code Section 1361(c)(5), labeled "Straight Debt Safe Harbor." This provision, which applies to tax years beginning after 1982, declares that "straight debt" is not treated as a second class of stock in an S corporation.

One final issue deserves mention with respect to Code Section 351. Even though there has been no express assumption of a predecessor entity's liabilities, is it possible that the successor corporation might be deemed to have impliedly assumed such liabilities? The rule appears to be that, mere succession to assets does not mean that there has been a corresponding assumption of liabilities, at least in a corporation-to-corporation transfer. [RJ Enstrom Corp v Interceptor Corp, 555 F 2d 277 (10th Cir 1977); Brown v Kleen-Kut Mfg Co, 238 Kan 642, 714 P 2d 942 (1986); Comstock v Great Lakes Dist Co, 209 Kan 306, 496 P 2d 1308 (1972)] The rule may be different, though, in a partnership-to-corporation situation. [Burwell v Commr, 1985 TC Memo 583]

Q 12:41 What else can be done to avoid some of the potential tax problems commonly associated with a PC?

Establishing Officers' Salaries. Another matter that should be worked out in advance of the first meeting of directors is the question of officers' salaries. Only reasonable salaries paid to officers and employees can be deducted on the tax return of the corporation. The test of reasonableness is a factual one, and the guidelines generally relate to what is being paid by other corporations in the same or similar businesses.

The reasonableness of salaries is rarely an issue in a newly formed corporation. The problem is most often faced by the very prosperous corporation, which is accused of trying to pay in tax deductible salaries what the IRS thinks should be paid out as nondeductible dividends. Personal service businesses, when virtually all income is from the services of shareholder-employees, present a special case.

Are unreasonable salaries a possible problem? Can there ever be an unreasonable salary when capital is not a material income-producing factor? Arguably, the answer is no, unless some of the profits can be attributed to goodwill. Very little authority exists about what might be a reasonable salary in the professional corporation context. In two cases involving doctors not all income was for personal medical services. The courts, in both cases, treated salaries paid to the doctors in excess of 100 percent of the doctor's billings as excessive, and hence a disguised dividend. [Klamath Medical Serv Bureau v Commr, 261 F 2d 842 (9th Cir 1958), *cert. denied*, 359 US 966 (1959); McClung Hosp, Inc, 19 CCH Tax Ct Mem 449 (1960)]

Some employment contracts require the officers to pay back to the corporation any amounts that the IRS, on audit, considers excessive compensation and disallows as a corporate deduction. If this works, it will produce a tax deduction for the officer in the year of repayment. [Rev Rul 79-311, 1979-2 CB 25; Ltr Rul 8148005] However, such a payback does not permit the corporation to readjust its income for the prior year under Code Section 1341. [Eugene Van Cleve, 82-1 USTC (CCH) ¶9166 (ED Mich 1981)] Many lawyers advise against these so-called *Oswald*-type agreements on ground that they increase the likelihood that the disallowance issue will be raised by IRS examiners. Such agreements have also been viewed by courts as a factor tending to show that the compensation paid was unreasonable. [See, e.g., Castle Ford, Inc, 37 TCM (CCH) 692 (1978)]

The IRS may approach the problem from another angle. Specifically, it may require that the corporation show, over several years at least, some reasonable return on invested capital, say 10 percent to 15 percent, to give proper recognition to the capital of the corporation. This approach was suggested by a former general counsel of the IRS in an interview entitled "The I.R.S. Sets Doctor Corporations Straight" [19 *Medical Economics*, 31–33 (July 20, 1970)], and received support in a nonprofessional corporation case, [Charles McCandless Tile Serv v US, 422 F 2d 1336, 70-1 USTC ¶9284 (Ct Cl 1970); but see Treas Reg § 1.1348-3(a)(3)(ii)] suggesting that capital is not normally a material income-producing factor when it is merely incident to a professional's practice. If the rule of *McCandless Tile* applies, some recognition of income at the corporate level will be required. *McCandless Tile* should pose no serious problem, however, if the corporation's assets consist of only office equipment, leasehold improvements, and a library. If it owns a business building or has some unamortizable goodwill on its books, then problems might arise.

Incorporation is most frequently undertaken by firms with one to 50 professionals. In such a case, the likelihood of salaries being in excess of 100 percent of a professional's billings, on any continuing basis, is not great. The goodwill of the firm will be relatively small and, with care, the firm may be able to have some control over its recognition. In larger firms, when goodwill is a considerable factor, and senior members regularly take out more in salaries than they bring in, incorporation will be unusual, partly because of the very real possibility of an unreasonable salary argument.

The major problem with salaries is how to establish them at levels high enough to facilitate maximum profit sharing contributions (to keep down corporate earnings), while insuring that the corporation has sufficient profits to make deductible contributions. This problem is compounded by the fact that the IRS frowns on year-end bonuses which the corporation attempts to count as compensation for purposes of contributions to profit sharing and pension plans. [Nor-Cal Adjusters v Commr, 503 F 2d 359 (9th Cir 1974)]

Richlands Medical Association [60 TCM 1572 660 (1990)] dealt with three Richlands, Virginia physicians who owned all of the stock and constituted the entire board of directors of a professional association, which owned a hospital and engaged in the practice of medicine. The professional association distributed all funds after the payment of hospital expenses as compensation to the physicians. The IRS proposed to disallow part of the compensation paid the three physicians for the years 1982 and 1983, producing corporate tax deficiencies of $637,000 and $602,000, respectively, in those two years. In addition to arguing that the compensation was reasonable, the physicians argued that there should be no corporate deficiency because the association was, for tax purposes, a partnership.

Having decided that Richlands was, in fact, a corporation for tax purposes, the court then dealt with the compensation issue. The parties each produced experts who testified as to reasonableness. The court allowed as deductible compensation:

1. 100 percent of each physician's collections attributable to his own patient services; *plus*

2. Compensation for the other medical responsibilities each doctor had at the hospital (e.g., director of intensive care, laboratory director, radiology director, stand-by and supervising emergency room physician, director of EKG, director of respiratory therapy, director of anesthesia, and chief of staff); *plus*

3. Additional compensation for administrative duties, including service as a corporate officer.

The IRS had allowed only an amount equal to item (1). The compensation of each of the doctors was two to three times collections for the years in question! Thus, this case is really a taxpayer victory (at least for other taxpayers), because only rarely is a professional compensation equal to one's collections. However, the court raised the question of how, if compensation consistently eliminated all earnings, the corporation "ever could have been expected to end up with a 'profit' at the corporate level."

The court also sustained negligence penalties on the unreasonable compensation issue, despite the corporation's argument that it relied on the professional advice of its CPA and, therefore, had a reasonable basis for what it did. "Petitioner has failed to present evidence," comments Judge Wells, "that its officers, who were well educated and highly-paid individuals, received any 'advice' from such CPA concerning allowable compensation deductions . . . and has failed to show that any advice received was based on all the facts." Thus, it would seem essential that practitioners make clear to their clients that mere preparation of a return by a CPA provides no insulation against the 20 percent accuracy-related penalties of Code Section 6662, absent specific advice from the CPA, after being furnished all the relevant facts as to the specific item involved.

Role of Employment Contracts. All professional corporations should have employment contracts with the major professional employees. In addition to express recognition by the professional of the corporation's right to direct his or her activities and control his or her actions, an employment contract can cover several areas of key importance. It may set forth a contractual bonus arrangement with the key employee. The IRS will recognize contractual bonuses, as well as bonuses paid pursuant to established policy, as qualifying compensation under a profit sharing or pension plan.

The agreement can also delineate, with some detail, exactly which employee business expenses, such as automobile, entertainment, and attendance at educational meetings, will be paid by the corporation and that will be the responsibility of the employee. If some expenses are to be paid by the employee without reimbursement from the corporation, the contract should expressly place the burden of those expenses upon the employee and state that he or she is not to be reimbursed. Such a contractual provision lays the foundation for deduction of these items as an employee business expense on the employee's return. A provision in the employment contract, or a written policy adopted by the corporation requiring a professional employee to pay his or her own automobile expenses, is probably necessary to permit a deduction for those expenses on the professional's personal tax return. [Charles v Fellrath, 42 TCM (CCH) 939 (1981); Robert O Eder, 42 TCM (CCH) 585 (1981)] However, such a written provision will not permit an employee to deduct five meals a week. [John D Moss, Jr, 758 F 2d 211, 85-1 USTC (CCH) ¶9285 (7th Cir 1985)]

Additionally, an employment contract can expressly bind the corporation to provide specified retirement plan payments, medical reimbursement, and other fringe benefits for the employee, as a supplement to the employee's specified regular salary. By such express agreement, some of the problems relating to deductibility of the fringe benefits and to employee reporting of additional salary or dividends may be avoided. [American Foundry, 59 TC 231 (1972)]

An employment contract may also provide for deferred compensation payments upon disability, voluntary and involuntary termination of employment, and even on death. A corporation can pay up to $5,000 to the estate of an employee or to the employee's beneficiary without the payment being taxed to the recipient if the amount is paid by reason of the death of the employee, and if the decedent did not possess, immediately before death, a nonforfeitable right to receive the amounts while living. [IRC § 101(b)]

Q 12:42 Can ERISA apply to PC severance pay or deferred compensation?

Yes. An employee *welfare* benefit plan covering a select group of management or highly compensated individuals is not subject to any voluntary reporting obligation. Rather, it is only required to furnish documents to the Department of Labor (DOL) upon request. [DOL Reg § 2520.104-24(b)] An employee *pension* benefit plan covering the same group of employees, on the other hand, is subject to limited reporting requirements. A top-hat pension plan must provide documents to the DOL on request and, in addition, file a statement with the DOL within 120 days of the plan's adoption that includes: (1) the employer's name, address, and employer identification number; (2) a declaration that the employer maintains the plan primarily for the purpose of providing deferred compensation for a select group of management or highly compensated employees; and (3) the number of plans and the number of employees in each plan. Failing to file a statement within the 120-day period will subject the plan to the normal ERISA filing requirements (i.e., annual Form 5500s) and the normal penalties for failing to file such reports (i.e., up to $1,000 a day).

Q 12:43   How can a "deferred compensation" arrangement be an employee pension benefit plan?

ERISA Section 3(2) defines an "employee pension benefit plan" to mean any plan, fund, or program that results in the deferral of income for periods extending to the termination of employment or beyond. Severance pay, however, is one of the benefits enumerated in the Section 3(1) definition of "employee welfare benefit plan." ERISA Section 3(2)(B) grants the DOL the authority to promulgate regulations providing for the exclusion of severance plans from the employee pension benefit plan definition.

The DOL has issued Regulations Section 2510.3-2(b). This regulation provides that, an arrangement paying severance benefits will not be deemed to be an employee pension benefit plan if it meets these three requirements:

1. The severance payments must not be contingent, directly or indirectly, upon the employee's retiring;
2. The total amount of the payments must not exceed the equivalent of twice the employee's annual compensation during the year immediately preceding the termination of service; and
3. The payments must generally be completed within 24 months after the termination of the employee's service.

Whether or not severance benefits are contingent upon an employee retiring has been the subject of various DOL advisory opinions. The DOL has generally concluded that severance benefits are indirectly contingent upon retirement if receipt of the benefits is conditioned upon reaching a certain age or completion of a certain period of service. In DOL Advisory Opinion 84-15A, by the nature of the plan, the only employees who would be eligible to receive payments constituted a group at or near retirement age; in DOL Advisory Opinion 83-47A, severance payments were available only when an employee accepted a distribution of his or her vested pension benefits; in DOL Advisory Opinion 80-37A, eligibility for severance benefits was based upon the completion of ten years of service and reaching age 55, provisions which mirrored the employer's pension plan provisions for early retirement; and in DOL Advisory Opinion 80-7A, severance benefits were available only to employees who were between age 60 and 65 and who waived any right to future employment upon receipt of the benefits.

Q 12:44 What is a personal holding company tax penalty?

The tax penalty, if the personal holding company provisions apply, is very severe: a 28 percent tax on undistributed income. However, the tax may be avoided by simply paying out all corporate earnings as dividends. But this subjects the earnings to double tax, unless the corporation has elected subchapter S status. A corporation may avoid this penalty tax by declaring a "deficiency dividend" [Treas Reg §§ 1.547-1 through 1.547-7], but this technique may not avoid the penalty entirely. A matter that gave much worry, at one time, was whether a professional corporation might be treated as a personal holding company under the tax law. The IRS might make this argument if substantial portions of the corporation's earnings were derived from "personal service contract income." [IRC § 543(a)(7)] A personal service contract exists only if an outsider has the right to designate who is to perform the services the corporation undertakes to provide, or if such a designation is made in the contract. The personal holding company issue was regarded as a much greater danger in the single shareholder-employee corporation than in larger corporations. If no individual owns 25 percent or more of the stock, this "personal services" provision is inapplicable. [IRC § 543(a)(7)]

Fortunately, the IRS has ruled that the personal holding company rules will not apply, even to a one-shareholder-employee professional corporation, unless there exists a written contract requiring the services to be performed by a specified individual. [Rev Rul 75-67, 1975-1 CB 169]

In *Thomas P. Byrnes, Inc.* [73 TC 416 (1979)] a manufacturer's representative incorporated his business. He was the principal shareholder and employee. He entered into a contract with the manufacturer, which specified that no other person would work the account without prior consultation with the manufacturer-client. Despite that provision, the Tax Court held that the income of the corporation was not personal holding company income. The court reasoned that, at most, this clause gave the customer veto power over new employees; it did not result in the designation of a particular person to perform services and thus did not trigger personal holding company treatment under Code Section 543(a)(7). In another example, a corporation owned by one radiologist who was a partner in a medical group was not a personal holding company. [Ltr Rul 8003010] The ruling concludes that the partnership agreement did not require the professional corporation to furnish the services of a particular individual, despite the fact that the corporation had only one employee. In another letter ruling, a clinic fired 13 physicians and then rehired their separate professional corporations. [See also Ltr Rul 8216057] The ruling states that this arrangement did not create "income from personal service contracts" within the meaning of Code Section 543(a)(7). However, some courts have held that personal holding company treatment is warranted when contracts provide for cancellation if named individuals terminate their interest in the corporation. [Able Metal Prod, Inc, 32 TC 1149 (1959); Allen Mach Corp, 31 TC 441 (1958)]

Q 12:45   Can the unreasonable accumulations tax apply to a PC?

Yes. It is doubtful that a professional corporation can be used to accumulate capital to any significant extent, even if the corporation is not a personal holding company. The tax on unreasonable accumulation of earnings applies to all earnings and profits of personal services corporations above the $150,000 basic exemption, unless there is a valid business purpose for the accumulation. [IRC § 535(c)(2)]

In *Earnest Booth, M.D., P.C.* [44 TCM (CCH) 595 (1982)] the Tax Court affirmed an IRS determination that a professional corporation that had accumulated $370,000 was subject to the unreasonable accumulations tax, despite the corporation's claim that the money was needed to cover possible malpractice liability in excess of insurance coverage, or to purchase equipment in the event that the pathology corporation's hospital contract was not renewed.

If a forced sale of one or more shareholders' stock upon death or retirement from the firm is contemplated, assets that are likely to substantially appreciate in value, such as an office building, should be kept out of the corporation. This avoids the problem of having to pay for such appreciation (via higher stock prices) without being able to write up the value of the assets for depreciation purposes.

The problem of buying out a deceased, retiring, or terminated professional's interest has not received much attention. Nor has much been said of the tax problems upon complete dissolution of a professional corporation. Partnerships may, by agreement, arrange to redeem a deceased or retiring partner's interest in a form cast as a capital transaction, giving rise to capital gain or loss, or as deferred compensation, which will be deductible to the firm and be ordinary income to the recipient. [IRC § 736]

If the corporation has no agreement and the stock must be redeemed upon death at some price established by a court under state law, the redemption will give rise to capital gain or loss. The corporation may find itself saddled with an item of goodwill upon its books that cannot be amortized, and that may cause problems in later unreasonable salary arguments with the IRS.

By agreement, however, corporations should be able to obtain the same results as are available to partnerships. The retiring or deceased shareholder's stock might be purchased at depreciated tax values, and any other payments made in the form of deferred compensation deductible by the corporation and taxable as ordinary income to the recipient. Code Section 101(b), giving income tax exemption to the first $5,000 in payments made on account of death, can be used as part of the arrangement. The IRS should not quarrel with this arrangement since it results in ordinary income treatment to any amounts taken from the corporation above the value of the shares.

Q 12:46 What are the other primary PC tax classification issues?

The following eight sets of tax rules must be considered by all personal service corporations. While the definition of a personal service corporation has some consistency, it is not uniform among the eight Internal Revenue Code sections dealing with personal service corporations. The areas in which personal service corporations are subject to special rules are:

1. *Code Section 11(b)(2)*. A flat 34 percent rate is imposed upon personal service corporations (PSCs), when: (a) substantially all of the corporation's activities are in any of the eight fields listed below; and (b) substantially all of the stock is owned by employees providing those services, retired employees, estates of deceased employees, and successors in interest (within two years of the employee's death). The eight fields are:

   i. Health

   ii. Law

   iii. Engineering

   iv. Architecture

   v. Accounting

   vi. Actuarial Science

   vii. Performing Arts

   viii. Consulting (a somewhat nebulous category that might create problems)

   The IRS, after years of study, finally issued its controversial veterinarian ruling, indicating that the term "health" deals with animals as well as people and that veterinarians who incorporate are, therefore, members of personal service corporations. [Rev Rul 91-30, 1991 CB 61]

2. *Code Section 269A*. If substantially all of the services of a PSC are performed for, or on behalf of, one other entity (or group of related entities), and the principal purpose for forming or availing of the PSC is avoiding or evading federal income tax by reducing the income of, or securing the benefit of any expense, deduction, credit, exclusion or other allowance for, any employee-owner that would otherwise not be available, then the IRS is given power to reallocate income and deductions.

3. *Code Section 280H*. Minimum distributions are required if a PSC is using a noncalendar fiscal year.

4. *Code Section 414(m)*. These rules are the "affiliated service group" rules, which apply to any organization engaged in

any of the eight activities listed in item (1) above, *plus* insurance activities *or* any other activities in which capital is not a material income-producing factor. Essentially, the rules of Code Section 414(m) are aggregation rules and require all members of an affiliated service group to be treated as one employer in discrimination testing for pension and nonpension employee welfare benefit plans.

5. *Code Section 441(i).* This subsection of the Code requires PSCs to be on a calendar year, except as provided in Code Section 444. A PSC is defined in the same way as in item (1) above.

6. *Code Section 448.* This provision generally limits the use of the cash method of accounting. A PSC is defined as in item (1), above. In general, PSCs can use the cash method of accounting as long as they are a qualified PSC, defined as corporations in which substantially all of the activities consist of the performance of services in the fields of health, law, engineering, architecture, accounting, actuarial science, the performing arts, or consulting, and in which substantially all the stock is owned directly or indirectly by employees performing such services for the corporation, certain retired employees, estates, or other persons within a prescribed two-year period after the death of qualified individuals. [IRC § 448(d)(2)]

7. *Code Section 469(j)(2).* Passive losses are disallowed. Here, a PSC is a corporation whose principal activity is the performance of services (in any of the eight fields listed in item (1) above and perhaps others—not now clear), if the services are substantially performed by employee-owners. Generally, this includes a corporation in which more than 10 percent of the stock is owned by employee-owners, directly or by attribution.

8. *Code Section 535(c)(2).* The maximum permissible accumulation of earnings without business purpose for a PSC is $150,000. For other corporations the limit is $250,000.

TEFRA, the 1982 tax law, enacted Code Section 269A, which overrules the *Keller* case for tax years beginning in 1983. Code Section 269A allows the IRS to reallocate corporate tax benefits to owners of more than 10 percent of a PSC when the "principal purpose for forming, or availing of such personal service corporation is the avoidance or evasion of Federal income tax by reducing the income of, or securing the benefit of any expense, deduction, credit, exclusion, or other allowance for any employee-owner which would not otherwise be available." [IRC § 269A(a)(2)] Under Proposed Treasury Regulations Section 1.269A-1, PSCs would generally escape IRS reallocation when the reduction in federal income tax liability is the lesser of $2,500 or 10 percent of the individual's tax or, for corporations in existence on September 3, 1982, when the reduction is attributable to qualified retirement plan deductions.

Code Section 269A applies only when "substantially all of the services of a personal service corporation are performed for, or on behalf of one other corporation, partnership or other entity." [IRC § 269A(a)(1)] Thus, it applies primarily to incorporated professional athletes and entertainers, partnerships of professional corporations, and hospital-based incorporated physicians, all businesses in which almost all of the corporation's income is derived from a single source. Code Section 269A appears not to apply to the ordinary incorporated medical or law practice, which serves many different patients or clients. Even if services are performed for only one other entity, this section should not apply if the individual can show that the incorporation was prompted by nontax business purposes.

Since many of the tax advantages of a partnership of professional corporations can be obtained by a single corporation, arguably a partnership of professional corporations is not formed for the principal purpose of securing tax advantages. Nevertheless, the proposed regulations indicate that the principal-purpose test of Code Section 269A(a)(2) is met when incorporation results in any reduction in income tax or in any increased tax benefit from the corporation that would not fit within the statutory framework or analogous rules under Code Section 269. [Treas Reg § 1.269-3(a)] Proposed Treasury Regulations Section 1.269A-1(b)(6) lists tax benefits that the IRS declares will trigger the reallocation rules of Code Section 269A. Many of the tax benefits listed there are clearly available to employees of a single corporation not subject to Code Section 269A.

Affiliated Service Groups and Employee Leasing. Code Section 414(m), dealing with affiliated service groups, was added to the law in 1980. It was designed to reverse the now infamous cases of *Floyd M. Garland, F.A.C.S., P.A.,* [73 TC 5 (1979)] and *Thomas Kiddie, M.D., Inc.* [69 TC 1055 (1978)], and to prevent incorporated professionals from securing for themselves better retirement plans than they provide for their rank and file personnel, by using one employer for the professional and another employer for the other personnel. Code Section 414(m) permits the aggregation of employees of certain otherwise separate organizations in applying the nondiscrimination tests for qualified retirement plans. All employees of "an affiliated service group" are treated as being employed by one employer for the pension rules. An affiliated service group consists of a service organization and the organization or organizations it serves. The statute is extremely complex and grammatically imprecise. The first IRS interpretation of the statute was Revenue Ruling 81-105 [1981-1 CB 256], which rendered obsolete Revenue Ruling 68-370. [1968-2 CB 174] The earlier ruling had provided guidelines for contributions to qualified plans by joint venturers or other employers who shared employees. Revenue Ruling 81-105 contains several useful illustrations of the operation of the rules of Code Section 414(m). [See also Prop Treas Reg §§ 1.414(m)-1 through 1.414(m)-4]

Despite the apparently broad sweep of the affiliated service group rules, it seems clear that expense-sharing arrangements that are not partnerships (because income is not shared) are beyond the scope of Code Section 414(m). There are unpublished IRS rulings to this effect. Similarly, of-counsel arrangements or other independent contractor arrangements should also be beyond the scope of Code Section 414(m), as long as the professionals are truly independent contractors and have no control over, or voting rights with respect to, the organization with which they contract. However, it is not now clear that the IRS will continue to follow this position.

TEFRA also added subsection (5) to Code Section 414(m). This subsection addresses organizations performing management functions. Its purpose is to remove the incentive for an executive of a corporation to terminate as an employee of the corporation, form a new executive management corporation, and then perform services for the former employer as an independent contractor. Subsection (5) precludes the use of this device to secure for the executive a qualified retirement plan more generous than that which is available for the other employees of the corporation. It accomplishes this result by providing that an organization whose principal purpose is performing, on a regular and continuing basis, management functions for one other organization, is in an affiliated service group with the organization for which it performs such management functions.

Employee leasing arrangements were also literally outside the scope of Code Section 414(m). However, TEFRA added Code Section 414(n), dealing with corporations that lease employees to other corporations; the lessee corporations are called recipient employers. Obviously, if corporations could give up their employees to leasing corporations and then contract for their services, they could drastically reduce their retirement plan costs. Code Section 414(n) removes this possibility. The purpose of Code Section 414(n) was to provide support personnel in long-term leasing arrangements — of which "Kelly Girl" or "Manpower" employees would be examples — some guaranteed minimum pension arrangements. If leased employees serve the recipient employer for more than one year, they must be counted as the recipient's employees for pension purposes. A leased employee could be included in both the recipient's plan and the leasing company's plan. However, the statute contains a safe harbor provision. Code Section 414(n)(5) provides that, if the leasing company provides a money purchase pension plan not integrated with social security, with a minimum contribution rate of at least 10 percent of compensation, immediate participation, and 100 percent vesting, the leasing company employees will be treated as employees of the leasing company for pension purposes regardless of the duration of their service with the recipient employer.

The effect of Code Section 414(n) on the common law rules in existence before the implementation of the statute is unclear. One of the major cases in this area is *Ronald C. Packard* [63 TC 621 (1975)] in which three unincorporated dentists excluded employees of a leasing company from their Keogh plan. The Tax Court approved this arrangement because the employees were truly leased and controlled by the leasing company and not by the dentists. On the other hand, in *Edward L. Burnetta, O.D., P.A.* [68 TC 387 (1977)] the recipient corporation leased employees from a leasing corporation in response to an advertisement by the leasing corporation that it would place the employees on its own payroll. Because the leasing corporation performed only payroll and recordkeeping functions, the Tax Court held that the leased personnel were really the employees of the recipient corporation and must be included in the recipient's retirement plans. [See also Bartles v Birmingham, 332 US 126 (1947); US v Silk, 331 US 704 (1947); Rev Rul 75-35, 1975-1 CB 131; Rev Rul 75-141, 1975-1 CB 195; Rev Rul 68-303, 1968-1 CB 165; Ltr Ruls 8125021, 8211045]

Fiscal Year, Medicare, Pensions, and Employee Benefits

Q 12:47 Are there restrictions on the tax year that may be used by a professional LLC or a professional corporation?

Yes. The Tax Reform Act of 1986 required all partnerships, S corporations, and PSCs to use a calendar year as their taxable year, unless they could establish a business purpose for a fiscal year. Before the ink was dry on that law, however, Congress passed the Revenue Act of 1987 and added Code Sections 444 and 280H. Under that law, a PSC, S corporation, or partnership that would otherwise have had to change to a calendar year may change to another fiscal year with a deferral period that does not exceed the lesser of: the previous deferral *or* three months. The "deferral period" is the period from the end of the entity's old fiscal year until December 31. For example, a new corporation, or an existing corporation with a fiscal year ending August 31 or before, may change to a fiscal year ending September 30, October 31, or November 30.

A partnership, other than one qualifying for the business-purpose exception must use the same tax year as that of its partners who own a majority interest in partnership profits and capital. If partners owning a majority interest have different tax years, the partnership must adopt the same year as its principal partners. [IRC § 706(b)(3)] S corporations [IRC § 1378(a)] and PSCs [IRC § 444(I)] are obligated to use a calendar year, unless they can come within the business-purpose exception or they make a fiscal-year election under Code Section 444.

For these rules, a PSC is defined as a corporation in which the principal activity is performance of personal services, the services are substantially performed by owner-employees, and the owner-employees own more than 10 percent of the fair market value of the stock on the last day of the tax year. [Temp Treas Reg § 1.441-4T(d)(1)] PSCs are those corporations performing services in the fields of health, law, engineering, architecture, accounting, actuarial science, performing arts, or consulting. [Temp Treas Reg § 1.441-4T(e)(1); IRC § 448(d)(2)(A)] The principal activity of a corporation is considered to be the performance of personal services, if the cost of the corporation's compensation for the testing period that is attributable to the performance of personal services exceeds 50 percent of its total compensation; moreover, 20 percent of the compensation costs must be attributable to personal services performed by employee-owners. [Temp Treas Reg § 1.441-4T(f)(1)] The term "employee-owner" is defined to mean any employee who owns, on any day during the tax year, any of the outstanding stock of the corporation, whether outright or by attribution. [Temp Treas Reg § 1.444-1T(c)(1)(ii)]

Special Rule for Certain S Corporations. A special rule applies to former regular C corporations that elected S status after September 18, 1986 but before January 1, 1988, and changed from a noncalendar fiscal year to a calendar year when they became S corporations. Such a corporation may change to a tax year with a deferral period of three months *or* the deferral period of its last taxable year as a C corporation.

Effect of Retaining Fiscal Year. S corporations and partnerships choosing not to use a calendar year must make estimated tax payments under Code Section 7159 on IRS Form 720.

PSCs choosing fiscal years as opposed to calendar years will need to make certain required payments under Code Section 280H, to avoid the loss of deductions. In light of the flat 35 percent tax on PSCs, it is important to follow the rules carefully, or there could be double taxation on certain income at a corporate 35 percent rate and at the personal rate (including federal and state taxes, deduction and exemption phaseouts, and medicare tax). In addition, if a fiscal year of a corporation or partnership is changed, consideration must be given to changing the retirement plan year.

Business Purpose Exception. A partnership, S corporation, or PSC may use a fiscal year, if it can establish to the satisfaction of the IRS that a business purpose exists for the use of such year. [IRC §§ 441(i)(1), 706(b)(1)(C), 1378(b)(2)] According to the Conference Committee Report to the 1986 Tax Reform Act, a business purpose generally exists if, in the last two months of the tax year that the business wants to use, the taxpayer receives at least 25 percent of its gross receipts, and has done so for three consecutive 12-month periods. [Rev Proc 83-25, 1983-1 CB 689]

Tiered Structures Must Use a Calendar Year. No election for retaining a fiscal year or using a three-month or less deferral period may be made by an entity that is part of a "tiered structure." The one exception to this rule is that an election may be made if all entities in the tiered structure consist entirely of partnerships or S corporations, or both, and all have the same tax year. A partnership, S corporation, or PSC is a member of a tiered structure if it directly owns any part of, or if directly owned in whole or in part by, a deferral entity (partnership, S corporation, PSC, and nongrantor or nonqualified subchapter S trusts). The IRS has provided two *de minimis* rules allowing certain tiered structures to retain fiscal years:

1. *Downstream rule.* An entity's ownership of any part of a deferral entity on the applicable date will be disregarded if, in the aggregate, all deferral entities accounted for not more than 5 percent of the entity's adjusted taxable income *or* not more than 2 percent of the entity's gross income.

2. *Upstream rule.* If an entity is directly owned by one or more deferral entities, ownership is disregarded if the deferral entities directly own in the aggregate 5 percent or less of an interest in the current profits of a partnership or stock value of a corporation.

Q 12:48 Are there other aspects of the status of a corporation versus a partnership or LLC that should be taken into account in deciding upon the form of entity to be used by a professional?

Yes. The fact of incorporation will also change certain other legal relationships between those who form professional or personal service corporations. For example, the Second Circuit has held that the decision by a group of doctors to operate as professional corporations undermines their argument that, in reality, they constitute a partnership for age discrimination purposes. The court held that a physician who owns as many shares in the corporation as the other doctors is an employee, not a "partner," and may pursue charges against the corporation under the Age Discrimination in Employment Act. [Hyland v New Haven Radiology Assoc, PC 794 F 2d 793 (2d Cir 1986); *contra*, EEOC v Dowd & Dowd, Ltd, 736 F 2d 1177 (7th Cir 1984) (holding that shareholders in a professional legal corporation are not employees under Title VII of the 1964 Civil Rights Act)]

In addition, it has been held that a physician is not personally obligated on amounts that the physician's professional corporation has agreed to pay on account of Medicare overpayments. While the trial court in this case ordered the physicians to personally pay the amounts, the appellate court reversed, holding that the corporation itself was the entity liable for payment. [Schreiber & Levinson, MD, PA v Zeig, 458 So 2d 872 (Fla App 1984)]

Q 12:49 Do the retirement plans of professional organizations structured as a regular professional corporation have advantages over qualified retirement plans of the general partnership, LLP, or LLC taxed as a partnership?

Yes, there are advantages. While none of the advantages are large enough to cause an organization to incorporate for these reasons alone, they should be taken into account in determining the structure to be used.

"Uncapped" Medicare Tax. Beginning in 1993, the medicare tax of 2.9 percent (1.45 percent to the employer and 1.45 percent to the employee in corporate form and 2.9 percent to self-employed individuals) applies without a dollar ceiling. It applies to all wages. In a professional corporation, structured as a regular C corporation, wages are only those payments of salary and bonus. Retirement plan contributions are not wages. In all other types of entities, such as S corporations and partnerships (including LLCs taxed as partnerships), the wages include the money that is used to contribute to the retirement plan because the retirement plan deduction is personally taken by each owner. Hence, if a $30,000 contribution is made for a professional each year, there is an extra $870 medicare tax to be paid each year. While 50 percent of that is deductible, the net effect is still to have an extra tax cost of about $640 per year per professional when a $30,000 contribution per professional is made into a qualified retirement plan. This is a significant annual cost.

No Deductions for Life Insurance. Payments attributable to medical insurance, life insurance, or disability insurance are not deductible for Keogh plans. [IRC § 404(e)] There is no prohibition against their deduction for corporate plans under IRC § 404.

No Income Averaging. Self-employed individuals are never separated from service for purposes of being able to receive benefits under a retirement plan before age $59\,^1/_2$. [IRC § 402(e)(4)] Thus, there can be no ten-year forward averaging before age $59\,^1/_2$ for self-employed individuals, except for distributions upon disability or death. [IRC § 402(e)(4)(A)] However, if a plan is terminated, there can be a rollover distribution into an IRA by a self-employed person. [Rev Rul 78-404, 1978-2 CB 156] Absent a plan termination, however, no rollover distribution is possible by a self-employed person to a qualified plan—only to an IRA (under a technical reading of the Code and would require five years of active participation for an IRA rollover by a self-employed person before age $59\,^1/_2$). Corporate employees who separate from service with a corporation may take their retirement benefits or may roll them over to an IRA or another corporate plan. [IRC §§ 402(a)(5)(E)(ii), 408(d)(3)(A)(iii)]

Special Note on Ten-Year Averaging Change Under TRA 1986. A recipient may elect income averaging treatment only if he or she has attained age $59\,^1/_2$ and elects to treat the distribution under the income averaging rules. [IRC § 402(e)(4)(B)]

For a lump distribution on account of a "triggering event" to a taxpayer who has not attained age $59\,^1/_2$, the income averaging election is available only if:

1. The taxpayer received the distribution before January 1, 1987; or

2. The taxpayer is an employee who separated from service before 1987, received the distribution by March 15, 1987, and elected to treat the distribution as received during 1986 [see TRA '86 § 1124 as modified by TAMRA § 1011A(d); Notice 87-13, 1987-1 CB 432, Q-24]; or

3. The recipient reached age 50 by January 1, 1986. [TRA, '86 § 1122(h)(3)(A)(ii)]

The age-50 transition rule applies to the estate, trust, or beneficiary of an employee eligible for this transition rule. [TRA, '86 § 1122(h)(3)(C), as amended by TAMRA § 1011A(b)(14)]

No Owner Borrowing. Employee-participants in a corporate plan can borrow from the plan, while owner-employees of Keogh plans and shareholder-employees of Subchapter S plans are forbidden from borrowing. [IRC § 4975(d)]

Tougher Rules on Payouts. The exemption from the 10 percent early distribution penalty for persons separated from service at or after age 55 does not literally apply to self-employed individuals. [IRC § 72(t)]

No Net Operating Loss Deduction. The funding of a Keogh plan cannot create a net operating loss, unlike the funding of a corporate plan.

No Tax-Free Disability. Tax-free disability payments are possible for corporate employees under Code Section 105(c) and the authority of the *Wood* and *Masterson* cases. [Wood v US, 590 F 2d 321 (9th Cir 1979); Masterson v US, 478 F Supp 454 (ND Ill 1979)] However, subsequent cases indicate that the IRS will contest this tax treatment absent special plan provisions.

Q 12:50   What are the other tax advantages that a professional corporation taxed as a regular C corporation provides that an entity taxed as a partnership will not provide?

Under the Tax Reform Act of 1986, numerous tax changes were made to limit the tax advantages of corporations, including professional corporations. However, several advantages still remain. The following is an example of tax savings, per year per professional, that might be achieved through the use of a regular C corporation.

Usual Items:		
Health insurance	$5,000	
Diagnostic medical/dental reimbursement	$1,000	
Disability insurance	$1,500	
Total	$7,500	
State taxes	@ 5%	
Federal taxes	@36%	
Savings		$3,075

Other Frequent Items:

Group term life insurance	$ 200
Automobile interest	$2,000
Total	$2,200
State taxes	@ 5%
Federal taxes	@36%
Savings	$ 902
Medicare tax on C or S corporation — savings	$ 870

Other Items:
Medical/dental reimbursement (expenses not
covered by insurance)
Withholding tax savings (pay tax later in year)

Medical/Dental Insurance and Reimbursement Plans

Regular C Corporations. Payments by the employer for hospital-ization and major medical insurance premiums on behalf of an employee, or payments made by the employer directly to the employee for reimbursement of uninsured medical expenses, are deductible by the employer and excluded from the employee's income. [IRC §§ 105(b), 106, 162]

Sole Proprietors, Partners, and 2 Percent (or More) S Corporation Shareholders. Self-employed individuals are not entitled to this benefit except to the extent of a deduction of 25 percent of the cost of health insurance. [TRA '86 § 1161, adding new § 162(l)]

IRS Position. Accident and health insurance premiums paid by a partnership on behalf of the partners qualify as Section 707(c) guaranteed payments, if they are paid for services in the capacity of a partner without regard to partnership income. These are deductible 100 percent by the partnership and taxable to the part-ners. The partnership reports the cost of premiums as guaranteed payments on Form 1065 and Schedule K-1, but is not obligated to file either a Form 1099 or W-2. While an S corporation follows the same general rule, it is required to file a Form W-2 for each 2 percent shareholder-employee who includes the cost of premiums as wages. In addition, these payments are not distributions for purposes of the single-class-of-stock requirement. [Rev Rul 91-26, 1991-1 CB 184]

Under Code Section 162(l), persons who are treated as employees under Code Section 401(c)(1) can deduct 60 percent of the amount paid for health insurance for themselves, their spouses and dependents.

Special Fringe Benefit Tax Rules for Regular C Corporations

Health and Dental Insurance and No Nondiscrimination Rules. A corporation may have a plan for the owners only, or may have a better plan for the owners than for the staff.

Medical Reimbursement. Medical reimbursement is available under Code Section 105(h) with deductible dollars, tax-free to employees (which includes owner-employees of a C corporation). Employees who fail to meet one or more of the following tests may be excluded: age 25, three years of service, and part-time employees (35/25 hours per week). Available dollar benefits for eligible employees must be the same annually.

Diagnostic Reimbursement. Discriminatory medical benefits for key employees may be applied for diagnostic procedures, including routine medical examinations, blood tests, x-rays (but excluding expenses for the treatment), and cure or testing of an unknown illness. This would include routine dental exam with x-rays. [Treas Reg § 1.105-11(g)]

Group-Term Life Insurance. Group-term life insurance is relatively inexpensive which makes it, when coupled with its preferential tax treatment, an attractive employee fringe benefit. The corporation's payments of premiums are deductible under Code Section 162, and no income is attributed to the employee for coverage up to $50,000 under Code Section 79(a). Premiums paid on behalf of self-employed individuals are taxable. [IRC § 79(b)(2)(A); Treas Reg § 1.79-0] All employees employed at least 20 hours per week after six months must be included, but benefits need only be proportionate to compensation.

Disability Income (Wage Continuation) Plans. The payment of disability insurance premiums by the corporation is deductible by the corporation under Code Section 162 and not includible in the income of the employee under Code Section 106; however, in the event of disability, the payment by the insurance company of disability benefits, as well as any direct payment by the corporation under a wage continuation plan on account of disability, would be income to the employee. [IRC § 105] Disability insurance premium payments made on behalf of partners and sole proprietors are not deductible by them, since they are self-employed persons. [IRC § 105(g)] Although payment of disability insurance premiums on behalf of an owner-employee (a self-employed person) is not deductible, the receipt of disability payments by the owner-employee, should he of she become disabled, would be tax free under Code Section 104(a)(3).

How Much Coverage? If the plan is insured, coverage is generally limited to approximately 60 percent of an employee's compensation, since insurance companies will typically not write in excess of that amount.

Need for Written Plan. In *Robert L. Harris v. U.S.* [77-1 USTC ¶9414 (ED Va 1977)], the taxpayer failed in his effort to prove there was a "plan." In *Bogene, Inc.* [27 TCM 730 (1968)], although a "plan" was not in writing, it was reflected in written corporate minutes before payments were made and, thus, held to exist. In *K.S. Rosen v U.S.* [87-1 USTC ¶9158 (WD Va 1987)], the court held the plan was established in the employee's employment agreement.

Nondiscrimination Rules. No tax nondiscrimination rules apply to disability plans. Thus, the insurance may be provided only to professionals so long as it covers them as employees and not as shareholders.

Cafeteria Plans. These are methods of legally reducing compensation to pay for fringe benefits, which allows the professional to have deductible fringe benefits without increasing employee staff overhead costs. The professional can have tax deductible health/dental insurance plans and, if medical reimbursement is unattractive due to the tax discrimination rules, the professional can use the cafeteria plan for medical reimbursement. The professionals as a group are limited to 25 percent of the total tax-free reimbursements in the cafeteria plans. Benefits that may be included are: medical/dental insurance, medical dental reimbursement, child care, disability and group term life insurance, and 401(k) contributions.

A Win-Win Tax Savings Program. Employees save federal and state income tax and social security. The employer saves social security, unemployment, and other payroll-based expenses. Not more than 25 percent of all tax-free benefits can go to "key employees." Child care benefits are available up to $5,000 per year, but key employees (5 percent or more owners) may only receive 25 percent of these benefits.

Best Plan Design for PC Fringe Benefits. Family health insurance should be provided through a separate plan for professional-shareholders only. A cafeteria plan should be established for staff for providing not only health insurance but all other fringe benefits. If these are provided at the employer's expense, simply "cancel" the benefits but increase salaries by the amount of benefits. Then, provide for medical reimbursement through a cafeteria plan (by salary reduction). Thus, this plan design costs the corporation nothing, and yet professionals can make substantial use of it because their health insurance is paid outside a cafeteria plan and not subject to a 25 percent rule.

Q 12:51 Can the tax problems of the professional corporation be solved so its benefits can be used effectively?

Yes, often they can be avoided. In those few cases when they cannot, with any certainty, the professional should use a partnership or S corporation type of practice rather than a regular C corporation. Specific PC problems are:

35 Percent Federal Flat Income Tax Bracket—Solved by Paying Out All Earnings Each Year so Corporation Pays No Tax. This disadvantage may be an advantage for very-high-income professionals, since they can be in a 50 percent aggregate marginal tax bracket (39.6 percent federal, plus state, plus personal deduction phase out, plus itemized deduction phase out, plus post-medicare tax). Thus, the corporate rate may be less, and may be a good place to accumulate funds with up to a 10 percent tax savings.

When this is not a factor, most PCs pay most of the compensation out as salary and bonuses, with properly structured employment contract arrangements. Beginning in 1988, Code Section 11(b)(2) was amended to provide for a flat tax bracket for PCs, which is now 35 percent.

With the inability of PCs to accumulate income at the lower corporate rates of 15 percent on earnings up to $50,000 (Code Section 11(b)(2) applies to taxable years beginning in 1988), it is no longer attractive to accumulate income in the corporation. This will undoubtedly result in efforts by many PCs to "zero out" (pay out all earnings) before the end of each taxable year, so that the corporation will have little or no accumulated income on which to pay tax at the top corporate rate of 34 percent. This will create even greater risks (from a tax standpoint) than presently exist in handling the operations of PCs. There are a number of ways the IRS can attach a PC and its shareholder-employees; however, in most situations, proper handling of the transactions and activities will eliminate (or significantly reduce) the risks involved.

Unreasonable Compensation—Seldom a Problem Except in Very Unusual Circumstances Because if Professionals Were Not There, Practice Would "Collapse." When a PC pays compensation to its professional employees, the IRS can claim that a portion of the compensation paid to a shareholder-employee is "unreasonable" and disallow the corporation's deduction for the compensation paid. [IRC § 162(a)(1); Treas Reg § 1.162-7] The "unreasonable" portion would then be taxed to the shareholder as a dividend. [Treas Reg §§ 1.162-7(b)(1), 1.162-8; Owensby & Kritikos, Inc v Commr, No 86-4073 (June 23, 1987); James H Rutter, 52 TCM 326 (1986)] For an "unreasonable compensation" case involving a law firm, see *Isaacson, Rosenbaum, Spiegleman & Friedman, PC v U.S.* [44 AFTR 2d 79-5382, 79-2 USTC § 1463 (Ct Cl 1979)]

Accumulated Earnings. Although a professional corporation can accumulate up to $150,000 without a business need, accumulation of income in excess of that amount must be based on valid business reasons. It is often difficult for a small professional corporation to establish a valid business reason for excess accumulations. [IRC § 535(c)(1)(B)]

Personal Holding Company. A professional corporation can become a "personal holding company" resulting in its undistributed "personal holding company income" being taxed at a rate of 50 percent. [IRC § 541] "Personal holding company income" includes amounts received under "personal service contracts" that permit the client to name the individual who is to perform the services. [IRC § 543(a)(7)] However, rulings by the IRS have practically eliminated the risk for most professional corporations by limiting the rule to only when the client has a legal right (rather than a mere "expectation") to name the person who will provide the services or when the professional services are so unique as to preclude a substitute provider. [Rev Ruls 75-249, 1975-1 CB 171; 75-67, 1975-1 CB 169; 75-250, 1975-1 CB 172]

Code Sections 482 and 269 and "Earner of Income" Problems. Even if the corporation is not a sham, the IRS has attempted to use the "assignment of income" doctrine and the "true earner of the income" theory under Code Section 61, together with attacks under Code Sections 482 and 269, to attribute the professional corporation's income to its professional employees. These attacks can be avoided by careful planning and adherence to formalities.

Chapter 13

Family Limited Partnerships

After outlining the basic characteristics of family limited partnerships (FLPs), this chapter discusses the protection against creditors offered by FLPs. It then analyzes the income tax advantages for both the business and the partners, as well as the gift and estate tax advantages of an FLP. Finally, this chapter examines valuation rules as they relate to FLPs.

Overview

Q 13:1   What is a family limited partnership?

A family limited partnership (FLP) is a partnership that includes as partners members of a family, such as grandparents, parents, children, and grandchildren. The partners may be trusts, custodianships, uniform transfers to minors arrangements, or other entities organized for the benefit of those family members.

When organizing an FLP, many questions about the organization of the entity must be answered, including:

- Who will be the partners?
- Where will the partnership be organized?
- What provisions will be included in the partnership agreement?

A partnership for purposes of the Internal Revenue Code (Code) includes any unincorporated organization or arrangement, regardless of form, used to conduct business or financial activities that is not classified as a corporation, trust, or estate under federal tax law. [IRC § 761(a)] The federal tax law definition of a partnership, in contrast with the Uniform Partnership Act, does not use explicit terms such as "two or more persons," "co-ownership of a business," or "division of profits." [IRC §§ 701, 704] The Internal Revenue Service (IRS) has issued guidelines under which limited partnerships can obtain letter rulings concerning their tax status. The requirements apply only when a taxpayer requests the IRS to issue an advance letter ruling on the tax classification of an organization as a partnership versus a trust or corporation. [Rev Proc 89-12, 1989-1 CB 798]

Q 13:2   For what purposes are an FLP useful?

An FLP is often the best choice to achieve the goals of (1) allocating income among family members, (2) making gifts, and planning for future estate taxes and (3) protecting assets from unnecessary liability exposure to creditors. It can provide substantial tax benefits, while allowing the family's business and assets to be transferred to succeeding generations in an orderly and cost-effective manner, with more protection from future creditors than that available to assets owned outright.

For example, use of an FLP can be very advantageous where the family business or other major assets make it impossible to divide the estate between the beneficiaries without dividing up the major assets. This is often the case where some children of the grantor want nothing to do with the family business yet the grantor wants to be fair to all children. In this situation, gifts of a limited partnership interest in an FLP would be an ideal solution. However, it must be kept in mind that the imposition of fiduciary duties by the general partner(s) to others may create its own set of problems.

Selecting the proper entity form is very important and requires balancing business and tax objectives. The process involves choosing among numerous tax, business, and owner alternatives and evaluating benefits versus burdens. When choosing the appropriate entity, the three most important considerations are: "the applicable commercial law, the tax treatment of the business form chosen, and the investment and business preferences of the parties involved." [Willis, *Partnership Taxation* (1994)] The issues include: how the entity and its owners will be taxed, management of the entity, succession of the entity's ownership, protection of the business assets from the owners' creditors, and the identity and character of the owners.

Creditor Protection

Q 13:3   Can an FLP be used for asset protection?

Yes. The ability to provide asset protection comes from the limited partnership statute. State statutes provide that an assignee of a partnership interest may receive, to the extent assigned, only the distribution to which the assignor would be entitled. [For example, see Idaho Code § 53-240] An assignee may become a limited partner only if: (1) the assignor gives the assignee that right and authority, and advance approval is provided in the partnership agreement, or (2) all other partners consent.

Therefore, if the partnership does not expand the statutory rights of an assignee, the assignee will not be able to become a partner and will only receive whatever distributions were to be made to the assignor.

A creditor can become a type of assignee by obtaining a charging order. If a creditor of a partner receives a judgment for money against the partner on application to a court of competent jurisdiction, the court may charge the partnership interest of the partner with payment of the unsatisfied amount of the judgment, with interest.

Q 13:4 What is a charging order?

A charging order is a statutory remedy of a creditor when the creditor is unable to force a partner to assign his or her partnership interest to the creditor. A charging order is neither an assignment nor an attachment. It is a court order, somewhat like a garnishment, that directs the partnership to make any distributions it would have made to the partner to the partner's creditors instead. The theory behind this rule is that, to allow a creditor access to the partnership assets and records as a result of the creditor's claim against one partner, would disrupt partnership business to the detriment of the other partners, especially if management rights were also involved. It is thus used to protect the partnership and the other partners.

It might be argued that this remedy is only appropriate in non-family situations; in family situations, in which every partner is presumably aware of each other's financial situation (and, indeed, the partnership may have been formed in response to such situation), the other partners are not entitled to the protection afforded by a charging order, and creditors should be allowed to reach the partnership assets. A charging order is, however, prescribed by statute. Accordingly, if the creditor attempts to reach any interest other than what is provided in the order, he or she must obtain court approval. This remedy, therefore, is costly to the creditor. As either an assignee or a holder of a charging order, the creditor may be treated as a partner for income tax purposes; if no distributions are forthcoming, he or she would have to pay tax on taxable income not distributed by the partnership, as discussed below.

Q 13:5 How is a charging order disadvantageous to a creditor?

A creditor with a charging order has the rights of an assignee of the partnership interest. The general partner can decide whether to distribute any money or property from the partnership to the partners. The assignee of the partnership interest does not have the power to force the general partner to make a distribution. However, the assignee may nevertheless still be liable for payment of taxes on the assignee's distributive share of income. If this occurs, the creditor may be willing to relinquish its interest in the partnership on terms more favorable than otherwise. [Henkel,

"How FLPs Can Protect Assets," *Estate Planning* (Jan–Feb 1993), p 3] The limited partnership, therefore, protects the assets by making assets—that would be desirable—undesirable for anyone else due to their inaccessibility and income tax burden.

Normally, a court limits a partner's creditor's remedy to a charging order. If, however, a creditor can establish that the claim may never be paid, a court may consider an order forcing the sale of the partner interest. Such an order is rare, however, since a sale could cause a material adverse disruption to the partnership. Even if such an order is obtained, the interest will have little value to an outside party, especially since the purchaser will merely become an assignee. Under most states' revised uniform limited partnership acts (RULPAs), a creditor cannot force the sale of a limited partner interest. [RULPA §§ 402(2), 402(4), 702, 801(4)] The partnership will not be dissolved if there is another general partner and the written provisions of the partnership agreement permit the partnership business to be carried on by him or her, and he or she does so. [RULPA § 801(4)] In addition, the partnership will not be dissolved if, within 90 days of the general partner's withdrawal, all parties agree in writing to continue the partnership business and to the appointment of a new general partner. [RULPA § 801(4)] Under many LLC statutes, a charging order is the only remedy a creditor possesses. [See also Q 6:12]

Q 13:6   What are the general partners' duties to an assignee or creditor with a charging order?

A limited partner, although restricted in the rights he or she has under the partnership agreement, still possesses certain rights and powers under RULPA. An assignee, however, has virtually none of those rights and powers. The assignee is only entitled to receive any distribution to which the assignor was entitled.

A general partner has very few, if any, fiduciary duties toward an assignee. Therefore, if a donee's assets are subject to creditor claims, the donor contemplating a gift of a limited partnership interest to a donee should consider retaining the limited partnership interest, preferably in a trust or another pass-through entity, such as a subsidiary limited partnership or LLC, and merely assigning the limited partnership interest to the donee without admitting the donee as a limited partner. However, in transferring only assignee interests, the donor may run afoul of Code Section 2038 for estate tax purposes, discussed hereafter. Notwithstanding the limited role of an assignee in a partnership, the assignee is considered a partner for tax purposes, thereby requiring the assignee to include the same amount in his or her taxable income as a limited partner holding the same distribution rights would have to include. [RULPA § 603]

Q 13:7   What right does a creditor have to reject the partnership agreement in bankruptcy?

Since federal bankruptcy law supersedes state law, it may be possible to obtain a federal bankruptcy order to sell a partnership interest, regardless of whether it is a general or limited partner interest. In neither case, however, could a creditor force the sale of the underlying partnership property, unless the claim was secured by the property, without an extraordinary court order.

A bankruptcy trustee, as the creditor's representative, may attempt to reject the partnership agreement as an executory contract and withdraw the debtor's interest from the partnership. Such an attempt should be addressed in the agreement by providing that, upon a withdrawal, the withdrawing partner should not receive fair value until the dissolution of the partnership. This must apply to any partner under any withdrawal in order to be supportable against a creditor.

Q 13:8   Can creditor protection of an FLP be lost through a "fraudulent conveyance?"

Yes. A problem arises if an owner subject to potential or actual claims wants to transfer an asset to an FLP in order to protect the asset.

If a transfer of property to an FLP is considered a "fraudulent conveyance" under state law or federal bankruptcy law, the creditors of the transferor may be able to reach the transferred property, and not just the transferor's interest in the partnership, by: voiding the transfer of the property to the partnership, attaching the transferred property, appointing a receiver to take charge of the transferred property, or levying on the transferred property. Although most statutes protect the recipients of the property who take in good faith and for fair market value, because of the family relationships of the FLP and the transferor, even if the transferor sold the property to the FLP for full and adequate consideration, it might not be possible to establish good faith.

Q 13:9 What is a fraudulent conveyance or transfer?

A *transfer* is generally defined as any direct or indirect disposition of property, whether or not consideration is received. [RULPA §§ 402(2), 702] A *fraudulent transfer,* however, is defined under state law or federal bankruptcy law. Generally, transfers are deemed fraudulent if made with the actual intent to delay, hinder, or defraud the transferor's creditors. [RULPA §§ 702, 704] Proof of actual intent may be found by one of two means. Either there is testimony as to the reasons for the transfer of the property that is unprotected by attorney-client privilege or there exist "badges of fraud," which are certain actions that are rebuttable evidence of intent. [RULPA §§ 703, 704] Five examples of badges of fraud that might be raised in the context of funding an FLP are:

1. Transfers to an "insider" that, when the transferor is an individual, includes a partnership in which the transferor is a general partner;
2. The indirect retention of the transferred property or control of the transferred property;
3. The transfer of all or substantially all of the transferor's property;
4. Transfers for less than adequate consideration; and
5. Transfers made when the transferor is insolvent at the time of the transfer or soon thereafter.

Q 13:10 Is it desirable to restrict the individual's ability to transfer a partnership interest?

Yes, to further protect against creditors and in order to keep the interest in the family. It is useful, therefore, to subject the limited partner interest to a buy-sell agreement.

If the limited partner is a minor, it is possible under the uniform transfers to minors statutes of most states to transfer the limited partner interest to a custodian who will hold the interest until the minor reaches age 18 or 21. Each state statute must be reviewed to ensure that a custodian is empowered under the statute to hold a limited partner interest. Under certain older uniform gifts to minors statutes, such an asset is not a permissible investment.

Use of a trust to hold the limited partner interest is recommended when a buy-sell agreement is not possible and the donor wants to restrict the donee's ability to transfer the limited partner interest. If held in an irrevocable trust, the limited partnership interest may be kept out of the donee's ownership for creditor purposes, including a divorce. Furthermore, if the limited partner interest is held by a trust, then future unborn beneficiaries of the trust may participate in the FLP.

Tax Advantages to the Business

Q 13:11 What are the entity-level tax advantages of an FLP?

Federal law determines the tests or standards applied in classifying an organization, but state law determines whether the legal relationships established by the organization's formation meet those standards. [Treas Reg § 301.7701-1(c)] The tax classification of an entity historically has turned on whether an entity has certain characteristics that cause it to be categorized as an association taxable as a corporation. [IRC § 7701(a)(3)] The term "corporation" includes associations and joint-stock companies.

In 1935, the U.S. Supreme Court identified the defining characteristics of an association in *Morrissey v. Commissioner.* [296 US 344 (1935)] According to the Court, the eight characteristics of an association properly taxable as a corporation are:

1. Associates in a common enterprise;
2. A purpose to transact business and share the profits;
3. Title to property being held by the business entity;
4. Centralized management;
5. Entity existence unaffected by the death of participants;

6. Transferability of the beneficial interest in the entity without affecting the continuity of the enterprise;

7. Large numbers of participants; and

8. Limited liability for participants.

[*Morrissey* at 356-359]

Six of the characteristics were later incorporated into Treasury regulations promulgated pursuant to Code Section 7701. Characteristic (3) and characteristic (5) were not included.

Corporate and noncorporate business forms share the attributes of being associates in a common enterprise and having a purpose to transact business and share the profits therefrom; therefore, those two characteristics are ignored when classifying entities for tax purposes. [Treas Reg § 301.7701-2(a)(2)] "In determining whether an organization has more corporate characteristics than noncorporate characteristics, all characteristics common to both types of organizations shall not be considered." [Treas Reg § 301.7701-2(a)(3)] The focus, therefore, is on the remaining six characteristics. Before the "check-the-box" regulations became effective, an entity had to possess a majority of the remaining characteristics to be classified as a corporation for federal tax purposes. [Treas Reg § 301.7701-2(a)(3)] Under "check-the-box" regulations, however, a noncorporate domestic entity is taxed as a partnership unless it makes an affirmative election to be taxed as a regular corporation.

Before January 1, 1997, the effective date of IRS "check-the-box" regulations, an entity was taxed as a corporation if the entity possessed more corporate than noncorporate characteristics. [Treas Reg § 301.7701-2(a)(3)] The "check-the-box" regulations allow many entities to elect partnership status without meeting the six-characteristics test.

Income Tax Advantages to the Partners

Q 13:12   How can family income taxes be reduced with an FLP?

The goal of reducing income taxes is realized by shifting family income from the parents' high marginal income tax bracket to the children's (and sometimes grandparents') lower marginal income tax bracket. If this is accomplished, the overall income taxes paid will be decreased.

The FLP provides beneficial rules when implementing a family income tax reduction plan. The FLP allows shifting of taxable income to lower-bracket taxpayers, while still maintaining ultimate control over the partnership's assets with others, generally the parents or entities they control, as the general partners. A limited partnership is a conduit or pass-through entity; as such, it files a tax return (Form 1065) but pays no tax. Each tax item passes through the partnership to the individual partners using a Form K-1.

Four methods can be employed in reducing family income taxes with an FLP.

Method 1. The easiest method is through a gifting program under which gifts are made annually by the parents to the children, using the annual gift tax exclusion. [IRC § 2503(b)] As gifts are made, the income that would have been reported on the parent's income tax return, at a high marginal income tax rate, is now reported on the children's income tax returns, at their lower marginal income tax rate. For children under the age of 14, Code Section 1(g) limits the amount of unearned income that would be received tax free or taxable at the child's lower marginal income tax rate. [See IRC § 1(g), known as the "kiddie tax"]

Method 2. The second method of lowering the family's overall income taxes is through the use of special allocations, subject to special family income tax rules discussed hereafter. A major advantage of using the limited partnership form is the ability to allocate tax items to the partners. In many instances, certain partners, usually the children, are not in a position to use specific tax items such as losses, depreciation, or amortization expenses. Therefore, if the partnership is properly organized and operated, the partners can allocate those specific items to the parents, thus allowing them to be used on the parents' individual income tax return to offset other income. Thus, the parents are able to lower their income taxes, reducing the family's overall income tax liability.

Method 3. The third method is for the FLP to pay reasonable salaries to children. A special allocation meets the standards of the Code if the allocation possesses substantial economic effect. [IRC § 704(b)(2)] The partner who receives the allocation must also receive the item's economic burden or benefit. [Treas Reg § 1.704-1(b)(2)(ii)(a)] This typically is reflected through the capital accounts. Capital accounts represent each partner's equity investment in the partnership. Under the capital account maintenance rules of the Treasury regulations, entries for recording the contributed assets and the contributing partners' capital accounts are similar to those used under financial accounting principles. [Treas Reg § 1.704-1(b)(2)(iv)] In drafting a valid allocation, the proper establishment and maintenance of capital accounts for each partner is required.

The partnership agreement must provide for the establishment and maintenance of the capital accounts throughout the full term of the partnership. [Treas Reg § 1.704-1(b)(2)(iv)(a)] The three requirements for a valid capital account are:

1. The capital account balances for each partner must be properly maintained and reflect increases and decreases based upon the nature of the allocations.

2. Upon the liquidation of the partnership, liquidating distributions to the partners must be made in accordance with the positive capital account balances of the partners.

3. Any partner with a deficit capital account balance must be required to restore the deficit balance to the partnership by the end of the taxable year in which the liquidation occurred or within 90 days after the date of the liquidation.

[Treas Reg § 1.704-1(b)(2)(ii)(b)(2), (iv)]

Even though an allocation may have substantial economic effect under the Code, such a determination is not conclusive; a deduction may be disallowed under other Code sections. The amount of deductions that may be taken is limited to the amount at risk in the venture. A partner's distributive share of loss is also limited to the extent of the adjusted basis of the partner's interest in the partnership at the end of the partnership year. Carryover losses may be used when the partner's outside basis has a positive balance, and an allocation may be reallocated under other provisions. [IRC § 482]

Method 4. Assets may be contributed to, or distributed from, the partnership without triggering capital gain recognition. Flexibility in future income tax planning is useful as the overall needs of the family change.

Q 13:13 Can an FLP deduct investment expenses under Code Section 162?

No. An individual who invests in securities and manages his or her investments seeking long-term gain is not "carrying on a trade or business" within the meaning of Section 162, regardless of the extent or continuity of the transactions or the work required in managing the portfolio. [See Higgins v Commissioner, 312 US 212, 218 (1941), *reh'g denied*, 312 US 714 (1941); Moller v United States, 721 F 2d 810, 814 (Fed Cir 1983)] While these cases address the issue with respect to individuals, they do not answer the question where a business entity, such as a partnership, is involved.

The IRS answered this question in Revenue Ruling 75-523. [1975-2 CB 257] In Revenue Ruling 75-523, the IRS stated that, like an individual, a partnership created solely for the purpose of investing in securities is not involved in "carrying on a trade or business" within the meaning of Section 162. Accordingly, the expenses incurred by the partnership during the taxable year for postage, stationery, safe deposit box rentals, bank charges, fees for accounting and investment services, and utility charges would only be deductible under Section 212. Thus, the deductions will be available to the individual only to the extent they (and other similar expenses) exceed two percent of the individual's adjusted gross income for the year in question. [IRC § 67(a)]

While the above ruling speaks to partnerships, it does not deal with the issue of the fiduciary duty of the general partner to act in the best interests of the partnership. Because the general partner in an FLP is arguably a fiduciary with respect to the partnership and the limited partner, can the FLP deduct these expenses as business expenses? Unfortunately, it has been held that where an estate or trust engages solely in investing activities, the estate or trust is not "carrying on a trade or business" within the meaning of Section 162. [See City of Bank Farmers Trust Co v Helvering, 313 US 121, 123-126 (1940), *aff'g* 112 F 2d 457 (2d Cir 1941)] A partnership would not be treated more favorably.

Q 13:14 Are there special family partnership income tax rules?

Yes. Income shifting is generally allowed under Code Section 704(e). The IRS may also distribute, allocate, or apportion income and deductions under the family rules if it determines that the taxpayer is evading taxes and if reallocation will more accurately reflect the taxpayer's income. [IRC § 704(e)(2)] The family partnership rules focus on halting abuse in situations not involving arm's-length bargaining.

If the donor gifts limited partner interests and remains the general partner, the general partner-donor will possibly run afoul of Code Section 2036(a). The IRS has ruled that, if the donor retains all of the income of a limited partnership, the value of the entire partnership will be includible in the donor's estate. In that situation, the donor has structured the partnership to pull out all of the income as salary or as a disproportionate distributive share. The safest type of income allocation is a straight pro rata distribution of income based on percentage interests in the partnership, although reasonable compensation for the general partner who manages the partnership property may be desirable — or even necessary.

Q 13:15 Can the IRS attempt to disregard an FLP using tax law doctrines such as substance over form, sham transaction, lack of business purpose or improper motives?

Yes, but only in unusual circumstances. In *Carriage Square, Inc. v. Commissioner* [69 TC 119 (1977)], the Tax Court, in holding certain trusts not to be bona fide limited partners to which income of a limited partnership was properly allocable, relied on Code Section 704(e), finding that the parties acted without a business purpose and without good faith. However, in *Friedlander Corporation v. Commissioner* [216 F2d 757 (5th Cir 1954)], the court held that it was erroneous, as a matter of law, to conclude that no partnership exists because the primary motive for forming the partnership was to reduce tax liability. This case allowed a business to change business form from a corporation to a partnership.

In *Merryman v. Commissioner* [873 F2d 879 (5th Cir 1989)], *Duhon v. Commissioner* [62 TCM 382 (CCH), TCM 91,369 at 1873 (RIA) (1991)], and *Cirelli v. Commissioner* [82 TC 335 (1984)], the courts relied on the economic substance and business purpose doctrines in disregarding a partnership formed to provide tax benefits to certain employees of an oil and gas drilling company. In *Cirelli*, however, it was not so much the lack of a business that mattered, since the operation of the oil rig unquestionably was a business, but rather a circular flow of funds within the company without any change in substance and a failure to adhere to the governing agreements.

In *Estate of Bischoff v. Commissioner* [69 TC 32, 40 (1977)], the Tax Court, in upholding the validity of a buy-sell agreement for an investment limited partnership holding stock in two active businesses and marketable securities, implied that the partnership itself was bona fide. The court brushed aside the IRS's objections that no legitimate business purpose could exist for a buy-sell agreement for a partnership that lacked any active business and that functioned solely as a holding company. Similarly, in *Estate of Harrison v. Commissioner* [52 TCM 1306 (CCH), TCM 87,008 at 42 (RIA) (1987)], the Tax Court gave short shrift to the IRS's assertion that an FLP holding real estate, oil, gas interests, and marketable securities should be ignored as an attempt to artificially depress the value of the decedent's property for estate tax purposes. The Tax Court ruled against the IRS and for the taxpayer.

In *LeFrak v. Commissioner* [66 TCM 1297 (1993)], a parent's attempt to transfer interests in real property to his children in the form of discounted partnership interests was disallowed. The children subsequently contributed the property to partnerships. The court, applying New York law, deemed the transfers to be mere interests in the real property of the parent. The parent's argument that he had created a one-person partnership with himself was rejected. Thus, the parent's 40 percent discount valuation, arrived at on the assumption of a valid partnership, was revalued by the court as a 20 percent discount rate in fractional real estate interests.

A partnership might be disregarded on account of: (1) a lack of bona fide co-partners, as in *Carriage Square*, or (2) other abuses, as in *Merryman*. The Treasury regulations, promulgated after the above cited cases were decided, provide that: "if a partnership is formed or availed in connection with a transaction or series of related transactions (individually or collectively, the transaction) with a principal purpose of substantially reducing the present value of the partners' aggregate federal tax liability in a manner that is inconsistent with the intent of Subchapter K, the Commissioner can disregard the form of the transaction. . . ." [Treas Reg § 1.701-2(b)] An initial draft of this regulation was published in the Federal Register, containing two examples of its application to

FLPs. These examples demonstrated the need for a bona fide business purpose consistent with the intent of Subchapter K in order to validate valuation discounts among family members. These examples, however, have been since deleted from the final regulation. This apparent retreat from business purpose or sham transaction scrutiny should not signal FLP immunity from IRS attack. As discussed through the case law above, the IRS, pursuant to Treasury Regulations Section 1.701-2(b), can still attack valuation discounts by other means.

Q 13:16 What are the tax consequences if the business purposes of an FLP are disregarded by the IRS?

If the IRS succeeded in asserting that a particular FLP had no valid business purpose, the relationship between the parties would be that of tenants in common holding undivided interests in the "partnership" property. Tenants in common have rights and obligations under state law, which would usually be the law of the state where the real property was located. They would also have rights and obligations under the partnership agreement, because it would be a contract entered into by the owners. The owners may also have the protections of the state limited partnership act as a partnership for state law purposes, even if they were not partners for federal income tax purposes. Thus, there may still be creditor protection and value discounts.

Q 13:17 What are valid business reasons for the formation of an FLP?

Some business purposes that should support FLPs for federal tax purposes are: (1) centralized management; (2) orderly development and management of the partnership property; (3) retention of the property in the family; (4) asset protection from creditors; (5) instruction to younger generation members about investments and the business involved; and (6) pass-through entity-level tax treatment.

The weight of authority indicating that an investment FLP ordinarily should be respected as a partnership for tax purposes, though a partnership in fact invested substantially in personal-use property, might still be viewed as pushing the legal principles to their extreme. Proposed Treasury Regulations Section 1.280A-1 suggests that there is no inherent problem in a partnership's ownership of a vacation home (or presumably any other personal-use property). In that proposed regulation, the IRS has set forth proposals for determining the personal use of a dwelling owned by a pass-through entity, including a partnership, under Code Section 280A.

Q 13:18 Can taxable gain be triggered upon the formation of the FLP?

Yes, in three situations.

Situation 1. Code Section 721(b) mandates recognition of gain on the transfer of appreciated property to a partnership more than 80 percent of whose assets consist of stocks, securities, options, cash, foreign currency, precious metals (unless used in the active conduct of a business), and an interest in an entity if its assets are substantially all from these categories (including RICs and REITs held for investment, but excluding real estate in the 80 percent calculation). The standards apply under Code Section 721(b) because of that section's notion of an "investment company." [See IRC § 351(e)(1); investment company is defined in Treas Reg § 1.351-1(c)] The IRS has ruled that diversification can exist even when one partner contributes securities and a second partner contributes only cash. [Rev Rul 87-9, 1987-1 CB 133]

The rule creates tax if the transfer to the partnership results, directly or indirectly, in diversification of the transferors' interests. The intent is to prevent the use of partnerships as a means to effect the tax-free exchange of interests in securities.

The diversification rule contains a *de minimis* exception. Some guidance about what constitutes an insignificant portion is provided in an example in the regulations, in which one-person transfers nonidentical securities equal in value to 1 percent of the value of identical stock contributed by two other persons. [Treas Reg § 1.351-1(c)(6), Ex 1]

Generally, partnerships do not recognize gain on a transfer of appreciated assets in exchange for an interest in the partnership. [IRC § 721(a)] However, if the partnership is classified as an "investment company," the rule of nonrecognition does not apply to contributions and gain may have to be recognized. [IRC § 721(b)]

The investment company regulations do not apply if the transfer of appreciated securities does not result in further diversification of the contributors' investments in marketable securities. [S Rep No 938, 94th Cong, 2d Sess, pt 2, at 43, 44 (1976)] Therefore, Code Section 721(b) is only a problem when family members contribute different marketable securities to the FLP. For example, diversification would exist if one family member contributed shares of stock in IBM and a second family member contributed shares of stock in Coca-Cola. Each partner would now have a partial interest in each stock, causing diversification to occur (each now owns a percentage of both stocks instead of complete ownership of their contribution). If each partner contributes shares of the same stock or stocks (e.g., shares of Coca-Cola and IBM), with no selling and purchasing of different companies stocks thereafter, then no diversification has occurred.

Situation 2. If a person transfers assets and liabilities to a partnership and is relieved of some of the liabilities, taxable gain is triggered to that extent. [IRC § 752]

Situation 3. A partner who receives a partnership interest for services rendered has taxable income to the extent of the fair market value of the interest, at least if it includes a capital and an income interest. [Sol Diamond v Commr, 492 F 2d 286 (7th Cir 1984)] If, however, a partner receives only a future profits interest and no capital partnership interest (i.e., the partner would not receive capital on liquidation), he or she does not have taxable income upon receipt of such interest. [Campbell v Commr, 943 F 2d 815 (8th Cir 1991)]

Q 13:19 What other tax issues do the partners have upon the creation of the FLP?

Upon the contribution of property to the partnership, the partnership will generally receive a basis equal to the adjusted basis of the property in the hands of the contributing partner. [IRC § 723] The contributing partner will take a basis in the partnership equal to the adjusted basis of the property contributed. [IRC § 722] Each partner's basis is increased by the partner's share of the partnership's liabilities. [IRC § 752] An increase in a partner's basis is beneficial since a partner may receive more distributions without recognizing gain. [IRC § 731(a)(1)] The amount of liabilities allocated to each partner depends on whether the liability is characterized as a recourse or nonrecourse liability. A liability of the partnership is considered to be recourse to the extent that any partner or related person bears the economic risk of loss. [Treas Reg § 1.752-1(a)(1)] Conversely, a liability is considered nonrecourse to the extent that no partner or related person bears the economic risk of loss. [Treas Reg § 1.752-1(a)(2)]

The allocation of recourse debt among the partners is designed to allocate the debt to the partner that will bear the ultimate economic risk of loss (see chapter 7). To determine the economic risk of loss, a constructive liquidation of the partnership is calculated. [Treas Reg § 1.752-2(b)] For example, assume that partner A has a basis of $100 and partner B has a basis of $50, and the partnership has a $25 recourse liability. If a constructive liquidation is performed, and it is determined that partner B would bear the economic risk of loss, then B's basis would be increased from $50 to $75. [IRC § 752(a)] After calculating the constructive liquidation, it can be determined which partner, or related person, would be obligated to make the payments necessary to satisfy the recourse obligations of the partnership.

Gift and Estate Tax Advantages

Q 13:20 What estate tax planning can be done with an FLP?

A taxpayer's gross estate upon death is subject to estate tax liability. The taxpayer can legally reduce the size of the estate in ways to reduce the estate tax. One goal of an estate plan may be to pass the family's business, investments, and financial operations to succeeding generations, with the lowest amount of transfer tax cost. The FLP offers an excellent way to reduce the size of a taxable estate and transfer the assets to the succeeding generation, with few negative side effects.

An FLP, done properly, allows the managing or general partner (usually the donor of the underlying assets of the FLP) to retain control of the business operations, control his or her salary, control the flow of income that is allocated to the other partnership interests, and, at the same time, reduce the income and estate taxes for the family.

Q 13:21   What are the basic gift and estate tax rules?

A gift tax is imposed on gifts of property made during life [IRC § 2501(a)], and upon transfers of property upon the death of the owner. [IRC § 2001(a)] The amount of gift or estate tax is based upon the fair market value of the transferred property on the date of receipt. Federal tax law determines the property to be included for gift and estate tax purposes; however, federal tax law might not coincide with other state laws of ownership. Federal law allows assets not owned at death to be taxed, for example, as assets given away or sold for less than fair market value shortly before death.

Estate planning, involving a closely held business or partnership, becomes a question of valuing the interest held by the decedent or donor. The IRS considers many factors in valuing an interest in a closely held business or a transferred interest at the death of an owner. The most important factor when valuing a transferred interest is control. If the IRS feels that the decedent maintains too much control over the transferred interest, then it may be added to the decedent's gross estate (see Q 13:41).

The Code provides for specific deductions and exemptions. Code Sections 2505(a) and 2010 provide a credit to offset the gift or estate tax liability of each individual taxpayer, allowing a transfer of $625,000 worth of property without gift (during life) or estate (at death) tax. The $625,000 limit applies per person during life and at death. This $625,000 amount increases in steps through 2006 to $1 million as a result of the Taxpayer Relief Act of 1997. If $300,000 of the credit equivalent is used by lifetime taxable gifts, only the balance ($325,000 in 1998) remains at death. The estate planner often designs an estate plan allowing the client to pay the least amount of gift and estate tax, while still maintaining the client's desires regarding the disposition of his or her property.

Property that remains in the taxpayer's estate and is transferred upon the taxpayer's death will receive a basis step up to fair market value in the hands of the donee. [IRC § 1014] As with all lifetime gifts, the Section 1014 step up in basis is lost for appreciated assets excluded from the gross estate. Therefore, any transfer tax savings of the gift must be weighed against the potential income tax detriment of the loss of the step up in basis. [IRC §§ 754, 1014]

Q 13:22 What are the basic gift tax goals?

The basic goals are to minimize the value of taxable gifts and to use gifts to reduce an individual's estate tax. A wealth-transfer program using an FLP works well, but an understanding of the estate and gift tax laws is essential. For purposes of the gift tax, a gift can occur whether the transfer is in trust or otherwise, whether the transfer is direct or indirect, and whether the property transferred is real or personal, tangible or intangible. [Treas Reg § 25.2511-1(a)] Donative intent on the part of the transferor is not an essential element in applying the gift tax on the transfer. [Treas Reg § 25.2511-1(g)(1)] The tax is applied based on the objective facts of the transfer and the circumstances under which it is made, rather than on the subjective motives of the donor.

The $10,000 Annual Gift Tax Exclusion Per Donee. In addition to the unified credit, the Code provides an annual gift tax exclusion of $10,000 per donee per year. [IRC § 2503(b)] When combined with gift splitting between spouses, spouses may transfer a total of $20,000 per donee, each year, without triggering any gift tax liability. [IRC §§ 2503(b), 2513]

The Present Interest Rule. The annual gift tax exclusion is available only when the gift consists of a present interest. [IRC § 2503(b); Treas Reg § 25.2503-3 (as amended in 1983)] The gift tax regulations recognize that an unrestricted life estate or term certain qualifies as a present interest: "an unrestricted right to the immediate use, possession, or enjoyment of property or the income from property (such as a life estate or term certain) is a present interest in property." [Treas Reg § 25-2503-3(b) (as amended in 1983); Ltr Rul 8906026] The issue of present interest in the context of minors and trusts was established in *Crummey v. Commissioner.* [397 F2d 82 (9th Cir 1968); see, e.g., Rev Rul 73-405, 1973-2 CB 321] If a donor makes a transfer to a trust and the trust instrument gives the beneficiary the power to demand immediate possession and enjoyment of the transferred property, the beneficiary has a present interest that is eligible for the annual gift tax exclusion, even if his or her demand right will lapse after a period of time. The IRS has ruled, however, that to qualify a transfer in trust for the annual exclusion, the demand right cannot be illusory. [Rev Rul 81-7, 1981-1 CB 474]

In *Cristofani Estate v. Commissioner* [97 TC 74 (1991)], the court concluded that the test of the existence of a present interest in trust corpus is not the likelihood that the beneficiaries will actually receive substantial benefits in the trust at some future time, but whether the beneficiaries have an unrestricted legal right to withdraw corpus. The Tax Court specifically stated that it did not believe that *Crummey* required a vested present interest or vested remainder interest in the trust corpus or income to qualify for the annual gift tax exclusion.

Outside of the trust context, the present interest rule is different for excludable $10,000 gifts to minors. No part of a transfer to a minor will be considered a future interest if the conditions of the transfer meet these two provisions of Code Section 2503(c):

1. The property and its income may be expended by, or for the benefit of, the minor donee before he or she reaches the age of 21. To the extent not so expended, it will pass to him or her at that time.

2. In the event of the donee's death before reaching 21, the property and income not expended will pass to his or her estate or to persons appointed by him or her under the exercise of a general power of appointment.

Marital Deduction. When a gift is made by one spouse to the other, the donor spouse may claim a gift tax marital deduction. [IRC § 2523] Unlimited deductible transfers may be made to the donor's spouse either during life or upon death, provided these four requirements are satisfied:

1. The parties are legally married at the time of the gift. (The annual gift tax exclusion is not available for a prenuptial gift.)

2. The donor is a U.S. citizen or resident.

3. The donee is a U.S. citizen.

4. The gift is not a nondeductible terminable interest (i.e., an interest in property that may terminate upon the passage of time or upon the occurrence or nonoccurrence of some event, with distribution thereafter to another person).

[IRC § 2523(f)(2)]

The annual exclusion for certain gifts made by U.S. citizens or residents to their non-U.S. citizen spouses is $100,000. [IRC § 2523(i)] Thus, when the donee spouse is not a U.S. citizen, the unlimited gift tax marital deduction is not allowed.

Basis. When a gift is made, the donee takes the tax basis in the partnership interest of the donor.

Q 13:23 Does a gift to family members using an FLP qualify for the $10,000 present interest gift tax exclusion?

Yes, generally. An interest in an FLP, even if stripped of distribution, liquidation, and sales rights, is not a future interest. No $10,000 per donee annual gift tax exclusion is permitted for future interests. [IRC § 2503(b)] The IRS addressed this issue in Technical Advice Memorandum 9131006 and in Letter Ruling 9415007. Both cases involved the gift of an interest in a partnership in which the limited partners had no right to present distributions, because distributions were subject to the discretion of the general partners. The IRS held the interests in the partnership to be present interests qualifying for the exclusion. In each case the IRS pointed to the ability of each partner to sell his or her interest, subject only to a right of first refusal held by the other partners.

Gifts of corporate stock have been held to constitute gifts of future interests when they were subject to a ten-year restriction on transfer. [Hutchinson v Commr, 47 TC 680, 686 (1967), *accord*, Rev Rul 76-360, 1976-2 CB 298] In its rulings on closely held stock, the IRS appears to have regularly approved as present interests outright gifts of stock that the donee might alienate, subject only to a right of first refusal, even though the present dividend prospects were bleak. [TAM 9346003; Ltr Rul 8121003]

Nothing in the rulings indicates there is any requirement that a permitted assignee be admissible automatically to the partnership as a substitute partner. (Such a requirement would be undesirable for purposes of entity classification, as it would evidence the corporate characteristic of free transferability.) There is generally no outside market for FLP interests not traded on a stock exchange.

Q 13:24   When does a gift of an interest in an FLP not qualify as a present interest for the $10,000 gift tax exclusion?

In Technical Advice Memorandum 9751003, the Internal Revenue Service ruled that gifts of interests in a limited partnership did not qualify for the annual exclusion for gifts because they constituted gifts of future interests in property. The reasoning in Technical Advice Memorandum 9751003 can be viewed as consistent with the Service's other rulings on this issue, even though it reaches a different conclusion than those other rulings.

Technical Advice Memorandum 9751003, when considered in conjunction with the prior rulings, indicates that the Service will rule that a gift of an interest in a limited partnership will not constitute a gift of a future interest in property, notwithstanding the vesting in the general partner of the sole discretion to determine the partnership's distribution policy, if the partnership agreement does not eliminate the general partner's fiduciary duty to the limited partners, and if the limited partners are permitted to sell or assign their interests in the partnership.

Under the Revised Uniform Partnership Act (RUPA), a partnership agreement may not eliminate a partner's fiduciary duties to the other partners and the partnership or unreasonably reduce a partner's duty of care. [RUPA § 103(b)(3), (4), (5) (partnership agreement may not eliminate the duty of loyalty, unreasonably reduce the duty of care or eliminate the obligation of good faith), applicable to limited partnerships under RULPA § 403] In interpreting the Uniform Partnership Act (UPA), which has been adopted by most states, courts strictly construe provisions in partnership agreements that would waive a partner's fiduciary duties. [See cases cited in 2 Alan R Bromberg and Larry E Ribstein, Bromberg and Ribstein on Partnership, § 6.07(h)(4), n. 145 (1997 and Supp), applicable to limited partnerships under RULPA § 403]

In states where no fiduciary duties exist, then fiduciary duties equivalent to those in RUPA should be part of the agreement.

In its rulings, the Service requires that the general partner must have strict fiduciary duties to the limited partner before it will rule that a gift of a limited partnership interest is not a gift of a future interest in property. The presence of fiduciary duties should arguably be irrelevant for purposes of the future interest determination. In many cases, a gift of a limited partnership interest should constitute a gift of a present interest in property.

The withdrawal rights of a limited partner are similar to the demand rights of a beneficiary who has been granted Crummey powers with respect to transfers to a trust. In *Crummey v. Commissioner* [397 F 2d 82 (9th Cir 1968)] the donor made gifts in the amount of the annual exclusion to an irrevocable family trust each year. Under the trust instrument, each beneficiary was entitled to withdraw immediately an amount in cash equal to the annual exclusion by making a written demand to the trustee before the end of the calendar year. The court held that the donor had made gifts of present interests in property because the trustee could not legally resist the beneficiary's demand for the withdrawal.

A partnership agreement, however, may eliminate a limited partner's withdrawal rights. [RULPA §§ 603, 604] Provisions restricting a limited partner's right to withdraw from the partnership are not uncommon. In fact, many states have amended their limited partnership statutes to provide that a limited partner may not withdraw at will from the partnership. The states that have eliminated withdrawal rights for limited partners include Alaska, California, Colorado, Delaware, Florida, Georgia, Montana, Missouri, Nevada, Ohio, Rhode Island, South Dakota, Tennessee, Texas, Virginia, and Washington. [See Alaska Stat § 32.11.260; Cal Corp Code § 15664; Colo Rev Stat Ann § 7-62-603; Del Code Ann tit 6, § 17-603; Fla Stat Ann § 620.143; Ga Code Ann § 14-9-603; Mo Ann Stat § 359.341; Mont Code Ann § 35-12-1003; Nev Rev Stat § 88.500; Ohio Rev Code § 1782.33(B); RI Gen Laws § 7-13-33; SD Codified Laws § 48-7-603; Tenn Code Ann § 61-2-603; Tex Rev Civ Stat Ann art 6132a-1 § 6.03; Va Code Ann § 50-73.38; Wash Rev Code Ann § 25.10.330]

Thus, a general partner may have complete control over whether and when partnership distributions may be made to the limited partners. While a limited partner will receive a distribution of partnership assets if and when the partnership is dissolved, [RULPA § 804] there is no guarantee that a limited partner will receive any distributions from the partnership prior to its dissolution.

RULPA provides that a limited partner may assign his or her interest in the partnership. [RULPA § 702] The interest that the limited partner may assign, however, is limited to the partner's right to receive distributions from the partnership. An assignment of a limited partner's interest does not entitle the assignee to become a partner in the partnership or to have any of the rights of a partner unless all of the other partners consent to admit the assignee as a partner or unless the partnership agreement provides otherwise. [RULPA §§ 702, 704(a)] The assignee will not succeed to the assignor's right to vote on partnership matters (if any), [see RULPA § 302 (partnership agreement may give voting rights to limited partners)] right to inspect partnership records, [See RULPA § 305 (limited partner's right to obtain information)] or any other right conferred on the limited partner under the partnership agreement. The fiduciary duties that a general partner owes to a limited partner in conducting partnership business do not extend to an assignee of a limited partner's interest. [See RULPA § 403 (except as otherwise provided in the partnership agreement, a general partner has the rights and powers and is subject to the restrictions of a partner in a partnership without limited partners); RUPA § 404 (partner owes fiduciary duties to the partnership and the partners); UPA § 21(1) (same); but see Kellis v Ring, 92 Cal App 3d 854, 155 Cal Rptr 297 (Cal App 1979) (general partner has no fiduciary duties to an assignee of a limited partnership interest; assignee may, however, sue for damages if the general partner has interfered with the assignee's right to partnership distributions)]

Nevertheless, the Service has ruled that a gift of a limited partnership interest did not constitute a gift of a future interest in property and, therefore, qualified for the annual gift exclusion, notwithstanding the partner's lack of withdrawal rights. [Ltr Rul 9415007; see also TAM 9131006 and TAM 8611004] In Letter Ruling 9415007, the transferor of limited partnership interests retained an interest as the sole general partner of the partnership. As the general partner, the transferor had exclusive management and control of the partnership, including full discretion to determine the amount and timing of distributions to the partners. The partnership agreement provided, however, that if the general partners directed the distribution of partnership funds to the partners, distributions had to be made to all partners at the same time in accordance with each partner's percentage interest in the partnership (based on each partner's capital account).

During the term of the partnership, no partner was entitled to demand a distribution or a return of the partner's capital account.

The Service ruled that the transfer of the limited partnership interests to the donees did not constitute a gift of a future interest in property because the general partner did not have the discretion of a trustee to distribute or withhold income (i.e., a power that generally results in the characterization of a gift to such a trust as a gift of a future interest in property). Instead, under the relevant partnership law, the general partner had a strict fiduciary duty to the limited partners to manage and operate the partnership to the best interests of the partnership and its partners.

Each limited partner in Letter Ruling 9415007 had the right to sell or assign its partnership interest, subject to a right of first refusal granted to the other partners. Accordingly, the Service concluded that each donee of a limited partnership interest would receive the immediate use, possession, and enjoyment of the interest (subject to a right of first refusal, which did not preclude a finding that the gift of the interest was a gift of a present interest in property). The other rulings in which the Service has ruled that a gift of a limited partnership interest qualified for the annual exclusion for gifts had similar fact patterns.

In Technical Advice Memorandum 9751003, the donor was a widow with no children who owned several acres of land with a leased industrial building ("Building") valued at approximately $2.4 million. The donor formed a limited partnership to which she transferred a 95 percent interest in Building in exchange for a limited partnership interest. The donor transferred the remaining 5 percent interest in Building to an S corporation in which she was the sole shareholder. The S corporation transferred its 5 percent interest in Building to the limited partnership in exchange for a general partnership interest. Over the next couple of years the donor gifted limited partnership interests to 35 family members and to trusts for the benefit of family members who were minors.

The Service determined that a provision permitting the general partner to retain income "for any reason whatsoever" eliminated the general partner's fiduciary duty to the limited partners because it allowed the general partner to withhold income for reasons unrelated to the conduct of the partnership. Because it was uncertain, at the time of the gifts, whether any income would be distributed to the limited partners and because the partnership agreement failed to require that, at the time of the gifts, there be a steady and ascertainable flow of income to a donee/limited partner, the Service concluded that the donees did not have a present interest in their income rights with respect to the limited partnership interests.

The Service also determined that the restrictions on the limited partners under the partnership agreement deprived them of the tangible and immediate economic benefit required for a present interest in property. The limited partners could not withdraw their capital contributions until 2022. The Service interpreted the partnership agreement to prohibit the limited partners other than the donor from transferring or assigning their interests. The fact that all partners consented to the intra-family assignments in December 1992 and March 1993 did not void this provision of the partnership agreement.

The limited partners could vote to liquidate the partnership. Partnership law permits the partnership agreement to grant voting rights to limited partners [RULPA § 302] and contemplates that limited partners will have the right to vote to dissolve and liquidate the partnership. [RULPA § 303(b)(6)(i)] It would seem that the ability of a limited partner to liquidate the partnership and obtain the partner's share of partnership assets would constitute a present economic right with respect to the partnership interest. Accordingly, a gift of such a partnership interest would seem to qualify as a gift of a present interest in property. However, in Technical Advice Memorandum 9751003, the Service explained that an economic right requiring joint action with others is a contingent right regarded as a future interest. [See, e.g., Ryerson v US, 312 US 405 (1941); Blasdel v Comm'r, 478 F2d 226 (5th Cir 1973); Chanin v United States, 393 F2d 972 (Ct Cl 1968)] Thus, the right of a limited partner to join with others to liquidate the partnership did not cause the interest to be a present interest in property. Accordingly, the Service ruled that the gifts of the limited partnership interests did not confer on the donees the substantial present economic benefit required by Code Section 2503(b) for a present interest.

Q 13:25 To what extent can asset values be frozen to prevent greater future estate tax?

Family partnerships were once used to "freeze" the value of the parents' interest in their estate and transfer the appreciation in the value of the estate to the children. Similarly, FLPs were once used to shift the growth interest in a corporation or other partnership to a younger family member, while keeping an "applicable retained interest," usually consisting of voting or liquidation rights. The objective of the parents is to freeze their interest while maintaining control of the assets. At the death of the parents, the control would then pass to the children free of transfer (estate) tax.

Chapter 14 of the Code (including Code Sections 2701-2704) was enacted in 1990 to limit such "estate freezes." Generally, the goal of Chapter 14 is to ignore or discount certain discretionary features in valuing a transferred interest, thereby increasing the value of the gift for gift tax purposes. However, outright gifts of the same type of interests retained by the donor will generally be future appreciation from the donor's estate, regardless of the enactment of Chapter 14. Thus, FLPs facilitate such gifts for estate planning purposes.

Chapter 14 includes four separate groups of rules:

1. Code Section 2701 applies to transfers of certain interests in partnerships and corporations.
2. Code Section 2702 applies to transfers of certain interests in trust (and certain similar nontrust transfers).
3. Code Section 2703 applies to option or buy-sell agreements.
4. Code Section 2704 applies to certain lapsing rights and restrictions.

While Code Sections 2701 and 2704 affect the valuation of closely held corporate and partnership interests, discounts based on minority interest and lack of marketability are not invalidated.

Under Code Section 2701, whenever an interest in a corporation or partnership is transferred to or for the benefit of a member of the transferor's family, and a senior interest is retained by the transferor or certain related persons, the value of the interest transferred is determined without regard to certain discretionary and variable rights inherent in the senior interest. Basically, the transferor must retain the equivalent of a "fixed rate cumulative preferred stock interest if the retained interest is to be given any value when valuing the transferred interest." [IRC 2701(c)(3); 346-2nd *Tax Management Portfolio (BNA)*, A-35] If no such interest is retained, the transfer is valued as if the parent transferred his or her entire interest (i.e., the retained interest will be treated as having a zero value); the value of the gift will be equal to the pre-transfer value of the transferor's interest.

Code Section 2704 provides that a lapse of any voting or liquidation right, created on or after October 9, 1990, in an entity controlled by the holder's family, constitutes a taxable gift or an increase in the value of the holder's gross estate if the lapse occurs at death. Code Section 2704 was enacted to correct certain perceived valuation abuses that resulted under case law regarding lapsing rights [52 TCM (CCH) 1306 (1987)] and liquidation restrictions not normally found in a partnership agreement or articles of incorporation.

Code Section 2703 addresses the use of buy-sell agreements and similar arrangements to freeze the value of interests in family corporations and partnerships. It states that the value of a decedent's interest in a corporation or partnership will be determined without regard to any option, agreement, or other right to acquire or use the property at less than its fair market value or any other restriction on the sale or disposition of the property, unless the agreement has a bona fide business purpose and is not a tax-avoidance device, and its terms are comparable to similar arrangements entered into by persons in arm's-length transactions.

Q 13:26   How does Chapter 14 specifically prevent estate freezes?

The most important concept of Code Sections 2701 and 2704 to understand is that they shift the focus away from an attempt to include previously transferred property in the decedent's estate to a determination of the proper gift tax valuation when the transfer is made. This requires the tax planner to evaluate the gift tax cost of making the transfer against the anticipated long-term benefit of excluding the transferred asset from one's estate.

Code Sections 2701 and 2704 of Chapter 14, enacted in 1990, subject gifts of interests in corporations, partnerships, and other entities to family members to special valuation rules for gift tax purposes. The special valuation rules require that the gifts be valued by the "subtraction" or "residual" method. Once a value for the entire entity is established, certain interests, usually the interests retained by the donor, are valued under those special valuation rules, which ignore the economic effect of certain rights or restrictions placed on the interests. The value of the retained interests is then subtracted from the value of the entire entity. What, if anything, remains determines the value, for gift tax purposes, of the interests in the entity that have been given away.

The special valuation rules of Code Section 2701 apply only if two requirements are present. First, there must be a transfer of a growth interest, usually referred to as a "subordinate equity interest" in a corporation or partnership to or for the benefit of a member of the transferor's family. [IRC § 2701(b); Treas Reg § 25.2701-3(a)(2)(iii)] Second, there must be a frozen "senior equity interest" with certain rights retained by the transferor immediately after the transfer.

Generally, Code Section 2701 is intended to reach only those interests in closely held businesses in which the transferor is in a position of control. For limited partnership purposes, control is defined as holding at least a 50 percent interest in the capital or profits of the partnership. [IRC § 2701(b)(2)(B)(i)] The rules of Code Section 2701 do not apply to any interest for which market quotations are readily available on established securities markets.

Even if the requirements of Code Section 2701 are complied with, Code Section 2701(a)(4) imposes a minimum valuation rule. Any junior equity interest transferred to the child must be valued at a minimum of 10 percent of the total equity interest owned by the parent, plus 10 percent of the total amount of any debt owed to the parent by the partnership.

Q 13:27 Does Code Section 2701 reach transfers to nonfamily members?

No. Code Section 2701 extends only to intra-family transfers of closely held interests. The term "member of the transferor's family" as used by Code Section 2701 is defined to include only the transferor's spouse, lineal descendants, and the spouses of the lineal descendants. The statute does not cover transfers to siblings, ancestors, or the descendants of either. If the family member criterion is not met, normal valuation techniques are used.

Q 13:28   Can a buy-sell agreement apply to further reduce value?

Yes, but it too can be impacted by Chapter 14, if family members are involved.

If a buy-sell agreement is binding on the parties, and stock is sold at below fair market value, the sale will be characterized as though an indirect transfer occurred with respect to the other owners. If one of those owners is the decedent's spouse, the estate may obtain a marital deduction for the spouse's proportionate share. [In re Cardinal Indus, Inc, 116 BR at 981, *contra,* Breeden v Catron (In re Catron), 158 BR 629 (ED Va 1993)] If, however, the unanticipated excess value of the asset does not pass to a spouse, it may absorb or exceed the deceased owner's unified credit for estate tax purposes.

A buy-sell agreement is often used in the family context to ensure that, upon the death (or a divorce) of a family member, the member's ownership interest in the entity does not pass outside the family. It can restrict the ability of any partner to transfer his or her interest, either during his or her lifetime or upon his or her death, outside of the family, even to a spouse. If the partner wants to sell the partner interest, it can provide a mechanism by which the family can buy the partner's interest before it is offered outside of the family.

The purpose of maintaining family control and protecting against creditors should be considered a valid purpose for the buy-sell agreement for federal estate and gift tax purposes.

Q 13:29   Are there other exceptions that allow a gift to be brought back into the taxable estate?

Yes. Code Section 2035 acts to bring back into the gross estate of a decedent any transfer that:

- Took place within three years before death; and
- Over which the donor relinquished a power or interest that would have caused inclusion under Code Section 2036, 2037, 2038, or 2042 if not relinquished.

Code Section 2035 extends the reach of these sections when they alone would not pull the transfer into the gross estate. Code

Section 2035 thus increases the reach of Code Sections 2036, 2037, 2038, and 2042 to three years before death.

Any interest given away by the donor is generally not considered part of the donor's estate for estate tax purposes (but may be included for gift tax purposes). However, Code Sections 2036-2038 provide for a reclassification of a gifted interest back into the estate of the donor if certain interests in and powers over are retained by the donor. Code Sections 2036-2038 define types of interests and powers that will trigger inclusion. Generally, the following types of transfers will be brought back into the doner's estate: a partnership interest gift which takes effect after the transferor's death, a gift of reversionary interests, and gifts with powers to revoke.

Under Code Section 2036(a)(1), if the donor gratuitously transfers legal title but retains the income interest over the transferred property, then the entire value of the property so transferred will be included in the decedent's gross estate. Code Section 2036(a)(2) operates to pull back transferred property into the estate of the donor when the donor retains the right to determine who gets the income derived from the property. Code Section 2036(b) was enacted to include in the donor's gross estate transferred stock when the donor retained voting rights in corporation.

Code Section 2036 applies only if the decedent retained an interest for a specified period of time. Three tests are used in determining if an interest has been retained for the prescribed period — if the donor retained an interest:

1. For his or her life;
2. For a period not ascertainable without reference to his or her death; or
3. For a period that does not in fact end before his or her death.

Code Section 2037 operates to bring certain conditioned transfers back into the gross estate of the decedent. This section applies if:

- The possession or enjoyment of the property is conditioned upon surviving the decedent; and
- The decedent has retained an interest in the property that may act to bring the property back to transferor's estate or, if living, to the transferor's power of disposition.

Stated another way, if the transferee obtains ownership while the transferor is living, Code Section 2037 does not apply.

Under Code Section 2038(a), if the donor makes a transfer in which the enjoyment of the transferred interest is subject to the donor's power to alter, amend, revoke, or terminate the transferred interest (such as the donor's power, as general partner, to control the distribution of partnership income), and the power does not end until the donor's death or is relinquished less than three years before the donor's death, the transferred property is includible in the donor's estate.

However, Code Sections 2036, 2037, and 2038 are not applicable to a bona fide sale for adequate and full consideration in money or money's worth.

Retention of voting rights in the stock of a publicly traded or closely held corporation triggers Code Sections 2036-2038. However, retention of control in a partnership does not. In *U.S. v. Byrum*, the decedent was a controlling shareholder in a close corporation. He transferred the stock of the corporation to an irrevocable trust, retaining the right to vote. The Supreme Court held that the stock was not included in his estate under Code Section 2036. The Court stated that, the power to vote did not include the right to designate the income from the transferred stock for purposes of Code Section 2036 because of the fiduciary duty a controlling shareholder has to promote the best interests of the corporation. Although the Revenue Act of 1978 amended Code Section 2036 to overrule *Byrum* when corporations are involved, *Byrum* is still good law for partnerships.

Relying on *Byrum*, the IRS has issued rulings stating that an individual, as a general partner, may retain control over certain assets contributed to an FLP without violating Code Sections 2036(a)(2) and 2038(a)(1). General partners are bound by the same fiduciary duty to act in the best interest of the FLP. Therefore, they must act in the best interest of the FLP in making and withholding distributions of income or assets. When drafting an FLP, attorneys may, therefore, include a provision stating that the general partner is bound by fiduciary duties to other partners in managing the business of the partnership, unless already required by state law.

However, as a result of the general partner's ability to control the management of the assets in an FLP, transferring voting stock in a closely held corporation in which 20 percent of the corporation is owned by the donor, can cause a problem under Code Section 2036(b). A transfer of such stock to an FLP, in which the donor would in his or her capacity as general partner continue to vote, may cause that portion of the partnership that includes the stock to be includible in the donor's estate, despite the gifts of the limited partner interests of the portion of the partnership under Code Section 2036(b).

Another IRS argument is that a minority interest, when combined with other ownership interests in the entity, may actually have enhanced value, because the interest represents the "swing vote" of the entity and its assets. [Curley v Brignoli Curley & Roberts Assoc, 746 F Supp 1208 (SDNY 1989), aff'd, 915 F2d 81 (2d Cir 1990), cert den; Mahon v Harst, 738 P 2d 1190 (Colo Ct App 1987); Lust v Kolbe, 356 A2d 592 (Md Ct Spec App 1976)] This position is highly questionable, particularly if the interests to be combined for this purpose are owned by siblings, in light of Revenue Ruling 93-12, in which the IRS conceded the family attribution argument. It is even more questionable when the interests are held by other-than-lineal ancestors or descendants.

Q 13:30 When do buy-sell agreements fix values for estate tax, and when does Code Section 2703 apply to negate that effect?

Buy-sell agreements among unrelated persons, if binding both during life and at death, generally are determinative for estate tax purposes. For gift tax purposes, assuming that this type of agreement meets certain requirements, it can also be taken into account in valuing the gifted asset. For estate tax purposes, if the agreement sets out a binding formula to establish the price of the stock upon death, fixes a value during life, and meets other requirements, the price established in the agreement is determinative in valuing the asset for estate tax purposes.

Under Treasury Regulations Section 20.2031-2(h), all three of these requirements must be met for agreements entered into before October 9, 1990:

1. For gift and estate tax purposes, the agreement must be a bona fide business arrangement, and not a device to pass the decedent's interest to natural objects of his or her bounty (such as children) for less than full and adequate consideration (i.e., a price below fair market value), in money or money's worth. Therefore, the agreement should document business motives, and the parties should create a history of strictly adhering to the terms of the agreement.

2. For estate tax purposes, the agreement must also restrict lifetime transfers of the asset by the decedent and must apply during the life as well as after the death of the owner.

3. For estate tax purposes, the agreement must require the decedent's estate to sell the asset.

Under case law, a right of first refusal, if the estate decides to sell the asset, does not meet the third requirement above. An option to purchase in the other parties' hands will, however, be sufficient for the second requirement. Clauses that release the estate's obligation upon the IRS's rejection of the agreement may be fatal to the tax benefit of fixing value. For estate tax purposes, the price must be specified or determinable according to a formula that is included in the agreement, and the price (or the formula) must have been reasonable when the agreement was entered into.

Code Section 2703 provides that, if family members are involved, the buy-sell agreement will be subject to greater scrutiny. However, Code Section 2703 is not limited solely to family members. It is applied to all transfers for estate, gift, and generation-skipping tax purposes. Code Section 2703(a) provides that buy-sell agreements will be ignored in value determination. To escape Code Section 2703(a), Code Section 2703(b) provides an exception if these three requirements are met:

1. The agreement must be a bona fide business arrangement;

2. It must not be a device to transfer the subject property to members of the decedent's family for less than full and adequate consideration; and

3. It must have terms that are comparable to similar arrangements entered into by persons in an arm's-length transaction.

Each requirement must be independently met, or Code Section 2703(a) applies. For purposes of Code Section 2703(b), the term "family members" is expanded to include not only "members of the family" as defined by Treasury Regulations Section 25.2701-2(b)(5) but also "any other individual who is a natural object of the transferors bounty." [Ltr Rul 9222043]

Valuation Discounts

Q 13:31   Does Code Section 2704(a) of Chapter 14 affect valuation discounts?

Yes, under certain circumstances. One of the major effects of using family limited partnerships is the existence of discounts against the value of the underlying assets that make up the partnership interests. Two recognized discounts are generally available to a family limited partnership. The first available discount is for the decrease in marketability of the partnership interest with no readily available public market. The second discount is a minority interest or lack of control discount.

Code Section 2704(a) must be consulted in determining the extent to which a partner's lack of control will contribute to any discount available in valuing his or her limited partnership interest. Before the enactment of Code Section 2704, taxpayers could make tax-free transfers of a property interest by making a gift of an interest in a corporation or partnership, retaining voting or liquidation rights in the entity, and then causing or allowing the rights to lapse. Upon lapse of the rights, value in the interest in the corporation or partnership would decrease and, thus, decrease the estate tax liability. Code Section 2704(a) and (b) were enacted to stop this type of arrangement.

In general, Code Section 2704(a) treats a lapse in voting or liquidation rights as a complete transfer by the person holding the right. If a lapse is found to occur during the holder's lifetime, the lapse is treated as a gift to the donee and taxed accordingly. If a lapse occurs upon the death of the holder, the transferred property is included in the gross estate of the decedent for estate tax purposes. Code Section 2704(a) applies if two conditions are true of the corporation or partnership. First, there must be a lapse in a voting or liquidation right. Second, the holder of the right at lapse, and members of the holder's family, must control the entity before and after the lapse. [IRC § 2704(a)(1); see also Treas Reg § 25.2704-1(f)] For purposes of Code Section 2704, members of the family include spouses, ancestral or lineal descendants of the transferor or spouse, siblings, and spouses thereof. [IRC § 2704(c)(2)] An individual controls a partnership when 50 percent or more of the capital or profit interests are held.

Voting rights grant the holder the right to vote on any matter concerning the entity. [Treas Reg § 25.2704-1(a)(2)(iv)] A liquidation right is the ability to force the entity to purchase all or a portion of the holder's equity interest. [Treas Reg § 25.2704-1(a)(2)(v)] A lapse of these rights occurs when one or both are restricted or eliminated with respect to the transferred interest. [Treas Reg § 25.2704-1(c)(1)] A transfer of voting or liquidation rights does not necessarily result in lapse. [Id] However, if the transfer causes the transferor to lose the ability to control liquidation of the interest retained and the interest is subordinate to the transferred interest, then the transfer results in lapse of the liquidation right of the subordinate interest. [Treas Reg § 25.2704-1(c)(1)] Lapse may also occur by operation of a state law, corporate charter, a partnership agreement, etc.

There are two general exceptions to Code Section 2704(a), even when there is a lapse of a liquidation right. First, Code Section 2704(a) does not apply if the holder of an interest, the holder's estate, or the members of the holder's family cannot, immediately after the lapse, liquidate an interest that the holder could have liquidated before the lapse. [Treas Reg § 25.2704-1(c)(2)(i)(A)] Whether the interest could be liquidated after lapse is determined by the partnership agreement or state law. [Treas Reg § 25.2704-1(c)(2)(i)(B)] The second exception to the applicability of Code Section 2704(a) arises when the lapse occurs by reason of a change in state law. [Treas Reg § 25.2704-1(c)(2)(iii)]

In the event Code Section 2704(a) is triggered, the amount included in the gross estate of the transferor equals the excess value of the interest held immediately before the lapse (valued as if neither voting nor liquidation rights lapsed), over the value of the interest immediately after the lapse. [Treas Reg § 25.2704-1(d)]

Q 13:32 Do Code Section 2704(b) or the existence of withdrawal rights affect valuation discounting?

Yes, under certain circumstances. Under the organizational documents, a member of an LLC or a limited partner in a limited partnership may not be entitled to withdraw from the entity and receive fair value for his or her interest until the date that the entity terminates. Accordingly, the value of the member or limited partner's interest upon withdrawal will be the going-concern value of the interest, which depends in part on anticipated cash distributions. In most closely held businesses, there are no predictable cash distributions because the money will be invested in the business.

However, if the state statute or the relevant FLP or LLC documents allow a member or limited partner to withdraw at any time or after notice and receive fair value for his or her interest, then under Code Section 2704(b) the value of the interest for gift tax purposes is its liquidation value. Moreover, the lack-of-marketability discount might not be allowed, because the IRS could take the position that establishing such a provision in the articles of organization is an applicable restriction that should be ignored under Code Section 2704. This should not affect the minority interest discount, however, since that discount is separate from the lack-of-marketability discount. Furthermore, the lack-of-marketability discount should not be lost entirely, in light of the lack of any consensus on the meaning of the term "fair value" in the case law, and because of the expense and delay of a lawsuit that the limited partner may have to bring to collect more than his or her discounted interest in the partnership. This contemplated litigation expense should support some portion of the lack-of-marketability discount. [E.g., see In re Phillips, 966 F 2d at 933-935 (general partner who has filed Chapter 11 petition on behalf of himself under Texas law may not file Chapter 11 petition on behalf of partnership; no conflict between federal and state law found)] Accordingly, Code Section 2704(b) may reduce the amount of discounts available for gifts of limited partner interests, but will not eradicate the discounts entirely.

Code Section 2704(b) may cause the value of any transferred interests to be based on the value of the entity without regard to any restrictions contained in the entity's agreement, depending on state law and the entity used. If stock in a corporation or an interest in a partnership or other entity is transferred to or for the benefit of a member of the transferor's family, and if immediately before the transfer the donor and the members of the donor's family controlled the entity, any restriction will be disregarded in determining the value of the transferred interest.

Under Code Section 2704(b)(1), an applicable restriction contained in the partnership agreement on the right of a donee to liquidate his or her interest may be disregarded for gift and estate tax purposes, thereby increasing the value of the gift or the size of the estate. An applicable restriction is a limitation on the ability to liquidate the entity (in whole or in part) that either lapses or partially lapses after the transfer or is removable, in whole or in part, by the transferor or any family member and is more restrictive than state law. If such a restriction exists, it is ignored for purposes of valuation, and the state law restrictions are used to determine the value.

Q 13:33   What are the exceptions to the application of Code Section 2704(b)?

There are four basic exceptions to the applicability of Code Section 2704(b). First, any reasonable commercial restriction that arises from any financing received by the entity from an outside source (not the transferor, transferee, or family member) is not included as an applicable restriction. Second, any restriction imposed by federal or state law is not an applicable restriction. Third, any agreement that is disregarded under Code Section 2703 is not included under Code Section 2704(b). Finally, the Secretary has the power to issue regulations that disregard a restriction for purposes of Code Section 2704(b).

For example, a creditor of the limited partner would not be able to force the limited partner to withdraw on six months' notice if the partnership agreement provided otherwise. For an LLC, if state law provides that, upon the death of a member, in the absence of an Operating Agreement, there must be unanimous consent by the remaining members to continue the LLC, the likelihood that the LLC will dissolve upon the death of one of the members may be high. Therefore, despite any provisions to the contrary in the Operating Agreement, under Code Section 2704(b) the likelihood that the members' creditors will be able to reach the LLC's underlying property is higher than when no such dissolution occurs. That likelihood may somewhat reduce the size of the lack-of-marketability discount that can be used to value the gift for gift tax purposes, since the actual provisions of the agreement will be ignored for purposes of valuation.

Q 13:34 Why do discounts exist when valuing a business enterprise?

Contributing money or other property to a legal entity in exchange for an interest in that entity will frequently result in a valuation disparity immediately after the transaction because the nature of the property rights has changed, often dramatically.

In organizing almost any new business, the individuals who contribute assets to an entity, be it a corporation, an FLP, or any other vehicle, experience an immediate diminution in value to the extent that the entity wraps a new set of legal rights and limitations around the assets and restricts the original owner's ability to deal with them unilaterally. [See Estate of Newhouse v Commr, 94 TC 193 *passim* (1990), *nonacq,* 1992-2 CB 1; for the discounting effect of incorporating an investment portfolio, see Gallum v Commr, 33 TCM 1316 (CCH), TCM 74,284 at 1246 (RIA) (1974), which allowed a 55 percent discount against the value of the corporation's underlying assets, whose value consisted predominantly of a portfolio of stocks and bonds, and only secondarily of a tannery business]

A discount should not be viewed as an artificial and undeserved tax benefit. If money or other assets contributed to an entity are successfully managed to create a profitable ongoing business, then, in many cases, the value of that operating business can become greater than the value of the underlying business assets. This difference in value is commonly referred to as the going-concern value or goodwill of the business.

The value of an entity, or an interest therein, will be the greater of going-concern value (the present value of the projected cash flow) or liquidation value in any situation when there is a liquidation power, that is, a legal or practical way to force a liquidation of the business. [See Estate of Watts v Commr, 823 F 2d 483 (1987)]

Q 13:35   What are the types of discounts for gift and estate tax when using an FLP?

There are two: a minority discount and a marketability discount.

Minority Discount. A minority discount is used when the person receiving the interest does not have a controlling interest in the entity. The theory behind a minority discount is that the owner does not own a majority or controlling interest and, therefore, cannot control the day-to-day operations of the entity or compel a sale or liquidation of the business assets. [Carr v Commr, 48 TCM (CCH) 507 (1985); Ward v Commr, 87 TC 78 (1986)] When the owner owns less than a controlling interest in the entity, that interest is worth less than a controlling interest, and his or her interest may be worth significantly less than the liquidation value of the interest. [Hall and Polacek, "Strategies for Obtaining the Largest Valuation Discounts," *Estate Planning* (Jan-Feb 1994), p 38]

When valuing an entity or an interest discount therein, each case must take into account the facts and circumstances of that particular situation. The discount applied in other cases, although similar, will not be determinative for use in any other situation. Thus, to provide a basis for the discount taken, the taxpayer should have the interest appraised.

In the past, the IRS vigorously opposed the concept of a minority discount with respect to closely held family businesses. [See Rev Rul 81-253, 1981-1 CB 187] However, in recent years, the IRS has conceded its position after having continually been unsuccessful. [Rev Rul 93-12; see Propstra Est v US, 680 F 2d 1248 (9th Cir 1982)]

The typical partnership agreement ensures that minority discounts will be available. The partnership agreement generally provides that only the general partner has the ability to control the day-to-day activities of the partnership, as well as making all other management decisions. This will, therefore, provide a minority discount, similar to nonvoting common stock, for all of the limited partnership interests.

Marketability Discount. A marketability discount is available for an interest that is not salable in an existing, publicly traded market, such as a stock exchange or commodities exchange. Due to the unavailability of a ready market, the value is discounted. This discount must be analyzed separately from any minority discount. A partial interest in a family-controlled entity can be extremely difficult to liquidate, thus reducing the interest's value in the market. Even if a taxpayer owns a controlling interest in the business, there may still be a marketability discount for the interest.

The partnership agreement often enhances a marketability discount. The partnership agreement will often provide that a new partner can only be admitted upon the consent of all other partners. In addition, no partner may have the right to withdraw and be paid for his or her interest. These provisions will restrict the market for the interests.

Q 13:36   Do the courts and the IRS allow discounts for partnership interests in family businesses?

Yes. Chapter 14 of the Code was enacted in 1990 to deal with certain estate tax issues, but it does not address minority discounts. In the legislative history of Code Section 2704, Congress expressly stated that the new provision was not intended to change existing law on minority discounts.

In early 1993 the IRS issued Revenue Ruling 93-12 [1993-1 CB 202] which expressly revoked Revenue Ruling 81-253 [1981-1 CB 187]. The IRS declared that it would no longer attempt automatically to apply a family attribution rule in valuing a transfer of shares in a family-owned business but instead would allow minority interests to be valued for gift tax purposes without regard to the family relationship of the parties. Revenue Ruling 93-12 further suggested that, even if a donor gives away a control block all at once, as long as each separate gift to each separate donee represents a minority interest, each gift should qualify for a minority discount.

The IRS views the estate tax, however, as standing on a different footing and does not permit a discount for minority interests passing from a control block to separate minority legatees. [See TAM 9449001, *contra* TAM 9432001] The IRS qualified this position in Technical Advice Memorandum 9436005, involving a donor who held 100 percent of the outstanding common stock of a corporation and made three simultaneous gifts of 30 percent of the corporate stock to each of his three children and a gift of 5 percent of the corporate stock to his spouse, while retaining a 5 percent interest in the corporation. The IRS observed that a small block of stock could command a premium value if its ownership could permit another minority shareholder (related or unrelated) to obtain control, and that this premium value could counterbalance the minority discount for the swing block to a greater or lesser extent. According to the IRS, the swing vote premium can be applicable whether the gifts of minority interests are simultaneous or sequential.

Technical Advice Memorandum 9436005 illustrates the fact that the valuation of interests in an entity is intimately related to the specific facts in the case. It raises the real, but hard-to-resolve, issue of how to treat indirect gifts. It also underscores the uncertainties that will accompany transfers of corporate stock that have attendant voting rights—something that is conspicuously absent when the interests being transferred are limited partnership interests in FLPs.

Treasury Regulations Section 1.701-2 is the partnership "anti-abuse" regulation in which the IRS included examples involving FLPs. The examples were then withdrawn less than a year later. FLP issues were addressed in the "final" regulations, but less than a month after their release, those examples using FLPs were withdrawn.

Q 13:37 Do these same valuation principles apply to an FLP that owns readily tradable securities?

Probably, although the exact answer is not clear. Generally, investment assets are often easily divided or distributed; hence, the amount of the discount applicable to an investment FLP may be less than the discount that would apply to an FLP holding other, less-liquid assets. For example, an investment FLP with five equal partners that owns 1,000 shares of Coca-Cola stock could liquidate and distribute 200 shares of stock to each partner without diminishing the aggregate value of the stock. On the other hand, if no withdrawal rights existed, a partner could not at the partner's request automatically sell his or her interest to the partnership. Nevertheless, a discount of 55 percent has been allowed for a non-marketable, minority interest of a corporation the primary assets of which were marketable securities. [Gallum v Comm'r, 33 TCM 1316 (CCH), TCM 74,284 at 1246 (RIA) 1974]

Many publicly traded closed end mutual funds sell at discounts to the value of their underlying assets, even though those interests are readily marketable. By contrast, if the same partnership held a single parcel of commercial real estate, it could not easily be subdivided into five separate property interests and, in any event, the subdivision of the property would likely diminish the aggregate value of the interests, since fractionalized real estate interests are often subject to significant discounts.

Q 13:38 Can assets other than an operating business be used in funding an FLP?

Yes, although tax issues are often important. Family members who contribute property or services to a partnership in exchange for partnership interests are subject to the same rules that apply to unrelated partners, with one exception discussed below. If the related parties deal with each other at arm's length, their partnership is recognized for tax purposes, and the terms of their partnership agreement will be adhered to in determining the gains and losses of the partnership and the partners. The terms of the partnership agreement determine the tax ramifications to the partners since: "[a] partner's distributive share of income, gain, loss, deduction, or credit shall, except as otherwise provided in this chapter [of the Code], be determined by the partnership agreement." [IRC § 704(a)] The FLP should be structured and operated in a business-like manner to receive the same tax treatment as if the partnership were owned by unrelated third parties.

Under the Code, a donee partner will be recognized as a partner "if he owns a capital interest in a partnership in which capital is a material income-producing factor." [IRC § 704(e)(1)] This safe-harbor rule applies whether the partner receives his or her interest by purchase or by gift. If the capital of the partnership is not a material income-producing factor, the partner must meet the test set out by the Supreme Court in *Culbertson v. United States* [337 US 733 (1949)], namely, whether, considering all of the facts—the agreement, the conduct of the parties in execution of its provisions, their statements, the testimony of disinterested persons, the relationship of the parties, their respective abilities and capital contributions, the actual control of income and the purposes for which it is used, and any other facts throwing light on the parties' true intent — the parties in good faith and acting with business purpose intended to join together in the present conduct of the enterprise. [Id at 742]

Whether capital is a material income-producing factor in the business of the partnership is determined based on all of the facts and circumstances. [Treas Reg § 1.704-1(e)(1)(iv)] The IRS will not issue a private letter ruling regarding the validity of the FLP, if capital is not a material income-producing factor. [Rev Proc 89-3, 1989-1 CB 761] The partner must also establish that he or she "owns" a capital interest in the partnership. A capital interest is "an interest in the assets of the partnership, which is distributable to the owner of the capital interest upon his withdrawal from the partnership or upon liquidation of the partnership." [Treas Reg § 1.704-1(e)(1)(v)]

The IRS will recognize the FLP if there are business or financial reasons for creating the limited partnership, even if there are substantial tax savings by creating the limited partnership. Substantial judicial authority exists supporting the concept that the IRS will recognize the FLP upon showing that the partnership was formed for a business, financial, or investment reason, or the partnership engaged in business, financial, or investment activities. [See Frank G Lyon Co v US, 435 US 561 (1978); Estate of McLendon v Commr, 66 TCM (CCH) 946 (1993); Sparks Farm, Inc v Commr, 56 TCM (CCH) 464 (1988); Estate of Harrison v Commr, 52 TCM (CCH) 1306 (1987); Estate of Bischoff v Commr, 69 TC 32 (1977)]

Q 13:39 Do the Code and Treasury regulations address valuation issues?

Yes, but only generally. For transfer tax purposes the value of property transferred to another is the price at which the property would change hands between a willing buyer and willing seller, neither being under any compulsion to buy or to sell and both having reasonable knowledge of relevant facts. [Treas Reg §§ 20.2031-1(b), 25.2512-1] As previously discussed, guidance on valuation of LLC and FLP interests is provided by both Treasury Regulations

Section 1.704-2(b) and case law (see Qs 13:15, 13:31-37). This previous discussion illustrates the IRS's scrutiny of valuation discounts applying the business purpose and sham transaction doctrines. In Revenue Ruling 59-60 and subsequent rulings, the IRS provided detailed guidance on the factors that govern the valuation of closely held business interests. [Rev Rul 59-60, 1959-1 CB 237, *modified by* Rev Rul 65-193, 1965-2 CB 370, *and further amplified by* Rev Ruls 77-287, 1977-2 CB 319 and 83-120, 1983-2 CB 170] The IRS provided eight factors:

1. The type of business and its background;
2. The economic forecast for the nation, in particular the company's industry;
3. The book value of the company and its financial condition;
4. The company's earnings and dividend capacity;
5. Goodwill and/or other intangible value;
6. Past stock sales and the size of the block of stock being valued;
7. Stock prices of similar publicly traded corporations; and
8. Any other relevant factors affecting fair market value.

The courts have applied these same eight principles in valuing partnership interests as well. [See Howard v Commr, 82 TC 239 (1984), *aff'd,* 786 F 2d 1174 (9th Cir 1984)]

In 1981, the IRS took the position that it ordinarily would not recognize a minority discount on transfers of stock "among family members where, at the time of the transfer, control (either majority voting control or de facto control) of the corporation exist[ed] in the family." [Rev Rul 81-253, 1981-1 CB 187] However, the IRS consistently lost on its argument that minority interests in family-controlled businesses should be valued at liquidation value or as part of a control group. The IRS threw in the towel and conceded this argument to taxpayers in 1993. [Rev Rul 93-12, 1993-1 CB 202]

Q 13:40 How great have valuation discounts been?

The cases allow valuation discounts for minority and marketability discounts together in a broad range of 20 percent to 60 percent. The cases are very fact specific, however, and it is difficult to draw broad conclusions. Studies by secondary-market analysts found that partnerships that are currently distributing, sell at a discount of 30 percent to 50 percent of net asset value. Partnerships not currently distributing were selling at discounts of over 50 percent. [CL Elliott and AW Howard, *Presentation of the Valuation Study Group on FLP and Related Subjects*] FLPs made up of 100 percent marketable securities can expect to receive less than the average discounts.

In *Estate of Watts v. Commissioner* [TC Memo 1985-595 (1985)], involving the valuation of a partnership interest for estate tax purposes, the decedent held a 15 percent interest in a general partnership engaged in an active business. The estate tax return valued the decedent's partnership interest at $2.55 million, while the IRS proposed a valuation of over $17 million. The Eleventh Circuit in *Watts* held that, because the interest held by the estate did not carry with it a liquidation right, the value of the interest should be determined using going-concern value rather than liquidation value. The Eleventh Circuit then affirmed the Tax Court's factual finding with respect to the value of the interest.

In *Estate of Harrison v. Commissioner* [52 TCM (CCH) 1306 (1987)], the decedent held both a 1 percent general partnership interest and 77.8 percent limited partnership interest in a partnership, which the decedent had received in exchange for contributing real estate and other property worth approximately $60 million.

Upon the decedent's death, the remaining general partners exercised their option to purchase the decedent's general partnership interest for approximately $757,000 and agreed within 90 days after the decedent's death to continue the partnership. The estate's position was that, after the death of the decedent, the estate did not have the power to force a dissolution of the partnership and thereby realize the value of the partnership assets. Instead, the estate had only the legal rights and property interests of a limited partner, which were valued by stipulation of the parties at $33 million. The IRS argued that the limited partnership interest should be valued at liquidation value of approximately $60 million. The Tax Court accepted and applied the estate's stipulated value, which represented approximately a 45 percent discount from its purported liquidation value.

In *Estate of McCormick v. Commissioner* [70 TCM 318 (CCH) (1995)], the Tax Court was presented with the issue of valuing partnership interests when a partner has the ability to dissolve the partnership as opposed to the value of the interests (for which the partner does not possess such dissolution power). As to the partners with dissolution capability, the court still allowed minority and marketability discounts. Partnership interests, even if valued by the ability (or inability) to liquidate, will still be eligible for valuation discounts.

In *Mandelbaum v. Commissioner* [69 TCM 2852 (CCH) (1995)] the court rejected a 30 percent marketability discount valuation rate applied to stock in a closely held corporation. The 30 percent rate was based on competing evaluations of a government appraiser and the taxpayer's expert. The court's disallowance of the proposed rate was based on the rule that the court will apply its own valuation calculation rather than simply dividing the difference between the competing parties.

In *Estate of Bennett v. Commissioner* [65 TCM 1816 (1993)], the Tax Court allowed a 15 percent lack-of-marketability discount upon the valuation of 100 percent of a corporation's stock. By allowing such a valuation discount, the court in essence deemed the value of the stock to be equal to 85 percent of the total corporate assets. In *Estate of Ford v. Commissioner* [53 F 3d 924 (8th Cir 1995)], the Tax Court again allowed a lack-of-marketability discount in the valuation of corporate stock. In *Ford,* the discount was used for the valuation of a decedent shareholder's stock for which he owned a controlling interest.

Q 13:41 Can the IRS use discounts to its advantage in estate tax cases?

Yes. The IRS has used discounts to reduce the value of property passing under the marital deduction. [Thomas v Price, 718 F Supp at 606, 607] When a decedent owned all of the stock, but only a minority interest passed under the marital bequest, the difference between 100 percent of the value of the stock includible in the taxable estate and the discounted value of the portion of the property passing under the marital deduction would be, to the extent it exceeded the decedent's available unified credit, subject to estate taxes.

Q 13:42   Must a person claiming a valuation discount notify the IRS?

Yes. Pursuant to IRS Form 709, the gift tax return, taxpayers claiming valuation discounts must so state. Form 709 provides a "yes" or "no" box on whether such a valuation discount is being claimed. Additionally, taxpayers claiming discounts must supply ample information about the discount. Therefore, it is important to adequately document the accompanying information.

Alternatives to the Family Limited Partnership

Q 13:43   Are there various entities other than the FLP to achieve similar results?

Yes. There are several, including the limited liability company (LLC), limited liability partnership (LLP), and limited liability limited partnership (LLLP). From a tax-planning standpoint, each has advantages and drawbacks depending on one's particular business needs.

Q 13:44   Does the limited partnership afford withdrawal flexibility similar to the general partnership?

No. The limited partnership is not as flexible with respect to the limited partners. The general partner may withdraw from a general partnership at the general partner's discretion under the Uniform Partnership Act. Similarly, in a limited partnership, the general partner may withdraw at the general partner's discretion. The limited partner, however, does not enjoy such freedom. States that follow the Revised Uniform Limited Partnership Act (RULPA) limit withdrawal of the limited partner or dissolution to a particular date or happening of events as specified in the partnership agreement. Moreover, if the partnership agreement provides no such date or events, the limited partner may withdraw only upon six months prior written notice. [Kan Stat Ann § 56-1a352]

Some statutes allow the limited partners a liquidation right, which, upon exercise, values the interest at that point in time even though the limited partner is not eligible to withdraw. A recent trend reflects deletion of this right from the statutes. [Colo Rev Stat § 7-62-603; Cal Corp Code § 15663; Fla Stat § 620-143; Ga Code § 14-11-603] Finally, some states have made withdrawal by the limited partner more difficult. These states have enacted statutes reflecting that a limited partner may withdraw only pursuant to the partnership agreement, and if the agreement is silent as to withdrawal, then the limited partner may not withdraw at all. [Colo Rev Stat § 7-62-603; Ga Code § 14-9-603]

Q 13:45 Is the general partner in a limited partnership subject to liability for exercising his or her right to withdraw?

Yes, in some cases. The general partner's right to withdraw forces the partnership to redeem his or her interest. This withdrawal, although permissible, may be wrongful. If the withdrawal violates the term of the partnership agreement, the partnership may seek damages. [RULPA § 602]

Q 13:46 Are all states similar in their treatment of member withdrawal in a limited liability company?

No. In fact, there are several approaches that states take as to procedure and effect of member withdrawal. Member withdrawal may cause dissolution of the LLC. In such states, the remaining members may, however, generally elect to continue the LLC. The variations of withdrawal treatment among states lie within the procedure for member withdrawal. Whether the LLC is classified as member-managed or manager-managed may also be an important distinction in this area. The most common approach taken is by states whose statutory codes mirror RULPA. These statutes treat LLCs similar to limited partnerships, allowing members to withdraw upon certain events or dates as governed by the partnership agreement or, in the absence of such agreement, the members may withdraw upon six months prior written notice. [See RULPA § 603]

Ohio, for example, provides separate rules depending on whether the LLC is manager or member managed. A member-managed LLC permits members to withdraw at anytime. [Ohio Rev

Code Ann § 1705.16.A] The manager-managed LCC is permitted to restrict withdrawal to the terms of the Operating Agreement, or six months written notice in the absence of such terms within the Operating Agreement. [Ohio Rev Code Ann § 1705.16B] Louisiana adds a "just cause" caveat to their statute. If the LLC Operating Agreement provides for a specific LLC expiration date, a member may withdraw before that date only for "just cause" as a result of another member's failure to perform his or her obligation. [La Rev Stat § 12.1325.A]

Other states allow LLC member withdrawal as if the members were general partners of a partnership. The LLC members, like general partners, have complete discretion to withdraw at any time, despite the terms of the Operating Agreement. [RULPA § 602] Recall, however, that a wrongful withdrawal can still trigger liability and such liability applies to an LLC as well. [Mo Rev Stat § 359.775 (member of LLC has power to withdraw, but right to withdraw is restricted); Okla Stat 18 § 2036.C]

Some states, such as North Dakota and Tennessee, view a withdrawing member as an assignee as to the redemption of his or her interests in the LLC. The member is free to withdraw from the LLC as permitted by statute, but if the LLC is not dissolved, then the withdrawing member is accorded assignee treatment. [Minn Stat § 322B.306.3(1); ND Cent Code § 10-32-30.3(a); Tenn Code Ann § 48A-16-101(c)(1)] Other states, such as Oregon and Virginia, opt for a "bright-line" approach. Here, withdrawal may only be done if provided in the Operating Agreement. If the agreement is silent as to withdrawal, then that member may not withdraw, and must wait until the LLC expires or is dissolved by an unrelated event. [Or Rev Stat § 63.205; Va Code Ann § 13.1-1032]

Arizona adds a restriction on family member withdrawal from a family-controlled LLC. Under the statute, if such a family member withdraws, that member will receive as distributions the "lesser of his right to share in distributions if the (LLC) had completed winding up . . . as of the date of withdrawal or his right to share in reasonably anticipated future distributions if the (LLC) were to continue for twenty-five years." [Ariz Rev Stat Ann § 29-707 D]

Challenges to the Family Limited Partnership

Q 13:47 Can restrictions upon a donee's right to transfer or liquidate his FLP interest warrant the donee being disregarded as a partner for income tax purposes?

Yes. "A person shall be recognized for partnership purposes . . . if he owns a capital interest in a partnership in which capital is a material income-producing factor. . . ." [IRC § 704(e)(1)] The "material income-producing factor" requirement will be met if a substantial portion of partnership income is attributable to partnership capital as opposed to the personal services of partners or employees. [IRC § 704(e)(2); Treas Reg § 1.704-1(e)(1)(iv)] However, restrictions on the donee's power to transfer or liquidate his interest can trigger the Service's setting aside of the donee's partner status due to a "lack of reality of ownership". [Treas Reg § 1.704-1(e)(2)(ix)]

In order to satisfy this "ownership" requirement, the Treasury regulations reflect the donee must acquire dominion and control of the partnership interests in order to satisfy Code Section 704(e). Specifically, the regulations list factors including: the degree to which the donee participates in management; whether a major portion of the donee's distributive share was actually distributed to the donee; retention of control of assets essential to the business; and whether the donee has held himself out publicly as a partner. [Treas Reg § 1.704-1(e)(2)]

Total control of management and operations of the partnership retained by the donor/general partner, however, will not require inclusion of the partnership interest in the donor's estate. The Service has issued private letter rulings favorable to the donor/general partner in the context of the family limited partnership. The common thread of these rulings is a scenario in which a general partner (parent) distributed limited partnership interests to the limited partners (children and grandchildren). The general partner retained total control over the partnership operations, and in one of the rulings, total control of distributions. Despite the complete control by the general partner, the Service ruled that such distributions would be respected for partnership purposes. The Service stated that the fiduciary duties of the parents as general partners requited that they not abuse their positions as general partners to the detriment of the limited partners. Absent this fiduciary duty, the "gifts" may have likely been taxed pursuant to Code Sections 2036 and 2038. [Ltr Ruls 9546007, 9131006] Alternatively, the gifts may not be treated as ones involving a present interest. [See Q 13:23]

Q 13:48   What are some of the other ways in which the IRS will challenge FLP transfers of partnership interests?

Among others, the IRS commonly employs a three alternative test to measure the transaction. Alternative 1 views the transaction as a single testamentary transaction despite the multiple transfers of the partnership interests to and through various individuals and entities. Alternative 2 values the partnership transfer without regard to any restriction under Code Section 2703(a)(2), unless the safe harbor of Section 2703(b) is satisfied. Alternative 3 applies Code Section 2704, which, similar to Alternative 2, disregards any "applicable restriction" in valuing the partnership interest transferred. [TAM 9730004; Ltr Rul 9723009]

The Service will also extend the traditional substance over form argument to FLP transfers. [Estate of Winkler, 73 TCM (CCH) 1657 (1997)] Here, the Service is trying to determine if the primary motive of the transaction is avoidance of tax.

The Service will also scrutinize the degree of retained control or power that the general partner possesses following the transfer. The closer the general partner's retained powers approach omnipotence, the more likely the attempted transfers of interests will be drawn back into the general partner's estate for Code Sections 2036 and 2038 purposes. [Estate of Shauerhamer, 73 TCM (CCH) 2855 (1997)]

Still another challenge is the gift upon formation of the entity approach. Here the Service reasons that a gift occurs if the property transferred exceeds the consideration received. As a result the Service will value the transfers to the FLP by family members separately and not in the aggregate. [Estate of Trenchard, 69 TCM (CCH) 2164 (1995); TAM 9842003]

The Service has also used the "swing vote" analysis in denying or reducing the extent of a limited partnership discount. Here the

Service measures the ability of shareholders to pool their minority interests to form a majority interest, which then may reduce the valuation discount. [See Estate of Bright v United States , 658 F2d 999 (1981)]

These weapons of the Service's arsenal will be discussed in greater depth in the immediate following questions. One should note the analysis of the separate arguments often seems similar. As will be seen, the Service will view whether the transaction was "arms-length," for a "bona fide" business purpose, or primarily motivated by tax avoidance, or some combination thereof when applying these arguments.

Q 13:49 What is the "three alternative test" used by the Service to void FLP discounts?

In viewing an FLP transfer, the Service applies three alternative hurdles for the taxpayer to clear. Alternative 1 reflects that the Service views the transaction as a single testamentary transaction. This view goes to the substance of the transfer despite the number of interim transfers between entities and individuals. Alternative 1 bears a close kinship to the traditional substance over form argument, due to its focus on the essence of the transfer. This "single testamentary transaction" probably takes on its own identity as a Service argument because it arises in intra-family situations where the limited partners have ultimately received partnership interests from the decedent via the limited partnership that they would have taken, in any event, under the will.

Alternative 2 involves the application of Code Section 2703(a)(2) which reflects that for gift and estate purposes the partnership interests transferred shall be valued without regard "to any restriction on the right to sell or use the property". Recall that restrictions on these interests often result in valuation discounts (See Q 13:34). The taxpayer may escape Code Section 2703(a)(2) if she can meet the safe harbor requirements of Code Section 2703(b). These requirements are that the transfer must (1) be a bona fide business arrangement; (2) not be a device to transfer such property to members of the decedent's family for less than full and adequate consideration; and (3) have terms that are comparable to similar arrangements entered into by persons in an arms'-length transaction. [IRC § 2703(b)(1), (2), (3)] Failure to satisfy the safe harbor will likely result in the loss of any valuation discount.

Alternative 3 applies Code Section 2704 to the transfer, which measures control of the transferor previous to the transfer. Similar to Alternative 2, Alternative 3 removes any restriction on a transferred interest for purposes of valuation. Specifically, where a transferor transfers an FLP interest to a member of the transferor's family, and the transferor and members of his family collectively hold, immediately prior to the transfer, control of the FLP, any applicable restriction will be disregarded for valuation purposes. [IRC § 2704(b)(1)(A), (B)] Such "applicable restriction" is one that (1) inhibits the ability of the partnership to liquidate, or (2) is one in which the transferor or his family members may alone or collectively remove in whole or in part subsequent to the transfer. [IRC § 2704(b)(2)] The thrust of this argument is that, despite the transfer, there is no real change in the control of the partnership. Thus, any valuation discount based on a lack of marketability/control is unwarranted. It may be helpful for the tax planner to think of the family attribution rules used by the Service in other areas of the Code to understand Alternative 3. [See IRC §§ 267, 318]

Q 13:50   Has the Service been successful in applying the three alternative test?

Yes, as to deathbed transfers. Where an FLP has been created a short time prior to death, and the decedent has, just prior to death, attempted transfers (with valuation discounts to the FLP's underlying assets) to family members, and the decedent's estate has claimed discounts upon the remaining FLP interests in the decedent's estate, the Service uses the three alternatives to attempt to void the discounts.

The three alternatives are not mutually exclusive. Deathbed intra-family transfers may fail all three alternatives in addition to failing other tests. The three alternatives are often referred to as "peeling the onion" or unwrapping the "partnership wrapper". This is so because if the purported discounts fail any of the alternatives, then the Service reasons, all transactions should be collapsed into one single testamentary transaction. In other words, the Service is attempting to unveil the substance of the transfer despite the layers or cloak of partnership status.

Q 13:51   How does the Service apply Alternative 1 in voiding an FLP discount?

A seminal case in this area of scrutiny of FLP minority interests discounts is *Estate of Murphy*. [60 TCM (CCH) 645 (1990)] The decedent in *Murphy* held a 51.41 percent controlling interest in a closely held corporation. A mere 18 days before her death, the decedent transferred enough shares in trust to her children to reduce her interest in the corporation to a minority status of 49.65 percent. The estate then attempted to apply minority discounts to the decedent's interests based on this newly acquired minority status. The Tax Court did recognize "that shares of corporate stock which represent a minority interest may be worth less than a proportionate share of the value of the assets of the corporation". [Id at 656] However, such minority discounts that are conceived from a plan with the sole purpose of obtaining such a discount will not be given credence. [Id at 658]

The *Murphy* court viewed dimly the facts that the closely held stock went to the children of the decedent leaving control of the corporation within the family, and that the scheme was devised suspiciously close to the date of death. Additional evidence was the fact that the decedent's attorney sent a letter to the decedent instructing her how this plan would allow her to receive minority discounts for estate tax purposes, while allowing her and the children to retain control. [Id at 648] In sum, the *Murphy* court viewed this as a single testamentary transaction, as the essence of the transfer was to give the children the interest in the corporation that they would have received by will.

In subsequent private letter rulings and technical advice memorandums, the Service used *Murphy* in attacking discounts, especially under Alternative 1. In Technical Advice Memorandum 9730004, the Service was presented with a situation wherein an FLP was created approximately two months before the death of the decedent. The decedent had been diagnosed with terminal cancer, and shortly thereafter set up an FLP on the subsequent advice of his son, an attorney who had published articles regarding FLP's. Following this advice the decedent issued a list of nontax reasons for creating the FLP. The decedent and son also created a corporation comprised of 100,000 shares, 50,000 of which went to the son, with another 1,000 shares going to a family friend, and the decedent retained 49,000 shares, which represented a minority interest in the corporation. The corporation was the general partner of the FLP. The decedent contributed his farmland valued at $400,000 to the partnership, and the corporation transferred capital of $4,040. The decedent in exchange took a 99 percent interest in the partnership, and promptly gave gifts amounting to 8 percent of the partnership to his son, daughter-in-law, and granddaughter. These 8 percent interests were then given minority discounts of 40 percent.

A mere 54 days later at the date of death, the estate contended that the decedent's remaining 91 percent interest should be given the same 40 percent minority discount based on the decedent's status as a minority shareholder in the closely held corporation. The Service, applying *Murphy*, concluded this scenario is a single testamentary transaction. Specifically, the Service noted the above took place within the span of 54 days and was an intra-family transfer. The Service, invoking the substance over form doctrine, reasoned that, despite the interim transfers, nothing of any substance changed. The family friend was unlikely to exercise his right to buy pro-rata shares of stock. The family of decedent essentially retained complete control of the corporation and partnership, which they would have done by will. In sum, the Service stated the "only discernible purpose for the partnership arrangement was to depress the value of the farmland as it passed through the Decedent's gross estate, into the control of Son, via the Partnership". [TAM 9730004]

In Technical Advice Memorandum 9723009, the Service again applied *Murphy* to find a single testamentary transaction. Similar to the above Memorandum, this was a situation in which an FLP was created less than two months prior to the decedent's death. The son of the decedent acting under a durable power of attorney transferred the bulk of decedent's estate valued at $692,050 to the partnership in exchange for a 98 percent limited partnership interest. A closely held corporation was formed to act as general partner for the partnership. The son, pursuant to his power of attorney, then transferred the decedent's 98 percent limited partnership interest and the decedent's shares in the corporation to a trust. The son and decedent were the trustees, with the decedent retaining the power to revoke or amend the trust. Following this transfer, the decedent became a minority shareholder of the corporation. As such, the estate claimed both minority as well as marketability discounts in valuing the decedent's partnership interest at $445,000, a 46 percent discount. The Service again deemed such actions a single testamentary transaction. The interim transfers between the FLP and the corporate general partner were dismissed as attempts to finesse the tax code for the decedent's benefit. The Service again noted the brief period within which all relevant events occurred, the retention of corporate control by the family, and that the son would have received the assets in any event under the will. The Service summarized their Alternative 1 argument using the same quote as in Technical Advice Memorandum 9730004 regarding the only discernible purpose of the FLP being the depression of the value of the estate. [TAM 9723009]

Q 13:52   How does the Service apply Alternative 2 to an FLP discount?

The Service, pursuant to Code Section 2703, for estate and gift purposes, values the property despite any "restriction on the right to sell the property" unless the taxpayer satisfies the safe harbor test of Section 2703(b). Since the restriction is the basis for the tax-payer's discounting the value of the limited partnership interest, its recognition under Code Section 2703(b) is crucial. Alternative 2 is concerned with the validity of each transaction leading up to the valuation discount. Because the FLP transactions at issue are often intra-family, the Service is skeptical of whether the transactions were at "arms' length", for a "bona fide" purpose, and with "adequate consideration", i.e., within the safe harbor. Moreover, each of these three requirements of the safe harbor must be inde-pendently satisfied for a right or restriction to meet the exception. [Treas Reg § 25.2703-1(b)(2)]

When applying Alternative 2, transactions within a family group are subject to special scrutiny, and the presumption is that such transfer is not at arms' length, thus failing the safe harbor of Code Section 2703(b). [TAM 9719006] In Technical Advice Memorandum 9719006, a terminally ill decedent formed an FLP two days prior to her death and after having been just removed from life support. Her assets to that point had been held in a revocable trust, and she was also a beneficiary of a marital trust. Decedent's assets in the marital trust were transferred to the FLP making the marital trust an approx-imate 82 percent limited partner. Her revocable trust did likewise becoming an approximate 16 percent limited partner. Her son and daughter were each named as 1 percent general partners. The marital trust then transferred two 30 percent limited partnership interests to son and daughter, leaving the marital trust as a 22 percent limited partner. In exchange the marital trust received $10,000 from the son and daughter each, and a 30-year promissory note from each in the amount of $485,731.84. After these transfers, the estate contended the $2,259,143.90 original asset value of the two trusts was entitled to a 48 percent minority discount for a value of $1,177,103 for estate tax purposes despite the mere two day period involved.

The Service held the above transactions did not satisfy the safe harbor. Such a transfer was not a bona fide business arrangement, but rather a device to transfer property to members of the decedent's family. The transaction was not at arms' length because the son and daughter, acting in their representative capacities, were essentially dealing with themselves on behalf of the trusts. There was not adequate and full consideration since the goal of the transfer was exclusively for the purpose of artificial devaluation. [TAM 9719006] The Service noted the brevity of events (two days), the terminally ill status of the decedent, and that the son and daughter would take the assets by will. The Service also deemed the above events to be a single testamentary transaction under Alternative 1.

In Technical Advice Memorandums 9723009 and 9730004, the Service held the minority discounts void as failing to satisfy the safe harbor. The Service again noted the special scrutiny warranted by intra-family transfers along with the presumption of a non-arms'-length transaction. The Service issued similar reasoning for its conclusions, as in Technical Advice Memorandum 9719006, citing the state of health of decedent, the doubtfulness of the decedent's recoupment of the immediate loss, and the brevity of events. The Service also noted that the family members were on both sides of the transactions, and would have taken the assets of the estate through inheritance but for the transfers at issue.

Q 13:53 How does the service apply Alternative 3 to an FLP discount?

In Technical Advice Memorandums 9730004 and 9723009, the Service applied Alternative 3 to the intra-family transfer finding the discount void. The common thread of the two Memorandums involved, as discussed, intra-family transfers of a minority interest with discounts of between 40-46 percent. These discounts reflected devaluation in assets over a period of less than two months. The family remained in control of the managing general partner, and the donees would have taken the decedents' assets through inheritance but for the transfers at issue.

Alternative 3 applies Code Section 2704 to these types of transactions. Pursuant to Section 2704(b)(1), a transfer of an interest in a partnership to a member of the transferor's family where the transferor's family is in control of the partnership immediately before such transfer warrants disregard of any "applicable restriction" in determining the value of the transferred interest. An "applicable restriction" means any restriction (1) which effectively limits the ability of the partnership to liquidate, and (2) with respect to which the transferor or any member of the transferor's family, either alone or collectively, has the right after such transfer to remove, in whole or in part, the restriction. [IRC § 2704(b)(2)] The term "applicable restriction" is fleshed out in the Treasury Regulations to mean a restriction more restrictive than applicable state law. Specifically, Treasury Regulations Section 25.2704-2(b) provides that an "applicable restriction" is a limitation on the ability to liquidate the entity (in whole or in part) that is more restrictive than the limitations that would apply under state law generally applicable to the entity in the absence of the restriction. [See Treas Reg § 25.2704-2(b); TAM 9730004, TAM 9723009]

In both Technical Advice Memorandums, the Service found that such "applicable restriction" existed. The applicable state law, in the absence of a withdrawal prohibition in the partnership agreement, permitted partner withdrawal or liquidation of interest upon six month's notice. However, both decedents at issue were permitted to withdraw or liquidate only upon unanimous consent by the partners under the existing partnership agreements. The Service found this to be more restrictive than the applicable state law, and as such, constituted an "applicable restriction." Hence the restriction was disregarded in determining the value of the partnership interest.

Q 13:54 Does the Service apply the three alternative test to limited liability company transfers?

Yes. The Service has applied the alternatives in the exact fashion as FLPs in the context of a limited liability company. [TAM 9736004] Here the Service was presented with a situation wherein the decedent executed a durable power of attorney naming her son as attorney-in-fact. This was done less than two months prior to her death. A few days later, the son formed two Michigan limited liability companies, "Farm Company" and "Company". As attorney-in-fact, the son terminated the marital trust of the decedent, transferring land previously held in trust to Farm Company with a fair market value of $432,000. The son transferred the remainder of decedent's assets held in trust, valued at $2.3 million to Company. Three days later, transfers of $500,000 to decedent's son and daughter were made from the decedent's capital account in Company. Decedent passed away approximately six weeks later.

The estate, based on an accounting firm's appraisal, claimed minority and marketability discounts for the above transfers. Specifically, the land was given a 75 percent discount to a figure of $110,000. The two $500,000 transfers were discounted 50 percent to $250,000. The remaining $1.32 million of assets in Company were discounted 50 percent to $660,000.

The Service, applying the three alternatives analysis, voided the discounts. The Service found the transfers to be a single testamentary transaction under Alternative 1 citing the similarity of the transfers at issue to those decided in *Murphy*. The son, as attorney-in-fact, was on both sides of the transactions, and the assets funneled through the LLCs would have been received through inheritance. Nothing of substance in terms of family control changed. In short, devaluation of assets was the only effect of the transfers.

Under Alternative 2, the Service held the transfers did not satisfy the safe harbor of Code Section 2703(b). The Service again noted the scrutiny of intra-family transfers with the presumption that such transfer is not arms' length. The son, as attorney-in-fact, was essentially dealing with himself, thus not arms' length. It was not a bona fide business transaction due to the inconceivable notion that the decedent would accept a partnership interest half the value of the assets she transferred. In view of the failure to reach the safe harbor, the estate is valued under Section 2703(a)(2), i.e., without regard to any restriction on the right to sell or use the property.

As to alternative 3, the Service noted the partnership operating agreement is somewhat unclear if it is more restrictive than the applicable state law. The Service stated that to the extent the operating agreement is more restrictive than the state law, such restriction will be ignored for valuing the estate pursuant to Code Section 2704(b)(1). [TAM 9736004]

Q 13:55 Is the Service generally successful in applying the traditional sham transaction or substance over form argument to an FLP intra-family transfer?

No. Courts have often, as discussed above, allowed the facts and circumstances of a transfer to warrant FLP valuation discount treatment. Indeed, this has been true even despite the lack of prior formality. [Estate of Winkler, 73 TCM (CCH) 1657 (1997)] In *Winkler*, the Service protested certain attempted family transfers of partnership interests. This case did not concern valuation discounts, but rather the Service claimed the purported transfers of partnership interests in lottery winnings were, in substance, gifts to partners (children). The Winklers were a married couple with five adult children. Collectively the family occasionally purchased Illinois lottery tickets with the tacit understanding that they would share in any and all lottery winnings. No FLP agreement was formally executed during this time. Mrs. Winkler purchased a winning lottery ticket entitling the bearer to $6,463,166 in winnings payable in 20 annual installments. On advice from their attorney, the Winklers formed an FLP with the two parents having a 25 percent interest each, and 10 percent interest per adult child. The Winklers then took receipt of the lottery winnings through the FLP.

The Service assessed gift tax deficiencies of $58,596 against both Mr. and Mrs. Winkler alleging that Mrs. Winkler purchased the lottery ticket on her behalf and made subsequent gifts of 10 percent interest to each child. The Service viewed the substance of the receipt by each child of his or her share of the lottery winnings as gifts despite their form as FLP interests in light of the fact that the FLP was not formed until after the winning lottery ticket had been ascertained.

The Tax Court, however, accepted the view of the Winklers that an oral partnership existed prior to purchase of the ticket. The Tax Court first viewed the definition of partnership under the Code as having a broad scope. [Estate of Winkler at 1662; IRC § 7701(a)(2); Treas Reg § 1.761-1(a)] In a sense, the substance over form argument did not fail the Service, but rather aided the Winklers in avoiding the assessed gift taxes. The Tax Court found testimony credible regarding the Winklers' pooling of money to purchase family lottery tickets. The fact that no such agreement existed reflecting specific division of winnings was not fatal. Thus despite the lack of form of a partnership agreement prior to the winning ticket, a partnership existed in substance.

Having found the existence of a partnership, the Tax Court then analyzed it under Code Section 704(e) (see Q 13:47) to determine proper tax treatment. The capital contributions to the partnership by the family members in the form of purchases of lottery tickets were each deemed to be a "material income-producing factor" under Treasury Regulations Section 1.704-1(e)(1)(iv). The income from the partnership was attributable to the lottery ticket purchases. The Court found that each child did in fact "own" this capital interest under Code Section 704(e)(1), since each child contributed capital in the form of dollar bills which purchased lottery tickets. [Estate of Winkler at 1664] Moreover, evidence was accepted that Mrs. Winkler only purchased the tickets in the presence of other family members, and kept the tickets grouped together with other family tickets. In sum, the Court found a prior oral partnership existed, and the purchases of the tickets were material income-producing factors. Therefore, the family members shared the winnings via their partnership interests and not as donees.

Q 13:56   Has the Service ever successfully challenged FLP transfers under the retained control view?

Yes. For estate tax purposes under Code Section 2036(a), a decedent's estate must include all property transferred during her lifetime in which the decedent retained a life estate. The Service is concerned with purported transfers in which the donor has continued to exercise dominion and control. Since the donee does not enjoy unfettered discretion, the property is really still in the donor's possession and should be taxed as such.

Where a donor purports to gift FLP interests, but the income from these interests is deposited into and commingled with the personal funds of the donor, such deposits are highly indicative of possession or enjoyment by the donor. [Estate of Shauerhamer, 73 TCM (CCH) 2855 (1997)] In *Estate of Shauerhamer*, the failure to include 66 limited partnership interests valued at $10,000 each along with income from other transferred assets was at issue. The decedent was diagnosed with colon cancer in late November 1990. Approximately one month later she formed three FLPs for each of her children naming the child the general partner. The decedent then contributed assets comprised of real property and interests in other partnerships to the FLPs in one-third shares.

The Court deemed the Service's assessment of a tax deficiency as to the decedent's estate for failing to include the limited interests and income from the contributed assets was valid. The evidence established an implied agreement between the family members as to ownership of the assets. The income generated by the FLP assets was deposited into and commingled with the decedent's personal funds from other sources. Such actions were the equivalent of a retained life estate in the FLP assets. [Estate of Shauerhamer at 2857-58] Therefore, the assets were included in the decedent's estate.

Q 13:57 Is the Service always successful under the retained control approach?

No. The Service has been unsuccessful in using the substance over form argument to show retained control of a purported FLP transfer so as to include the assets in the estate of the transferor. [Estate of Frank, 69 TCM (CCH) 2254 (1995)] In *Estate of Frank*, the decedent, prior to his failing health, appointed his son as attorney-in-fact. As attorney-in-fact, the son had the power to make gifts in any amount and to anyone. The son, acting under this power, transferred 91 shares of closely held stock to the decedent's spouse. This transfer occurred a mere two days prior to the decedent's death. Moreover, the donee (decedent's spouse) died just seventeen days following the receipt of the shares. The family owned all of the stock of Magton Corporation, a closely held corporation that owned and managed motel properties. The 91 shares had been in a revocable trust of the decedent wherein the decedent retained the lone power to alter, amend or revoke the trust. Following the transfer, the family members each possessed only a minority interest in Magton Corporation.

The Service, using the substance over form argument, attacked the transfer. The Service felt that such a transfer represented in substance a relinquishment of the decedent's powers over the property transferred. Therefore the Service argued that the Tax Court should disregard the form of the transaction where the son purported to withdraw the shares and then retitle them in the name of decedent's spouse. If the Tax Court accepted this view, the shares would then be included in the decedent's estate under Code Sections 2035 and 2038 since the decedent's power of revocation (i.e., retained control) over the shares would have still existed up to the date of his death. [Id at 2258]

The Court, however, sided with the decedent's estate, rejecting the substance over form argument and finding no retained control. Specifically the Service found that the attorney-in-fact powers of the son were exercised in a legitimate manner. The son was granted such authority to withdraw from the trust and make gifts of the income or corpus of the trust to anyone with or without consideration. As such, the transaction was a legitimate gift thus removing the share from the estate of decedent. [Id at 2259]

The remaining issue was then the valuation of the minority interests and lack of marketability of interests in Magton Corporation. The Service and the Frank family stipulated to a 20 percent minority interest. The sub-issue here was the determination of the fair market value of Magton Corporation in order to apply the discount. The lack of marketability discount was set at 30 percent (the midpoint between the parties' suggested percentages of 35 percent and 25 percent, respectively) by the court. Thus the net asset value of nearly $5 million was discounted to a value of approximately $2.8 million in order to determine the value per share.

Q 13:58 Do the *Murphy* and *Frank* decisions leave the tax planner in a quandary?

Yes. These decisions both involved transfers of interests of closely held stock in a intra-family disposition (see Qs 13:50 and 13:54 for a discussion of the facts involved). The transfers took place within a short period of time prior to the death of the transferor. However, the Tax Court allowed the *Frank* transfer, but rejected the *Murphy* transfer, despite similar substance over form arguments marshalled by the Service. The tax planner is ill advised to assume that the more recent *Frank* decision has overruled the *Murphy* decision. *Murphy* is routinely trumpeted by the Service in post-*Frank* Tax Court cases, technical advice memorandums, and private letter rulings. Moreover, the fact that both decisions are Tax Court cases obviates any forum shopping considerations.

The proximity of the transfers to the date of death of the transferor is not a distinguishable factor in these cases. The Tax Court in *Murphy* rejected the validity of the discounts in part due to the fact such transfer was done a mere eighteen days prior to the death of the transferor. [Id at 658] The *Frank* court, however, allowed the discounts even though the transfer was executed just two days prior to the death of the transferor.

One could surmise that the degree of retained stock ownership by the decedent following the transfer is a crucial distinguishment between the two cases. In *Murphy*, the decedent dipped just below 50 percent stock ownership to a 49.65 percent minority shareholder. In *Frank*, the decedent's prior majority ownership dropped to 32.1 percent following the transfer. Moreover, the decedent's estate in *Frank* argued that such a substantial drop evidenced that tax avoidance was not the sole motive of the transfer. However, the Tax Court focused more on control remaining within the family than the stock ownership percentage in finding the *Murphy* transfer not subject to a valuation discount. [Id at 660] The *Frank* Court did not even address the estate's argument as to the substantial drop in stock ownership, deciding instead that motive for the transfer was irrelevant. [Id at 2259] Therefore post-transfer stock ownership is probably not a relevant distinction. These decisions are further muddled by the fact that the family in *Frank* retained control of the business entity just as the family in *Murphy*, but such family control was not detrimental to *Frank*.

The tax planner is also ill advised to assume that attorney-in-fact powers as in *Frank* will not be scrutinized by the Service. The Court in *Frank* was persuaded that the attorney-in-fact powers exercised by the son were valid and proper which precluded any substance over form scrutiny. However, subsequent Technical Advice Memorandums 9736004 and 9723009 expressly state that such attorney-in-fact powers allow the attorney-in-fact/child to operate on both sides of the transaction. Because the child as attorney-in-fact is essentially dealing with himself, the Service reasons the safe harbor of Code Section 2703(b) cannot be met because such a transaction could not be bona fide or at arms' length. [TAMs 9736004, 9723009, and 9719006] Such self-dealing transactions also evidence a single testamentary transaction. [TAM 9719006]

The *Murphy* Court was also persuaded by the letter from the decedent's attorney explaining how the transfer would result in valuation discounts yet allowing the family to retain control. [Estate of Murphy at 665] This evidence bolstered the Court's use of substance over form to void the discounts. *Frank* may have been free of such blatant evidence, but as stated above, the Court did not reach the substance over form issue finding the validity of the son's attorney-in-fact status precluded any substance over form argument. [Estate of Frank at 2259]

In sum, *Murphy* and *Frank* are difficult to reconcile with one another. The tax planner who orchestrates an FLP transfer based on *Frank* should be prepared to do battle with the Service using *Murphy* as its weapon.

Q 13:59 How does the Service apply the "swing vote" analysis to reduce or void a minority discount?

The swing vote analysis is a situation where the Service, viewing the stock ownership in isolation, recognizes a legitimate minority interest. The Service then, viewing stock ownership in the aggregate, searches to see if the minority interest at issue can be coupled with another minority interest to form majority ownership, i.e., to form the swing vote in corporate decision-making.

The Service bases the swing vote analysis on the willing buyer/willing seller rule for determining fair market value. This rule, of course, is the touchstone for receiving minority discounts since a willing buyer would not pay a pro rata share of the entire enterprise for only a minority interest. Naturally, the swing vote analysis arises often in the context of families. Recall that in the three alternative analysis, courts look to see if control has remained within the family following a transfer. Similarly, the swing vote analysis looks to see if related family members, individually owning minority interests, can pool these interests to derive the benefits of majority ownership.

The Fifth Circuit for the U.S. Court of Appeals has, to an extent, recognized the swing vote analysis. [Estate of Bright v United States, 658 F 2d 999 (1981)] In *Estate of Bright*, the sole issue was the value of the decedent wife's stock. The decedent and her husband collectively had 55 percent stock ownership in each of several affiliated corporations. The remaining 45 percent of the stock was owned by unrelated parties. Both parties stipulated to the fact that, under Texas law, the stock was the community property of the married couple, and that upon death, the decedent can exercise testamentary disposition as to her half.

The Service's primary argument regarding family attribution was rejected. The Service then argued that the swing vote value of the stock should be factored into the fair market valuation. The fair market value is the "price at which the property would change hands between a willing buyer and a willing seller, neither being under any compulsion to buy or to sell and both having knowledge of relevant facts." [Treas Reg § 20.2031-1(b)] The Service argued that although the buyer and seller under this rule are hypothetical, they still have "knowledge of relevant facts". These relevant facts are that a husband and wife each owning 27.5 percent of the stock allows them to combine their ownership into majority status, thus casting the swing vote. In other words, no minority discount should be given because although its a minority share viewed in isolation, such ownership is, nevertheless, majority ownership when viewed in the aggregate. The Court of Appeals noted that such an argument had been recognized by courts, however, since the Service failed to raise this issue at the District Court level, the Court of Appeals declined to entertain the issue. [Estate of Bright at 1008]

The Service has subsequently expressed the view that swing vote potential is a factor to be taken into consideration when valuing closely held stock. [TAM 9436005] The Service was faced with the scenario in which a father, who had been a 100 percent shareholder of a closely held corporation, transferred 30 percent blocks of shares to each of his three children. Each 30 percent interest is, of course, a minority interest. However, the Service cited to authority subsequent to *Estate of Bright* that holds swing vote potential can reduce the minority discount percentage. Specifically, in *Estate of Winkler v. Commissioner* [TC Memo 1989-232] (unrelated to the *Estate of Winkler* case discussed in Q 13:54), the Tax Court was faced with the valuation of a 10 percent minority interest in a closely held corporation.

The 10 percent interest was owned by Clara Winkler with the Winkler family owning another 40 percent. The Simmons family owned the remaining 50 percent. The court held that because neither family had majority ownership, such 10 percent ownership has enhanced value because an outside purchaser could pool this interest with the 50 percent owned by the Simmons family to effect a majority interest.

Technical Advice Memorandum 9436005 also cited persuasive authority found in published media including Shannon P. Pratt's book entitled *Valuing Small Businesses and Professional Practices*, 527 (2d ed. 1994). In this book, Pratt writes "if two stockholders own 49 percent [of the stock] and a third owns 2 percent, the 49 percent stockholders may be on par with each other. . . . The 2 percent stockholder may be able to command a premium over the pro-rata value for that particular block of stock because of the swing vote power."

In view of *Estate of Winkler* and the expert commentary, the Service ruled that the 30 percent interests must have their swing vote potential factored into their individual valuations since two 30 percent shareholders can aggregate their interests and cast the swing vote.

In Technical Advice Memorandum 9436005, the Service distinguished Revenue Ruling 93-12. [1993-1 CB 202] Here a donor transferred all outstanding stock of a closely held corporation in equal 20 percent interests to each of his five children. The ruling concludes the factor of corporate control in the family is not considered in valuing each transferred interest for purposes of Code Section 2512. Moreover, a minority discount will not be disallowed solely because a transferred interest, when aggregated with interests held by other family members, would be part of a controlling interest. However, the essence of Technical Advice Memorandum 9436005 is not an automatic disallowance of the minority discount, but rather that swing vote potential is a factor to be taken into consideration in valuing a minority interest.

Q 13:60   How does the Service utilize the gift upon formation of the entity attack?

In *Estate of Trenchard* [69 TCM (CCH) 2164 (1995)], the Service used this argument to assess significant gift taxes upon intra-family transfers to a closely held corporation. The Trenchards, their daughter, and their three grandchildren all transferred property to a newly formed closely held corporation. The properties were exchanged for debt and stock of the closely held corporation. The Trenchards retained approximately 61 percent majority status of the corporation. The daughter received stock equaling 35 percent voting power and the three grandchildren each received 1 percent interest in the voting stock of the corporation. The Trenchards both eventually passed away, and their estates were consolidated for gift tax determination purposes. In all, Mr. and Mrs. Trenchard transferred property, including farmland, in the amount of $2,952,748 to the corporation. In exchange, they received debt (debentures) and stock of the corporation collectively valued at $1,281,951.

The Service contended that the transfers of property to the corporation by the Trenchards were actually gifts to their daughter and grandchildren. Specifically, "[w]here the property is transferred for less than an adequate and full consideration in money or money's worth, then the amount by which the value of the property exceeded the value of the consideration shall be deemed a gift, and shall be included in computing the amount of gifts made during the calendar year." [IRC § 2512(b)] The Tax Court stated that the "breadth of the Federal gift tax provisions may exceed the reach of the term 'gift' under the common law." [Estate of Trenchard at 2170] Moreover, "a gift for Federal gift tax purposes encompasses sales and other exchanges of property in which the value of the property transferred is more than the value of the consideration received". [Estate of Trenchard at 2170, citing Treas Reg § 25.2512-8]

The daughter, acting as executrix for the estates of the Trenchards, argued that the gift tax provisions of the Code were inapplicable because the transfers of property were genuine business transactions. The daughter issued a list of reasons supporting her argument including: that she initiated the corporation to manage the family business after the deaths of the Trenchards; the corporation simplified the allocations of the income and expenses connected to the farmland; the corporation allowed business assets to remain consolidated; and it afforded Mr. and Mrs. Trenchard protection against decline in the real estate market. [Estate of Trenchard at 2170]

The Tax Court agreed with the Service, holding that the excess of the transferred property's value over the value of the debt and stock received should be taxed as gifts. The Tax Court stated that "[w]e closely scrutinize a transfer involving related parties, such as family members and their closely held corporation, to determine whether the transfer is a gift. We presume such transfer is a gift." [Id] The Tax Court found that the estates failed to overcome this presumption as there was not "meaningful arms' length bargaining" nor was the bargaining "bona fide". [Id] (Note the similar reasoning of the Tax Court here compared to the reasoning of Alternative 2 in Q 13:51.)

Moreover, the Tax Court noted Mr. Trenchard's long history of gifting parcels of land to his family. The executrix was recently divorced and dependent on the income from the family farm. None of the others, save Mr. Trenchard, engaged in farming; and Mr. Trenchard was conscious of estate planning. The Court found incredible the notion that the Trenchards would have made such transfers had the shareholders been unrelated, since in return they received unsecured notes, noncumulative preferred stock that paid no dividends or current income, and they consummated an exchange of property that would significantly reduce their current income received from such property. [Id at 2171]

In Technical Advice Memorandum 9842003, the IRS again attacked an FLP where the partnership was formed or funded soon before death in an effort to reduce transfer taxes. In TAM 9842003, the decedent formed a limited partnership with two of her children. Each of the children transferred $50 to the partnership in exchange for a one half of one percent general partnership interest and the decedent transferred $9,900 to the partnership in exchange for a 99 percent limited partnership interest. Within six weeks of the decedent's death, the decedent transferred to the partnership $2,261,607 of assets, consisting of securities, cash and real estate including the decedent's personal residence. On the decedent's estate tax return, the limited partnership interest was valued at $1,356,964, or 60 percent of the fair market value of the assets the decedent had contributed.

The IRS asserted a number of different arguments, including a number of the same arguments it has made in other rulings to disallow the valuation discounts claimed by the estate in valuing the decedent's partnership interest. In addition, the IRS adopted a new alternative for imposing transfer taxes with respect to the transfer of property to an FLP. This new theory asserted by the IRS is that the transfer of the property to the partnership by the decedent constituted a gift to the other partners.

The TAM first concluded that the entire transaction, including the transfer of assets to the partnership, was a single testamentary transaction occurring at the decedent's death. The result is that any decrease in value of the assets resulting from the creation of the partnership is to be disregarded. Alternatively, the TAM concluded that the property passing from the decedent was the underlying partnership assets, subject to the partnership agreement, and the value of these assets is determined without regard to the partnership agreement under Code Section 2703(a)(2). Further, the TAM said that any restrictions on the decedent's ability to liquidate the partnership interest are disregarded in valuing the limited partnership interest under Code Section 2704(b)(2).

Under this new alternative gift theory, the IRS reasoned that the decedent made a gift to the other partners by the transfer of assets to the partnership. Relying on *Trenchard,* the IRS ruled that the transfer to the partnership constituted a gift to the other partners in an amount equal to the difference between the fair market value of the transferred assets and the fair market value of the partnership interest received in the exchange.

In light of the IRS's position in TAM 9842003, careful planning is essential when a taxpayer transfers property to an FLP. First, a transfer of property for consideration does not constitute a gift if the property is transferred in the ordinary course of business. However, it may be very difficult to prove that such a transfer to a family owned entity is in the ordinary course of business (i.e., at arm's length and lacking donative intent). Alternatively, the taxpayer may be in a better position to argue that the ordinary course of business test is satisfied if the taxpayer transfers business assets in exchange for a general partnership interest in an FLP and the other family members transfer a pro rata share of property to the FLP in the same transaction. This will result in the transferors asserting a business purpose for forming or increasing the capitalization of the entity. In addition, a transfer should not constitute a gift where the transferors receive all of the general partnership interests and subsequently transfer limited partnership interests to other family members. Of course, later gifts of partnership interests could be subject to the gift tax.

Q 13:61   What is the "unity of ownership" doctrine?

This doctrine is a means once used by the Service to question the validity of a valuation discount in the family context. A seminal case in this area is *Propstra v. United States* [680 F 2d 1248 (9th Cir 1982)] In *Propstra*, the decedent's estate took a 15 percent minority interest discount upon a one-half community property interest in several parcels of real property. The Service argued that no such discount was warranted pursuant to their unity of ownership argument. The decedent's spouse retained the other one-half community property interest. The Service argued that "not only must the estate prove the value of the interest if sold separately, but it must also prove that the interests in question were likely to be sold apart from the other undivided one-half interest in the property." [Propstra at 1251] Moreover, this unity of ownership theory holds one may "reasonably assume that the interest held by the estate will ultimately be sold with the other undivided interest and that interest's proportionate share of the market value of the whole will thereby be realized." [Id]

The Court of Appeals, however, rejected the unity of ownership argument, and allowed the minority interest discount. The court expressly rejected any imputation of unity of ownership principles for purposes of applying Code Sections 2031 and 2033 in property valuations of one's estate. The court then stated the definition of "fair market value" under the regulations (see Q 13:57). Specifically the court held "[b]y no means is this language an explicit directive from Congress to apply unity of ownership principles to estate valuations. In comparison, Congress has made explicit its desire to have unity of ownership or family attribution principles apply in other areas of the federal tax law." [Id] The court also noted that the Fifth Circuit and U.S. Tax Court had previously rejected the unity of ownership argument. [Propstra at 1252-53]

In response to these multiple defeats the Service issued Revenue Ruling 93-12. [1993-1 CB 202] This revenue ruling expresses that the Service will abide by the above courts' decisions. Specifically, the Ruling states:

> After further consideration of the position taken in Rev. Rul. 81-253, and in light of the cases noted above, the Service has concluded that, in the case of a corporation with a single class of stock, notwithstanding the family relationship of the

> donor, the donee, and other shareholders, the shares of other family members will not be aggregated with the transferred shares to determine whether the transferred shares should be valued as part of a controlling interest. . . .

If a donor transfers shares in a corporation to each of the donor's children, the factor of corporate control in the family is not considered in valuing each transferred interest for purposes of section 2512 of the Code. For gift and estate tax purposes the Service will follow *Bright, Propstra, Andrews,* and *Lee* in not assuming that all voting power held by family members may be aggregated for purposes of determining whether the transferred shares should be valued as part of a controlling interest. Consequently, a minority discount will not be disallowed solely because a transferred interest, when aggregated with interests held by family members, would be a part of a controlling interest. This would be the case whether the donor held 100 percent or some lesser percentage of the stock immediately before the gift.

Accordingly, Revenue Ruling 93-12 revoked Revenue Ruling 81-253. [1981-1 CB 187] Although this 1993 ruling has put an end to the unity of ownership argument, this does not signal an end to challenges by the Service with respect to valuation discounts. The bevy of possible Service arguments discussed in this section evidences the Service's close scrutiny of intra-family transfers. In fact, as seen in the three alternative analysis, the retention of control of the business entity by the family following a transfer on ownership interest is a strong factor used to void a minority discount.

Q 13:62 Is a transfer of stock in order to become a minority shareholder followed by an immediate redemption of the then remaining stock an effective tax planning technique?

No. In this situation, a taxpayer is a majority shareholder. As such, he or she cannot, of course, qualify for a minority discount. So this taxpayer reasons he or she can transfer a portion of the shares to another party which in turn leaves the taxpayer a minority shareholder. The shareholder then takes a minority discount upon the remaining shares and has them redeemed by the corporation. The Tax Court has ruled, however, that such a bifurcation of the stock should be collapsed into one transaction and viewed as a transfer of a majority interest. [Estate of Cidulka, TC Memo 1996-149]

In *Cidulka*, the taxpayer owned a 52 percent majority interest in a closely held corporation. The remaining shares were mostly owned by the taxpayer's son and the son's family. On the advice of the taxpayer's attorneys and accountant, the taxpayer, on January 25, 1982, transferred 40 shares to his son and son's family collectively. The corporation then redeemed the entire remainder of the taxpayer's shares of stock. This transfer left the son as the majority shareholder. The taxpayer contended that the 40 shares and the redeemed shares should both be viewed as separate transactions and that both transfers should receive a minority discount. The Tax Court disagreed, finding instead that the two transactions should be collapsed into a single transaction and viewed as a transfer of a majority interest. As such, the 40 shares gifted and the subsequent redemption were revalued applying a majority ownership valuation. Specifically the Tax Court stated:

> This record is clear that decedent (taxpayer) discussed with his accountant and two lawyers a plan to dispose of his interest in SOAI to his son John Cidulka by gift in a manner that would avoid all gift taxes and estate taxes. The underlying plan was that minority interests would be valued at book value and, therefore, each gift made to each individual would be an amount that would be less than $10,000, in 1982 and less than $3,000 in prior years when that was the exclusion for gift taxes.

Moreover, the *Cidulka* court offered precedent and reasoning of the Tax Court and the Court of Appeals for the Seventh Circuit stating "that a hypothetical bifurcation of stock for the purpose of its valuation as a minority interest will not be recognized since it would be an easy method of implementing a tax avoidance scheme". [Estate of Cidulka citing Northern Trust Co v Commissioner, 87 TC 349, 386-88 (1986); see also Estate of Curry v United States, 706 F 2d 1424, 1426-30 (7th Cir 1983)]

Although *Cidulka* did not involve an FLP, this case is representative of how the Service will attack an entity-based transfer where there is a transfer of some stock followed by a simultaneous redemption of some or all of the remaining stock effected for minority discount purposes. Moreover, the Service will attack such a transfer where the motive is one of tax avoidance via a bifurcation of the stock and attempted minority discounts taken on the divided sets of stock.

Q 13:63 Should a taxpayer use an unbiased and thoroughly qualified individual when computing a minority discount?

Yes. A taxpayer is treading upon thin ice if he or she uses an individual with a stake in the outcome as a valuation expert, or has no thorough valuation at all. The case of *Estate of McCormick* [TC Memo 1995-371] is emblematic of such a situation. In *McCormick*, the appropriate minority discount percentages for various partnership interests were at issue. *McCormick* shows the importance of using unbiased outside sources in arriving at minority discount percentiles. In *McCormick*, the taxpayer attempted minority discounts of various partnership interests ranging from 30 to 40 percent. The Service contended the appropriate range was between 10 to 25 percent.

The Tax Court adjudged minority discounts to be within the range proffered by the Service. The fair market values of several underlying properties were in dispute upon which the minority discounts would be determined. As to certain unimproved parcels of land, the taxpayer/petitioner proffered his son, an integral member of the family business, as his expert. Although the son possessed a real estate sales and broker's license, the Tax Court did not recognize him as an expert. Specifically, the Tax Court noted that the son had a financial interest in the outcome rendering his testimony incapable of being impartial and disinterested. As such, the son, under the federal rules of evidence, was allowed only to testify as a lay or fact witness. [See, e.g., United States v Abel, 469 US 45, 51-52 (1984)]

As to certain development realty, the taxpayer offered a certified public accountant (CPA) as an expert for valuation purposes. Although the CPA did use his own judgment and expertise in deriving a minority discount, the Tax Court was not impressed by his testimony. The Tax Court noted that the CPA exercised his judgment and performed computations based solely on estimates and other information provided by the taxpayer/petitioner and his family. In rejecting the CPA's testimony and accepting the Service's expert testimony the Tax Court stated:

[P]etitioners have not provided an adequate foundation for the distinction they make. Also, petitioners' value, as was the case of the undeveloped realty, was based on estimates without sufficient supporting data to determine its correctness, whereas respondent's (the Service) analysis was well documented and utilized an accepted method of valuation employed by a qualified expert.

In view of *McCormick*, it is incumbent upon the taxpayer to use an unrelated third party, with no pecuniary interest in the outcome of a given minority discount case, as an expert to derive a minority discount. Furthermore, this third party must be allowed to perform an independent review of the asset values and arrive at his own conclusions. As seen in *McCormick*, an otherwise qualified expert's opinion is tainted if he uses data solely furnished by a taxpayer and without conducting his own independent examination of the assets.

Q 13:64 Who bears the burden of proof in valuation cases?

The taxpayer did before the 1998 IRS Reform and Restructuring Act. An example of this burden of proof is provided in *Estate of Scanlon*. [TCM 1996-331] In *Scanlon*, the appropriate marketability discount to be taken on nonpublicly traded stock was at issue. The taxpayer called an expert who opined that a 35 percent marketability discount was appropriate based on internal documents of the corporation and other financial worksheets. The Service did not offer an expert to dispute the valuation discount. The taxpayer argued that he must prevail in view of the absence of any conflicting testimony from an expert offered by the Service. The Tax Court flatly rejected this reasoning stating:

> [t]he fact that (the Service) did not call an expert at trial to support her determination does not mean that (the taxpayer) has met its burden of proof. Although Mr. Chaffe testified as an expert in this case on (the taxpayer's) behalf, we will not follow his opinion if it is contrary to our judgment. We may adopt or reject his opinion in its entirety, if we believe it appropriate to do so, or we may select the portions of his opinion that we choose to adopt.

Thus, even though the burden is after the 1998 Act initially with the IRS, by introducing some evidence, the burden will shift to the taxpayer. The ultimate decision, however, will remain with the court.

Appendix A

Registration of Foreign LLCs

State	LLC Act Specifically Recognizes Foreign LLCs	Statutory Registration Procedures	Initial Filing Fee
Alabama	Yes. § 10-12-46	Yes. § 10-12-47	$75
Alaska	Yes. § 10.50.600	Yes. § 10.50.605	$250
Arizona	Yes. § 29-801	Yes. § 29-802	$150
Arkansas	Yes. § 4-32-1001	Yes. § 4-32-1002	$300
California	Yes. § 17450	Yes. § 17451	$70
Colorado	Yes. § 7-80-901	Yes. § 7-80-904(1)	$75
Connecticut	Yes. § 51	Yes. § 52	$60
Delaware	Yes. § 18-901	Yes. § 18-902	$50 plus $20 copy fee
District of Columbia	Yes. § 29-1352	Yes. § 29-1353	$150

State	LLC Act Specifically Recognizes Foreign LLCs	Statutory Registration Procedures	Initial Filing Fee
Florida[1]	Yes. § 608.505. Statute does not refer to state of organization's laws for liability protection, but states that LLC has the same rights and privileges of domestic LLC. Also provides Florida does not regulate the organizational or internal affairs of the LLC.[2]	Yes. § 608.501(1)	$100
Georgia	Yes. § 14-11-1	Yes. § 14-11-702	$200
Hawaii	Yes. §1-1001	Yes. §1-1002	$100
Idaho	Yes. § 53.650	Yes. § 53.651	$100
Illinois	Yes. § 180/45-1	Yes. § 180/50-5-10	$400
Indiana	Yes. § 23-18-11-1	Yes. § 23-18-11-2	$90
Iowa	Yes. § 490A.1401	Yes. § 490A.1407	$100
Kansas	Yes. § 17-7636	Yes. § 17-7637	$150
Kentucky	Yes. § 275.385(1)	Yes. § 275.395	$90
Louisiana	Yes. § 12:1342	Yes. § 12:1342	$100
Maine	Yes. § 711	Yes. §§ 712, 713	$250
Maryland	Yes. § 4A-1001	Yes. § 4A-1002	$50

State	LLC Act Specifically Recognizes Foreign LLCs	Statutory Registration Procedures	Initial Filing Fee
Massa-chusetts	Yes. $47. Foreign LLCs cannot do business that is prohibited in Mass. The Mass. LLC's organization, internal affairs, and the liability of its members and managers are governed by the law of the state in which it is organized	Yes. §§ 12, 48	$500
Michigan	Yes. § 450.5001	Yes. § 450.5002	$50
Minnesota	Yes. § 322B.90	Yes. § 322B.91	$185
Mississippi	Yes. § 79-27-1001	Yes. § 79-29-1002	$250
Missouri	Yes. § 347.151	Yes. § 347.153	$100
Montana	Yes. § 35-8-1001. Statute does not provide state of organization's law applies, but does provide that Montana is not authorized to regulate the organizational or internal affairs of a foreign LLC.[3]	Yes. § 35-8-1003	$70
Nebraska	Yes. § 21-2637	Yes. § 21-2638	$110, plus recording fee
Nevada	Yes. § 88.570	Yes. § 86.551	$125
New Hampshire	Yes. § 304-C:62	Yes. § 304-C:64	$200
New Jersey	Yes. § 42:2B-52	Yes. § 42:2B-53	$100

State	LLC Act Specifically Recognizes Foreign LLCs	Statutory Registration Procedures	Initial Filing Fee
New Mexico	Yes. § 53-19-47	Yes. § 53-19-48	$100
New York	Yes. § 801	Yes. § 802	$250
North Carolina	Yes. § 57C-7-01	Yes. § 57C-7-02(a)	$250
North Dakota	Yes. § 10-32-135	Yes. § 10-32-138	$125
Ohio	Yes. § 1705.53	Yes. § 1705.54	$85
Oklahoma	Yes. § 2042	Yes. § 2043	$300
Oregon	Yes. § 63.714	Yes. § 63.707	$440
Pennsylvania	Yes. § 8981. Statute provides that foreign LLC is subject to the same liabilities, restrictions, duties, and penalites now in force or hereafter imposed upon a domestic LLC, to the same extent as if it had been organized under Pennsylvania law.[4]	Yes.	$180
Rhode Island	Yes. § 7-16-48	Yes. § 7-16-49	$150
South Carolina	Yes. § 33-43-1001. Statute does not provide the laws of the state of formation govern the liability of members. Does provide they govern organizational and internal affairs.[5]	Yes. § 33-43-1008. Foreign LLC that renders a professional service is not required to obtain a certificate of authority, unless the LLC maintains an office in the state. § 33-43-1008(c). But see § 33-43-1101 relicensing requirements	$110

State	LLC Act Specifically Recognizes Foreign LLCs	Statutory Registration Procedures	Initial Filing Fee
South Dakota	Yes. § 47-34-45	Yes. § 47-34-47	$90 and up, based on capital
Tennessee	Yes. § 48A-45-101	Yes. § 48A-45-301 $50/ member — $300 minimum	$3,000 maximum
Texas	Yes. § 7.02	Yes. § 7.05	$500
Utah	Yes. § 48-2b-143. Does not provide that the law of the state of formation governs liability, but does provide that Utah law does not apply to the organizational and internal affairs of the foreign LLC.[6]	Yes. § 48-2b-144	$50
Vermont	Yes. § 3131	Yes. § 3132	$100
Virginia	Yes. § 13.1-1051	Yes. § 13.1-1052	$100
Washington	Yes. § 901	Yes. § 902	$175
West Virginia	Yes. § 31B-10-1001	Yes. § 31B-11-1002	$150
Wisconsin	Yes. § 183.1001	Yes. § 183.1002	$100
Wyoming	No provision	Although the fees section, § 17-15-132, describes fees applicable to the Certificate of Authority issued for foreign LLCs.[7]	$100 and up, based on capital, but not to exceed $25,000

---

1. Florida requires members of a foreign LLC to sign an affidavit disclosing member's name and contributions. Section [608.412]

2. If Florida law governs the liability of members, Section 608.436 provides that no member or manager is liable under a judgment, decree, court order, or any other manner for a debt, obligation, or liability of the LLC. There are exceptions to this rule, including liability for a manager or managing member's breach of a fiduciary duty, violation of criminal law, etc. [Section 608.4362] Examples in the statute include violations of "corporate" opportunities, and conduct and conscious disregard of the LLC's best interest or willfulness conduct. Florida also provides that members are liable for a period of one year to return any capital distribution received from the LLC, for the benefit of creditors who extended credit to the LLC before that distribution was made. If the distribution was wrongful (e.g., rendered the LLC insolvent at the time of the distribution), a member is liable for the return of that distribution for six years. [Section 608.428]

3. If Montana law applies to determine the liability of a member, Section 35-8-304 provides that no person is liable, solely by reason of being a member or manager, or both, for any liability of the LLC, whether arising in contract, tort, or otherwise or for the acts or omissions of any other member, manager, agent, or employee of the LLC. This applies to liabilities under a judgment, decree, court order, or in any other manner for a debt, obligation, or other liability of the LLC. In the context of professional services, Section 35-8-1306 provides that an employee of a professional LLC is not liable for the conduct of other employees unless the employee is at fault in appointing, supervising, or cooperating with the employee who is negligent or commits another wrongful act or omission.

4. The Pennsylvania statute provides broad protection for the liability of members and managers, with a provision similar to that of Montana. [Section 8922]

5. Section 33-43-304 specifically provides that no member or manager is liable for the obligations of the LLC, or for the acts or omissions of any other manager, member, agent, or employee, unless he or she is at fault in appointing, supervising, or cooperating with them in any wrongful or negligent act or omission.

6. If Utah law applies to the liability of members, Section 48-2b-109 provides that no member, manager, or employee is personally liable for the LLC's debts, obligations, or other liability. In addition, Section 48-2b-111 provides that no member, manager, or employee of an LLC is personally liable for the acts or omissions of any other member, manager, or employee of the LLC. Thus, Utah law provides maximum protection for the acts or omissions of any other person, regardless of the supervision or control of the other member.

7. If Wyoming law applies to determine the liability of a member, Section 17-15-113 provides that no member or manager is liable for the LLC's debts, obligations, or liabilities. Nothing in the statute discusses liability for acts or omissions of other members.

Appendix B

Analysis of LLCs by State

Note: The state laws that govern the contents of this schedule are constantly changing; therefore, this appendix should be used merely as a guide.

State	State Income Tax Classification of LLC	Entity Level Tax on LLC	Tax Form and Filing Date*	Composite Filing Available	Annual Report Required	Other Tax Information
Alabama	Follows federal	No	Form 65 due April 15	No	No	Nonresident passive corporate owners will be subject to income tax on their distributive share of the flow-through entities' income.
Alaska	Follows federal	$100/year–domestic; $200/year–foreign	No tax return required	N/A	Yes. Due Jan 2 every two years.	
Arizona	Follows federal	No	Form 165 due April 15; Single member LLCs use Form 120 due April 15	Yes		Arizona provides that a non-resident corporate partner of a partnership doing business in Arizona is subject to Arizona income tax.

*Assumes the LLC qualifies as a partnership in those states that follow federal and LLC is filing on a calendar year basis.

State	State Income Tax Classification of LLC	Entity Level Tax on LLC	Tax Form and Filing Date*	Composite Filing Available	Annual Report Required	Other Tax Information
Arkansas	Follows federal	Annual $103 franchise tax	Form AR1050 due May 15	Yes	Yes. Due June 1 ($109 fee)	
California	Follows federal	$800 LLC minimum franchise tax and maximum gross receipts tax of $4,500	Form 568 due April 15	Yes	Yes. Due in anniversary month ($5 fee)	In addition to the $800 minimum tax, an annual LLC fee is imposed based upon total income from all sources reportable to California (range from $500 to $4,000). Non-resident members may either (1) file a group non-resident return and pay California income tax; or (2) file a Form 3832 consenting to the jurisdiction of California. If any LLC member fails to sign Form 3832, the LLC is required to pay tax on the member's distributive share at the highest marginal rate (11%).
Colorado	Taxed as partnerships	No	Form 106 due October 15	Yes	Yes. Due every two years	An LLC may file a Form 107 for each non-resident member to consent to file a Colorado income tax return. If a non-resident member fails to sign, the LLC must submit Form 108 and remit 5% of the member's Colorado source income.
Connecticut	Follows federal	No	Form CT-1065 due April 15	Yes	Yes. Due on anniversary date ($10 fee)	Foreign corporate limited partnerships and limited liability companies are subject to Connecticut's Corporation Business Tax.

*Assumes the LLC qualifies as a partnership in those states that follow federal and LLC is filing on a calendar year basis.

State	State Income Tax Classification of LLC	Entity Level Tax on LLC	Tax Form and Filing Date*	Composite Filing Available	Annual Report Required	Other Tax Information
Delaware	Follows federal	$100 annual tax on domestic & foreign LLCs	Form 300 due April 15	No	No	
District of Columbia	Follows federal	9.975% franchise tax on D.C. source income for an unincorporated business ($100 minimum tax)	Form D-30 due April 15	No	Yes. Due June 16 ($50 fee)N/A	If the D.C. franchise tax liability exceeds $1,000, estimated payments must be made to avoid a penalty. If more than 80% of gross income is derived from personal services rendered by individuals and capital is not a material income-producing factor, a franchise tax return is not required. Instead, the LLC must file a partnership return (Form D-65).
Florida	Follows federal (SB 704; eff. 7/1/98) (no state personal income tax)	Until 7/1/98	5.5% tax	Form F-1120 FT due April 1	N/A	Yes. Due May 1, Florida treats nonresident corporate limited partners as having a taxable nexus and therefore imposes a corporate income tax on them.
Georgia	Follows federal	4% withholding tax for nonresident members, with exceptions	Form 700 due April 15	Yes	Yes. Due April 1 ($25 fee)	If composite return is filed, with holding is not required. Georgia requires that an LLC pay a withholding tax on behalf of nonresident members' distributive share of income of the LLC.

*Assumes the LLC qualifies as a partnership in those states that follow federal and LLC is filing on a calendar year basis.

State	State Income Tax Classification of LLC	Entity Level Tax on LLC	Tax Form and Filing Date*	Composite Filing Available	Annual Report Required	Other Tax Information
Hawaii	Follows federal	No	Form N-20 due April 20	No	Yes. Due June 30 ($25 Fee)	
Idaho	Follows federal	No	Form 65 due April 15	Yes	No	
Illinois	Follows federal	1.5% partnership tax	Form IL-1065 due April 15	Yes	Yes. Due within 60 days following first day of anniversary month ($300 fee)	Foreign corporate partners of partnerships doing business in Illinois will be taxed on their distributive shares of any income received from the partnership. This rule is applied to both general and limited partners.
Indiana	Follows federal	Withholding tax on nonresident member's distributive share of Indiana income at highest state rate	Form IT-65 due April 15	Yes	Yes. (Biennial Report) Due in anniversary month every two years ($30 fee)	The tax withheld and paid by the LLC may be applied towards the tax on the composite return.
Iowa	Taxed as partnership	Withholding tax on nonresident member's distributive share of Iowa income at highest state rate	Form IA-1065 due May 1	Yes	No	
Kansas	Follows federal	Franchise tax on net capital accounts	Form K-65 due April 15	Yes	Yes. Due April 15 (fee equals $1 for each $1,000 of net capital accounts; minimum fee of $20 and maximum of $2,500)	

*Assumes the LLC qualifies as a partnership in those states that follow federal and LLC is filing on a calendar year basis.

State	State Income Tax Classification of LLC	Entity Level Tax on LLC	Tax Form and Filing Date*	Composite Filing Available	Annual Report Required	Other Tax Information
Kentucky	Follows federal	No	Form 765 due April 15	Yes	Yes. Due June 30 ($15 fee)	Must have 15 or more full-year nonresident members to receive special permission to file a composite return.
Louisiana	Follows federal	No	Form IT-565 due May 15	No	No	
Maine	Follows federal	"Financial institutions" are taxed at a rate of 1% of Maine net income and 8 cents per $1,000 of Maine assets	Form TR due April 15	Yes	Yes ($60 fee)	
Maryland	Follows federal	5% withholding tax for non-residents	Form 510 due April 15	Yes		Non-resident members may apply the amount withheld and paid by the LLC to their Maryland individual income tax.
Massachusetts	Follows federal	No	Form 3 due April 15	No	Yes. ($500 fee)	A nonresident corporate limited partner of a limited partnership will be subject to a corporate excise tax unless the corporate limited partner owns less than a five percent interest in the limited partnership and the value of that interest is less than $10,000.
Michigan	Subject to single business tax; members taxed	2.3375% of LLC tax base	Form C-8000 due April 30	No	Yes for professional LLCs only; Due Feb 15 ($50 fee)	Legislation has been passed phasing out the Single Business Tax if certain requirements are met. Mich. H.B. 4745 (1999).

*Assumes the LLC qualifies as a partnership in those states that follow federal and LLC is filing on a calendar year basis.

State	State Income Tax Classification of LLC	Entity Level Tax on LLC	Tax Form and Filing Date*	Composite Filing Available	Annual Report Required	Other Tax Information
Minnesota	Follows federal	8.5% withholding tax for non-residents	Form M-3 due April 15	No	Yes. Due by anniversary date every two years	If Schedule A of Form M-3 has Minnesota receipts of at least $500,000, then a fee between $100 and $5,000 will be assessed.
Mississippi	Follows federal	No	Form 86-105 due April 15	Yes	No	LLC may withhold and pay 5% of net profit to avoid joint and several liability. Non-resident members may apply any amount withheld to the non-resident Mississippi individual income tax return.
Missouri	Follows federal	Withholding tax on nonresident member's distributive share of Missouri income at highest state rate	Form MO-1065 due April 15	Yes	No	Net profits earned in the City of Kansas City subject to 1% earnings tax.
Montana	Follows federal	No	Form PR-1 due April 15	Yes	Yes. Due April 15	
Nebraska	Follows federal	No	Form 1065N due April 15	No	No	Non-resident members may file Form 12N to avoid the tax withholding but member must file a Nebraska non-resident income tax return. If the LLC withholds tax for non-resident member, the member is not required to file a Nebraska non-resident income tax return unless there was a refund.

*Assumes the LLC qualifies as a partnership in those states that follow federal and LLC is filing on a calendar year basis.

State	State Income Tax Classification of LLC	Entity Level Tax on LLC	Tax Form and Filing Date*	Composite Filing Available	Annual Report Required	Other Tax Information
Nevada	No state income tax	N/A	N/A	N/A	Yes. Due last day of anniversary month ($85 fee)	
New Hampshire	Follows federal	5% tax on dividends and interest of partnership; 7% tax on business profits; .0025% Business Enterprise Tax; however a dollar-for-dollar credit is allowed against the business profits tax for the amount of the business enterprise tax owed	Forms NH-1065, BET, BT Summary and DP-10 due April 15	No	Yes. Due April 1 ($100 fee)	7% tax due on business profits if gross receipts (earned everywhere) are greater than $50,000. 5% tax due on interest and dividends if 1) such amount is over $1,200; 2) LLC has a usual place of business in New Hampshire; 3) LLC has at least one New Hampshire member, and 4) LLC has non-transferable shares. .0025% Enterprise tax due on dividends, interest and wages paid, if gross receipts are more than $100,000 or the enterprise value tax base is more than $50,000.
New Jersey	Follows federal	No	Form NJ-1065 due April 15	Yes	No	Non-resident passive corporate owners of flow-through entities doing business in New Jersey will be subject to the Corporate Business Tax only if they exercise some form of control over the entity.

*Assumes the LLC qualifies as a partnership in those states that follow federal and LLC is filing on a calendar year basis.

State	State Income Tax Classification of LLC	Entity Level Tax on LLC	Tax Form and Filing Date*	Composite Filing Available	Annual Report Required	Other Tax Information
New Mexico	Follows federal	No	No tax return required	Yes	No	New Mexico now requires pass through entities to file an annual informational return with the State Taxation and Revenue Department. The return is due on or before the due date of the entity's federal tax return. The enactment also requires withholding for the owner's share of net income multiplied by a rate set by the department. (Ch. 14 (H. 487), laws 1999)
New York	Follows federal	$50 per member annual fee (fee cannot be less than $325 or more than $10,000)	Form IT-204 and IT-204-LL due April 15	Yes	No	Net income earned in New York City subject to 4% business income tax.
North Carolina	Follows federal	No	Form D-403 due April 15	Yes	Yes. Due within 60 days following the last day of anniversary month ($200 fee)	Non-resident members (who are individuals) are not required to file a North Carolina individual income tax return if the LLC income is their only North Carolina source income and the LLC paid the required tax for non-residents. However, a foreign corporate limited partner (or member) would be subject to the state's income and franchise tax.
North Dakota	Follows federal	No	Form 58 due April 15	Yes	Yes. Due Nov 15 ($50 fee)	

*Assumes the LLC qualifies as a partnership in those states that follow federal and LLC is filing on a calendar year basis.

State	State Income Tax Classification of LLC	Entity Level Tax on LLC	Tax Form and Filing Date*	Composite Filing Available	Annual Report Required	Other Tax Information
Ohio	Follows federal	5% withholding tax for nonresidents	Form IT-4708 due April 15	Yes	No	LLC may be subject to city taxes for income earned in Cincinnati, Cleveland or Columbus.
Oklahoma	Follows federal	No	Form 514 due April 15	Yes	Yes for foreign LLCs only; Due July 1 ($100 fee)	
Oregon	Follows federal	No	Form 65 due April 15	Yes	Yes. Due by anniversary date	LLC subject to 1.45% business income tax for income earned in Multnomah County. LLC subject to 2.2% license fee ($100 minimum) for income earned in the City of Portland. A foreign corporate limited partner is liable for paying the income tax on its share of the limited partnership's income.
Pennsylvania	Follows federal (Act 97-7, eff. 1/1/98)	Until 1/1/98, state taxed LLCs as corporations except for "restricted professional companies"; RPC pays withholding tax on member's distributive share of PA income at highest state rate ($300/PA member annual fee)	Form PA-54 due April 15 (partnership); Form RCT-101 due April 15 (corporation)	Yes	Yes	Effective January 1, 1998, the Pennsylvania Corporate Income Tax does not apply to LLCs classified as partnerships under the check the box regulations.

*Assumes the LLC qualifies as a partnership in those states that follow federal and LLC is filing on a calendar year basis.

State	State Income Tax Classification of LLC	Entity Level Tax on LLC	Tax Form and Filing Date*	Composite Filing Available	Annual Report Required	Other Tax Information
Rhode Island	Follows federal		Form RI-1065 due April 15	No	Yes. Due between Sept 1 and Nov 1 ($50 fee)	Non-resident members must sign an agreement to file a Rhode Island individual tax return and the LLC must attach these agreements to the LLC tax return. If a nonresident fails to file an income tax return the limited liability company is responsible for paying the tax itself.
South Carolina	Follows federal	5.5% withholding tax for non-residents	Form SC1065 due April 15	Yes	Yes	Withholding is not required if a composite return is filed or non-resident member consents to jurisdiction of South Carolina.
South Dakota	No state income tax	N/A	N/A	N/A		
Tennessee	Follows federal	$50 per member annual fee with $3,000 cap	No tax return required	N/A	Yes. Due 4 months after fiscal year closing ($50 per member; minimum fee of $300 and maximum of $3,000)	
Texas	No state income tax; subject to corporate franchise tax	Greater of .25% of capital or 4.5% of earned surplus	Form 05-144 due May 15	N/A	No	
Utah	Follows federal	No	Form TC-65 due April 15	Yes	Yes. Due during anniversary month	

*Assumes the LLC qualifies as a partnership in those states that follow federal and LLC is filing on a calendar year basis.

State	State Income Tax Classification of LLC	Entity Level Tax on LLC	Tax Form and Filing Date*	Composite Filing Available	Annual Report Required	Other Tax Information
Vermont	Follows federal	Annual $250 entity tax; LLC must make estimated tax payments at highest marginal rate on nonresident member's distributive share	Form 106 due April 15	Yes	Yes due 2-1/2 months after fiscal year ($15 fee for domestic LLC, $100 fee for foreign LLC)	
Virginia	Follows federal	$50 Annual Registration Fee	No tax return required	N/A	No	
Washington	No state income tax	Business and Occupation Tax of .011% to 3.3% of gross income	N/A	N/A	Yes. Due last day of anniversary month ($50 fee)	
West Virginia	Follows federal	4% withholding for non-residents; greater of $50 or .75% business franchise tax on capital accounts	Forms IT-165 and BFT-120 due April 15	No	Yes. Due between January 1 and April 1 ($10 fee)	Non-resident member may consent to the jurisdiction of West Virginia to avoid the required withholding by filing Form NRW-4
Wisconsin	Follows federal	If treated as partnership, subject to temporary surcharge tax of up to $9,800	Form 3 due April 15	Yes	No	
Wyoming	No state income tax	N/A	N/A	N/A	Yes. Due Jan 2 ($50 fee)	

*Assumes the LLC qualifies as a partnership in those states that follow federal and LLC is filing on a calendar year basis.

B-11

Appendix C

Comparison Chart: Regular and S Corporations, LLC, Limited Partnership (LP), General Partnership (GP), and LLP

	C Corp	S Corp	LLC*	LP	GP	LLP
Number of Owners	No restrictions	No more than 75 shareholders	No restrictions, but need at least two members to be considered a partnership for tax purposes	Must have at least one general partner and at least one limited partner and they must be at least two different partners	Must have at least two partners	Must have at least two partners

*Assumes LLC is a partnership for tax purposes.

	C Corp	S Corp	LLC*	LP	GP	LLP
Type of Owners	No restrictions	May not have shareholders other than individuals, certain trusts, estates, and certain exempt organizations (including charitable organizations and qualified retirement trusts). May not include regular corporations, S corporations (except for 100% owned S corporation subsidiaries), or nonresident aliens as shareholders	No restrictions	No restrictions	No restrictions	Professionals (except in a few states)
Classes of Ownership Interests	Permitted	One class only, but can have differences in voting rights	Permitted	Permitted	Permitted	Permitted
Liability of Owners	Limited	Limited	Limited	General partners have joint and several liability; limited partners have limited liability except in unusual circumstances	General partners have joint and several liability	Joint and several liability except generally not liable for malpractice of other partners
Owner Participation in Management	Permitted	Permitted	Permitted	Participation by limited partners generally restricted	Permitted	Permitted

*Assumes LLC is a partnership for tax purposes.

	C Corp	S Corp	LLC*	LP	GP	LLP
Organization Costs	Filing fee	Filing fee	Filing fee	Filing fee	None	Filing fee
Formation Requirements	File articles of incorporation with state; adopt bylaws; initial minutes of organizers or directors	Same as for regular corporation; file S election with IRS	File articles of organization with state; adopt operating agreement	File certificate of limited partnership; adopt partnership agreement	None. Partnership may exist in the absence of any written agreement	None but must register with state
Conduct of Business in Other States	Most states have foreign corporation qualification provisions	Same as for regular corporation	Most states have foreign LLC qualification provisions	Most states have foreign limited partnership qualification provisions	Typically no mechanism for qualification of foreign partnerships	Unclear as to liability; probably determined by state where lawsuit is filed
Name	Must contain "corporation," "limited," "incorporated," "company," or an abbreviation thereof	Same as for regular corporation	Must contain "L.C.," or "LLC" or words Limited Company or Limited Liability Company	Must contain "Limited," "Limited Partnership," "Ltd.," or "L.P."	No requirements	No requirements
Interests Transferable with Full Substitution of Transferee	Yes, subject to agreements among shareholders	Same as for regular corporation	Only if permitted by articles of organization, regulations or operating agreement; possible tax issue if freely transferable	Only if permitted by partnership agreement; possible tax issue if freely transferable	As permitted by partnership agreement	As permitted by partnership agreement
Term	Typically perpetual unless otherwise limited in articles of incorporation	Same as for regular corporation	May not exceed term specified in operating agreement	Typically limited by partnership agreement	Typically limited by partnership agreement	Typically limited by partnership agreement

*Assumes LLC is a partnership for tax purposes.

	C Corp	S Corp	LLC*	LP	GP	LLP
Dissolution on Death, Retirement, Withdrawal, etc., of Owner	No	No	Determined by operating agreement unless state law requires	No for limited partner(s); yes for general partners unless partnership agreement provides otherwise (but possible tax issue)	Yes	Yes
Level of Income Taxes	At corporate and shareholder level	At shareholder level only, except certain items can be taxed at corporate level	At member level only, if structured to be taxed as partnership	At partner level only	At partner level	At partner level
Special Allocations of Tax Items	Permitted if provided as stock classes	Pro rata according to stock ownership	Permitted	Permitted	Permitted	Permitted
Contributions on Formation	Taxable, unless transferors meet 80% control test of § 351 of IRC and adjusted basis of assets exceeds liabilities	Same as regular corporation	Nontaxable unless disguised sale or member is relieved from debt	Nontaxable unless disguised sale or partner is relieved from debt	Same as limited partnership	Same as limited partnership
Deductibility of losses by owners	No, except upon sale/exchange of stock if § 1244 applies	Yes, subject to basis limitations; corporate debt not included in basis but shareholder debt to corporation is included	Yes, subject to basis limitations; LLC debt included in basis if taxed as partnership	Same as LLC	Same as limited partnership	Same as limited partnership
At-Risk Limitations	Applicable, if closely held or PSC	Applicable	Applicable	Applicable	Applicable	Applicable

*Assumes LLC is a partnership for tax purposes.

	C Corp	S Corp	LLC*	LP	GP	LLP
Passive Activity Limitations	Applicable, if closely held or PSC	Applicable	Applicable	Applicable	Applicable	Applicable
Distributions	Taxable to extent of earnings and profits	Nontaxable to extent of shareholder's tax basis in stock or debt	Nontaxable to extent of member's tax basis in LLC interest	Nontaxable to extent of partner's tax basis in partnership interest	Nontaxable to extent of partner's tax basis in partnership interest	Nontaxable to extent of partner's tax basis in partnership interest
Liquidation	Taxable to both corporation and shareholders	Taxable at shareholder level via flow-through of corporate items	Nontaxable to extent of member's tax basis in LLC interest	Nontaxable to extent of partner's tax basis in partnership interest	Nontaxable to extent of partner's tax basis in partnership interest	Nontaxable to extent of partner's tax basis in partnership interest
"Employee" Fringe Benefits for Owners	Permitted	Not permitted if 2% shareholder	Not permitted	Not permitted	Not permitted	Not permitted
Medicare Tax on Retirement Plan for Owners' Contributions	No	No	Yes	Yes	Yes	Yes

*Assumes LLC is a partnership for tax purposes.

C-5

Appendix D

Limited Liability Company Checklist

ARTICLES OF ORGANIZATION

1. State of Organization: _____

2. Name of Limited Liability Company: _____

   _____

   Phone call clearance from Secretary of State

   Date: _____

3. Name of Organizer(s) — persons who will sign Articles of Organization: _____

   _____

4. Period of Duration: _____ Years
                        OR
                        will remain in existence until _____

5. Purpose and Type of Business: _____

   _____

   _____

   Indicate specific business purpose in Articles?

   _____ Yes

OR

_____ No — use general language.

6. Name & Address of Registered Agent and Office:

Name: _____

Street and City: _____

State: _____ Zip: _____-_____

Telephone: (____) _____ Fax: (____) _____

7. Names and Addresses of Initial Members:

_____

_____

_____

8. May new members be admitted to the LLC? Yes _____ No _____

   If yes, what are the terms and conditions of the admission?

   _____

   OR

   _____ upon the unanimous consent of all members

9. Termination of Existence, upon the death, insanity, retirement, resignation, expulsion, bankruptcy, or dissolution of a member, or upon the occurrence of any other event which terminates the continued membership of a member in the LLC, unless the business of the LLC is continued by the consent of:

   _____ at least a majority in interest

   OR

   _____ all the remaining members

10. Taxation as: _____ Partnership _____ Corporation

11. Date that the existence of the LLC shall commence:

   _____(usually the date of filing the articles of organization)

INFORMATION FOR OPERATING AGREEMENT AND ORGANIZATIONAL MINUTES

OPERATING AGREEMENT

1. Address and Telephone Number of *PRINCIPAL* OFFICE of LLC, if different from registered office:

   Street and City: _____

   State: _____ County: _____ Zip: _____-_____

   Telephone Number: (____) _____

2. Will LLC have Manager(s)? _____ Yes _____ No

   (If No Manager(s), skip to Item 3)

   If Yes, Number of Managers:

   _____ no less than _____ nor more than _____

   OR

   _____ initial number of Managers: _____

   OR

   _____ One Manager

   Name of Manager(s): _____

   _____ Manager need NOT be resident of state

   _____ (OPTION) Manager need NOT be a Member or Affiliate of Member

   _____ (OPTION) Remove Manager for Cause, on:

   _____ (STANDARD OPTION) Majority Vote;

   OR

   _____ 2/3 Vote;

   OR

   _____ 75% Vote

   _____ Manager Action by Majority Vote

OR

____ Manager Action by Majority of Quorum

____ (OPTION) Manager may not usurp business opportunity of LLC

____ (OPTION) Business Ventures—Manager may have conflict of interest—Indicate one:

    ____ OK but may not compete with LLC

    OR

    ____ OK and may compete with LLC

3. Member Action:

    ____ (STANDARD OPTION) Member Majority Vote

    OR

    ____ Vote of Majority of Quorum

    ____ Veto power by Name: _____

    Secondary person having veto power: _____

    ____ 2/3 Vote required for:

        ____ Sale of substantially all assets

        ____ Merger or consolidation

4. May Member Have Conflict of Interest with LLC?

    ____ Yes ____ No

    If yes: Indicate one:

    ____ OK but may not compete with LLC

    OR

    ____ OK and may compete with LLC

5. ____ Transactions with Affiliates—LLC may have transactions with Members or Affiliates of Members

6. Member Vote for Removal of Officers (or Manager(s), if any):

    ____ Member Majority Vote—Unanimous

OR

_____ Majority of Quorum

OR

_____ 2/3 Vote

7. Names and Addresses of Initial Members (see same under Articles of Organization); Number and Percentage of Units.

   a. The initial Capital Contributions to be made at time of organization (may be property, services, cash (include description/agreed value of property if other than cash)):

Name and Address	Amount/ No. Units	% Owned
_____	_____	_____
_____		
_____	_____	_____
_____		
_____	_____	_____
_____		

   b. May any additional contributions be required to be made by any members? Yes _____ No _____

   If yes, at what times and upon what events shall they be made?

   _____

   _____

   c. Each Initial Member has made a Capital Contribution for Initial Units of (mark one):

   _____ $1.00;

   _____ cash and other property reflected on the LLC's books;

   _____ their interest in certain land and cash contributions reflected in the LLC's books;

   _____ other: _____

8. ____ (NONSTANDARD OPTION) Units granted in connection w/separate Financing Agreement

9. Additional Capital

____ Short form language (additional contributions as required for operation of LLC)

OR

____ Long form language (includes remedies for default)

10. Additional Members

____ Preemptive rights of members to acquire additional interest to maintain % ownership.

11. Capital Accounts

____ Short form (general)

OR

____ Long form (detailed)

12. Allocation of Net Profits & Losses:

____ On liquidation; and/or

____ Upon other significant capital event

13. ____ (NONSTANDARD OPTION) Special Rules Regarding Contributed and Distributed Property = Capital Accounts adjusted and Income and Loss allocated for variation between adjusted tax basis of a Property and its initial Book Value.

14. Annual Meeting Date and Time: _____

15. Quorum: ____ Majority = quorum

____ 50.1% or greater = quorum

16. Tax Elections

Name Tax Matters Member: _____

____ (OPTION) The parties agree that the LLC shall make Section 734, 743 and 754 elections under the 1986 Code, as amended, at the request of any Member.

17. ____ (OPTION) Group State Tax Returns — LLC to file

18. Buy-Sell Provision—Transfer of Interest must be approved by vote of non-transferring Members:

    ____ Majority;

OR

    ____ All;

OR

    ____ 2/3 Vote

19. Substitute Members—persons to whom Interests transferred may not become Substitute Members except on vote of Members:

    ____ Unanimous;

OR

    ____ Majority;

OR

    ____ 2/3 Vote

20. Dissolution (must agree with Articles) upon certain events, unless continued by consent of:

    ____ Majority in Interest;

OR

    ____ All remaining members
    (must be at least two remaining members)

    OR

    ____ 2/3 Vote

21. Amendment of Operating Agreement:

    ____ Unanimous Vote of Members

OR

    ____ 2/3 Vote

OR

    ____ Majority in Interest

22. Remedies:

   _____ (OPTION) Attorneys Fees Assessed in Favor of Prevailing Party

   _____ (OPTION) Specific Performance

23. _____ (OPTION) Waiver of Jury Trial

24. _____ (OPTION) Power of Attorney to: _____ to act for Members

25. May the remaining members of the LLC continue the business on the death, retirement, resignation, expulsion, bankruptcy or dissolution of a member or the occurrence of any other event which terminates continued membership of a member in the LLC?

   _____ No

OR

   _____ Yes
      (must be at least two remaining members)

26. Voting by Members (except as specified above):

   _____ Vote of majority present at meeting

OR

   _____ Vote of majority present IF 51% of members present

   _____ (OPTION) 2/3 Vote required for:

      _____ Sale of substantially all assets

      _____ Merger or consolidation

27. Officers (May have none, any or all of the following — Standard is to have Secretary and Treasurer only) mark & give names:

   _____ INCLUDE all officer descriptions for possible future use, even if not going to elect all

OR

   _____ INCLUDE ONLY following descriptions:

*INDICATE NAME OF INITIAL PERSON HOLDING EACH EXISTING OFFICE

____ (STANDARD) Secretary: _____ *

____ (STANDARD) Treasurer: _____ *

____ (OPTIONAL) Chairman: _____ *

____ (OPTIONAL) Vice-Chairman: _____ *

____ (OPTIONAL) Chief Executive Officer: _____ *

____ (OPTIONAL) Chief Financial Officer: _____ *

____ (OPTIONAL) Assistant Secretary: _____ *

____ (OPTIONAL) Assistant Treasurer: _____ *

____ (OPTIONAL) Founders (2) — no rights, duties or authority but invited to meetings to provide advice, etc.:

28. Will there be any restrictions on transferability of a member's interest? ____ Yes ____ No

   If yes, what are they? _____

   _____

   _____

   _____

29. Tax year (generally should be December 31 unless the majority of the members of the LLC have other fiscal years):

   _____ Calendar Year

   OR

   _____ Fiscal Year: (beg) _____ and (end) _____

30. How may the operating agreement be amended?

   _____ By the managers

   OR

   _____ By the members
   If by members, percentage vote required to so amend:

   ____ Unanimous consent

   OR

   ____ % voting interest

31. BANK WITH WHICH LLC WILL HAVE CHECKING ACCOUNT:

   Bank: _____

   Address: _____

   WHO MAY SIGN CHECKS. (If more than one signature is required, indicate specifics.)

   Names: _____

   Specifics: _____

   If LLC wants BORROWING POWER from the above bank, designate officers authorized to borrow (if more than one signature is required, indicate specifics).

   Names: _____

   Specifics: _____

   Name of any additional bank from which borrowings may be made:

   _____

32. Are you converting a Partnership to an LLC? Yes _____ No _____

33. Tax Numbers: Do you want us to prepare applications for?

   *Federal I.D. # (SS-4) _____ Yes _____ No, accountant will do

   *State tax application? _____ Yes _____ No, accountant will do

   NOTE: A partnership forming an LLC may keep its partnership Federal I.D. number and, if applicable, state tax numbers.

34. How many employees will the LLC have? _____

35. Will LLC be doing business in any state other than the state of organization? _____Yes _____ No

   If yes, name State(s): _____

36. Members' Buy/Sell Agreement to be prepared?

   _____Yes _____ No

Appendix E

Articles of Organization

ARTICLES OF ORGANIZATION OF (NAME)

The undersigned, for the purpose of forming a limited liability company under the [STATE] Limited Liability Company Act (the "Act"), does hereby make, acknowledge and file the following Articles of Organization:

ARTICLE I
Name

The name of the limited liability company shall be [NAME OF COMPANY], (the "Company").

ARTICLE II
Duration

The Company shall commence its existence on the date these Articles of Organization are filed by the [STATE] Secretary of State. The Company's existence [shall be perpetual] or [shall terminate _____ years after its commencement, unless the Company is earlier dissolved as provided in these Articles of Organization, the Operating Agreement, or under the Act].

ARTICLE III

Purposes and Powers

The general purpose for which the Company is organized is to transact any lawful business for which a limited liability company may be organized under the laws of the State of [STATE], and the Company shall have all the powers granted to a limited liability company under the laws of the State of [STATE]. [OPTIONAL: Specify the specific purpose of the limited liability company to limit the scope of activities for which LLC assets can be expended. Check the appropriate state statutes to determine if a limited liability company is allowed to be organized for that purpose.]

ARTICLE IV

Registered Office and Agent

The name and street address of the registered agent and the registered office of the Company in the State of [STATE] is _____, _____.

ARTICLE V

Capital Contributions

The members of the Company shall contribute to the capital of the Company in the amounts agreed by the members.

ARTICLE VI

Members; Admission of New Members

The names and addresses of the members of the Company are as follows:

[Names and Addresses]

No additional members shall be admitted to the Company except with the written consent of all [OPTIONAL: two-thirds in interest] [OPTIONAL: a majority in interest] the members of the Company and upon such terms and conditions as shall be determined by all the members. A member may transfer his or her interest in the Company as set forth in the Operating Agreement

of the Company, but the transferee shall have no right to participate in the management of the business and affairs of the Company or become a member unless the transferee is approved to
be a member.

ARTICLE VII
Termination of Existence

The Company shall be dissolved upon [STANDARD: the greater
of a Member Majority Vote or a Majority in Interest (as those terms
are defined in the Operating Agreement)] **OR** [OPTIONAL: Member
Two-Thirds Vote] **OR** [OPTIONAL: all] the remaining members.

ARTICLE VIII
Management

[OPTION 1: If Managed by Members]

The Company shall be managed by its members, who shall be
entitled to vote in person or by proxy, in accordance with the
Operating Agreement adopted by the members, which may contain provisions not inconsistent with the laws of this state or
these Articles. Each member shall have a number of votes (including fractions) equal to such member's Units in the Company,
with the total number of votes of all members totalling One Hundred (100).

[OPTION 2: If Managed by Manager(s)]

The Company shall be managed by its designated manager or
managers, who shall be elected by the majority vote of the members.
For all elections of manager(s), each member shall be entitled to vote
in person or by proxy, in accordance with the Operating Agreement
adopted by the members, which may contain provisions not inconsistent with the laws of this state or these Articles. Each member
shall have a number of votes (including fractions) equal to such
member's Units in the Company, with the total number of votes of
all members totalling One Hundred (100). The name and mailing
address of each person who is to serve as manager until the first
annual meeting of members or until his or her successor is elected
and qualified are:

[NAME(S) AND ADDRESS(ES)]

ARTICLE IX
Organizer

The name and address of the organizer is:

[NAME AND ADDRESS]

IN WITNESS WHEREOF, the undersigned has made and subscribed these Articles of Organization, pursuant to the Act, under penalties of perjury and does hereby declare and certify that the facts stated herein are true, and accordingly has hereunto signed these Articles of Organization as of this ___ day of _____, 199__.

[Check the state statute to determine who must sign the Articles of Organization.]

_____

_____

STATE OF [STATE]   )
) SS:
COUNTY OF_____)

Before me personally appeared [NAME(S)], to me well known to be the organizer[s] of the above Limited Liability Company and who subscribed the above Articles of Organization, and [THEY/HE/SHE] freely and voluntarily acknowledged before me according to law that [THEY/HE/SHE] made the same for the uses and purposes therein mentioned and set forth.

IN WITNESS WHEREOF, I have hereunto set my hand and affixed my official seal this ____day of_____, 199__.

_____

Notary Public, State of [STATE]

My commission expires:_____

Appendix F

Member-Managed LLC Operating Agreement

OPERATING AGREEMENT
OF
[NAME LLC]
A [STATE] LIMITED LIABILITY COMPANY
Managed by Its Members

[**Note.** This Model Operating Agreement should be used only as a guide as many provisions might not apply or should be redrafted to apply to a particular state law or limited liability company design.]

TABLE OF CONTENTS

INTRODUCTION

The person signing the Articles of Organization has acted as organizer to form a [NAME LLC] (the "Company"), a limited liability company under the laws of the State of [State] on behalf of the Members named below and any Additional Member. The Company's business shall be conducted under such name until such time as the Members shall hereafter designate otherwise and file amendments to the Articles in accordance with applicable law. The parties hereto agree to the provisions hereof in order to define their rights, liabilities, restrictions and limitations with respect to the Company.

* * * * * *

ARTICLE I
DEFINITIONS

The following terms used in this Operating Agreement shall have the following meanings (unless otherwise expressly provided herein):

(a) *"Act"* shall mean the Limited Liability Company Act of the State of [State] and all amendments thereto.

(b) *"Additional Member"* shall mean any Person or Entity who or that is admitted to the Company as an Additional Member pursuant to this Operating Agreement.

(c) *"Affiliate"* shall mean a lineal descendant, ascendant or spouse of a Member and any Entity in which the Member of a lineal descendant, ascendant or spouse of a Member has a direct or indirect beneficial ownership interest.

(d) *"Articles"* shall mean the Articles of Organization, or such other documents as are filed with the Secretary of State under the Act, as amended from time to time.

(e) *"Book Value"* shall mean the net book value as calculated on a cash basis for Federal income tax purposes, of the net assets (which shall be the amount of cash, and for other assets, the original cost, less depreciation, less liabilities) of the Company as of the end of the calendar month during which a Member withdraws from the Company, multiplied by the Percentage of Units owned by that Member. The definition of Book Value shall not include any value representing goodwill, except goodwill purchased by the Company.

(f) *"Capital Account"* shall mean the individual account maintained for each Member as provided hereafter.

(g) *"Capital Contribution"* shall mean any contribution to the capital of the Company in cash, property, services, or the obligation to contribute cash, property or services by a Member whenever made.

(h) *"Code"* shall mean the Internal Revenue Code of 1986, as amended from time to time.

(i) *"Company"* shall mean this Limited Liability Company.

(j) *"Deficit Capital Account"* shall mean with respect to any Member, the deficit balance, if any, in such Member's Capital Account as of the end of the taxable year, after giving effect to the following adjustments:

  (1) credit to such Capital Account any amount which Member is obligated to restore under Section 1.704-1(b)(2)(ii)(c) of the Treasury Regulations, as well as any addition thereto pursuant to the next to last sentence of Sections 1.704-1(b)(4)(iv)(f) and (h)(5) of the Treasury Regulations, after taking into account thereunder any changes during such year in the Company's Minimum Gain and in the Member Nonrecourse Debt Minimum Gain attributable to any Member nonrecourse debt; and

  (2) debit to such Capital Account the items described in Sections 1.704-1(b)(2)(ii)(d)(4), (5) and (6) of the Treasury Regulations.

(k) *"Dissolution"* shall occur on any event provided herein.

(l) *"Distributable Cash"* shall mean all cash, revenues and funds received by the Company from Company operations, less the sum of the following to the extent paid or set aside by the Company: (i) all principal and interest payments on indebtedness of the Company and all other sums paid to lenders; (ii) all cash expenditures incurred incident to the normal operation of the Company's business; (iii) such cash reserves as the Members deem reasonably necessary to the proper operation of the Company's business.

(m) *"Effective Date"* shall be the date the Company is first effective under the Act, as may be further provided in the Articles.

(n) *"Entity"* shall mean any general partnership, limited partnership, limited liability partnership, limited liability company, corporation, joint venture, trust, business trust, cooperative or association.

(o) *"Initial Members"* shall mean those Members named hereafter.

(p) *"Initial Units"* shall mean those Units owned by the Initial Members.

(q) *"Majority in Interest"* shall mean those Members (other than a Member who has suffered a dissolution event or is seeking approval for a Transfer) owning a majority of the profits interest and a majority of the capital interest in the Company at the time the approval of which is required under this Operating Agreement. [Leave in for Rev. Proc. 95-10 even if use Member Two-Thirds Vote]

(r) *"Member"* shall mean the Initial Members, Persons or Entities becoming Members hereunder, including Additional Members and Substitute Members, but shall not include transferees or assignees unless they become Members.

(s) *"Member Majority Vote"* shall mean an affirmative vote by Members holding at least a majority of all outstanding Units that are present, in person or by proxy, at a duly-called meeting where a Quorum is present.

[OPTIONAL]

(t) *"Member Two-Thirds Vote"* shall mean an affirmative vote by Members holding at least two-thirds of all outstanding Units that are present, in person or by proxy, at a duly-called meeting where a Quorum is present.

(u) *"Member Nonrecourse Debt Minimum Gain"* shall have the meaning set forth in Treasury Regulations Section 1.704-2(i)(3).

(v) *"Minimum Gain"* shall have the meaning set forth in Treasury Regulations Section 1.704-2(d).

(w) *"Net Profits"* shall mean, for each Year, the income and gains of the Company determined in accordance with accounting principles consistently applied from year to year under the method of accounting and as reported, separately or in the aggregate, as appropriate, on the Company's information tax return filed for Federal income tax purposes, plus any income described in Section 705(a)(1)(B) of the Code and any income exempt from tax.

(x) *"Net Losses"* shall mean, for each Year, the losses and deductions of the Company determined in accordance with accounting principles consistently applied from year to year under the method of accounting and as reported, separately or in the aggregate, as appropriate, on the Company's information tax return filed for Federal income tax purposes, plus any expenditures described in Section 705(a)(2)(B) of the Code.

(y) *"Officer(s)"* shall mean those officers of the Company, if any, designated hereafter.

(z) *"Operating Agreement"* shall mean this Operating Agreement, as originally executed and as amended.

(aa) *"Person"* shall mean any individual or entity, and the heirs, executors, administrators, legal representatives, successors, and assigns of such *"Person,"* where applicable.

(ab) *"Quorum"* shall mean the presence in person, or by proxy, or by telephone conference, of the Members holding at least fifty and one-tenth percent (50.1%) or more of the outstanding Units.

(ac) *"Substitute Member"* shall mean any Person or Entity who or which is admitted to the Company as a Substitute Member as provided hereafter.

(ad) *"Transfer(s)"* shall mean (i) when used as a verb, to give, gift, sell, exchange, assign, redeem, transfer, pledge, hypothecate, encumber, bequeath, devise or otherwise dispose of and (ii) when used as a noun, the nouns corresponding to such verbs, in either case voluntarily or involuntarily, by operation of law or otherwise.

(ae) *"Transferee"* shall mean a person or entity to which the economic rights and benefits of a Member's Interest has been transferred but where such person or entity has not been made a Substitute Member.

(af) *"Units"* shall mean the ownership interests held by Members in the Company.

(ag) *"Year"* shall mean the Company's fiscal year for income tax purposes as determined pursuant to Section 706 of the Code.

ARTICLE II
OFFICES

2.1 *Principal Office.* The principal office for the transaction of the business of the Company is hereby located at [full address].

2.2 *Registered Office.* The registered office and resident agent shall be as identified in the Company's Articles. The Company may change the location of its registered office and/or the identity of its resident agent. Upon making such a change, a certificate certifying the change shall be executed, acknowledged and filed with the Secretary of State.

2.3 *Other Offices.* Branch or subordinate offices may at any time be established by the Company at any place or places where the Company is qualified to do business.

ARTICLE III
PERMITTED BUSINESSES OF COMPANY

The business of the Company shall be as stated in the Articles unless otherwise determined by the Members by unanimous consent, in which case the Articles must be amended. In addition the Company is permitted:

(a) To exercise all other powers necessary to or reasonably connected with the Company's business which may be legally exercised by limited liability companies under the Act.

(b) To engage in all activities necessary, customary, convenient, or incident to any of the foregoing.

ARTICLE IV
MANAGEMENT AND OFFICERS

4.1 *Management.* The business and affairs of the Company shall be managed by the Members. The Members shall direct, manage and control the business of the Company to the best of their ability and shall have full and complete authority, power and discretion to make any and all decisions and to do any and all things which the Members shall deem to be reasonably required in light of the Company's business and objectives.

4.2 *Certain Powers of Members.* Without limiting the generality of the previous sections of this Operating Agreement, the Members shall have power and authority, on behalf of the Company:

(a) To purchase, hold, improve, lease or make any other acquisition, own use and otherwise deal with real and/or tangible and intangible personal properties from any Person or Entity as the Members may determine, in the name of the Company or a nominee;

(b) To sell, convey, mortgage, pledge, lease, exchange, and otherwise dispose of real and/or tangible and intangible personal properties from any Person or Entity as the Members may determine;

(c) To borrow money for the Company from banks, other lending institutions, the Members, Affiliates of the Members, and other persons or entities on such terms as they deem appropriate, and in connection therewith, issue evidence of indebtedness to hypothecate, encumber and grant security interests in the assets of the Company to secure repayment of the borrowed sums; and to assume or refinance existing indebtedness;

(d) To purchase liability and other insurance to protect the Company, and its Members' property and business;

(e) To invest any Company funds (by way of example and not by limitation) in time deposits, short-term governmental obligations, commercial paper or other investments;

(f) To open bank accounts in the name of the Company, and to determine the signatories thereon;

(g) To execute, negotiate and deliver, on behalf of the Company, or delegate to the Officers to execute, all instruments and documents, including, without limitation, contracts, checks, drafts, notes and other negotiable instruments, mortgages or deeds of trust, security agreements, financing statements, deeds, bills of sale or other documents providing for the acquisition, mortgage or disposition of the Company's property, assignments, leases, partnership agreements, and any other instruments or documents necessary or appropriate, to the business of the Company;

(h) To employ accountants, legal counsel, managing agents, managing Members, or others to perform services for the Company and to compensate them from Company funds;

(i) To enter into other agreements on behalf of the Company, with any other Person or Entity for any purpose, in such forms as the Members may approve;

(j) To execute and file any bankruptcy petition, on behalf of the Company, pursuant to applicable Federal laws; and

(k) To do and perform all other acts as may be necessary or appropriate to the conduct of the Company's business, including but not limited to establishment of funds or reserves, prepay, recast, increase, modify, extend or otherwise amend existing debt, commitments, contracts or other obligations in whole or in part.

Unless authorized to do so by this Operating Agreement or by the Members, no Member, agent, or employee of the Company shall have any power or authority to bind the Company in any way, to pledge its credit or to render it liable pecuniarily for any purpose.

4.3 *Action by Members.* Only the decisions and actions of a Member on behalf of the Company within the scope of the Member's authority shall bind the Company. Except as otherwise specifically provided herein or by the Act, all actions and decisions of the Members shall require a Member Majority Vote [OPTIONAL: Member Two-Thirds Vote] **OR** [OPTIONAL: unanimous vote of all Members]. The Members may make any decision or take any action at a meeting, by conference telephone call, by written consent, by oral agreement or any other method they elect; provided that, at the request of any Member with respect to a decision or action, such decision or action must be made or taken by written consent signed by the number of Members required to approve such decision or action. [OPTIONAL: A Member Two-Thirds Vote of Units that are present, in person or by proxy, at a duly-called meeting where a Quorum is present, shall be required for the following:

(a) To sell or otherwise dispose of all or substantially all of the assets of the Company as part of a single transaction or plan so long as such disposition is not in violation of or a cause of a default under any other agreement to which the Company may be bound; and

(b) Merger or consolidation of the Company with another Entity or Entities.]

4.4 *Amendment.* Any amendment of this Operating Agreement requires the written action of a [OPTION 1: Member Majority Vote] **OR** [OPTION 2: Member Two-Thirds Vote] **OR** [OPTION 3: unanimous vote of all Members].

4.5 *Member Has No Exclusive Duty to Company.* No Member shall be required to manage the Company as his or her sole and exclusive function. Each Member shall devote reasonable time and effort to management duties, *if any.*

[STANDARD]

4.6 *Other Business Ventures of Member.* Any Member or Affiliate of a Member may engage independently or with others in other business ventures of every nature and description, except as provided hereafter. As a general matter, neither the Company nor any Member shall have any right by virtue of this Operating Agreement or the relationship created hereby in or to any other ventures or activities in which any Member or Affiliate of a Member is involved or to the income or proceeds derived therefrom.

[OPTION 1: However, no Member or Affiliate shall take advantage of a business opportunity, unless the Company elects to forego same, nor shall any Member own, manage, consult with, or be employed by any venture or entity that competes with the Company's business.]

[OPTION 2: The pursuit of business and investments by Members or Affiliates of a Member, even if directly competitive with the Company's business, is hereby consented to by the Members and shall not be deemed wrongful or improper.]

[OPTIONAL]

4.7 *Transactions with Affiliates.* Each Member shall disclose any and all direct or indirect affiliation or interest in any entity with which the Company does business or proposes to do business. The

Company may enter into agreements with one or more Members or Affiliates of a Member to provide leasing, management, legal, accounting, architectural, development, or other services to the Company, provided that any such services shall be at rates at least as favorable to the Company as those available from unaffiliated parties. The validity of any transaction, agreement or payment involving the Company and any Member or Affiliate of a Member otherwise permitted hereunder shall not be affected by reason of the relationship between such Person and the Company or any of its Members.

[OPTIONAL]

4.8 *Indemnity of Members and Officers.* The Company shall indemnify and hold harmless each Member and/or Officer from and against any and all claims or liabilities of any nature whatsoever arising out of or resulting from any such act or omission in connection with the Company, including, without limitation, reasonable costs and expenses of litigation and appeal (including reasonable fees and expenses of attorneys engaged by a Member and/or Officer in defense of such act or omission), but these Persons shall not be entitled to be indemnified or held harmless due to, or arising from, their gross negligence or willful misconduct.

4.9 *Resignation.* Any Officer of the Company may resign at any time by giving written notice to the other Members of the Company. The resignation of any Officer shall take effect upon receipt of notice thereof or at such later time as shall be specified in such notice (but not before the notice is mailed, delivered, or sent by facsimile transmission (fax, etc.)); and, unless otherwise specified therein, the acceptance of such resignation shall not be necessary to make it effective.

4.10 *Removal of Officers.* At a meeting called expressly for that purpose, all or any lesser number of Officers may be removed at any time, with or without cause, by a Member Majority Vote.

4.11 *Salaries.* Members shall not initially receive compensation for their services as such, but the Members may authorize the reimbursement of expenses, including expenses incurred to attend meetings of the Members; provided, that nothing herein contained shall be construed to preclude the Company from establishing compensation for Members as such, and provided further that nothing herein contained shall preclude any Member from receiving compensation for services to the Company in any other capacity.

4.12 *Election of Officers.* The Members may designate as Officers any or all of the following: a Chairman, Vice Chairman, Chief Executive Officer, Chief Operating Officer (who may also have the title of President), Chief Financial Officer, Secretary and Treasurer at the first meeting of the Members, to serve such terms as the Members determine. Each such Officer shall hold office until he or she shall resign, shall be removed or is otherwise disqualified to serve, or his or her successor shall be elected and qualified. The Company may also have, at the discretion of the Members, one or more vice presidents, founders, assistant secretaries, assistant treasurers or other Officers. Any number of offices may be held by the same person. The duties of such Officers shall be as follows:

(a) *The Chairman.* The Chairman shall be a non-executive chairman. He or she shall preside at meetings of the Members and shall perform such other duties as may be assigned to him or her by this Operating Agreement or the Members. In the absence of the Chairman, the Vice-Chairman shall have and may exercise all of the powers of the Chairman.

(b) *The Vice-Chairman.* The Vice-Chairman shall perform the duties of the Chairman when the Chairman is unavailable.

(c) *Chief Executive Officer.* Subject to the direction and under the supervision of the Members, the Chief Executive Officer shall generally direct the policy and management of the Company and shall have general charge of the business, affairs and property of the Company and control over its Officers, agents and employees; and shall do and perform such other duties and may exercise such other powers as from time to time may be assigned to him or her by this Operating Agreement or by the Members.

(d) *Chief Operating Officer.* The Chief Operating Officer shall perform such duties as are customary for such office subject to the direction of the Members and the Chief Executive Officer.

(e) *Chief Financial Officer.* The Chief Financial Officer shall perform such duties as are customary for such office subject to the direction of the Members and the Chief Executive Officer.

(f) *Secretary.* The Secretary shall keep, or cause to be kept, a book of minutes at the principal office or such other place as the Members may order, of all meetings of Members, with the time and place of holding, whether regular or special, and if special, how authorized, the notice thereof given, the names of those present at Members' meetings, and the proceedings thereof. The Secretary shall have such other powers and perform such other duties as may be prescribed by the Members or this Operating Agreement. The Secretary may seek assistance for these duties as to the annual minutes from the Company's attorneys.

(g) *Treasurer.* The Treasurer shall keep and maintain or cause to be kept and maintained, accounts of the properties and business transactions of the Company, including accounts of its assets, liabilities, receipts, disbursements, gains, losses, and capital, to the extent agreed by the Members. The Treasurer shall deposit all monies and other valuables in the name and to the credit of the Company with such depositories as may be designated by the Members. He or she shall disburse the funds of the Company as may be ordered by the Members, shall render to the Members upon request an account of all of the transactions as Treasurer and of the financial condition of the Company, and shall have such other powers and perform such other duties as may be prescribed by the Members or this Operating Agreement. He or she shall be bonded, if required by the Members.

(h) *The Assistant Secretary and Assistant Treasurer.* The Assistant Secretary and Assistant Treasurer (or in the event there be more than one Assistant Secretary or Assistant Treasurer, in the order of their seniority, designation or election) shall, in the absence of or disability of the Secretary or Treasurer, respectively, perform the duties and exercise the powers of the Secretary or Treasurer and shall perform such other duties as may be prescribed by the Members or this Operating Agreement.

(i) *Founders.* The Members may recognize and appoint two individuals as Founders of the Company. The Founders shall have no rights, duties or authorities as a result of their position as Founder, but shall be invited to all meetings of the Officers and/or Members to provide such advice and counsel to the Company as the Members deem appropriate.

4.13 *Business Expenses of Members.* From time to time, a Member will be required to incur certain expenses related to the trade or business of the Company for which the Company will not reimburse that Member. These expenses include, but are not limited to: [OPTIONAL: (1) use of the Member's personal automobile for Company business; (2) meals and entertainment of persons who are clients or prospective clients of the Company; (3) professional dues, licenses, publications, etc. . . . , for the Member related to the Company's business; (4) use of a Member's personal computer (including software purchased for business purposes) or other office equipment on behalf of the Company; (5) conventions; (6) charitable contributions; and (7) club dues.]

Each Member is accountable to the Company for substantiating expenses incurred by such Member and reimbursed by the Company. Such expenses must be either actually substantiated to the Company or must be deemed substantiated pursuant to the Internal Revenue Service per diem arrangements. The Member shall include in the expense request for reimbursement the time, place, date, business purpose and other individuals involved, as well as a brief description of the specific business being transacted or discussed. In the event that any reimbursement from the Company, whether paid before or after the expense is incurred, cannot be substantiated and documented by the Member, the unsubstantiated amounts (except IRS approved per diem arrangements) must be returned by the Member to the Company.

ARTICLE V
CAPITAL CONTRIBUTIONS; RIGHTS AND MEETINGS OF MEMBERS

5.1 *Initial Members*. The Initial Members [their addresses,] the value of their Capital Contribution and the number of Units each owns ("Initial Units") are as follows:

Name of Member	Value of Capital Contribution	No. of Units
[————————]	[————]	[——]%
[————————]	[————]	[——]%

[OPTIONAL—SHORT FORM ADDITIONAL CAPITAL]

5.2 *Additional Capital*. The Members acknowledge that the Company may require from time to time funds, in addition to funds available from the operation of the Company's business with which to operate the Company, including the payment of taxes, insurance, debt service and other operating expenses of the Company. The Members may from time to time contribute in cash or in kind to the capital of the Company such additional funds as are required for the purposes set forth above, or for any other purpose relating to the Company business, in amounts in proportion to their respective Units, if they agree, but no Member shall be required to do so.

[OPTIONAL—LONG FORM ADDITIONAL CAPITAL]

5.2 *Additional Capital Contribution May Be Required.*

(a) The Members acknowledge that the Company may require from time to time funds, in addition to funds available from the operation of the Company with which to own and operate the Company, including the maintenance and renovation of the Company's property and the payment of the taxes, insurance, debt service and other carrying charges and the operating expenses of the Company. The Members shall from time to time contribute cash to the capital of the Company the additional funds as determined pursuant to a Member Majority Vote required for the purposes set forth above, or for any other purpose relating to the business of the Company, in accordance with their respective Units.

(b) If any Member fails or refuses for any reason to contribute the share of the additional cash capital required to be contributed by him or her pursuant to this Operating Agreement within ten (10) days after approved by the Members, then any Member not in default hereunder may (but shall not be required to) rectify that default by contributing all or any part thereof for and on behalf of that defaulting Member, and any amounts so contributed by that Member, together with interest thereon from the date of the advance at the rate of __ percent (__%), shall immediately become due and owing and shall be a debt due by the defaulting Member to the Member so contributing said sum, and the Member so rectifying that default, in whole or in part, shall have (i) a security interest in the defaulting Member's Units to secure the aggregate of said Capital Contribution made by him or her on behalf of the defaulting Member, together with interest thereon as stated above and (ii) the right to enforce such debt and exercise his or her interest in the security as provided in the Uniform Commercial Code. If more than one Member desires to rectify a default as set forth in this Section 5.2(b), those Members shall be entitled to contribute on a pro rata basis in proportion to their Units, excluding the Units of the Member in default and those Members not so contributing to rectification of the default. The exercise by a Member of his or her right to cure a defaulting Member's default as provided above, and the exercise by the Member of the remedies applicable thereto, as set forth in clauses (i) and (ii) of this paragraph, shall be without prejudice to the Member's other rights and remedies.

5.3 *Additional Members*. From time to time the Company may issue additional Units to any Persons and Entities (including to existing Members) for such Capital Contributions and on such terms and conditions as the Members may determine, and such additional Units may have different rights regarding voting, profit and loss allocations and distribution, whether subordinate or preferred, as the Members may determine. Persons or Entities that purchase additional Units pursuant to this Section shall be Additional Members and no consent is needed to issue Units to them or for them to become Additional Members because such consent is hereby given.

5.4 *Preemptive Rights*. Provided, however, issuance of such additional Units shall be subject to the following preemptive rights: A Member shall [OPTIONAL: not] have the right (but not the obligation) to purchase a share of any additional Units so issued to maintain his or her pro rata ownership of all Units of the Company, at the same price, time and terms as for all other Members.

5.5 *Limitation of Liability*. Each Member's liability shall be limited as set forth in the Act. No Member will be personally liable for any debts or losses of the Company beyond his or her respective Capital Contributions, except as otherwise required by the Act or by written signed agreement.

5.6 *Annual Meeting*. The annual meeting of the Members shall be held on the last Friday of December in each year, at 10:00 a.m., or at such other time as shall be determined by the Members, for the purpose of electing the Officers for the upcoming year and the transaction of such business as may come before the meeting. If the day fixed for the annual meeting shall be a legal holiday, such meeting shall be held on the next succeeding business day.

5.7 *Special Meetings.* Special meetings of the Members, for any purpose or purposes, unless otherwise prescribed by statute, may be called by any Officer, or by any Member or Members holding at least twenty percent (20%) of the outstanding Units. Business transacted at a special meeting of Members shall be confined to the purpose or purposes stated in the notice of the meeting.

5.8 *Place of Meetings.* The Members may designate any place in the United States as the place of meeting for any meeting of the Members. If no designation is made, or if a special meeting be otherwise called, the place of meeting shall be held at the Company's principal place of business.

5.9 *Duly Called Meetings.* If all of the Members shall meet at any time and place, and consent to the holding of a meeting at such time and place, such meeting shall be a duly-called meeting without call or notice, and at such meeting lawful action may be taken. Otherwise, written notice stating the place, day and hour of the meeting and the purpose or purposes for which the meeting is called shall be delivered not less than ten (10) nor more than sixty (60) days before the date of the meeting, either personally or by mail, by or at the direction of the person calling the meeting, to each Member. If mailed, such notice shall be deemed to be delivered after being deposited in the United States mail, in a sealed envelope addressed to the Member at his or her address as it appears on the books of the Company, or as given by the Member to the Company for purposes of notice, with postage thereon prepaid. If transmitted by way of facsimile, such notice shall be deemed to be delivered on the date of such facsimile transmission to the facsimile number, if any, for the respective Member which has been supplied by such Member to each other Member and identified as such Member's facsimile number.

5.10 *Record Date.* For the purpose of determining Members entitled to notice of or to vote at any meeting of Members or any adjournment thereof, or Members entitled to receive payment of any distribution, or in order to make a determination of Members for any other purpose, the date on which notice of the meeting is mailed or the date on which the resolution declaring such distribution is adopted, as the case may be, shall be the record date for such determination of Members. When a determination of Members entitled to vote at any meeting of Members has been made as provided in this Section, such determination shall apply to any adjournment thereof.

5.11 *Quorum.* In the absence of a Quorum at any such meeting, a majority of the Units so represented may adjourn the meeting from time to time for a period not to exceed ninety (90) days without further notice. However, if the adjournment is for more than ninety (90) days, or if after the adjournment a new record date is fixed for the adjourned meeting, a notice of the adjourned meeting shall be given to each Member. At such adjourned meeting at which a Quorum shall be present, any business may be transacted which might have been transacted at the meeting as originally noticed. The Members present at a duly-called meeting may continue to transact business until adjournment, notwithstanding the withdrawal during such meeting of Members whose absence would cause less than a Quorum.

5.12 *Proxies.* At all meetings of Members, a Member may vote the Units held by such Member in person or by proxy executed in writing by the Member or by a duly authorized attorney-in-fact. Such proxy shall be filed with the Secretary of the Company before or at the time of the meeting. No proxy shall be valid after three (3) years from the date of its execution, unless otherwise provided in the proxy.

5.13 *Action by Members Without a Meeting.* Action required or permitted to be taken at a meeting of Members may be taken without a meeting if the action is evidenced by one or more written consents describing the action taken, signed by each Member and delivered to the Secretary for inclusion in the minutes or for filing with the Company records. Action taken under this Section is effective when all Members have signed the consent, unless the consent specifies a different effective date.

5.14 *Waiver of Notice.* When any notice is required to be given to any Member, a waiver thereof in writing signed by the Person entitled to such notice, whether before, at, or after the time stated therein, shall be equivalent to the giving of such notice.

5.15 *List of Members.* Upon written request of any Member, the Secretary shall provide a list showing the names, addresses and Units of all Members in the Company.

5.16 *Maintenance of Company Books.* The Treasurer shall maintain and preserve, during the term of the Company, and for six (6) years thereafter, all accounts, books, and other relevant Company documents.

5.17 *Inspection of Company Books.* The Company shall provide Members and their agents and attorneys access to any of its books and records at the principal place of business. The Company shall provide former Members and their agents and attorneys access for proper purposes to books and records pertaining to the period during which they were Members. The right of access provides the opportunity to inspect and copy books and records during ordinary business hours. The Company may impose a reasonable charge, limited to the costs of labor and material, for copies of records furnished.

5.18 *Information to Be Furnished.* The Company shall furnish to a Member, and to the legal representative of a deceased Member or Member under legal disability:

(a) *Without demand,* information concerning the Company's business or affairs reasonably required for the proper exercise of the Member's rights and performance of the Member's duties under this Operating Agreement and the Act; and

(b) *On demand,* other information concerning the Company's business or affairs, except to the extent the demand or the information demanded is unreasonable or otherwise improper under the circumstances.

A Member has the right upon signed request given to the Company to obtain at the Company's expense a copy of the current and any prior Operating Agreements.

ARTICLE VI
ALLOCATIONS, DISTRIBUTIONS, AND REPORTS

6.1 *Capital Accounts.*

[OPTIONAL—SHORT PROVISION]

(a) Throughout the term of the Company, a Capital Account shall be maintained at all times for each Member in accordance with Code Section 704(b) and all regulations thereunder.

[OPTIONAL—LONG PROVISION]

(a) A separate Capital Account will be maintained for each Member. Each Member's Capital Account will be increased by the amount of money contributed (but not loans) by such Member to the Company; the fair market value of property contributed by such Member to the Company (net of liabilities secured by such contributed property that the Company is considered to assume or take subject to under Code Section 752); allocations to such Member of Company income and gain; and allocations to such Member of income described in Code Section 705(a)(1)(B). Each Member's Capital Account will be decreased by the amount of money distributed to such Member by the Company (but not any payment of interest or principal on loans made to the Company); the fair market value of property distributed to such Member by the Company (net of liabilities secured by such distributed property that such Member is considered to assume or take subject to under Code Section 752); allocations to such Member of expenditures described in Code Section 705(a)(2)(B); and allocations to the account of such Member of the Company's losses and deductions as set forth in the Treasury Regulations, taking into account adjustments to reflect Book Value.

(b) In the event of a permitted sale or exchange of a Unit in the Company, the Capital Account of the transferor shall become the Capital Account of the transferee to the extent it relates to the transferred Unit.

(c) The manner in which Capital Accounts are to be maintained pursuant to this Section is intended to comply with the requirements of Code Section 704(b) and the Treasury

Regulations promulgated thereunder. If in the opinion of the Company's accountants the manner in which Capital Accounts are to be maintained pursuant to the preceding provisions of this Section should be modified in order to comply with Code Section 704(b) and the Treasury Regulations thereunder, then notwithstanding anything to the contrary contained in the preceding provisions of this Section, the method in which Capital Accounts are maintained shall be so modified; provided, however, that any change in the manner of maintaining Capital Accounts shall not materially alter the economic agreement between or among the Members.

6.2 *Allocations of Profits and Losses.* The Net Profits and Net Losses of the Company for each fiscal year will be allocated to the Members pro rata by their Units.

[OPTIONAL: Use if special allocations provided in Section 6.2]

Notwithstanding this Section:

(a) No allocations of loss, deduction and/or expenditures described in Code Section 705(a)(2)(B) shall be charged to the Capital Accounts of any Member if such allocation would cause such Member to have a Deficit Capital Account (in excess of any limited dollar amount of such deficit balance that such Member is obligated to restore). The amount of the loss, deduction and/or Code Section 705(a)(2)(B) expenditure which would have caused a Member to have such a Deficit Capital Account shall instead be charged to the Capital Account of any Members which would not have such a Deficit Capital Account as a result of the allocation, in proportion to their Units, or, if no such Members exist, then to the Members in proportion to the number of Units held by such Members.

(b) If any Member unexpectedly receives any adjustments, allocations, or distributions described in Treasury Regulations Section 1.704-1(b)(2)(ii)(d)(4), (5), or (6), which create or increase a Deficit Capital Account of such Member, then items of Company income and gain (consisting of a pro rata portion of each item of Company income, including gross income, and gain for such year and, if necessary, for subsequent years) shall be specially credited to the Capital

Account of such Member in an amount and manner sufficient to eliminate, to the extent required by the Treasury Regulations, the Deficit Capital Account so created as quickly as possible. It is the intent that this Section be interpreted as a Qualified Income Offset to comply with the alternate test for economic effect set forth in Treasury Regulations Section 1.704-1(b)(2)(ii)(d).

(c) If there is a net decrease in Company Minimum Gain for a Year, then there shall be allocated to each Member items of income and gain for that Year equal to that Member's share of the net decrease in Minimum Gain (as determined under Treasury Regulations Section 1.704-2(g)(2)), subject to the exceptions set forth in Treasury Regulations Section 1.704-2(f)(2), (3), and (5), *provided*, that if the Company has any discretion as to an exception set forth pursuant to Treasury Regulations Section 1.704-2(f)(5), the Tax Matters Member may exercise such discretion on behalf of the Company. The Tax Matters Member shall, if the application of the Minimum Gain chargeback requirement would cause a distortion in the economic arrangement among the Members, ask the Commissioner to waive the Minimum Gain chargeback requirement pursuant to Treasury Regulations Section 1.704-2(f)(4). The foregoing is intended to be a "Minimum Gain Chargeback" provision as described in Treasury Regulations Section 1.704-2(f) and shall be interpreted and applied in all respects in accordance with that Regulation.

(d) If during a fiscal year there is a net decrease in Member Nonrecourse Debt Minimum Gain, then, in addition to the amounts, if any, allocated pursuant to the preceding paragraph, any Member with a share of that Member Nonrecourse Debt Minimum Gain (as determined under Treasury Regulations Section 1.704-2(i)(5)) as of the beginning of the fiscal year shall, subject to the exceptions set forth in Treasury Regulations Section 1.704-2(i)(4), be allocated items of income and gain for the year (and, if necessary, for succeeding years) equal to that Member's share of the net decrease in the Member Nonrecourse Debt Minimum Gain. The Tax Matters Member shall, if the application of the Member Nonrecourse Debt Minimum Gain chargeback requirement would cause a distortion in the economic arrangement among the Members, ask the Commissioner to waive the Minimum Gain chargeback requirement pursuant to Treasury Regulations Section 1.704-2(f)(4) and (i)(4). The foregoing is intended to be the "chargeback of Member Nonrecourse Debt Minimum Gain" required by Treasury Regulations Section 1.704-2(i)(4) and shall be interpreted and applied in all respects in accordance with that Regulation.

(e) Notwithstanding anything to the contrary in this Article VI, Company losses, deductions, or Code Section 705(a)(2)(B) expenditures that are attributable to a particular Member nonrecourse liability shall be allocated to the Member that bears the economic risk of loss for the liability in accordance with the rules of Treasury Regulations Section 1.704-2(i).

(f) Beginning in the first taxable year in which there are allocations of "nonrecourse deductions" (as defined in Section 1.704-2(b)(i) of the Treasury Regulations) attributable to nonrecourse liabilities of the Company, and thereafter throughout the full term of the Company, nonrecourse deductions shall be allocated to the Members in accordance with, and as a part of, the allocations of Company profit or loss for such period.

(g) Any credit or charge to the Capital Accounts of the Members shall be taken into account in computing subsequent allocations of profits and losses pursuant to Section 6.1, so that the net amount of any items charged or credited to Capital Accounts shall, to the extent possible, be equal to the net amount that would have been allocated to the Capital Account of each Member pursuant to the provisions of this Article if the special allocations required by this Section had not occurred.

6.3 *Mid-Year Allocations.* When a Member, Additional Member, or Substitute Member is admitted, or the number of a Member's Units changes, the allocations of Net Profits or Net Losses for that Year shall be allocated [OPTION 1: by the interim closing of the books method at the end of the prior month] **OR** [OPTION 2: pro rata mid-year], for that portion of the Company's tax year in which the Member, Additional Member, or Substitute Member was admitted or the Units changed, in accordance with the provisions of Code Section 706(d) and the Treasury Regulations promulgated thereunder.

6.4 *Special Rules Regarding Contributed and Distributed Property.* Notwithstanding the prior provisions, to the extent required by and in accordance with Code Section 704(b) and Treasury Regulations Section 1.704-1(b)(2)(iv)(g) and (i) or Code Section 704(c) and Treasury Regulations Section 1.704-1(c), Capital Accounts shall be adjusted and Income and Loss shall be allocated among the Members to take account of any variation between the adjusted tax basis of a property and its initial Book Value. Capital Accounts shall be adjusted to reflect revaluation of a property in all cases required by Treasury Regulations Section 1.704-1(b) and in all optional circumstances to the extent allowed by Treasury Regulations Section 1.704-1(b)(2)(iv)(f) unless the Company determines such would not be beneficial and fair under the circumstances. Solely for the purposes of adjusting the Member's Capital Accounts, and not for tax purposes, if any property is distributed in kind to any Member, the difference between its fair market value and its Book Value at the time of the distribution shall be treated as a gain or loss recognized by the Company and allocated as Net Profit or Loss under this Article.

6.5 *Distributions.*

(a) Except as provided in (b) below, distributions from the Company to Members shall be made at the times and in the amounts determined by the Members. It is anticipated that Distributable Cash shall be distributed at least quarterly. All distributions shall be made to all the Members in proportion to their Units, except as otherwise above provided. All amounts withheld pursuant to the Code or any provisions of state or local tax law with respect to any payment or distribution to the Members from the Company shall be treated as amounts distributed to the relevant Member or Members pursuant to this Section.

(b) Upon liquidation of the Company (or any Member's interest), liquidating distributions will be made in accordance with the positive Capital Account balances of the Members, as determined after taking into account all Capital Account adjustments for the Company's taxable year during which the liquidation occurs. Liquidation proceeds will be paid within sixty (60) days of the end of the taxable year (or, if later, within ninety (90) days after the date of the liquidation).

6.6 *Limitation Upon Distributions.* No distribution shall be made unless, after the distribution is made, the assets of the Company are in excess of all liabilities of the Company, except liabilities to Members on account of their contributions. No Member shall be entitled to interest on his or her Capital Contribution or to return of his or her Capital Contribution, whether in cash or in property, except as otherwise specifically provided for herein.

6.7 *Accounting Method.* The books and records of account of the Company shall be maintained in accordance with the method of accounting utilized for the Company's Federal income tax return unless the Members determine otherwise.

6.8 *Returns.* The Treasurer shall cause the preparation and timely filing of all tax returns required to be filed by the Company pursuant to the Code and all other tax returns deemed necessary and required in each jurisdiction in which the Company does business. Copies of such returns, or pertinent information therefrom, shall be furnished to the Members within a reasonable time after the end of the Company's Year.

6.9 *Tax Elections; Tax Matters Member.* All elections permitted to be made by the Company under Federal or state laws shall be made by the Members. The Members shall designate a Tax Matters Member, who initially shall be [NAME], and at any time the Members can remove the Tax Matters Member, appoint a new one, or fill any vacancy, by a proper meeting.

[OPTIONAL: The parties agree that the Company shall make Section 734, 743 and 754 elections under the Code, at the request of any Member.]

6.10 *Tax Status.* Each party hereto acknowledges that it is the Members' intention that the Company will be classified as a partnership for Federal income tax purposes and subject to all provisions of Subchapter K of Chapter 1 of Subtitle A of the Code; *PROVIDED, HOWEVER,* the filing of Federal and state income tax returns shall not be construed to extend the purposes or expand the obligations or liabilities of the Company nor shall it be construed to create a partnership (other than for tax purposes) or other agency or other relationship between the Members.

6.11 *Priority and Return of Capital.* No Member shall have priority over any other Member, either as to the return of Capital Contributions or as to Net Profits, Net Losses or distributions; provided that this Section shall not apply to loans (as distinguished from Capital Contributions) which a Member has made to the Company. No Member shall be entitled to the return of his or her Capital Contribution or interest thereon except by way of distribution of cash or other assets of the Company pursuant to the terms of this Operating Agreement.

6.12 *Group State Tax Returns.* The Company shall withhold tax and file "group" or "composite" state income tax returns on behalf of nonresident Members where the Company conducts business, to the extent applicable state law requires such withholding and/or returns. To the extent the Company withholds such tax and/or files a group or composite state income tax return, the Company shall notify each Member of his or her share of tax paid with such return, which share shall be determined pursuant to any reasonable method chosen by the Members in accordance with applicable law. The Company is authorized to withhold from distributions hereunder to the Members and to pay over to the appropriate taxing authorities any amounts required to be so withheld, which shall nevertheless be treated as distributions hereunder to such Member.

ARTICLE VII
RESTRICTIONS ON TRANSFERABILITY

7.1 *Buy-Sell Provisions.* If a Member attempts to Transfer any or all of his or her Units, the parties shall follow the terms of any existing Member's Agreement. If there is no existing Member's Agreement, no Member may Transfer, either voluntarily or involuntarily, any interest in this Company without the prior written consent of not less than [STANDARD: Member Majority Vote] **OR** [OPTIONAL: Member Two-Thirds Vote] **OR** [OPTIONAL: All of the Members who are not transferring their Units in the Company] (which may be withheld by their discretion).

7.2 *Substitute Members.* No one to whom any Units are Transferred, whether or not Section 7.1 is complied with, can become a Substitute Member unless the other Members (other than the transferor) approve of the Transfer by [STANDARD: the greater of a

Member Majority Vote or a Majority in Interest] **OR** [OPTION 1: all of the Members who are not transferring their Units in the Company] **OR** [OPTION 2: the greater of a Member Two-Thirds Vote or a Majority in Interest] **OR** [OPTION 3: unanimous] written consent (which may be withheld in their discretion), and the transferee has signed a copy of this Operating Agreement agreeing to be bound by its provisions. A Substitute Member has the rights and powers, and is subject to the restrictions and liabilities, of a Member under the Operating Agreement and the Act. A Substitute Member is liable for the transferor member's obligations to make contributions and for obligations to return unlawful distributions, but a Transferee or Substitute Member is not obligated for the transferor member's liabilities unknown to the Transferee or Substitute Member at the time the Transferee becomes a Substitute Member. A Substitute Member is not personally liable for any obligation of the Company incurred before admission as a Substitute Member.

7.3 *Transferees*. A Transferee who has not received such approval shall have no right to vote or participate in the management of the business and affairs of the Company or to become a Member, and shall only be entitled to receive the share of profits or other distributions and the return of contributions to which the transferor Member would otherwise be entitled. A Transferee who does not become a Substitute Member is not entitled to access to information concerning Company transactions, or to inspect or copy any of the Company's books and other records. A Transferee who does not become a Substitute Member is entitled to:

(a) Receive, upon dissolution and winding up of the Company business, a statement of account only from the date of the latest statement of account agreed to by all Members; and

(b) Seek a judicial determination that it is equitable to wind up Company business if the Company was a term limited liability company at the time of the transfer or entry of the charging order that gave rise to the transfer and the duration stated in the Articles has expired.

7.4 *Termination of Member's Status as Member*. A Member ceases to be a Member upon transfer of all of the Member's distributional interest, other than a transfer for security purposes, or a court order charging the Member's distributional interest, which has not been foreclosed.

7.5 *Remaining Liability.* Whether or not a Transferee of a distributional interest becomes a Substitute Member, the transferor Member is not released from liability to the Company under the Operating Agreement or the Act.

7.6 *Time of Transfer.* The Company need not give effect to a transfer until it has notice of the transfer.

ARTICLE VIII
DISSOLUTION AND TERMINATION

8.1 *Dissolution.*

(a) The Company shall be dissolved upon the occurrence of any of the following events:

  (i) when the period fixed for the duration of the Company, if any, shall expire;

  (ii) by the unanimous written agreement of all Members or the number or percentage specified herein for decisions by Members generally;

  (iii) [No longer required in most states] upon the death, insanity, retirement, resignation, expulsion, bankruptcy, dissolution of a Member or occurrence of any other event which terminates the continued Membership of a Member in the Company unless the business of the Company is continued by the consent of [STANDARD: the greater of a Member Majority Vote and at least a Majority in Interest] **OR** [OPTION 1: all of the remaining Members] **OR** [OPTION 2: a Member Two-Thirds Vote] within ninety (90) days;

  (iv) an event that makes it unlawful for all or substantially all of the business of the Company to be continued, but any cure of illegality within 90 days after notice to the Company of the event is effective retroactively to the date of the event for purposes of this section;

  (v) on application by a Member, and upon entry of a judicial decree that:

    (A) The economic purpose of the Company is likely to be unreasonably frustrated,

(B) Another Member has engaged in conduct relating to the Company's business that makes it not reasonably practicable to carry on the Company's business with that Member,

(C) It is not otherwise reasonably practicable to carry on the Company's business in conformity with the Articles and this Operating Agreement,

(D) A disassociated Member has the right to have the Company dissolved and its business wound up for failure to cause the Member's distributional interest to be purchased, or

(E) The Managers or Members in control of the Company have acted, are acting, or will act in a manner that is illegal, oppressive, fraudulent or unfairly prejudicial to the petitioning Member; or

(vi) on application by a Transferee of a Member's interest, a judicial determination that it is equitable to wind up the Company's business:

(A) After the expiration of the specified term, if the Company was for a specified term at the time the applicant became a transferee by Member disassociation, transfer, or entry of a charging order that gave rise to the transfer, or

(B) At any time, if the Company was at will at the time the applicant became a transferee by Member dissociation, transfer, or entry of a charging order that gave rise to the transfer.

(b) As soon as possible following the occurrence of any of the events specified in this Section effecting the Dissolution of the Company, the Company shall execute a statement of intent to dissolve in such form as shall be prescribed by the appropriate Secretary of State, file same with the Secretary of State's office, and within twenty (20) days after the filing mail notice of such to each creditor of the Company. Upon the filing by the appropriate Secretary of State of a statement of intent to dissolve, the Company shall cease to carry on its business, except insofar as may be necessary for the winding up of its business, but its separate existence shall continue until a Certificate of Dissolution has been issued by the

Secretary of State or until a decree dissolving the Company has been entered by a court of competent jurisdiction.

8.2 *Winding Up, Liquidation and Distribution.*

(a) Upon the filing of the statement of intent to dissolve, the Members shall proceed to wind up and liquidate the Company as follows:

   (i) proceed to collect its assets;

   (ii) convey and dispose of such of its assets as are not to be distributed in kind to its Members;

   (iii) if the Members have determined that any assets of the Company are to be distributed in kind, the net fair market value of such assets as of the date of dissolution shall be determined by agreement of the Members, or if they cannot agree, by an independent appraiser selected by the Members;

   (iv) pay, satisfy, or discharge its liabilities and obligations or make adequate provisions for the payment or discharge thereof; and

   (v) do all other acts required to liquidate the Company's business and affairs.

(b) After paying or discharging all its obligations or making adequate provisions for payment or discharge thereof, the remaining assets shall be distributed as provided herein.

(c) If, upon the dissolution and liquidation (as defined in Treasury Regulations Section 1.704-1(b)(2)(ii)(g)) of the Company, after giving effect to all contributions, distributions, allocations and other Capital Account adjustments for all taxable years, including the year during which the liquidation occurs, any Member has a negative Capital Account, then that Member shall be obligated to contribute to the Company an amount equal to the negative Capital Account for distribution to Members with positive Capital Account balances, by the end of the taxable year during which liquidation occurs (or, if later, within ninety (90) days after the date of such liquidation); but in no event shall a Member be required to contribute capital to satisfy any liability of the Company, except as required by law or herein.

8.3 *Articles of Dissolution.* When all debts, liabilities and obligations of the Company have been paid or discharged, or adequate provisions have been made therefor, and all of the remaining assets of the Company have been distributed to the Members, articles of Dissolution shall be executed in duplicate and verified by the person signing the articles, which articles shall set forth the information required by the Act, and shall be filed with the Secretary of State. Upon such filing the existence of the Company shall cease, except as provided in the Act.

8.4 *Return of Contribution Nonrecourse to Other Members.* Except as provided by law, upon Dissolution, each Member shall look solely to the assets of the Company for the return of his or her Capital Contribution. If the Company property remaining after the payment or discharge of the debts and liabilities of the Company is insufficient to return the cash or other property contribution of one or more Members, such Member or Members shall have no recourse against any other Member.

ARTICLE IX
MISCELLANEOUS PROVISIONS

9.1 *Notices.* Any notice, demand, or communication required or permitted to be given by any provision of this Operating Agreement shall be deemed to have been sufficiently given or served for all purposes if sent by facsimile transmission to the party's number, mailed as provided hereafter, or delivered personally to the party to whom the same is directed, so long as sent by registered or certified mail, postage and charges prepaid, addressed to the Member's and/or Company's address, as appropriate, which is set forth in this Operating Agreement. Except as otherwise provided herein, any such notice shall be deemed to be given three (3) business days after the date on which the same was deposited in a regularly maintained receptacle for the deposit of United States mail, addressed and sent as aforesaid.

9.2 *Governing Law.* This Operating Agreement, and the substantive application and interpretation hereof, shall be governed exclusively by the law of the state of the Act.

9.3 *Entire Agreement*. This Operating Agreement is the entire agreement between the parties hereto with respect to the subject matter hereof and shall not be amended, altered or modified in any manner whatsoever, except as provided herein by a written instrument. This Operating Agreement supersedes all prior agreements between the parties with respect to the subject matter hereof and all such prior agreements shall be void and of no further force or effect as of the date thereof.

9.4 *Execution of Additional Instruments*. Each Member hereby agrees to execute such other and further statements of interest and holdings, designations, powers of attorney and other instruments necessary to comply with any laws, rules or regulations.

9.5 *Construction*. Whenever the singular number is used in this Operating Agreement and when required by the context, the same shall include the plural, and the masculine gender shall include the feminine and neuter genders and vice versa; and the word "person" or "party" shall include a corporation, firm, partnership, proprietorship or other form of association.

9.6 *Headings*. The headings in this Operating Agreement are inserted for convenience only and are in no way intended to describe, interpret, define, or limit the scope, extent or intent of this Operating Agreement or any provision hereof.

9.7 *Waivers*. The failure of any party to seek redress for violation of or to insist upon the strict performance of any covenant or condition of this Operating Agreement shall not prevent a subsequent act, which would have originally constituted a violation, from having the effect of an original violation.

9.8 *Rights and Remedies Cumulative*. The rights and remedies provided by this Operating Agreement are cumulative and the use of any one right or remedy by any party shall not preclude or waive the right to use any or all other remedies. Said rights and remedies are given in addition to any other rights the parties may have by law, statute, ordinance or otherwise.

9.9 *Severability*. If any provision of this Operating Agreement or the application thereof to any person or circumstance shall be invalid, illegal or unenforceable to any extent, the remainder of this Operating Agreement and the application thereof shall not be affected and shall be enforceable to the fullest extent permitted by law.

9.10 *Heirs, Successors and Assigns.* Each and all of the covenants, terms, provisions and agreements herein contained shall be binding upon and inure to the benefit of the parties hereto and, to the extent permitted by this Operating Agreement, their respective heirs, legal representatives, successors and assigns.

9.11 *Creditors.* None of the provisions of this Operating Agreement shall be for the benefit of or enforceable by any creditors of the Company.

9.12 *Rule Against Perpetuities.* The parties hereto intend that the Rule against Perpetuities (and any similar rule of law) not be applicable to any provisions of this Operating Agreement. However, notwithstanding anything to the contrary in this Operating Agreement, if any provision in this Operating Agreement would be invalid or unenforceable because of the Rule against Perpetuities or any similar rule of law but for this Section, the parties hereto hereby agree that any future interest which is created pursuant to said provision shall cease if it is not vested within twenty-one (21) years after the death of the survivor of the group composed of all who are Members of the Company and their issue who are living on the date of this Operating Agreement and their issue, if any, who are living on the effective date of this Operating Agreement.

9.13 *No Partition.* Each Member irrevocably waives during the term of the Company the right, if any, such Member may have, if any, to maintain any action for partition with respect to the real property of the Company.

9.14 *Counterparts.* This Operating Agreement may be executed in counterparts, each of which shall be deemed an original but all of which shall constitute one and the same instrument.

9.15 *Remedies.*

[OPTIONAL]

    (a) *Attorneys' Fees Assessed in Favor of Prevailing Party.* If the Company or any party obtains a judgment against any other party by reason of breach of this Operating Agreement, reasonable attorneys' fee and costs, as determined by the court, shall be included in such judgment, to compensate the prevailing party for its reasonable legal fees and costs. Any Member shall be entitled to maintain, on its own behalf or on behalf of the Company, any action or proceeding against any other Member, successor, or the Company (including any action for damages, specific performance or declaratory relief) for or by reason of breach by such party of this Operating Agreement, or any other agreement entered into in connection with the same, notwithstanding the fact that any or all of the parties to such proceeding may then be Members in the Company, and without dissolving the Company as a limited liability company.

[OPTIONAL]

(b) *Specific Performance.* Each party to this Operating Agreement agrees that the Members would be irreparably damaged if any of the provisions of this Operating Agreement are not performed in accordance with their specific terms and that monetary damages would not provide an adequate remedy in such event. Accordingly, except as otherwise provided in the Act, it is agreed that, in addition to any other remedy to which the nonbreaching Members may be entitled, at law or in equity, the nonbreaching Members shall be entitled to injunctive relief to prevent breaches of the provisions of this Operating Agreement and specifically to enforce the terms and provisions hereof in any action instituted in any court of the United States or any state thereof having subject matter jurisdiction thereof.

9.16 *Dispute Resolution.*

[OPTIONAL]

(a) *Waiver of Jury Trial.* THE PARTIES HERETO WAIVE TRIAL BY JURY IN ANY ACTION, PROCEEDING OR COUNTERCLAIM BROUGHT BY ANY PARTY(IES) AGAINST ANY OTHER PARTY(IES) ON ANY MATTER ARISING OUT OF OR IN ANY WAY CONNECTED WITH THIS OPERATING AGREEMENT OR THE RELATIONSHIP OF THE PARTIES CREATED HEREUNDER.

[OPTIONAL]

(b) **Agreement to Submit to Arbitration.** The parties and their successors shall strive to settle amicably any dispute, controversy or claim arising out of or relating to the Company or this Agreement or a breach thereof. The parties recognize the value of mediation and encourage its use where appropriate. However, any dispute, controversy or claim related to this Agreement or breach thereof, status as a Member, and the business or management of the Company, shall be submitted to arbitration and upon demand, any such dispute, controversy or claim shall be settled by arbitration in accordance with the Commercial Arbitration Rules of the American Arbitration Association, and judgment upon the award rendered by the arbitrators may be entered in any court of competent jurisdiction as provided in Section 9.2. The parties contemplate and agree that the award of the arbitrators shall be final and binding upon the parties hereto and their successors.

The parties hereto agree that (i) three arbitrators shall be selected pursuant to the rules and procedures of the American Arbitration Association, (ii) all arbitrators shall be licensed attorneys, in good standing, (iii) the Company may at its option request arbitrators who are not licensed in Kansas, (iv) the arbitrators shall have the power to award injunctive relief or to direct specific performance, (v) the arbitrators will not have the authority to award punitive damages, (vi) each of the parties shall bear its own attorneys' fees, costs and expenses and an equal share of the arbitrators' and administrative fees of arbitration, provided, however, the arbitrators shall have the power to award to the prevailing party a sum equal to that party's reasonable attorney's fees, costs and expenses and that party's share of the arbitrators' and administrative fees of arbitration.

[OPTIONAL]

9.17 *Securities Law Investment Intent, Representations, and Warranties.* Each Member warrants, represents, agrees and acknowledges: (a) that he or she has adequate means of providing for his or her current needs and foreseeable future contingencies, and anticipates no need now or in the foreseeable future to sell his or her Units; (b) that he or she is acquiring his or her Units or his or her own account as a long-term investment and without a present view to make any distribution, resale or fractionalization thereof; (c) that he or she and his or her independent counselors have such knowledge and experience in financial and business matters that they are capable of evaluating the merits and risks of the investment involved in his or her acquisition of his or her Units and they have evaluated the same; (d) that he or she is able to bear the economic risks of such investment; (e) that he or she and his or her independent counselors have made such investigation of the Company (including its business prospects and financial condition) and the Members, have had access to all information regarding the Company and the Members, and have had an opportunity to ask all of the questions regarding the Company and the Members as they deem necessary to fully evaluate his or her investment therein; (f) that in connection with his or her acquisition of a Unit, he or she has been fully informed by his or her independent counsel as to the applicability of the requirements of the Securities Act of 1933 and all applicable state securities or "blue sky" laws to his or her Units; (g) that he or she understands that (1) his or her Units are not registered under the Securities Act or any state securities law, (2) there is no market for his or her Units and that he or she will be unable to transfer his or her Units unless such is so registered or unless the transfer complies with an exemption from such registration (evidence of which must be satisfactory to counsel for the Company), (3) such Units cannot be expected to be readily transferred or liquidated, and (4) his or her acquisition of a Unit in the Company involves a high degree of risk; and (h) that no representations are or have been made to him or her by any Member or its representatives as to any tax advantages which may inure to his or her benefit or as to the Company's status for tax purposes, and that he or she has relied upon his or her independent counsel with respect to such matters.

[OPTIONAL]

9.18 *Power of Attorney.*

(a) Each Member hereby irrevocably makes, constitutes and appoints [NAME] as his or her true and lawful attorney-in-fact to make, execute, sign, acknowledge and file with respect to this or any successor Company:

1. Such amendments to or restatements of the Company's Articles of Organization as may be required or appropriate pursuant to the provisions of this Operating Agreement, or otherwise under the Act;

2. Any and all amendments or changes to this Operating Agreement and the instruments described in (a), as

now or hereafter amended, which the Members may deem necessary or appropriate to (a) effect a change or modification of the Company approved in accordance with the terms of this Operating Agreement, including amendments, or (b) reflect (i) the exercise by any of any power granted to it under this Operating Agreement; (ii) any amendments adopted by the Members in accordance with the terms of this Operating Agreement; (iii) the admission of any substituted Member in accordance with Section 7.2; and (iv) the disposition by any Member of his or her Units in compliance herewith;

3. All statements of intent to dissolve, notices, articles of dissolution or cancellations of foreign registration and other documents or instruments which may be deemed necessary or desirable by the Members to effect the dissolution and liquidation of the Company after its termination as provided herein; and

4. All such other instruments, documents and certificates which may from time to time be required by the laws of the State of [State], the United States of America or any political subdivision or agency thereof, to effectuate, implement, continue and defend the valid and subsisting existence of the Company and any other instruments, documents or certificates required to qualify the Company to do business in any other State where it is required to so qualify.

(b) The Members hereby agree that the grant of the foregoing power of attorney is coupled with an interest and survives the death, disability, legal incapacity, bankruptcy, insolvency, dissolution, or cessation of existence of a Member and shall survive the delivery of an assignment by any Member of the whole or any part of his or her Units, except that where an assignee of such Units has been admitted as a substitute Member, as provided in Section 7.2, then the foregoing power of attorney of the assignor Member shall survive the delivery of such assignment for the sole purpose of enabling the Company to execute, acknowledge and file any and all instruments necessary to effectuate such substitution.

[OPTIONAL]

9.19 *Confidentiality.* The parties hereto agree that the Company has an interest in maintaining the confidentiality of its Confidential Information. "Confidential Information" means information disclosed or known to a party as a consequence of or through the party's relationship with the Company and related to the Company's business, internal affairs, client relationships or work product arising out of client relationships. "Confidential Information" is intended to include trade secrets as defined in the Restatement Second of Torts. The parties hereto agree that the Company shall be entitled to seek injunctive relief in the courts against any action of a party which threatens the confidentiality of the Confidential Information, as a provisional remedy pending arbitration of any claims arbitrable under this Article.

IN WITNESS WHEREOF, the parties have caused this Operating Agreement to be duly executed on _____, 19_.

ALL MEMBERS

_____

_____

_____

_____

[OPTIONAL]

9.20 *Spousal Consent to Operating Agreement.*

SPOUSAL CONSENT
to
OPERATING AGREEMENT

_____, 19__

Each of the undersigned, being the spouse of a Member who has signed the foregoing Agreement, hereby acknowledges that the undersigned has read and is familiar with the provisions of said Agreement and agrees to be bound thereby and join therein to the extent, if any, that the undersigned's agreement and joinder may be necessary. The undersigned hereby agrees that his or her spouse may join in any future amendment or modifications of said Agreement without any further signature, acknowledgement, agreement or consent on his or her part; and he or she hereby further agrees that any community interest which he or she may have in his or her spouse's LLC Interest in the Company shall be subject to the provisions of the Agreement.

_____

_____

_____

_____

Appendix G

Manager-Managed LLC Operating Agreement

OPERATING AGREEMENT OF
[NAME LLC]
A [STATE] LIMITED LIABILITY COMPANY
Managed by Managers

[**Note.** This Model Operating Agreement should be used only as a guide as many provisions might not apply or should be redrafted to apply to a particular state law or LLC design. **An Operating Agreement for a manager-managed LLC would be the same as that for a member-managed LLC (see Appendix F), with the exception of Article IV, included here.**]

TABLE OF CONTENTS

OPERATING AGREEMENT

INTRODUCTION

The person signing the Articles of Organization has acted solely as organizer to form _____ (the "Company"), a limited liability company under the laws of the State of _____ on behalf of its Members. The Company's business shall be conducted under such name until such time as the Articles are amended in accordance with applicable law and this Operating Agreement. The Company's term, puropse, powers, registered office, and registered agent shall be as stated in the Articles until such time as they are amended in accordance with applicable law and this Operating Agreement. The parties hereto agree to the provisions hereof in order to define their rights, liabilities, duties, restrictions, and limitations with respect to the Company.

****

ARTICLE I
DEFINITIONS

The followings terms used in this Operating Agreement shall have the following meanings (unless otherwise expressly provided herein);

"Act" shall mean the Limited Liability Company Act of the State of _____ and all amendments thereto.

"Additional Member" shall mean any Person who or that is admitted to the Company as an Additional Member pursuant to this Operating Agreement.

"Affiliate" shall mean a lineal descendant, ascendant, or spouse of a Member or Manager and any entity in which the Member, the Manager, or a lineal descendant, ascendant, or spouse of a Member or Manager has a 10 percent or more direct beneficial ownership interest.

"Articles" shall mean the Articles of Organization, or such other documents as are filed with the Secretary of State Under the Act, as amended from time to time.

"Assignee" shall mean a Person to whom the economic rights and benefits of a Member's ownership interest have been transferred but where such Person has not been made a Substitute Member.

"Capital Account" shall mean the individual account maintained for each Member as provided hereafter.

"Capital Contribution" shall mean any contribution to the capital of the Company in cash, property, services, or the obligation to contribute cash, property, or services by a Member whenever made.

"Code" shall mean the Internal Revenue Code, as amended from time to time.

"Company" shall mean this Limited Liability Company.

[OPTIONAL: Use if special allocations in 6.2.]

"Deficit Capital Account" shall mean with respect to any Member, the deficit balance, if any, in such Member's Capital Account as of the end of the taxable year, after giving effect to the following adjustments:

a. Credit to such Capital Account any amount which Member is obligated to restore under Section 1.704-1(b)(2)(ii)(c) of the Treasury regulations, as well as any addition thereto pursuant to the next to last sentence of Sections 1.704-1(b)(4)(iv)(f) and (h)(5) of the Treasurey regulations, after taking into account thereunder any changes during such year in the Company's Minimum Gain and in the Member Nonrecourse Debt Minimum Gain attributable to any Member nonrecourse debt; and

b. Debit to such Capital Account the items described in Sections 1.704-1(b)(2)(ii)(d)(4), (5), and (6) of the Treasury regulations.

[OPTIONAL: Use if distributions referenced to this term.]

"Distributable Cash" shall mean all cash, revenues, and funds received by the Company from Company operations, less the sum of the following to the extent paid or set aside by the Company: (i) all principal and interest payments on indebtedness of the Company and all other sums paid to lenders; (ii) all cash expenditure incurred incident to the normal operation of the Company's business; and (iii) such cash reserves as the Members deem reasonably necessary to the proper operation of the Company's business.

[OPTIONAL: Use if provisions reference effective date of Company.]

"Effective Date" shall be the date the Company is first effective, as may be further provided in the Articles.

"Initial Members" shall mean those Members named hereafter.

"Initial Units" shall mean those Units owned by the Initial Members.

"Manager(s)" shall mean the Person or Persons elected and qualified as Managers as provided herein.

"Members" shall mean the Initial Members and Persons becoming Members hereunder, including Additional Members and Substitute Members, but shall not include Assignees unless they become Members, nor shall it include Members who have assigned all of their economic interest in their Unit(s).

"Member Majority Vote" shall mean, if used herein, an affirmative vote by Members holding at least a majority of all outstanding units that are present, in person or by proxy or telephone conference, at a duly called meeting where a Quorum is present; provided, however, when used to continue the business on dissolution or in Article VI, Restrictions on Transferability, shall mean an affirmative vote by Members holding at least a majority of all outstanding Units held by Members other than by any Member who has suffered a dissolution event or whose Units are proposed to be transferred, respectively.

"Member Two-Thirds Vote" shall mean, if used herein, an affirmative vote by Members holding at least two thirds of all outstanding Units that are present, in person or by proxy or telephone conference, at a duly called meeting where a Quorum is present.

[OPTIONAL: Use if special allocations in 6.2.]

"Member Nonrecourse Debt Minimum Gain" shall have the meaning set forth in Treasury Regulation Section 1.704-2(i)(3).

[OPTIONAL: Use if special allocations in 6.2.]

"Minimum Gain" shall have the meaning set forth in Treasury Regulations Section 1.704-2(d).

"Net Profits" shall mean, for each Year, the income and gains of the Company determined in accordance with accounting principles consistently applied from year to year under the method of accounting and as reported, separately or in the aggregate, as appropriate, on the Company's information tax return filed for federal income tax purposes, plus any income described in Section 705(a)(1)(B) of the Code and any income exempt from tax.

"Net Losses" shall mean, for each Year, the losses and deductions of the Company determined in accordance with accounting principles consistently applied from year to year under the method of accounting and as reported, separately or in the aggregate, as appropriate, on the Company's information tax return filed for federal income tax purposes, plus any expenditures described in Section 705(a)(2)(B) of the Code.

"Officer(s)" shall mean those officers of the Company, if any, designated hereafter.

"Operating Agreement" shall mean this Operating Agreement, as originally executed and as amended.

"Person" shall mean any individual or any general partnership, limited partnership, limited liability partnership, limited liability company, corporation, joint venture, trust, business trust, cooperative or association, and any other entity and the heirs, executors, administrators, legal representatives, successors, and assigns of such Person, where applicable.

"Quorum" shall mean the presence in person, proxy, or by telephone conference of the Members holding at least 50.1% or more of the outstanding Units held by Members.

"Substitute Member" shall mean any Person who or that is admitted to the Company as a Substitute Member as provided hereafter.

"Transfer(s)" shall mean (i) when used as a verb, to give, gift, sell, exchange, assign, redeem, transfer, pledge, hypothecate, encumber, bequeath, devise, or otherwise dispose of, including an amendment to a "living trust" that is treated as a Transfer as provided hereafter, and (ii) when used as a noun, the nouns corresponding to such verbs, in either case voluntarily or involuntarily, by operation of law or otherwise.

If a corporation or other business entity is the Member, a Transfer of ownership interest in such entity or any reorganization of such entity that results in the individual(s) who own the controlling interest in the entity no longer owning a controlling interest shall be a Transfer under this Operating Agreement. If a trust is the Member, a change in the terms of the trust or circumstances either of which results in the individual(s) who are the primary beneficiary(ies) of the trust no longer being the primary beneficiary(ies) shall be a Transfer under this Operating Agreement.

"Units" shall mean the ownership interests in the Company.

"Year" shall mean the Company's fiscal year for income tax purposes as determined pursuant to Section 706 of the Code.

ARTICLE II
OFFICES

2.1 *Principal Office.* The principal office for the transaction of the business of the Company is hereby located at [*full address*].

2.2 *Other Offices.* Branch or subordinate offices may at any time be established by the Company at any place or places where the Company is qualified to do business.

ARTICLE III
MANAGEMENT AND OFFICERS

3.1 *Management.* The business and affairs of the Company shall be managed by a Manager or Managers. The Managers shall direct, manage, and control the business of the Company to the best of their ability and shall have full and complete authority, power, and discretion to make any and all decisions and to do any and all things that the Managers shall deem to be reasonably required in light of the Company's business and objectives.

3.2 *Number, Tenure, and Qualification of Managers.* [OPTION 1: The initial Managers of the Company shall be named in the Company's Articles of Organization. Thereafter, the Managers shall be elected by the Members at the Company's annual meeting of Members.] **OR** [OPTION 2: The number of Managers shall be not less than ___ (_) and not more than ___ (_), with the number to be fixed from time to time by a Member Majority Vote, but in no instance shall there be less than one Manager. The initial number of Managers of the Company shall be ___ (_)]. **OR** [OPTION 3: There shall at all times during the term of the Company be one Manager. _____ is hereby appointed as the initial Manager.]

Each Manager shall hold office until the next annual meeting of Members or until his or her successor shall have been elected and qualified or until earlier death, resignation, or removal. [OPTION 4: Managers need not be residents of the state of _____.] **OR** [OPTION 5: Managers need not be Members of the Company (or an owner of an entity that is a Member).]

The Manager [OPTION (select one) may/may not] be a Person that is any entity.

3.3 *Resignation, Removal, and Replacement of Managers.* A Manager shall discharge his or her duties as Manager until (1) he or she resigns or is removed pursuant to the provisions hereof, and (2) a successor Manager is approved if necessary to have at least one Manager.

    (a) *Resignation.* A Manager of the Company may resign at any time by giving written notice to the other Managers, if any, and to the Members of the Company. The resignation of any Manager shall take effect upon receipt of notice thereof or at such later time as shall be specified in such notice (but not before the notice is mailed, delivered, or sent by facsimile transmission; and, unless otherwise specified therein, the acceptance of such resignation shall not be necessary to make it effective).

    (b) *Removal.* At a meeting called expressly for that purpose, a Manager may be removed for cause [OPTIONAL: or without cause] at any time by a decision to do so approved by [OPTION 1: Member Majority Vote] **OR** [OPTION 2: Member Two-Thirds Vote].

    (c) *Vacancy.* Any vacancy in a Manager's position occurring for any reason, including the resignation, death, removal, incapacity, or inability to act of a Manager, may be filled by [Member Majority Vote]. A Manager elected to fill a vacancy shall be elected until his or her successor shall be elected and shall qualify or until his or her earlier death, resignation, or removal. Upon the approval of a successor Manager in accordance with this Section, the Manager or his or her legal representative shall execute such documents and take such action as may be required to permit the successor Manager to act as a Manager in accordance with the provisions hereof.

3.4 *Certain Powers of Members.* Only the Managers and agents of the Company authorized by the Managers shall have the authority to bind the Company. The Managers may obligate the Company only as to matters within the scope of the authority granted hereunder, subject to the written direction of the Members. The Managers have the power and authority, on behalf of the Company, to do the following to carry out the business and affairs of the Company:

(a) To purchase, hold, improve, lease, acquire, own, use, and otherwise deal with real, tangible, and intangible personal properties from any Person as the Managers may determine, in the name of the Company, or as a nominee;

(b) To sell, convey, mortgage, pledge, lease, exchange, and otherwise dispose of real, tangible, and intangible personal properties from any Person as the Managers may determine;

(c) To borrow money for the Company from banks, other lending institutions, the Members, Affiliates of the Members, and other Persons on such terms as they deem appropriate, and to assume or refinance existing indebtedness; and, in connection therewith, issue evidence of indebtedness to hypothecate, encumber, and grant security interests in the assets of the Company to secure repayment of the borrowed sums;

(d) To purchase liability and other insurance to protect the Company and its property and business;

(e) To invest any Company funds (by way of example and not by limitation) in time deposits, short-term governmental obligations, commercial paper, or other investments;

(f) To open bank accounts in the name of the Company, and to determine the signatories thereon;

(g) To execute, negotiate, and deliver, on behalf of the Company, all instruments and documents, including, without limitation, contracts, checks, drafts, notes and other negotiable instruments, mortgages or deeds of trust, security agreements, financing statements, deeds, bills of sale or other documents providing for the acquisition, mortgage, or disposition of the Company's property, assignments, leases, partnership agreements, and any other instruments or documents necessary or appropriate to the business of the Company;

(h) To employ accountants, legal counsel, managing agents, Members, or others to perform services for the Company and to compensate them from Company funds;

(i) To enter into other agreements on behalf of the Company, with any other Person for any purpose, in such forms as the Managers may approve;

(j) To execute and file any bankruptcy petition, on behalf of the Company, pursuant to applicable federal laws; and

(k) To do and perform all other acts as may be necessary or appropriate to the conduct of the Company's business, including but not limited to establishment of funds or reserves, prepay, recast, increase, modify, extend, or otherwise amend existing debt, commitments, contracts, or other obligations in whole or in part.

Unless authorized to do so by this Operating Agreement or by the Managers, no Member who is not a Manager of the Company and no agent or employee of the Company shall have any power or authority to bind the Company in any way to pledge its credit or to render it liable pecuniarily for any purpose. Each Member shall indemnify the Company for any costs or damages incurred by the Company as a result of the unauthorized action of such Member.

3.5 *Action by Members.* Except as otherwise specifically provided herein or by the Act, all actions and decisions of the Managers shall require [OPTION 1: a vote of a majority by number of the Managers] **OR** [OPTION 2: a vote of two thirds by number of the Managers] **OR** [OPTION 3: a unanimous vote of the Managers]. The Managers may make any decision or take any action at a meeting, by conference telephone call, by unanimous written consent, by oral agreement, or by any other method they elect. [OPTIONAL: A Member Two-Thirds Vote shall be required for the following:

(a) To sell or otherwise dispose of all or substantially all of the assets of the Company as part of a single transaction or plan so long as such disposition is not in violation of or a cause of a default under any other agreement to which the Company may be bound; and

(b) Merger or consolidation of the Company with another entity or entities.]

3.6 *Manager Has No Exclusive Duty to Company.* No Manager shall be required to manage the Company as his or her sole and exclusive function. Each Member shall devote reasonable time and effort to management duties.

[STANDARD]

3.7 *Other Business Ventures of Managers and Members.* Any Manager, Member or Affiliate of a Member or Manager may engage independently or with others in other business ventures of every nature and description, except as provided hereafter.

[OPTION 1: However, no Manager, Member, or Affiliate shall take advantage of a business opportunity in the same line of business with the Company, unless the Company elects to forgo same, nor shall any Manager or Member own, manage, consult with, or be employed by any venture or entity that competes with the Company's business.]

[OPTION 2: The pursuit of business and investments by Managers, Members, or Affiliates of a Member or Manager, even if directly competitive with the Company's business, is hereby consented to by the Members and shall not be deemed wrongful or improper.]

[OPTIONAL]

3.8 *Transactions with Affiliates.* Unless otherwise agreed in writing by all Members, each Manager and each Member shall disclose any and all direct or indirect affiliation with or interest in any Person with which the Company proposes to do business or enter into any financial transactions. The Company may enter into agreements with one or more Managers, Members, or Affiliates of a Member or Manager provided that any such agreement shall be at rates and terms at least as favorable to the Company as those available from unaffiliated parties.

[OPTIONAL]

3.9 *Indemnity.* The Company shall indemnify and hold harmless each Manager and each Member [and any Officers] from and against any and all claims or liabilities of any nature whatsoever arising out of or resulting from any such act or omission in connection with the Company, including, without limitation, reasonable costs and expenses of litigation and appeal (including reasonable fees and expenses of attorneys engaged by a Manager or a Member [and any Officers] in defense of such act or omission), but these Persons shall not be entitled to be indemnified or held harmless because of, or arising from, their gross negligence or willful misconduct.

3.10 *Salaries.* Managers [and any Officers] shall not initially receive compensation for their services as such, but the Managers may authorize the reimbursement of expenses, including expenses incurred to attend meetings of the Managers or Members; provided, however, that nothing herein contained shall be construed to preclude the Members from establishing compensation for Managers [or any Officers] as such, and provided further that nothing herein contained shall preclude any Manager [or any Officers] from receiving compensation for services to the Company in any other capacity.

3.11 *Election, Resignation, and Removal of Officers.* The Managers may designate any Officers of the Company, including without limitation any or all of the following: a Chair, Vice-Chair, Chief Executive Officer, President, Chief Operating Officer (who may also have the title of President), Chief Financial Officer, Secretary, Treasurer, and one or more vice presidents, assistant secretaries, or assistant treasurers.

The Officers shall serve such terms as the Members determine. Any number of offices may be held by the same Person. Any Officer may resign at any time by giving written notice to the Managers. The resignation of any Officer shall take effect upon receipt of notice thereof or at such later time as shall be specified in such notice (but not before the notice is mailed, delivered, or sent by facsimile transmission); and, unless otherwise specified therein, the acceptance of such resignation shall not be necessary to make it effective. All or any lesser number of Officers may be removed at any time, with or without cause, by a [OPTION 1: majority vote by number of the Managers] **OR** [OPTION 2: two-thirds vote by number of the Managers].

The duties of such Officers shall be as follows:

(a) *The Chair.* He or she shall preside at meetings of the Managers and the Members and shall perform such other duties as may be assigned to him or her by this Operating Agreement or the Managers. In the absence of the Chair, the Vice-Chair shall have and may exercise all of the powers of the Chair.

(b) *The Vice-Chair.* The Vice-Chair shall perform the duties of the Chair when the Chair is unavailable.

(c) *Chief Executive Officer/President.* Subject to the direction and under the supervision of the Managers, the Chief Executive Officer (also called "CEO" or "President") shall generally direct the policy and management of the Company and shall have general charge of the business, affairs, and property of the Company and control over its Officers, agents, and employees; and shall do and perform such other duties and may exercise such other powers as from time to time may be assigned to him or her by this Operating Agreement or by the Managers. The CEO shall serve as Chair if no Chair is elected.

(d) *Chief Operating Officer/Vice President.* The Chief Operating Officer ("COO") shall perform such duties as are customary for such office subject to the direction of the Managers and the Chief Executive Officer. The COO shall perform the duties of the CEO if the CEO is incapacitated or otherwise unable to do so. The COO may also be called the Vice President.

(e) *Chief Financial Officer.* The Chief Financial Officer ("CFO") shall perform such duties as are customary for such office subject to the direction of the Managers and the Chief Executive Officer.

(f) *Secretary.* The Secretary shall keep, or cause to be kept, a book of minutes at the principal office or such other place as the Managers may order of all meetings of Managers and Members, with the time and place of holding, whether regular or special, and if special, how authorized, the notice thereof given, the names of those present at such meetings, and the proceedings thereof. The Secretary shall have such other powers and perform such other duties as may be prescribed by the Managers or this Operating Agreement. The Secretary may seek assistance for these duties as to the annual minutes from the Company's attorneys.

(g) *Treasurer.* The Treasurer shall keep and maintain or cause to be kept and maintained accounts of the properties and business transactions of the Company, including accounts of its assets, liabilities, receipts, disbursements, gains, losses, and capital, to the extent agreed by the Members. The Treasurer shall deposit all moneys and other valuables in the name and to the credit of the Company with such depositories as may be designated by the Managers. He or she shall disburse the funds of the Company as may be ordered by the Members, shall render to the Members upon request an account of all of the transactions as Treasurer and of the financial condition of the Company, and shall have such other powers and perform such other duties as may be prescribed by the Members or this Operating Agreement. He or she shall be bonded, if required by the Members.

(h) *The Assistant Secretary and Assistant Treasurer.* The Assistant Secretary and Assistant Treasurer (or in the event there be more than one Assistant Secretary or Assistant Treasurer, in the order of their seniority, designation, or election) shall, in the absence of or disability of the Secretary or Treasurer, respectively, perform the duties and exercise the powers of the Secretary or Treasurer and shall perform such other duties as may be prescribed by the Managers or this Operating Agreement.

[OPTIONAL]

3.12 *Business Expenses of Managers and Members.* From time to time, a Manager or Member will be required to incur certain expenses related to the trade or business of the Company for which the Company will not reimburse that Manager or Member. [OPTIONAL: These expenses include, but are not limited to (1) use of the Manager's or the Member's personal automobile for Company business; (2) meals and entertainment of persons who are clients or prospective clients of the Company; (3) professional dues, licenses, publications, and so forth, for the Manager or Member related to the Company's business; (4) use of a Manager's or Member's personal computer (including software purchased for business purposes) or other office equipment on behalf of the Company; (5) conventions; (6) charitable contributions; or (7) club dues.]

Each Manager and Member is accountable to the Company for substantiating expenses incurred by such Manager or Member that are eligible to be reimbursed by the Company. Such expenses must be either actually substantiated to the Company or must be deemed substantiated pursuant to the Internal Revenue Service per diem arrangements. The Manager or Member shall include in the expense request for reimbursement the time, place, date, business purpose, and names of other individuals involved, as well as a brief description of the specific business being transacted or discussed. In the event that any reimbursement from the Company, whether paid before or after the expense is incurred, cannot be substantiated and documented by the Manager or Member, the unsubstantiated amounts (except IRS-approved per diem arrangements) must be returned by the Manager or Member to the Company.

ARTICLE IV
MANAGEMENT AND OFFICERS

4.1 *Management.* The business and affairs of the Company shall be managed by an individual Manager or the Managers. The Managers shall direct, manage and control the business of the Company. They shall have full and complete authority, power and discretion to make any and all decisions and to do any and all things which the Managers believe to be reasonably required in light of the Company's business and objectives.

4.2 *Number, Tenure and Qualifications of Managers.* [OPTION 1: The initial Manager(s) of the Company shall be named in the Company's Articles of Organization. Thereafter, the Managers shall be elected by the Members at the Company's annual meeting.] **OR** [OPTION 2: The number of Managers shall be not less than ( ) and not more than ( ), with the number to be fixed from time to time by a Member Majority Vote, but in no instance shall there be less than one Manager. The initial number of Managers of the Company shall be ( )]. **OR** [OPTION 3: There shall at all times during the term of the Company be one Manager. is hereby appointed as the initial Manager.]

Each Manager shall hold office until the next meeting of Members or until his or her successor shall have been elected and qualified or until earlier death, resignation or removal. [OPTION 4: Managers need not be residents of the state of [State]] **OR** [OPTION 5: Members of the Company (or an owner of an Entity which is a Member)].

The Manager [OPTION (select one) may/may not] be a Person which is any entity.

[OPTIONAL]

4.3 *Removal, Replacement of Manager.* The Manager shall discharge his or her duties as the Manager until (1) the manager resigns or is removed pursuant to the provisions hereof, and (2) a successor Manager is approved. A Manager may resign as such at any time. A Manager may be removed for cause [OPTIONAL: or without cause] at any time by a decision to do so approved by a [OPTION 1: Member Majority Vote] **OR** [OPTION 2: Member Two-Thirds Vote] of the Units collectively held by Members entitled to vote hereunder at such time.

In the event of the resignation, death, removal, incapacity or inability to act as a Manager, another Member shall be designated as successor Manager by [OPTION 1: Member Majority Vote] **OR** [OPTION 2: Member Two-Thirds Vote] of the Units collectively held by Members entitled to vote hereunder at such time. Upon the selection of a successor Manager in accordance with this Section, the Manager or his or her legal representative shall execute such documents and take such action as may be required to permit the successor Manager to act as a Manager in accordance with the provisions hereof.

4.4 *Authority of Manager.* Only the Manager(s) and agents of the Company authorized by the Manager(s) shall have the authority to bind the Company. The Manager(s) may obligate the Company only as to matters within the scope of the authority granted hereunder, subject to the written direction of the Members. No Member who is not either a Manager or otherwise authorized as an agent shall take any action to bind the Company, and each Member shall indemnify the Company for any costs or damages incurred by the Company as a result of the unauthorized action of such Member. Each Manager has the power, on behalf of the Company, to do all things reasonably required to carry out the business and affairs of the Company, including without limitation:

    (a) To purchase, lease or make any other acquisition, ownership, holding, improvement, use and other dealing with, real and/or personal properties in the name of the Company from any Person or Entity as the Manager(s) may determine. The fact that a Member is directly or indirectly affiliated or connected with any such Person or Entity shall not prohibit the Manager(s) from dealing with that Person or Entity;

(b) To sell, convey, mortgage, pledge, lease, exchange, and make any other disposition of real and/or personal properties in the name of the Company from any Person or Entity as the Manager(s) may determine. The fact that a Member is directly or indirectly affiliated or connected with any such Person or Entity shall not prohibit the Manager(s) from dealing with that Person or Entity;

(c) To borrow money for the Company from banks, other lending institutions, the Members, or Affiliates of the Members on such terms as it deems appropriate, and in connection therewith, to hypothecate, encumber and grant security interests in the assets of the Company to secure repayment of the borrowed sums. Except as otherwise provided in the Act, no debt shall be contracted or liability incurred by or on behalf of the Company except by the Company's Manager(s);

(d) To purchase liability and other insurance to protect the Company's property and business;

(e) To invest any Company funds temporarily (by way of example but not limitation) in time deposits, short-term governmental obligations, commercial paper or other investments;

(f) To open bank accounts in the name of the Company, and the Managers shall be the sole signatories thereon, unless the Manager(s) designates otherwise;

(g) To execute on behalf of the Company, or delegate to the Officers to execute, all instruments and documents, including, without limitation, checks; drafts; notes and other negotiable instruments; mortgages or deeds of trust; security agreements; financing statements; documents providing for the acquisition, mortgage or disposition of the Company's property; assignments, bills of sale; leases; partnership agreements; and any other instruments or documents necessary, in the opinion of the Manager(s), to the business of the Company;

(h) To employ accountants, legal counsel, managing agents or other experts to perform services for the Company and to compensate them from Company funds;

    (i) To enter into any and all other agreements on behalf of the Company, with any other Person or Entity for any purpose, in such forms as the Manager(s) may approve;

    (j) To execute and file any bankruptcy petition, on behalf of the Company, pursuant to applicable Federal laws;

    (k) To do and perform all other acts as may be necessary or appropriate to the conduct of the Company's business;

    (l) To perform all other duties and functions provided herein to be performed by the Manager; and

    (m) Any Person dealing with the Company or the Manager may rely upon a certificate signed by the Manager as to the identity and authority of the Manager or any other Member.

4.5 *Action by Manager(s).* Except as otherwise specifically provided herein, all actions and decisions of the Manager(s) shall require a vote of a [majority][a majority of a Quorum] of the number of Managers. The Manager(s) may make any decision or take any action at a meeting, by conference telephone call, by written consent, by oral agreement or any other method the Manager(s) elect; provided that, at the request of any Manager with respect to a decision or action of the Managers, such decision or action must be made or taken by written consent signed by the number of Managers required to approve such decision or action.

4.6 *Manager Has No Exclusive Duty to Company.* A Manager shall not be required to manage the Company as his or her sole and exclusive function; and he or she may have other business interests and may engage in other activities in addition to those relating to the Company [OPTION: so long as the Manager does not compete with the Company or usurp a Company business opportunity].

Each Manager shall devote reasonable time and effort to management duties.

[OPTIONAL]

4.7 *Other Business Ventures of Manager or Member.* Any Manager, Member or affiliate of a Member may engage independently or with others in other business ventures of every nature and description, except as limited hereby. Neither the Company nor any Manager or [OPTION: Member] shall have any right to any other such ventures or activities in which any Manager, Member or affiliate of a Member is involved or to the income or proceeds derived therefrom, except as limited hereby.

[OPTION 1: The pursuit of other ventures and activities by Managers, Members or affiliates of a Member is hereby consented to by the Members and shall not be deemed wrongful or improper; *provided however*, no Manager, Member or Affiliate shall own, manage, consult with, or be employed by any venture or entity that competes with the Company's business.] No Manager, Member or Affiliate shall utilize any business or investment opportunity if such opportunity is of a character which, if presented to the Company could be taken by the Company. Any Manager, Member or Affiliate shall have the right to take for his or her or its own account (individually or as a member or fiduciary), or to recommend to others, any such particular opportunity only if the Company in writing declines to pursue such business or investment opportunity. [OPTION 2: The pursuit of other ventures and activities by Managers, Members or Affiliates of a Member, even if directly competitive with the Company's business, is hereby consented to by the Members and shall not be deemed wrongful or improper.]

[OPTIONAL]

4.8 *Transactions with Affiliates.* The Company may enter into agreements with one or more Members or Affiliates of a Member to provide leasing, management, legal, accounting, architectural, development, or other services to the Company, provided that any such services shall be at rates at least as favorable to the Company as those available from unaffiliated parties. The validity of any transaction, agreement or payment involving the Company and any Member or Affiliate of a Member otherwise permitted hereunder shall not be affected by reason of the relationship between such Person and the Company or any of its Members. Notwithstanding anything to the contrary herein, each Member shall disclose any and all direct or indirect affiliation or interest in any entity with which the Company does business or proposes to do business.

[OPTIONAL]

4.9 *Indemnity of Manager and Officers.* The Company shall indemnify and hold harmless each Manager and/or Officer from and against any and all claims or liabilities of any nature whatsoever arising out of or resulting from any such act or omission in connection with the Company, including, without limitation, reasonable costs and expenses of litigation and appeal (including reasonable fees and expenses of attorneys engaged by a Manager and/or Officer in defense of such act or omission), but these Persons shall not be entitled to be indemnified or held harmless due to, or arising from, their gross negligence or willful misconduct.

4.10 *Reliance upon Others.* In discharging its duties, a Manager shall be fully protected in relying in good faith upon such information, opinions, reports or statements by any of its other Members, Managers, Officers, or agents, or by any other person, as to matters the Manager reasonably believes are within such other Person's professional or expert competence and who has been selected with reasonable care by or on behalf of the Company, including information, opinions, reports or statements as to the value and amount of the assets, liabilities, profits or losses of the Company or any other facts pertinent to the existence and amount of assets from which distributions to members might properly be paid.

4.11 *Resignation.* Any Manager or Officer of the Company may resign at any time by giving written notice to the Members of the Company. The resignation of any Manager or Officer shall take effect upon receipt of notice thereof or at such later time as shall be specified in such notice (but not before the notice is mailed, delivered, or sent by facsimile transmission) and, unless otherwise specified therein, the acceptance of such resignation shall not be necessary to make it effective.

4.12 *Salaries.* Managers shall not initially receive compensation for their services as such, but the Manager(s) may authorize the payment of Managers' fees and reimbursement of expenses of attendance; provided, that nothing herein contained shall be construed to preclude the Members, by a Member Majority Vote, from establishing compensation for Managers as such, and provided further that nothing herein contained shall preclude any Manager from receiving compensation for services to the Company in any other capacity.

4.13 *Election of Officers.* The Managers may designate as Officers any or all of the following: a Chairman, Vice Chairman, Chief Executive Officer, Chief Operating Officer (who may also have the title of President), Chief Financial Officer, Secretary and a Treasurer at the first meeting of the Managers, to serve such terms as the Managers determine. Each such Officer shall hold office until he or she shall resign, shall be removed or is otherwise disqualified to serve, or his or her successor shall be elected and qualified. The Company may also have, at the discretion of the Managers, one or more vice presidents, founders, assistant secretaries, assistant treasurers or other Officers. Any number of offices may be held by the same person. The duties of such Officers shall be as follows:

(a) *The Chairman.* The Chairman shall be a non-executive chairman. He or she shall preside at meetings of the Members and Managers and shall perform such other duties as may be assigned to him or her by this Operating Agreement or the Managers. In the absence of the Chairman, the Vice-Chairman shall have and may exercise all of the powers of the Chairman.

(b) *The Vice-Chairman.* The Vice-Chairman shall perform the duties of the Chairman when the Chairman is unavailable.

(c) *Chief Executive Officer.* Subject to the direction and under the supervision of the Managers, the Chief Executive Officer shall generally direct the policy and management of the Company and shall have general charge of the business, affairs and property of the Company and control over its Officers, agents and employees; and shall do and perform such other duties and may exercise such other powers as from time to time may be assigned to him or her by this Operating Agreement or by the Managers.

(d) *Chief Operating Officer.* The Chief Operating Officer shall perform such duties as are customary for such office subject to the direction of the Managers and the Chief Executive Officer.

(e) *Chief Financial Officer.* The Chief Financial Officer shall perform such duties as are customary for such office subject to the direction of the Managers and the Chief Executive Officer.

(f) *Secretary.* The Secretary shall keep, or cause to be kept, a book of minutes at the principal office or such other place as the Members or Managers may designate of all meetings of Members or Managers, with the time and place of holding, whether regular or special, and if special, how authorized, the notice thereof given, the names of those present at Members' and Managers' meetings, and the proceedings thereof. The Secretary shall have such other powers and perform such other duties as may be prescribed by the Members or Managers or this Operating Agreement. The Secretary may seek assistance for these duties as to the annual minutes from the Company's attorneys.

(g) *Treasurer.* The Treasurer shall keep and maintain or cause to be kept and maintained, accounts of the properties and business transactions of the Company, including accounts of its assets, liabilities, receipts, disbursements, gains, losses, and capital, to the extent agreed by the Members or Managers. The Treasurer shall deposit all monies and other valuables in the name and to the credit of the Company with such depositories as may be designated by the Members or Managers. He or she shall disburse the funds of the Company as may be ordered by the Members or Managers, shall render to the Members and Managers upon request an account of all of the transactions as Treasurer and of the financial condition of the Company, and shall have such other powers and perform such other duties as may be prescribed by the Members, Managers, or this Operating Agreement. He or she shall be bonded, if required by the Managers.

(h) *The Assistant Secretary and Assistant Treasurer.* The Assistant Secretary and Assistant Treasurer (or in the event there be more than one Assistant Secretary or Assistant Treasurer, in the order of their seniority, designation or election) shall, in the absence of or disability of the Secretary or Treasurer, respectively, perform the duties and exercise the powers of the Secretary or Treasurer and shall perform such other duties as may be prescribed by the Members or Managers or this Operating Agreement.

(i) *Founders.* The Members or Managers may recognize and appoint two individuals as Founders of the Company. The Founders shall have no rights, duties or authorities as a result of their position as Founder, but shall be invited to all meetings of the Manager(s) to provide such advice and counsel to the Company as the Members or Managers deem appropriate.

4.14 *Unreimbursed Business Expenses of Members or Managers.* From time to time, a Member or Manager will be required to incur certain expenses related to the trade or business of the Company for which the Company will not reimburse that Member or Manager. These expenses include, but are not limited to: (1) use of the Member's or Manager's personal automobile for Company business; (2) meals and entertainment of persons who are clients or prospective clients of the Company; (3) professional dues, licenses, publications, etc., for the Member or Manager related to the Company's business; (4) use of a Member's or Manager's personal computer (including software purchased for business purposes) or other office equipment on behalf of the Company; (5) conventions; (6) charitable contributions; and (7) club dues.

Any Member or Manager who has incurred unreimbursed expenditures which that Member or Manager has determined are appropriately documented and deductible as expenses related to the trade or business of the Company, shall notify the Treasurer of the Company of the total amount of these expenditures that that Member or Manager intends to deduct on his or her individual return.

The unreimbursed business expenses paid from the personal funds of a Member will be treated, for purposes of this Operating Agreement, as a contribution to the capital of the Company with a corresponding allocation of the Company's deductions back to the capital of the contributing Member. It is the responsibility of the Member or Manager to maintain records to support any such expenditures.

ARTICLE V
CAPITAL CONTRIBUTIONS, ALLOCATIONS, AND DISTRIBUTIONS

5.1 *Initial Members.* The Initial Members, their addresses, [the value of their Capital Contribution,] and the number of Units each owns ("Initial Units") are set forth on Exhibit A, attached hereto.

5.2 *Additional Capital Contribution May Be Required.*

(a) The Members acknowledge that the Company may require from time to time funds in addition to funds available from the operation of the Company with which to own and operate the Company, including the maintenance and renovation of the Company's property and the payment of the taxes, insurance, debt service, other carrying charges, and operating expenses of the Company. The Members and any Assignees shall from time to time contribute in U.S. dollars to the capital of the Company the additional funds required for the purposes set forth above, or for any other purpose relating to the business of the Company, in accordance with their respective Units, as determined pursuant to [OPTION 1: a Member Majority Vote] **OR** [OPTION 2: Member Two-Thirds Vote] **OR** [OPTION 3: a unanimous vote of the Members] **OR** [OPTION 4: an affirmative vote of Members holding at least ___ percent of the outstanding Units].

(b) If any Member or Assignee fails or refuses for any reason to contribute his or her share of the additional cash capital required to be contributed by him or her pursuant to this Operating Agreement within 10 days after approval by the Members, then any Member not in default hereunder may (but shall not be required to) rectify that default by contributing all or any part thereof for and on behalf of that defaulting Member or Assignee, and any amounts so contributed by the rectifying Member, together with interest thereon from the date of the advance at the rate of ___ percent, shall immediately become due and owing and shall be a debt due by the defaulting Member or Assignee to the Member so contributing said sum, and the Member so rectifying that default, in whole or in part, shall have (i) a security interest in the defaulting Member's (or Assignee's) Units to secure the aggregate of said Capital Contribution made by him or her on behalf of the defaulting Member or Assignee, together with interest thereon as stated above and (ii) the right to enforce such debt and exercise his or her interest in the security as provided in the Uniform Commercial Code. If more than one Member desires to rectify a default as set forth in this Section, those Members shall be entitled to contribute on a pro rate basis in proportion to their Units, excluding the Units of the Member or Assignee in default and those Members not so contributing to rectification of the default. The exercise by a Member of his or her right to cure a defaulting Member's or Assignee's default as provided above, and the exercise by the Member of the remedies applicable thereto, as set forth in clause (i) and (ii) of this paragraph, shall be without prejudice to the Members' other rights and remedies.

5.3 *Additional Members.* From time to time the Company may issue additional Units to any Persons (including to existing Members) for such Capital Contributions and on such terms and conditions as the Members determined by [OPTION 1: a Member Majority Vote] **OR** [OPTION 2: a Member Two-Thirds Vote] **OR** [OPTION 3: a unanimous vote of the Members], and such additional Units may have different rights regarding voting, profit and loss allocations, and distribution, whether subordinate or preferred, as the Members determine by such vote. Persons that purchase additional Units pursuant to this Section shall be Additional Members.

5.4 *Preemptive Rights.* Provided, however, issuance of such additional Units shall be subject to the following preemptive rights. A Member shall have the right (but not the obligation) to purchase a share of any additional Units so issued to maintain such Member's pro rata ownership of all Units, at the same price, time, and terms as for all other Persons.

5.5 *Capital Accounts.*

[STANDARD OPTION]

(a) Throughout the term of the Company, a Capital Account shall be maintained at all times for each Member in accordance with Code Section 704(b) and all Treasury regulations promulgated thereunder.

[OPTIONAL LONG PROVISION: Use to "spell out" rules for client/ accountant.]

(a) A separate Capital Account will be maintained for each Member. Each Member's Capital Account will be increased by the amount of money contributed (but not loans) by such Member to the Company; the fair market value of property contributed by such Member to the Company (net of liabilities secured by such contributed property that the Company is considered to assume or take subject to under Code Section 752); allocations to such Member of Company income and gain; and allocations to such Member of income described in Code Section 705(a)(1)(B). Each Member's Capital Account will be decreased by the amount of money distributed to such Member by the Company (but not any payment of interest or principal on loans made to the Company); the fair market value of property distributed to such Member by the

Company (net of liabilities secured by such distributed property that such Member is considered to assume or take subject to under Code Section 752); allocations to such Member of expenditures described in Code Section 705(a)(2)(B); and allocations to the account of such Member of the Company's losses and deductions as set forth in the Treasury regulations, taking into account adjustments to reflect book value.

(b) In the event of a permitted sale or exchange of a Unit in the Company, the Capital Account of the transferor shall become the Capital Account of the transferee to the extent it relates to the transferred Unit.

(c) The manner in which Capital Accounts are to be maintained pursuant to this Section is intended to comply with the requirements of Code Section 704(b) and the Treasury regulations promulgated thereunder. If in the opinion of the Company's accountants the manner in which Capital Accounts are to be maintained pursuant to the preceding provisions of this Section should be modified in order to comply with Code Section 704(b) and the Treasury regulations thereunder, then notwithstanding anything to the contrary contained in the preceding provisions of this Section, the method in which Capital Accounts are maintained shall be so modified; provided, however, that any change in the manner of maintaining Capital Accounts shall not materially alter the economic agreement between or among the Members.

[STANDARD]

5.6 *Allocations of Profits and Losses.* The Net Profits and Net Losses of the Company for each fiscal year will be allocated to the Capital Accounts of the Members and any Assignees in proportion to their Units.

[OPTION: Use if special allocations.]

5.6 *Allocations of Profits and Losses.* The Net Profits and Net Losses of the Company for each fiscal year will be allocated to the Capital Accounts of the Members as follows.

Notwithstanding the above provisions of this Section:

(a) No allocations of loss, deduction and/or expenditures described in Code Section 705(a)(2)(B) shall be charged to the Capital Accounts of any Member if such allocation would cause such Member to have a Deficit Capital Account in excess of any limited dollar amount of such deficit balance that such Member is obligated to restore. The amount of the loss, deduction, and/or Section 705(a)(2)(B) expenditure that would have caused a Member to have such a Deficit Capital Account shall instead be charged to the Capital Account of any Members that would not have such a Deficit Capital Account as a result of the allocation, in proportion to their Units, or, if no such Members exist, then to the Members in proportion to the number of Units held by such Member.

(b) If any Member unexpectedly receives any adjustments, allocations, or distributions described in Treasury Regulation Sections 1.704-1(b)(2)(ii)(d)(4), (5), or (6), which create or increase a Deficit Capital Account of such Member, then items of Company income and gain (consisting of a pro rata portion of each item of Company income, including gross income, and gain for such year and, if necessary, for subsequent years) shall be specially credited to the Capital Account of such Member in an amount and manner sufficient to eliminate, to the extent required by the Treasury regulations, the Deficit Capital Account so created as quickly as possible. It is the intent that this Section be interpreted as a Qualified Income Offset to comply with the alternate test for economic effect set forth in Treasury Regulations Section 1.704-1(b)(2)(ii)(d).

(c) If there is a net decrease in Company Minimum Gain for a Year, then there shall be allocated to each Member items of income and gain for that Year equal to that Member's share of the net decrease in Minimum Gain (as determined under Treasury Regulations Section 1.704-2(g)(2)), subject to the exceptions set for in Treasury Regulations Section 1.704-2 (f)(2), (3), and (5), *provided*, that if the Company has any discretion as to an exception set forth pursuant to Treasury Regulations Section 1.704-2(f)(5), the Tax Matters Member may exercise such discretion on behalf of the Company. The Tax Matters Member shall, if the application of the Minimum Gain chargeback requirement would cause a distortion in the economic arrangement among the Members, ask the Commissioner to waive the Minimum Gain chargeback requirement pursuant to Treasury Regulations Section 1.704-2(f)(4). The foregoing is intended to be a "Minimum Gain Chargeback" provision as described in Treasury Regulations Section 1.704-2(f) and shall be interpreted and applied in all respects in accordance with that regulation.

(d) If during a fiscal year there is a net decrease in Member Nonrecourse Debt Minimum Gain, then, in addition to the amounts, if any, allocated pursuant to the preceding paragraph, any Member with a share of that Member Nonrecourse Debt Minimum Gain (as determined under Treasury Regulations Section 1.704-2(i)(5)) as of the beginning of the fiscal year shall, subject to the exceptions set forth in Treasury Regulations Section 1.704-2(i)(4), be allocated items of income and gain for the year (and, if necessary, for succeeding years) equal to that Member's share of the net decrease in the Member Nonrecourse Debt Minimum Gain. The Tax Matters Member shall, if the application of the Member Nonrecourse Debt Minimum Gain chargeback requirement would cause a distortion in the economic arrangement among the Members, ask the Commissioner to waive the Minimum Gain chargeback requirement pursuant to Treasury Regulations Sections 1.704-2(f)(4) and 1.704-2(i)(4). The foregoing is intended to be the "chargeback of Member Nonrecourse Debt Minimum Gain" required by Treasury Regulations Section 1.704-2(i)(4) and shall be interpreted and applied in all respects in accordance with that regulation.

(e) Notwithstanding anything to the contrary in this Article, Company losses, deductions, or Section 705(a)(2)(B) expenditures that are attributable to a particular Member nonrecourse liability shall be allocated to the Member that bears the economic risk of loss for the liability in accordance with the rules of Treasury Regulations Section 1.704-2(i).

(f) Beginning in the first taxable year in which there are allocations of "nonrecourse deductions" (as defined in Section 1.704-2(b)(i) of the Treasury regulations) attributable to nonrecourse liabilities of the Company, and thereafter throughout the full term of the Company, nonrecourse deductions shall be allocated to the Members in accordance with, and as a part of, the allocations of Company profit or loss for such period.

(g) Any credit or charge to the Capital Accounts of the Members shall be taken into account in computing subsequent allocations of profits and losses, so that the net amount of any items charged or credited to Capital Accounts shall, to the extent possible, be equal to the net amount that would have been allocated to the Capital Account of each Member pursuant to the provisions of this Article if special allocations are required by this Section.

5.7 *Mid-Year Allocations.* When a Member, Additional Member, or Substitute Member is admitted, or the number of a Member's Units changes, the allocations of Net Profits or Net Losses for that Year shall be allocated [OPTION 1: by the interim closing-of-the-books method at the end of the prior month] **OR** [OPTION 2: pro rata] for that portion of the Company's tax year in which the Member, Additional Member, or Substitute Member was admitted or the Units changed in accordance with the provisions of Code Section 706(d) and the Treasury regulations promulgated thereunder.

5.8 *Special Rules Regarding Contributed and Distributed Property.* Notwithstanding the prior provisions, to the extent required by and in accordance with Code Section 704(b) and Treasury Regulations Section 1.704-1(b)(2)(iv)(g) and (i) or Code Section 704(c) and Treasury Regulations Section 1.704-1(c), Capital Accounts shall be adjusted and Net Profits and Net Losses shall be allocated among the Members to take account of any variation between the adjusted tax basis of a property and its initial book value. Capital Accounts shall be adjusted to reflect revaluation of a property in all cases required by Treasury Regulations Section 1.704-1(b) and in all optional circumstances to the extent allowed by Treasury Regulations Section 1.704-1(b)(2)(iv)(f) unless the Company determines such would not be beneficial and fair under the circumstances. Solely for the purposes of adjusting the Member's Capital Accounts, and not for tax purposes, if any property is distributed in kind to any Member, the difference between its fair market value and its book value at the time of the distribution shall be treated as a gain or loss recognized by the Company and allocated as Net Profits or Net Losses under this Article.

5.9 *Distributions.*

(a) Except as provided in (b) below, distributions from the Company to Members and any Assignees shall be made at the times and in the amounts determined by [OPTION 1: a Member Majority Vote] **OR** [OPTION 2: a Member Two-Thirds Vote] **OR** [OPTION 3: unanimous vote of Members]. All distributions shall be made to the Members and any Assignees in proportion to their positive Capital Accounts balance.

(b) Upon liquidation of the Company (or any Member's interest), liquidating distributions will be made in accordance with the positive Capital Account balances of the Members and any Assignees, as determined after taking into account all Capital Account adjustments for the Company's taxable year during which the liquidation occurs. Liquidation proceeds will be paid within 60 days of the end of the taxable year (or, if later, within 90 days after the date of the liquidation).

(c) All amounts withheld pursuant to the Code or any provisions of state or local tax law with respect to any payment or distribution to the Members or any Assignees from the Company shall be treated as amounts distributed to the relevant Member(s) or Assignee(s) pursuant to this Section.

5.10 *Limitation Upon Distributions.* No distribution shall be made unless, after the distribution is made, the assets of the Company are in excess of all liabilities of the Company, except liabilities to Members on account of their contributions.

5.11 *Accounting Method.* The books and records of account of the Company shall be maintained in accordance with the method of accounting used for the Company's federal income tax return unless the Members determine otherwise.

(a) *Tax Returns.* The Company shall prepare and timely file all tax returns required to be filed by the Company pursuant to the Code and all other tax returns deemed necessary and required in each jurisdiction in which the Company does business. Copies of such returns, or pertinent information therefrom, shall be furnished to the Members within a reasonable time after the end of the Company's Year.

(b) *Elections.* All elections permitted to be made by the Company under Federal or state laws may be made by the Company. [OPTIONAL: The Company shall make Section 734, 743, and 754 elections under the Code, at the request of any Member.]

(c) *Tax Matters Member.* The Members shall designate a Tax Matters Member, who initially shall be ___, and at any time the Members can remove the Tax Matters Member, appoint a new one, or fill any vacancy, by a proper meeting.

5.12 *Tax Status.* Each party hereto acknowledges that it is the Members' intention that the Company will be classified as a partnership for federal income tax purposes and subject to all provisions of Subchapter K of Chapter 1 of Subtitle A of the Code; *PROVIDED, HOWEVER,* the filing of Federal and state income tax returns shall not be construed to extend the purposes or expand the obligations or liabilities of the Company nor shall it be construed to create a partnership (other than for tax purposes) or other agency or other relationship between the Members.

5.13 *Priority and Return of Capital.* No Member shall have priority over any other Member, either as to the return of Capital Contributions or as to Net Profits, Net Losses, or distributions; provided that this Section shall not apply to loans (as distinguished from Capital Contributions) that a Member has made to the Company. No Member shall be entitled to the return of his or her Capital Contribution or interest thereon except by way of distribution of cash or other assets of the Company pursuant to the terms of this Operating Agreement.

5.14 *Group State Tax Returns.* The Company shall withhold tax and file "group" or "composite" state income tax returns on behalf of nonresident Members or any nonresident Assignees where the Company conducts business, to the extent applicable state law requires such withholding and/or returns. To the extent the Company withholds such tax and/or files a group or composite state income tax return, the Company shall notify each Member or any Assignee of his or her share of tax paid with such return, which share shall be determined pursuant to any reasonable method chosen by the Members in accordance with applicable law. The Company is authorized to withhold from distributions hereunder to the Members and any Assignee and to pay over to the appropriate taxing authorities any amounts required to be so withheld, which shall nevertheless be treated as distributions hereunder to such Member or Assignee.

ARTICLE VI
RESTRICTIONS ON TRANSFERABILITY; BUY-SELL PROVISIONS

6.1 *Restriction on Transfer.* If a Member or any Assignee attempts to Transfer any or all of his or her Units or any right or interest therein, the parties shall follow the terms of any existing Members' Agreement. If there is no existing Members' Agreement, no Member or Assignee may Transfer, either voluntarily or involuntarily, any or all of his or her Units or any right or interest therein (a) without prior approval by [STANDARD: Member Majority Vote (provided, however, a Transfer resulting in a deemed termination of the Company under Code Section 708 shall require the approval of all other Members)] **OR** [OPTIONAL: Member Two-Thirds Vote] **OR** [OPTIONAL: all of the Members who are not transferring their Units in the Company] (such approval of Transfer must be evidenced in writing and may be withheld or granted in the Members' sole discretion) or (b) without complying with the provisions of the right of first refusal as set forth in Section 6.2.

6.2 *Right of First Refusal.* A Member or Assignee may Transfer any or all of his or her Units or any right or interest in them without the prior approval specified in Section 6.1, provided that unless the following terms are complied with:

(a) *Notice of Transfer.* If a Member or Assignee (the "Offeree") intends to Transfer any Units, the Offeree shall give written notice of such intention to each of the other Members. Such written notice, in addition to stating the intention to Transfer, shall state (i) the number of Units to be transferred ("Offered Units"); (ii) the name, business, and residence address of the proposed Assignee; and (iii) whether or not the Transfer is for valuable consideration, and, if so, the amount of the consideration and the other material terms of the Transfer. If the intended Transfer is for valuable consideration, (i) the intended Transfer must be pursuant to a legally enforceable offer in writing, made and signed by an offeror who is not an Affiliate of the Offeree and who is a Person financially capable of carrying out the terms of such Offer, and (ii) a copy of the written offer must be attached to the notice. In the event of an involuntary Transfer, notice shall be deemed given and received on the date the Members have actual notice of such involuntary Transfer if the Offeree does not given written notice. The written notice given by a Member or an Assignee in accordance with this provision or actual notice of an involuntary Transfer shall hereinafter be referred to as "Notice," and the date of receipt of the Notice shall be the last date the Notice is received by any other Member.

(b) *Option to Purchase.*

  (i) *First Option to Purchase.* Within 60 days of the receipt of Notice, the Company may exercise an option to purchase all or any portion of the Offered Units. The Company, by [OPTION 1: Member Majority Vote] **OR** [OPTION 2: Member Majority Vote and action of the Managers], shall exercise such option by giving written notice both to the Offeree and each other Member within such 60-day period. Should the Company fail to give written notice within such 60-day period, the Company shall be deemed to have waived such option.

  (ii) *Second Option to Purchase.* If the Company does not exercise its option to purchase all of the Offered Units, each Member other than the Offeree, within 80 days of the receipt of Notice, may exercise an option to purchase a number of the unpurchased Offered Units equal to the total number of unpurchased Offered Units multiplied by a fraction, the numerator of which is the number of the Units owned by such other Member at the time of the receipt of Notice and the denominator of which is the total number of the Units owned by all Members other than the Offeree. The other Members shall exercise such options by giving written notice both to the Offeree and each other Member within such 80-day period. Should a Member fail to give written notice within such 80-day period, the Member shall be deemed to have waived such option.

  (iii) *Third Option to Purchase.* If neither the Company nor an other Member shall exercise his or her option to purchase all of the Offered Units, each other Member who exercises in full a Second Option may, within 10 days after the expiration of the 80-day option period, exercise an option to purchase the remaining Offered Units.

In the case of a single Member, his or her option shall be to purchase all of the remaining Offered Units. In the case of two or more other Members, each such other Member's option shall be to purchase the amount all such other Members may determine by agreement among themselves, or if they cannot agree, by one or more successive allocations in the proportion that the number of Units owned by each of the eligible other Members bears to the total number of Units owned by all such eligible other Members. Such other Members shall exercise such options by giving written notice both to the Offeree and each other Member within such 90-day period. Should a Member fail to give written notice within such 90-day period, the Member shall be deemed to have waived such option.

(iv) *Forfeiture of Options.* The Company and the other Members must in the aggregate exercise their options to purchase all of the Offered Units, otherwise, their options shall be forfeited.

(c) *Effect of Non-Exercise of Options.* If the purchase options are forfeited or waived, then:

    (i) in the event of an involuntary Transfer, after the expiration of the last option period (90 days from the receipt of Notice) granted above, the purported Assignee shall then own the Offered Units and shall be subject to the terms of this Operating Agreement; or

    (ii) within 10 days after the expiration of the last option period (90 days from the receipt of Notice) granted above, the Offeree may Transfer the Offered Units to the Assignee named in the Notice upon the terms specified therein, which Assignee shall be subject to the terms of this Operating Agreement. No such Transfer shall be valid unless it is completed within such time period upon the terms and to the Assignee stated in the Notice.

(d) *Transfer to Family Member.* Any Member may, without complying with the prior provisions of this Section, Transfer his or her Units or an interest therein if such Transfer is made to a Family Member or to any trust primarily for such Member's benefit and/or for the benefit of a Family

Member. The term "Family Member" means any spouse of a Member, any descendants of a Member, or any spouse of a descendant of a Member. If the Member is a trust, then the determination of a Family Member shall be based on the relationship to the primary beneficiary of the trust. If the Member is a corporation or other entity, the determination of a Family Member will be based on the relationship to the individual owning the controlling interest.

6.3 *Terms of Sale.*

(a) *Purchase Price.* The purchase price for Units purchased pursuant to this Article shall be equal to the fair market value of the Company on the effective date of the purchase multiplied by a percent, which is the percent the number of Units being purchased is to all the outstanding Units. The fair market value shall be determined by an appraiser who is selected and agreed to by the parties to the purchase. If the parties cannot agree upon an appraiser by the effective date of the purchase, the purchasing party shall select one appraiser and the selling party shall select one appraiser, and those two appraisers shall select a third appraiser and the three appraisals shall be averaged. The cost of such ppraisals shall be borne one-half by the selling party and one-half by the purchasing party. Each party must notify the other of its choice of appraiser within ten days after the effective date of the purchase; otherwise, if one party fails to do so then the appraiser selected by the party who gave timely notification shall be the sole appraiser. Provided, however, if the Notice specifies that the Transfer is for valuable consideration, then the purchase price shall be the amount set out in the Notice, if less.

(b) *Payment in Cash or Note.* The purchase price for Units purchased pursuant to this Article shall be payable in cash, or, at the option of the purchaser, 20 percent in cash and the balance of the purchase price by a negotiable promissory note of the purchaser for a term determined by the purchaser, not to exceed five years after the closing. The promissory note shall bear interest at the prime rate, plus 1 percent, in effect on the first day of each calendar year at a bank selected by the purchaser. Principal and acrued interest shall be payable in equal quarterly payments, with the first payment due at the end of the quarter first occurring after the closing. The promissory note shall be secured by a security interest in the purchased Units. If closing occurs after the effective date of the purchase, the purchase price shall include interest from the effective date of the purchase until closing, calculated as provided above for a promissory note. Provided, however, if the Notice specifies that the Transfer is for valuable consideration, the purchaser has the option to use the terms set out in the Notice.

(c) *Closing and Effective Date of Purchase.* The effective date of the purchase shall be the date determined by the purchaser, but in no event later than 100 days following the receipt of the Notice. The closing shall occur on the effective date unless the appraisal(s) cannot be completed by such date, in which case, closing shall be held within 10 days after the appraisal(s) is completed. The purchasing party shall become the owner of the Units as of the effective date of the purchase for all purposes, notwithstanding the closing occurring later. The closing shall take place at the location specified by the purchaser.

6.4 *Remedy for Failure of Seller to Convey Units.* In the event that a Member or his or her representative or successor-in-interest, or an Assignee ("Transferring Person"), fails to Transfer his or her Units to the Company or to other Members as required by the provisions of this Operating Agreement, the purchaser of such Units may deposit the purchase price for such Units (by certified or cashier's check, promissory note, or both, as the case may be under the applicable provisions of this Operating Agreement) with any bank doing business within 25 miles of the Company's principal office, or with the Company's certified public accountants, as agent or trustee, in escrow for such Transferring Person, to be held by such bank or accountant until withdrawn by such Transferring Person. Upon such deposit by the purchaser of such Units and upon written notice to the Transferring Person, the Units to be transferred pursuant to the applicable provisions of this Opearating Agreement shall at such time be deemed to have been sold, assigned, transferred, and conveyed to such purchaser, such Transferring Person shall have no further rights thereto and the Company shall record such Transfer in its books of account.

6.5 *Warranties on Transfer.* The Transferring Person, by transferring Units of the Company pursuant to this Operating Agreement,
shall be deemed to warrant that such Units are transferred free and
clear of all liens, encumbrances, and claims of others of every kind
and character. In the event that any Units to be purchased are
found to be subject to any lien, encumbrance, or claim, the pur-
chaser(s) shall have the election to (a) postpone payment of the
purchase price for such Units until such time as such lien, encumbrance, or claim has been discharged; or (b) disburse directly to
such lienholder, encumbrancer, or claimant, if the amount of such
claim be liquidated, such part of the purchase price as may be adequate to discharge said lien, encumbrance, or claim. In the event
that any lien, encumbrance, or claim is in excess of the amount of
the purchase price the purchaser(s) may, but shall not be obligated
to, disburse the entire purchase price to such lienholder, encumbrancer, or claimant and thereupon any lien, encumbrance, or
charge against the Units shall be fully released and discharged and
such Units shall be transferred into the name of the purchaser(s),
free and clear of all liens, encumbrances, charges, and claims.

6.6 *Substitute Members.* No one to whom any Units are Transferred, whether or not Section 6.1 is complied with, can become
a Substitute Member unless the other Members (other than the
transferror) approve of the Transfer by [STANDARD: a Member
Majority Vote] **OR** [OPTION 1: unanimous vote] **OR** [OPTION 2: a
Member Two-Thirds Vote] (which approval may be withheld or
granted in their sole discretion), and the Person to whom such
Units are Transferred has signed a copy of this Operating Agreement agreeing to be bound by its provisions. A Substitute Member
has the rights and powers, and is subject to the restrictions and
liabilities, of a Member under the Operating Agreement and the
Act. [OPTIONAL: A Substitute Member is liable for the transferor
Member's obligations to make contributions and for obligations to
return unlawful distributions, but an Assignee or Substitute Member is not obligated for the transferor Member's liabilities unknown
to the Assignee or Substitute Member at the time the transferee
becomes a Substitute Member. A Substitute Member is not personally liable for any obligation of the Company incurred before
admission as a Substitute Member.]

6.7 *Assignee.* An Assignee shall have no right to vote or
participate in the management of the business and affairs of the

Company or to become a Member, and shall only be entitled to receive the share of profits or other distributions and the return of contributions to which the transferor Member would otherwise be entitled. An Assignee is not entitled to access to information concerning Company transactions, or to inspect or copy any of the Company's books and other records.

6.8 *Termination of Member's Status as Member.* A Member ceases to be a Member upon Transfer of all of the Member's Units, other than a Transfer for security purposes or a court order charging the Member's Units that have not been foreclosed.

6.9 *Remaining Liability.* Whether or not a Person to whom Units are transferred becomes a Substitute Member or remains an Assignee, the transferor Member is not released from liability to the Company under the Operating Agreement or the Act.

6.10 *Time of Transfer.* The Company need not give effect to a Transfer until it has notice of the Transfer and it has been approved as provided herein.

6.11 *Transfer to a Living Trust.* Any Transfer by a Member of his or her Units in the Company to a living trust, as defined below, shall be permitted without consent, and the living trust shall become a Substitute Member. For all purposes of this Operating Agreement, the Units shall still be considered as owned by the individual Member, and all references such as to the death or disability of a Member, or any other provision that would apply to an individual and not a trust, shall be considered as applying to the individual who is the grantor of the living trust, and, in turn, to such living trust. However, all payments shall be made to the living trust. For this purpose, a "living trust" shall mean a trust of which the individual Member is the sole grantor and sole initial trustee over which the individual Member has the full right of revocation, and which will function during the Member's life primarily for the benefit of the Member. However, a subsequent amendment to the living trust that would do either of the following: (i) remove the grantor Member as a trustee even though the Member is still alive and competent, or (ii) cause the living trust to function during the Member's life other than primarily for the Member's benefit, shall be treated as a Transfer restricted as provided above.

ARTICLE VII
DISSOLUTION AND TERMINATION

7.1 *Dissolution.*

(a) The Company shall be dissolved upon the occurrence of any of the following events:

   (i) when the period fixed for the duration of the Company shall expire;

   (ii) by the unanimous written agreement of all Members;

   (iii) upon the death, insanity, retirement, resignation, expulsion, bankruptcy, dissolution of a Member, or occurrence of any other event that terminates the continued Membership of a Member in the Company unless the business of the Company is continued by a provision in the Articles or by [STANDARD: a Member Majority Vote] **OR** [OPTION 1: a Member Two-Thirds Vote] **OR** [OPTION 2: unanimous vote of all Members] within 90 days;

   (iv) any other event of dissolution specified in the Act.

(b) As soon as possible following the occurrence of any of the events specified in this Section effecting the dissolution of the Company, the Company shall execute a [OPTION 1: statement of intent to dissolve] **OR** [OPTION 2: notice of winding up business] in such form as shall be prescribed by the Secretary of State, file same with the Secretary of State's office, and [OPTIONAL: within 20 days] after the filing, mail notice of such to each creditor of the Company. Upon the filing by the Secretary of State of a [OPTION 1: statement of intent to dissolve] **OR** [OPTION 2: notice of winding up business], the Company shall cease to carry on its business, except insofar as may be necessary for the winding up of its business, but its separate existence shall continue until [OPTION 1: Articles of Termination have been filed with] **OR** [OPTION 2: a Certificate of Dissolution has been issued by] the Secretary of State or until a decree dissolving the Company has been entered by a court of competent jurisdiction.

7.2 *Winding Up, Liquidation, and Distribution.*

(a) Upon the filing of the [OPTION 1: statement of intent to dissolve] **OR** [OPTION 2: notice of winding up business], the Managers, or if none, the Members, shall proceed to wind up and liquidate the Company as follows:

(i) Proceed to collect its assets;

(ii) Convey and dispose of such of its assets as are not to be distributed in kind to its Members;

(iii) If the Managers, or if none, the Members, have determined that any assets of the Company are to be distributed in kind, the net fair market value of such assets as of the date of dissolution shall be determined by agreement of the Members, or if they cannot agree, by an independent appraiser selected by the Members.

(iv) Pay, satisfy, or discharge its liabilities and obligations or make adequate provisions for the payment or discharge thereof; and

(v) Do all other acts required to liquidate the Company's business and affairs.

(b) After paying or discharging all its obligations or making adequate provisions for payment or discharge thereof, the remaining assets shall be distributed as provided herein.

(c) If, upon the dissolution and liquidation (as defined in Treasury Regulations Section 1.704-1(b)(2)(ii)(g)) of the Company, after giving effect to all contributions, distributions, allocations, and other Capital Account adjustments for all taxable years, including the year during which the liquidation occurs, any Member has a negative Capital Account, that Member shall be obligated to contribute to the Company an amount equal to the negative Capital Account for distribution to Members with positive Capital Account balances by the end of the taxable year during which liquidation occurs (or, if later, within 90 days after the date of such liquidation); but in no event shall a Member be required to contribute capital to satisfy any liability of the Company, except as required by law or herein.

7.3 Articles of [OPTION 1: *Dissolution*] **OR** [OPTION 2: *Termination*]. When all debts, liabilities, and obligations of the Company have been paid or discharged, or adequate provisions have been made therefor, and all of the remaining assets of the Company have been distributed to the Members, Articles of [OPTION 1: Dissolution] **OR** [OPTION 2: Termination] shall be executed in duplicate and verified by the Person signing the articles, which articles shall set forth the information required by the Act, and shall be filed with the Secretary of State. Upon such filing, the existence of the Company shall cease, except as provided in the Act.

7.4 *Return of Contribution Non-recourse to Other Members.* Except as provided by law, upon dissolution, each Member shall look solely to the assets of the Company for the return of his or her Capital Contribution. If the Company property remaining after the payment or discharge of the debts and liabilities of the Company is insufficient to return the cash or other property contribution of one or more Members, such Member or Members shall have no recourse against any other Member.

ARTICLE VIII
MISCELLANEOUS PROVISIONS

8.1 *Notices.* Any notice, demand, or communication required or permitted to be given by any provision of this Operating Agreement shall be in writing and deemed to have been sufficiently given or served for all purposes if (a) sent by facsimile transmission to the party's facsimile number as it appears on the records of the Company (such transmission shall be evidenced by a confirmation report showing the date of transmission), (b) delivered personally to the party to whom the same is directed, or (c) mailed by first-class U.S. mail, postage and charges prepaid, addressed to the party's address (as it appears on the records of the Company). Any Member may change his or her address or facsimile number for notice by giving notice in writing, stating his or her new address or facsimile number for notices to the other Members of the Company. Except as otherwise provided herein, any such notice delivered by mail shall be deemed to be given three business days after the date on which the same was deposited in a regularly maintained receptacle for the deposit of U.S. mail, addressed and sent as aforesaid, except that any notice or other communication mailed to the Company that is not received by the Company within three business days after the date of its mailing or transmission shall be deemed to have been given as of the date actually received by the Company.

8.2 *Governing Law.* This Operating Agreement, and the substantive application and interpretation hereof, shall be governed exclusively by the law of the state of the Act.

8.3 *Entire Agreement.* This Operating Agreement is the entire agreement between the parties hereto with respect to the subject matter hereof and shall not be amended, altered, or modified in any manner whatsoever, except as provided herein by a written instrument. This Operating Agreement supersedes all prior agreements between the parties with respect to the subject matter hereof and all such prior agreements shall be void and of no further force or effect as of the date thereof.

8.4 *Execution of Additional Instruments.* Each Member hereby agrees to execute such other and further statements of interest and holdings, designations, powers of attorney, and other instruments necessary to comply with any laws, rules, or regulations.

8.5 *Construction.* Whenever the singular number is used in this Operating Agreement and when required by the context, the same shall include the plural, and the masculine gender shall include the feminine and neuter genders and vice versa.

8.6 *Headings.* The headings in this Operating Agreement are inserted for convenience only and are in no way intended to describe, interpret, define, or limit the scope, extent, or intent of this Operating Agreement or any provision hereof.

8.7 *Waivers.* The failure of any party to seek redress for violation of or to insist upon the strict performance of any covenant or condition of this Operating Agreement shall not prevent a subsequent act, which would have originally constituted a violation, from having the effect of an original violation.

8.8 *Rights and Remedies Cumulative.* The rights and remedies provided by this Operating Agreement are cumulative and the use of any one right or remedy by any party shall not preclude or waive the right to use any or all other remedies. Said rights and remedies are given in addition to any other rights the parties may have by law, statute, ordinance, or otherwise.

8.9 *Severability.* If any provision of this Operating Agreement or the application thereof to any Person or circumstance shall be invalid, illegal, or unenforceable to any extent, the remainder of this Operating Agreement and the application thereof shall not be affected and shall be enforceable to the fullest extent permitted by law.

8.10 *Heirs, Successors, and Assigns.* Each and all of the covenants, terms, provisions, and agreements herein contained shall be binding upon and inure to the benefit of the parties hereto and, to the extent permitted by this Operating Agreement, their respective heirs, legal representatives, successors, and assigns.

8.11 *Creditors.* None of the provisions of this Operating Agreement shall be for the benefit of or enforceable by any creditors of the Company.

8.12 *Rule Against Perpetuities.* The parties hereto intend that the Rule against Perpetuities (and any similar rule of law) not be applicable to any provisions of this Operating Agreement. However, notwithstanding anything to the contrary in this Operating Agreement, if any provision in this Operating Agreement would be invalid or unenforceable because of the Rule against Perpetuities or any similar rule of law but for this Section, the parties hereto hereby agree that any future interest that is created pursuant to said provision shall cease if it is not vested within 21 years after the death of the survivor of the group composed of all who are Members of the Company and their issue who are living on the date of this Operating Agreement and their issue, if any, who are living on the effective date of this Operating Agreement.

8.13 *No Partition.* Each Member irrevocably waives during the term of the Company the right, if any, such Member may have, if any, to maintain any action for partition with respect to the real property of the Company.

8.14 *Counterparts.* This Operating Agreement may be executed in counterparts, each of which shall be deemed an original but all of which shall constitute one and the same instrument.

8.15 *Remedies.*

[OPTIONAL]

(a) *Attorneys' Fees Assessed in Favor of Prevailing Party.* If the Company or any party obtains a judgment against any other party by reason of breach of this Operating Agreement, reasonable attorneys' fee and costs, as determined by the court, shall be included in such judgment to compensate the prevailing party for its reasonable legal fees and costs. Any Member shall be entitled to maintain, on its own behalf or on behalf of the Company, any action or proceeding against any other Member, successor, or the Company (including any action for damages, specific performance, or declaratory relief) for or by reason of breach by such party of this Operating Agreement, or any other agreement entered into in connection with the same, notwithstanding the fact that any or all of the parties to such proceeding may then be Members in the Company, and without dissolving the Company as a limited liability company.

[STANDARD]

(b) *Specific Performance.* Each party to this Operating Agreement agrees that the Members would be irreparably damaged if any of the provisions of this Operating Agreement are not performed in accordance with their specific terms and that monetary damages would not provide an adequate remedy in such event. Accordingly, except as otherwise provided in the Act, it is agreed that, in addition to any other remedy to which the nonbreaching Members may be entitled, at law or in equity, the nonbreaching Members shall be entitled to injunctive relief to prevent breaches of the provisions of this Operating Agreement and specifically to enforce the terms and provisions hereof in any action instituted in any court of the United States or any state thereof having subject matter jurisdiction thereof.

8.16 *Dispute Resolution.*

[OPTIONAL]

(a) *Waiver of Jury Trial.* The parties hereto waive trial by jury in any action, proceeding or counterclaim brought by any party(ies) against any other party(ies) on any matter arising out of or in any way connected with this operating agreement or the relationship of the parties created hereunder.

[OPTIONAL]

(b) *Agreement to Submit to Arbitration.* The parties and their successors shall strive to settle amicably any dispute, controversy, or claim arising out of or relating to the Company or this Agreement or a breach thereof. The parties recognize the value of mediation and encourage its use where appropriate. However, any dispute, controversy, or claim related to this Agreement or breach thereof, status as a Member of Manager, and the business or management of the Company shall be submitted to arbitration and upon demand, any such dispute, controversy, or claim shall be settled by arbitration in accordance with the Commercial Arbitration Rules of the American Arbitration Association, and judgment upon the award rendered by the arbitrators may be entered in any court of competent jurisdiction. The parties contemplate and agree that the award of the arbitrators shall be final and binding upon the parties hereto and their successors.

The parties hereto agree that (i) arbitrator(s) shall be selected pursuant to the rules and procedures of the American Arbitration Association; (ii) the arbitrator(s) shall be licensed attorneys, in good standing; (iii) the Company may at its option request arbitrators who are licensed in outside the state of _____; (iv) the arbitrators shall have the power to award injunctive relief or to direct specific performance; (v) the arbitrators will not have the authority to award punitive damages; and (vi) each of the parties shall bear its own attorneys' fees, costs, and expenses and an equal share of the arbitrator(s) decide to award to the prevailing party a sum equal to that party's reasonable attorneys' fees, costs and expenses and that party's share of the arbitrator and administrative fees of arbitration. For this purpose, any expert witness fees shall be an eligible cost.

[STANDARD]

8.17 *Securities Law Investment Intent, Representations, and Warranties.* Each Member warrants, represents, agrees, and acknowledges: (a) that he or she has adequate means of providing for his or her current needs and foreseeable future contingencies and anticipates no need now or in the foreseeable future to sell his or her Units; (b) that he or she is acquiring his or her Units or his or her own account as a long-term investment and without a present view to make any distribution, resale, or fractionalization thereof; (c) that he or she and his or her independent counselors have such knowledge and experience in financial and business matters that they are capable of evaluating the merits and risks of the investment involved in his or her acquisition of his or her Units and they have evaluated the same; (d) that he or she is able to bear the economic risks of such investment; (e) that he or she and his or her independent counselors have made such investigation of the Company (including its business prospects and financial condition) and the Members, have had access to all information regarding the Company and the Members and have had an opportunity to ask all of the questions regarding the Company and the Members as they deem necessary to fully evaluate his or her investment therein; (f) that in connection with his or her acquisition of a Unit, he or she has been fully informed by his or her independent counsel as to the applicability of the requirements of the Securities Act of 1933 and all applicable state securities or blue sky laws to his or her Units; (g) that he or she understands that (1) his or her Units are not registered under the Securities Act or any state securities law, (2) there is no market for his or her Units and that he or she will be unable to Transfer his or her Units unless such is so registered or unless the Transfer complies with an exemption from such registration (evidence of which must be satisfactory to counsel for the Company), (3) such Units cannot be expected to be readily transferred or liquidated, and (4) his or her acquisition of a Unit in the Company involves a high degree of risk; and (h) that no representations are or have been made to him or her by any Member or its representatives as to any tax advantages that may inure to his or her benefit or as to the Company's status for tax purposes and that he or she has relied upon his or her independent counsel with respect to such matters.

[OPTIONAL]

8.18 *Power of Attorney.*

(a) Each Member hereby irrevocably makes, constitutes and appoints [NAME] as his or her true and lawful attorney-infact to make, execute, sign, acknowledge and file with respect to this or any successor Company:

(i) Such amendments to or restatements of the Company's Articles as may be required or appropriate pursuant to the provisions of this Operating Agreement, or otherwise under the Act;

(ii) Any and all amendments or changes to this Operating Agreement and the instruments described in ___, as now or hereafter amended, which the Members may deem necessary or appropriate to (a) effect a change or modification of the Company approved in accordance with the terms of this Operating Agreement, including amendments, or (b) reflect (1) the exercise by any of any power granted to it under this Operating Agreement, (2) any amendments adopted by the Members in accordance with the terms of this Operating Agreement, (3) the admission of any Substitute Member in accordance with Section _____, and (4) the disposition by any Member of his or her Units in compliance herewith;

(iii) All statements of intent to dissolve, notices, articles of dissolution or cancellations of foreign registration, and other documents or instruments that may be deemed necessary or desirable by the Members to effect the dissolution and liquidation of the Company after its termination as provided herein; and

(iv) All such other instruments, documents, and certificates that may from time to time be required by the laws of the State of _____, the United States of America, or any political subdivision or agency thereof to effectuate, implement, continue, and defend the valid and subsisting existence of the Company and any other instruments, documents, or certificates required to qualify the Company to do business in any other State where it is required to so qualify.

(b) The Members hereby agree that the grant of the foregoing power of attorney is coupled with an interest and survives the death, disability, legal incapacity, bankruptcy, insolvency, dissolution, or cessation of existence of a Member and shall survive the delivery of an assignment by any Member of the whole or any part of his or her Units, except that where an assignee of such Units has been admitted as a Substitute Member, as provided in Section ___, then the foregoing power of attorney of the assignor Member shall survive the delivery of such assignment for the sole purpose of enabling the Company to execute, acknowledge, and file any and all instruments necessary to effectuate such substitution.

[OPTIONAL]

8.19 *Confidentiality.* The parties hereto agree that the Company has an interest in maintaining the confidentiality of its Confidential Information. "Confidential Information" means information disclosed or known to a party as a consequence of or through the party's relationship with the Company and related to the Company's business, internal affairs, client relationships, or work product arising out of client relationships. "Confidential Information" is intended to include trade secrets as defined in the Restatement Second of Torts. The parties hereto agree that the Company shall be entitled to seek injunctive relief in the courts against any action of a party which threatens the confidentiality of the Confidential Information, as a provisional remedy pending arbitration of any claims arbitrable under this Article.

IN WITNESS WHEREOF, the parties have caused this Operating Agreement to be duly executed on _____, 19___.

ALL MEMBERS

_____

_____

_____

_____

[OPTIONAL]

SPOUSAL CONSENT
to
OPERATING AGREEMENT
_____, 19__

Each of the undersigned, being the spouse of a Member who has signed the foregoing Agreement, hereby acknowledges that the undersigned has read and is familiar with the provisions of said Agreement and agrees to be bound thereby and join therein to the extent, if any, that the undersigned's agreement and joinder may be necessary. The undersigned hereby agrees that his or her spouse may join in any future amendment or modifications of said Agreement without any further signature, acknowledgement, agreement, or consent on his or her part; and he or she hereby further agrees that any community interest that he or she may have in his or her spouse's LLC Interest in the Company shall be subject to the provisions of the Agreement.

_____

_____

_____

_____

EXHIBIT A

INITIAL MEMBERS

Members	Value of Capital Contribution	Number of Initial Units
(Name and address)	$_____	__ _____
(Name and address)	$_____	_____
(Name and address)	$_____	_____

MEMBERS

Dated: _____

_____

_____

_____

Appendix H

Partnership Agreement for Professional Firm

XYZ LLP
Partnership Agreement for Professional Firm
Two Classes of Partners;
Executive Committee; and Managing Partner

TABLE OF CONTENTS

PARTNERSHIP AGREEMENT

This Agreement is made and entered into by and between those parties whose signatures appear at the end hereof or sign an addendum thereto. This Agreement is in full substitution of and revokes all prior partnership agreements. This Agreement shall be effective as of _____, 1997.

ARTICLE I
DEFINITIONS

"Act" means the Uniform Partnership Act, Revised Statutes of _____ and any amendments thereto.

"Agreement" means this partnership agreement, as amended from time to time.

"Capital Account" means the individual account maintained for each Partner pursuant to Section 4.4.

"Capital Contribution" means the amount of cash or the agreed value of other property contributed to the Partnership by a Partner.

"Class I Capital" means capital contributed other than Class II Capital.

"Class II Capital" means the capital contributed pursuant to Section 4.3.

"Class II Capital Fund" means all Class II Capital and income earned thereon, and the segregated accounts which hold all Class II Capital contributions and all income earned thereon.

"Class II Capital Fund Income" means the income earned by the Class II Capital Fund; "Class II Capital Fund Expenses" means any expenses directly associated with the Class II Capital Fund, including interest paid to Withdrawn Partners on their Class II Capital Account balances; and "Class II Capital Fund Net Income" means the amount by which the Class II Capital Fund Income exceeds Class II Capital Fund Expenses.

"Class II Capital Fund Percentages" means the percent a Partner's Class II Capital Account balance is of all Class II Capital Account balances, excluding any amounts owed Withdrawn Partners for their Class II Capital Account balances.

"Code" means the Internal Revenue Code of 1986, as amended from time to time, or any similar provision of succeeding law; and "Reg." the regulations thereunder.

"Designated Successor" means the person designated by a Partner in writing to the Managing Partner (or the Managing Partner's designee) in _____ prior to death to succeed to his or her Partnership Interest upon such death. In the event any Partner gives more than one such designation, the last one shall control. In the absence of such written designation the Designated Successor shall be the deceased Partner's estate.

"Duly Called Meeting" means a meeting called by written notice or voice mail to all Partners at the meeting at least five days in advance of the meeting, giving the time, location, and proposed agenda of the meeting.

"Executive Committee" means the committee selected as provided in Section 3.2.1.

"Income" and "Losses," respectively, mean the net income or net losses of the Partnership as determined for federal income tax purposes, as adjusted to take into account income exempt from tax and Section 705 (a)(2)(B) of the Code expenditures, and all items required to be separately stated by Section 702 of the Code and the regulations thereunder.

"Managing Partner" means the Partner selected as provided in Section 3.3.1.

"Net Book Value" means the assets (less allowable depreciation and amortization) minus liabilities as shown on the most recent balance sheet of the Partnership prepared according to the Partnership's standard accounting practices, except there shall be subtracted the Class II Capital Fund, with other adjustments made as the Managing Partner determines is appropriate, including taking into account planned distributions of capital or the prior Year's Income and amounts to be paid to any Withdrawn Partner.

"Partner(s)" means those persons signing this Agreement and any person admitted as an additional Partner as provided herein, but excludes any Withdrawn Partner.

"Partnership" means the partnership created by this Agreement.

"Partnership Interest" means the entire ownership interest of a Partner in the Partnership, including but not limited to rights to distributions, rights to share in profits and losses, rights to capital, rights to guaranteed payments, and any other such rights and obligations.

"Partnership Percentage" means the percentage given to a Partner from time to time, which decision when made and reduced to writing in the books and records of the Partnership is incorporated by reference herein. Distributions, allocations, contributions, or any other matters to be done in accordance with the Partnership Percentages shall be based upon the Partnership Percentages at that time, except as otherwise specifically provided herein.

"Partnership Rate" means a rate equal to the prime lending rate at Citibank, N.A., of New York, New York, or any successor institution, plus 2%, to be adjusted each calendar quarter.

"Retired Partner" means a Partner who voluntarily leaves the Partnership because of age or disability with no intent to thereafter pursue, either full time or part time, a law-related career.

"Successor" means an agent (under a power of attorney or otherwise), conservator, guardian, executor, administrator, personal representative, legal representative, estate, heirs, assigns, legatees, devisees, Designated Successor, trustee, successor-in-interest, or any other person succeeding to the Partnership Interest of or acting on behalf of a Partner.

"Total Disability" means the inability to practice law due to a mental or physical disease or condition, which continues for more than six consecutive months, and which is anticipated to continue on a permanent basis.

"Withdrawn Partner," "Withdraws" or "Withdrawal" mean, as applicable, anyone who is no longer a Partner, including one who has died, retired (whether voluntarily or mandatorily), voluntarily left the Partnership, becomes an employee of the Partnership, or has been removed from the Partnership, including a Retired Partner, and the date of "Withdrawal" shall be the date of death or the effective date of any retirement, leaving, becoming an employee, or removal.

"Year" means a calendar year.

ARTICLE II
THE PARTNERSHIP

Section 2.1 *Registered Limited Liability Partnership.* The Partners have previously formed a _____ general partnership pursuant to the Act. From and after the effective date of this Agreement, the Partnership shall be a _____ registered limited liability partnership formed under and governed by the provisions of the Act. The Partners hereby authorize the Managing Partner to sign on behalf of the Partnership the application to register the Partnership as a registered limited liability partnership under the Act, and to file the same with the _____ Secretary of State, and to sign and file any other applications or forms necessary or desirable to form and maintain the Partnership's status as a registered limited liability partnership in _____ and in any state in which the Partnership does business or otherwise may find it desirable to be so registered. The rights and liabilities of the Partners shall be as provided in the Act except as modified by this Agreement.

Section 2.2 *Name.* The business of the Partnership shall be conducted under the name "XYZ LLP," or such other name as the Partnership may decide.

Section 2.3 *Registered Office and Agent.* The registered office of the Partnership, as required by the Act, shall be _____. The registered agent for service of process, as required by the Act, shall be XYZ Registered Agent, Inc.

Section 2.4 *Business of the Partnership.* The business of the Partnership is the practice of _____ and any and all activities related or incidental thereto.

Section 2.5 *Term.* The Partnership shall continue as long as the Partners practice law, or until dissolved as provided in Article IX.

Section 2.6 *Place of Business.* The principal place of business of the Partnership shall be _____, or such other place as the Partnership may decide.

ARTICLE III
MANAGEMENT AND VOTING

Section 3.1 *The Partnership.*

Subsection 3.1.1 *Authority of the Partnership.* The Partnership has ultimate authority for all aspects of the operation, administration and governance of the Firm. However, the Partnership hereby delegates such authority to the Executive Committee and Managing Partner as set out in this Article III (subject only to the terms of this Agreement), retaining the right to make decisions only as to the following matters:

(a) Establish, modify or rescind the means of governing the Partnership;

(b) Approval or disapproval of the Executive Committee's recommendation regarding Managing Partner;

(c) Removal of the Managing Partner;

(d) Election of the Executive Committee as provided in Section 3.2.1;

(e) Admittance and approval of removal of Partners;

(f) Dissolution of the Partnership;

(g) Approval of mergers, acquisitions, the opening of or closing of offices, and the location of the Partnership's principal place of business;

(h) Approval or disapproval of the Executive Committee's recommendations regarding the Partnership Percentage for each Partner; and

(i) Any other matter specifically required by this Agreement to be made by the Partnership.

It is anticipated that the Partnership will make decisions from time to time regarding these matters, including decisions supplementing the matters addressed in this Agreement. The validity and effect of all decisions of the Partnership made before the effective date of this Agreement are not affected by this Agreement, unless they are contrary to the terms of this Agreement, and any such prior decision of the Partnership shall continue as such and shall be binding on the Partnership and all Partners and their Successors until revoked, modified or amended.

Subsection 3.1.2 *Partnership Voting.* Each Partner shall have one vote. Provided, however, if a Partner has materially breached the terms of this Agreement or any decision of the Partnership as determined by the Partnership, then he or she shall have no right to vote and the calculation of Majority Vote, quorum, Super-Majority Vote, Two-Thirds Vote, or any other voting requirement in this Agreement shall exclude such Partner.

All decisions to be made by the Partnership, whether arising as to ordinary matters connected with the Partnership business or not, shall be by Majority Vote, unless otherwise specified in this Agreement.

A vote may be taken at a Duly Called Meeting, or however else the Managing Partner determines, as long as there is the required percent of affirmative votes. If a vote is to be taken at a Duly Called Meeting, then there must be present (in person or by proxy), at the time of the vote, a quorum. A quorum shall be at least 35% of all Partners entitled to vote on the issue.

The use of proxies in voting shall be allowed for all Two-Thirds Votes and all Super-Majority Votes, and may be allowed for a Majority Vote as decided by the Managing Partner.

A "Majority Vote" shall be either (i) an affirmative vote of at least 51% of all Partners who are present (in person or by proxy) at a Duly Called Meeting, but no less than 33% of all Partners; or (ii) an affirmative vote of at least 51% of all Partners, however taken.

A "Two-Thirds Vote" shall be either (i) an affirmative vote of at least 66% of all Partners who are present (in person or by proxy) at a Duly Called Meeting, but no less than 51% of all Partners; or (ii) an affirmative vote of at least 66% of all Partners, however taken.

A "Super-Majority Vote" shall be either (i) an affirmative vote of at least 90% of all Partners who are present (in person or by proxy) at a Duly Called Meeting, but no less than 75% of all Partners; or (ii) an affirmative vote of at least 90% of all Partners, however taken.

Subsection 3.1.3 *Review of Managing Partner and Executive Committee Decisions.* The Partnership also expressly reserves the right to: (i) review and modify decisions or proposed decisions made by the Managing Partner or the Executive Committee, (ii) initiate the making of decisions, or (iii) modify the provisions of this Agreement to transfer back to the Partnership authority delegated herein to the Executive Committee and or Managing Partner (each referred to herein as an "Issue"), pursuant to the following procedures:

(a) Forty percent (40%) of all Partners may, either in writing or by a vote at a Duly Called Meeting, request that a specific Issue be considered and voted upon by the Partnership.

(b) When such a request is made, the Managing Partner will convene a special Partnership meeting not less than ten (10) days after the date of the request. The purpose of the meeting will be for the Partnership to consider and vote on the Issue. Proxies for any such meeting shall be allowed.

(c) At the meeting, the Partnership will consider and vote on the Issue. No action will be taken on the Issue unless more than fifty percent (50%) of all Partners (not just those present at the meeting in person or by proxy) vote in favor of such action.

Subsection 3.1.4 *Agenda Items.* Any Partner may request that the Managing Partner place an item regarding that issue on the agenda for a regularly scheduled Partnership meeting of the Partners entitled to vote on that issue. The Managing Partner shall accommodate such requests by placing the item on the agenda for the next such Partnership meeting where discussion of such an item can be reasonably accommodated.

Subsection 3.1.5 *Amendment of Agreement.* This Agreement may be amended by the Partnership from time to time. Such amendment shall require a Two-Thirds Vote; provided, however, to amend this Agreement to lower a Super-Majority Vote requirement shall require a Super-Majority Vote.

Section 3.2 *The Executive Committee.*

Subsection 3.2.1 *Election of the Executive Committee.* The Partners shall elect an Executive Committee by Majority Vote. The Executive Committee shall consist of six members, plus the Managing Partner. The members of the Executive Committee shall be Partners. Executive Committee members shall serve three-year terms, staggered so that two positions shall be up for reelection each Year. If a Partner has served on the Executive Committee for at least six consecutive years, that Partner shall be ineligible for reelection to the Executive Committee for one year after his or her term ends. If both Executive Committee members whose terms end would otherwise be ineligible under this provision, then only the member with the most seniority shall be ineligible for reelection. If seniority is equal between the two members whose terms have ended, then they shall flip a coin, and only the loser of the coin toss shall be ineligible for reelection. "Seniority" for this purpose means longest time of consecutive service on the Executive Committee.

Subsection 3.2.2 *Authority and Responsibilities of the Executive Committee.* The Executive Committee shall communicate with the Managing Partner on matters relating to the management and operations of the Partnership. In addition, the Executive Committee shall have the authority and be required to make decisions regarding the following specific responsibilities delegated by the Partnership:

(a) Recommend a Managing Partner to the Partners;

(b) Recommend to the Partners the Partnership Percentage for each Partner;

(c) Recommend to the Partners the removal of any Partner pursuant to Section 6.2(ii);

(d) Approval or disapproval of a long-range plan for the Partnership and a strategic plan for implementing the long-range plan of the Partnership;

(e) Approval or disapproval of the budget for the Partnership recommended by the Managing Partner;

(f) Approval of Partnership expenditures, commitments and borrowings in excess of $100,000; and

(g) Undertake the specific responsibilities of the Managing Partner in the event the Managing Partner is incapacitated or the Managing Partner position is vacant.

In connection with any matter delegated to the Executive Committee, a third party may rely on the signature of a majority of the Executive Committee members, and may rely on the identity of the Executive Committee as set out in writing by the Managing Partner, dated within three months prior to the date of reliance thereon.

Section 3.3 *The Managing Partner.*

Subsection 3.3.1 *Election and Removal of Managing Partner.* The Executive Committee shall make a recommendation to the Partners regarding who should serve as Managing Partner. The Partners by

Majority Vote shall approve or disapprove the person so recommended for Managing Partner. The Managing Partner must be a Partner in the Partnership. The Managing Partner shall serve for such term as selected by the Executive Committee.

The Managing Partner may be removed at any time by a vote of the entire Executive Committee with not more than one dissenting vote (exclusive of the Managing Partner) or by a Two-Thirds Vote of the Partners (exclusive of the Managing Partner).

Subsection 3.3.2 *Authority of the Managing Partner.* The Managing Partner has authority to make all decisions for the Partnership not specifically reserved to the Partnership or required to be made by the Executive Committee.

In connection with any matter within the Managing Partner's authority, a third party may rely on the signature of the Managing Partner alone and need not require signatures of any other Partner or the Executive Committee, and may rely on the identity of the Managing Partner as set out in writing by a resolution of the Executive Committee, signed by a majority of the members thereof, dated within three months prior to the date of reliance thereon.

Subsection 3.3.3 *Responsibilities of the Managing Partner.* The Managing Partner's primary responsibility is to supervise the administration and operation of the Partnership and make long-range plans for the Partnership. The Managing Partner will consult, as necessary, with the Partners and Executive Committee with regard to the foregoing. The Managing Partner shall devote full time and attention to the responsibilities of the position.

The Managing Partner shall have the following specific responsibilities:

(a) Prepare, for approval by the Executive Committee, a long-range plan for the Partnership and a strategic plan for implementing the long-range plan and implement and monitor the long-range plan;

(b) Prepare, for approval by the Executive Committee, the budget for the Partnership and implement and monitor the budget;

(c) Approval of Partnership expenditures, commitments and borrowings in amounts less than $100,000;

(d) Recommend to the Partners the removal of any Partner pursuant to Section 6.2(i);

(e) Act regarding the removal, death, disability and retirement of Partners;

(f) Supervise and direct the administration and management of the Partnership and carry out decisions of the Partnership and Executive Committee;

(g) Schedule and chair regular meetings of the Partners and the Executive Committee;

(h) Engage in civic activities, meetings with clients and generally act as the representative and spokesman of the Partnership; and

(i) Any other matter specifically required by this Agreement to be done by the Managing Partner.

Section 3.4 *Acts by an Individual Partner.* No Partner shall have the power to act on behalf of the Partnership for any purpose or shall have the authority to bind the Partnership in any way, except as specifically set forth in this Agreement or except for actions on behalf of the Partnership in connection with rendering normal legal services within the guidelines established by the Managing Partner.

ARTICLE IV
CAPITAL CONTRIBUTIONS

Section 4.1 *Class I Capital Contributions.* Upon becoming a Partner, that Partner shall contribute to the Class I Capital of the Partnership cash equal to his or her initial Partnership Percentage times the Net Book Value. At the beginning of every Year thereafter, a Partner's Partnership Percentage shall be multiplied times the Net Book Value. If the resulting number exceeds that Partner's current Class I Capital Account balance, he or she shall contribute cash to the Class I Capital equal to the excess. If the resulting number is less than that Partner's current Class I Capital Account balance, the Partnership shall pay to the Partner from the Class I Capital the difference in cash. The current Class I Capital Account balance shall be calculated taking into account all events which would adjust that account up to the effective date of the change. The due date for any contribution or payment hereunder may be delayed as decided by the Managing Partner. Upon Withdrawal of a Partner, the provisions of Article VII shall govern, however.

Section 4.2 *Additional Class I Capital Contributions.* All Partners shall contribute additional cash to the Class I Capital of the Partnership at the times and in the amounts recommended by the Managing Partner and approved by the Partnership from time to time. All additional contributions shall be made by the Partners in proportion to their Partnership Percentages at the time any additional such contribution is due.

Section 4.3 *Class II Capital Contributions.* All Partners shall contribute to the Class II Capital of the Partnership. The total amount to be contributed each Year, if any, shall be decided by the Managing Partner; provided, however, if the amount for any one Year would exceed $500,000, then the amount must be recommended by the Managing Partner and approved by the Partners. Each Partner shall contribute his or her Partnership Percentage for that Year times the Class II Capital contribution amount for that Year.

This contribution shall be made by withholding from distributions to the Partners the amount of the contribution at the time or times decided by the Managing Partner. If a Partner Withdraws from the Partnership prior to when such Class II Capital contribution is made in full, that Partner shall not be obligated to make the remaining Class II Capital contribution.

All Class II Capital contributions shall be kept in accounts segregated from other Partnership funds, which accounts and income earned thereon shall be known collectively as the Class II Capital Fund. Distributions of income of the Class II Capital Fund as provided in Article V, and of Class II Capital as provided in this Article or Article VII, shall be made as provided therein from the Class II Capital Fund. In addition, the Managing Partner may make distributions to the Partners in proportion to their Class II Capital Fund Percentages from the Class II Capital Fund. The Class II Capital Fund may be used in addition only for the following purposes, and for no other purposes:

(a) As collateral for borrowings for expenditures which have previously been decided upon by the Executive Committee or Managing Partner, as applicable.

(b) To cover cash shortfalls at the end of the Year to make distributions to the Partners as decided by the Executive Committee. (A cash shortfall for this purpose shall occur only if the Managing Partner decides to make a distribution for that Year in excess of cash then available for distribution.) However, in the event funds are used for this purpose, those amounts must be reimbursed within 60 days even if the Partnership must borrow to do so.

(c) To make loans to incoming Partners for the purpose of assisting them in making their Class I Capital contribution on such terms as decided by the Managing Partner from time to time.

(d) Any other purpose as recommended by the Managing Partner and approved by a Two-Thirds Vote of the Partners.

Any reimbursement to the Class II Capital Fund shall be with interest at a per annum rate not less than the prime lending rate charged by First National Bank as of the first day of any calendar month during which such funds are used, but not yet reimbursed. If the assets and current Income (other than the Class II Capital Fund or Income thereon) of the Partnership are not sufficient to reimburse the Class II Capital Fund, and therefore the Partners who have Class II Capital account balances bear more of a liability than their share as provided in Article VIII, those Partners shall be entitled to contribution from the other Partners as provided in that Article.

Section 4.4 *Capital Accounts.* Throughout the term of the Partnership, a Capital Account shall be maintained at all times for each Partner in accordance with Section 704(b) of the Code and all regulations thereunder, including Reg. 1.704-1(b). Each Partner's Capital Account shall consist of two parts, Class I and Class II. All adjustments to the Capital Accounts shall be reflected in the Class I part, except those to be specifically reflected in the Class II part as set forth below. The Class II part shall reflect contributions and return of Class II Capital, distributions of Class II Capital Fund Net Income, allocations of Class II Capital Fund Income and Class II Capital Fund Expenses, and any other Capital Account adjustments connected directly with the Class II Capital and Class II Capital Fund.

Section 4.5 *Withdrawal and Return of Capital Contributions.* No Partner shall be entitled to be repaid or withdraw any part of his or her Capital Contribution, or to receive any distributions from the

Partnership, except as provided by this Agreement. No Partner shall be paid interest on any Capital Contribution, except from and after the date the same is due and payable under the terms of this Agreement or as specifically provided in this Agreement.

Section 4.6 *Default in Payment of Capital Contributions.* The payment of any Capital Contributions a Partner is obligated to pay under this Agreement, or any obligation a Partner may owe to the Partnership or any of the Partnership's affiliates (regardless of in what capacity that obligation arose), is secured by the Partner's Partnership Interest, and each Partner by execution of this Agreement expressly grants the Partnership this security interest and all rights of a secured party under the Uniform Commercial Code, and agrees to the operations of this provision. If any Partner fails to pay all or any portion of a contribution required under Section 4.1 or 4.2, within 60 days after it is due ("Defaulting Partner"), the Partnership has the following rights or options, to be exercised as the Managing Partner decides, none of which shall be exclusive or mandatory:

(a) To pursue the Defaulting Partner for the amount owed, plus interest at the Partnership Rate, plus any other damages including but not limited to incidental and consequential damages, plus attorneys' fees incurred in the collection of any such amounts, and/or to foreclose the Partnership's security interest.

(b) To offset amounts otherwise to be distributed or paid to a Defaulting Partner from the Partnership against any amounts owed by the Defaulting Partner as set out in Subsection (a) above.

(c) To reduce the Defaulting Partner's Partnership Percentage to the percent that (i) his or her total Class I Capital Contribution less any amount of Class I Capital previously returned to him or her is of (ii) the total Class I Capital Contributions of all current Partners less any amounts of Class I Capital previously returned to them.

(d) To require all non-Defaulting Partners to contribute the amount the Defaulting Partner's unpaid contribution to the Partnership based on their respective Partnership Percentages, and treat that either as (i) loans to the Partnership at the Partnership Rate, or (ii) a loan to the Defaulting Partner at the Partnership Rate (secured by a security interest in the

Defaulting Partner's Partnership Interest and all the rights the Partnership has under this Section 4.5(a) and (b)) and a subsequent contribution by the Defaulting Partner to the Partnership.

(e) To expel the Defaulting Partner pursuant to Section 6.2 and other related provisions of this Agreement.

ARTICLE V
ALLOCATIONS AND DISTRIBUTIONS

Section 5.1 *Allocations.* First, Class II Capital Fund Income and Class II Capital Fund Expenses shall be allocated to the Partners in accordance with their Class II Capital Fund Percentages. Second, Income shall be allocated to all Partners in accordance with their respective Partnership Percentages. Any Losses shall be allocated among the Partners in accordance with their respective Partnership Percentages.

In the Year a Partner Withdraws, that Partner shall be allocated Income or Losses up through the last day of the month prior to the month in which the Withdrawal occurs, or if withdrawal occurs on the last day of the month, up through the last day of that month.

Section 5.2 *Change in Partner's Interest.* Subject to the provisions of Section 5.1, in the event there is a change in a Partner's interest in the Partnership during any Year of the Partnership, the Partners' respective shares of Class II Capital Fund Income and Class II Capital Fund Expenses, Income and Losses shall be determined by such method as the Partnership decides is consistent with income tax rules and the Partnership's accounting practice. If Section 706(c) or (d) of the Code requires an item to be allocated differently than otherwise allocated under this Article V at the applicable time, the allocation shall be done in accordance with Section 706(c) or (d).

Section 5.3 *Non-Liquidating Distributions.* All Class II Capital Fund Net Income for a Year shall be distributed to the Partners in accordance with their respective Class II Capital Fund Percentages by February 28th of the following Year. Any other non-liquidating distributions (whether of Income or Capital) shall be made as decided by the Managing Partner. Notwithstanding the prior provisions, if a

Partner Withdraws from the Partnership, no distributions shall be made to the Withdrawn Partner after Withdrawal except as provided in Article VII.

Section 5.4 *Tax Status.* For federal income tax purposes this Partnership will be subject to the provisions of Sub-Chapter K of Chapter 1 of Subtitle A of the Code, and each Partner agrees to file any federal, state or local income tax return required due to income received from the Partnership, and that any such return shall be consistent with the Partnership's federal, state and local tax returns.

Section 5.5 *Business Expenses.* Each Partner shall incur ordinary and necessary business expenses, and pay for them with such Partner's own funds, in connection with the law practice, including but not limited to automobile, entertainment, promotion, continuing legal education (including travel, tuition, meals and lodging), home, office and related equipment and furniture expenses (including fax, telephone and car phone), professional/business meetings and dues, professional/business books and journals, professional/business equipment, and moving expenses. A Partner shall have no right to be reimbursed for any such ordinary and necessary expenses except for those expenses for which the Partnership has specifically set out in written policies that Partners will be reimbursed. This Agreement constitutes a plan whereby each Partner is accountable to the Partnership for substantiating expenses covered by any reimbursement arrangement. Such expenses must be either actually substantiated to the Partnership or must be deemed substantiated pursuant to the Internal Revenue Service per diem arrangements. Each Partner shall include in the expense request for reimbursement the time, place, date, business purpose and other individuals involved, as well as a brief description of the specific business being transacted or discussed.

ARTICLE VI
ADDITIONAL AND WITHDRAWN PARTNERS

Section 6.1 *Additional Partners.* The Partnership may admit to the Partnership additional Partners upon a Super-Majority Vote. Before becoming a Partner, each admittee shall agree in writing to be bound by the terms of this Agreement and any amendments thereto.

Section 6.2 *Removal.* The Partnership may remove from the Partnership any Partner (i) upon recommendation by the Managing

Partner and approval by a Two-Thirds Vote of the Partners, or (ii) upon recommendation by the Executive Committee and approval by a Majority Vote of the Partners. Which procedure is being used shall be set out in the minutes of the Partnership meeting at which the vote is taken. The effective date of any removal shall be the date determined by the Managing Partner.

Section 6.3 *Mandatory Retirement.* A Partner shall retire from the Partnership and cease to be a Partner hereunder as of the end of the Year during which such Partner reaches the age of 75. The effective date of such retirement shall be the end of the Year in which he or she reaches age 75. Provided, however, the Partnership may decide to exempt any Partner from this requirement under extraordinary circumstances.

Section 6.4 *Voluntary Retirement or Leaving.* Any Partner may retire from or leave the Partnership upon giving prior written notice to the Partnership of his or her intention to retire or leave. The effective date of such voluntary retirement or leaving shall be the date determined by the Managing Partner.

Section 6.5 *Transfer by a Partner.* Except with regard to the grant of the security interest set out in Section 4.6, no Partner may sell, assign, convey, pledge, encumber, or otherwise transfer (whether voluntarily or involuntarily) any part or all of his or her Partnership Interest, without the prior written consent of the Managing Partner. Any transfer in contravention of this Section shall give the Partnership the option at any time after the transfer to redeem all of the Partner's Partnership Interest in the same manner as a Partner who leaves, and thereafter such transferring Partner shall be treated as a Withdrawn Partner for all purposes hereunder.

Section 6.6 *Rights of Withdrawn Partner, Successor or Assignee.* A Withdrawn Partner or Successor of a Partner shall have no rights in the Partnership (including but not limited to rights to any accounting or information, to inspect books or records, to attend meetings, or to participate in management of the Partnership or Partnership business), whether under the Agreement, the Act or other law, or decision of the Partnership, except the right to receive payments otherwise due the Partner hereunder. Provided, however, this shall not change the rights specifically set forth in _____ the Act. Provided, further, the Partnership has no obligation to make any payments to a Successor until such time as it is notified in writing and has been given such documentation and information as it deems appropriate to establish the legal right of the Successor to payment.

Section 6.7 *Files of Departing Partner.* When a Partner withdraws, such Partner shall not be entitled to take any client files except upon written request signed by the client asking for the file(s) to be transferred to that attorney, in which case the Partnership may make copies of the file(s) prior to the transfer at its expense. Further, if requested by the Managing Partner, that attorney shall allow the Managing Partner (or his or her designee) to review all of that attorney's files or materials relating to the practice of law, including, but not limited to, reference materials or work product of that attorney, and whether or not such were produced or completed while employed by or a Partner in the Partnership, and the Partnership may at its expense copy any such files or materials.

Section 6.8 *Suspension.* The Managing Partner shall have the right to suspend a Partner. Upon notice to the Partner of such suspension, the Partner is immediately suspended from all duties on behalf of the Partnership and, if requested by the Managing Partner, shall no longer be physically present at any Partnership office. Such suspension shall not affect allocation of income or distributions to such Partner. Provided, however, such suspension cannot continue beyond sixty (60) days without a decision by the Executive Committee to so continue it.

ARTICLE VII
PAYMENTS TO WITHDRAWN PARTNERS

Section 7.1 *Death.* Upon the death of a Partner, the Partner's Designated Successor shall succeed to the deceased Partner's Partnership Interest. The Partnership shall pay the Designated Successor in complete liquidation of the deceased Partner's Partnership Interest an amount equal to the deceased Partner's Capital Account on the date of death (using values determined according to the Partnership's standard accounting practices for the end of the month prior to the month in which death occurs), after adjustment for all events occurring up through the date of death, including any allocation of Income or Losses for all periods prior to the date of death (but only as provided in Section 5.1), plus the deceased Partner's

Designated Successor shall be released from liability as set forth in Section 8.4. This amount is a payment in exchange for the Partner's interest in Partnership property, and shall be a distribution by the Partnership pursuant to Section 736(b) of the Code. This payment shall be made to the Designated Successor no later than June 30th of the Year following the Year in which death occurs. The Class II part of the Capital Account shall be paid from the Class II Capital Fund.

The Partners agree that the amounts to be paid hereunder represent the total redemption price for the entire Partnership Interest of a deceased Partner. No additional amounts shall be due the Designated Successor for a share in profits, guaranteed payment, or any other distribution, as the amounts received prior to death shall be the only payments due in that regard for the Year of death (except for any payments that may become due under the terms of any separate plan adopted by the Partnership from time to time, and entitlements to payment under any such plan shall depend on its terms). No payments shall be made for goodwill.

The Partnership may accomplish the redemption hereunder without any action being required by the Designated Successor. If the Designated Successor will not accept payment or is for some reason unavailable, it shall be sufficient for the funds to be deposited in a bank account in the name of the deceased Partner or the Designated Successor until such time as the Designated Successor will accept such or is available. The Partnership has no obligation to make any payments to the Designated Successor until such time as it knows of the death and has been given such documentation and information as it deems appropriate to establish the legal right of the Designated Successor to payment.

Section 7.2 *Withdrawal Other Than Death.* On Withdrawal other than death, including the retirement, removal, or leaving of a Partner, the Partnership shall pay the Withdrawn Partner in complete liquidation of his or her Partnership Interest an amount equal to his or her Capital Account on the date of Withdrawal (using values determined according to the Partnership's standard accounting practices for the end of the month prior to the month in which Withdrawal occurs), after adjustment for all events occurring up through the date of Withdrawal, including any allocation of Income or Losses for all periods prior to the date of Withdrawal (but only as provided in Section 5.1), plus the Withdrawn Partner may be released from liability as set forth in Section 8.4. This amount is a payment in exchange for the Partner's interest in Partnership property, and shall be a distribution by the Partnership pursuant to Section 736(b) of the Code. The Class II part of the Capital Account shall be paid from the Class II Capital Fund to the Withdrawn Partner no later than June 30th of the Year following the Year in which Withdrawal occurs; the Class I part of the Capital Account shall be paid at the following times: (i) if the payment is due to a Retired Partner who Withdraws at age 70 or later, or a Partner who Withdraws due to Total Disability, then the payment shall be made no later than June 30th of the Year following the Year in which Withdrawal occurs; (ii) If the payment is due any other Partner, then the payment shall be made in two equal annual installments, no later than June 30th of the Year following the Year in which Withdrawal occurs and June 30th of the following Year. Provided, however, for a Partner who has been removed pursuant to Section 6.2(ii), both Class I and Class II parts of the Capital Account shall be paid no later than June 30th of the year in which the effective date of the removal occurs.

The Partners agree that the amounts to be paid hereunder represent the total redemption price for the entire Partnership Interest of a Withdrawn Partner. No additional amounts shall be due the Withdrawn Partner for a share in profits, guaranteed payment, or any other distribution, as the amounts received prior to Withdrawal shall be the only payments due in that regard for the Year of Withdrawal (except for any payments that may become due under the terms of any separate plan adopted by the Partnership from time to time, and entitlement to payment under any such plan shall depend on its terms). No payments shall be made for goodwill.

The Partnership may accomplish the redemption hereunder without any action being required by the Withdrawn Partner. If the Withdrawn Partner will not accept payment or is for some reason unavailable, it shall be sufficient for the funds to be deposited in a bank account in the name of the Withdrawn Partner until such time as the Withdrawn Partner will accept such or is available.

Section 7.3 *Limitation on Capital Payments to Partners.* Notwithstanding the provisions of Sections 7.1 and 7.2 to the contrary, payments to Withdrawn Partners in connection with their Capital Account balance shall be delayed under the following circumstances. No more than 20% of the Class II Capital Fund, based on the balance on December 31st of the Year prior to the Year in which payment is made, and excluding income earned in the prior Year not yet distributed, may be paid to such Partners for their Class II Capital in that Year, and not more than 20% of the Net Book Value of the Partnership, based on the balance sheet for December 31st of the Year prior to the Year in which payment is made, may be paid to such Partners for their Class I Capital. The limits shall be applied separately for Class I and Class II.

If the amount that would otherwise be paid to all such Partners for Class I or Class II Capital under provisions of Sections 7.1 and 7.2 would exceed such 20%, only such 20% shall be paid, and the payments shall be by category in the following order of priority:

(a) Payments due because of the death of a Partner, in the order death occurs.

(b) Payment to Partners who have been removed pursuant to Section 6.2(ii).

(c) Payments due a Retired Partner who Withdraws at age 68 or later.

(d) Payments due a Partner who Withdraws due to Total Disability.

(e) Payments due a Retired Partner who Withdraws at the beginning of the Year in which he or she will reach the age of 63, or later, and who has been with the firm for at least 10 years prior to retiring.

(f) Payments due a Partner who Withdraws for any other reason.

Except as provided in (a) above, if a category can only be partially paid under this limitation, then payments due for prior Years, delayed because of this limitation, shall be paid, earliest Years first, pro rata among payments due for each Year if payments for a given Year can only be partially made. Each Year the limitation applies, the priority of payments shall begin again for all payments due for that Year and for prior Years. After making all payments due in order of this priority within such 20% limit, if there are payments that have been due for more than 24 months which are not paid, then 10% of the amount of such payments shall be paid, even though that exceeds the 20%.

Provided, however, nothing herein shall delay the payment of Class II Capital Fund Net Income or interest on Class II Capital as provided in Section 7.4.

The Partners by Majority Vote can permit exceptions to any of these payment restrictions and allow any payments of Class I Capital or Class II Capital or interest thereon to be paid earlier than provided in this Agreement.

Section 7.4 *Interest on Payments of Capital Accounts.* No interest shall be paid on any payment of Class I Capital to a Withdrawn Partner, unless payment is not made at the time for payment set out in this Agreement after taking into account delays due to Section 7.3.

Interest shall be paid on the outstanding amount due for Class II Capital from the date of Withdrawal as provided herein. The interest shall be paid no later than June 30th following each Year in which any Class II Capital is outstanding and unpaid, on the amount so outstanding during that Year. (Provided, however, for the purpose of interest calculations, all amounts paid on or before June 30th shall be deemed paid at the end of the prior Year.) The amount of interest to be paid is as follows: (i) for payments due no later than June 30th after the Year in which Withdrawal occurs, the interest shall be the same amount as the Class II Capital Fund Net Income that would have been distributed to the Withdrawn Partner if he or she had been a Partner through the end of the Year, after subtracting the Class II Capital Fund Income, less Class II Capital Fund Expense, allocated to the Withdrawn Partner for that Year; and (ii) for payments due in following Years, interest shall be calculated the same for each following Year, except the Withdrawn Partner's share of Class II Capital Fund Net Income shall be based on the Class II Capital Account balance for that Year (as reduced by the payment due no later than June 30th that Year), there shall be excluded from the calculation of Class II Capital Fund Net Income for this purpose the interest paid to the Withdrawn Partner, and of course there would be no subtraction for Class II Capital Fund Income less Class II Capital Fund Expense allocated to the Withdrawn Partner.

Section 7.5 *Adjustment of Partnership Percentages.* A Withdrawn Partner's Partnership Percentage shall be allocated among the remaining Partners in the Year of Withdrawal in accordance with their then respective Partnership Percentages.

Section 7.6 *Optional Calculation of Capital Accounts.* Notwithstanding the prior provisions to the contrary, if Partners having Partnership Percentages exceeding 20 percent in the aggregate

Withdraw from the Partnership in any one twelve-month period, then the Managing Partner, in his or her sole discretion, may elect to value the Capital Account of the Withdrawn Partners under this section by written notice to the Withdrawn Partners within 12 months after the Withdrawal occurs. (Provided, however, any amounts paid to a Withdrawn Partner after Withdrawal and before the election is made need not be repaid.) If such election is made, the Managing Partner shall cause the Net Book Value of the Partnership as of the end of the Year prior to when the Withdrawal occurs to be adjusted as follows:

(a) Any client advances included in such Net Book Value that have been written off after the date of Withdrawal and before the election is made, shall be subtracted from such Net Book Value.

(b) The value of the tangible assets of the Partnership as reflected in such Net Book Value shall be changed to fair market value as determined by an appraiser selected by the Managing Partner in his or her sole discretion, provided the appraiser must not be a Partner in the Partnership or related by blood to a Partner, and must have some experience in appraising similar assets.

No change shall be made in such Net Book Value from cash basis to accrual basis, however. The Withdrawn Partner's Partnership Percentage at the end of the Year prior to Withdrawal shall be multiplied times this adjusted Net Book Value, the Withdrawn Partner's Class II Capital account balance shall be added, and that figure shall be then adjusted for all events occurring in the Year of Withdrawal up through the date of Withdrawal that affect a Partner's Capital Account, and the result shall be the value of the Capital Account on the date of Withdrawal for all purposes under this Agreement.

ARTICLE VIII
INDEMNIFICATION

Section 8.1 *Indemnification for Acts in Professional Capacity.* The Partnership shall indemnify and hold harmless each Partner from and against any damages, including reasonable attorneys' fees, that he or she may individually sustain by reason of any act, omission or alleged acts or omissions committed by the Partner, or by someone acting under such Partner's direct supervision or control, while acting in his or her Professional Capacity. (For this purpose, "Professional Capacity" shall mean acting in his or her professional capacity as attorney, counselor at law, notary and including as administrator, executor, trustee, guardian, committee for incompetent, or other fiduciary, or similar agent or advisor, whether or not in the name of the Partnership, provided that a portion of the fee (if a fee is charged and regardless of whether such fee is actually collected) accruing from such work shall inure to the benefit of the Partnership.)

Provided, however, this indemnification shall not apply to (i) damages to the extent covered by insurance or reimbursed through some other source, (ii) damages caused by such Partner's own acts or omissions done wrongfully and intentionally without just cause or excuse, or that are found to be in complete indifference to, or in conscious disregard for, the safety and property of others, or (iii) damages caused by acts or omissions which would be excluded from coverage under any professional liability insurance policy in force now or hereafter naming the Partnership as an insured.

This indemnity shall not apply after a person ceases to be a Partner, unless the Partners otherwise decide. Provided, however, this indemnity shall apply to damages (other than professional negligence or other tort liability except to the extent of any deductible on insurance policies naming the Partnership as an insured) incurred by the following: (i) the Designated Successor of a person who dies while a Partner, (ii) a Retired Partner, unless the Retired Partner has, in fact, pursued, either full time or part time, a law-related career between leaving the Partnership and the date or dates the Partnership would otherwise provide an indemnity under this Section, or (iii) the estate, heirs, devisees, legatees, or personal representatives of a Retired Partner who dies.

This indemnification shall not be a personal obligation of the Partners and shall be limited to the net assets of the Partnership. This indemnification is personal to the Partner, is not for the benefit of and cannot be enforced by any third party to whom the Partner owes any obligation, and is not assignable. This indemnity shall only apply to damages that an indemnified Partner pays from his or her own funds and is intended as a one time only payment in connection with a particular activity. If any amount is paid to such Partner pursuant to this indemnification and subsequently such Partner pays additional amounts as damages in connection with the activity, there shall be no right to indemnification hereunder as to those additional amounts.

Any right to indemnity or contribution for any damages that a Partner may individually incur for the acts, omissions, or alleged acts and omissions of his or herself or others incurred, created, or assumed while the Partnership is not a registered limited liability partnership and thus the limited liability provisions of Section 358.150(2) do not apply, shall be governed by any prior applicable partnership agreement and by the Act as it applies to a partnership which is not a registered limited liability partnership to the extent that Act is not superseded by any such prior applicable partnership agreement.

Section 8.2 *Indemnification for Acts as Executive Committee Member and Managing Partner.* The Partnership shall indemnify and hold harmless each Partner from and against any damages, including reasonable attorneys' fees, that he or she may individually sustain by reason of serving as an Executive Committee Member or the Managing Partner. Provided, however, this indemnification shall not apply to (a) damages to the extent covered by insurance or reimbursed through some other source, or (b) damages caused by such Partner's own acts or omissions done wrongfully and intentionally without just cause or excuse, or that are found to be in complete indifference to, or in conscious disregard for, the safety and property of others. This indemnification shall not be a personal obligation of the Partners and shall be limited to the net assets of the Partnership. This indemnification is personal to the Partner, is not for the benefit of and cannot be enforced by any third party to whom the Partner owes any obligation, and is not assignable. This indemnity shall only apply to damages that an indemnified Partner pays from his or her own funds and is intended as a one time only payment in connection with a particular activity. If any amount is paid to such Partner pursuant to this indemnification and subsequently such Partner pays additional amounts as damages in connection with the activity, there shall be no right to indemnification hereunder as to those additional amounts.

Section 8.3 *Responsibility for Acts.* Notwithstanding any other provision of this Article, if the Partnership, or any Partner, incurs damage due, in whole or in part, to any act or omission by a Partner for which the Partner is not entitled to be indemnified under Sections 8.1 and 8.2, (regardless of whether such act or omission occurred before, during or after such person was a Partner) such Partner (whether still a Partner or not) shall, upon request by the Executive Committee, reimburse the Partnership and any Partner for any such damage (including reasonable attorneys' fees), sustained by them, except to the extent of any insurance or other third-party reimbursement received by the Partnership or Partner for such damages.

ARTICLE IX
DISSOLUTION AND LIQUIDATION

Section 9.1 *Dissolution.* Upon the Withdrawal or bankruptcy of a Partner, or any other action or circumstance which would constitute a dissolution under the Act (except for a decision by the Partners to dissolve), the Partnership shall be deemed automatically reconstituted between the remaining Partners and the business of the Partnership shall be continued without interruption and without the execution of any confirmatory agreement as a new partnership under the same name and under the same terms and provisions as are set forth in this Agreement, and no Partner shall have the right to have Partnership property applied to discharge liabilities. The Partnership may be dissolved by Majority Vote, and upon such dissolution no one shall have the right to continue the business, but the Partnership shall be wound up and liquidated as set forth below.

Section 9.2 *Winding Up and Liquidation.* If the Partnership is dissolved and its business is not continued as provided in Section 9.1, the Partners then serving on the Executive Committee, or if none, the Partners selected by the Majority Vote of the Partners, ("Liquidating Partners") shall commence to wind up the affairs of the Partnership and to liquidate the Partnership's assets. No distributions shall be made after dissolution if the business is not continued except as set forth below; provided, however, the Liquidating Partners shall be entitled to reasonable compensation for the time spent in winding up and liquidation. The assets of the Partnership shall be sold to the extent possible over a reasonable period of time.

The Liquidating Partners shall make decisions regarding any issues on how pending work shall be handled, or other matters that come up in the dissolution. Sales may be made to Partners as long as the price and terms are substantially fair market value, determined by the Liquidating Partners in their discretion. No Partner or group of Partners shall have the right to use any phone number previously used by the Partnership; rather those phone numbers shall be used to provide call forwarding to all Partners on a fair basis. The right to client files and mailing lists shall be determined pursuant to Section 9.5. The Liquidating Partners shall pursue any Partners whose share of liability as set forth in Article VIII has not been fully paid or borne, to the extent feasible. After winding up, the proceeds of the liquidation and any other assets of the Partnership shall be distributed in the following order:

(a) To creditors, in the order of priority as provided by law, except those liabilities to Partners in their capacities as Partners.

(b) To the Partners for amounts owed them by the Partnership other than for capital and profits.

(c) To set up such reserves as the Liquidating Partners reasonably deem necessary for any contingent liabilities or obligations of the Partnership, for such periods as they deem advisable, with any balance of such reserves to be distributed on the expiration of such periods as provided herein.

(d) To the Partners in proportion to their respective positive Capital Accounts balances, as determined after taking into account all Capital Account adjustments for the Year during which such liquidation occurs, including the allocation of Income and Losses on any sale or disposition, by the end of such Year (or, if later, within 90 days after the date of such liquidation).

(e) Any excess to the Partners in accordance with their Partnership Percentages as of the date of dissolution.

Section 9.3 *Final Reports*. Within a reasonable time following the completion of the liquidation of the Partnership's properties, the Liquidating Partners shall supply to each of the other Partners a statement that shall set forth the assets and liabilities of the Partnership as of the date of dissolution and complete liquidation, application of the proceeds of liquidation, each Partner's portion of distributions and the amounts paid to the Liquidating Partners pursuant to Section 9.2, and any other significant information.

Section 9.4 *Files and Mailing Lists.* Upon liquidation of the Partnership, client files shall be given to the attorney listed as "responsible attorney" on the file; provided, however, upon written request signed by the client asking the file(s) to be transferred to another attorney, the person holding that file shall transfer it to that attorney, but that person may make copies of the file(s) prior to the transfer at his or her expense. Notwithstanding the foregoing, any attorney or his or her Successor shall be entitled to copy any file on which the attorney did any work upon showing a need therefor related to the defense of any litigation brought concerning matters reflected in that file, to the extent not a violation of the attorney-client privilege or ethical principle of confidentiality, and upon payment of copying charges in making such copies. Any Partner on liquidation may receive a copy of any mailing list maintained by the Partnership upon written request no later than three months after liquidation, and upon payment of standard copying charges in making such copies.

Section 9.5 *Termination.* Upon the completion of the liquidation of the Partnership and the distribution of all Partnership funds, the Partnership shall terminate.

ARTICLE X
ARBITRATION AND GOVERNING LAW

Section 10.1 *Agreement to Submit to Arbitration.* The parties and their Successors shall strive to settle amicably any dispute, controversy or claim arising out of or relating to the business of the Partnership or this Agreement or a breach thereof. The parties recognize the value of mediation and encourage its use where appropriate. However, any dispute, controversy or claim arising out of or related to this Agreement or breach thereof, status as a Partner, business or management of the Partnership, or claimed discrimination, harassment, retaliation or other grievance of any kind shall be submitted to arbitration, and upon demand, any such dispute, controversy or claim shall be settled by arbitration in accordance with the Commercial Arbitration Rules of the American Arbitration Association. The parties agree that the award of the Arbitrators shall be final and binding upon the parties and their Successors.

The parties hereto agree that (i) three arbitrators shall be selected pursuant to the rules and procedures of the American

Arbitration Association, (ii) all arbitrators shall be licensed attorneys, in good standing, (iii) the Partnership may at its option request arbitrators who are not licensed in _____ _____, (iv) the arbitrators shall have the power to award injunctive relief or to direct specific performance, (v) the arbitrators will not have the authority to award punitive damages, (vi) each of the parties shall bear its own attorneys' fees, costs and expenses and an equal share of the arbitrators' and administrative fees of arbitration, (vii) the arbitrators will not have the authority to award attorneys' fees other than to direct or confirm in the award that each party shall pay its own fees, except if attorneys' fees are otherwise specifically provided for under the terms of this Agreement, and (viii) the arbitrators shall award to the prevailing party a sum equal to that party's share of the arbitrators' and administrative fees of arbitration.

Section 10.2 *Confidentiality.* The parties agree that the Partnership has an interest in maintaining the confidentiality of its Confidential Information. "Confidential Information" means information disclosed or known to a party as a consequence of or through the party's relationship with the Partnership and related to the Partnership's business, internal affairs, client relationships or work product arising out of client relationships. "Confidential Information" is intended to include trade secrets as defined in the Restatement Second of Torts.

Section 10.3 *Court Action.* The Partnership shall be entitled to seek injunctive relief in court against any action of a party which threatens the confidentiality of the Confidential Information, and as a provisional remedy pending arbitration of any claims arbitrable under this Article, and to enter a judgment upon any award entered by the Arbitrators and enforce the same.

Section 10.4 *Governing Law and Site.* The parties agree that the Federal Arbitration Act, currently at 9 U.S.C. § 1, *et seq.* and the federal substantive law promulgated relative thereto shall be the applicable governing law regarding the application, implementation, interpretation and enforcement of the rights to arbitration set forth in this Article. The parties agree that any arbitration conducted pursuant to this Agreement shall be conducted in _____, _____, at the offices of the American Arbitration Association, and if no such offices are available, at a site in _____, _____, selected by the Managing Partner.

Any legal dispute, controversy or claim arising out of or relating to this Agreement or breach thereof, status as a Partner, business or management of the Partnership, or claimed discriminations, harassment, retaliation, or other grievance of any kind shall be governed under the laws of the State of _____ (excluding the conflicts of laws provisions thereof). Subject to the prior provisions of this Article regarding arbitration, any suit regarding such dispute, controversy or claim shall be brought only in the United States District Court for the _____, or if appropriate the Circuit Court of _____, and the parties hereto hereby irrevocably consent to personal jurisdiction in _____, and acknowledge the convenience and propriety of the venue.

ARTICLE XI
MISCELLANEOUS

Section 11.1 *Use of Name.* The Partnership shall have the right to continue to use the name of any deceased or Retired Partner in the Partnership name and to assign the rights to any name the Partnership uses.

Section 11.2 *Corporate Partners.* If any Partner is a corporation, the provisions hereunder regarding the death, disability, or retirement of a Partner, insurance on a Partner, or any other provision applicable to an individual rather than a corporation, shall be applied to the corporate Partner as though the principal shareholder was the Partner. If the principal shareholder of a corporate Partner dies, that shall constitute an automatic withdrawal of the corporate Partner from the Partnership on the date of such death.

Section 11.3 *Service on Boards of Directors.* No Partner shall serve on a board of directors or as an officer for any corporation, or in any similar capacity for any other entity, other than an affiliate of the Partnership, without prior written approval of the Managing Partner.

Section 11.4 *Payment and Satisfaction.* If a Partner (in any capacity) owes the Partnership or any affiliate any amounts, the Partnership is hereby authorized by such Partner to pay any amounts the Partnership owes such Partner under this Agreement or otherwise to the Partnership or any affiliate, and that shall be treated for all purposes as a deemed payment by the Partnership to such Partner, and then by the Partner to such Partnership or affiliate.

Section 11.5 *Binding Effect and Assignment.* This Agreement shall be binding upon the Partners, their spouses (now or in the future), and Successors. This Agreement and all rights and benefits hereunder are personal to the Partners and neither this Agreement nor any of the rights hereunder shall be voluntarily or involuntarily transferred or assigned to any other person or inure to the benefit of any person not a party hereto. This Agreement and all rights and obligations of the Partnership shall be binding upon and inure to the benefit of its successors and assigns. The term "Successor" shall mean only any person that, by any voluntary merger, consolidation, purchase of assets, liquidation, or other voluntary assignment acquires a substantial part of the assets of the Partnership.

Section 11.6 *Notices.* Unless otherwise provided herein, all notices, requests, demands, and other communications under this Agreement shall be in writing. Unless otherwise provided herein, notice shall be deemed to have been duly given on the date of service if served personally on the party to whom notice is to be given, or within seven (7) calendar days after mailing, if mailed to the party to whom notice is to be given, by registered or certified mail, return receipt requested, postage prepaid, and properly addressed, or within three (3) calendar days after deposit with a delivery service, if sent to the party to whom notice is to be given by a service guaranteeing overnight delivery, costs prepaid, and properly addressed:

(a) If to the Partnership, to XYZ LLP, _____ Attn: Managing Partner; and

(b) If to a Partner, to such Partner's office at XYZ LLP, or if no longer at any offices of XYZ LLP to the Partner's last known address as set forth in the records of the Partnership, or any other address that any party may designate by written notice to the others.

Any notice which is required to be made within a stated period of time shall be considered timely if delivered, mailed or deposited before midnight of the last day of such period.

Section 11.7 *Books and Records.* Proper and complete records and books of account shall be kept by the Partnership at any location that the Managing Partner decides, in which shall be entered fully and accurately all transactions and other matters relative to the Partnership's business. Information needed by each Partner for preparation of his or her income tax return shall be prepared and delivered to each Partner on a timely basis.

Section 11.8 *Survival of Rights and Obligations.* The provisions of this Agreement regarding the rights and obligations of the Partners between each other shall survive and remain in full force and effect notwithstanding the Withdrawal of a Partner, any termination of the Partnership or this Agreement.

Section 11.9 *Entire Agreement.* This Agreement is the entire agreement between the parties hereto with respect to the subject matter hereof and shall not be amended, altered or modified in any manner whatsoever, except by a written instrument executed by the parties hereto as provided in Section 3.1.5. This Agreement supersedes all prior agreements between the parties with respect to the subject matter hereof and all such prior agreements shall be void and of no further force or effect as of the date thereof.

Section 11.10 *Severability.* If any one or more of the provisions of this Agreement, as applied to any party or any circumstance, shall, for any reason, be held to be invalid, illegal or unenforceable in any respect, then such provision shall be deemed limited to the extent that such court determines it enforceable, and as so limited, shall remain in full force and effect. In the event that such court shall determine any such provision, or portion thereto, wholly invalid, illegal or unenforceable, such invalidity, illegality or unenforceability shall not affect any other provision of this Agreement and this Agreement shall be construed as if such invalid, illegal or unenforceable provision shall have never been contained herein.

Section 11.11 *Captions.* Captions or section headings contained in this Agreement are inserted only as a matter of convenience and in no way define, limit, or extend the scope or intent of this Agreement or any provision hereof.

Section 11.12 *Execution.* This Agreement may be executed in one or more counterparts, each of which shall be deemed an original, but all of which together shall constitute one in the same instrument. Any counterpart may be used in connection with the proof of this Agreement.

Appendix I

"Check the Box" Treasury Regulations

§ *1.581-1 Banks.*

    (a) In order to be a bank as defined in section 581, an institution must be a corporation for federal tax purposes. See § 301.7701-2(b) of this chapter for the definition of a corporation.

    (b) This section is effective as of January 1, 1997.

§ *1.581-2 Mutual savings banks, building and loan associations, and cooperative banks.*

    (a) * * * See section 593 for special rules concerning reserves for bad debts. * * * See also section 594 and § 1.594-1 for special rules governing the taxation of a mutual savings bank conducting a life insurance business.

§ *1.761-1 Terms defined.*

    (a) *Partnership.* The term partnership means a partnership as determined under §§ 301.7701-1, 301.7701-2, and 301.7701-3 of this chapter.

* * * * * **PART 301 — PROCEDURE AND ADMINISTRATION**

§ *301.6109-1 Identifying numbers.*

    * * * * *

    (b) * * *

        (2) * * *

(v) A foreign person that makes an election under § 301.7701-3(c);

* * * * *

(h) Special rules for certain entities under § 301.7701-3 — (1) General rule. Any entity that has an employer identification number (EIN) will retain that EIN if its federal tax classification changes under § 301.7701-3.

(2) Special rules for entities that are disregarded as entities separate from their owners — (i) When an entity becomes disregarded as an entity separate from its owner. Except as otherwise provided in regulations or other guidance, a single owner entity that is disregarded as an entity separate from its owner under § 301.7701-3, must use its owner's taxpayer identifying number (TIN) for federal tax purposes.

(ii) When an entity that was disregarded as an entity separate from its owner becomes recognized as a separate entity. If a single owner entity's classification changes so that it is recognized as a separate entity for federal tax purposes, and that entity had an EIN, then the entity must use that EIN and not the TIN of the single owner. If the entity did not already have its own EIN, then the entity must acquire an EIN and not use the TIN of the single owner.

(3) Effective date. The rules of this paragraph (h) are applicable as of January 1, 1997.

* * * * *

§ *301.7701-1 Classification of organizations for federal tax purposes.*

(a) *Organizations for federal tax purposes* — (1) *In general.* The Internal Revenue Code prescribes the classification of various organizations for federal tax purposes. Whether an organization is an entity separate from its owners for federal tax purposes is a matter of federal tax law and does not depend on whether the organization is recognized as an entity under local law.

(2) *Certain joint undertakings give rise to entities for federal tax purposes.* A joint venture or other contractual arrangement may create a separate entity for federal tax

purposes if the participants carry on a trade, business, financial operation, or venture and divide the profits therefrom. For example, a separate entity exists for federal tax purposes if co-owners of an apartment building lease space and in addition provide services to the occupants either directly or through an agent. Nevertheless, a joint undertaking merely to share expenses does not create a separate entity for federal tax purposes. For example, if two or more persons jointly construct a ditch merely to drain surface water from their properties, they have not created a separate entity for federal tax purposes. Similarly, mere co-ownership of property that is maintained, kept in repair, and rented or leased does not constitute a separate entity for federal tax purposes. For example, if an individual owner, or tenants in common, of farm property lease it to a farmer for a cash rental or a share of the crops, they do not necessarily create a separate entity for federal tax purposes.

(3) *Certain local law entities not recognized.* An entity formed under local law is not always recognized as a separate entity for federal tax purposes. For example, an organization wholly owned by a State is not recognized as a separate entity for federal tax purposes if it is an integral part of the State.

Similarly, tribes incorporated under section 17 of the Indian Reorganization Act of 1934, as amended, 25 U.S.C. 477, or under section 3 of the Oklahoma Indian Welfare Act, as amended, 25 U.S.C. 503, are not recognized as separate entities for federal tax purposes.

(4) *Single owner organizations.* Under §§ 301.7701-2 and 301.7701-3, certain organizations that have a single owner can choose to be recognized or disregarded as entities separate from their owners.

(b) *Classification of organizations.* The classification of organizations that are recognized as separate entities is determined under §§ 301.7701-2, 301.7701-3, and 301.7701-4 unless a provision of the Internal Revenue Code (such as section 860A addressing Real Estate Mortgage Investment Conduits (REMICs)) provides for special treatment of that organization. For the classification of organizations as trusts, see § 301.7701-4. That section provides that trusts generally do not have associates or an objective to carry on business for profit. Section § 301.7701-2 and 301.7701-3 provide rules for classifying organizations that are not classified as trusts.

(c) *Qualified cost sharing arrangements.* A qualified cost sharing arrangement that is described in § 1.482-7 of this chapter and any arrangement that is treated by the Commissioner as a qualified cost sharing arrangement under § 1.482-7 of this chapter is not recognized as a separate entity for purposes of the Internal Revenue Code. See § 1.482-7 of this chapter for the proper treatment of qualified cost sharing arrangements.

(d) *Domestic and foreign entities.* For purposes of this section and §§ 301.7701-2 and 301.7701-3, an entity is a domestic entity if it is created or organized in the United States or under the law of the United States or of any State; an entity is foreign if it is not domestic. See sections 7701(a)(4) and (a)(5).

(e) *State.* For purposes of this section and § 301.7701-2, the term State includes the District of Columbia.

(f) *Effective date.* The rules of this section are effective as of January 1, 1997.

§ *301.7701-2 Business entities; definitions.*

(a) *Business entities.* For purposes of this section and § 301.7701-3, a business entity is any entity recognized for federal tax purposes (including an entity with a single owner that may be disregarded as an entity separate from its owner under § 301.7701-3) that is not properly classified as a trust under § 301.7701-4 or otherwise subject to special treatment under the Internal Revenue Code. A business entity with two or more members is classified for federal tax purposes as either a corporation or a partnership. A business entity with only one owner is classified as a corporation or is disregarded; if the entity is disregarded, its activities are treated in the same manner as a sole proprietorship, branch, or division of the owner.

(b) *Corporations.* For federal tax purposes, the term corporation means —

(1) A business entity organized under a Federal or State statute, or under a statute of a federally recognized Indian tribe, if the statute describes or refers to the entity as incorporated or as a corporation, body corporate, or body politic;

(2) An association (as determined under § 301.7701-3);

(3) A business entity organized under a State statute, if the statute describes or refers to the entity as a joint-stock company or joint-stock association;

(4) An insurance company;

(5) A State-chartered business entity conducting banking activities, if any of its deposits are insured under the Federal Deposit Insurance Act, as amended, 12 U.S.C. 1811 et seq., or a similar federal statute;

(6) A business entity wholly owned by a State or any political subdivision thereof;

(7) A business entity that is taxable as a corporation under a provision of the Internal Revenue Code other than section 7701(a)(3); and

(8) *Certain foreign entities* — (i) *In general.* Except as provided in paragraphs (b)(8)(ii) and (d) of this section, the following business entities formed in the following jurisdictions:

American Samoa, Corporation

Argentina, Sociedad Anonima

Australia, Public Limited Company

Austria, Aktiengesellschaft

Barbados, Limited Company

Belgium, Societe Anonyme

Belize, Public Limited Company

Bolivia, Sociedad Anonima

Brazil, Sociedade Anonima

Canada, Corporation and Company

Chile, Sociedad Anonima

People's Republic of China, Gufen Youxian Gongsi

Republic of China (Taiwan), Ku-fen Yu-hsien Kung-szu

Colombia, Sociedad Anonima

Costa Rica, Sociedad Anonima
Cyprus, Public Limited Company
Czech Republic, Akciova Spolecnost
Denmark, Aktieselskab
Ecuador, Sociedad Anonima or Compania Anonima
Egypt, Sharikat Al-Mossahamah
El Salvador, Sociedad Anonima
Finland, Julkinen Osakeyhtio/ Publikt Aktiebolag
France, Societe Anonyme
Germany, Aktiengesellschaft
Greece, Anonymos Etairia
Guam, Corporation
Guatemala, Sociedad Anonima
Guyana, Public Limited Company
Honduras, Sociedad Anonima
Hong Kong, Public Limited Company
Hungary, Reszvenytarsasag
Iceland, Hlutafelag
India, Public Limited Company
Indonesia, Perseroan Terbuka
Ireland, Public Limited Company
Israel, Public Limited Company
Italy, Societa per Azioni
Jamaica, Public Limited Company
Japan, Kabushiki Kaisha
Kazakstan, Ashyk Aktsionerlik Kogham
Republic of Korea, Chusik Hoesa
Liberia, Corporation
Luxembourg, Societe Anonyme
Malaysia, Berhad
Malta, Public Limited Company
Mexico, Sociedad Anonima
Morocco, Societe Anonyme

Netherlands, Naamloze Vennootschap
New Zealand, Limited Company
Nicaragua, Compania Anonima
Nigeria, Public Limited Company
Northern Mariana Islands, Corporation
Norway, Allment Aksjeselskap
Pakistan, Public Limited Company
Panama, Sociedad Anonima
Paraguay, Sociedad Anonima
Peru, Sociedad Anonima
Philippines, Stock Corporation
Poland, Spolka Akcyjna
Portugal, Sociedade Anonima
Puerto Rico, Corporation
Romania, Societe pe Actiuni
Russia, Otkrytoye Aktsionernoy Obshchestvo
Saudi Arabia, Sharikat Al-Mossahamah
Singapore, Public Limited Company
Slovak Republic, Akciova Spolocnost
South Africa, Public Limited Company
Spain, Sociedad Anonima
Surinam, Naamloze Vennootschap
Sweden, Publika Aktiebolag
Switzerland, Aktiengesellschaft
Thailand, Borisat Chamkad (Mahachon)
Trinidad and Tobago, Limited Company
Tunisia, Societe Anonyme
Turkey, Anonim Sirket
Ukraine, Aktsionerne Tovaristvo Vidkritogo Tipu
United Kingdom, Public Limited Company
United States Virgin Islands, Corporation
Uruguay, Sociedad Anonima
Venezuela, Sociedad Anonima or Compania Anonima

(ii) Clarification of list of corporations in paragraph (b)(8)(1) of this section-(A) *Exceptions in certain cases.*

    (1) With regard to Canada, a Nova Scotia Unlimited Liability Company (or any other company or corporation all of whose owners have unlimited liability pursuant to federal or provincial law).

    (2) With regard to India, a company deemed to be a public limited company solely by operation of Section 43A(1) (relating to corporate ownership of the company), section 43A(1A) (relating to annual average turnover), or section 43A(1B) (relating to ownership interests in other companies) of the Companies Act, 1956 (or any combination of these), provided that the organizational documents of such deemed public limited company continue to meet the requirements of section 3(1)(iii) of the Companies Act, 1956.

    (3) With regard to Malaysia, a Sendirian Berhad.

(B) *Inclusions in certain cases.* With regard to Mexico, the term Sociedad Anonima includes a Sociedad Anomia that chooses to apply the variable capital provision of Mexican corporate law (Sociedad Anomia de Capital Variable).

(iii) *Public companies.* For purposes of paragraph (b)(8)(1) of this section, with regard to Cyprus, Hong Kong, and Jamaica the term Public Limited Company includes any Limited Company that is not defined as a private company under the corporate laws of those jurisdictions. In all other cases, where the term Public Limited Company is not defined, that term shall include any Limited Company defined as a public company under the corporate laws of the relevant jurisdiction.

(iv) *Limited companies.* For purposes of paragraph (b)(8), any reference to a limited company includes, as the case may be, companies limited by shares and companies limited by guarantee.

(v) *Multilingual countries.* Different linguistic renderings of the name of an entity listed in paragraph (b)(8)(i) of this section shall be disregarded. For example, an entity formed under the laws of Switzerland as a Societe Anonyme will be a corporation and treated in the same manner as an Aktiengesellschaft.

(c) *Other business entities.* For federal tax purposes —

(1) The term partnership means a business entity that is not a corporation under paragraph (b) of this section and that has at least two members.

(2) *Wholly owned entities* — (i) *In general.* A business entity that has a single owner and is not a corporation under paragraph (b) of this section is disregarded as an entity separate from its owner.

(ii) *Special rule for certain business entities.* If the single owner of a business entity is a bank (as defined in section 581), then the special rules applicable to banks will continue to apply to the single owner as if the wholly owned entity were a separate entity.

(d) *Special rule for certain foreign business entities* — (1) *In general.* Except as provided in paragraph (d)(3) of this section, a foreign business entity described in paragraph (b)(8)(i) of this section will not be treated as a corporation under paragraph (b)(8)(i) of this section if —

(i) The entity was in existence on May 8, 1996;

(ii) The entity's classification was relevant (as defined in § 301.7701-3(d)) on May 8, 1996;

(iii) No person (including the entity) for whom the entity's classification was relevant on May 8, 1996, treats the entity as a corporation for purposes of filing such person's federal income tax returns, information returns, and withholding documents for the taxable year including May 8, 1996;

(iv) Any change in the entity's claimed classification within the sixty months prior to May 8, 1996, occurred solely as a result of a change in the organizational documents of the entity, and the entity and all members of the entity recognized the federal tax consequences of any change in the entity's classification within the sixty months prior to May 8, 1996;

(v) A reasonable basis (within the meaning of section 6662) existed on May 8, 1996, for treating the entity as other than a corporation; and

(vi) Neither the entity nor any member was notified in writing on or before May 8, 1996, that the classification of the entity was under examination (in which case the entity's classification will be determined in the examination).

(2) *Binding contract rule.* If a foreign business entity described in paragraph (b)(8)(i) of this section is formed after May 8, 1996, pursuant to a written binding contract (including an accepted bid to develop a project) in effect on May 8, 1996, and all times thereafter, in which the parties agreed to engage (directly or indirectly) in an active and substantial business operation in the jurisdiction in which the entity is formed, paragraph (d)(1) of this section will be applied to that entity by substituting the date of the entity's formation for May 8, 1996.

(3) *Termination of grandfather status* — (i) *In general.* An entity that is not treated as a corporation under paragraph (b)(8)(i) of this section by reason of paragraph (d)(1) or (d)(2) of this section will be treated permanently as a corporation under paragraph (b)(8)(i) of this section from the earliest of:

(A) The effective date of an election to be treated as an association under § 301.7701-3;

(B) A termination of the partnership under section 708(b)(1)(B) (regarding sale or exchange of 50 percent or more of the total interest in an entity's capital or profits within a twelve month period); or

(C) A division of the partnership under section 708(b)(2)(B).

(ii) *Special rule for certain entities.* For purposes of paragraph (d)(2) of this section, paragraph (d)(3)(i)(B) of this section shall not apply if the sale or exchange of interests in the entity is to a related person (within the meaning of sections 267(b) and 707(b)) and occurs no later than twelve months after the date of the formation of the entity.

(e) *Effective date.* Except as otherwise provided in this paragraph (e), the rules of this section apply as of January 1, 1997. The reference to the Finnish, Maltese, and Norwegian entities in paragraph (b)(8)(i) of this section is applicable on November 29, 1999. The reference to the Trinidadian entity in paragraph (b)(8)(i) of this section applies to entities formed on or after November 29, 1999. Any Maltese or Norwegian entity that becomes an eligible entity as a result of paragraph (b)(8)(i) of this section in effect on November 29, 1999 may elect by February 14, 2000 to be classified for federal tax purposes as an entity other than a corporation retroactive to any period from and including January 1, 1997. Any Finnish entity that becomes an eligible entity as a result of paragraph (b)(8)(i) of this section in effect on November 29, 1999 may elect by February 14, 2000 to be classified for federal tax purposes as an entity other than a corporation retroactive to any period from and including September 1, 1997.

§ 301.7701-3 Classification of certain business entities.

(a) *In general.* A business entity that is not classified as a corporation under § 301.7701-2(b) (1), (3), (4), (5), (6), (7), or (8) (an eligible entity) can elect its classification for federal tax purposes as provided in this section. An eligible entity with at least two members can elect to be classified as either an association (and thus a corporation under § 301.7701-2(b)(2)) or a partnership, and an eligible entity with a single owner can elect to be classified as an association or to be disregarded as an entity separate from its owner. Paragraph (b) of this section provides a default classification for an eligible entity that does not make an election. Thus, elections are necessary only when an eligible entity chooses to be classified initially as other than the default classification or when an eligible entity chooses to change its classification. An entity whose classification is determined under the default classification retains that classification (regardless of any changes in the members' liability that occurs at any time during the time that the entity's classification is relevant as defined in paragraph (d) of this section) until the entity makes an election to change that classification under paragraph (c)(1) of this section. Paragraph (c) of this section provides rules for making express elections. Paragraph (d) of this section provides special rules for foreign eligible entities. Paragraph (e) of this section provides special rules for classifying entities resulting from partnership terminations and divisions under section 708(b). Paragraph (f) of this section sets forth the effective date of this section and a special rule relating to prior periods.

(b) Classification of eligible entities that do not file an election — (1) *Domestic eligible entities.* Except as provided in paragraph (b)(3) of this section, unless the entity elects otherwise, a domestic eligible entity is —

   (i) A partnership if it has two or more members; or

   (ii) Disregarded as an entity separate from its owner if it has a single owner.

(2) *Foreign eligible entities* — (i) *In general.* Except as provided in paragraph (b)(3) of this section, unless the entity elects otherwise, a foreign eligible entity is —

   (A) A partnership if it has two or more members and at least one member does not have limited liability;

   (B) An association if all members have limited liability; or

   (C) Disregarded as an entity separate from its owner if it has a single owner that does not have limited liability.

(ii) *Definition of limited liability.* For purposes of paragraph (b)(2)(i) of this section, a member of a foreign eligible entity has limited liability if the member has no personal liability for the debts of or claims against the entity by reason of being a member. This determination is based solely on the statute or law pursuant to which the entity is organized, except that if the underlying statute or law

allows the entity to specify in its organizational documents whether the members will have limited liability, the organizational documents may also be
relevant. For purposes of this section, a member has
personal liability if the creditors of the entity may
seek satisfaction of all or any portion of the debts or
claims against the entity from the member as such.
A member has personal liability for purposes of this
paragraph even if the member makes an agreement
under which another person (whether or not a
member of the entity) assumes such liability or
agrees to indemnify that member for any such liability.

(3) *Existing eligible entities* — (i) *In general.* Unless the entity elects otherwise, an eligible entity in existence prior
to the effective date of this section will have the same
classification that the entity claimed under §§ 301.7701-
1 through 301.7701-3 as in effect on the date prior to the
effective date of this section; except that if an eligible
entity with a single owner claimed to be a partnership
under those regulations, the entity will be disregarded
as an entity separate from its owner under this paragraph (b)(3)(i). For special rules regarding the classification of such entities for periods prior to the effective
date of this section, see paragraph (f)(2) of this section.

(ii) *Special rules.* For purposes of paragraph (b)(3)(i) of
this section, a foreign eligible entity is treated as
being in existence prior to the effective date of this
section only if the entity's classification was relevant (as defined in paragraph (d) of this section) at
any time during the sixty months prior to the effective date of this section. If an entity claimed different classifications prior to the effective date of this
section, the entity's classification for purposes of
paragraph (b)(3)(i) of this section is the last classification claimed by the entity. If a foreign eligible
entity's classification is relevant prior to the effective date of this section, but no federal tax or information return is filed or the federal tax or information return does not indicate the classification of
the entity, the entity's classification for the period

prior to the effective date of this section is determined under the regulations in effect on the date prior to the effective date of this section.

(c) *Elections* — (1) *Time and place for filing* — (i) *In general.* Except as provided in paragraphs (c)(1)(iv) and (v) of this section, an eligible entity may elect to be classified other than as provided under paragraph (b) of this section, or to change its classification, by filing Form 8832, Entity Classification Election, with the service center designated on Form 8832. An election will not be accepted unless all of the information required by the form and instructions, including the taxpayer identifying number of the entity, is provided on Form 8832. See § 301.6109-1 for rules on applying for and displaying Employer Identification Numbers.

> (ii) *Further notification of elections.* An eligible entity required to file a federal tax or information return for the taxable year for which an election is made under paragraph (c)(1)(i) of this section must attach a copy of its Form 8832 to its federal tax or information return for that year. If the entity is not required to file a return for that year, a copy of its Form 8832 must be attached to the federal income tax or information return of any direct or indirect owner of the entity for the taxable year of the owner that includes the date on which the election was effective. An indirect owner of the entity does not have to attach a copy of the Form 8832 to its return if an entity in which it has an interest is already filing a copy of the Form 8832 with its return. If an entity, or one of its direct or indirect owners, fails to attach a copy of a Form 8832 to its return as directed in this section, an otherwise valid election under paragraph (c)(1)(i) of this section will not be invalidated, but the non-filing party may be subject to penalties, including any applicable penalties if the federal tax or information returns are inconsistent with the entity's election under paragraph (c)(1)(i) of this section.

> (iii) *Effective date of election.* An election made under paragraph (c)(1)(i) of this section will be effective

on the date specified by the entity on Form 8832 or on the date filed if no such date is specified on the election form. The effective date specified on Form 8832 can not be more than 75 days prior to the date on which the election is filed and can not be more than 12 months after the date on which the election is filed. If an election specifies an effective date more than 75 days prior to the date on which the election is filed, it will be effective 75 days prior to the date it was filed. If an election specifies an effective date more than 12 months from the date on which the election is filed, it will be effective 12 months after the date it was filed. If an election specifies an effective date before January 1, 1997, it will be effective as of January 1, 1997. If a purchasing corporation makes an election under section 338 regarding an acquired subsidiary, an election under paragraph (c)(1)(i) of this section for the acquired subsidiary can be effective no earlier than the day after the acquisition date (within the meaning of section 338(h)(2)).

(iv) *Limitation.* If an eligible entity makes an election under paragraph (c)(1)(i) of this section to change its classification (other than an election made by an existing entity to change its classification as of the effective date of this section), the entity cannot change its classification by election again during the sixty months succeeding the effective date of the election. However, the Commissioner may permit the entity to change its classification by election within the sixty months if more than fifty percent of the ownership interests in the entity as of the effective date of the subsequent election are owned by persons that did not own any interests in the entity on the filing date or on the effective date of the entity's prior election. An election by a newly formed eligible entity that is effective on the date of formation is not considered a change for purposes of this paragraph (c)(1)(iv).

(v) *Deemed elections* — (A) *Exempt organizations.* An eligible entity that has been determined to be, or claims to be, exempt from taxation under section 501(a) is treated as having made an election under this section to be classified as an association. Such election will be effective as of the first day for which exemption is claimed or determined to apply, regardless of when the claim or determination is made, and will remain in effect unless an election is made under paragraph (c)(1)(i) of this section after the date the claim for exempt status is withdrawn or rejected or the date the determination of exempt status is revoked.

(B) *Real estate investment trusts.* An eligible entity that files an election under section 856(c)(1) to be treated as a real estate investment trust is treated as having made an election under this section to be classified as an association. Such election will be effective as of the first day the entity is treated as a real estate investment trust.

(vi) *Examples.* The following examples illustrate the rules of this paragraph (c)(1):

Example 1. On July 1, 1998, X, a domestic corporation, purchases a 10% interest in Y, an eligible entity formed under Country A law in 1990. The entity's classification was not relevant to any person for federal tax or information purposes prior to X's acquisition of an interest in Y. Thus, Y is not considered to be in existence on the effective date of this section for purposes of paragraph (b)(3) of this section. Under the applicable Country A statute, all members of Y have limited liability as defined in paragraph (b)(2)(ii) of this section. Accordingly, Y is classified as an association under paragraph (b)(2)(i)(B) of this section unless it elects under this paragraph (c) to be classified as a partnership. To be classified as a partnership as of July 1, 1998, Y must file a Form 8832 by September 13, 1998. See paragraph (c)(1)(i) of this section. Because an election cannot be effective more than 75 days prior to the date on which it is filed, if Y files its Form 8832 after September 13, 1998, it will be classified as an association from July 1, 1998, until the effective date of the election. In that case, it could not change its classification by election under this paragraph (c) during the sixty months succeeding the effective date of the election.

Example 2. (i) Z is an eligible entity formed under Country B law and is in existence on the effective date of this section within the meaning of paragraph (b)(3) of this section. Prior to the effective date of this section, Z claimed to be classified as an association. Unless Z files an election under this paragraph (c), it will continue to be classified as an association under paragraph (b)(3) of this section.

(ii) Z files a Form 8832 pursuant to this paragraph (c) to be classified as a partnership, effective as of the effective date of this section. Z can file an election to be classified as an association at any time thereafter, but then would not be permitted to change its classification by election during the sixty months succeeding the effective date of that subsequent election.

(2) *Authorized signatures* — (i) *In general.* An election made under paragraph (c)(1)(i) of this section must be signed by —

    (A) Each member of the electing entity who is an owner at the time the election is filed; or

    (B) Any officer, manager, or member of the electing entity who is authorized (under local law or the entity's organizational documents) to make the election and who represents to having such authorization under penalties of perjury.

  (ii) *Retroactive elections.* For purposes of paragraph (c)(2)(i) of this section, if an election under paragraph (c)(1)(i) of this section is to be effective for any period prior to the time that it is filed, each person who was an owner between the date the election is to be effective and the date the election is filed, and who is not an owner at the time the election is filed, must also sign the election.

  (iii) *Changes in classification.* For paragraph (c)(2)(i) of this section, if an election under paragraph (c)(1)(i) of this section is made to change the classification of an entity, each person who was an owner on the date that any transactions under paragraph (g) of this section are deemed to occur, and who is not an owner at the time the election is filed, must also sign the election. This paragraph (c)(2)(iii) applies to elections filed on or after November 29, 1999.

(d) *Special rules for foreign eligible entities* — (1) *Definition of relevance.* For purposes of this section, a foreign eligible entity's classification is relevant when its classification affects the liability of any person for federal tax or information purposes. For example, a foreign entity's classification would be relevant if U.S. income was paid to the entity and the determination by the withholding agent of the amount to be withheld under chapter 3 of the Internal Revenue Code (if any) would vary depending upon whether the entity is classified as a partnership or as an association. Thus, the classification might affect the documentation that the withholding agent must receive from the entity, the type of tax or information return to file, or how the return must be prepared. The date that the classification of a foreign eligible entity is relevant is the date an event occurs that creates an obligation to file a federal tax return, information return, or statement for which the classification of the entity must be determined. Thus, the classification of a foreign entity is relevant, for example, on the date that an interest in the entity is acquired which will require a U.S. person to file an information return on Form 5471.

(2) *Special rule when classification is no longer relevant.* — If the classification of a foreign eligible entity which was previously relevant for federal tax purposes ceases to be relevant for sixty consecutive months, the entity's classification will initially be determined under the default classification when the classification of the foreign eligible entity again becomes relevant. The date that the classification of a foreign entity ceases to be relevant is the date an event occurs that causes the classification to no longer be relevant, or, if no event occurs in a taxable year that causes the classification to be relevant, then the date is the first day of that taxable year.

(e) *Coordination with section* 708(b). Except as provided in § 301.7701-2(d)(3) (regarding termination of grandfather status for certain foreign business entities), an entity resulting from a transaction described in section 708(b)(1)(B) (partnership termination due to sales or exchanges) or section 708(b)(2)(B) (partnership division) is a partnership.

(f) *Changes in number of members of an entity*—(1) *Associations.* The classification of an eligible entity as an association is not affected by any change in the number of members of the entity.

    (2) *Partnerships and single member entities.* An eligible entity classified as a partnership becomes disregarded as an entity separate from its owner when the entity's membership is reduced to one member. A single member entity disregarded as an entity separate from its owner is classified as a partnership when the entity has more than one member. If an elective classification change under paragraph (c) of this section is effective at the same time as a membership change described in this paragraph (f)(2), the deemed transactions in paragraph (g) of this section resulting from the elective change preempt the transactions that would result from the change in membership.

    (3) *Effect on sixty month limitation.* A change in the number of members of an entity does not result in the creation of a new entity for purposes of the sixty month limitation on elections under paragraph (c)(1)(iv) of this section.

    (4) *Examples.* The following examples illustrate the application of this paragraph (f):

    Example 1. A, a U.S. person, owns a domestic eligible entity that is disregarded as an entity separate from its owner. On January 1, 1998, B, a U.S. person, buys a 50 percent interest in the entity from A. Under this paragraph (f), the entity is classified as a partnership when B acquires an interest in the entity. However, A and B elect to have the entity classified as an association effective on January 1, 1998. Thus, B is treated as buying shares of stock on January 1, 1998. (Under paragraph (c)(1)(iv) of this section, this election is treated as a change in classification so that the entity generally cannot change its classification by election again during the sixty months succeeding the effective date of the election.) Under paragraph (g)(1) of this section, A is treated as contributing the assets and liabilities of the entity to the newly formed association immediately before the close of December 31, 1997. Because A does not retain control of the association as required by section 351, A's contribution will be a taxable event. Therefore, under section 1012, the association will take a fair market value basis in the assets contributed by A, and A will have a fair market value basis in the stock received. A will have no additional gain upon the sale of stock to B, and B will have a cost basis in the stock purchased from A.

Example 2. (i) On April 1, 1998, A and B, U.S. persons, form X, a foreign eligible entity. X is treated as an association under the default provisions of paragraph (b)(2)(i) of this section, and X does not make an election to be classified as a partnership. A subsequently purchases all of B's interest in X. (ii) Under paragraph (f)(1) of this section, X continues to be classified as an association. X, however, can subsequently elect to be disregarded as an entity separate from A. The sixty month limitation of paragraph (c)(1)(iv) of this section does not prevent X from making an election because X has not made a prior election under paragraph (c)(1)(i) of this section.

Example 3. (i) On April 1, 1998, A and B, U.S. persons, form X, a foreign eligible entity. X is treated as an association under the default provisions of paragraph (b)(2)(i) of this section, and X does not make an election to be classified as a partnership. On January 1, 1999, X elects to be classified as a partnership effective on that date. Under the sixty month limitation of paragraph (c)(1)(iv) of this section, X cannot elect to be classified as an association until January 1, 2004 (i.e., sixty months after the effective date of the election to be classified as a partnership). (ii) On June 1, 2000, A purchases all of B's interest in X. After A's purchase of B's interest, X can no longer be classified as a partnership because X has only one member. Under paragraph (f)(2) of this section, X is disregarded as an entity separate from A when A becomes the only member of X. X, however, is not treated as a new entity for purposes of paragraph (c)(1)(iv) of this section. As a result, the sixty month limitation of paragraph (c)(1)(iv) of this section continues to apply to X, and X cannot elect to be classified as an association until January 1, 2004 (i.e., sixty months after January 1, 1999, the effective date of the election by X to be classified as a partnership).

(5) *Effective date.* This paragraph (f) applies as of November 29, 1999.

(g) *Elective changes in classification* — (1) *Deemed treatment of elective change* — (i) *Partnership to association.* If an eligible entity classified as a partnership elects under paragraph (c)(1)(i) of this section to be classified as an association, the following is deemed to occur: The partnership contributes all of its assets and liabilities to the association in exchange for stock in the association, and immediately thereafter, the partnership liquidates by distributing the stock of the association to its partners.

(ii) *Association to partnership.* If an eligible entity classified as an association elects under paragraph (c)(1)(i) of this section to be classified as a partnership, the following is deemed to occur: The association distributes all of its assets and liabilities to its shareholders in liquidation of the association, and immediately thereafter, the shareholders contribute all of the distributed assets and liabilities to a newly formed partnership.

(iii) *Association to disregarded entity.* If an eligible entity classified as an association elects under paragraph (c)(1)(i) of this section to be disregarded as an entity separate from its owner, the following is deemed to occur: The association distributes all of its assets and liabilities to its single owner in liquidation of the association.

(iv) *Disregarded entity to an association.* If an eligible entity that is disregarded as an entity separate from its owner elects under paragraph (c)(1)(i) of this section to be classified as an association, the following is deemed to occur: The owner of the eligible entity contributes all of the assets and liabilities of the entity to the association in exchange for stock of the association.

(2) *Effect of elective changes.* The tax treatment of a change in the classification of an entity for federal tax purposes by election under paragraph (c)(1)(i) of this section is determined under all relevant provisions of the Internal Revenue Code and general principles of tax law, including the step transaction doctrine.

(3) *Timing of election* — (i) *In general.* An election under paragraph (c)(1)(i) of this section that changes the classification of an eligible entity for federal tax purposes is

treated as occurring at the start of the day for which the election is effective. Any transactions that are deemed to occur under this paragraph (g) as a result of a change in classification are treated as occurring immediately before the close of the day before the election is effective. For example, if an election is made to change the classification of an entity from an association to a partnership effective on January 1, the deemed transactions specified in paragraph (g)(1)(ii) of this section (including the liquidation of the association) are treated as occurring immediately before the close of December 31 and must be reported by the owners of the entity on December 31. Thus, the last day of the association's taxable year will be December 31 and the first day of the partnership's taxable year will be January 1.

(ii) *Coordination with section 338 election.* A purchasing corporation that makes a qualified stock purchase of an eligible entity taxed as a corporation may make an election under section 338 regarding the acquisition if it satisfies the requirements for the election, and may also make an election to change the classification of the target corporation. If a taxpayer makes an election under section 338 regarding its acquisition of another entity taxable as a corporation and makes an election under paragraph (c) of this section for the acquired corporation (effective at the earliest possible date as provided by paragraph (c)(1)(iii) of this section), the transactions under paragraph (g) of this section are deemed to occur immediately after the deemed asset purchase by the new target corporation under section 338.

(iii) *Application to successive elections in tiered situations.* When elections under paragraph (c)(1)(i) of this section for a series of tiered entities are effective on the same date, the eligible entities may specify the order of the elections on Form 8832. If no order is specified for the elections, any transactions that are deemed to occur in this paragraph (g) as a result of the classification change will be treated as occurring first for the highest tier entity's classification change, then for the next highest tier entity's classification change, and so forth down the chain of entities until all the transactions under this paragraph (g) have occurred. For example, Parent, a corporation, wholly owns all of the interest of an eligible entity classified as an association (S1), which wholly owns another eligible entity classified as an association (S2), which wholly owns another eligible entity classified as an association (S3). Elections under paragraph (c)(1)(i) of this section are filed to classify S1, S2, and S3 each as disregarded as an entity separate from its owner effective on the same day. If no order is specified for the elections, the following transactions are deemed to occur under this paragraph (g) as a result of the elections, with each successive transaction occurring on the same day immediately after the preceding transaction S1 is treated as liquidating into Parent, then S2 is treated as liquidating into Parent, and finally S3 is treated as liquidating into Parent.

(4) *Effective date.* This paragraph (g) applies to elections that are filed on or after November 29, 1999. Taxpayers may apply this paragraph (g) retroactively to elections filed before November 29, 1999 if all taxpayers affected by the deemed transactions file consistently with this paragraph (g).

(h) *Effective date* — (1) *In general.* Except as otherwise provided in this section, the rules of this section are applicable as of January 1, 1997.

(2) *Prior treatment of existing entities.* In the case of a business entity that is not described in § 301.7701-2(b)(1), (3), (4), (5), (6), or (7), and that was in existence prior to January 1, 1997, the entity's claimed classification(s) will be respected for all periods prior to January 1, 1997, if —

(i) The entity had a reasonable basis (within the meaning of section 6662) for its claimed classification;

(ii) The entity and all members of the entity recognized the federal tax consequences of any change in the entity's classification within the sixty months prior to January 1, 1997; and

(iii) Neither the entity nor any member was notified in writing on or before May 8, 1996, that the classification of the entity was under examination (in which case the entity's classification will be determined in the examination).

§ *301.7701-4 Trusts.*

(b) *Business trusts.* The fact that any organization is technically cast in the trust form, by conveying title to property to trustees for the benefit of persons designated as beneficiaries, will not change the real character of the organization if the organization is more properly classified as a business entity under § 301.7701-2.

(c) * * *

(1) An investment trust with multiple classes of ownership interests ordinarily will be classified as a business entity under § 301.7701-2; however, an investment trust with multiple classes of ownership interests, in which there is no power under the trust agreement to vary the investment of the certificate holders, will be classified as a trust if the trust is formed to facilitate direct investment in the assets of the trust and the existence of multiple classes of ownership interests is incidental to that purpose.

(2) * * *

Example 1. As a consequence, the existence of multiple classes of trust ownership is not incidental to any purpose of the trust to facilitate direct investment, and, accordingly, the trust is classified as a business entity under § 301.7701-2.

Example 2. Accordingly, the trust is classified as a business entity under § 301.7701-2.

(f) *Effective date.* The rules of this section generally apply to taxable years beginning after December 31, 1960. Paragraph (e)(5) of this section contains rules of applicability for paragraph (e) of this section. In addition, the last sentences of paragraphs (b), (c)(1), and (c)(2), Example 1 and

Example 3 of this section, are effective as of January 1, 1997.

§ *301.7701-5 Domestic, foreign, resident, and nonresident persons.*

A domestic corporation is one organized or created in the United States, including only the States (and during the periods when not States, the Territories of Alaska and Hawaii), and the District of Columbia, or under the law of the United States or of any State or Territory. A foreign corporation is one which is not domestic. A domestic corporation is a resident corporation even though it does no business and owns no property in the United States. A foreign corporation engaged in trade or business within the United States is referred to in the regulations in this chapter as a resident foreign corporation, and a foreign corporation not engaged in trade or business within the United States, as a nonresident foreign corporation. A partnership engaged in trade or business within the United States is referred to in the regulations in this chapter as a resident partnership, and a partnership not engaged in trade or business within the United States, as a nonresident partnership. Whether a partnership is to be regarded as resident or nonresident is not determined by the nationality or residence of its members or by the place in which it was created or organized.

§ *301.7701-6 Definitions; person, fiduciary.*

(a) *Person.* The term person includes an individual, a corporation, a partnership, a trust or estate, a joint-stock company, an association, or a syndicate, group, pool, joint venture, or other unincorporated organization or group. The term also includes a guardian, committee, trustee, executor, administrator, trustee in bankruptcy, receiver, assignee for the benefit of creditors, conservator, or any person acting in a fiduciary capacity.

(b) *Fiduciary* — (1) *In general.* Fiduciary is a term that applies to persons who occupy positions of peculiar confidence toward others, such as trustees, executors, and administrators. A fiduciary is a person who holds in trust an estate to which another has a beneficial interest, or receives and controls income of another, as in the case of receivers. A committee or guardian of the property of an incompetent person is a fiduciary.

(2) *Fiduciary distinguished from agent.* There may be a fiduciary relationship between an agent and a principal,

but the word agent does not denote a fiduciary. An agent having entire charge of property, with authority to effect and execute leases with tenants entirely on his own responsibility and without consulting his principal, merely turning over the net profits from the property periodically to his principal by virtue of authority conferred upon him by a power of attorney, is not a fiduciary within the meaning of the Internal Revenue Code. In cases when no legal trust has been created in the estate controlled by the agent and attorney, the liability to make a return rests with the principal.

(c) *Effective date.* The rules of this section are effective as of January 1, 1997.

§ *301.7701-7 Trusts — domestic and foreign.*

(a) *In general.* (1) A trust is a United States person if —

    (i) A court within the United States is able to exercise primary supervision over the administration of the trust (court test); and

    (ii) One or more United States persons have the authority to control all substantial decisions of the trust (control test).

(2) A trust is a United States person for purposes of the Internal Revenue Code (Code) on any day that the trust meets both the court test and the control test. For purposes of the regulations in this chapter, the term domestic trust means a trust that is a United States person. The term foreign trust means any trust other than a domestic trust.

(3) Except as otherwise provided in part I, subchapter J, chapter 1 of the Code, the taxable income of a foreign trust is computed in the same manner as the taxable income of a nonresident alien individual who is not present in the United States at any time. Section 641(b). Section 7701(b) is not applicable to trusts because it only applies to individuals. In addition, a foreign trust is not considered to be present in the United States at any time for purposes of section 871(a)(2), which deals with capital gains of nonresident aliens present in the United States for 183 days or more.

(b) *Applicable law.* The terms of the trust instrument and applicable law must be applied to determine whether the court test and the control test are met.

(c) *The court test* — (1) *Safe harbor.* A trust satisfies the court test if —

    (i)   The trust instrument does not direct that the trust be administered outside of the United States;

    (ii) The trust in fact is administered exclusively in the United States; and

    (iii) The trust is not subject to an automatic migration provision described in paragraph (c)(4)(ii) of this section.

(2) *Example.* The following example illustrates the rule of paragraph (c)(1) of this section:

Example. A creates a trust for the equal benefit of A's two children, B and C. The trust instrument provides that DC, a State Y corporation, is the trustee of the trust. State Y is a state within the United States. DC administers the trust exclusively in State Y and the trust instrument is silent as to where the trust is to be administered. The trust is not subject to an automatic migration provision described in paragraph (c)(4)(ii) of this section. The trust satisfies the safe harbor of paragraph (c)(1) of this section and the court test.

(3) Definitions. The following definitions apply for purposes of this section:

    (i)   *Court.* The term court includes any federal, state, or local court.

    (ii) *The United States.* The term the United States is used in this section in a geographical sense. Thus, for purposes of the court test, the United States includes only the States and the District of Columbia. See section 7701(a)(9). Accordingly, a court within a territory or possession of the United States or within a foreign country is not a court within the United States.

    (iii) *Is able to exercise.* The term is able to exercise means that a court has or would have the authority under applicable law to render orders or judgments resolving issues concerning administration of the trust.

(iv) *Primary supervision.* The term primary supervision means that a court has or would have the authority to determine substantially all issues regarding the administration of the entire trust. A court may have primary supervision under this paragraph (c)(3)(iv) notwithstanding the fact that another court has jurisdiction over a trustee, a beneficiary, or trust property.

(v) *Administration.* The term administration of the trust means the carrying out of the duties imposed by the terms of the trust instrument and applicable law, including maintaining the books and records of the trust, filing tax returns, managing and investing the assets of the trust, defending the trust from suits by creditors, and determining the amount and timing of distributions.

(4) *Situations that cause a trust to satisfy or fail to satisfy the court test.* (i) Except as provided in paragraph (c)(4)(ii) of this section, paragraphs (c)(4)(i)(A) through (D) of this section set forth some specific situations in which a trust satisfies the court test. The four situations described are not intended to be an exclusive list.

(A) *Uniform Probate Code.* A trust meets the court test if the trust is registered by an authorized fiduciary or fiduciaries of the trust in a court within the United States pursuant to a state statute that has provisions substantially similar to Article VII, Trust Administration, of the Uniform Probate Code, 8 Uniform Laws Annotated 1 (West Supp. 1998), available from the National Conference of Commissioners on Uniform State Laws, 676 North St. Clair Street, Suite 1700, Chicago, Illinois 60611.

(B) *Testamentary trust.* In the case of a trust created pursuant to the terms of a will probated within the United States (other than an ancillary probate), if all fiduciaries of the trust have been qualified as trustees of the trust by a court within the United States, the trust meets the court test.

(C) *Inter vivos trust.* In the case of a trust other than a testamentary trust, if the fiduciaries and/or beneficiaries take steps with a court within the United States that cause the administration of the trust to be subject to the primary supervision of the court, the trust meets the court test.

(D) A United States court and a foreign court are able to exercise primary supervision over the administration of the trust. If both a United States court and a foreign court are able to exercise primary supervision over the administration of the trust, the trust meets the court test.

(ii) *Automatic migration provisions.* Notwithstanding any other provision in this section, a court within the United States is not considered to have primary supervision over the administration of the trust if the trust instrument provides that a United States court's attempt to assert jurisdiction or otherwise supervise the administration of the trust directly or indirectly would cause the trust to migrate from the United States. However, this paragraph (c)(4)(ii) will not apply if the trust instrument provides that the trust will migrate from the United States only in the case of foreign invasion of the United States or widespread confiscation or nationalization of property in the United States.

(5) *Examples.* The following examples illustrate the rules of this paragraph (c):

Example 1. A, a United States citizen, creates a trust for the equal benefit of A's two children, both of whom are United States citizens. The trust instrument provides that DC, a domestic corporation, is to act as trustee of the trust and that the trust is to be administered in Country X, a foreign country. DC maintains a branch office in Country X with personnel authorized to act as trustees in Country X. The trust instrument provides that the law of State Y, a state within the United States, is to govern the interpretation of the trust. Under the law of Country X, a court within Country X is able to exercise primary supervision over the administration of the trust. Pursuant to the trust instrument, the Country X court applies the law of State Y to the trust. Under the terms of the trust instrument the trust is administered in Country X. No court within the United States is able to exercise primary supervision over the administration of the trust. The trust fails to satisfy the court test and therefore is a foreign trust.

Example 2. A, a United States citizen, creates a trust for A's own benefit and the benefit of A's spouse, B, a United States citizen. The trust instrument provides that the trust is to be administered in State Y, a state within the United States, by DC, a State Y corporation. The trust instrument further provides that in the event that a creditor sues the trustee in a United States court, the trust will automatically migrate from State Y to Country Z, a foreign country, so that no United States court will have jurisdiction over the trust. A court within the United States is not able to exercise primary supervision over the administration of the trust because the United States court's jurisdiction over the administration of the trust is automatically terminated in the event the court attempts to assert jurisdiction. Therefore, the trust fails to satisfy the court test from the time of its creation and is a foreign trust.

(d) *Control test* — (1) *Definitions* — (i) *United States person.* The term United States person means a United States person within the meaning of section 7701(a)(30). For example, a domestic corporation is a United States person, regardless of whether its shareholders are United States persons.

   (ii) *Substantial decisions.* The term substantial decisions means those decisions that persons are authorized or required to make under the terms of the trust instrument and applicable law and that are not ministerial. Decisions that are ministerial include decisions regarding details such as the bookkeeping, the collection of rents, and the execution of investment decisions. Substantial decisions include, but are not limited to, decisions concerning —

   (A) Whether and when to distribute income or corpus;

   (B) The amount of any distributions;

   (C) The selection of a beneficiary;

   (D) Whether a receipt is allocable to income or principal;

(E) Whether to terminate the trust;

(F) Whether to compromise, arbitrate, or abandon claims of the trust;

(G) Whether to sue on behalf of the trust or to defend suits against the trust;

(H) Whether to remove, add, or replace a trustee;

(I) Whether to appoint a successor trustee to succeed a trustee who has died, resigned, or otherwise ceased to act as a trustee, even if the power to make such a decision is not accompanied by an unrestricted power to remove a trustee, unless the power to make such a decision is limited such that it cannot be exercised in a manner that would change the trust's residency from foreign to domestic, or vice versa; and

(J) Investment decisions; however, if a United States person under section 7701(a)(30) hires an investment advisor for the trust, investment decisions made by the investment advisor will be considered substantial decisions controlled by the United States person if the United States person can terminate the investment advisor's power to make investment decisions at will.

(iii) *Control.* The term control means having the power, by vote or otherwise, to make all of the substantial decisions of the trust, with no other person having the power to veto any of the substantial decisions. To determine whether United States persons have control, it is necessary to consider all persons who have authority to make a substantial decision of the trust, not only the trust fiduciaries.

(iv) *Treatment of certain employee benefit trusts.* Provided that United States fiduciaries control all of the substantial decisions made by the trustees or fiduciaries, the following types of trusts are deemed to satisfy the control test set forth in paragraph (a)(1)(ii) of this section—

(A) A qualified trust described in section 401(a);

    (B) A trust described in section 457(g);

    (C) A trust that is an individual retirement account described in section 408(a);

    (D) A trust that is an individual retirement account described in section 408(k) or 408(p);

    (E) A trust that is a Roth IRA described in section 408A;

    (F) A trust that is an education individual retirement account described in section 530;

    (G) A trust that is a voluntary employees' beneficiary association described in section 501(c)(9);

    (H) Such additional categories of trusts as the Commissioner may designate in revenue procedures, notices, or other guidance published in the Internal Revenue Bulletin (see § 601.601(d)(2)(ii)(b)).

 (v) *Examples.* The following examples illustrate the rules of paragraph (d)(1) of this section:

Example 1. Trust has three fiduciaries, A, B, and C. A and B are United States citizens and C is a nonresident alien. No persons except the fiduciaries have authority to make any decisions of the trust. The trust instrument provides that no substantial decisions of the trust can be made unless there is unanimity among the fiduciaries. The control test is not satisfied because United States persons do not control all the substantial decisions of the trust. No substantial decisions can be made without C's agreement.

Example 2. Assume the same facts as in Example 1, except that the trust instrument provides that all substantial decisions of the trust are to be decided by a majority vote among the fiduciaries. The control test is satisfied because a majority of the fiduciaries are United States persons and therefore United States persons control all the substantial decisions of the trust.

Example 3. Assume the same facts as in Example 2, except that the trust instrument directs that C is to make all of the trust's investment decisions, but that A and B may veto C's investment decisions. A and B cannot act to make the investment decisions on their own. The control test is not satisfied because the United States persons, A and B, do not have the power to make all of the substantial decisions of the trust.

Example 4. Assume the same facts as in Example 3, except A and B may accept or veto C's investment decisions and can make investments that C has not recommended. The control test is satisfied because the United States persons control all substantial decisions of the trust.

(2) *Replacement of any person who had authority to make a substantial decision of the trust* — (i) *Replacement within 12 months.* In the event of an inadvertent change in any person that has the power to make a substantial decision of the trust that would cause the domestic or foreign residency of the trust to change, the trust is allowed 12 months from the date of the change to make necessary changes either with respect to the persons who control the substantial decisions or with respect to the residence of such persons to avoid a change in the trust's residency. For purposes of this section, an inadvertent change means the death, incapacity, resignation, change in residency or other change with respect to a person that has a power to make a substantial decision of the trust that would cause a change to the residency of the trust but that was not intended to change the residency of the trust. If the necessary change is made within 12 months, the trust is treated as retaining its pre-change residency during the 12-month period. If the necessary change is not made within 12 months, the trust's residency changes as of the date of the inadvertent change.

(ii) *Request for extension of time.* If reasonable actions have been taken to make the necessary change to prevent a change in trust residency, but due to circumstances beyond the trust's control the trust is unable to make the modification within 12 months, the trust may provide a written statement to the district director having jurisdiction over the trust's return setting forth the reasons for failing to make the necessary change within the required time period. If the district director determines that the failure was due to reasonable cause, the district director may grant the trust an extension of time to make the necessary change. Whether an extension of time is granted is in the sole discretion of the district director and, if granted, may contain such terms with respect to assessment as may be necessary to ensure that the correct amount of tax will be collected from the trust, its owners, and its beneficiaries. If the district director does not grant an extension, the trust's residency changes as of the date of the inadvertent change.

(iii) *Examples.* The following examples illustrate the rules of paragraphs (d)(2)(i) and (ii) of this section:

Example 1. A trust that satisfies the court test has three fiduciaries, A, B, and C. A and B are United States citizens and C is a nonresident alien. All decisions of the trust are made by majority vote of the fiduciaries. The trust instrument provides that upon the death or resignation of any of the fiduciaries, D, is the successor fiduciary. A dies and D automatically becomes a fiduciary of the trust. When D becomes a fiduciary of the trust, D is a nonresident alien. Two months after A dies, B replaces D with E, a United States person. Because D was replaced with E within 12 months after the date of A's death, during the period after A's death and before E begins to serve, the trust satisfies the control test and remains a domestic trust.

Example 2. Assume the same facts as in Example 1 except that at the end of the 12-month period after A's death, D has not been replaced and remains a fiduciary of the trust. The trust becomes a foreign trust on the date A died unless the district director grants an extension of the time period to make the necessary change.

(3) *Automatic migration provisions.* Notwithstanding any other provision in this section, United States persons are not considered to control all substantial decisions of the trust if an attempt by any governmental agency or creditor to collect information from or assert a claim against the trust would cause one or more substantial decisions of the trust to no longer be controlled by United States persons.

(4) *Examples.* The following examples illustrate the rules of this paragraph (d):

Example 1. A, a nonresident alien individual, is the grantor and, during A's lifetime, the sole beneficiary of a trust that qualifies as an individual retirement account (IRA). A has the exclusive power to make decisions regarding withdrawals from the IRA and to direct its investments. The IRA's sole trustee is a United States person within the meaning of section 7701(a)(30). The control test is satisfied with respect to this trust because the special rule of paragraph (d)(1)(iv) of this section applies.

Example 2. A, a nonresident alien individual, is the grantor of a trust and has the power to revoke the trust, in whole or in part, and revest assets in A. A is treated as the owner of the trust under sections 672(f) and 676. A is not a fiduciary of the trust. The trust has one trustee, B, a United States person, and the trust has one beneficiary, C. B has the discretion to distribute corpus or income to C. In this case, decisions exercisable by A to have trust assets distributed to A are substantial decisions. Therefore, the trust is a foreign trust because B does not control all substantial decisions of the trust.

Example 3. A trust, Trust T, has two fiduciaries, A and B. Both A and B are United States persons. A and B hire C, an investment advisor who is a foreign person, and may terminate C's employment at will. The investment advisor makes the investment decisions for the trust. A and B control all other decisions of the trust. Although C has the power to make investment decisions, A and B are treated as controlling these decisions. Therefore, the control test is satisfied.

Example 4. G, a United States citizen, creates a trust. The trust provides for income to A and B for life, remainder to A's and B's descendants. A is a nonresident alien and B is a United States person. The trustee of the trust is a United States person. The trust instrument authorizes A to replace the trustee. The power to replace the trustee is a substantial decision. Because A, a nonresident alien, controls a substantial decision, the control test is not satisfied.

(e) *Effective date*—(1) *General rule.* Except for the election to remain a domestic trust provided in paragraph (f) of this section, this section is applicable to trusts for taxable years ending after February 2, 1999. This section may be relied on by trusts for taxable years beginning after December 31,

1996, and also may be relied on by trusts whose trustees have elected to apply sections 7701(a)(30) and (31) to the trusts for taxable years ending after August 20, 1996, under section 1907(a)(3)(B) of the Small Business Job Protection Act of 1996, (the SBJP Act) Public Law 104-188, 110 Stat. 1755 (26 U.S.C. 7701 note).

(2) *Trusts created after August 19, 1996.* If a trust is created after August 19, 1996, and before April 5, 1999, and the trust satisfies the control test set forth in the regulations project REG-251703-96 published under section 7701(a)(30) and (31) (1997-1 C.B. 795) (See § 601.601(d)(2) of this chapter), but does not satisfy the control test set forth in paragraph (d) of this section, the trust may be modified to satisfy the control test of paragraph (d) by December 31, 1999. If the modification is completed by December 31, 1999, the trust will be treated as satisfying the control test of paragraph (d) for taxable years beginning after December 31, 1996, (and for taxable years ending after August 20, 1996, if the election under section 1907(a)(3)(B) of the SBJP Act has been made for the trust).

(f) *Election to remain a domestic trust* — (1) *Trusts eligible to make the election to remain domestic.* A trust that was in existence on August 20, 1996, and that was treated as a domestic trust on August 19, 1996, as provided in paragraph (f)(2) of this section, may elect to continue treatment as a domestic trust notwithstanding section 7701(a)(30)(E). This election is not available to a trust that was wholly-owned by its grantor under subpart E, part I, subchapter J, chapter 1, of the Code on August 20, 1996. The election is available to a trust if only a portion of the trust was treated as owned by the grantor under subpart E on August 20, 1996. If a partially-owned grantor trust makes the election, the election is effective for the entire trust. Also, a trust may not make the election if the trust has made an election pursuant to section 1907(a)(3)(B) of the SBJP Act to apply the new trust criteria to the first taxable year of the trust ending after August 20, 1996, because that election, once made, is irrevocable.

(2) *Determining whether a trust was treated as a domestic trust on August 19, 1996* — (i) *Trusts filing Form 1041 for*

the taxable year that includes August 19, 1996. For purposes of the election, a trust is considered to have been treated as a domestic trust on August 19, 1996, if: the trustee filed a Form 1041, "U.S. Income Tax Return for Estates and Trusts," for the trust for the period that includes August 19, 1996 (and did not file a Form 1040NR, "U.S. Nonresident Alien Income Tax Return," for that year); and the trust had a reasonable basis (within the meaning of section 6662) under section 7701(a)(30) prior to amendment by the SBJP Act (prior law) for reporting as a domestic trust for that period.

(ii) *Trusts not filing a Form 1041.* Some domestic trusts are not required to file Form 1041. For example, certain group trusts described in Rev. Rul. 81-100 (1981-1 C.B. 326) (See § 601.601(d)(2) of this chapter) consisting of trusts that are parts of qualified retirement plans and individual retirement accounts are not required to file Form 1041. Also, a domestic trust whose gross income for the taxable year is less than the amount required for filing an income tax return and that has no taxable income is not required to file a Form 1041. Section 6012(a)(4). For purposes of the election, a trust that filed neither a Form 1041 nor a Form 1040NR for the period that includes August 19, 1996, will be considered to have been treated as a domestic trust on August 19, 1996, if the trust had a reasonable basis (within the meaning of section 6662) under prior law for being treated as a domestic trust for that period and for filing neither a Form 1041 nor a Form 1040NR for that period.

(3) *Procedure for making the election to remain domestic* — (i) *Required Statement.* To make the election, a statement must be filed with the Internal Revenue Service in the manner and time described in this section. The statement must be entitled "Election to Remain a Domestic Trust under Section 1161 of the Taxpayer Relief Act of 1997," be signed under penalties of perjury by at least one trustee of the trust, and contain the following information —

(A) A statement that the trust is electing to continue to be treated as a domestic trust under section 1161 of the Taxpayer Relief Act of 1997;

(B) A statement that the trustee had a reasonable basis (within the meaning of section 6662) under prior law for treating the trust as a domestic trust on August 19, 1996. (The trustee need not explain the reasonable basis on the election statement.);

(C) A statement either that the trust filed a Form 1041 treating the trust as a domestic trust for the period that includes August 19, 1996, (and that the trust did not file a Form 1040NR for that period), or that the trust was not required to file a Form 1041 or a Form 1040NR for the period that includes August 19, 1996, with an accompanying brief explanation as to why a Form 1041 was not required to be filed; and

(D) The name, address, and employer identification number of the trust.

(ii) *Filing the required statement with the Internal Revenue Service.* (A) Except as provided in paragraphs (f)(3)(ii)(E) through (G) of this section, the trust must attach the statement to a Form 1041. The statement may be attached to either the Form 1041 that is filed for the first taxable year of the trust beginning after December 31, 1996 (1997 taxable year), or to the Form 1041 filed for the first taxable year of the trust beginning after December 31, 1997 (1998 taxable year). The statement, however, must be filed no later than the due date for filing a Form 1041 for the 1998 taxable year, plus extensions. The election will be effective for the 1997 taxable year, and thereafter, until revoked or terminated. If the trust filed a Form 1041 for the 1997 taxable year without the statement attached, the statement should be attached to the Form 1041 filed for the 1998 taxable year.

(B) If the trust has insufficient gross income and no taxable income for its 1997 or 1998 taxable year, or both, and therefore is not required to file a Form 1041 for either or both years, the trust must make the election by filing a Form 1041 for either the 1997 or 1998 taxable year with the statement attached (even though not otherwise required to file a Form 1041 for that year). The trust should only provide on the Form 1041 the trust's name, name and title of fiduciary, address, employer identification number, date created, and type of entity. The statement must be attached to a Form 1041 that is filed no later than October 15, 1999.

(C) If the trust files a Form 1040NR for the 1997 taxable year based on application of new section 7701(a)(30)(E) to the trust, and satisfies paragraph (f)(1) of this section, in order for the trust to make the election the trust must file an amended Form 1040NR return for the 1997 taxable year. The trust must note on the amended Form 1040NR that it is making an election under section 1161 of the Taxpayer Relief Act of 1997. The trust must attach to the amended Form 1040NR the statement required by paragraph (f)(3)(i) of this section and a completed Form 1041 for the 1997 taxable year. The items of income, deduction and credit of the trust must be excluded from the amended Form 1040NR and reported on the Form 1041. The amended Form 1040NR for the 1997 taxable year, with the statement and the Form 1041 attached, must be filed with the Philadelphia Service Center no later than the due date, plus extensions, for filing a Form 1041 for the 1998 taxable year.

(D) If a trust has made estimated tax payments as a foreign trust based on application of section 7701(a)(30)(E) to the trust, but has not yet filed a Form 1040NR for the 1997 taxable year, when the trust files its Form 1041 for the 1997 taxable year it must note on its Form 1041 that it made estimated tax payments based on treatment as a foreign trust. The Form 1041 must be filed with the Philadelphia Service Center (and not with the service center where the trust ordinarily would file its Form 1041).

(E) If a trust forms part of a qualified stock bonus, pension, or profit sharing plan, the election provided by this paragraph (f) must be made by attaching the statement to the plan's annual return required under section 6058 (information return) for the first plan year beginning after December 31, 1996, or to the plan's information return for the first plan year beginning after December 31, 1997. The statement must be attached to the plan's information return that is filed no later than the due date for filing the plan's information return for the first plan year beginning after December 31, 1997, plus extensions. The election will be effective for the first plan year beginning after December 31, 1996, and thereafter, until revoked or terminated.

(F) Any other type of trust that is not required to file a Form 1041 for the taxable year, but that is required to file an information return (for example, Form 5227) for the 1997 or 1998 taxable year must attach the statement to the trust's information return for the 1997 or 1998 taxable year. However, the statement must be attached to an information return that is filed no later than the due date for filing the trust's information return for the 1998 taxable year, plus extensions. The election will be effective for the 1997 taxable year, and thereafter, until revoked or terminated.

(G) A group trust described in Rev. Rul. 81-100 consisting of trusts that are parts of qualified retirement plans and individual retirement accounts (and any other trust that is not described above and that is not required to file a Form 1041 or an information return) need not attach the statement to any return and should file the statement with the Philadelphia Service Center. The trust must make the election provided by this paragraph (f) by filing the statement by October 15, 1999. The election will be effective for the 1997 taxable year, and thereafter, until revoked or terminated.

(iii) *Failure to file the statement in the required manner and time.* If a trust fails to file the statement in the manner or time provided in paragraphs (f)(3)(i) and (ii) of this section, the trustee may provide a written statement to the district director having jurisdiction over the trust setting forth the reasons for failing to file the statement in the required manner or time. If the district director determines that the failure to file the statement in the required manner or time was due to reasonable cause, the district director may grant the trust an extension of time to file the statement. Whether an extension of time is granted shall be in the sole discretion of the district director. However, the relief provided by this paragraph (f)(3)(iii) is not ordinarily available if the statute of limitations for the trust's 1997 taxable year has expired. Additionally, if the district director grants an extension of time, it may contain terms with respect to assessment as may be necessary to ensure that the correct amount of tax will be collected from the trust, its owners, and its beneficiaries.

(4) *Revocation or termination of the election* — (i) *Revocation of election.* The election provided by this paragraph (f) to be treated as a domestic trust may only be revoked with the consent of the Commissioner. See sections 684, 6048, and 6677 for the federal tax consequences and reporting requirements related to the change in trust residence.

(ii) *Termination of the election.* An election under this paragraph (f) to remain a domestic trust terminates if changes are made to the trust subsequent to the effective date of the election that result in the trust no longer having any reasonable basis (within the meaning of section 6662) for being treated as a domestic trust under section 7701(a)(30) prior to its amendment by the SBJP Act. The termination of the election will result in the trust changing its residency from a domestic trust to a foreign trust on the effective date of the termination of the election. See sections 684, 6048, and 6677 for the federal tax consequences and reporting requirements related to the change in trust residence.

(5) *Effective date.* This paragraph (f) is applicable beginning on February 2, 1999.

Appendix J

Uniform Limited Liability Company Act (1996)

Drafted by the
NATIONAL CONFERENCE OF COMMISSIONERS
ON UNIFORM STATE LAWS
and by it
APPROVED AND RECOMMENDED FOR ENACTMENT
IN ALL THE STATES
at its
ANNUAL CONFERENCE
MEETING IN ITS ONE-HUNDRED-AND-FIFTH YEAR
SAN ANTONIO, TEXAS
JULY 12–JULY 19, 1996
WITH PREFATORY NOTE AND COMMENTS
COPYRIGHT 1996
By
NATIONAL CONFERENCE OF COMMISSIONERS
ON UNIFORM STATE LAWS
UNIFORM LIMITED LIABILITY COMPANY ACT (1996)

The Committee that acted for the National Conference of Commissioners on Uniform State Laws in preparing the Uniform Limited Liability Company Act (1996) was as follows:

EDWARD I. CUTLER, P.O. Box 3239, Tampa, FL 33601, *Chair*

RICHARD E. FORD, 203 West Randolph Street, Lewisburg, WV 24901

HARRY J. HAYNSWORTH, IV, William Mitchell College of Law, 875 Summit Avenue, St. Paul, MN 55105

CHARLES G. KEPLER, P.O. Box 490, 1135 14th Street, Cody, WY 82414

WAYNE C. KREUSCHER, 1313 Merchants Bank Building, 11 South Meridian Street, Indianapolis, IN 46204

REED L. MARTINEAU, P.O. Box 45000, 10 Exchange Place, Salt Lake City, UT 84145

RICHARD F. MUTZEBAUGH, State Capitol Building, 200 East Colfax Avenue, Denver, CO 80203

GLEE S. SMITH, P.O. Box 360, 111 East 8th, Larned, KS 67550

HOWARD J. SWIBEL, Suite 1200, 120 South Riverside Plaza, Chicago, IL 60606

CARTER G. BISHOP, Suffolk University Law School, 41 Temple Street, Boston, MA 02114, *Reporter*

EX OFFICIO

RICHARD C. HITE, 200 West Douglas Avenue, Suite 600, Wichita, KS 67202, *President*

JOHN P. BURTON, P.O. Box 1357, Suite 101, 123 East Marcy Street, Santa Fe, NM 87501, *Chair, Division E*

EXECUTIVE DIRECTOR

FRED H. MILLER, University of Oklahoma, College of Law, 300 Timberdell Road, Norman, OK 73019, *Executive Director*

WILLIAM J. PIERCE, 1505 Roxbury Road, Ann Arbor, MI 48104, *Executive Director Emeritus*

REVIEW COMMITTEE

JAMES M. BUSH, Suite 2200, Two North Central Avenue, Phoenix, AZ 85004, *Chair*

FRANCIS J. PAVETTI, P.O. Box 829, Court House Square Building, New London, CT 06320

DONALD JOE WILLIS, Suites 1600-1950, Pacwest Center, 1211 S.W. 5th Avenue, Portland, OR 97204

ADVISORS

ROBERT R. KEATINGE, *American Bar Association*

STEVEN G. FROST, *American Bar Association, Section of Taxation*

THOMAS EARL GEU, *American Bar Association, Section of Real Property, Probate and Trust Law, Probate and Trust Division*

JAMES W. REYNOLDS, *American Bar Association, Section of Business Law*

SANFORD J. LIEBSCHUTZ, *American Bar Association, Section of Real Property, Probate and Trust Law, Real Property Division*

Copies of this Act may be obtained from:

**NATIONAL CONFERENCE OF COMMISSIONERS
ON UNIFORM STATE LAWS
211 East Ontario Street, Suite 1300
Chicago, Illinois 60611
312/915-0195**

UNIFORM LIMITED LIABILITY COMPANY ACT (1996)

TABLE OF CONTENTS

UNIFORM LIMITED LIABILITY COMPANY ACT (1996)

PREFATORY NOTE

Borrowing from abroad, Wyoming initiated a national movement in 1977 by enacting this country's first limited liability company act. The movement started slowly as the Internal Revenue Service took more than ten years to announce finally that a Wyoming limited liability company would be taxed like a partnership. Since that time, every State has adopted or is considering its own distinct limited liability company act, many of which have already been amended one or more times.

The allure of the limited liability company is its unique ability to bring together in a single business organization the best features of all other business forms — properly structured, its owners obtain both a corporate-styled liability shield and the pass-through tax benefits of a partnership. General and limited partnerships do not offer their partners a corporate-styled liability shield. Corporations, including those having made a Subchapter S election, do not offer their shareholders all the pass-through tax benefits of a partnership. All state limited liability company acts contain provisions for a liability shield and partnership tax status.

Despite these two common themes, state limited liability company acts display a dazzling array of diversity. Multistate activities of businesses are widespread. Recognition of out-of-state limited liability companies varies. Unfortunately, this lack of uniformity manifests itself in basic but fundamentally important questions, such as: may a company be formed and operated by only one owner; may it be formed for purposes other than to make a profit; whether owners have the power and right to withdraw from a company and receive a distribution of the fair value of their interests; whether a member's dissociation threatens a dissolution of the company; who has the apparent authority to bind the company and the limits of that authority; what are the fiduciary duties of owners and managers to a company and each other; how are the rights to manage a company allocated among its owners and managers; do the owners have the right to sue a company and its other owners in their own right as well as derivatively on behalf of the company; may general and limited partnerships be converted to limited liability companies and may limited liability companies merge with other limited liability companies and other business organizations; what is the law governing foreign limited liability companies; and are any or all of these and other rules simply default rules that may be modified by agreement or are they nonwaivable.

Practitioners and entrepreneurs struggle to understand the law governing limited liability companies organized in their own State and to understand the burgeoning law of other States. Simple questions concerning where to organize are increasingly complex. Since most state limited liability company acts are in their infancy, little if any interpretative case law exists. Even when case law develops, it will have limited precedential value because of the diversity of the state acts.

Accordingly, uniform legislation in this area of the law appeared to have become urgent.

After a Study Committee appointed by the National Conference of Commissioners in late 1991 recommended that a comprehensive project be undertaken, the Conference appointed a Drafting Committee which worked on a Uniform Limited Liability Company Act (ULLCA) from early 1992 until its adoption by the Conference at its Annual Meeting in August 1994. The Drafting Committee was assisted by a blue ribbon panel of national experts and other interested and affected parties and organizations. Many, if not all, of those assisting the Committee brought substantial experience from drafting limited liability company legislation in their own States. Many are also authors of leading treatises and articles in the field. Those represented in the drafting process included an American Bar Association (ABA) liaison, four advisors representing the three separate ABA Sections of Business Law, Taxation, and Real Property, Trust and Probate, the United States Treasury Department, the Internal Revenue Service, and many observers representing several other organizations, including the California Bar Association, the New York City Bar Association, the American College of Real Estate Lawyers, the National Association of Certified Public Accountants, the National Association of Secretaries of State, the Chicago and Lawyers Title Companies, the American Land Title Association, and several university law and business school faculty members.

The Committee met nine times and engaged in numerous national telephonic conferences to discuss policies, review over fifteen drafts, evaluate legal developments and consider comments by our many knowledgeable advisers and observers, as well as an ABA subcommittee's earlier work on a prototype. In examining virtually every aspect of each state limited liability company act, the Committee maintained a single policy vision — to draft a flexible act with a comprehensive set of default rules designed to substitute as the essence of the bargain for small entrepreneurs and others.

This Act is flexible in the sense that the vast majority of its provisions may be modified by the owners in a private agreement. Only limited and specific fundamental matters may not be altered by private agreement. To simplify, those nonwaivable provisions are set forth in a single subsection. Helped thereby, sophisticated parties will negotiate their own deal with the benefit of counsel.

The Committee also recognized that small entrepreneurs without the benefit of counsel should also have access to the Act. To that end, the great bulk of the Act sets forth default rules designed to operate a limited liability company without sophisticated agreements and to recognize that members may also modify the default rules by oral agreements defined in part by their own conduct. Uniquely, the Act combines two simple default structures which depend upon the presence of designations in the articles of organization. All default rules under the Act flow from these two designations.

First, unless the articles reflect that a limited liability company is a term company and the duration of that term, the company will be an at-will company. Generally, the owners of an at-will company may demand a payment of the fair value of their interests at any time. Owners of a term company must generally wait until the expiration of the term to obtain the value of their interests. Secondly, unless the articles reflect that a company will be managed by managers, the company will be managed by its members. This designation controls whether the members or managers have apparent agency authority, management authority, and the nature of fiduciary duties in the company.

In January of 1995 the Executive Committee of the Conference adopted an amendment to harmonize the Act with new and important Internal Revenue Service announcements, and the amendment was ratified by the National Conference at its Annual Meeting in August of 1995. Those Internal Revenue Service announcements generally provide that a limited liability company will not be taxed like a corporation regardless of its organizational structure. Freed from the old tax classification restraints, the amendment modifies the Act's dissolution provision by eliminating member dissociation as a dissolution event. This important amendment significantly increases the stability of a limited liability company and places greater emphasis on a limited liability company's required purchase of a dissociated member's interest.

The adoption of ULLCA will provide much needed consistency among the States, with flexible default rules, and multistate recognition of limited liability on the part of company owners. It will also promote the development of precedential case law.

UNIFORM LIMITED LIABILITY COMPANY ACT (1996)

(ARTICLE)
GENERAL PROVISIONS

Section 101. Definitions.
Section 102. Knowledge and Notice.
Section 103. Effect of Operating Agreement; Nonwaivable Provisions.
Section 104. Supplemental Principles of Law.
Section 105. Name.
Section 106. Reserved Name.
Section 107. Registered Name.
Section 108. Designated Office and Agent for Service of Process.
Section 109. Change of Designated Office or Agent for Service of Process.
Section 110. Resignation of Agent for Service of Process.
Section 111. Service of Process.
Section 112. Nature of Business and Powers.

SECTION 101. DEFINITIONS

In this [Act]:

(1) "Articles of organization" means initial, amended, and restated articles of organization and articles of merger. In the case of a foreign limited liability company, the term includes all records serving a similar function required to be filed in the office of the [Secretary of State] or other official having custody of company records in the State or country under whose law it is organized.

(2) "At-will company" means a limited liability company other than a term company.

(3) "Business" includes every trade, occupation, profession, and other lawful purpose, whether or not carried on for profit.

(4) "Debtor in bankruptcy" means a person who is the subject of an order for relief under Title 11 of the United States Code or a comparable order under a successor statute of general application or a comparable order under federal, state, or foreign law governing insolvency.

(5) "Distribution" means a transfer of money, property, or other benefit from a limited liability company to a member in the member's capacity as a member or to a transferee of the member's distributional interest.

(6) "Distributional interest" means all of a member's interest in distributions by the limited liability company.

(7) "Entity" means a person other than an individual.

(8) "Foreign limited liability company" means an unincorporated entity organized under laws other than the laws of this State which afford limited liability to its owners comparable to the liability under Section 303 and is not required to obtain a certificate of authority to transact business under any law of this State other than this [Act].

(9) "Limited liability company" means a limited liability company organized under this [Act].

(10) "Manager" means a person, whether or not a member of a manager-managed company, who is vested with authority under Section 301.

(11) "Manager-managed company" means a limited liability company which is so designated in its articles of organization.

(12) "Member-managed company" means a limited liability company other than a manager-managed company.

(13) "Operating agreement" means the agreement under Section 103 concerning the relations among the members, managers, and limited liability company. The term includes amendments to the agreement.

(14) "Person" means an individual, corporation, business trust, estate, trust, partnership, limited liability company,

association, joint venture, government, governmental sub-division, agency, or instrumentality, or any other legal or commercial entity.

(15) "Principal office" means the office, whether or not in this State, where the principal executive office of a domestic or foreign limited liability company is located.

(16) "Record" means information that is inscribed on a tangible medium or that is stored in an electronic or other medium and is retrievable in perceivable form.

(17) "Sign" means to identify a record by means of a signature, mark, or other symbol, with intent to authenticate it.

(18) "State" means a State of the United States, the District of Columbia, the Commonwealth of Puerto Rico, or any territory or insular possession subject to the jurisdiction of the United States.

(19) "Term company" means a limited liability company in which its members have agreed to remain members until the expiration of a term specified in the articles of organization.

(20) "Transfer" includes an assignment, conveyance, deed, bill of sale, lease, mortgage, security interest, encumbrance, and gift.

Comment

Uniform Limited Liability Company Act ("ULLCA") definitions, like the rest of the Act, are a blend of terms and concepts derived from the Uniform Partnership Act ("UPA"), the Uniform Partnership Act (1994) ("UPA 1994", also previously known as the Revised Uniform Partnership Act or "RUPA"), the Revised Uniform Limited Partnership Act ("RULPA"), the Uniform Commercial Code ("UCC"), and the Model Business Corporation Act ("MBCA"), or their revisions from time to time; some are tailored specially for this Act.

"Business." A limited liability company may be organized to engage in an activity either for or not for profit. The extent to which contributions to a nonprofit company may be deductible for Federal income tax purposes is determined by federal law. Other state law determines the extent of exemptions from state and local income and property taxes.

"Debtor in bankruptcy." The filing of a voluntary petition operates immediately as an "order for relief." See Sections 601(7)(i) and 602(b)(2)(iii).

"Distribution." This term includes all sources of a member's distributions including the member's capital contributions, undistributed profits, and residual interest in the assets of the company after all claims, including those of third parties and debts to members, have been paid.

"Distributional interest." The term does not include a member's broader rights to participate in the management of the company. See Comments to Article 5.

"Foreign limited liability company." The term is not restricted to companies formed in the United States.

"Manager." The rules of agency apply to limited liability companies. Therefore, managers may designate agents with whatever titles, qualifications, and responsibilities they desire. For example, managers may designate an agent as "President."

"Manager-managed company." The term includes only a company designated as such in the articles of organization. In a manager-managed company agency authority is vested exclusively in one or more managers and not in the members. See Sections 101(10) (manager), 203(a)(6) (articles designation), and 301(b) (agency authority of members and managers).

"Member-managed limited liability company." The term includes every company not designated as "manager-managed" under Section 203(a)(6) in its articles of organization.

"Operating agreement." This agreement may be oral. Members may agree upon the extent to which their relationships are to be governed by writings.

"Principal office." The address of the principal office must be set forth in the annual report required under Section 211(a)(3).

"Record." This Act is the first Uniform Act promulgated with a definition of this term. The definition brings this Act in conformity with the present state of technology and accommodates prospective future technology in the communication and storage of information other than by human memory. Modern methods of communicating and storing information employed in commercial practices are no longer confined to physical documents.

The term includes any writing. A record need not be permanent or indestructible, but an oral or other unwritten communication must be stored or preserved on some medium to qualify as a record. Information that has not been retained other than through human memory does not qualify as a record. A record may be signed or may be created without the knowledge or intent of a particular person. Other law must be consulted to determine admissibility in evidence, the applicability of statute of frauds, and other questions regarding the use of records. Under Section 206(a), electronic filings may be permitted and even encouraged.

SECTION 102. KNOWLEDGE AND NOTICE

(a) A person knows a fact if the person has actual knowledge of it.

(b) A person has notice of a fact if the person:

    (1) knows the fact;

    (2) has received a notification of the fact; or

    (3) has reason to know the fact exists from all of the facts known to the person at the time in question.

(c) A person notifies or gives a notification of a fact to another by taking steps reasonably required to inform the other person in ordinary course, whether or not the other person knows the fact.

(d) A person receives a notification when the notification:

    (1) comes to the person's attention; or

    (2) is duly delivered at the person's place of business or at any other place held out by the person as a place for receiving communications.

(e) An entity knows, has notice, or receives a notification of a fact for purposes of a particular transaction when the individual conducting the transaction for the entity knows, has notice, or receives a notification of the fact, or in any event when the fact would have been brought to the individual's attention had the entity exercised reasonable diligence. An entity exercises reasonable diligence if it maintains reasonable routines for communicating significant information to the individual conducting the transaction for the entity and there is reasonable compliance with the routines. Reasonable diligence does not require an individual acting for the entity to communicate information unless the communication is part of the individual's regular duties or the individual has reason to know of the transaction and that the transaction would be materially affected by the information.

Comment

Knowledge requires cognitive awareness of a fact, whereas notice is based on a lesser degree of awareness. The Act imposes constructive knowledge under limited circumstances. See Comments to Sections 301(c), 703, and 704.

SECTION 103. EFFECT OF OPERATING AGREEMENT; NONWAIVABLE PROVISIONS

(a) Except as otherwise provided in subsection (b), all members of a limited liability company may enter into an operating agreement, which need not be in writing, to regulate the affairs of the company and the conduct of its business, and to govern relations among the members, managers, and company. To the extent the operating agreement does not otherwise provide, this [Act] governs relations among the members, managers, and company.

(b) The operating agreement may not:

(1) unreasonably restrict a right to information or access to records under Section 408;

(2) eliminate the duty of loyalty under Section 409(b) or 603(b)(3), but the agreement may:

(i) identify specific types or categories of activities that do not violate the duty of loyalty, if not manifestly unreasonable; and

(ii) specify the number or percentage of members or disinterested managers that may authorize or ratify, after full disclosure of all material facts, a specific act or transaction that otherwise would violate the duty of loyalty;

(3) unreasonably reduce the duty of care under Section 409(c) or 603(b)(3);

(4) eliminate the obligation of good faith and fair dealing under Section 409(d), but the operating agreement may determine the standards by which the performance of the obligation is to be measured, if the standards are not manifestly unreasonable;

(5) vary the right to expel a member in an event specified in Section 601(6);

(6) vary the requirement to wind up the limited liability company's business in a case specified in Section 801(a)(3) or(a)(4); or

(7) restrict rights of a person, other than a manager, member, and transferee of a member's distributional interest, under this [Act].

Comment

The operating agreement is the essential contract that governs the affairs of a limited liability company. Since it is binding on all members, amendments must be approved by all members unless otherwise provided in the agreement. Although many agreements will be in writing, the agreement and any amendments may be oral or may be in the form of a record. Course of dealing, course of performance and usage of trade are relevant to determine the meaning of the agreement unless the agreement provides that all amendments must be in writing.

This section makes clear that the only matters an operating agreement may not control are specified in subsection (b). Accordingly, an operating agreement may modify or eliminate any rule specified in any section of this Act except matters specified in subsection (b). To the extent not otherwise mentioned in subsection (b), every section of this Act is simply a default rule, regardless of whether the language of the section appears to be otherwise mandatory. This approach eliminates the necessity of repeating the phrase "unless otherwise agreed" in each section and its commentary.

Under subsection (b)(1), an operating agreement may not unreasonably restrict the right to information or access to any records under Section 408. This does not create an independent obligation beyond Section 408 to maintain any specific records. Under subsections (b)(2) to (4), an irreducible core of fiduciary responsibilities survive any contrary provision in the operating agreement. Subsection (b)(2)(i) authorizes an operating agreement to modify, but not eliminate, the three specific duties of loyalty set forth in Section 409(b)(1) to (3) provided the modification itself is not manifestly unreasonable, a question of fact. Subsection (b)(2)(ii) preserves the common law right of the members to authorize future or ratify past violations of the duty of loyalty provided there has been a full disclosure of all material facts. The authorization or ratification must be unanimous unless otherwise provided in an operating agreement, because the authorization or ratification itself constitutes an amendment to the agreement. The authorization or ratification of specific past or future conduct may sanction conduct that would have been manifestly unreasonable under subsection (b)(2)(i).

SECTION 104. SUPPLEMENTAL PRINCIPLES OF LAW

(a) Unless displaced by particular provisions of this [Act], the principles of law and equity supplement this [Act].

(b) If an obligation to pay interest arises under this [Act] and the rate is not specified, the rate is that specified in [applicable statute].

Comment

Supplementary principles include, but are not limited to, the law of agency, estoppel, law merchant, and all other principles listed in UCC Section 1-103, including the law relative to the capacity to contract, fraud, misrepresentation, duress, coercion, mistake, bankruptcy, and other validating and invalidating clauses. Other principles such as those mentioned in UCC Section 1-205 (Course of Dealing and Usage of Trade) apply as well as course of performance. As with UPA 1994 Section 104, upon which this provision is based, no substantive change from either the UPA or the UCC is intended. Section 104(b) establishes the applicable rate of interest in the absence of an agreement among the members.

SECTION 105. NAME

(a) The name of a limited liability company must contain "limited liability company" or "limited company" or the abbreviation "L.L.C.", "LLC", "L.C.", or "LC". "Limited" may be abbreviated as "Ltd.", and "company" may be abbreviated as "Co.".

(b) Except as authorized by subsections (c) and (d), the name of a limited liability company must be distinguishable upon the records of the [Secretary of State] from:

    (1) the name of any corporation, limited partnership, or company incorporated, organized or authorized to transact business, in this State;

    (2) a name reserved or registered under Section 106 or 107;

    (3) a fictitious name approved under Section 1005 for a foreign company authorized to transact business in this State because its real name is unavailable.

(c) A limited liability company may apply to the [Secretary of State] for authorization to use a name that is not distinguishable upon the records of the [Secretary of State] from one or more of the names described in subsection (b). The [Secretary of State] shall authorize use of the name applied for if:

    (1) the present user, registrant, or owner of a reserved name consents to the use in a record and submits an undertaking in form satisfactory to the [Secretary of State] to change the name to a name that is distinguishable upon the records of the [Secretary of State] from the name applied for; or

    (2) the applicant delivers to the [Secretary of State] a certified copy of the final judgment of a court of competent jurisdiction establishing the applicant's right to use the name applied for in this State.

(d) A limited liability company may use the name, including a fictitious name, of another domestic or foreign company which is used in this State if the other company is organized or authorized to transact business in this State and the company proposing to use the name has:

    (1) merged with the other company;

    (2) been formed by reorganization with the other company; or

(3) acquired substantially all of the assets, including the name, of the other company.

SECTION 106. RESERVED NAME

(a) A person may reserve the exclusive use of the name of a limited liability company, including a fictitious name for a foreign company whose name is not available, by delivering an application to the [Secretary of State] for filing. The application must set forth the name and address of the applicant and the name proposed to be reserved. If the [Secretary of State] finds that the name applied for is available, it must be reserved for the applicant's exclusive use for a nonrenewable 120-day period.

(b) The owner of a name reserved for a limited liability company may transfer the reservation to another person by delivering to the [Secretary of State] a signed notice of the transfer which states the name and address of the transferee.

Comment

A foreign limited liability company that is not presently authorized to transact business in the State may reserve a fictitious name for a nonrenewable 120-day period. When its actual name is available, a company will generally register that name under Section 107 because the registration is valid for a year and may be extended indefinitely.

SECTION 107. REGISTERED NAME

(a) A foreign limited liability company may register its name subject to the requirements of Section 1005, if the name is distinguishable upon the records of the [Secretary of State] from names that are not available under Section 105(b).

(b) A foreign limited liability company registers its name, or its name with any addition required by Section 1005, by delivering to the [Secretary of State] for filing an application:

(1) setting forth its name, or its name with any addition required by Section 1005, the State or country and date of its organization, and a brief description of the nature of the business in which it is engaged; and

(2) accompanied by a certificate of existence, or a record of similar import, from the State or country of organization.

(c) A foreign limited liability company whose registration is effective may renew it for successive years by delivering for filing in the office of the [Secretary of State] a renewal application complying with subsection (b) between October 1 and December 31 of the preceding year. The renewal application renews the registration for the following calendar year.

(d) A foreign limited liability company whose registration is effective may qualify as a foreign company under its name or consent in writing to the use of its name by a limited liability company later organized under this [Act] or by another foreign company later authorized to transact business in this State. The registered name terminates when the limited liability company is organized or the foreign company qualifies or consents to the qualification of another foreign company under the registered name.

SECTION 108. DESIGNATED OFFICE AND AGENT FOR SERVICE OF PROCESS

(a) A limited liability company and a foreign limited liability company authorized to do business in this State shall designate and continuously maintain in this State:

(1) an office, which need not be a place of its business in this State; and

(2) an agent and street address of the agent for service of process on the company.

(b) An agent must be an individual resident of this State, a domestic corporation, another limited liability company, or a foreign corporation or foreign company authorized to do business in this State.

Comment

Limited liability companies organized under Section 202 or authorized to transact business under Section 1004 are required to designate and continuously maintain an office in the State. Although the designated office need not be a place of business, it most often will be the only place of business of the company. The company must also designate an agent for service of process within the State and the agent's street address. The agent's address need not be the same as the company's designated office address. The initial office and agent designations must be set forth in the articles of organization, including the address of the designated office. See Section 203(a)(2) to (3). The current office and agent designations must be set forth in the company's annual report. See Section 211(a)(2). See also Section 109 (procedure for changing the office or agent designations), Section 110 (procedure for an agent to resign), and Section 111(b) (the filing officer is the service agent for the company if it fails to maintain its own service agent).

SECTION 109. CHANGE OF DESIGNATED OFFICE OR AGENT FOR SERVICE OF PROCESS

A limited liability company may change its designated office or agent for service of process by delivering to the [Secretary of State] for filing a statement of change which sets forth:

(1) the name of the company;

(2) the street address of its current designated office;

(3) if the current designated office is to be changed, the street address of the new designated office;

(4) the name and address of its current agent for service of process; and

(5) if the current agent for service of process or street address of that agent is to be changed, the new address or the name and street address of the new agent for service of process.

SECTION 110. RESIGNATION OF AGENT FOR SERVICE OF PROCESS

(a) An agent for service of process of a limited liability company may resign by delivering to the [Secretary of State] for filing a record of the statement of resignation.

(b) After filing a statement of resignation, the [Secretary of State] shall mail a copy to the designated office and another copy to the limited liability company at its principal office.

(c) An agency is terminated on the 31st day after the statement is filed in the office of the [Secretary of State].

SECTION 111. SERVICE OF PROCESS

(a) An agent for service of process appointed by a limited liability company or a foreign limited liability company is an agent of the company for service of any process, notice, or demand required or permitted by law to be served upon the company.

(b) If a limited liability company or foreign limited liability company fails to appoint or maintain an agent for service of process in this State or the agent for service of process cannot with reasonable diligence be found at the agent's address, the [Secretary of State] is an agent of the company upon whom process, notice, or demand may be served.

(c) Service of any process, notice, or demand on the [Secretary of State] may be made by delivering to and leaving with the [Secretary of State], the [Assistant Secretary of State], or clerk having charge of the limited liability company department of the [Secretary of State's] office duplicate copies of the process, notice, or demand. If the process, notice, or demand is served on the [Secretary of State], the [Secretary of State] shall forward one of the copies by registered or certified mail, return receipt requested, to the company at its designated office. Service is effected under this subsection at the earliest of:

   (1) the date the company receives the process, notice, or demand;

   (2) the date shown on the return receipt, if signed on behalf of the company; or

   (3) five days after its deposit in the mail, if mailed postpaid and correctly addressed.

(d) The [Secretary of State] shall keep a record of all processes, notices, and demands served pursuant to this section and record the time of and the action taken regarding the service.

(e) This section does not affect the right to serve process, notice, or demand in any manner otherwise provided by law.

Comment

Service of process on a limited liability company and a foreign company authorized to transact business in the State must be made on the company's agent for service of process whose name and address should be on file with the filing office. If for any reason a company fails to appoint or maintain an agent for service of process or the agent cannot be found with reasonable diligence at the agent's address, the filing officer will be deemed the proper agent.

SECTION 112. NATURE OF BUSINESS AND POWERS

(a) A limited liability company may be organized under this [Act] for any lawful purpose, subject to any law of this State governing or regulating business.

(b) Unless its articles of organization provide otherwise, a limited liability company has the same powers as an individual to do all things necessary or convenient to carry on its business or affairs, including power to:

    (1) sue and be sued, and defend in its name;

    (2) purchase, receive, lease, or otherwise acquire, and own, hold, improve, use, and otherwise deal with real or personal property, or any legal or equitable interest in property, wherever located;

    (3) sell, convey, mortgage, grant a security interest in, lease, exchange, and otherwise encumber or dispose of all or any part of its property;

    (4) purchase, receive, subscribe for, or otherwise acquire, own, hold, vote, use, sell, mortgage, lend, grant a security interest in, or otherwise dispose of and deal in and with, shares or other interests in or obligations of any other entity;

    (5) make contracts and guarantees, incur liabilities, borrow money, issue its notes, bonds, and other obligations, which may be convertible into or include

the option to purchase other securities of the limited liability company, and secure any of its obligations by a mortgage on or a security interest in any of its property, franchises, or income;

(6) lend money, invest and reinvest its funds, and receive and hold real and personal property as security for repayment;

(7) be a promoter, partner, member, associate, or manager of any partnership, joint venture, trust, or other entity;

(8) conduct its business, locate offices, and exercise the powers granted by this [Act] within or without this State;

(9) elect managers and appoint officers, employees, and agents of the limited liability company, define their duties, fix their compensation, and lend them money and credit;

(10) pay pensions and establish pension plans, pension trusts, profit sharing plans, bonus plans, option plans, and benefit or incentive plans for any or all of its current or former members, managers, officers, employees, and agents;

(11) make donations for the public welfare or for charitable, scientific, or educational purposes; and

(12) make payments or donations, or do any other act, not inconsistent with law, that furthers the business of the limited liability company.

Comment

A limited liability company may be organized for any lawful purpose unless the State has specifically prohibited a company from engaging in a specific activity. For example, many States require that certain regulated industries, such as banking and insurance, be conducted only by organizations that meet the special requirements. Also, many States impose restrictions on activities in which a limited liability company may engage. For example, the practice of certain professionals is often subject to special conditions.

A limited liability company has the power to engage in and perform important and necessary acts related to its operation and function. A company's power to enter into a transaction is distinguishable from the authority of an agent to enter into the transaction. See Section 301 (agency rules).

(ARTICLE) 2
ORGANIZATION

SECTION 201. LIMITED LIABILITY COMPANY AS LEGAL ENTITY

A limited liability company is a legal entity distinct from its members.

Comment

A limited liability company is legally distinct from its members who are not normally liable for the debts, obligations, and liabilities of the company. See Section 303. Accordingly, members are not proper parties to suits against the company unless an object of the proceeding is to enforce members' rights against the company or to enforce their liability to the company.

SECTION 202. ORGANIZATION

(a) One or more persons may organize a limited liability company, consisting of one or more members, by delivering articles of organization to the office of the [Secretary of State] for filing.

(b) Unless a delayed effective date is specified, the existence of a limited liability company begins when the articles of organization are filed.

(c) The filing of the articles of organization by the [Secretary of State] is conclusive proof that the organizers satisfied all conditions precedent to the creation of a limited liability company.

Comment

Any person may organize a limited liability company by performing the ministerial act of signing and filing the articles of organization. The person need not be a member. As a matter of flexibility, a company may be organized and operated with only one member to enable sole proprietors to obtain the benefit of a liability shield. New and important Internal Revenue Service announcements clarify that a one-member limited liability company will not be taxed like a corporation. Nor will it be taxed like a partnership since it lacks at least two members. Rather, a one-member limited liability company is disregarded for Federal tax purposes and its operations are reported on the return of its single owner.

The existence of a company begins when the articles are filed. Therefore, the filing of the articles of organization is conclusive as to the existence of the limited liability shield for persons who enter into transactions on behalf of the company. Until the articles are filed, a firm is not organized under this Act and is not a "limited liability company" as defined in Section 101(9). In that case, the parties' relationships are not governed by this Act unless they have expressed a contractual intent to be bound by the provisions of the Act. Third parties would also not be governed by the provisions of this Act unless they have expressed a contractual intent to extend a limited liability shield to the members of the would-be limited liability company.

SECTION 203. ARTICLES OF ORGANIZATION

(a) Articles of organization of a limited liability company must set forth:

(1) the name of the company;

(2) the address of the initial designated office;

(3) the name and street address of the initial agent for service of process;

(4) the name and address of each organizer;

(5) whether the company is to be a term company and, if so, the term specified;

(6) whether the company is to be manager-managed, and, if so, the name and address of each initial manager; and

(7) whether one or more of the members of the company are to be liable for its debts and obligations under Section 303(c).

(b) Articles of organization of a limited liability company may set forth:

(1) provisions permitted to be set forth in an operating agreement; or

(2) other matters not inconsistent with law.

(c) Articles of organization of a limited liability company may not vary the nonwaivable provisions of Section 103(b). As to all other matters, if any provision of an operating agreement is inconsistent with the articles of organization:

(1) the operating agreement controls as to managers, members, and members' transferees; and

(2) the articles of organization control as to persons, other than managers, members and their transferees, who reasonably rely on the articles to their detriment.

Comment

The articles serve primarily a notice function and generally do not reflect the substantive agreement of the members regarding the business affairs of the company. Those matters are generally reserved for an operating agreement which may be unwritten. Under Section 203(b), the articles may contain provisions permitted to be set forth in an operating agreement. Where the articles and operating agreement conflict, the operating agreement controls as to members but the articles control as to third parties. The articles may also contain any other matter not inconsistent with law. The most important is a Section 301(c) limitation on the authority of a member or manager to transfer interests in the company's real property.

A company will be at-will unless it is designated as a term company and the duration of its term is specified in its articles under Section 203(a)(5). The duration of a term company may be specified in any manner which sets forth a specific and final date for the dissolution of the company. For example, the period specified may be in the form of "50 years from the date of filing of the articles" or "the period ending on January 1, 2020." Mere specification of a particular undertaking of an uncertain business duration is not sufficient unless the particular undertaking is within a longer fixed period. An example of this type of designation would include "2020 or until the building is completed, whichever occurs first." When the specified period is incorrectly specified, the company will be an at-will company. Notwithstanding the correct specification of a term in the articles, a company will be an at-will company among the members under Section 203(c)(1) if an operating agreement so provides. A term company that continues after the expiration of its term specified in its articles will also be an at-will company.

A term company possesses several important default rule characteristics that differentiate it from an at-will company. An operating agreement may alter any of these rules. Generally, a member of an at-will company may rightfully dissociate at any time whereas a dissociation from a term company prior to the expiration of the specified term is wrongful. See Comments to Section 602(b). Accordingly, a dissociated member of an at-will company is entitled to have the company purchase that member's interest for its fair value determined as of the date of the member's dissociation. A dissociated member of a term company must generally await the expiration of the agreed term to withdraw the fair value of the interest determined at as of the date of the expiration of the agreed term. Thus, a dissociated member in an at-will company receives the fair value of their interest sooner than in a term company and also does not bear the risk of valuation changes for the remainder of the specified term. See Comments to Section 701(a).

A company will be member-managed unless it is designated as manager-managed under Section 203(a)(6). Absent further designation in the articles, a company will be a member-managed at-will company. The designation of a limited liability company as either member-or manager-managed is important because it defines who are agents and have the apparent authority to bind the company under Section 301. In a member-managed company, the members have the agency authority to bind the company. In a manager-managed company only the managers have that authority. New and important Internal Revenue Service announcements clarify that the agency structure of a limited liability company will not cause it to be taxed like a corporation. The agency designation relates only to agency and does not preclude members of a manager-managed company from participating in the actual management of company business. See Comments to Section 404(b).

SECTION 204. AMENDMENT OR RESTATEMENT OF ARTICLES OF ORGANIZATION

(a) Articles of organization of a limited liability company may be amended at any time by delivering articles of amendment to the [Secretary of State] for filing. The articles of amendment must set forth the:

   (1) name of the limited liability company;

   (2) date of filing of the articles of organization; and

   (3) amendment to the articles.

(b) A limited liability company may restate its articles of organization at any time. Restated articles of organization must be signed and filed in the same manner as articles of amendment. Restated articles of organization must be designated as such in the heading and state in the heading or in an introductory paragraph the limited liability company's present name and, if it has been changed, all of its former names and the date of the filing of its initial articles of organization.

Comment

An amendment to the articles requires the consent of all the members unless an operating agreement provides for a lesser number. See Section 404(c)(3).

SECTION 205. SIGNING OF RECORDS

(a) Except as otherwise provided in this [Act], a record to be filed by or on behalf of a limited liability company in the office of the [Secretary of State] must be signed in the name of the company by a:

(1) manager of a manager-managed company;

(2) member of a member-managed company;

(3) person organizing the company, if the company has not been formed; or

(4) fiduciary, if the company is in the hands of a receiver, trustee, or other court-appointed fiduciary.

(b) A record signed under subsection (a) must state adjacent to the signature the name and capacity of the signer.

(c) Any person may sign a record to be filed under subsection (a) by an attorney-in-fact. Powers of attorney relating to the signing of records to be filed under subsection (a) by an attorney-in-fact need not be filed in the office of the [Secretary of State] as evidence of authority by the person filing but must be retained by the company.

Comment

Both a writing and a record may be signed. An electronic record is signed when a person adds a name to the record with the intention to authenticate the record. See Sections 101(16) ("record" definition) and 101(17) ("signed" definition).

Other provisions of this Act also provide for the filing of records with the filing office but do not require signing by the persons specified in clauses (1) to (3). Those specific sections prevail.

SECTION 206. FILING IN OFFICE OF (SECRETARY OF STATE)

(a) Articles of organization or any other record authorized to be filed under this [Act] must be in a medium permitted by the [Secretary of State] and must be delivered to the office of the [Secretary of State]. Unless the [Secretary of State] determines that a record fails to comply as to form with the filing requirements of this [Act], and if all filing fees have been paid, the [Secretary of State] shall file the record and send a receipt for the record and the fees to the limited liability company or its representative.

(b) Upon request and payment of a fee, the [Secretary of State] shall send to the requester a certified copy of the requested record.

(c) Except as otherwise provided in subsection (d) and Section 207(c), a record accepted for filing by the [Secretary of State] is effective:

    (1) at the time of filing on the date it is filed, as evidenced by the [Secretary of State's] date and time endorsement on the original record; or

    (2) at the time specified in the record as its effective time on the date it is filed.

(d) A record may specify a delayed effective time and date, and if it does so the record becomes effective at the time and date specified. If a delayed effective date but no time is specified, the record is effective at the close of business on that date. If a delayed effective date is later than the 90th day after the record is filed, the record is effective on the 90th day.

Comment

The definition and use of the term "record" permits filings with the filing office under this Act to conform to technological advances that have been adopted by the filing office. However, since Section 206(a) provides that the filing "must be in a medium permitted by the [Secretary of State]", the Act simply conforms to filing changes as they are adopted.

SECTION 207. CORRECTING FILED RECORD

(a) A limited liability company or foreign limited liability company may correct a record filed by the [Secretary of State] if the record contains a false or erroneous statement or was defectively signed.

(b) A record is corrected:

    (1) by preparing articles of correction that:

        (i) describe the record, including its filing date, or attach a copy of it to the articles of correction;

        (ii) specify the incorrect statement and the reason it is incorrect or the manner in which the signing was defective; and

(iii) correct the incorrect statement or defective signing; and

(2) by delivering the corrected record to the [Secretary of State] for filing.

(c) Articles of correction are effective retroactively on the effective date of the record they correct except as to persons relying on the uncorrected record and adversely affected by the correction. As to those persons, articles of correction are effective when filed.

SECTION 208. CERTIFICATE OF EXISTENCE OR AUTHORIZATION

(a) A person may request the [Secretary of State] to furnish a certificate of existence for a limited liability company or a certificate of authorization for a foreign limited liability company.

(b) A certificate of existence for a limited liability company must set forth:

(1) the company's name;

(2) that it is duly organized under the laws of this State, the date of organization, whether its duration is at-will or for a specified term, and, if the latter, the period specified;

(3) if payment is reflected in the records of the [Secretary of State] and if nonpayment affects the existence of the company, that all fees, taxes, and penalties owed to this State have been paid;

(4) whether its most recent annual report required by Section 211 has been filed with the [Secretary of State];

(5) that articles of termination have not been filed; and

(6) other facts of record in the office of the [Secretary of State] which may be requested by the applicant.

(c) A certificate of authorization for a foreign limited liability company must set forth:

(1) the company's name used in this State;

(2) that it is authorized to transact business in this State;

(3) if payment is reflected in the records of the [Secretary of State] and if nonpayment affects the authorization of the company, that all fees, taxes, and penalties owed to this State have been paid;

(4) whether its most recent annual report required by Section 211 has been filed with the [Secretary of State];

(5) that a certificate of cancellation has not been filed; and

(6) other facts of record in the office of the [Secretary of State] which may be requested by the applicant.

(d) Subject to any qualification stated in the certificate, a certificate of existence or authorization issued by the [Secretary of State] may be relied upon as conclusive evidence that the domestic or foreign limited liability company is in existence or is authorized to transact business in this State.

SECTION 209. LIABILITY FOR FALSE STATEMENT IN FILED RECORD

If a record authorized or required to be filed under this [Act] contains a false statement, one who suffers loss by reliance on the statement may recover damages for the loss from a person who signed the record or caused another to sign it on the person's behalf and knew the statement to be false at the time the record was signed.

SECTION 210. FILING BY JUDICIAL ACT

If a person required by Section 205 to sign any record fails or refuses to do so, any other person who is adversely affected by the failure or refusal may petition the [designate the appropriate court] to direct the signing of the record. If the court finds that it is proper for the record to be signed and that a person so designated has failed or refused to sign the record, it shall order the [Secretary of State] to sign and file an appropriate record.

SECTION 211. ANNUAL REPORT FOR (SECRETARY OF STATE)

(a) A limited liability company, and a foreign limited liability company authorized to transact business in this State, shall deliver to the [Secretary of State] for filing an annual report that sets forth:

    (1) the name of the company and the State or country under whose law it is organized;

    (2) the address of its designated office and the name and address of its agent for service of process in this State;

    (3) the address of its principal office; and

    (4) the names and business addresses of any managers.

(b) Information in an annual report must be current as of the date the annual report is signed on behalf of the limited liability company.

(c) The first annual report must be delivered to the [Secretary of State] between [January 1 and April 1] of the year following the calendar year in which a limited liability company was organized or a foreign company was authorized to transact business. Subsequent annual reports must be delivered to the [Secretary of State] between [January 1 and April 1] of the ensuing calendar years.

(d) If an annual report does not contain the information required in subsection (a), the [Secretary of State] shall promptly notify the reporting limited liability company or foreign limited liability company and return the report to it for correction. If the report is corrected to contain the information required in subsection (a) and delivered to the [Secretary of State] within 30 days after the effective date of the notice, it is timely filed.

Comment

Failure to deliver the annual report within 60 days after its due date is a primary ground for administrative dissolution of the company under Section 809. See Comments to Sections 809 to 812.

(ARTICLE) 3
RELATIONS OF MEMBERS AND MANAGERS
TO PERSONS DEALING WITH
LIMITED LIABILITY COMPANY

SECTION 301. AGENCY OF MEMBERS AND MANAGERS

(a) Subject to subsections (b) and (c):

(1) Each member is an agent of the limited liability company for the purpose of its business, and an act of a member, including the signing of an instrument in the company's name, for apparently carrying on in the ordinary course the company's business or business of the kind carried on by the company binds the company, unless the member had no authority to act for the company in the particular matter and the person with whom the member was dealing knew or had notice that the member lacked authority.

(2) An act of a member which is not apparently for carrying on in the ordinary course the company's business or business of the kind carried on by the company binds the company only if the act was authorized by the other members.

(b) Subject to subsection (c), in a manager-managed company:

(1) A member is not an agent of the company for the purpose of its business solely by reason of being a member. Each manager is an agent of the company for the purpose of its business, and an act of a manager, including the signing of an instrument in the company's name, for apparently carrying on in the ordinary course the company's business or business of the kind carried on by the company binds the company, unless the manager had no authority to act for the company in the particular matter and the person with whom the manager was dealing knew or had notice that the manager lacked authority.

(2) An act of a manager which is not apparently for carrying on in the ordinary course the company's business or business of the kind carried on by the company binds the company only if the act was authorized under Section 404.

(c) Unless the articles of organization limit their authority, any member of a member-managed company or manager of a manager-managed company may sign and deliver any instrument transferring or affecting the company's interest in real property. The instrument is conclusive in favor of a person who gives value without knowledge of the lack of the authority of the person signing and delivering the instrument.

Comment

Members of a member-managed and managers of manager-managed company, as agents of the firm, have the apparent authority to bind a company to third parties. Members of a manager-managed company are not as such agents of the firm and do not have the apparent authority, as members, to bind a company. Members and managers with apparent authority possess actual authority by implication unless the actual authority is restricted in an operating agreement. Apparent authority extends to acts for carrying on in the ordinary course the company's business and business of the kind carried on by the company. Acts beyond this scope bind the company only where supported by actual authority created before the act or ratified after the act.

Ordinarily, restrictions on authority in an operating agreement do not affect the apparent authority of members and managers to bind the company to third parties without notice of the restriction. However, the restriction may make a member or manager's conduct wrongful and create liability to the company for the breach. This rule is subject to three important exceptions. First, under Section 301(c), a limitation reflected in the articles of organization on the authority of any member or manager to sign and deliver an instrument affecting an interest in company real property is effective when filed, even to persons without knowledge of the agent's lack of authority. New and important Internal Revenue Service announcements clarify that the agency structure of a limited liability company will not cause it to be taxed like a corporation. Secondly, under Section 703, a dissociated member's apparent authority terminates two years after dissociation, even to persons without knowledge of the dissociation. Thirdly, under Section 704, a dissociated member's apparent authority may be terminated earlier than the two years by filing a statement of dissociation. The statement is effective 90 days after filing, even to persons without knowledge of the filing. Together, these three provisions provide constructive knowledge to the world of the lack of apparent authority of an agent to bind the company.

SECTION 302. LIMITED LIABILITY COMPANY LIABLE FOR MEMBER'S OR MANAGER'S ACTIONABLE CONDUCT

A limited liability company is liable for loss or injury caused to a person, or for a penalty incurred, as a result of a wrongful act or omission, or other actionable conduct, of a member or manager acting in the ordinary course of business of the company or with authority of the company.

Comment

Since a member of a manager-managed company is not as such an agent, the acts of the member are not imputed to the company unless the member is acting under actual or apparent authority created by circumstances other than membership status.

SECTION 303. LIABILITY OF MEMBERS AND MANAGERS

(a) Except as otherwise provided in subsection (c), the debts, obligations, and liabilities of a limited liability company, whether arising in contract, tort, or otherwise, are solely the debts, obligations, and liabilities of the company. A member or manager is not personally liable for a debt, obligation, or liability of the company solely by reason of being or acting as a member or manager.

(b) The failure of a limited liability company to observe the usual company formalities or requirements relating to the exercise of its company powers or management of its business is not a ground for imposing personal liability on the members or managers for liabilities of the company.

(c) All or specified members of a limited liability company are liable in their capacity as members for all or specified debts, obligations, or liabilities of the company if:

    (1) a provision to that effect is contained in the articles of organization; and

    (2) a member so liable has consented in writing to the adoption of the provision or to be bound by the provision.

Comment

A member or manager, as an agent of the company, is not liable for the debts, obligations, and liabilities of the company simply because of the agency. A member or manager is responsible for acts or omissions to the extent those acts or omissions would be actionable in contract or tort against the member or manager if that person were acting in an individual capacity. Where a member or manager delegates or assigns the authority or duty to exercise appropriate company functions, the member or manager is ordinarily not personally liable for the acts or omissions of the officer, employee, or agent if the member or manager has complied with the duty of care set forth in Section 409(c).

Under Section 303(c), the usual liability shield may be waived, in whole or in part, provided the waiver is reflected in the articles of organization and the member has consented in writing to be bound by the waiver. The importance and unusual nature of the waiver consent requires that the consent be evidenced by a writing and not merely an unwritten record. See Comments to Section 205. New and important Internal Revenue Service announcements clarify that the owner liability structure of a limited liability company (other than a foreign limited liability company formed outside the United States) will not cause it to be taxed like a corporation.

(ARTICLE) 4
RELATIONS OF MEMBERS TO EACH OTHER AND TO LIMITED LIABILITY COMPANY

Section 401. Form of Contribution.
Section 402. Member's Liability for Contributions.
Section 403. Member's and Manager's Rights to Payments and Reimbursement.

SECTION 401. FORM OF CONTRIBUTION

A contribution of a member of a limited liability company may consist of tangible or intangible property or other benefit to the company, including money, promissory notes, services performed, or other agreements to contribute cash or property, or contracts for services to be performed.

Comment

Unless otherwise provided in an operating agreement, admission of a member and the nature and valuation of a would-be member's contribution are matters requiring the consent of all of the other members. See Section 404(c)(7). An agreement to contribute to a company is controlled by the operating agreement and therefore may not be created or modified without amending that agreement through the unanimous consent of all the members, including the member to be bound by the new contribution terms. See 404(c)(1).

SECTION 402. MEMBER'S LIABILITY FOR CONTRIBUTIONS

(a) A member's obligation to contribute money, property, or other benefit to, or to perform services for, a limited liability company is not excused by the member's death, disability, or other inability to perform personally. If a member does not make the required contribution of property or services, the member is obligated at the option of the company to contribute money equal to the value of that portion of the stated contribution which has not been made.

(b) A creditor of a limited liability company who extends credit or otherwise acts in reliance on an obligation described in subsection (a), and without notice of any compromise under Section 404(c)(5), may enforce the original obligation.

Comment

An obligation need not be in writing to be enforceable. Given the informality of some companies, a writing requirement may frustrate reasonable expectations of members based on a clear oral agreement. Obligations may be compromised with the consent of all of the members under Section 404(c)(5), but the compromise is generally effective only among the consenting members. Company creditors are bound by the compromise only as provided in Section 402(b).

SECTION 403. MEMBER'S AND MANAGER'S RIGHTS TO PAYMENTS AND REIMBURSEMENT

(a) A limited liability company shall reimburse a member or manager for payments made and indemnify a member or manager for liabilities incurred by the member or manager in the ordinary course of the business of the company or for the preservation of its business or property.

(b) A limited liability company shall reimburse a member for an advance to the company beyond the amount of contribution the member agreed to make.

(c) A payment or advance made by a member which gives rise to an obligation of a limited liability company under subsection (a) or (b) constitutes a loan to the company upon which interest accrues from the date of the payment or advance.

(d) A member is not entitled to remuneration for services performed for a limited liability company, except for reasonable compensation for services rendered in winding up the business of the company.

Comment

The presence of a liability shield will ordinarily prevent a member or manager from incurring personal liability on behalf of the company in the ordinary course of the company's business. Where a member of a member-managed or a manager of a manager-managed company incurs such liabilities, Section 403(a) provides that the company must indemnify the member or manager where that person acted in the ordinary course of the company's business or the preservation of its property. A member or manager is therefore entitled to indemnification only if the act was within the member or manager's actual authority. A member or manager is therefore not entitled to indemnification for conduct that violates the duty of care set forth in Section 409(c) or for tortious conduct against a third party. Since members of a manager-managed company do not possess the apparent authority to bind the company, it would be more unusual for such a member to incur a liability for indemnification in the ordinary course of the company's business.

SECTION 404. MANAGEMENT OF LIMITED LIABILITY COMPANY

(a) In a member-managed company:

    (1) each member has equal rights in the management and conduct of the company's business; and

    (2) except as otherwise provided in subsection (c), any matter relating to the business of the company may be decided by a majority of the members.

(b) In a manager-managed company:

    (1) each manager has equal rights in the management and conduct of the company's business;

    (2) except as otherwise provided in subsection (c), any matter relating to the business of the company may be exclusively decided by the manager or, if there is more than one manager, by a majority of the managers; and

    (3) a manager:

        (i) must be designated, appointed, elected, removed, or replaced by a vote, approval, or consent of a majority of the members; and

        (ii) holds office until a successor has been elected and qualified, unless the manager sooner resigns or is removed.

(c) The only matters of a member or manager-managed company's business requiring the consent of all of the members are:

(1) the amendment of the operating agreement under Section 103;

(2) the authorization or ratification of acts or transactions under Section 103(b)(2)(ii) which would otherwise violate the duty of loyalty;

(3) an amendment to the articles of organization under Section 204;

(4) the compromise of an obligation to make a contribution under Section 402(b);

(5) the compromise, as among members, of an obligation of a member to make a contribution or return money or other property paid or distributed in violation of this [Act];

(6) the making of interim distributions under Section 405(a), including the redemption of an interest;

(7) the admission of a new member;

(8) the use of the company's property to redeem an interest subject to a charging order;

(9) the consent to dissolve the company under Section 801(b)(2);

(10) a waiver of the right to have the company's business wound up and the company terminated under Section 802(b);

(11) the consent of members to merge with another entity under Section 904(c)(1); and

(12) the sale, lease, exchange, or other disposal of all, or substantially all, of the company's property with or without goodwill.

(d) Action requiring the consent of members or managers under this [Act] may be taken without a meeting.

(e) A member or manager may appoint a proxy to vote or otherwise act for the member or manager by signing an appointment instrument, either personally or by the member's or manager's attorney-in-fact.

Comment

In a member-managed company, each member has equal rights in the management and conduct of the company's business unless otherwise provided in an operating agreement. For example, an operating agreement may allocate voting rights based upon capital contributions rather than the subsection (a) per capita rule. Also, member disputes as to any matter relating to the company's business may be resolved by a majority of the members unless the matter relates to a matter specified in subsection (c) (unanimous consent required). Regardless of how the members allocate management rights, each member is an agent of the company with the apparent authority to bind the company in the ordinary course of its business. See Comments to Section 301(a). A member's right to participate in management terminates upon dissociation. See Section 603(b)(1).

In a manager-managed company, the members, unless also managers, have no rights in the management and conduct of the company's business unless otherwise provided in an operating agreement. If there is more than one manager, manager disputes as to any matter relating to the company's business may be resolved by a majority of the managers unless the matter relates to a matter specified in subsection (c) (unanimous member consent required). Managers must be designated, appointed, or elected by a majority of the members. A manager need not be a member and is an agent of the company with the apparent authority to bind the company in the ordinary course of its business. See Sections 101(10) and 301(b).

To promote clarity and certainty, subsection (c) specifies those exclusive matters requiring the unanimous consent of the members, whether the company is member- or manager-managed. For example, interim distributions, including redemptions, may not be made without the unanimous consent of all the members. Unless otherwise agreed, all other company matters are to be determined under the majority of members or managers rules of subsections (a) and (b).

SECTION 405. SHARING OF AND RIGHT TO DISTRIBUTIONS

(a) Any distributions made by a limited liability company before its dissolution and winding up must be in equal shares.

(b) A member has no right to receive, and may not be required to accept, a distribution in kind.

(c) If a member becomes entitled to receive a distribution, the member has the status of, and is entitled to all remedies available to, a creditor of the limited liability company with respect to the distribution.

Comment

Recognizing the informality of many limited liability companies, this section creates a simple default rule regarding interim distributions. Any interim distributions made must be in equal shares and approved by all members. See Section 404(c)(6). The rule assumes that: profits will be shared equally; some distributions will constitute a return of contributions that should be shared equally rather than a distribution of profits; and property contributors should have the right to veto any distribution that threatens their return of contributions on liquidation. In the simple case where the members make equal contributions of property or equal contributions of services, those assumptions avoid the necessity of maintaining a complex capital account or determining profits. Where some members contribute services and others property, the unanimous vote necessary to approve interim distributions protects against unwanted distributions of contributions to service contributors. Consistently, Section 408(a) does not require the company to maintain a separate account for each member, the Act does not contain a default rule for allocating profits and losses, and Section 806(b) requires that liquidating distributions to members be made in equal shares after the return of contributions not previously returned. See Comments to Section 806(b).

Section 405(c) governs distributions declared or made when the company was solvent. Section 406 governs distributions declared or made when the company is insolvent.

SECTION 406. LIMITATIONS ON DISTRIBUTIONS

(a) A distribution may not be made if:

   (1) the limited liability company would not be able to pay its debts as they become due in the ordinary course of business; or

   (2) the company's total assets would be less than the sum of its total liabilities plus the amount that would be needed, if the company were to be dissolved, wound up, and terminated at the time of the distribution, to satisfy the preferential rights upon dissolution, winding up, and termination of members whose preferential rights are superior to those receiving the distribution.

(b) A limited liability company may base a determination that a distribution is not prohibited under subsection (a) on financial statements prepared on the basis of accounting practices and principles that are reasonable in the circumstances or on a fair valuation or other method that is reasonable in the circumstances.

(c) Except as otherwise provided in subsection (e), the effect of a distribution under subsection (a) is measured:

   (1) in the case of distribution by purchase, redemption, or other acquisition of a distributional interest in a limited liability company, as of the date money or other property is transferred or debt incurred by the company; and

   (2) in all other cases, as of the date the:

      (i) distribution is authorized if the payment occurs within 120 days after the date of authorization; or

      (ii) payment is made if it occurs more than 120 days after the date of authorization.

(d) A limited liability company's indebtedness to a member incurred by reason of a distribution made in accordance with this section is at parity with the company's indebtedness to its general, unsecured creditors.

(e) Indebtedness of a limited liability company, including indebtedness issued in connection with or as part of a distribution, is not considered a liability for purposes of determinations under subsection (a) if its terms provide that payment of principal and interest are made only if and to the extent that payment of a distribution to members could then be made under this section. If the indebtedness is issued as a distribution, each payment of principal or interest on the indebtedness is treated as a distribution, the effect of which is measured on the date the payment is made.

Comment

This section establishes the validity of company distributions, which in turn determines the potential liability of members and managers for improper distributions under Section 407. Distributions are improper if the company is insolvent under subsection (a) at the time the distribution is measured under subsection (c). In recognition of the informality of many limited liability companies, the solvency determination under subsection (b) may be made on the basis of a fair valuation or other method reasonable under the circumstances.

The application of the equity insolvency and balance sheet tests present special problems in the context of the purchase, redemption, or other acquisition of a company's distributional interests. Special rules establish the time of measurement of such transfers. Under Section 406(c)(1), the time for measuring the effect of a distribution to purchase a distributional interest is the date of payment. The company may make payment either by transferring property or incurring a debt to transfer property in the future. In the latter case, subsection (c)(1) establishes a clear rule that the legality of the distribution is tested when the debt is actually incurred, not later when the debt is actually paid. Under Section 406(e), indebtedness is not considered a liability for purposes of subsection (a) if the terms of the indebtedness itself provide that payments can be made only if and to the extent that a payment of a distribution could then be made under this section. The effect makes the holder of the indebtedness junior to all other creditors but senior to members in their capacity as members.

SECTION 407. LIABILITY FOR UNLAWFUL DISTRIBUTIONS

(a) A member of a member-managed company or a member or manager of a manager-managed company who votes for or assents to a distribution made in violation of Section 406, the articles of organization, or the operating agreement is personally liable to the company for the amount of the distribution which exceeds the amount that could have been distributed without violating Section 406, the articles of organization, or the operating agreement if it is established that the member or manager did not perform the member's or manager's duties in compliance with Section 409.

(b) A member of a manager-managed company who knew a distribution was made in violation of Section 406, the articles of organization, or the operating agreement is personally liable to the company, but only to the extent that the distribution received by the member exceeded the amount that could have been properly paid under Section 406.

(c) A member or manager against whom an action is brought under this section may implead in the action all:

(1) other members or managers who voted for or assented to the distribution in violation of subsection (a) and may compel contribution from them; and

(2) members who received a distribution in violation of subsection (b) and may compel contribution from the member in the amount received in violation of subsection (b).

(d) A proceeding under this section is barred unless it is commenced within two years after the distribution.

Comment

Whenever members or managers fail to meet the standards of conduct of Section 409 and vote for or assent to an unlawful distribution, they are personally liable to the company for the portion of the distribution that exceeds the maximum amount that could have been lawfully distributed. The recovery remedy under this section extends only to the company, not the company's creditors. Under subsection (a), members and managers are not liable for an unlawful distribution provided their vote in favor of the distribution satisfies the duty of care of Section 409(c).

Subsection (a) creates personal liability in favor of the company against members or managers who approve an unlawful distribution for the entire amount of a distribution that could not be lawfully distributed. Subsection (b) creates personal liability against only members who knowingly received the unlawful distribution, but only in the amount measured by the portion of the actual distribution received that was not lawfully made. Members who both vote for or assent to an unlawful distribution and receive a portion or all of the distribution will be liable, at the election of the company, under either but not both subsections.

A member or manager who is liable under subsection (a) may seek contribution under subsection (c)(1) from other members and managers who also voted for or assented to the same distribution and may also seek recoupment under subsection (c)(2) from members who received the distribution, but only if they accepted the payments knowing they were unlawful.

The two-year statute of limitations of subsection (d) is measured from the date of the distribution. The date of the distribution is determined under Section 406(c).

SECTION 408. MEMBER'S RIGHT TO INFORMATION

(a) A limited liability company shall provide members and their agents and attorneys access to its records, if any, at the company's principal office or other reasonable locations specified in the operating agreement. The company shall provide former members and their agents and attorneys access for proper purposes to records pertaining to the period during which they were members. The right of access provides the opportunity to inspect and copy records during ordinary business hours. The company may impose a reasonable charge, limited to the costs of labor and material, for copies of records furnished.

(b) A limited liability company shall furnish to a member, and to the legal representative of a deceased member or member under legal disability:

(1) without demand, information concerning the company's business or affairs reasonably required for the proper exercise of the member's rights and performance of the member's duties under the operating agreement or this [Act]; and

(2) on demand, other information concerning the company's business or affairs, except to the extent the demand or the information demanded is unreasonable or otherwise improper under the circumstances.

(c) A member has the right upon written demand given to the limited liability company to obtain at the company's expense a copy of any written operating agreement.

Comment

Recognizing the informality of many limited liability companies, subsection (a) does not require a company to maintain any records. In general, a company should maintain records necessary to enable members to determine their share of profits and losses and their rights on dissociation. If inadequate records are maintained to determine those and other critical rights, a member may maintain an action for an accounting under Section 410(a). Normally, a company will maintain at least records required by state or federal authorities regarding tax and other filings.

The obligation to furnish access includes the obligation to insure that all records, if any, are accessible in intelligible form. For example, a company that switches computer systems has an obligation either to convert the records from the old system or retain at least one computer capable of accessing the records from the old system.

The right to inspect and copy records maintained is not conditioned on a member or former member's purpose or motive. However, an abuse of the access and copy right may create a remedy in favor of the other members as a violation of the requesting member or former member's obligation of good faith and fair dealing. See Section 409(d).

Although a company is not required to maintain any records under subsection (a), it is nevertheless subject to a disclosure duty to furnish specified information under subsection (b)(1). A company must therefore furnish to members, without demand, information reasonably needed for members to exercise their rights and duties as members. A member's exercise of these duties justifies an unqualified right of access to the company's records. The member's right to company records may not be unreasonably restricted by the operating agreement. See Section 103(b)(1).

SECTION 409. GENERAL STANDARDS OF MEMBER'S AND MANAGER'S CONDUCT

(a) The only fiduciary duties a member owes to a member-managed company and its other members are the duty of loyalty and the duty of care imposed by subsections (b) and (c).

(b) A member's duty of loyalty to a member-managed company and its other members is limited to the following:

    (1) to account to the company and to hold as trustee for it any property, profit, or benefit derived by the member in the conduct or winding up of the company's business or derived from a use by the member of the company's property, including the appropriation of a company's opportunity;

    (2) to refrain from dealing with the company in the conduct or winding up of the company's business as or on behalf of a party having an interest adverse to the company; and

    (3) to refrain from competing with the company in the conduct of the company's business before the dissolution of the company.

(c) A member's duty of care to a member-managed company and its other members in the conduct of and winding up of the company's business is limited to refraining from engaging in grossly negligent or reckless conduct, intentional misconduct, or a knowing violation of law.

(d) A member shall discharge the duties to a member-managed company and its other members under this [Act] or under the operating agreement and exercise any rights consistently with the obligation of good faith and fair dealing.

(e) A member of a member-managed company does not violate a duty or obligation under this [Act] or under the operating agreement merely because the member's conduct furthers the member's own interest.

(f) A member of a member-managed company may lend money to and transact other business with the company. As to each loan or transaction, the rights and obligations of the member are the same as those of a person who is not a member, subject to other applicable law.

(g) This section applies to a person winding up the limited liability company's business as the personal or legal representative of the last surviving member as if the person were a member.

(h) In a manager-managed company:

    (1) a member who is not also a manager owes no duties to the company or to the other members solely by reason of being a member;

    (2) a manager is held to the same standards of conduct prescribed for members in subsections (b) through (f);

    (3) a member who pursuant to the operating agreement exercises some or all of the rights of a manager in the management and conduct of the company's business is held to the standards of conduct in subsections (b) through (f) to the extent that the member exercises the managerial authority vested in a manager by this [Act]; and

    (4) a manager is relieved of liability imposed by law for violation of the standards prescribed by subsections (b) through (f) to the extent of the managerial authority delegated to the members by the operating agreement.

Comment

Under subsections (a), (c), and (h), members and managers, and their delegatees, owe to the company and to the other members and managers only the fiduciary duties of loyalty and care set forth in subsections (b) and (c) and the obligation of good faith and fair dealing set forth in subsection (d). An operating agreement may not waive or eliminate the duties or obligation, but may, if not manifestly unreasonable, identify activities and determine standards for measuring the performance of them. See Section 103(b)(2) to (4).

Upon a member's dissociation, the duty to account for personal profits under subsection (b)(1), the duty to refrain from acting as or representing adverse interests under subsection (b)(2), and the duty of care under subsection (c) are limited to those derived from matters arising or events occurring before the dissociation unless the member participates in winding up the company's business. Also, the duty not to compete terminates upon dissociation. See Section 603(b)(3) and (b)(2). However, a dissociated member is not free to use confidential company information after dissociation. For example, a dissociated member of a company may immediately compete with the company for new clients but must exercise care in completing on-going client transactions and must account to the company for any fees from the old clients on account of those transactions. Subsection (c) adopts a gross negligence standard for the duty of care, the standard actually used in most partnerships and corporations.

Subsection (b)(2) prohibits a member from acting adversely or representing an adverse party to the company. The rule is based on agency principles and seeks to avoid the conflict of opposing interests in the mind of the member agent whose duty is to act for the benefit of the principal company. As reflected in subsection (f), the rule does not prohibit the member from dealing with the company other than as an adversary. A member may generally deal with the company under subsection (f) when the transaction is approved by the company.

Subsection (e) makes clear that a member does not violate the obligation of good faith under subsection (d) merely because the member's conduct furthers that member's own interest. For example, a member's refusal to vote for an interim distribution because of negative tax implications to that member does not violate that member's obligation of good faith to the other members. Likewise, a member may vote against a proposal by the company to open a shopping center that would directly compete with another shopping center in which the member owns an interest.

SECTION 410. ACTIONS BY MEMBERS

(a) A member may maintain an action against a limited liability company or another member for legal or equitable relief, with or without an accounting as to the company's business, to enforce:

(1) the member's rights under the operating agreement;

(2) the member's rights under this [Act]; and

(3) the rights and otherwise protect the interests of the member, including rights and interests arising independently of the member's relationship to the company.

(b) The accrual, and any time limited for the assertion, of a right of action for a remedy under this section is governed by other law. A right to an accounting upon a dissolution and winding up does not revive a claim barred by law.

Comment

During the existence of the company, members have under this section access to the courts to resolve claims against the company and other members, leaving broad judicial discretion to fashion appropriate legal remedies. A member pursues only that member's claim against the company or another member under this section. Article 11 governs a member's derivative pursuit of a claim on behalf of the company.

A member may recover against the company and the other members under subsection (a)(3) for personal injuries or damage to the member's property caused by another member. One member's negligence is therefore not imputed to bar another member's action.

SECTION 411. CONTINUATION OF TERM COMPANY AFTER EXPIRATION OF SPECIFIED TERM

(a) If a term company is continued after the expiration of the specified term, the rights and duties of the members and managers remain the same as they were at the expiration of the term except to the extent inconsistent with rights and duties of members and managers of an at-will company.

(b) If the members in a member-managed company or the managers in a manager-managed company continue the business without any winding up of the business of the company, it continues as an at-will company.

Comment

A term company will generally dissolve upon the expiration of its term unless either its articles are amended before the expiration of the original specified term to provide for an additional specified term or the members or managers simply continue the company as an at-will company under this section. Amendment of the articles specifying an additional term requires the unanimous consent of the members. See Section 404(c)(3). Therefore, any member has the right to block the amendment. Absent an amendment to the articles, a company may only be continued under subsection (b) as an at will company. The decision to continue a term company as an at-will company does not require the unanimous consent of the members and is treated as an ordinary business matter with disputes resolved by a simple majority vote of either the members or managers. See Section 404. In that case, subsection (b) provides that the members' conduct amends or becomes part of an operating agreement to "continue" the company as an at-will company. The amendment to the operating agreement does not alter the rights of creditors who suffer detrimental reliance because the company does not liquidate after the expiration of its specified term. See Section 203(c)(2).

Preexisting operating-agreement provisions continue to control the relationship of the members under subsection (a) except to the extent inconsistent with the rights and duties of members of an at-will company with an operating agreement containing the same provisions. However, the members could agree in advance that, if the company's business continues after the expiration of its specified term, the company continues as a company with a new specified term or that the provisions of its operating agreement survive the expiration of the specified term.

(ARTICLE) 5
TRANSFEREES AND CREDITORS
OF MEMBER

Section 501.   Member's Distributional Interest.
Section 502.   Transfer of Distributional Interest.
Section 503.   Rights of Transferee.
Section 504.   Rights of Creditor.

SECTION 501. MEMBER'S DISTRIBUTIONAL INTEREST

(a) A member is not a co-owner of, and has no transferable interest in, property of a limited liability company.

(b) A distributional interest in a limited liability company is personal property and, subject to Sections 502 and 503, may be transferred in whole or in part.

(c) An operating agreement may provide that a distributional interest may be evidenced by a certificate of the interest issued by the limited liability company and, subject to Section 503, may also provide for the transfer of any interest represented by the certificate.

Comment

Members have no property interest in property owned by a limited liability company. A distributional interest is personal property and is defined under Section 101(6) as a member's interest in distributions only and does not include the member's broader rights to participate in management under Section 404 and to inspect company records under Section 408.

Under Section 405(a), distributions are allocated in equal shares unless otherwise provided in an operating agreement. Whenever it is desirable to allocate distributions in proportion to contributions rather than per capita, certification may be useful to reduce valuation issues. New and important Internal Revenue Service announcements clarify that certification of a limited liability company will not cause it to be taxed like a corporation.

SECTION 502. TRANSFER OF DISTRIBUTIONAL INTEREST

A transfer of a distributional interest does not entitle the transferee to become or to exercise any rights of a member. A transfer entitles the transferee to receive, to the extent transferred, only the distributions to which the transferor would be entitled.

Comment

Under Sections 501(b) and 502, the only interest a member may freely transfer is that member's distributional interest. A member's transfer of all of a distributional interest constitutes an event of dissociation. See Section 601(3). A transfer of less than all of a member's distributional interest is not an event of dissociation. A member ceases to be a member upon the transfer of all that member's distributional interest and that transfer is also an event of dissociation under Section 601(3). Relating the event of dissociation to the member's transfer of all of the member's distributional interest avoids the need for the company to track potential future dissociation events associated with a member no longer financially interested in the company. Also, all the remaining members may expel a member upon the transfer of "substantially all" the member's distributional interest. The expulsion is an event of dissociation under Section 601(5)(ii).

SECTION 503. RIGHTS OF TRANSFEREE

(a) A transferee of a distributional interest may become a member of a limited liability company if and to the extent that the transferor gives the transferee the right in accordance with authority described in the operating agreement or all other members consent.

(b) A transferee who has become a member, to the extent transferred, has the rights and powers, and is subject to the restrictions and liabilities, of a member under the operating agreement of a limited liability company and this [Act]. A transferee who becomes a member also is liable for the transferor member's obligations to make contributions under Section 402 and for obligations under Section 407 to return unlawful distributions, but the transferee is not obligated for the transferor member's liabilities unknown to the transferee at the time the transferee becomes a member.

(c) Whether or not a transferee of a distributional interest becomes a member under subsection (a), the transferor is not released from liability to the limited liability company under the operating agreement or this [Act].

(d) A transferee who does not become a member is not entitled to participate in the management or conduct of the limited liability company's business, require access to information concerning the company's transactions, or inspect or copy any of the company's records.

(e) A transferee who does not become a member is entitled to:

  (1) receive, in accordance with the transfer, distributions to which the transferor would otherwise be entitled;

  (2) receive, upon dissolution and winding up of the limited liability company's business:

    (i) in accordance with the transfer, the net amount otherwise distributable to the transferor;

    (ii) a statement of account only from the date of the latest statement of account agreed to by all the members;

(3) seek under Section 801(a)(5) a judicial determination that it is equitable to dissolve and wind up the company's business.

(f) A limited liability company need not give effect to a transfer until it has notice of the transfer.

Comment

The only interest a member may freely transfer is the member's distributional interest. A transferee may acquire the remaining rights of a member only by being admitted as a member of the company by all of the remaining members. New and important Internal Revenue Service announcements clarify that the transferability of membership interests of a limited liability company in excess of these default rules will not cause it to be taxed like a corporation. In many cases a limited liability company will be organized and operated with only a few members. These default rules were chosen in the interest of preserving the right of existing members in such companies to determine whether a transferee will become a member.

A transferee not admitted as a member is not entitled to participate in management, require access to information, or inspect or copy company records. The only rights of a transferee are to receive the distributions the transferor would otherwise be entitled, receive a limited statement of account, and seek a judicial dissolution under Section 801(a)(5).

Subsection (e) sets forth the rights of a transferee of an existing member. Although the rights of a dissociated member to participate in the future management of the company parallel the rights of a transferee, a dissociated member retains additional rights that accrued from that person's membership such as the right to enforce Article 7 purchase rights. See and compare Sections 603(b)(1) and 801(a)(4) and Comments.

SECTION 504. RIGHTS OF CREDITOR

(a) On application by a judgment creditor of a member of a limited liability company or of a member's transferee, a court having jurisdiction may charge the distributional interest of the judgment debtor to satisfy the judgment. The court may appoint a receiver of the share of the distributions due or to become due to the judgment debtor and make all other orders, directions, accounts, and inquiries the judgment debtor might have made or which the circumstances may require to give effect to the charging order.

(b) A charging order constitutes a lien on the judgment debtor's distributional interest. The court may order a foreclosure of a lien on a distributional interest subject to the charging order at any time. A purchaser at the foreclosure sale has the rights of a transferee.

(c) At any time before foreclosure, a distributional interest in a limited liability company which is charged may be redeemed:

    (1) by the judgment debtor;

    (2) with property other than the company's property, by one or more of the other members; or

    (3) with the company's property, but only if permitted by the operating agreement.

(d) This [Act] does not affect a member's right under exemption laws with respect to the member's distributional interest in a limited liability company.

(e) This section provides the exclusive remedy by which a judgment creditor of a member or a transferee may satisfy a judgment out of the judgment debtor's distributional interest in a limited liability company.

Comment

A charging order is the only remedy by which a judgment creditor of a member or a member's transferee may reach the distributional interest of a member or member's transferee. Under Section 503(e), the distributional interest of a member or transferee is limited to the member's right to receive distributions from the company and to seek judicial liquidation of the company.

(ARTICLE) 6
MEMBER'S DISSOCIATION

SECTION 601. EVENTS CAUSING MEMBER'S DISSOCIATION

A member is dissociated from a limited liability company upon the occurrence of any of the following events:

(1) the company's having notice of the member's express will to withdraw upon the date of notice or on a later date specified by the member;

(2) an event agreed to in the operating agreement as causing the member's dissociation;

(3) upon transfer of all of a member's distributional interest, other than a transfer for security purposes or a court order charging the member's distributional interest which has not been foreclosed;

(4) the member's expulsion pursuant to the operating agreement;

(5) the member's expulsion by unanimous vote of the other members if:

　(i) it is unlawful to carry on the company's business with the member;

　(ii) there has been a transfer of substantially all of the member's distributional interest, other than a transfer for security purposes or a court order charging the member's distributional interest which has not been foreclosed;

　(iii) within 90 days after the company notifies a corporate member that it will be expelled because it has filed a certificate of dissolution or the equivalent, its charter has been revoked, or its right to conduct business has been suspended by the jurisdiction of its incorporation, the member fails to obtain a revocation of the certificate of dissolution or a reinstatement of its charter or its right to conduct business; or

　(iv) a partnership or a limited liability company that is a member has been dissolved and its business is being wound up;

(6) on application by the company or another member, the member's expulsion by judicial determination because the member:

     (i) engaged in wrongful conduct that adversely and materially affected the company's business;

    (ii) willfully or persistently committed a material breach of the operating agreement or of a duty owed to the company or the other members under Section 409; or

    (iii) engaged in conduct relating to the company's business which makes it not reasonably practicable to carry on the business with the member;

(7) the member's:

    (i) becoming a debtor in bankruptcy;

    (ii) executing an assignment for the benefit of creditors;

    (iii) seeking, consenting to, or acquiescing in the appointment of a trustee, receiver, or liquidator of the member or of all or substantially all of the member's property; or

    (iv) failing, within 90 days after the appointment, to have vacated or stayed the appointment of a trustee, receiver, or liquidator of the member or of all or substantially all of the member's property obtained without the member's consent or acquiescence, or failing within 90 days after the expiration of a stay to have the appointment vacated;

(8) in the case of a member who is an individual:

    (i) the member's death;

    (ii) the appointment of a guardian or general conservator for the member; or

    (iii) a judicial determination that the member has otherwise become incapable of performing the member's duties under the operating agreement;

(9) in the case of a member that is a trust or is acting as a member by virtue of being a trustee of a trust, distribution of the trust's entire rights to receive distributions from the company, but not merely by reason of the substitution of a successor trustee;

(10) in the case of a member that is an estate or is acting as a member by virtue of being a personal representative of an estate, distribution of the estate's entire rights to receive distributions from the company, but not merely the substitution of a successor personal representative; or

(11) termination of the existence of a member if the member is not an individual, estate, or trust other than a business trust.

Comment

The term "dissociation" refers to the change in the relationships among the dissociated member, the company and the other members caused by a member's ceasing to be associated in the carrying on of the company's business. Member dissociation from either an at-will or term company, whether member- or manager-managed is not an event of dissolution of the company unless otherwise specified in an operating agreement. See Section 801(a)(1). However, member dissociation will generally trigger the obligation of the company to purchase the dissociated member's interest under Article 7.

A member may be expelled from the company under paragraph (5)(ii) by the unanimous vote of the other members upon a transfer of "substantially all" of the member's distributional interest other than for a transfer as security for a loan. A transfer of "all" of the member's distributional interest is an event of dissociation under paragraph (3).

Although a member is dissociated upon death, the effect of the dissociation where the company does not dissolve depends upon whether the company is at-will or term. Only the decedent's distributional interest transfers to the decedent's estate which does not acquire the decedent member's management rights. See Section 603(b)(1). Unless otherwise agreed, if the company was at-will, the estate's distributional interest must be purchased by the company at fair value determined at the date of death. However, if a term company, the estate and its transferees continue only as the owner of the distributional interest with no management rights until the expiration of the specified term that existed on the date of death. At the expiration of that term, the company must purchase the interest of a dissociated member if the company continues for an additional term by amending its articles or simply continues as an at-will company. See Sections 411 and 701(a)(2) and Comments. Before that time, the estate and its transferees have the right to make application for a judicial dissolution of the company under Section 801(b)(5) as successors in interest to a dissociated member. See Comments to Sections 801, 411, and 701. Where the members have allocated management rights on the basis of contributions rather than simply the number of members, a member's death will result in a transfer of management rights to the remaining members on a proportionate basis. This transfer of rights may be avoided by a provision in an operating agreement extending the Section 701(a)(1) at-will purchase right to a decedent member of a term company.

SECTION 602. MEMBER'S POWER TO DISSOCIATE; WRONGFUL DISSOCIATION

(a) Unless otherwise provided in the operating agreement, a member has the power to dissociate from a limited liability company at any time, rightfully or wrongfully, by express will pursuant to Section 601(1).

(b) If the operating agreement has not eliminated a member's power to dissociate, the member's dissociation from a limited liability company is wrongful only if:

    (1) it is in breach of an express provision of the agreement; or

    (2) before the expiration of the specified term of a term company:

       (i) the member withdraws by express will;

       (ii) the member is expelled by judicial determination under Section 601(6);

       (iii) the member is dissociated by becoming a debtor in bankruptcy; or

       (iv) in the case of a member who is not an individual, trust other than a business trust, or estate, the member is expelled or otherwise dissociated because it willfully dissolved or terminated its existence.

(c) A member who wrongfully dissociates from a limited liability company is liable to the company and to the other members for damages caused by the dissociation. The liability is in addition to any other obligation of the member to the company or to the other members.

(d) If a limited liability company does not dissolve and wind up its business as a result of a member's wrongful dissociation under subsection (b), damages sustained by the company for the wrongful dissociation must be offset against distributions otherwise due the member after the dissociation.

Comment

A member has the power to withdraw from both an at-will company and a term company although the effects of the withdrawal are remarkably different. See Comments to Section 601. At a minimum, the exercise of a power to withdraw enables members to terminate their continuing duties of loyalty and care. See Section 603(b)(2) to (3).

A member's power to withdraw by express will may be eliminated by an operating agreement. New and important Internal Revenue Service announcements clarify that alteration of a member's power to withdraw will not cause the limited liability company to be taxed like a corporation. An operating agreement may eliminate a member's power to withdraw by express will to promote the business continuity of an at-will company by removing member's right to force the company to purchase the member's distributional interest. See Section 701(a)(1). However, such a member retains the ability to seek a judicial dissolution of the company. See Section 801(a)(4).

If a member's power to withdraw by express will is not eliminated in an operating agreement, the withdrawal may nevertheless be made wrongful under subsection (b). All dissociations, including withdrawal by express will, may be made wrongful under subsection (b)(1) in both an at-will and term company by the inclusion of a provision in an operating agreement. Even where an operating agreement does not eliminate the power to withdraw by express will or make any dissociation wrongful, the dissociation of a member of a term company for the reasons specified under subsection (b)(2) is wrongful. The member is liable to the company and other members for damages caused by a wrongful dissociation under subsection (c) and, under subsection (d), the damages may be offset against all distributions otherwise due the member after the dissociation. Section 701(f) provides a similar rule permitting damages for wrongful dissociation to be offset against any company purchase of the member's distributional interest.

SECTION 603. EFFECT OF MEMBER'S DISSOCIATION

(a) Upon a member's dissociation:

    (1) in an at-will company, the company must cause the dissociated member's distributional interest to be purchased under [Article] 7; and

    (2) in a term company:

        (i) if the company dissolves and winds up its business on or before the expiration of its specified term, [Article] 8 applies to determine the dissociated member's rights to distributions; and

        (ii) if the company does not dissolve and wind up its business on or before the expiration of its specified term, the company must cause the dissociated member's distributional interest to be purchased under [Article] 7 on the date of the expiration of the term specified at the time of the member's dissociation.

(b) Upon a member's dissociation from a limited liability company:

    (1) the member's right to participate in the management and conduct of the company's business terminates, except as otherwise provided in Section 803, and the member ceases to be a member and is treated the same as a transferee of a member;

    (2) the member's duty of loyalty under Section 409(b)(3) terminates; and

    (3) the member's duty of loyalty under Section 409(b)(1) and (2) and duty of care under Section 409(c) continue only with regard to matters arising and events occurring before the member's dissociation, unless the member participates in winding up the company's business pursuant to Section 803.

Comment

Member dissociation is not an event of dissolution of a company unless otherwise specified in an operating agreement. See Section 801(a)(1). Dissociation from an at-will company that does not dissolve the company causes the dissociated member's distributional interest to be immediately purchased under Article 7. See Comments to Sections 602 and 603. Dissociation from a term company that does not dissolve the company does not cause the dissociated member's distributional interest to be purchased under Article 7 until the expiration of the specified term that existed on the date of dissociation.

Subsection (b)(1) provides that a dissociated member forfeits the right to participate in the future conduct of the company's business. Dissociation does not however forfeit that member's right to enforce the Article 7 rights that accrue by reason of the dissociation. Similarly, where dissociation occurs by death, the decedent member's successors in interest may enforce that member's Article 7 rights. See and compare Comments to Section 503(e).

Dissociation terminates the member's right to participate in management, including the member's actual authority to act for the company under Section 301, and begins the two-year period after which a member's apparent authority conclusively ends. See Comments to Section 703. Dissociation also terminates a member's continuing duties of loyalty and care, except with regard to continuing transactions, to the company and other members unless the member participates in winding up the company's business. See Comments to Section 409.

(ARTICLE) 7
MEMBER'S DISSOCIATION WHEN
BUSINESS NOT WOUND UP

SECTION 701. COMPANY PURCHASE OF DISTRIBUTIONAL INTEREST

(a) A limited liability company shall purchase a distributional interest of a:

    (1) member of an at-will company for its fair value determined as of the date of the member's dissociation if the

member's dissociation does not result in a dissolution and winding up of the company's business under Section 801; or

(2) member of a term company for its fair value determined as of the date of the expiration of the specified term that existed on the date of the member's dissociation if the expiration of the specified term does not result in a dissolution and winding up of the company's business under Section 801.

(b) A limited liability company must deliver a purchase offer to the dissociated member whose distributional interest is entitled to be purchased not later than 30 days after the date determined under subsection (a). The purchase offer must be accompanied by:

(1) a statement of the company's assets and liabilities as of the date determined under subsection (a);

(2) the latest available balance sheet and income statement, if any; and

(3) an explanation of how the estimated amount of the payment was calculated.

(c) If the price and other terms of a purchase of a distributional interest are fixed or are to be determined by the operating agreement, the price and terms so fixed or determined govern the purchase unless the purchaser defaults. If a default occurs, the dissociated member is entitled to commence a proceeding to have the company dissolved under Section 801(a)(4)(iv).

(d) If an agreement to purchase the distributional interest is not made within 120 days after the date determined under subsection (a), the dissociated member, within another 120 days, may commence a proceeding against the limited liability company to enforce the purchase. The company at its expense shall notify in writing all of the remaining members, and any other person the court directs, of the commencement of the proceeding. The jurisdiction of the court in which the proceeding is commenced under this subsection is plenary and exclusive.

(e) The court shall determine the fair value of the distributional interest in accordance with the standards set forth in

Section 702 together with the terms for the purchase. Upon making these determinations, the court shall order the limited liability company to purchase or cause the purchase of the interest.

(f) Damages for wrongful dissociation under Section 602(b), and all other amounts owing, whether or not currently due, from the dissociated member to a limited liability company, must be offset against the purchase price.

Comment

This section sets forth default rules regarding an otherwise mandatory company purchase of a distributional interest. Even though a dissociated member's rights to participate in the future management of the company are equivalent to those of a transferee of a member, the dissociation does not forfeit that member's right to enforce the Article 7 purchase right. Similarly, if the dissociation occurs by reason of death, the decedent member's successors in interest may enforce the Article 7 rights. See Comments to Sections 503(e) and 603(b)(1).

An at-will company must purchase a dissociated member's distributional interest under subsection (a)(1) when that member's dissociation does not result in a dissolution of the company under Section 801(a)(1). The purchase price is equal to the fair value of the interest determined as of the date of dissociation. Any damages for wrongful dissociation must be offset against the purchase price.

Dissociation from a term company does not require an immediate purchase of the member's interest but the operating agreement may specify that dissociation is an event of dissolution. See Section 801(a)(1). A term company must only purchase the dissociated member's distributional interest under subsection (a)(2) on the expiration of the specified term that existed on the date of the member's dissociation. The purchase price is equal to the fair value of the interest determined as of the date of the expiration of that specified term. Any damages for wrongful dissociation must be offset against the purchase price.

The valuation dates differ between subsections (a)(1) and (a)(2) purchases. The former is valued on the date of member dissociation whereas the latter is valued on the date of the expiration of the specified term that existed on the date of dissociation. A subsection (a)(2) dissociated member therefore assumes the risk of loss between the date of dissociation and the expiration of the then stated specified term. See Comments to Section 801 (dissociated member may file application to dissolve company under Section 801(a)(4)).

The default valuation standard is fair value. See Comments to Section 702. An operating agreement may fix a method or formula for determining the purchase price and the terms of payment. The purchase right may be modified. For example, an operating agreement may eliminate a member's power to withdraw from an at-will company which narrows the dissociation events contemplated under subsection (a)(1). See Comments to Section 602(a). However, a provision in an operating agreement providing for complete forfeiture of the purchase right may be unenforceable where the power to dissociate has not also been eliminated. See Section 104(a).

The company must deliver a purchase offer to the dissociated member within 30 days after the date determined under subsection (a). The offer must be accompanied by information designed to enable the dissociated member to evaluate the fairness of the offer. The subsection (b)(3) explanation of how the offer price was calculated need not be elaborate. For example, a mere statement of the basis of the calculation, such as "book value," may be sufficient.

The company and the dissociated member must reach an agreement on the purchase price and terms within 120 days after the date determined under subsection (a). Otherwise, the dissociated member may file suit within another 120 days to enforce the purchase under subsection (d). The court will then determine the fair value and terms of purchase under subsection (e). See Section 702. The member's lawsuit is not available under subsection (c) if the parties have previously agreed to price and terms in an operating agreement.

SECTION 702. COURT ACTION TO DETERMINE FAIR VALUE OF DISTRIBUTIONAL INTEREST

(a) In an action brought to determine the fair value of a distributional interest in a limited liability company, the court shall:

(1) determine the fair value of the interest, considering among other relevant evidence the going concern value of the company, any agreement among some or all of the members fixing the price or specifying a formula for determining value of distributional interests for any other purpose, the recommendations of any appraiser appointed by the court, and any legal constraints on the company's ability to purchase the interest;

(2) specify the terms of the purchase, including, if appropriate, terms for installment payments, subordination of the purchase obligation to the rights of the company's other creditors, security for a deferred purchase price, and a covenant not to compete or other restriction on a dissociated member; and

(3) require the dissociated member to deliver an assignment of the interest to the purchaser upon receipt of the purchase price or the first installment of the purchase price.

(b) After the dissociated member delivers the assignment, the dissociated member has no further claim against the company, its members, officers, or managers, if any, other than a claim to any unpaid balance of the purchase price and a claim under any agreement with the company or the remaining members that is not terminated by the court.

(c) If the purchase is not completed in accordance with the specified terms, the company is to be dissolved upon application under Section 801(a)(4)(iv) [MCA, 35-8-902(1)(d)]. If a limited liability company is so dissolved, the dissociated member has the same rights and priorities in the company's assets as if the sale had not been ordered.

(d) If the court finds that a party to the proceeding acted arbitrarily, vexatiously, or not in good faith, it may award one or more other parties their reasonable expenses, including attorney's fees and the expenses of appraisers or other experts, incurred in the proceeding. The finding may be based on the company's failure to make an offer to pay or to comply with Section 701(b).

(e) Interest must be paid on the amount awarded from the date determined under Section 701(a) to the date of payment.

Comment

The default valuation standard is fair value. Under this broad standard, a court is free to determine the fair value of a distributional interest on a fair market, liquidation, or any other method deemed appropriate under the circumstances. A fair market value standard is not used because it is too narrow, often inappropriate, and assumes a fact not contemplated by this section — a willing buyer and a willing seller.

The court has discretion under subsection (a)(2) to include in its order any conditions the court deems necessary to safeguard the interests of the company and the dissociated member or transferee. The discretion may be based on the financial and other needs of the parties.

If the purchase is not consummated or the purchaser defaults, the dissociated member or transferee may make application for dissolution of the company under subsection (c). The court may deny the petition for good cause but the proceeding affords the company an opportunity to be heard on the matter and avoid dissolution. See Comments to Section 801(a)(4).

The power of the court to award all costs and attorney's fees incurred in the suit under subsection (d) is an incentive for both parties to act in good faith. See Section 701(c).

SECTION 703. DISSOCIATED MEMBER'S POWER TO BIND LIMITED LIABILITY COMPANY

For two years after a member dissociates without the dissociation resulting in a dissolution and winding up of a limited liability company's business, the company, including a surviving company under [Article] 9, is bound by an act of the dissociated member which would have bound the company under Section 301 before dissociation only if at the time of entering into the transaction the other party:

(1) reasonably believed that the dissociated member was then a member;

(2) did not have notice of the member's dissociation; and

(3) is not deemed to have had notice under Section 704.

Comment

Member dissociation will not dissolve the company unless otherwise specified in an operating agreement. See Section 801(a)(1). A dissociated member of a member-managed company does not have actual authority to act for the company. See Section 603(b)(1). Under Section 301(a), a dissociated member of a member-managed company has apparent authority to bind the company in ordinary course transactions except as to persons who knew or had notice of the dissociation. This section modifies that rule by requiring the person to show reasonable reliance on the member's status as a member provided a Section 704 statement has not been filed within the previous 90 days. See also Section 804 (power to bind after dissolution).

SECTION 704. STATEMENT OF DISSOCIATION

(a) A dissociated member or a limited liability company may file in the office of the [Secretary of State] a statement of dissociation stating the name of the company and that the member is dissociated from the company.

(b) For the purposes of Sections 301 and 703, a person not a member is deemed to have notice of the dissociation 90 days after the statement of dissociation is filed.

(ARTICLE) 8
WINDING UP COMPANY'S BUSINESS

Section 801.   Events Causing Dissolution and Winding Up of Company's Business.
Section 802.   Limited Liability Company Continues After Dissolution.
Section 803.   Right to Wind Up Limited Liability Company's Business.
Section 804.   Member's or Manager's Power and Liability as Agent After Dissolution.
Section 805.   Articles of Termination.
Section 806.   Distribution of Assets in Winding Up Limited Liability Company's Business.
Section 807.   Known Claims Against Dissolved Limited Liability Company.
Section 808.   Other Claims Against Dissolved Limited Liability Company.
Section 809.   Grounds for Administrative Dissolution.

SECTION 801. EVENTS CAUSING DISSOLUTION AND WINDING UP OF COMPANY'S BUSINESS

(a) A limited liability company is dissolved, and its business must be wound up, upon the occurrence of any of the following events:

(1) an event specified in the operating agreement;

(2) consent of the number or percentage of members specified in the operating agreement;

(3) an event that makes it unlawful for all or substantially all of the business of the company to be continued, but any cure of illegality within 90 days after notice to the company of the event is effective retroactively to the date of the event for purposes of this section;

(4) on application by a member or a dissociated member, upon entry of a judicial decree that:

  (i) the economic purpose of the company is likely to be unreasonably frustrated;

  (ii) another member has engaged in conduct relating to the company's business that makes it not reasonably practicable to carry on the company's business with that member;

  (iii) it is not otherwise reasonably practicable to carry on the company's business in conformity with the articles of organization and the operating agreement;

  (iv) the company failed to purchase the petitioner's distributional interest as required by Section 701; or

  (v) the managers or members in control of the company have acted, are acting, or will act in a manner that is illegal, oppressive, fraudulent, or unfairly prejudicial to the petitioner; or

(5) on application by a transferee of a member's interest, a judicial determination that it is equitable to wind up the company's business:

    (i) after the expiration of the specified term, if the company was for a specified term at the time the applicant became a transferee by member dissociation, transfer, or entry of a charging order that gave rise to the transfer; or

    (ii) at any time, if the company was at will at the time the applicant became a transferee by member dissociation, transfer, or entry of a charging order that gave rise to the transfer.

Comment

The dissolution rules of this section are mostly default rules and may be modified by an operating agreement. However, an operating agreement may not modify or eliminate the dissolution events specified in subsection (a)(3) (illegal business) or subsection (a)(4) (member application). See Section 103(b)(6).

The relationship between member dissociation and company dissolution is set forth under subsection (a)(1). Unless member dissociation is specified as an event of dissolution in the operating agreement, such dissociation does not dissolve the company. New and important Internal Revenue Service announcements clarify that the failure of member dissociation to cause or threaten dissolution of a limited liability company will not cause the company to be taxed like a corporation.

A member or dissociated member whose interest is not required to be purchased by the company under Section 701 may make application under subsection (a)(4) for the involuntary dissolution of both an at-will company and a term company. A transferee may make application under subsection (a)(5). A transferee's application right, but not that of a member or dissociated member, may be modified by an operating agreement. See Section 103(b)(6). A dissociated member is not treated as a transferee for purposes of an application under subsections (a)(4) and (a)(5). See Section 603(b)(1). For example, this affords reasonable protection to a dissociated member of a term company to make application under subsection (a)(4) before the expiration of the term that existed at the time of dissociation. For purposes of a subsection (a)(4) application, a dissociated member includes a successor in interest, e.g., surviving spouse. See Comments to Section 601.

In the case of applications under subsections (a)(4) and (a)(5), the applicant has the burden of proving either the existence of one or more of the circumstances listed under subsection (a)(4) or that it is equitable to wind up the company's business under subsection (a)(5). Proof of the existence of one or more of the circumstances in subsection (a)(4), may be the basis of a subsection (a)(5) application. Even where the burden of proof is met, the court has the discretion to order relief other than the dissolution of the company. Examples include an accounting, a declaratory judgment, a distribution, the purchase of the distributional interest of the applicant or another member, or the appointment of a receiver. See Section 410.

A court has the discretion to dissolve a company under subsection (a)(4)(i) when the company has a very poor financial record that is not likely to improve. In this instance, dissolution is an alternative to placing the company in bankruptcy. A court may dissolve a company under subsections (a)(4)(ii), (a)(4)(iii), and (a)(4)(iv) for serious and protracted misconduct by one or more members. Subsection (a)(4)(v) provides a specific remedy for an improper squeeze-out of a member.

In determining whether and what type of relief to order under subsections (a)(4) and (a)(5) involuntary dissolution suits, a court should take into account other rights and remedies of the applicant. For example, a court should not grant involuntary dissolution of an at-will company if the applicant member has the right to dissociate and force the company to purchase that member's distributional interest under Sections 701 and 702. In other cases, involuntary dissolution or some other remedy such as a buy-out might be appropriate where, for example, one or more members have (i) engaged in fraudulent or unconscionable conduct, (ii) improperly expelled a member seeking an unfair advantage of a provision in an operating agreement that provides for a significantly lower price on expulsion than would be payable in the event of voluntary dissociation, or (iii) engaged in serious misconduct and the applicant member is a member of a term company and would not have a right to have the company purchase that member's distributional interest upon dissociation until the expiration of the company's specified term.

SECTION 802. LIMITED LIABILITY COMPANY CONTINUES AFTER DISSOLUTION

(a) Subject to subsection (b), a limited liability company continues after dissolution only for the purpose of winding up its business.

(b) At any time after the dissolution of a limited liability company and before the winding up of its business is completed, the members, including a dissociated member whose dissociation caused the dissolution, may unanimously waive the right to have the company's business wound up and the company terminated. In that case:

(1) the limited liability company resumes carrying on its business as if dissolution had never occurred and any liability incurred by the company or a member after the dissolution and before the waiver is determined as if the dissolution had never occurred; and

(2) the rights of a third party accruing under Section 804(a) or arising out of conduct in reliance on the dissolution before the third party knew or received a notification of the waiver are not adversely affected.

Comment

The liability shield continues in effect for the winding up period because the legal existence of the company continues under subsection (a). The company is terminated on the filing of articles of termination. See Section 805.

SECTION 803. RIGHT TO WIND UP LIMITED LIABILITY COMPANY'S BUSINESS

(a) After dissolution, a member who has not wrongfully dissociated may participate in winding up a limited liability company's business, but on application of any member, member's legal representative, or transferee, the [designate the appropriate court], for good cause shown, may order judicial supervision of the winding up.

(b) A legal representative of the last surviving member may wind up a limited liability company's business.

(c) A person winding up a limited liability company's business may preserve the company's business or property as a going concern for a reasonable time, prosecute and defend actions and proceedings, whether civil, criminal, or administrative, settle and close the company's business, dispose of and transfer the company's property, discharge the company's liabilities, distribute the assets of the company pursuant to Section 806, settle disputes by mediation or arbitration, and perform other necessary acts.

SECTION 804. MEMBER'S OR MANAGER'S POWER AND LIABILITY AS AGENT AFTER DISSOLUTION

(a) A limited liability company is bound by a member's or manager's act after dissolution that:

(1) is appropriate for winding up the company's business; or

(2) would have bound the company under Section 301 before dissolution, if the other party to the transaction did not have notice of the dissolution.

(b) A member or manager who, with knowledge of the dissolution, subjects a limited liability company to liability by an act that is not appropriate for winding up the company's business is liable to the company for any damage caused to the company arising from the liability.

Comment

After dissolution, members and managers continue to have the authority to bind the company that they had prior to dissolution provided that the third party did not have notice of the dissolution. See Section 102(b) (notice defined). Otherwise, they have only the authority appropriate for winding up the company's business. See Section 703 (agency power of member after dissociation).

SECTION 805. ARTICLES OF TERMINATION

(a) At any time after dissolution and winding up, a limited liability company may terminate its existence by filing with the [Secretary of State] articles of termination stating:

(1) the name of the company;

(2) the date of the dissolution; and

(3) that the company's business has been wound up and the legal existence of the company has been terminated.

(b) The existence of a limited liability company is terminated upon the filing of the articles of termination, or upon a later effective date, if specified in the articles of termination.

Comment

The termination of legal existence also terminates the company's liability shield. See Comments to Section 802 (liability shield continues in effect during winding up). It also ends the company's responsibility to file an annual report. See Section 211.

SECTION 806. DISTRIBUTION OF ASSETS IN WINDING UP LIMITED LIABILITY COMPANY'S BUSINESS

(a) In winding up a limited liability company's business, the assets of the company must be applied to discharge its obligations to creditors, including members who are creditors. Any surplus must be applied to pay in money the net amount distributable to members in accordance with their right to distributions under subsection (b).

(b) Each member is entitled to a distribution upon the winding up of the limited liability company's business consisting of a return of all contributions which have not previously been returned and a distribution of any remainder in equal shares.

SECTION 807. KNOWN CLAIMS AGAINST DISSOLVED LIMITED LIABILITY COMPANY

(a) A dissolved limited liability company may dispose of the known claims against it by following the procedure described in this section.

(b) A dissolved limited liability company shall notify its known claimants in writing of the dissolution. The notice must:

(1) specify the information required to be included in a claim;

> (2) provide a mailing address where the claim is to be sent;
>
> (3) state the deadline for receipt of the claim, which may not be less than 120 days after the date the written notice is received by the claimant; and
>
> (4) state that the claim will be barred if not received by the deadline.

(c) A claim against a dissolved limited liability company is barred if the requirements of subsection (b) are met, and:

> (1) the claim is not received by the specified deadline; or
>
> (2) in the case of a claim that is timely received but rejected by the dissolved company, the claimant does not commence a proceeding to enforce the claim within 90 days after the receipt of the notice of the rejection.

(d) For purposes of this section, "claim" does not include a contingent liability or a claim based on an event occurring after the effective date of dissolution.

Comment

A known claim will be barred when the company provides written notice to a claimant that a claim must be filed with the company no later than at least 120 days after receipt of the written notice and the claimant fails to file the claim. If the claim is timely received but is rejected by the company, the claim is nevertheless barred unless the claimant files suit to enforce the claim within 90 days after the receipt of the notice of rejection. A claim described in subsection (d) is not a "known" claim and is governed by Section 808. This section does not extend any other applicable statutes of limitation. See Section 104. Depending on the management of the company, members or managers must discharge or make provision for discharging all of the company's known liabilities before distributing the remaining assets to the members. See Sections 806(a), 406, and 407.

SECTION 808. OTHER CLAIMS AGAINST DISSOLVED LIMITED LIABILITY COMPANY

(a) A dissolved limited liability company may publish notice of its dissolution and request persons having claims against the company to present them in accordance with the notice.

(b) The notice must:

(1) be published at least once in a newspaper of general circulation in the [county] in which the dissolved limited liability company's principal office is located or, if none in this State, in which its designated office is or was last located;

(2) describe the information required to be contained in a claim and provide a mailing address where the claim is to be sent; and

(3) state that a claim against the limited liability company is barred unless a proceeding to enforce the claim is commenced within five years after publication of the notice.

(c) If a dissolved limited liability company publishes a notice in accordance with subsection (b), the claim of each of the following claimants is barred unless the claimant commences a proceeding to enforce the claim against the dissolved company within five years after the publication date of the notice:

(1) a claimant who did not receive written notice under Section 807;

(2) a claimant whose claim was timely sent to the dissolved company but not acted on; and

(3) a claimant whose claim is contingent or based on an event occurring after the effective date of dissolution.

(d) A claim not barred under this section may be enforced:

(1) against the dissolved limited liability company, to the extent of its undistributed assets; or

(2) if the assets have been distributed in liquidation, against a member of the dissolved company to the extent of the member's proportionate share of the claim or the company's assets distributed to the member in liquidation, whichever is less, but a member's total liability for all claims under this section may not exceed the total amount of assets distributed to the member.

Comment

An unknown claim will be barred when the company publishes notice requesting claimants to file claims with the company and stating that claims will be barred unless the claimant files suit to enforce the claim within five years after the date of publication. The procedure also bars known claims where the claimant either did not receive written notice described in Section 807 or received notice, mailed a claim, but the company did not act on the claim.

Depending on the management of the company, members or managers must discharge or make provision for discharging all of the company's known liabilities before distributing the remaining assets to the members. See Comment to Section 807. This section does not contemplate that a company will postpone member distributions until all unknown claims are barred under this section. In appropriate cases, the company may purchase insurance or set aside funds permitting a distribution of the remaining assets. Where winding up distributions have been made to members, subsection (d)(2) authorizes recovery against those members. However, a claimant's recovery against a member is limited to the lesser of the member's proportionate share of the claim or the amount received in the distribution. This section does not extend any other applicable statutes of limitation. See Section 104.

SECTION 809. GROUNDS FOR ADMINISTRATIVE DISSOLUTION

The [Secretary of State] may commence a proceeding to dissolve a limited liability company administratively if the company does not:

(1) pay any fees, taxes, or penalties imposed by this [Act] or other law within 60 days after they are due; or

(2) deliver its annual report to the [Secretary of State] within 60 days after it is due.

Comment

Administrative dissolution is an effective enforcement mechanism for a variety of statutory obligations under this Act and it avoids the more expensive judicial dissolution process. When applicable, administrative dissolution avoids wasteful attempts to compel compliance by a company abandoned by its members.

SECTION 810. PROCEDURE FOR AND EFFECT OF ADMINISTRATIVE DISSOLUTION

(a) If the [Secretary of State] determines that a ground exists for administratively dissolving a limited liability company, the [Secretary of State] shall enter a record of the determination and serve the company with a copy of the record.

(b) If the company does not correct each ground for dissolution or demonstrate to the reasonable satisfaction of the [Secretary of State] that each ground determined by the [Secretary of State] does not exist within 60 days after service of the notice, the [Secretary of State] shall administratively dissolve the company by signing a certification of the dissolution that recites the ground for dissolution and its effective date. The [Secretary of State] shall file the original of the certificate and serve the company with a copy of the certificate.

(c) A company administratively dissolved continues its existence but may carry on only business necessary to wind up and liquidate its business and affairs under Section 802 and to notify claimants under Sections 807 and 808.

(d) The administrative dissolution of a company does not terminate the authority of its agent for service of process.

Comment

A company's failure to comply with a ground for administrative dissolution may simply occur because of oversight. Therefore, subsections (a) and (b) set forth a mandatory notice by the filing officer to the company of the ground for dissolution and a 60 day grace period for correcting the ground.

SECTION 811. REINSTATEMENT FOLLOWING ADMINISTRATIVE DISSOLUTION

(a) A limited liability company administratively dissolved may apply to the [Secretary of State] for reinstatement within two years after the effective date of dissolution. The application must:

(1) recite the name of the company and the effective date of its administrative dissolution;

(2) state that the ground for dissolution either did not exist or have been eliminated;

(3) state that the company's name satisfies the requirements of Section 105; and

(4) contain a certificate from the [taxing authority] reciting that all taxes owed by the company have been paid.

(b) If the [Secretary of State] determines that the application contains the information required by subsection (a) and that the information is correct, the [Secretary of State] shall cancel the certificate of dissolution and prepare a certificate of reinstatement that recites this determination and the effective date of reinstatement, file the originai of the certificate, and serve the company with a copy of the certificate.

(c) When reinstatement is effective, it relates back to and takes effect as of the effective date of the administrative dissolution and the company may resume its business as if the administrative dissolution had never occurred.

SECTION 812. APPEAL FROM DENIAL OF REINSTATEMENT

(a) If the [Secretary of State] denies a limited liability company's application for reinstatement following administrative dissolution, the [Secretary of State] shall serve the company with a record that explains the reason or reasons for denial.

(b) The company may appeal the denial of reinstatement to the [name appropriate] court within 30 days after service of the notice of denial is perfected. The company appeals by petitioning the court to set aside the dissolution and attaching to the petition copies of the [Secretary of State's] certificate of dissolution, the company's application for reinstatement, and the [Secretary of State's] notice of denial.

(c) The court may summarily order the [Secretary of State] to reinstate the dissolved company or may take other action the court considers appropriate.

(d) The court's final decision may be appealed as in other civil proceedings.

(ARTICLE) 9
CONVERSIONS AND MERGERS

SECTION 901. DEFINITIONS.

In this [article]:

(1) "Corporation" means a corporation under [the State Corporation Act], a predecessor law, or comparable law of another jurisdiction.

(2) "General partner" means a partner in a partnership and a general partner in a limited partnership.

(3) "Limited partner" means a limited partner in a limited partnership.

(4) "Limited partnership" means a limited partnership created under [the State Limited Partnership Act], a predecessor law, or comparable law of another jurisdiction.

(5) "Partner" includes a general partner and a limited partner.

(6) "Partnership" means a general partnership under [the State Partnership Act], a predecessor law, or comparable law of another jurisdiction.

(7) "Partnership agreement" means an agreement among the partners concerning the partnership or limited partnership.

(8) "Shareholder" means a shareholder in a corporation.

Comment

Section 907 makes clear that the provisions of Article 9 are not mandatory. Therefore, a partnership or a limited liability company may convert or merge in any other manner provided by law. However, if the requirements of Article 9 are followed, the conversion or merger is legally valid. Article 9 is not restricted to domestic business entities.

SECTION 902. CONVERSION OF PARTNERSHIP OR LIMITED PARTNERSHIP TO LIMITED LIABILITY COMPANY

(a) A partnership or limited partnership may be converted to a limited liability company pursuant to this section.

(b) The terms and conditions of a conversion of a partnership or limited partnership to a limited liability company must be approved by all of the partners or by a number or percentage of the partners required for conversion in the partnership agreement.

(c) An agreement of conversion must set forth the terms and conditions of the conversion of the interests of partners of a partnership or of a limited partnership, as the case may be, into interests in the converted limited liability company or the cash or other consideration to be paid or delivered as a result of the conversion of the interests of the partners, or a combination thereof.

(d) After a conversion is approved under subsection (b), the partnership or limited partnership shall file articles of organization in the office of the [Secretary of State] which satisfy the requirements of Section 203 and contain:

    (1) a statement that the partnership or limited partnership was converted to a limited liability company from a partnership or limited partnership, as the case may be;

    (2) its former name;

    (3) a statement of the number of votes cast by the partners entitled to vote for and against the conversion and, if the vote is less than unanimous, the number or percentage required to approve the conversion under subsection (b); and

    (4) in the case of a limited partnership, a statement that the certificate of limited partnership is to be canceled as of the date the conversion took effect.

(e) In the case of a limited partnership, the filing of articles of organization under subsection

(d) cancels its certificate of limited partnership as of the date the conversion took effect.

(f) A conversion takes effect when the articles of organization are filed in the office of the [Secretary of State] or at any later date specified in the articles of organization.

(g) A general partner who becomes a member of a limited liability company as a result of a conversion remains liable as a partner for an obligation incurred by the partnership or limited partnership before the conversion takes effect.

(h) A general partner's liability for all obligations of the limited liability company incurred after the conversion takes effect is that of a member of the company. A limited partner who becomes a member as a result of a conversion remains liable only to the extent the limited partner was liable for an obligation incurred by the limited partnership before the conversion takes effect.

Comment

Subsection (b) makes clear that the terms and conditions of the conversion of a general or limited partnership to a limited liability company must be approved by all of the partners unless the partnership agreement specifies otherwise.

SECTION 903. EFFECT OF CONVERSION; ENTITY UNCHANGED

(a) A partnership or limited partnership that has been converted pursuant to this [article] is for all purposes the same entity that existed before the conversion.

(b) When a conversion takes effect:

(1) all property owned by the converting partnership or limited partnership vests in the limited liability company;

(2) all debts, liabilities, and other obligations of the converting partnership or limited partnership continue as obligations of the limited liability company;

(3) an action or proceeding pending by or against the converting partnership or limited partnership may be continued as if the conversion had not occurred;

(4) except as prohibited by other law, all of the rights, privileges, immunities, powers, and purposes of the converting partnership or limited partnership vest in the limited liability company; and

(5) except as otherwise provided in the agreement of conversion under Section 902(c), all of the partners of the converting partnership continue as members of the limited liability company.

Comment

A conversion is not a conveyance or transfer and does not give rise to claims of reverter or impairment of title based on a prohibited conveyance or transfer. Under subsection (b)(1), title to all partnership property, including real estate, vests in the limited liability company as a matter of law without reversion or impairment.

SECTION 904. MERGER OF ENTITIES

(a) Pursuant to a plan of merger approved under subsection (c), a limited liability company may be merged with or into one or more limited liability companies, foreign limited liability companies, corporations, foreign corporations, partnerships, foreign partnerships, limited partnerships, foreign limited partnerships, or other domestic or foreign entities.

(b) A plan of merger must set forth:

(1) the name of each entity that is a party to the merger;

(2) the name of the surviving entity into which the other entities will merge;

(3) the type of organization of the surviving entity;

(4) the terms and conditions of the merger;

(5) the manner and basis for converting the interests of each party to the merger into interests or obligations of the surviving entity, or into money or other property in whole or in part; and

(6) the street address of the surviving entity's principal place of business.

(c) A plan of merger must be approved:

(1) in the case of a limited liability company that is a party to the merger, by all of the members or by a number or percentage of members specified in the operating agreement;

(2) in the case of a foreign limited liability company that is a party to the merger, by the vote required for approval of a merger by the law of the State or foreign jurisdiction in which the foreign limited liability company is organized;

(3) in the case of a partnership or domestic limited partnership that is a party to the merger, by the vote required for approval of a conversion under Section 902(b); and

(4) in the case of any other entities that are parties to the merger, by the vote required for approval of a merger by the law of this State or of the State or foreign jurisdiction in which the entity is organized and, in the absence of such a requirement, by all the owners of interests in the entity.

(d) After a plan of merger is approved and before the merger takes effect, the plan may be amended or abandoned as provided in the plan.

(e) The merger is effective upon the filing of the articles of merger with the [Secretary of State], or at such later date as the articles may provide.

Comment

This section sets forth a "safe harbor" for cross-entity mergers of limited liability companies with both domestic and foreign: corporations, general and limited partnerships, and other limited liability companies. Subsection (c) makes clear that the terms and conditions of the plan of merger must be approved by all of the partners unless applicable state law specifies otherwise for the merger.

SECTION 905. ARTICLES OF MERGER

(a) After approval of the plan of merger under Section 904(c), unless the merger is abandoned under Section 904(d), articles of merger must be signed on behalf of each limited liability company and other entity that is a party to the merger and delivered to the [Secretary of State] for filing. The articles must set forth:

(1) the name and jurisdiction of formation or organization of each of the limited liability companies and other entities that are parties to the merger;

(2) for each limited liability company that is to merge, the date its articles of organization were filed with the [Secretary of State];

(3) that a plan of merger has been approved and signed by each limited liability company and other entity that is to merge;

(4) the name and address of the surviving limited liability company or other surviving entity;

(5) the effective date of the merger;

(6) if a limited liability company is the surviving entity, such changes in its articles of organization as are necessary by reason of the merger;

(7) if a party to a merger is a foreign limited liability company, the jurisdiction and date of filing of its initial articles of organization and the date when its application for authority was filed by the [Secretary of State] or, if an application has not been filed, a statement to that effect; and

(8) if the surviving entity is not a limited liability company, an agreement that the surviving entity may be served with process in this State and is subject to liability in any action or proceeding for the enforcement of any liability or obligation of any limited liability company previously subject to suit in this State which is to merge, and for the enforcement, as provided in this [Act], of the right of members of any limited liability company to receive payment for their interest against the surviving entity.

(b) If a foreign limited liability company is the surviving entity of a merger, it may not do business in this State until an application for that authority is filed with the [Secretary of State].

(c) The surviving limited liability company or other entity shall furnish a copy of the plan of merger, on request and without cost, to any member of any limited liability company or any person holding an interest in any other entity that is to merge.

(d) Articles of merger operate as an amendment to the limited liability company's articles of organization.

SECTION 906. EFFECT OF MERGER

(a) When a merger takes effect:

 (1) the separate existence of each limited liability company and other entity that is a party to the merger, other than the surviving entity, terminates;

 (2) all property owned by each of the limited liability companies and other entities that are party to the merger vests in the surviving entity;

 (3) all debts, liabilities, and other obligations of each limited liability company and other entity that is party to the merger become the obligations of the surviving entity;

 (4) an action or proceeding pending by or against a limited liability company or other party to a merger may be continued as if the merger had not occurred or the surviving entity may be substituted as a party to the action or proceeding; and

 (5) except as prohibited by other law, all the rights, privileges, immunities, powers, and purposes of every limited liability company and other entity that is a party to a merger vest in the surviving entity.

(b) The [Secretary of State] is an agent for service of process in an action or proceeding against the surviving foreign entity to enforce an obligation of any party to a merger if the surviving foreign entity fails to appoint or maintain an agent designated for service of process in this State or the agent for service of process cannot with reasonable diligence be found at the designated office. Upon receipt of process, the [Secretary of State] shall send a copy of the process by registered or certified mail, return receipt requested, to the surviving entity at the address set forth in the articles of merger. Service is effected under this subsection at the earliest of:

(1) the date the company receives the process, notice, or demand;

(2) the date shown on the return receipt, if signed on behalf of the company; or

(3) five days after its deposit in the mail, if mailed postpaid and correctly addressed.

(c) A member of the surviving limited liability company is liable for all obligations of a party to the merger for which the member was personally liable before the merger.

(d) Unless otherwise agreed, a merger of a limited liability company that is not the surviving entity in the merger does not require the limited liability company to wind up its business under this [Act] or pay its liabilities and distribute its assets pursuant to this [Act].

(e) Articles of merger serve as articles of dissolution for a limited liability company that is not the surviving entity in the merger.

SECTION 907. (ARTICLE) NOT EXCLUSIVE

This [article] does not preclude an entity from being converted or merged under other law.

(ARTICLE) 10
FOREIGN LIMITED LIABILITY COMPANIES

SECTION 1001. LAW GOVERNING FOREIGN LIMITED LIABILITY COMPANIES

(a) The laws of the State or other jurisdiction under which a foreign limited liability company is organized govern its organization and internal affairs and the liability of its managers, members, and their transferees.

(b) A foreign limited liability company may not be denied a certificate of authority by reason of any difference between the laws of another jurisdiction under which the foreign company is organized and the laws of this State.

(c) A certificate of authority does not authorize a foreign limited liability company to engage in any business or exercise any power that a limited liability company may not engage in or exercise in this State.

Comment

The law where a foreign limited liability company is organized, rather than this Act, governs that company's internal affairs and the liability of its owners. Accordingly, any difference between the laws of the foreign jurisdiction and this Act will not constitute grounds for denial of a certificate of authority to transact business in this State. However, a foreign limited liability company transacting business in this State by virtue of a certificate of authority is limited to the business and powers that a limited liability company may lawfully pursue and exercise under Section 112.

SECTION 1002. APPLICATION FOR CERTIFICATE OF AUTHORITY

(a) A foreign limited liability company may apply for a certificate of authority to transact business in this State by delivering an application to the [Secretary of State] for filing. The application must set forth:

(1) the name of the foreign company or, if its name is unavailable for use in this State, a name that satisfies the requirements of Section 1005;

    (2) the name of the State or country under whose law it is organized;

    (3) the street address of its principal office;

    (4) the address of its initial designated office in this State;

    (5) the name and street address of its initial agent for service of process in this State;

    (6) whether the duration of the company is for a specified term and, if so, the period specified;

    (7) whether the company is manager-managed, and, if so, the name and address of each initial manager; and

    (8) whether the members of the company are to be liable for its debts and obligations under a provision similar to Section 303(c).

(b) A foreign limited liability company shall deliver with the completed application a certificate of existence or a record of similar import authenticated by the secretary of state or other official having custody of company records in the State or country under whose law it is organized.

Comment

As with articles of organization, the application must be signed and filed with the filing office. See Sections 105, 107 (name registration), 205, 206, 209 (liability for false statements), and 1005.

SECTION 1003. ACTIVITIES NOT CONSTITUTING TRANSACTING BUSINESS

(a) Activities of a foreign limited liability company that do not constitute transacting business in this State within the meaning of this [article] include:

    (1) maintaining, defending, or settling an action or proceeding;

    (2) holding meetings of its members or managers or carrying on any other activity concerning its internal affairs;

    (3) maintaining bank accounts;

(4) maintaining offices or agencies for the transfer, exchange, and registration of the foreign company's own securities or maintaining trustees or depositories with respect to those securities;

(5) selling through independent contractors;

(6) soliciting or obtaining orders, whether by mail or through employees or agents or otherwise, if the orders require acceptance outside this State before they become contracts;

(7) creating or acquiring indebtedness, mortgages, or security interests in real or personal property;

(8) securing or collecting debts or enforcing mortgages or other security interests in property securing the debts, and holding, protecting, and maintaining property so acquired;

(9) conducting an isolated transaction that is completed within 30 days and is not one in the course of similar transactions of a like manner; and

(10) transacting business in interstate commerce.

(b) For purposes of this [article], the ownership in this State of income-producing real property or tangible personal property, other than property excluded under subsection (a), constitutes transacting business in this State.

(c) This section does not apply in determining the contacts or activities that may subject a foreign limited liability company to service of process, taxation, or regulation under any other law of this State.

SECTION 1004. ISSUANCE OF CERTIFICATE OF AUTHORITY

Unless the [Secretary of State] determines that an application for a certificate of authority fails to comply as to form with the filing requirements of this [Act], the [Secretary of State], upon payment of all filing fees, shall file the application and send a receipt for it and the fees to the limited liability company or its representative.

SECTION 1005. NAME OF FOREIGN LIMITED LIABILITY COMPANY

(a) If the name of a foreign limited liability company does not satisfy the requirements of Section 105, the company, to obtain or maintain a certificate of authority to transact business in this State, must use a fictitious name to transact business in this State if its real name is unavailable and it delivers to the [Secretary of State] for filing a copy of the resolution of its managers, in the case of a manager-managed company, or of its members, in the case of a member-managed company, adopting the fictitious name.

(b) Except as authorized by subsections (c) and (d), the name, including a fictitious name to be used to transact business in this State, of a foreign limited liability company must be distinguishable upon the records of the [Secretary of State] from:

(1) the name of any corporation, limited partnership, or company incorporated, organized, or authorized to transact business in this State;

(2) a name reserved or registered under Section 106 or 107; and

(3) the fictitious name of another foreign limited liability company authorized to transact business in this State.

(c) A foreign limited liability company may apply to the [Secretary of State] for authority to use in this State a name that is not distinguishable upon the records of the [Secretary of State] from a name described in subsection (b). The [Secretary of State] shall authorize use of the name applied for if:

(1) the present user, registrant, or owner of a reserved name consents to the use in a record and submits an undertaking in form satisfactory to the [Secretary of State] to change its name to a name that is distinguishable upon the records of the [Secretary of State] from the name of the foreign applying limited liability company; or

(2) the applicant delivers to the [Secretary of State] a certified copy of a final judgment of a court establishing the applicant's right to use the name applied for in this State.

(d) A foreign limited liability company may use in this State the name, including the fictitious name, of another domestic or foreign entity that is used in this State if the other entity is incorporated, organized, or authorized to transact business in this State and the foreign limited liability company:

(1) has merged with the other entity;

(2) has been formed by reorganization of the other entity; or

(3) has acquired all or substantially all of the assets, including the name, of the other entity.

(e) If a foreign limited liability company authorized to transact business in this State changes its name to one that does not satisfy the requirements of Section 105, it may not transact business in this State under the name as changed until it adopts a name satisfying the requirements of Section 105 and obtains an amended certificate of authority.

SECTION 1006. REVOCATION OF CERTIFICATE OF AUTHORITY

(a) A certificate of authority of a foreign limited liability company to transact business in this State may be revoked by the [Secretary of State] in the manner provided in subsection (b) if:

(1) the company fails to:

    (i) pay any fees, taxes, and penalties owed to this State;

    (ii) deliver its annual report required under Section 211 to the [Secretary of State] within 60 days after it is due;

    (iii) appoint and maintain an agent for service of process as required by this [article]; or

    (iv) file a statement of a change in the name or business address of the agent as required by this [article]; or

(2) a misrepresentation has been made of any material matter in any application, report, affidavit, or other record submitted by the company pursuant to this [article].

(b) The [Secretary of State] may not revoke a certificate of authority of a foreign limited liability company unless the

[Secretary of State] sends the company notice of the revocation, at least 60 days before its effective date, by a record addressed to its agent for service of process in this State, or if the company fails to appoint and maintain a proper agent in this State, addressed to the office required to be maintained by Section 108. The notice must specify the cause for the revocation of the certificate of authority. The authority of the company to transact business in this State ceases on the effective date of the revocation unless the foreign limited liability company cures the failure before that date.

SECTION 1007. CANCELLATION OF AUTHORITY

A foreign limited liability company may cancel its authority to transact business in this State by filing in the office of the [Secretary of State] a certificate of cancellation. Cancellation does not terminate the authority of the [Secretary of State] to accept service of process on the company for [claims for relief] arising out of the transactions of business in this State.

SECTION 1008. EFFECT OF FAILURE TO OBTAIN CERTIFICATE OF AUTHORITY

(a) A foreign limited liability company transacting business in this State may not maintain an action or proceeding in this State unless it has a certificate of authority to transact business in this State.

(b) The failure of a foreign limited liability company to have a certificate of authority to transact business in this State does not impair the validity of a contract or act of the company or prevent the foreign limited liability company from defending an action or proceeding in this State.

(c) Limitations on personal liability of managers, members, and their transferees are not waived solely by transacting business in this State without a certificate of authority.

(d) If a foreign limited liability company transacts business in this State without a certificate of authority, it appoints the [Secretary of State] as its agent for service of process for [claims for relief] arising out of the transaction of business in this State.

SECTION 1009. ACTION BY (ATTORNEY GENERAL)

The [Attorney General] may maintain an action to restrain a foreign limited liability company from transacting business in this State in violation of this [article].

(ARTICLE) 11
DERIVATIVE ACTIONS

Section 1101. Right of Action.
Section 1102. Proper Plaintiff.
Section 1103. Pleading.
Section 1104. Expenses.

SECTION 1101. RIGHT OF ACTION

A member of a limited liability company may maintain an action in the right of the company if the members or managers having authority to do so have refused to commence the action or an effort to cause those members or managers to commence the action is not likely to succeed.

Comment

A member may bring an action on behalf of the company when the members or managers having the authority to pursue the company recovery refuse to do so or an effort to cause them to pursue the recovery is not likely to succeed. See Comments to Section 411(a) (personal action of member against company or another member).

SECTION 1102. PROPER PLAINTIFF

In a derivative action for a limited liability company, the plaintiff must be a member of the company when the action is commenced; and:

(1) must have been a member at the time of the transaction of which the plaintiff complains; or

(2) the plaintiff's status as a member must have devolved upon the plaintiff by operation of law or pursuant to the terms of the operating agreement from a person who was a member at the time of the transaction.

SECTION 1103. PLEADING

In a derivative action for a limited liability company, the complaint must set forth with particularity the effort of the plaintiff to secure initiation of the action by a member or manager or the reasons for not making the effort.

Comment

There is no obligation of the company or its members or managers to respond to a member demand to bring an action to pursue a company recovery. However, if a company later decides to commence the demanded action or assume control of the derivative litigation, the member's right to commence or control the proceeding ordinarily ends.

SECTION 1104. EXPENSES

If a derivative action for a limited liability company is successful, in whole or in part, or if anything is received by the plaintiff as a result of a judgment, compromise, or settlement of an action or claim, the court may award the plaintiff reasonable expenses, including reasonable attorney's fees, and shall direct the plaintiff to remit to the limited liability company the remainder of the proceeds received.

(ARTICLE) 12
MISCELLANEOUS PROVISIONS

SECTION 1201. UNIFORMITY OF APPLICATION AND CONSTRUCTION

This [Act] shall be applied and construed to effectuate its general purpose to make uniform the law with respect to the subject of this [Act] among States enacting it.

SECTION 1202. SHORT TITLE

This [Act] may be cited as the Uniform Limited Liability Company Act (1996).

SECTION 1203. SEVERABILITY CLAUSE

If any provision of this [Act] or its application to any person or circumstance is held invalid, the invalidity does not affect other provisions or applications of this [Act] which can be given effect without the invalid provision or application, and to this end the provisions of this [Act] are severable.

SECTION 1204. EFFECTIVE DATE

This [Act] takes effect [_____].

SECTION 1205. TRANSITIONAL PROVISIONS

(a) Before January 1, 199__, this [Act] governs only a limited liability company organized:
   (1) after the effective date of this [Act], unless the company is continuing the business of a dissolved limited liability company under [Section of the existing Limited Liability Company Act]; and
   (2) before the effective date of this [Act], which elects, as provided by subsection (c), to be governed by this [Act].

(b) On and after January 1, 199__, this [Act] governs all limited liability companies.

(c) Before January 1, 199__, a limited liability company voluntarily may elect, in the manner provided in its operating agreement or by law for amending the operating agreement, to be governed by this [Act].

Comment

Under subsection (a)(1), the application of the Act is mandatory for all companies formed after the effective date of the Act determined under Section 1204. Under subsection (a)(2), the application of the Act is permissive, by election under subsection (c), for existing companies for a period of time specified in subsection (b) after which application becomes mandatory. This affords existing companies and their members an opportunity to consider the changes effected by this Act and to amend their operating agreements, if appropriate. If no election is made, the Act becomes effective after the period specified in subsection (b). The period specified by adopting States may vary, but a period of five years is a common period in similar cases.

SECTION 1206. SAVINGS CLAUSE

This [Act] does not affect an action or proceeding commenced or right accrued before the effective date of this [Act].

Appendix K

Family Limited Partnership Agreement

TABLE OF CONTENTS

AGREEMENT OF
_____ FAMILY
LIMITED PARTNERSHIP

This Limited Partnership Agreement (the "Agreement"), dated as of the _____ day of _____ , 19__, is made and entered into by and among [name of General Partner], the General Partner [or Partners], and those parties listed in Exhibit 1 as Limited Partners.

ARTICLE I
DEFINITIONS

When used in this Agreement, the following terms shall have the meanings set forth below except as otherwise specifically provided herein:

Section 1.1 "Assignee" shall mean any assignee, transferee or other successor in interest to an interest in this Partnership who has not been admitted as a substitute Limited Partner or General Partner as provided herein.

Section 1.2 "Income" and "Loss" shall mean all items of income and gain, including tax-exempt income, and of loss and deduction, including IRC § 705(a)(2)(B) expenditures, on a net basis for each fiscal period.

Section 1.3 "IRC §" or "Reg." means the applicable Section of the Internal Revenue Code or Treasury Regulation, respectively, and any amendments or additions thereto.

Section 1.4 "Partner(s)" means the General Partner and Limited Partners, collectively, and does not include an Assignee.

Section 1.5 "Partner Approval" means the affirmative vote of Partners whose Partnership Percentages are more than 50% of the Partnership Percentages of all Partners; provided, however, when used in Article VIII, **Transfer of Partnership Interests,** means the affirmative vote of Partners whose Partnership Percentages are more than 50% of the Partnership Percentages of all Partners other than the Partner whose interest in the Partnership is subject to a Transfer.

Section 1.6 "Partnership" means this partnership.

Section 1.7 "Partnership Percentages" means the percentages established in Section 5.1.

Section 1.8 "Person" shall mean any individual or any general partnership, limited partnership, limited liability partnership, limited liability company, corporation, joint venture, trust, business trust, cooperative or association, and any other entity, and the heirs, executors, administrators, legal representatives, successors, and assigns of such "Person," where applicable.

Section 1.9 "Transfer" means (i) when used as a verb, to gift, sell, exchange, assign, redeem, transfer, pledge, hypothecate, encumber, bequeath, devise, or otherwise dispose of, whether voluntarily or involuntarily or whether arising from a divorce, separation, death, attachment, execution, bankruptcy, foreclosure, judicial order, operation of law or otherwise and (ii) when used as a noun, the nouns corresponding to such verbs.

If a corporation or other business entity is the Partner, then a Transfer of ownership interest in such entity or any reorganization of such entity which results in the individual(s) who own the controlling interest in the entity no longer owning a controlling interest shall be a "Transfer" under this Agreement. If a trust is the Partner, then a change in the terms of the trust or in circumstances which results in the individual(s) who are the primary beneficiary(ies) of the trust no longer being the primary beneficiary(ies), then that change shall be a "Transfer" under this Agreement.

ARTICLE II
THE LIMITED PARTNERSHIP

Section 2.1 Formation of Partnership. The parties hereto agree to form and by execution of this Agreement do hereby enter into a partnership (hereinafter "Partnership") under the Uniform Limited Partnership Act of the State of _____ ("Act"), which Act shall govern the rights and liabilities of the parties hereto, except as otherwise herein expressly stated.

Section 2.2 Partnership Name and Certificate. The name of the Partnership is "_____ Family Limited Partnership," and it shall conduct business under such name. The General Partner in its sole discretion may change the name at any time and from time to time. The General Partner shall promptly execute and file with the Secretary of State, or any other applicable office, a certificate of limited partnership (hereinafter the "Certificate") in accordance with the Act.

Section 2.3 Business Purpose of the Partnership. The Partnership's purpose is to conduct any business that is legal for a limited partnership to conduct, including without limitation, the investment and management of property held by the Partnership [and _____].

Section 2.4 Resident Agent and Registered Office. The resident agent and registered office shall be as stated in the Certificate. The General Partner may change the registered agent and registered office from time to time, provided that the General Partner shall notify the Limited Partners of any such change in writing.

Section 2.5 Term of Partnership. The Partnership shall commence on the date on which the Certificate has been filed in accordance with the provisions of the Act and shall continue until 40 years after the date the Certificate is recorded, unless it is sooner dissolved or terminated pursuant to the provisions of this Agreement.

Section 2.6 Nature of Partners' Interests. The interests of the Partners in the Partnership shall be personal property for all purposes. Legal title to all Partnership assets shall be held in the name of the Partnership. No Partner shall have any right, title or interest in or to any Partnership property; any Partnership property shall be subject to the terms of this Agreement.

Section 2.7 Use of Real Estate. All the Partners have the right to use any real estate owned by the Partnership which is available for personal use by the Partners. Such use shall be as the Partners agree among themselves. If the Partners cannot agree among themselves regarding this use, then the General Partner shall reasonably determine each Partner's use based on all the facts and circumstances, including each Partner's Partnership Percentage.

ARTICLE III
THE GENERAL PARTNER

Section 3.1 Identity of General Partner. "General Partner" means _____, in its capacity as General Partner of the Partnership and any Person becoming a successor or additional general partner pursuant to the provisions of this Agreement.

Section 3.2 Management Power. If more than one Person is serving as General Partner, all actions and/or decisions to be made by the General Partner shall be made by the affirmative vote of a majority of all such Persons. [Provided, however, while _____ is serving as General Partner, or a trust of which _____ is both the sole trustee and primary beneficiary is serving as General Partner, then decisions of the General Partner shall be made solely by _____. Provided further, if neither _____ or a trust of which he [she] is both sole trustee and primary beneficiary is serving as General Partner, then while _____ is serving as General Partner, or a trust of which _____ is both the sole trustee and primary beneficiary is serving as General Partner, then decisions of the General Partner shall be made solely by _____.]

The General Partner shall devote such time and attention to the business of the Partnership as may reasonably be necessary to the conduct of such business. The General Partner shall have full, exclusive and complete discretion in the management and control of the Partnership, shall make all decisions affecting the business of the Partnership and may take such action as he or she deems necessary or appropriate to accomplish the purposes of the Partnership as set forth herein, including but not limited to the powers and authority granted by law and to:

A. Maintain records of all rights and interests acquired or disposed of by the Partnership, all correspondence relating to the Partnership business and the original records of all statements, bills, and other instruments furnished the Partnership in connection with its business. Such records, together with receipts, vouchers and other supporting evidence thereof, shall be kept in the principal office of the Partnership for such periods as are customary in the industry and shall be made available at reasonable times to Limited Partners for inspection or copying;

B. Make, execute, assign, acknowledge and file on behalf of the Partnership and/or each Limited Partner, any and all documents or instruments of any kind that the General Partner may deem appropriate in carrying out the purposes and business of the Partnership, including, without limitation, powers of attorney, sales contracts, marketing agreements, documents or instruments of any kind or character, or amendments thereto. No Person, firm or corporation dealing with the General Partner shall be required to determine or inquire into the authority and power of the General Partner to bind the Partnership and execute, acknowledge and deliver any and all documents in connection therewith;

C. Purchase, acquire, hold, maintain, operate, sell, exchange, dispose of, or otherwise invest in any property;

D. Manage, administer, conserve, improve, develop, operate, lease, use, and defend the Partnership's assets directly or through third parties;

E. Quitclaim, release, or abandon any Partnership assets with or without consideration;

F. Sue and be sued, complain and defend in the Partnership's name, of and on its behalf;

G. Borrow money or obtain credit on such terms and conditions as the General Partner deems appropriate, from lending institutions or individuals, including the General Partner, for any Partnership purpose, and in connection with such loans, mortgage, pledge, assign or otherwise encumber or alienate any or all of the properties and assets owned by the Partnership, including any income therefrom, to secure or provide repayment thereof;

H. Enter into operating agreements or other transactions with others including the General Partner and its affiliates with respect to the assets owned by the Partnership or services to the Partnership, or with respect to any business or venture in which this Partnership may engage, containing such terms, provisions and conditions as the General Partner shall approve;

I. Employ all types of agents and employees (including lawyers and accountants) as may seem proper;

J. Incur any reasonable expense for travel, telephone, facsimile, insurance, taxes, and such other things, in carrying on the Partnership's business;

K. Invest Partnership cash not being used to acquire property in any manner the General Partner deems appropriate, including but not limited to bank time deposits, banker's acceptances and other acceptances and other interest-bearing obligations; and

L. Make any election on behalf of the Partnership that is required or may be permitted under the Internal Revenue Code of 1986, as amended from time to time, and supervise the preparation and filing of all tax and information returns that the Partnership may be required to file.

Section 3.3 Fees and Expenses of the General Partner. The General Partner shall not be entitled to any compensation except in connection with services performed by the General Partner for the Partnership other than in its capacity as a Partner. The General Partner shall be reimbursed for all out-of-pocket expenses and costs incurred in the performance of its responsibility to the Partnership.

Section 3.4 Change in Interest Upon Event of Withdrawal. When a Person serving as a General Partner of the Partnership ceases to serve as General Partner upon an event of withdrawal (as provided in the Act), the Person's interest in the Partnership shall become a Limited Partner interest and such Person shall be an Assignee unless admitted as a substitute Limited Partner as provided herein.

Section 3.5 Resignation of General Partner. Either _____ or _____ [or trusts or entities which may become a substitute General Partner without consent (as provided in Section 8.6),] may, upon notice to all of the other Partners resign as General Partner, provided that such resignation would not result in a dissolution as provided in Article IX, Dissolution and Liquidation.

Section 3.6 Additional General Partner. Additional General Partners may be admitted as decided by and upon such terms and conditions as specified by the General Partner with Partner Approval. Provided, however, if there is no Person serving as General Partner, or if the General Partner is not _____, _____ [or a trust or entity which may become a substitute General Partner without consent (as provided in Section 8.6),] no consent of the General Partner is required to admit an additional General Partner.

ARTICLE IV
THE LIMITED PARTNERS

Section 4.1 Limited Partners. The Limited Partners are those Persons whose names appear on Exhibit I attached hereto, those Persons who become substitute Limited Partners, and additional Limited Partners pursuant to the provisions of this Agreement.

Section 4.2 Limited Liability. No Limited Partner shall be personally liable for any of the debts or obligations of the Partnership or for any Partnership losses beyond the amount of his or her capital contribution and share of the undistributed Partnership profits, as provided by law.

Section 4.3 Restrictions on Limited Partners. No Limited Partner shall participate in the management and control of the business of the Partnership, transact any business for the Partnership, or attempt to do so, and no Limited Partner shall have the power to represent, sign for or bind the General Partner or the Partnership.

Section 4.4 Rights of the Limited Partners. The Limited Partners shall have the powers and rights given to Limited Partners by the terms of this Agreement and the Act, and the exercise of these rights and powers are deemed to be matters affecting the basic structure of the Partnership and not the control of Partnership business.

Section 4.5 Additional Limited Partners. A Person may be admitted as an additional Limited Partner as decided by and upon such terms and conditions as specified by the General Partner with Partner Approval.

ARTICLE V
CAPITAL CONTRIBUTIONS

Section 5.1 Capital Contributions and Percentages. The capital contributed to the Partnership by each Partner, and the agreed value of those contributions, and each Partner's Partnership Percentage is listed in Exhibit 1. Future capital shall be contributed in the amounts and times determined by the General Partner with Partner Approval, and shall be contributed by each Partner in accordance with their current Partnership Percentage. No Partner shall be required to contribute additional capital without that Partner's consent. A Partner's Partnership Percentage shall be the percent that Partner's capital account balance is to the capital account balances of all Partners at any given time. Exhibit I shall be revised as necessary to reflect any additional capital contributions and revised Partnership Percentages, and additional or substitute Partners.

Section 5.2 Capital Accounts. Throughout the term of the Partnership, a Capital Account shall be maintained at all times for each Partner in accordance with IRC § 704(b) and (c) and all regulations thereunder, including Treas. Reg. § 1.704-l(b).

Section 5.3 Return of Capital Contributions and Withdrawal. No Partner or Assignee shall be entitled to withdraw from the Partnership, or to the return of his or her capital contribution, or receive any other distribution for his or her interest in the Partnership, or interest thereon, prior to liquidation of the Partnership, except as determined by the General Partner with Partner Approval.

Section 5.4 Additional Capital and Additional Partners. A Partner may contribute additional capital in exchange for an additional interest in the Partnership, but only as decided by and on such terms and conditions as specified by the General Partner with Partner Approval.

ARTICLE VI
ALLOCATIONS AND DISTRIBUTIONS

Section 6.1 Allocation of Income and Loss. Income and Loss of the Partnership shall be allocated to the Partners or Assignees in proportion to their Partnership Percentages, subject to the provision of IRC § 704(c) regarding contributed property with a tax basis that is less than its fair market value.

Section 6.2 Distributions. No distributions shall be made prior to liquidation except as determined by the General Partner with Partner Approval. Distributions prior to or on liquidation of the Partnership (or upon liquidation of a Partner's interest in the Partnership), shall be made pro rata according to the positive capital account balances, as determined after taking into account all capital account adjustments for the Partnership taxable year during which such liquidation occurs, by the end of such taxable year (or, if later, within 90 days after the date of such liquidation).

Section 6.3 Book-Up. Immediately prior to: (a) an additional capital contribution by an existing or new Partner of more than a de minimis amount which results in a shift in the Partnership Percentages; (b) the liquidation of the Partnership within the meaning of Treasury Regulation 1.704-1(b)(2)(ii)(g); or (c) a purchase to be made under the terms of Article VIII, the basis of the Partnership's assets and liabilities shall be adjusted in accordance with Treasury Regulation 1.704-1(b)(2)(iv) to the value thereof (which shall be determined as provided in Section 8.4(A)), and the capital accounts of all the Partners shall be adjusted simultaneously to reflect the aggregate net adjustment to basis as if the Partnership recognized capital gain and loss equal to the amount of such aggregate net adjustment. Such deemed recognized capital gain or loss shall be allocated as provided in Section 6.1 above.

Section 6.4 Change in Partner's Interest. In the event there is a change in Partnership Percentages during any taxable year of the Partnership (whether by contribution, distribution, transfer or otherwise), the respective shares of Income and Loss shall be determined by using the "interim closing of the books" method using a monthly convention, or such other method as the General Partner determines is consistent with income tax rules and the Partnership's accounting practice. If IRC § 706(d) requires an item to be allocated differently than otherwise allocated under this Article at the applicable time, the allocation shall be done in accordance with IRC § 706(d).

Section 6.5 Interpretation of Allocations. This Article shall be interpreted under and is intended to comply with IRC § 704 and Reg. 1.704-1 and any amendments or additions thereto. In the event the

General Partner determines it is prudent to modify the manner in which the Capital Accounts are maintained or Income and Loss are allocated hereunder in order to comply with such statute and regulation or to accomplish the Partners' intent regarding division of distributions in accordance with such, the General Partner may make such modification, provided, however, that it is not likely to have a material effect on the amounts taxed or distributed to any Partner. Further, any allocation hereunder shall be an allocation of book items, and the tax items allocated shall follow the book items allocated.

ARTICLE VII
ACCOUNTING AND REPORTS

Section 7.1 Fiscal Year and Method of Accounting. The fiscal year of the Partnership and the method of accounting shall be determined by the General Partner.

Section 7.2 Books and Records. The General Partner shall maintain complete and accurate books and records reflecting the nature and extent of the assets, liabilities and contractual commitments of the Partnership and all receipts and disbursements of the Partnership. In addition, the General Partner shall maintain all other records necessary for documenting and recording the business and affairs of the Partnership. Any Limited Partner or his or her duly authorized representative may, at his or her own expense, inspect the books of the Partnership at reasonable times during ordinary business hours.

Section 7.3 Bank Accounts. The Partnership shall establish and maintain accounts in financial institutions (including federal and state banks, trust companies, or savings and loan institutions) in such amounts as the General Partner may deem necessary from time to time. Checks may be drawn on and withdrawals of funds may be made from any such accounts for Partnership purposes and may be signed by either the General Partner or the duly authorized personnel of the Partnership.

Section 7.4 Tax Matters Partner. The General Partner shall from time to time designate a Tax Matters Partner pursuant to IRC § 6231(a)(7). The initial Tax Matters Partner shall be the General Partner (or if more than one Person is serving as General Partner, the Person named first).

ARTICLE VIII
TRANSFER OF PARTNERSHIP INTERESTS

Section 8.1 Assignment. A Partner or Assignee may not Transfer his or her interest in the Partnership except in accordance with this Article. Any purported Transfer of an interest in the Partnership which is consummated other than as set forth in this Article shall be null and void and shall not be binding upon the General Partner or the Partnership. No Transfer permitted under this Article shall be effective until the General Partner has received a copy of the instrument of assignment, which shall be effective only as of the last day of the month in which the assignment is received, executed by the transferor and the transferee and an instrument, in form prescribed by the General Partner, duly executed, which is effective to transfer the Partnership interest under applicable local law and makes the transferee subject to the terms of this Agreement.

No Transfer shall relieve the transferor from any liabilities which, by law, survive such Transfer, and the Assignee shall be bound by the terms of this Agreement.

Section 8.2 Right of First Refusal. A Partner or Assignee may not Transfer his or her interest in the Partnership to any Person, without the consent of the General Partner with Partner Approval, unless the following is complied with:

A. *Notice of Transfer.* If a Partner or Assignee (the "Offeree") intends to Transfer any interest in the Partnership, the Offeree shall give written notice of such to each of the other Partners, which shall state (i) the intention to Transfer, (ii) the interest to be transferred ("Offered Interest"), (iii) the name, business and residence address of the proposed transferee, and (iv) whether or not the Transfer is for a valuable consideration, and, if so, the amount of the consideration and the other material terms of the Transfer (the "Notice"). If it is an involuntary Transfer, "Notice" shall be deemed received by the General Partner when the General Partner has actual notice of such involuntary Transfer, if no such written notice is given by an Offeree.

B. *Option to Purchase.*

1. *First Option to Purchase.* Within sixty (60) days of the General Partner's receipt of the Notice, the Partnership

may exercise an option to purchase all or any portion of the Offered Interest for the price and terms as established under Section 8.4. The General Partner shall exercise such option by giving written notice both to the Offeree and each other Partner within the sixty (60) day period provided in this Subsection "1". Should the General Partner fail to give written notice within such sixty (60) day period, the Partnership shall be deemed to have waived such option.

2. *Second Option to Purchase.* If the Partnership does not exercise its option to purchase all of the Offered Interest, each other Partner, within eighty (80) days of the General Partner's receipt of the Notice, may exercise an option to purchase a percentage of the unpurchased Offered Interest equal to a fraction, the numerator of which is the Partnership Percentage owned by such other Partner at the time of the General Partner's receipt of the Notice and the denominator of which is the total Partnership Percentages then owned by all Partners other than the Offeree. The other Partners shall exercise such options by giving written notice both to the Offeree and each other Partner within such eighty (80) day period. Should a Partner fail to give written notice within such eighty (80) day period, the Partner shall be deemed to have waived such option.

3. *Third Option to Purchase.* If neither the Partnership nor an other Partner shall fully exercise his or her option to purchase set out above, each other Partner who exercises in full a Second Option may, within ten (10) days after the expiration of the eighty (80) day option period provided for in Subsection "2", exercise an option to purchase the remaining Offered Interest. In the case of a single Partner, his or her option shall be to purchase all of the remaining Offered Interest. In the case of two or more other Partners, each such other Partner's option shall be to purchase the amount all such other Partners may by agreement among themselves determine, or if they cannot agree, as determined by the General Partner. Such other Partners shall exercise such options by giving written notice both to the Offeree and each other Partner within such ninety (90) day period. Should a Partner fail to give written notice

within such ninety (90) day period, the Partner shall be deemed to have waived such option.

4. *Forfeiture of Options.* The Partnership and the other Partners must in the aggregate exercise their options to purchase all of the Offered Interest or their options shall be forfeited.

C. *Effect of Non-Exercise of Options.* If the purchase options are forfeited or not exercised, then the Offered Interest may be transferred by the Offeree, within 100 days after receipt by the General Partner of the Notice to the transferee named in the Notice upon the terms therein stated, which transferee shall be subject to the terms of this Agreement. No such Transfer shall be valid unless it is completed within such time period upon the terms and to the transferee stated in the Notice.

D. *Transfer to Family Member.* Any Partner may, without complying with the prior provisions of this Section, Transfer an interest in the Partnership if such Transfer is made to a Family Member or to any trust primarily for the Partner's benefit and/or for the benefit of a Family Member. The term "Family Member" means _____ [name of parent(s)] and their descendants.

Section 8.3 Removal of Partners. Any Partner or Assignee may be removed from the Partnership on the decision of the General Partner with Partner Approval. Upon such removal, the Partnership shall buy such Person's entire interest in the Partnership at the price and terms set out in Section 8.4.

Section 8.4 Terms of Sale.

A. *Purchase Price.* The purchase price for an interest in the Partnership purchased pursuant to this Article shall be the fair market value of such Partnership interest. The fair market value shall be determined by an appraisal performed by the certified public accountant regularly employed to prepare the tax returns of the Partnership or, if there be no such certified public accountant, by any certified public accountant selected by the General Partner, whose decision in this matter shall be conclusive. Provided, however, for a purchase pursuant to Section 8.2, the purchase price shall be the amount set out in the Notice, if less.

B. *Payment in Cash or Note.* The purchase price for a Partnership interest purchased pursuant to this Article VIII shall be payable in cash, or at the option of the purchaser, 20% in cash, and the balance of the purchase price by a negotiable promissory note of the purchaser for a term determined by the purchaser, not to exceed 5 years after the Closing, payable in equal quarterly payments, with the first payment due at the end of the quarter first occurring after the Closing, bearing interest at the prime rate, plus 1%, in effect at a bank selected by the purchaser on the first day of each calendar year. Provided, however, for a purchase pursuant to Section 8.2, the purchaser has the option to use the terms set out in the Notice.

C. *Closing.* The Closing of any purchase hereunder shall be the date and place determined by the purchaser, but no later than 100 days after the receipt by the General Partner of the Notice, or the date of removal, as applicable, at 10:00 a.m. at the registered office of the Partnership.

Section 8.5 Substitute Partner. A Person to whom a Partner or Assignee has made a Transfer or purported Transfer (whether or not in compliance with this Article), shall have the status of an Assignee only, and may become a substitute Limited Partner or General Partner only upon decision by the General Partner with Partner Approval; provided, however, a transferee who receives an interest pursuant to Section 8.2D shall become a substitute Limited Partner if the interest being transferred is a Limited Partner interest, or a substitute General Partner if the interest being transferred is a General Partner interest, without the need for a decision by the General Partner or Partner Approval.

ARTICLE IX
DISSOLUTION AND LIQUIDATION

Section 9.1 Dissolution. The Partnership shall be dissolved at the expiration of the term of the Partnership set forth in the Certificate; provided, however, the Partnership shall be dissolved prior thereto without breach of this Agreement upon occurrence of one of the following:

A. By written consent of all the Partners.

B. An event of withdrawal of a Person serving as General Partner (as defined in the Act), but the Partnership shall not be dissolved:

1. If there is at least one other Person serving as General Partner, in which case the business of the Partnership shall be carried on by the remaining Person(s) serving as General Partner; or

2. If, within 90 days after such withdrawal, all Partners agree in writing to continue the business of the Partnership and to the appointment, effective as of the date of withdrawal, of one or more additional general partners, if necessary or desired.

C. Entry of a decree of judicial dissolution under the Act.

Section 9.2 Winding Up and Liquidation. Upon dissolution, the Partnership shall be wound up and liquidated as rapidly as business circumstances will permit. The assets may be sold or distributed in kind at the discretion of the General Partner; provided, however, any assets distributed in kind shall be distributed pro rata among the Partners and Assignees according to the percent of the total distribution each is entitled to receive. The assets of the Partnership shall be applied as follows:

A. To payment of debts and liabilities of the Partnership and the expenses of liquidation according to the priorities established by law; provided, however, to the extent permitted by law, liabilities with respect to which any Partner is or may be personally liable shall be paid first;

B. To the setting up of such reserves as the General Partner may reasonably deem necessary for any contingent liabilities or obligations of the Partnership, provided that any such reserve shall be paid over by such Person to an independent escrow agent, to be held by such agent or his or her successor for such period as such Person shall deem advisable for the purpose of applying such reserves to the payment of such liabilities or obligations and, at the expiration of such period, the balance of such reserves, if any, shall be distributed as herein provided; and

C. Then, as provided in Section 6.2.

ARTICLE X
MISCELLANEOUS PROVISIONS

Section 10.1 Notices. All notices or other communications required or permitted to be given pursuant to this Agreement, in the case of notice or communications required or permitted to be given to Limited Partners or Assignees, shall be in writing and considered as properly given if personally delivered or if mailed by the United States first-class mail, postage prepaid, and addressed to such Limited Partner's or Assignee's address for notices as it appears on the records of the Partnership, and shall, in the case of notices or communications required or permitted to be given to the General Partner, be in writing and shall be considered as properly given if personally delivered or mailed by the United States certified or registered mail, return receipt requested, postage prepaid, addressed to the General Partner. Any Partner or Assignee may change his or her address for notice by giving notice in writing, stating his or her new address for notices, to the other Partners. Any notice or other communication shall be deemed to have been given as of the date on which it is personally delivered or, if mailed, the date on which it is deposited in the United States mails in compliance with the terms of this Section.

Section 10.2 Governing Law. This Agreement and all rights and liabilities of the parties hereto with reference to the Partnership shall be subject to, governed by and construed in accordance with the laws of the State of _____.

Section 10.3 Certificate of Limited Partnership. Each Limited Partner hereby agrees to execute, acknowledge and file or deliver (either individually or by virtue of the power of attorney granted the General Partner) all such certificates (including the Certificate), amendments, instruments, documents, or counterparts thereof as may be required to comply with the laws of the state in which the Partnership is formed, or any other jurisdiction in which the Partnership does business, and provide any information required to complete such documents. An amendment to the Certificate of Limited Partnership to reflect a change in the General Partner will be validly made if signed only by the new General Partner. The General Partner shall have no obligation to provide any Partner with a copy of the Certificate or any Certificate of Amendment.

Section 10.4 Power of Attorney. Each Limited Partner and Assignee does hereby appoint and empower the General Partner as his or her true and lawful attorney-in-fact, in such Limited Partner's name and behalf, to prepare any and every amendment to this Agreement and to the Certificate and to sign, certify under oath and acknowledge any and every such amendment to this Agreement and to the Certificate (such power of attorney shall be deemed to be irrevocable and a power coupled with an interest so long as the General Partner remains as a general partner of the Partnership and shall survive the assignment by any Limited Partner of the whole or any part of its Partnership interest), where such an amendment has been approved in accordance with the provisions of this Agreement and is necessary to reflect:

A. A change in the name of the Partnership, the registered office or registered agent, or in the amount or character of the capital contribution of any Limited Partner;

B. The admission of a General Partner pursuant to this Agreement; or

C. A change in the time stated in this Agreement or in the Certificate (or any amendment of either or both of them) for the expiration of the term or for the return of the Capital Account of any Partner.

Section 10.5 Amendments. Amendments to this Agreement which are of an inconsequential nature and do not affect the rights of the Limited Partners in any material respect, or as specifically authorized in this Agreement, may be made by the General Partner. Any other amendment to this Agreement may be proposed to the Partners by the General Partner or by Limited Partners owning not less than ten percent (10%) of the Partnership. The General Partner shall submit to the Limited Partners any such proposed amendment and the recommendation of the General Partner as to its adoption. A proposed amendment shall become effective at such time as it has been approved in writing by the General Partner, with Partner Approval. The General Partner shall give written notice to the Limited Partners promptly after any amendment has become effective or has been rejected.

Section 10.6 Voting. On all matters requiring action, decision, vote or consent of the Partners, the signatures of the Partners owning the required Partnership Percentages is sufficient and no meeting or other formality is required.

Section 10.7 Section Headings. The headings in this Agreement are inserted for convenience and identification only and are in no way intended to describe, interpret, define or limit the scope, extent or intent of this Agreement or any provision hereof.

Section 10.8 Sole Agreement. This Agreement constitutes the entire understanding of the parties hereto with respect to the subject matter hereof.

Section 10.9 Effect of Agreement. Subject to the restrictions contained herein, each and all of the covenants, terms, provisions and agreements herein contained shall be binding upon and inure to the benefit of the parties hereto and their successors.

Section 10.10 Gender and Number. Whenever the context requires, the gender of all words used herein shall include the masculine, feminine and the neuter and the plural of all words shall include the singular and plural.

Section 10.11 Severability. If any provision of this Agreement, or the application thereof, shall, for any reason and to any extent, be invalid or unenforceable, the remainder of this Agreement and the application of such provision to other Persons or circumstances shall not be affected thereby, but rather shall be enforced to the maximum extent permissible under applicable law.

IN WITNESS WHEREOF, the undersigned have executed this Agreement on the date first written above.

GENERAL PARTNER:

_____

_____

LIMITED PARTNERS:

_____

_____

Exhibit 1. The Parties

_____ FAMILY LIMITED PARTNERSHIP

Date: _____, 19__

GENERAL PARTNERS

Name of Partner	Address	Partnership Percentage	Capital Contribution

LIMITED PARTNERS

Name of Partner	Address	Partnership Percentage	Capital Contribution

Appendix L

Sample Estate Planning Provisions and Comments

TABLE OF CONTENTS

I. Preference to Continue Business

"Without imposing any legal limitation on the broad powers given to my executor and trustees in this will, I request that ABC Investments, L.L.C. be retained and continued until its liquidation in accordance with the provisions of the operating agreement of such entity."

Comment: If the estate plan calls for the LLC's business to be continued after the testator's death, such preference can be put in the will, as done above, as a request rather than a requirement. This gives the fiduciary the option of selling the testator's interest if circumstances change after the testator's death.

II. Special Provisions to Operate Business in an Estate or Trust

"Each Trustee and Executor is specifically authorized to continue any business (whether a proprietorship, corporation, partnership, limited partnership, limited liability company or other business entity) which I may own or in which I may be financially interested at the time of my death for such time as my Executor or Trustee may deem it to be in the best interests of my estate or of the trusts; to employ in the conduct of such business such capital out of my general estate or out of any of the trusts as my executor or Trustee may deem proper; to borrow money for use in any such business alone or with other persons financially interested in such business, and to secure such loan or loans by a mortgage, pledge or any other manner of encumbrance of, not only my property and interest in such business, but also such portion of my general estate or of the trust outside of such business as my Executor or Trustee may deem proper; to employ any officers, managers, employees or agents that it may deem advisable in the management of the business, including electing directors, officers or employees of the Trustee or Executor to take part in the management of the business as directors, managers or officers; to receive compensation for the services of the trustee, whether as directors, managers, officers or otherwise, to be paid by it from the business or from other assets or from both as the Trustee or Executor in its discretion may deem advisable; to organize, either alone or jointly with others, new corporations, partnerships, limited partnerships, limited liability companies or other business entities; and generally to exercise with respect to the continuance, management, sale or liquidation of any business which I may own or in which I may be financially interested at the time of my death, or of any new business or business interest, all the powers which I could have exercised during my lifetime."

Comment: This Provision gives authority to the fiduciary to continue, manage, liquidate, incorporate or sell the testator's interest in the LLC.

III. Powers to Use General Estate Assets and Business Income in the Business

"Notwithstanding any rule of law to the contrary, in the conduct of any business interest of mine which I have directed or authorized my Executors and Trustees to retain and continue to manage, they shall in their discretion make use of whatever amounts they deem advisable from my general estate, notwithstanding any other provisions of this will relating to distributions or profits from the business. My Executors and Trustees shall also retain in the business as much of the cash realized by the business that they deem advisable from the working capital needs of the business, including reserves for improvements, additional machinery, real estate additions, and other needs."

Comment: If the business will require or can profitably use additional funds, this provision authorizes the fiduciary to invest estate assets and business profits in the business.

IV. Request that Testator's Interest Be Sold to Child at Specified Age

"My expressed preference is for the continuation of ABC Investments, L.L.C. (the 'business'). I request that a part of my interest in the business be offered for sale to my children upon each child's reaching 30 years of age, upon terms that are compatible with the provisions of the operating agreement of the business and that shall be fair to all the beneficiaries under this will. My entire interest in the business may be owned by my children when the youngest reaches 30 years of age. In carrying out this preference, I request that due consideration be given to the valuation method employed in the operating agreement, or if none, the fair market value, and the inclination and aptitudes of such of my children for the operation of the business."

Comment: This provision is useful if the testator desires to offer his interest in the LLC for sale to his children when they reach a specified age, but again flexibility is offered to the fiduciary because the preference is expressed in terms of a request. The last sentence of the provision is intended to avoid problems with IRC § 2703.

V. Business to Be Managed by Children and Not by Executor or Trustee

"If at my death I own any interest in ABC Investments, L.L.C. (the 'business'), then I authorize and direct that such interest be managed, represented and directed by my children, W, X, Y and Z, and neither my Executor, during the period that my estate is being administered, nor my Trustee, during the continuance of any trust provided for or created in this will, shall have any voice or right in the management or direction of the business, and the sole right of my Executor, during the period that my estate is being administered, shall be to receive my share of the distribution or profits from the business, and the sole right of the Trustee of any trust shall be to receive the distributions or profits from the share or portion of the business which is held in trust."

> **Comment:** This provision is an alternative to provision II which gives the fiduciary the power to manage the testator's interest in the LLC, and can be used when the testator would prefer to grant such power to other parties such as the testator's children.

VI. Direction to Dispose of Business Interest but with Powers to Continue the Business if Necessary

"While it is my desire that my interest in ABC Investments, L.L.C. (the "business") shall be terminated as soon as may be deemed advisable by my Executor and Trustee, nevertheless should my interest not be disposed of prior to the settlement of my estate, I give to my Executor and Trustee the fullest powers and authorities concerning the business including the power, in my Executor's or Trustee's sole and absolute discretion, to conduct, manage and carry on the business, or to join in it, at the risk of the general assets of the estate or of any trust of which such interest is a part, in the same manner and to the same intent and purpose as I might or could do if living and continuing to be engaged in the business, without any personal liability on the part of my Executor and Trustee to any person or persons. Nothing in this section shall be construed to prohibit my Executor or Trustee from disposing at any time, either in whole or in part, of my interest in the business or the interest of any trust in the business, for any price or prices and upon any terms of payment that my Executor or Trustee, in such Executor's or Trustee's sole and absolute discretion, may deem advisable."

Comment: This provision expresses the testator's desire that the testator's interest in the LLC be sold, but gives the fiduciary the authority to manage the business before it is sold.

Appendix M

State Formation and Ownership Requirements

State	Minimum Number Required to Form LLC,	Minimum Members Required
Alabama	One. § 10-12-9	One. § 10-12-9
Alaska	One. § 10.50.070	One. § 10.50.070
Arizona	One. § 29-631	One. § 29-631
Arkansas	One. § 4-32-201	One. § 4-32-201
California	One. § 17050	One. § 17050
Colorado	One. § 7-80-203	One. § 7-80-203
Connecticut	One. § 34-120	One. § 34-101(9)
Delaware	One. § 18-201(a)	One. § 18-101(6)
District of Columbia	One. § 29-1302	Two. § 29-1301(16)
Florida	One. § 608.405	One. § 608.407
Georgia	One. § 14-11-203	One. § 14-11-101(12)
Hawaii	One. § 428-202	One. § 428-202
Idaho	One. § 53.607	One. § 53.607
Illinois	One. § 5-1(a)	One. § 5-1(b)
Indiana	One. § 23-18-2-4	One. § 23-18-2-4
Iowa	One. § 490A.301	One. § 490A.102(13)
Kansas	One. § 17-7605	One. § 17-7605
Kentucky	One. § 275.020	One. § 275.015(8)
Louisiana	One. § 12:1304	One. § 12:1301(10)
Maine	One. § 621	One. § § 621
Maryland	One. § 4A-202	One. § 4A-202

State	Minimum Number Required to Form LLC,	Minimum Members Required
Massachusetts	One. § 12	Two. §§ 2(5), a certificate of cancellation is required if number of members falls below two
Michigan	One. § 450.4202	One. § 450.4202
Minnesota	One. § 322B.105	One. § 322B.11
Mississippi	One. § 79-29-201	One. § 79-29-201
Missouri	One. § 347.037	One. § 347.017
Montana	One. § 35-8-201	One. § 35-8-201
Nebraska	One. § 21-2605	One. § 21-2605
Nevada	One. § 86.151	One. § 86.151(3)
New Hampshire	One. § 304-C:12	One. § 304-C:1(V)
New Jersey	One. § 42:2B-11	One. § 42:2B-2
New Mexico	One. § 53-19-7	One. § 53-19-7
New York	One. § 203(a)	One. § 203(c)
North Carolina	One. § 57C-2-20	One. § 57C-2-20
North Dakota	One. § 10-32-05	One. § 10-32-06
Ohio	One. § 1705.04(A)	One. § 1705.04(A)
Oklahoma	One. § 2004	One. § 2001.11
Oregon	One. § 63.044	One. § 63.001(13)
Pennsylvania	One. § 8912	One. § 8912
Rhode Island	One. § 7-16-5	One. § 7-16-5
South Carolina	One. § 33-44-202	One. § 33-44-202
South Dakota	One. § 47-34A-202.1(a)	One. § 47-34A-202.1(a)
Tennessee	One. § 48-203-102	One. § 48-205-101
Texas	One. § 3.01	One. § 4.01
Utah	One. § 48-2b-103	One. § 48-2b-103(2)(a)
Vermont	One. § 3022	One. § 3022
Virginia	One. § 13.1-1010	One. § 13.1-1010
Washington	One. § 25.15.070	One. § 25.15.270
West Virginia	One. § 31B-2-202	One. § 31B-2-202(a)
Wisconsin	One. § 183.0201	One. § 183.0201
Wyoming	One. § 17-15-106	One § 17-15-144

Appendix N

OPERATING AGREEMENT
OF
[NAME] L.L.C.
A [STATE] LIMITED LIABILITY COMPANY
Managed by Its Member

[**Note.** This One Person Model Operating Agreement should be
used only as a guide as many provisions might not apply or should
be redrafted to apply to a particular state law or LLC design.]

TABLE OF CONTENTS

OPERATING AGREEMENT OF (NAME LLC)

INTRODUCTION

The Articles of Organization of [Name LLC] were filed with the [State] Secretary of State on [Date]. The Company's business shall be conducted under such name until such time as the Articles of Organization are amended in accordance with applicable law and this Operating Agreement. The Company's term, purpose, powers, registered office, and registered agent shall be as stated in the Articles of Organization. The Articles of Organization have been reproduced and are attached as Exhibit A. Pursuant to the Act and this Agreement, the [Initial Member] does hereby organize the [Name LLC].

* * * * * *

ARTICLE I
DEFINITIONS AND GENERAL PROVISIONS

The following terms used in this Operating Agreement shall have the following meanings (unless otherwise expressly provided herein):

"*Act*" shall mean the Limited Liability Company Act of the State of [State] and all amendments thereto.

"*Agreement*" shall mean this agreement and all amendments thereto.

"*Additional Member*" shall mean any Person who or which is admitted to the Company as an Additional Member pursuant to this Operating Agreement.

"*Articles*" shall mean the Articles of Organization or such other documents as are filed with the Secretary of State under the Act, as amended from time to time.

"*Capital Account*" shall mean the individual account maintained for each Member as provided hereafter.

"*Capital Contribution*" shall mean any contribution to the capital of the Company in cash, property, services, or the obligation to contribute cash, property or services by a Member whenever made.

"*Code*" shall mean the Internal Revenue Code of 1986, as amended from time to time.

"*Company*" shall mean this limited liability company, [Name LLC].

"*Member*" shall mean the initial Member identified in Section 4.1 hereof and Persons becoming Members as provided in this Operating Agreement (including Additional Members and Substitute Members) and who will be identified on an Exhibit B attached hereto.

"*Net Profits*" shall mean, for each Year, the income and gains of the Company determined in accordance with accounting principles consistently applied from year to year under the method of accounting and as reported, separately or in the aggregate, as appropriate, for Federal income tax purposes, plus any income described in Section 705(a)(1)(B) of the Code and any income exempt from tax.

"*Net Losses*" shall mean, for each Year, the losses and deductions of the Company determined in accordance with accounting principles consistently applied from year to year under the method of accounting and as reported, separately or in the aggregate, as appropriate, for Federal income tax purposes, plus any expenditures described in Section 705(a)(2)(B) of the Code.

"*Operating Agreement*" shall mean this Operating Agreement, as originally executed and as amended.

"*Person*" shall mean any individual or any general partnership, limited partnership, limited liability partnership, limited liability company, corporation, joint venture, trust, business trust, cooperative or association, and any other entity, and the heirs, executors, administrators, legal representatives, successors, and assigns of such "*Person*," where applicable.

"*Principal Office*" The principal office for the transaction of the business of the Company is hereby located at [*full address*], or any other place(s) established by the Company.

"*Substitute Member*" shall mean any Person who or which is admitted to the Company as a Substitute Member as provided hereafter.

"*Transfer(s)*" shall mean (i) when used as a verb, to give, gift, sell, exchange, assign, redeem, transfer, pledge, hypothecate, encumber, bequeath, devise or otherwise dispose of, which is treated as a Transfer as provided hereafter, and (ii) when used as a noun, the nouns corresponding to such verbs, in either case voluntarily or involuntarily, by operation of law or otherwise.

If a corporation or other business entity is a Member, then a Transfer of ownership interest in such entity or any reorganization of such entity which results in the individual(s) who own the controlling interest in the entity no longer owning a controlling interest, shall be a "Transfer" under this Operating Agreement.

If a trust is a Member, then a change in the terms of the trust or circumstances either of which results in (i) the individual(s) who are the primary beneficiary(ies) of the trust no longer being the primary beneficiary(ies) or (ii) the Person(s) who is the trustee(s) of the trust no longer being the sole trustee(s), then such change shall be a "Transfer" under this Operating Agreement.

"*Units*" shall mean the ownership interests in the Company.

"*Year*" shall mean the Company's fiscal year for income tax purposes as determined pursuant to Section 706 of the Code.

ARTICLE II
MANAGEMENT

2.1 *Powers.* The business and affairs of the Company shall be managed solely by the Member(s). The Member(s) shall direct, manage and control the business of the Company to the best of their ability and shall have full and complete authority, power and discretion to make any and all decisions and to do any and all things which the Member(s) shall deem to be reasonably required in light of the Company's business and objectives. However, the Member(s) is under no obligation to perform services for the Company by the mere fact that the person is a Member. The Member(s) shall have power and authority, on behalf of the Company:

(a) To purchase, hold, improve, lease, acquire, own, use, and otherwise deal with real property, tangible personal property, and/or intangible personal property from any Person as the Member(s) may determine, in the name of the Company, or as a nominee;

(b) To sell, convey, mortgage, pledge, lease, exchange, and otherwise dispose of real and/or tangible and/or intangible personal properties from any Person as the Member(s) may determine;

(c) To borrow money for the Company from banks, other lending institutions, the Member(s), affiliates of the Member(s), and other Persons on such terms as the Member(s) deem appropriate, and to assume or refinance existing indebtedness; and in connection therewith, issue evidence of indebtedness to hypothecate, encumber and grant security interests in the assets of the Company to secure repayment of the borrowed sums;

(d) To purchase liability and other insurance to protect the Company and its property and business;

(e) To invest any Company funds (by way of example and not by limitation) in time deposits, short-term governmental obligations, commercial paper or other investments;

(f) To open bank accounts in the name of the Company and to determine the signatories thereon;

(g) To execute, negotiate and deliver, on behalf of the Company, all instruments and documents, including, without limitation, contracts, checks, drafts, notes and other negotiable instruments, mortgages or deeds of trust, security agreements, financing statements, deeds, bills of sale or other documents providing for the acquisition, mortgage or disposition of the Company's property, assignments, leases, partnership agreements, and any other instruments or documents necessary or appropriate, to the business of the Company;

(h) To employ accountants, legal counsel, managing agents or others to perform services for the Company and to compensate them from Company funds;

(i) To enter into other agreements on behalf of the Company, with any other Person for any purpose, in such forms as the Members may approve;

(j) To execute and file any bankruptcy petition, on behalf of the Company, pursuant to applicable Federal laws;

(k) To determine, to the extent allowed by law, the taxable year and method of accounting of the Company;

(l) To determine, to the extent allowed by law, the method the Company will be taxed (as a separate or disregarded entity) under the Code.

(m) To do and perform all other acts as may be necessary or appropriate to the conduct of the Company's business, including but not limited to establishment of funds or reserves, prepay, recast, increase, modify, extend or otherwise amend existing debt, commitments, contracts or other obligations in whole or in part.

2.2 *Agent Authority.* Unless authorized to do so by this Operating Agreement or by the Member(s), no agent or employee of the Company shall have any power or authority to bind the Company in any way, to pledge its credit or to render it liable pecuniarily for any purpose. Only the decisions and actions of the Member(s) on behalf of the Company shall bind the Company.

2.3 *Member's Liability.* A Member shall not be personally liable for any acts performed for the Company by the Member concerning Company matters or be liable solely by virtue of being a Member unless the Member engaged in fraud.

2.4 *Member's Indemnification.* A Member shall be indemnified by the Company for any act performed for the Company by the Member concerning Company matters unless the Member engaged in fraud.

ARTICLE III
COMPANY ACTIONS AND RECORDS

3.1 *Action by Member(s).* The Member(s) may make any decision or take any action on behalf of the Company.

3.2 *Amendment.* Any amendment of this Operating Agreement shall be set forth in writing and signed by each Member(s).

3.3 *Maintenance of Company Books.* The Company shall maintain and preserve for seven (7) years all accounts, books, and other relevant Company documents.

ARTICLE IV
CAPITAL CONTRIBUTIONS, ALLOCATIONS
AND DISTRIBUTIONS

4.1 *Initial Member.* The Company shall initially have only one Member, who shall be [Initial Member's Name] and shall own 100 Units in the Company.

4.2 *Initial Capital Contribution.* The Initial Member shall contribute to the Company all of the property listed on Exhibit C attached hereto after the execution of this Agreement and prior to Company commencing of business.

4.3 *Additional Capital Contribution.* The Member(s) shall only be required to make additional capital contributions to the Company upon prior approval and consent of the Member(s), and is under no other obligation to make any additional contributions to the Company.

4.4 *Additional Members.* The Company may issue additional Units to any Person for such Capital Contributions and on such terms and conditions as the Member(s) determine and such additional Units may have different rights regarding voting, profit and loss allocations and distributions, whether subordinate or preferred, as the Members determine. Persons that purchase additional Units pursuant to this Section shall be Additional Members. This Operating Agreement shall be amended to reflect the addition of any new Member.

4.5 *Capital Accounts.* Throughout the term of the Company, a Capital Account will be maintained for each Member. Each Member's Capital Account will be increased by the amount of capital contributions (but not loans) by such Member to the Company, and income and will be decreased by distributions and losses. The manner in which Capital Accounts are to be maintained pursuant to this Section is intended to comply with the requirements of Code Section 704(b) and the Treasury Regulations promulgated thereunder.

4.6 *Allocations of Profits and Losses.* The Net Profits and Net Losses of the Company for each fiscal year shall be allocated to the Capital Accounts of the Member(s) and any Assignees in proportion to their Units.

4.7 *Mid-Year Allocations.* Upon the admission of any Additional Member or the Transfer of less than all of the initial Member's Units, the allocations of Net Profits or Net Losses for that Year shall be allocated pro rata for that portion of the Company's tax year in which the Additional Member was admitted or the Units changed in accordance with the provisions of Code Section 706(d) and the Treasury Regulations promulgated thereunder.

4.8 *Distributions.*

(a) Except as provided in (b) below, distributions from the Company to the Member(s) shall be in proportion to their Units and shall be made at the times and in the amounts determined by the Member(s).

(b) Upon liquidation of the Company, liquidating distributions will be made to the Member or the Members in accordance with their positive Capital Account balances, as determined after taking into account all Capital Account adjustments for the Company's taxable year during which the liquidation occurs. Liquidation proceeds will be paid within sixty (60) days of the end of the taxable year (or, if later, within ninety (90) days after the date of the liquidation).

4.9 *Limitation Upon Distributions.* No distribution shall be made unless, after the distribution is made, the assets of the Company are in excess of all liabilities of the Company, except liabilities to any Member on account of a capital contribution.

ARTICLE V
TRANSFERABILITY

5.1 *Initial Member May Transfer; Restrictions on Transfer.* The initial Member may voluntarily Transfer any portion of the Member's Units to one or more Persons without prior written approval from any other Member or Person. No Member other than the initial Member nor an Assignee may Transfer, either voluntarily or involuntarily, any or all of his or her Units or any right or interest therein without the prior written approval of all Member(s) who are not transferring their Units in the Company (such approval may be withheld or granted in the Member(s)' sole discretion). Any purported Transfer without compliance with the provisions of this Article shall be null and void, shall not be binding on the Members, and shall not be recorded on the books of the Company.

5.2 *Substitute Members.* A Person to whom the initial Member voluntarily Transfers all or a portion of its Units shall automatically become a Substitute Member upon such Person signing a copy of this Operating Agreement agreeing to be bound by its provisions. However, no Person to whom any Units are Transferred by any

Member other than the initial Member or by any Assignee of the initial Member, whether or not this Article V is complied with, can become a Substitute Member unless all of the Members who are not transferring their Units approve of the Transfer by written consent (which may be withheld in their discretion), and such Person has signed a copy of this Operating Agreement agreeing to be bound by its provisions. A Substitute Member has the rights and powers, and is subject to the restrictions and liabilities, of a Member under the Operating Agreement and the Act.

5.3 *Assignees.* An Assignee shall have no right to vote or participate in the management of the business and affairs of the Company or to become a Member, and shall only be entitled to receive the share of profits or other distributions and the return of contributions to which the transferor Member would otherwise be entitled. An Assignee shall be subject to all restrictions and liabilities of a Member under the Operating Agreement and the Act. An Assignee is not entitled to access to information concerning Company transactions, or to inspect or copy any of the Company's books and other records.

5.4 *Termination of Member's Status As Member.* A Member ceases to be a Member upon Transfer of all of the Member's Units, other than a Transfer for security purposes or a court order charging the Member's Units.

5.5 *Remaining Liability.* Whether or not a Person to whom Units are transferred becomes a Substitute Member or remains an Assignee, the transferor Member is not released from liability to the Company, if any, under the Operating Agreement or the Act.

5.6 *Time of Transfer.* The Company need not give effect to a Transfer until it has received written notice of the Transfer and such Transfer has been approved as provided herein.

ARTICLE VI
DISSOLUTION AND TERMINATION

The Company shall be dissolved upon the occurrence of any of the following events:

(i) by the unanimous written agreement of the Member(s);

(ii) upon the death, resignation, bankruptcy, dissolution, judicial declaration of incompetence or occurrence of such other event which constitutes an event of withdrawal with respect to the sole remaining Member of the Company;

(iii) upon the entry of a decree of judicial dissolution as specified in the Act; or

(iv) at the time specified in the Company's Articles, if any.

As soon as possible following the occurrence of any of the events specified in this Section effecting the dissolution of the Company, the Company shall execute such forms as shall be prescribed by the Secretary of State and file same with the Secretary of State's office as necessary to wind up the Company's business. The Company shall cease to carry on its business, except insofar as may be necessary for the winding up of its business, and its separate existence shall continue until Articles of Termination have been filed with the Secretary of State or until a decree dissolving the Company has been entered by a court of competent jurisdiction. During this "winding up" period, the Company shall take all appropriate and necessary steps to first satisfy the claims of the known and unknown creditors as required by the Act. When this process is completed, then the Company will satisfy all of the claims of the Members and any assignees proportionally to their interests.

ARTICLE VII
MISCELLANEOUS PROVISIONS

7.1 *Governing Law.* This Operating Agreement, and the substantive application and interpretation hereof, shall be governed exclusively by the law of the state of [State].

7.2 *Entire Agreement.* This Operating Agreement is the entire agreement with respect to the subject matter hereof and shall not be amended, altered or modified in any manner whatsoever, except as provided herein by a written instrument. The Attached Exhibits and Articles of Organization are hereby incorporated into this Agreement. Should there by any inconsistencies with respect to the Articles and this Agreement, this Agreement shall prevail. This Operating Agreement supersedes all prior agreements with respect to the subject matter hereof and all such prior agreements shall be void and of no further force or effect as of the date thereof.

7.3 *Construction.* Whenever the singular number is used in this Operating Agreement and when required by the context, the same shall include the plural, and the masculine gender shall include the feminine and neuter genders and vice versa.

7.4 *Headings.* The headings in this Operating Agreement are inserted for convenience only and are in no way intended to describe, interpret, define, or limit the scope, extent or intent of this Operating Agreement or any provision hereof.

7.5 *Waivers.* The failure of any party to seek redress for violation of or to insist upon the strict performance of any covenant or condition of this Operating Agreement shall not prevent a subsequent act, which would have originally constituted a violation, from having the effect of an original violation.

7.6 *Rights and Remedies Cumulative.* The rights and remedies provided by this Operating Agreement are cumulative and the use of any one right or remedy by any party shall not preclude or waive the right to use any or all other remedies. Said rights and remedies are given in addition to any other rights the parties may have by law, statute, ordinance or otherwise.

7.7 *Severability.* If any provision of this Operating Agreement or the application thereof to any Person or circumstance shall be invalid, illegal or unenforceable to any extent, the remainder of this Operating Agreement and the application thereof shall not be affected and shall be enforceable to the fullest extent permitted by law.

7.8 *Heirs, Successors and Assigns.* Each and all of the covenants, terms, provisions and agreements herein contained shall be binding upon and inure to the benefit of the parties hereto and, to the extent permitted by this Operating Agreement, their respective heirs, legal representatives, successors and assigns.

7.9 *Creditors.* None of the provisions of this Operating Agreement shall be for the benefit of or enforceable by any creditors of the Company.

IN WITNESS WHEREOF, the initial Member has caused this Operating Agreement to be duly executed on _____, _____ .

_____
Member

Appendix O

Family Limited Partnership Documents Requested by IRS in Estate Tax Audits

[**Note.** The following is a list of documents that in the past have been requested by the IRS in the estate tax audit of a family limited partnership. This is list is by no means exclusive, but rather a guide as to what kinds of documents should be kept on hand in the case of an audit.]

1. All documents relating to the creation of the partnership (including bills) from any attorney, accountant or firm involved in recommending the creation of the partnership or in drafting the partnership agreement.

2. Original partnership agreement and all amendments thereto.

3. Articles of incorporation of the general partner, if the general partner is a corporation.

4. All documents that were prepared to meet state law requirements on the formation and operation of the partnership (i.e. certificate of limited partnership which has the filing date stamp on it and all amendments thereto; stamped copies of annual reports; supplemental affidavits on capital contributions, etc.)

5. All partnership financial statements and tax returns prepared and/or filed since inception.

6. All of the partnership's bank and other records (i.e. general ledger, cash receipts and disbursement journals, check registers, etc.) which reflect the amount and nature of all deposits and distributions, including distributions to partners,

for the period since the partnership was formed to the date of gift/current date.

7. Minutes of all partnership meetings; if none, indicate the dates of all meetings and the business discussed.

8. Evidence showing how the value of each partnership asset was arrived at as of the date:

   a. it was contributed to the partnership;

   b. of each gift of a partnership interest; provide all appraisals and supporting work papers obtained of the partnership's assets, including partnership interests and any discounts;

9. Evidence to substantiate all initial and subsequent capital contributions and the source of all contributions by partners of than the donor.

10. For any partnership asset that has been sold or offered for sale since the formation of the partnership, provide evidence which documents the sale or attempted sale (i.e. sale agreement, listing agreement, escrow statement, etc.).

11. For each partnership asset, explain/provide:

    a. evidence that the partnership owns the asset (i.e. deeds, bills of sale, other title changes, account statements, the date the transfer of the asset to the partnership was complete);

    b. when the donor acquired the asset;

    c. how the asset was used by the donor since its acquisition and how the partnership has used the asset since (i.e. held for rent, personal residence, investment, etc.); and

    d. who managed the asset prior to and after its contribution; explain in detail what the management consisted of and how it changed after the partnership was formed.

12. Brokerage statements reflecting the ownership and activity of the securities and mutual funds contributed to the partnership for the period beginning one year prior to the formation of the partnership and continuing through the current date, and copies of any other tax returns and financial statements which reflect the activity of the partnership assets, if different from the foregoing.

13. For each gift or transfer of a partnership interest, provide:
    a. evidence that the partnership interest was legally transferred under state law and under the partnership agreement;
    b. any assignment of partnership interest prepared;
    c. the terms of the assignment, if not indicated in a written assignment;
    d. the amount and source of any consideration paid;
    e. an explanation of how the amount of the consideration was arrived at.

14. Provide the following with respect to the donor, all other original partners and any recipients of gifts or transfers of partnership interests:
    a. date of birth;
    b. education, occupation, and their residence addresses;
    c. experience and expertise in dealing with partnerships, real estate, financial affairs and investments; provide tangible evidence thereof;
    d. extent of the donor's investments as of the date of the formation of the partnership, including a summary of assets that were not contributed to the partnership; provided tangible evidence thereof; and
    e. any personal financial statements and credit applications which were prepared in connection with loan applications after the partnership was created.

15. Indicate whether the partnership is currently in existence, and, if so, provide the current ownership interests.

16. Provide a summary of any other transfers of partnership interests not reflected in the gift tax returns filed.

17. A statement describing the donor's state of health at the time of the formation of the partnership and for the six month period prior thereto, including a description of any serious illnesses. Please also provide the names, addresses and telephone numbers of all doctors who would have knowledge of the donor's state of health during this period to the present date and provide these doctors with authorization to respond to the Service's future requests for

information, including a copy of the medical records, if necessary.

18. The donor's revocable trust, and any executed power of attorney, if not submitted with the return.

19. A statement including the identity of the parties recommending the use of the partnership, when the recommendations were made, and the reasons set forth in support of the partnership.

20. Names, addresses, and current telephone numbers of the representatives of the Donor/Estate, all donees/beneficiaries, all partners, accountants/bookkeepers, and brokers/investment advisors.

Internal Revenue Code

[All references are made to question numbers.]

Internal Revenue Code

[All references are made to question numbers.]

[All references are made to question numbers.]

Treasury Regulations Sections

[All references are made to question numbers.]

[All references are made to question numbers.]

Treasury Regulations Sections

[All references are made to question numbers.]

Administrative Announcement Table

[All references are made to question numbers.]

Revenue Ruling

Rev Rul

[All references are made to question numbers.]

Revenue Procedure

Rev Proc

Letter Rules

Ltr Rul

Administrative Announcement Table

[All references are made to question numbers.]

Table of Cases

[All references are made to question numbers.]

[All references are made to question numbers.]

Table of Cases

[All references are made to question numbers.]

[All references are made to question numbers.]

Table of Cases

[All references are made to question numbers.]

[All references are made to question numbers.]

Table of Cases

[All references are made to question numbers.]

[All references are made to question numbers.]

Index

[References are to question numbers.]

Index

References are to question numbers.

Index

[References are to question numbers.]

[References are to question numbers.]

U